The Gospel of John

An Initiatory Pathway Translation and Commentary

Adrian Anderson   PhD

Revealing a veiled layer of meaning in the
Greek text which presents spiritual
truths that transcend religion.

Distributed by Ebooks Alchemy
Prahran East VIC 3198
Australia

© Copyright 2022 Adrian Anderson
Threshold Publishing
Australia

All rights reserved

ISBN 9780645195415   Paperback

ISBN 9780645195422   Hardback

Cover image: courtesy of M. Swann

CONTENTS

Foreword
The Initiatory Intention Path or the Initiatory Quest Path

Introduction 5
The Canon: esoteric texts withheld from it

PART ONE

Section 1 10
The esoteric-initiatory context of the life of Jesus
Nazareth - Nazarites
The Essenes and "the Jesus movement".
The common themes of the Essenes and the Gospels
The Essenes' presence in the Gospels
A parable of Jesus against a feature of Essenism
Bethphage, an esoteric community ?
Christians: the people of The Nazaritic-Essene Way

Section 2 24
The Odes of Solomon
The Son of Man
The Son of God
The Katabasis or Journey to the Underworld

Section 3 43
Various ranks of spiritual beings
Pre-existence and Post-existence
Transmigration or reincarnation and the Bible
Repeated lives on Earth? The cultural context of Jesus
If reincarnation is a valid concept, why did Jesus not confirm this?
The dynamics and structure of Creation and of the human being

Section 4 61
The cosmic nature of Christ
Jesus or Christ ?
The events on Golgotha hill
What is 'eternal life' ?

Section 5 71
The cosmic Christ and the Sun
Origenes and the two aspects of Christ or Logos
The nature of the Logos
Jesus as a person, permeated by the 'Christ-Logos'
Life contrasted with 'eternal life'

Section 6 79
An expanded understanding of the concept of God.
The different meanings of God in the Gospels

Section 7 87
Identifying another meaning of 'faith': the ability
to be spiritually-intuitively perceiving
'Faith' with Theophrastos, Basilides and
Valentinos

Section 8 96
Codex Bezae: the most valuable ancient Greek text
of the Gospels, preserving esoteric teachings
Some key terms in the Gospel of John

PART TWO
Chapter One
The Gospel of John: a New Translation 114

Chapter Two
The Gospel of John: Commentary 187

Appendices

1 Luke 16: 1-12: The Essenes and The Parable of the unsatisfactory estate manager	527
2 The two 'Logoi' in Origenes	545
3 Faith: its second meaning in 'Pistis Sophia'	554
4 Texts viewed as showing Jesus to be the Logos	556
5 Christ as a cosmic deity of the Sun-sphere	563
6 Verse 5 of the Prologue as starting with "and the light shone"	571
7 Photius against Clement of Alexandria regarding the Logos	572
8 Verse 1:18: attempts to identify the Logos as God and also as Jesus.	575
9 Steiner interpreting 1:14 as about Jesus	576
10 Rudolf Steiner's commentary on v. 18	579
11 The Naasseni Hymn	581
12 8:25 the confusion around this verse	582
13 The complex Greek in 8:28	584
14 13:1 he loved them with regard to the goal	586
15 13:18 the Initiatory Level: Christ as the Earth-spirit	589
16 17:3 Here Jesus is named by the Christ	612
17 The sequence of events in the first Easter	615
18 Concerning Mary Magdalene	616

Bibliography
INDEX 632
Books by this author

ACKNOWLEDGEMENTS

I would like to express my gratitude to
M. Swann & D. Skewes
for their many helpful comments and support
during the demanding process of writing this book.

Foreword

Offered here is a new translation of the Gospel of John, in which many previously unknown teachings about the Christ and the initiatory path in the early years of the Christian era are revealed. It also presents a cosmic aspect to Christianity which is made possible through a new approach to assessing the Greek text of the Gospel.

Jesus is understood in this 'esoteric' Christianity to be the vessel of the Divine; which I refer to as 'the cosmic Christ', a term which will be considered in detail later. The group of disciples in the movement which grew up around Jesus were probably oriented, informally, towards the initiatory spirituality of the Essenes.

This translation and commentary is firmly based on a study of the ancient Greek texts of the Gospel, and also incorporates insights derived from merging academic scholarship with understanding of the esoteric spirituality. Esoteric mystical pursuits were widespread through various initiatory groups active in the Hellenistic Age. These movements were an integral part of the Hellenized Judaic people, amongst whom 'the Jesus movement' arose.

The new insights presented here are the result of discerning that a second layer of meaning was specifically but discreetly embedded in the Gospel, and that Jesus had a connection to various people involved in esoteric spiritual movements of his times.

This second esoteric layer of meaning as revealed in the commentary, is not grafted by me onto the Gospel; it was placed there by the Gospel writer, but veiled from the general reader. To achieve this, the evangelist utilized complex grammatical features of the ancient Greek language in a sophisticated way.

This principle of always veiling the deeper, more potent, esoteric truths was a common feature in the religions or cults of the Hellenistic Age, and long before then. So the experiences which acolytes underwent in the Mysteries were kept secret. The new translation presented here confirms that a similar approach existed in early Christianity.

This approach to Gospel interpretation could be called *the Initiatory Quest critical pathway*. (In theology, a 'critical pathway', or 'exegetical method' means the interpretative approach that one is using when reading the Bible). This approach or pathway to contemplating the Gospel will now be referred to as **"the Initiatory Quest approach"**. The appropriateness of this description for the approach used here will become evident later.

A major outcome of this work is that it becomes evident that the editorial work carried out by the Evangelist as he wrote the Gospel, was underpinned by spiritual insights and experiences, often deriving from his own seership. He consequently incorporated deep and awe-inspiring truths about a 'cosmic Christ', and about the significance of what could be called 'the Christ-reality' for the spiritual development of the human soul far into the future.

The discerning of this veiled level of meaning in the Gospel required insight into the evangelist's use of complex and subtle nuances of the Greek language. My task then was to academically validate these new insights, as far as possible. I believe my work has revealed profound truths which have been lying hidden, in plain sight, for many centuries.

In contrast to this, modern theological viewpoints are often a projection onto the Gospel of disinterest in, or non-awareness of, an esoteric spiritual dimension to life. This is because it is informed by a humanistic approach to Gospel understanding. This approach is not the basis of my work, yet the contribution made by such scholarship to assessing the Gospels is not in any way under-valued here. The use of such pathways as Source analysis, Form analysis, Textual analysis, etc, have all brought to light important perspectives which revealed the limitations of an earlier purely emotive or sentimental view of the New Testament.

These analytical 'pathways' to studying Biblical texts undertaken by scholars since the mid-19th century, have opened up many important techniques for encountering Scripture. But the modern humanistic incompatibility with the deeply esoteric spiritual worldview and initiatory strivings of the Jewish and Greek peoples in the Hellenistic Age, which is discreetly present in the Gospels, has often resulted in an arid perspective on these texts, unaware of their deeper message.

If a person already has reverence for the Gospels, the result of my new approach makes possible a deeper and wider perspective. A heightened understanding in turn deepens the feeling of holiness about this text. But such insights require acceptance that the perspective of Jesus and of all Biblical texts, is that the human being is part of a larger, spiritual cosmos and purpose.

This implies such concepts as a life-force sustaining living creatures, and the existence of diverse spiritual realms, and of various divine beings in those realms who are deeply involved in humanity's inner life.

If the reader is not interested in religion as such, these discoveries may awaken astonishment and awe at the cosmic nature of the 'Christ' – a deity known under various names to the priesthoods of earlier religions. The new discoveries revealed in this work also show the far-reaching purpose of the events recorded in this Gospel; a deepened understanding of Jesus, and of 'Christ' emerges.

My research into, and meditative engagement with these texts, which commenced in the 1970's, was enriched by a study of many esoteric Jewish or Christian texts from the Hellenistic world. This included many esoteric mystical texts known to academics as Apocryphal and Pseudepigraphic texts, as well as Gnostic texts. Also included in the research were the works of Origenes and Clement (both of Alexandria), the Nag Hammadi Library, the Dead Sea Scrolls, the Odes of Solomon, and other texts.

A commentary on most of the verses in the Gospels is an integral part of this work. It informs the reader as to the context of an event or statement, and above all, discusses veiled messages within a given verse. An invaluable help for my work was found in the research of the scholar and spiritual researcher, Rudolf Steiner (1861-1925), whose teachings I assessed for academia some years ago.¹ Various of the 360 volumes in his Complete Works (in German), together with archive documents, were consulted for this book.

Steiner's contribution to modernity, deriving from his scholarship and spiritual insights, is unique in that his contributions have been established as of significant value to many specialist fields of expertise, such as educational, agricultural and medical-pharmaceutical work. For example there are eight hospitals in Europe, and many clinics within mainstream hospitals, which are staffed by doctors who, in addition to their mainstream medical qualifications are also trained in Steiner's approach to medicine.

Seeking understanding of the Gospel message from esoteric insights acquired from a study of esoteric non-Biblical documents and the work of Rudolf Steiner, results in a higher level of understanding and enhanced clarity. But precisely this new understanding brings into question many previously held religious convictions, which are in themselves coherent and comforting. So this can be a challenging experience, but the rewards for those who persevere are substantial as a new, spiritually profound, comprehension of the Gospel emerges.

---

[1] In 2005 my PhD thesis (Monash Univ.), "Dramatic Anthroposophy", is formally described as a world-first assessment of the 'anthroposophy' of Rudolf Steiner.

Introduction

The veiled esoteric-initiatory aspect of early Christianity

The great third century scholar Origenes, in his *On First Principles*, had already alluded to the existence of deeper esoteric truths concerning Christ which were viewed as a precious heritage, and thus not to be revealed to the general members of the church. They were to be taught only to those people who were assessed as capable of benefiting from them, and of honouring the elevated spiritual capacities needed by the initiated teacher to perceive them.

His comments establish that in the early church there was some form of initiatory training, involving experiencing spiritual realities. This spiritual discipline was not unique to the new religion, since all the religions and cults of the time had this feature, which became known as "The Mysteries". There were for example, those of the Persian deity Mithra, the Egyptian god Serapis and the Greco-Latin goddess Artemis or Diana.

It was the goal of the Mysteries to assist people dedicated to the spiritual-esoteric quest, to develop advanced spirituality and thereby attain higher cognitional abilities. For some millennia, acolytes in the Mysteries underwent a similar three-day 'death' sleep, known as a 'katabasis', leaving their body to experience realms of spirit, until the hierophant awakened them.

The remarks of Origenes, made when he was discussing the forming of 'the Canon' need to be understood against this background. The canon is that selection of Christian texts which would later be defined, by the fourth century, as 'sacred Scripture', to eventually become "The New Testament". In the words of Origenes, writing about AD 250, the origin of those texts which later became the Canon, came about through a process of making available to the church in general, only those texts which were considered suitable for the wider church community,

"......most of what is circulating around (in public) for interpretation of Christian truths, is adapted to the wider community, and edifies the person who is not able to understand the higher meanings (of Christian texts)..."[2]

It is difficult to know which documents were regarded as genuine in the lifetime of Origenes, as the Christian Scriptures or New Testament was not formally defined until the fourth century.

Clement of Alexandria and initiatory Christianity
The implication of these words from Origenes, of an approach to Scripture which kept some texts away from wider circulation, is supported by another document, from Flavius Clement of Alexandria, (ca. 220 AD). It was discovered in the 20th century, and confirms the existence of an esoteric-initiatory side to the early Christian church: a 'secret Gospel of Mark". It was discovered in a monastery in Mar Saba in Judea. It is in the form of a letter written by Clement, in which a secret Gospel written by St. Mark is mentioned.

Some sentences from this otherwise unknown Gospel are quoted by Clement, and reference is also made to a seven-stage initiatory process. Clement possessed a copy of this secret Gospel which he says was only made accessible by the church in Alexandria, to those on the initiatory path. What is also of great importance is that in his letter, reference is made to 'hierophantic teachings' of Jesus.[3] For example, "As for Mark then, during Peter's stay in Rome, he wrote an account of the Lord's actions, not however declaring all of them, nor

---

[2] Origenes, Περὶ ἀρχῶν (*On First Principles*) 4:2,6 #170, Tome 3, p.371, Sources Chrêtiennes....πλεῖσται δὲ περιφερομεναι τοῖς πλήθεσιν ἁρμόζουσαι ἑρμηνεῖαι καὶ οἰκοδομοῦσαι τοὺς ὑψηλοτέρων ἀκούειν μὴ δυναμένους τὸν αὐτόν πως ἔχουσι χαρακτῆρα...
[3] It was discovered by Prof. M. Smith, *Clement of Alexandria and a Secret Gospel of St. Mark*, (1973, Harvard UP). Unfortunately scholars, other than the discoverer, have never been able to see the original letter, and its whereabouts is unknown, as all attempts to find it have been unsuccessful.

yet hinting at the secrets (ones)....he composed a more spiritual Gospel for those being initiated. Nevertheless, he did not divulge the words not be uttered, nor did he write down the hierophantic teachings of the Lord...."

In addition, Clement intimates in one of his books, using the language of the Mysteries, that Christianity also has initiatory processes for those who seek to develop their higher spiritual potential. Here he is addressing a man yearning for Egyptian Mystery wisdom,

"Teiresias - you *shall* have sight ! For Christ - he by whom the blind gain sight - shines upon you more brightly than the Sun. Night will flee from you, fire will fear you; death shall depart from you. Old man, you who cannot see Thebes, you shall see the Heavens ! O truly sacred mysteries ! O unsullied light !

My path is illumined by torches and I survey the heavens and God. Through being initiated, I become holy.[4] The Lord is the hierophant; he places his seal upon the mystae,[5] illumining him. He presents the one who believes (in Christ) to the Father, to be kept for safe for ever. Such are the revelries of *my* Mysteries ! If you so wish, be initiated ! And you shall [then] dance with the Angels,[6] around the un-begotten, indestructible One, the only God with true being;[7] the Word of God joining us in our hymn singing." [8]   (trans. A.A.)

In our modern religious traditions, there has been little acceptance of a secret, esoteric dimension to

---

[4] Through being initiated, I become holy: ἅγιος γίνομαι μυούμενος.

[5] A Mystae is an acolyte seeking to journey along the initiatory path at a Mystery Centre.

[6] 'Dancing with Angels': χορεύσεις μετ ἀγγελων

[7] 'only God with true being': μόνον ὄντος Θεὸν

[8] At the end of his book, *Exhortation to the Heathen* (Chapt. 12) in ΚΛΗΜΕΝΤΟΣ ΤΟΓ ΑΛΕΞΑΝΔΡΕΩΣ ·Λογος Προτρεπτικος in *Die Griechischen Christlichen Schriftsteller der erste drei Jahrhunderte*; J.C. Hinrich'sche Vlg, Leipzig,1906.

Christianity, preserving initiatory teachings Jesus.⁹ But already with the discovery of the Nag Hammadi papyri in Egypt and the Dead Sea Scrolls, last century, some glimmers of directly esoteric-spiritual truths associated with Gospels were revealed.

Yet these glimpses remain on the periphery of Biblical studies; for a focus on an initiatory, esoteric aspect to the Gospels did not survive the first centuries. The time has arrived for this missing core element of the Gospels to be presented to those seeking spirituality, and eventually, to be re-admitted to Scriptural studies.

But modern theology is not oriented towards specifically esoteric insights, or knowledge gained by inspired seership, that is, enhanced consciousness of transcendent realities. Theological studies are mostly unaware of deeper esoteric-holistic nuances of many events and teachings in the Gospels. For such studies are lacking knowledge of the spiritual framework or structure of the cosmos and of the human being's soul and spirit. Yet this knowledge is essential, as these two realities are pivotal to the esoteric side of Christianity, and are deeply intertwined.

The new translations offered here are not fanciful ideas imposed onto the texts. I have endeavoured to demonstrate, for scholars of Greek, in foot-notes or in separate Appendices, that my alternative translations are correct to the Greek text. A careful study of the alternative versions of Gospel passages, found in various ancient papyrus or parchments texts, has been undertaken. As a result of this, the text of the great codex Bezae Cantabrigiensis has been carefully assessed, as it preserves unique and genuine records, deriving from the first century CE, of words or deeds of Jesus. (The same attention was given to those very early, valuable documents, Papyrus 66 and 75).

My work revealing a second deeper layer of meaning in the Gospels, began in the mid-1990's and was academically validated at that time. The additional technical grammatical notes provided in the book seek

---

⁹ As one Professor of New Testament studies said me, about this *Secret Gospel of Mark*, "We didn't know what to do with it."

to validate the different translations I offer here. These notes are suitable both for those who are learning ancient Greek and those who are scholars in this language.

The veiled messages in the Gospels allude to teachings about similar deep cosmic realities that the ancient Mysteries for millennia had been exploring in various lands, and which in the time of Christ, show some affiliation to the view of Gnostics and the Essenes. But the Gospel writers understood these ancient truths in a new light, from their insights and experiences of Jesus and the cosmic Christ. Examples of this will be pointed out in the commentary on relevant Gospel verses.

To find the veiled meaning of the Gospel, the person with a traditional Christian background needs to rise above most of the conclusions of non-esoteric theology regarding the spiritual context of the New Testament.

Whereas the person with no religious background, and a modern humanistic education, and perhaps some dislike of religious texts, needs to have a capacity to feel reverence for experiential spiritual wisdom. Both groups need knowledge of the structure of Creation and of the human being, mentioned earlier. For this is the esoteric context of the Gospel teachings.

Section 1
The esoteric-initiatory context of the life and work of Jesus

Before the new translation of the Gospels is considered, the spiritual-cultural context of the life of Jesus needs to be considered. The substantial role of Jewish esoteric-initiatory movements within early Christianity has not been acknowledged by the humanistic attitude which has been the prevailing attitude in the Christian church. The view has always been that Christianity arose entirely from within normal Jewish culture. But this is not the case; it was deeply interwoven with, and made possible by, Nazaritic and Essene influences. (See below for a description of the Nazaritic life.)

Nazareth – Nazarites

The Nazaritic way of life had a major influence in the life of Jesus. It was into a Nazaritic family and community that Jesus was born and lived his childhood: he lived in Nazareth. The famous words in the Gospel of St. Luke, (1:26) about God sending the Archangel Gabriel to 'the city of Nazareth' is an unfortunate translation. For it appears that Nazareth was not a city, not even a town, because, as historians are aware, no such city or town, existed in the time of Jesus; or at least was not noted in Jewish records.

As far as these historical records are concerned, there is no mention of a 'Nazareth', from centuries before, and right up to, the time of Jesus. That is, there were no references to Nazareth in the Hebrew Scriptures, in the Talmud, nor in the works of Josephus. This has led some people to conclude, incorrectly, that the historical basis of the entire life of Jesus is questionable. It was not until two or three centuries after the time of Jesus, that 'Nazareth' enters historical records.

Steiner's contribution here is interesting; he taught that Nazareth was not a town nor a hamlet, but rather a small, secluded community established by people within the esoteric-mystical streams of Judaism.[10] The word

---

[10] GA 123, *The Gospel of Matthew*, lect. 6. Sept. 1910.

used in the Gospel of St. Luke for "the city of Nazareth", (polis) need not always mean a town or city; it also meant a community. This was one of its meanings in Classical Greek, and this is what Luke intended it to mean; he was strongly inclined towards the use of Classical-Attic Greek.[11]

Steiner had concluded that the leader of the Qumran Essenes had been brutally murdered, about 63 BC, causing other members to flee to the area of Damascus. He reports that some time after the Essenes fled from Qumran, some of those who survived the massacre, returned to Palestine.

Scholars are aware that sometime after 40 BC, some of these Essenes did re-settle in Palestine.[12] These people would have had a less formal Essene lifestyle, hence one which was similar to the Nazarites; the age-old, more esoteric Jewish tradition. So one may conclude that the social fabric behind the life of Jesus, helping him in his mission included reclusive esoteric-mystical groups: these could be called Essene-Naziritic people. This cultural background to the life of Jesus has been ignored, and yet it played a crucial role in the work of Jesus.

The first affirmation about this social context, is that John the Baptist was a Nazirite, as declared in Luke 1:15, and significantly he was related to Jesus. Secondly, Jesus lived in Nazareth, this reclusive mystic-esoteric colony. So the parents of Jesus, his family and childhood friends were probably all from Essene-Naziritic groups. This includes John the Baptist, who would have grown up in an Essene-Naziritic settlement, similar to Nazareth. This was the cultural context of Jesus, of he who would become the Messiah.

---

[11] This is partly due to his affinity with the writing style of Josephus: H.J. Cadbury, *The Style and Literary Method of Luke*, (2001, Wipf and Stock-Harvard UP), and partly due to his knowledge of Classical Greek medical texts (R. Knowling, *The Medical Language of St. Luke*, in The Biblical World journal, 1902, Chicago.

[12] A. Dupont-Sommers, *The Essene Writings from Qumran*, World Publ. Co. Cleveland, 1962, p.339.

The episode in the Gospel of St. John, Chapt. 1, where Nathanael meets Jesus is very striking in this connection. For when Andrew tells Nathanael that Jesus is the son of "that Joseph who is from Nazareth", Nathanael voices doubt that any thing good can come from that settlement. But this means that Nathanael not only had been in this secluded place, he had also met the father of Jesus, and moreover he has perceived the disappointing 'inner tone' of the group.

As a result he concluded that people there – but probably not all – were failing to live up to the standards expected of a true esoteric-mystical group. This scepticism is validated by the miserable response to Jesus from the people of Nazareth as reported in the Gospels. (This is considered further in the relevant Gospel verses.)

Nazarites
So who were the Nazarites? These people could be either free Jewish men or women, (or their slaves), who sought to dedicate their lives to God. That is, to become especially involved in the inner life, and thus to observe the requirements of Judaism. But in addition, they had to abstain from wine or any other intoxicating liquors produced from grapes; and their hair would not be shorn, and they had to avoid any ceremonial uncleanness with especial care.

So they became drawn to the quest for a higher spirituality and therefore a higher consciousness. These people were defined in the Book of Amos as 'prophets'; this term means that they were actively seeking to develop higher cognitional capacity (i.e., seership). The first formal records about the Nazarites appear in the *Book of Ruth* (written some centuries after the Israelites had arrived in the Holy Land, but referring back to earlier centuries).

However the Hebrew Scriptures indicate that such a Nazaritic mystical-esoteric inner life was nurtured for many centuries before the arrival in the Promised Land, indeed, even prior to the ancestors of the Hebrews settling in Egypt, from Mesopotamia. For example, *Deuteronomy* refers to Joseph, a son of Jacob, as a

'Nazir' amongst his people; this is very significant, since Joseph possessed a form of seership, which gave him dream-interpretation abilities. The translators have to struggle with this word 'Nazir', and may translate it either as "the *prince* among his people" or as "one *separated from* his people". This reflects the fact that this same word is used for 'Nazirite' and means a person who is 'consecrated' (to God) and therefore separated from the general community.

Otherwise only Samson and the Rechabites (a nomadic people, forming a sub-section of tribe of Judah) are specifically mentioned as being Nazarites in the Hebrew Scriptures (or the 'Old Testament'). But no doubt there were many others; in fact Nazarites appear again in the Christian Scriptures (or the 'New Testament').

Jesus' followers became Nazarites
That 'the Jesus movement' existed within an esoteric cultural context has been ignored for millennia. But Jesus was raised in a Nazarite-Essene colony, and this is a fact that needs to be far more emphasized than it has been. In addition, this spiritual background to the early life of Jesus also played a part in the life of many of the first Christians; as Luke indicates in the *Book of Acts*, these people often became 'short-term' Nazarites (21:17).

A 'short-term' Nazarite is a person who decides to enter into the strict devout way of life that the Nazarites had developed, but not for life, only for some weeks or months. This vow of taking up a short-term temporary commitment to the Nazarite way of life, had long been a feature of the Jewish people, and references to this are recorded in the Hebrew Scriptures.

It is a highly significant fact that followers of Jesus made this vow, as detailed in the *Book of Acts*, without Luke specifying that the vows and other acts of these people were in fact, Nazaritic. As all scholars are aware, it was not necessary for Luke, the author of Acts, to specify this, as it was common knowledge. But the Essenes were the most significant esoteric movement with a prominent role in the life of Jesus.

The Essenes and "the Jesus movement".
The Essenes were the most significant group in the esoteric-initiatory life in Judaism. Consequently they were discussed by noted historians of the Hellenistic Age: Pliny the Elder, Philo and Josephus. Already in the 18th century, German scholars concluded that the Essenes played a major role in the 'Jesus movement'. But with the discovery of the Dead Sea Scrolls, and their gradual, much-delayed publication, starting in the 1950's, many scholars began to realize that there was obviously an association of sorts between Jesus and the Essenes.

But before assessing these sources of information, it will be helpful to consciously engage with the evidence about the role of the Essenes in the work of Jesus as given in the Gospels themselves. This is evidence which has only recently been considered in theological studies.

The Essene movement
Although not all of the information from Pliny, Philo and Josephus is regarded as accurate, they have provided an invaluable record of this group. It was in the mid-20th century, that the Dead Sea Scrolls were found in caves in Palestine; most of these were written in Hebrew.

These scrolls contain some texts which were written by the Essenes, and some texts which are what we now know as the Hebrew Scriptures (or the 'Old Testament'). Other texts are the more mystical or non-canonical Hebrew religious writings, such as the *Book of Enoch*, of *Jubilees*, and of *Tobit*. The scrolls were found at Qumran, in Palestine, which was a settlement located about one mile from the Dead Sea. The picture that emerges from all of the above writers is that the Essenes commenced in the 2nd century BCE; and had some similarities to the obscure Therapeutae; who were an older esoteric-initiatory group. The Essenes had a very lofty soul as their founding leader, Jeshua Ben-Pandira. His high spirituality endowed him with a majestic seership.

This leader is referred to as the 'Teacher of Righteousness' in the scrolls. The group was subject to a violent attack from opponents about 63 BCE, which led to them dispersing, but they later gradually returned to Palestine, as noted above. They fade from historical records by the late 1st century CE. They were dedicated to an esoteric-initiatory monastic life, within the general context of Judaism.

Some were celibate, and lived apart at Qumran, and perhaps elsewhere; whilst others had families and lived in the towns. Their life was dedicated to a striving to develop cognition of the spiritual realms and its deities. This demanded a disciplined life aimed at overcoming earthly desires, and resulted in an inner distance from the normal world in general.

They contemplated their religious books, undertook meditation towards developing a higher consciousness, and followed detailed hygiene laws and purification rituals, living a strictly regulated ascetic life. This led to some of them attaining to a higher consciousness or seership.

This is shown in their writings which are about higher spirit realms and the various beings in these. The *Book of Enoch* is a prime example of this, and was probably written, at least in part, by the Essenes (by their initiate leader, Jeshua Ben Pandira). But parts of other texts have been found which are the result of seership.

One fragmentary text, *The Tree of Evil*, (4Q458) refers to an Angel being sent by God to the Earth. The entire theme of another fragment, *The Angels of Mastemoth and the Rule of Belial*, (4Q390) is the activity of various spirit beings. Another text, *The Vision of the Four Kingdoms*, (4Q457) refers multiple times to the Angels, and how brilliantly radiant they appear to clairvoyant vision.[13]

There are still other significant texts showing an acute awareness of spiritual beings amongst the Essenes. *The Testament of Amram* (4Q543, 545-548), directly refers to "The Watchers"; that is, stern, high spiritual beings who are guardians of the various spirit realms, and watch over the human souls in their realm.

---

[13] These fragmentary texts, with Q4 numbers, are published in *The Dead Sea Scrolls Uncovered* (Ref. 6)

Two of these beings are described as battling over the soul of the Essene initiate who is recording this clairvoyant experience.

Another relevant point here is the report from Flavius Josephus the ancient Roman historian, that a person who is admitted to the Essene Order is "expressly forbidden to reveal the names of the Angels".[14]

The common themes of the Essenes and the Gospels

Professor Charlesworth, amongst other scholars, has identified about a dozen themes in Essene writings and in the Gospels, which don't occur elsewhere, or very rarely. These include references to the Holy Spirit, to the Spirit of Truth, to 'sons of light, and to 'he who walks in darkness', and also striking statements about 'living water'. In the Gospels, Jesus is the source of 'living water'. In John (4:13-14), when Jesus is speaking to the Samaritan woman at a well, he declares,

"Everyone who drinks this water will be thirsty again, but whoever drinks the water I give him will never thirst. Indeed, the water I give him will become in him a spring of water welling up to eternal life."

There is a similar theme in the Qumran *Hymn Scroll*, where the Teacher of Righteousness is a vessel for this living water, which God gives to him. He says,
"And Thou O God, has put into my mouth as it were, an autumn rain for all (the sons of men), and a spring of living waters which shall not run dry." [15]

The Essenes' presence in the Gospels

There are several passages in the Gospels which may be interpreted as indicating the existence of a network of people with close links to the Essenes, who worked behind the scenes to assist Jesus. That is, people who were devoted to the initiatory quest. A feature which shows a direct link to the Essenes occurs as the time of the arrest of Jesus draws near. Jesus wishes to celebrate a new kind of Passover meal with his disciples: the

---

[14] Josephus, *The Jewish War*, BK. chapt. 8.
[15] DSS, *The Hymn Scroll*, sect. 16, in Dupont-Sommers, p.228.

famous Last Supper. He instructs two of them to go into Jerusalem and look out for a man carrying a water pitcher (Lk.22:10). They are to ask that man to show them a room wherein the Last Supper can take place.

As scholars are aware, this is a very unusual situation, because almost without exception, carrying water pitchers back to one's dwelling was the task for the womenfolk to do, not men. There are but three possibilities here: one is that a manservant was doing this; a very rare occurrence, but possible. The second is the remote possibility that the head of the household carried the water as a special act of devotion in preparation for the Passover festival – but this would be an even more rare occurrence than a male servant doing this work.

The third possibility is much more likely – that an Essene, a male member of a celibate Essene group, was carrying the water. This work had to be done by a man, because there were no women in their enclave. It is most likely that he was an Essene, because this person gave the disciples access to a special room for the Last Supper.[16] It is unlikely that an especially devout Jew, the head of the household, would be giving help to Jesus and his Disciples – unless that person was a devout Essene who was not celibate, and thus had a family.

It is also unlikely because any head of a household, whether an Essene or a normal devout Jew, who assisted Jesus would be invoking serious danger not only himself but also on his family and his servants. For the same reasons, a male servant in a household would not risk offering such help. It was well known to the Essenes and the public in general, that the Sanhedrin were fiercely opposed to Jesus.

The danger is all the more serious if the circumstances indicated in the Gospel of St. John apply: that the Passover meal was celebrated on a Thursday, which is a day too early, the day before the Passover festival – for such an action leaves the people doing this open to the charge of blasphemy. Moreover if there were

---

[16] Rudolf Steiner regarded this room as an initiatory room of the Essenes.

no cooked lamb on the table, as the Greek text seems to be indicating – this (apparent) even more serious blasphemy would incur the most severe penalty.

A parable of Jesus cautioning against a feature of Essenism

Another strong instance of the Essenes being an important feature in the spiritual landscape of the times is the caution Jesus gave in a parable to his Disciples against the Essenes' attitude with regard to the world and its realities.

The parable occurs in Luke, chapter 16, and is known as the Parable of the Unjust Steward. It is this parable which has remained a confronting enigma throughout the history of theological engagement with the Gospel of Luke. In this text, Jesus refers to "the Sons of Light" – a term which is used specifically by the Essenes as a name for their Order.

At least one academic, David Flusser, argues that it must be referring to the Essenes. He concludes that it was cautioning the Disciples to avoid the exclusive, isolationist approach to economic transactions with the general populace.[17]

But when this parable is assessed using the Initiatory Quest approach, the conclusion that it is directly referring to the Essenes is not only confirmed, its actual meaning is substantially deepened, far beyond that of economic exclusivity. See Appendix 1 where my new translation and commentary of Luke 16:1-12 is included. This cautioning by Jesus against a too narrow, or rather a too 'world-alienated' mindset, developed by the Essenes, demonstrates that, despite their goal of developing seership and thereby gaining a resonance with divine beings, the Order did have failings in some aspects. That Jesus would seek to educate his disciples about this, establishes just how close was the interaction between 'the Jesus movement' and the Essenes.

---

[17] *The Parable of the Unjust Steward: Jesus' criticism of the Essenes*, in Jesus and the Dead Sea Scrolls, edit. J. Charlesworth, Doubleday, N.Y. 1992.

Bethphage
Bethphage had a significant role in the work of Jesus. It appears to have been another Essene-Nazaritic colony; the place that the disciples were sent to by Jesus to obtain a donkey for his triumphal ride into Jerusalem. This is why Jesus can say to his disciples (Matt. 21:2):
'If someone objects to you untying and taking away a donkey, just explain, "The Master needs it", and they will allow you to bring the animal to me.'

Obviously, the people in Bethphage were supporters and students of Jesus, the Messiah, who was their Master. And these inhabitants recognized the disciples as colleagues. But what are the indications that the people in Bethphage were involved in the initiatory-mystical path, seeking higher consciousness? The name, Bethphage is an indicator; it means in Aramaic, 'unripe figs". Although this meaning can be seen as a normal agricultural word, here, according to Rudolf Steiner it is the name of an esoteric-mystical colony, and so functions as a veiled reference to the quest for higher consciousness.[18]

He taught his students that the fig was a symbol of the 'eyes of the soul'. These 'eyes' are vortices in the soul-body (or aura) which, once developed, bestow higher cognition or seership on the purified, sanctified acolyte. Every Hindu temple has a fig-tree, and some Egyptian pharaohs were depicted as meditating under a fig-tree.

For similar reasons in Palestine, the word 'fig', apart from everyday usage, was also used where spiritual-esoteric development was undertaken. (The third eye on the forehead of the Buddha symbolizes the soul-eye in the forehead area). If the figs are unripe, this means that 'the eyes of the soul' are not developed, so efforts are underway to develop them, by those in Bethphage.

It is also relevant that Lazaros and his sisters Mary and Martha lived in Bethany, just a short distance away from Bethphage. It is also significant that, in the opinion of many scholars, Lazaros had been a disciple of John

---

[18] GA 139, lect. 22. Sept., 1912.

the Baptist (see Commentary on 1:41). One sees that a network of esoteric-mystical people, not far from each other, had formed around the Messiah.

Christians: The people of the Nazaritic-Essene Way

So closely intertwined were the Essenes and the people in 'the Jesus movement', that in Palestine and beyond its borders, the first Christians were understood by the general community to be an informal offshoot of the Essenes. One can draw this conclusion from passages in the *Book of Acts* which establish that, in the minds of people generally of the Middle East, and their rulers appointed by Rome, the early Christians were members of "The Way" and that this was a "Nazarene sect".

Acts records that Paul was a strict Pharisee, and at first he was persecuting the Christians; he was called Saul at this time. Luke reports that before Saul (later Paul) became a Christian through his clairvoyant encounter with the Saviour on the road to Damascus, he went to the high priest in Jerusalem,

> "and asked him for letters to the synagogues in Damascus, so that if he found any people there **who belonged to 'The Way'**, whether men or women, he might take them as prisoners to Jerusalem." (9:1,2)   (emphasis mine, AA)

Then Luke reports, about the Christian missionary activity which was later taken up so extensively by Paul,

> "Paul entered the synagogue and spoke boldly there for three months, arguing persuasively about the kingdom of God. But some of them became obstinate; they refused to believe and **publicly maligned 'The Way'**. So Paul left them."

These intriguing references to Christians being known at first as members of Essene path, "The Way", have rarely been discussed in the light of the Dead Sea Scrolls. Although the Essenes called themselves "The Sons of Light", in the Scrolls, they referred to their ascetic, initiatory movement as "The Way". This was the title the Essenes gave to their own spiritual-religious path in *The Community Rule* scroll:

"the men of holiness....walk in The Way of perfection".
"...he shall impart true knowledge and righteous judgement to those who have chosen The Way."
"He will deliver my soul from the Pit (Sheol)
and will direct my steps to The Way."
"If you turn from The Way, then evil will meet you".[19]

So one concludes, in view of all the evidence presented above, that the first Christians were in fact understood by the general community to be in effect, Nazaritic-Essenes in a general way, not in a strict sense.

The Christians as Nazirites

For in addition to having these references to "The Way", Luke later reports on the actions taken by the Sanhedrin against Paul, which led him to being tried in a courtroom setting, before a Roman governor. What the Sanhedrin declares to the Roman authority (Felix) about Paul, is very significant,

> "We have found this man to be a troublemaker, stirring up riots among the Jews all over the world. He is a **ringleader of the Nazarene sect**."

Shortly after this accusation Paul denies much of what he is accused of, but adds,

> ".....However, I admit that I worship the God of our fathers, **as a follower of 'The Way'**, which they call a sect." (24:14)

So Paul is acknowledging that he is a Nazarene, that is, a person who is 'Nazaritic' in terms of his spiritual affiliations, and that the people of Nazareth were also, in general terms, Essenes, or members of 'the Way', and that these people were also truly worshippers of 'God' (Jahve).

Now to fully realize the significance of Paul's words, we need to consider the words of Jesus himself, as the Risen Saviour, speaking some years earlier, when he met the angry Saul on the road to Damascus, who was seeking to persecute these people of 'The Way'. As Saul

---

[19] *Dead Sea Scrolls Uncovered*, 4Q 397-99.

is enveloped in a blinding light, as part of the ensuing dialogue, he asks this glorious being whom He is, and receives this answer,
"I am Jesus the Nazarene, whom you are persecuting", he replied.

Jesus Christ identified himself as a Nazarene directly to Saul. So before the term 'Christian' came into existence, the human definition of Jesus, (aside from the divine status of Messiah or Son of God) was that of a Nazaritic-Essene person; a 'Nazarene'.

In fact, this point was emphasized at the beginning of Matthew's Gospel, connecting to the fact that when the Holy Family returned from Egypt, they avoided Judea, and settled in Nazareth;

> Having been warned in a dream, he withdrew to the district of Galilee, and he went and lived in a town called Nazareth. So was fulfilled what was said through the prophets: "He will be called a Nazarene." (2:22-23)

There are actually no clear prophecies directly to this effect, but Matthew nevertheless makes this emphatic statement.[20] In fact, this identifying of Jesus as a Nazarene, was also emphasized at the end of Mark's Gospel, by the Angel who speaks with the two Marys at the opened tomb:

> "Don't be alarmed," he said. "You are looking for Jesus the Nazarene who was crucified. He has risen! He is not here."

One can also note that demons defined Jesus as a member of the esoteric Nazarene colony,

---

[20] Some scholars see a link to words of Isaiah (11:1) "A shoot will come up from the stump of Jesse; from his roots a Branch will bear fruit." Rudolf Steiner has further insights (his commentary on this verse is in his lectures on Matthew's Gospel).

"What do you want with us, Jesus of Nazareth? Have you come to destroy us? I know who you are the Holy One of God!" (Mk.1:24 and Lk. 4:34)

So the 'Jesus movement' arose from within the vitally important initiatory Nazaritic-Essene group, and consequently was viewed generally in the community as part of this group of people.

SECTION 2

The esoteric-spiritual literary background

The Odes of Solomon
Another striking example of the presence of an initiatory, mystical landscape of Palestine, created by the widespread interest in the initiatory path, is a collection of 42 mystical-initiatory poetic texts, known as *The Odes of Solomon*. These were found amongst a collection of ancient texts in 1909, and are now in the John Rylands Library (University of Manchester). They are written in the Syriac language, although a few have also been found in ancient Greek.

The author, his spiritual context, the date and the original language of these Odes, is unknown. Most scholars now believe that they date from late first century or mid-second century CE. Others conclude that they are from a 'mainstream' Jewish writer with a deep engagement in the mystical traditions of Judaism, or perhaps a Jew who became a Christian.

But very significantly, some scholars including myself, conclude that the writer was an Essene. The text is perplexing, firstly because the meaning of some phrases and words in the Syriac is not clear. But secondly, unknown to those working out of a humanistic interpretation, and hence unfamiliar with esoteric knowledge, many of the Odes are directly referring to initiatory experiences and knowledge.

Thirdly, these Odes may have been altered later by a Christian editor, but additionally, some of the actions and teachings of Christ have similarities to what initiates in the Mysteries experienced. The deep esoteric basis of these Odes, and the consequent difficulty that they present to a theological translator, is highlighted with Ode 36, which is about attaining a higher degree of initiation; this was known as becoming 'a Son of God'.

This term is discussed below. The entire message of the Ode is not seen without awareness of this context. It is written from the 'clairvoyant' or higher consciousness state of an initiate; hence most translations usually do not convey the meaning of various phrases. This difficulty is exemplified by the phrase which is translated as, "and my mouth was opened, like cloud of dew"; and "like his (God's) own newness, he renewed me". Below is my version of this Ode, based on a study of five translations (English or German), with their comments on the Syriac text. But I have paraphrased the text, so as to clarify the intended esoteric meaning of various obscure phrases.

Ode 36
The Spirit of the Lord rested upon me,[21]
and this Spirit raised me to high realms
and enabled me to be inwardly upright
in the Lord's high place,
before the fullness of His being and His glory,
where I glorified Him, composing
songs of praise to Him.
Begotten was I by the Spirit
before the countenance of the Lord,
and, because I was a Son of Man,
I was named 'The Illumined One',
The Son of God,
as I gave praise amidst the Praising Ones.
Thus was I exalted – amidst the Mighty Ones.[22]
The Spirit formed me like unto
the greatness of the Most High.
The eternally renewing Lord
re-created me as a self-renewing one, and [23]

---

[21] Normally translated as "I rested upon the Spirit of the Lord", but M. Lattke has pointed out that there is a variant text, which has the opposite meaning; I have concluded that this is the more accurate version. (M. Lattke, "*Eine übersehene Textvariante in den Oden Salomos*, in the Zeitschrift für Antikes Christentum 8[2] Jan. 2004.)

[22] Instead of "I was the *most* glorified (or *most* praised) ..." adopting the interpretation of Rendel Harris, M. Lattke, H. Grimme) that the superlative is not meant here, despite the repetition in the Syriac text of the same key word, which can indicate a superlative function in intended.

[23] The "eternally renewing Lord": investing here the literal "newness of the Lord", with a meaning that is appropriate to the ageless-ness or perpetually self-renewing nature of a high spiritual being,

he anointed me from the fullness of His own being.
Thus I became one whose
inner nature draws close to Him.
And like the descending dew materializing,
from my mouth words emerged,
as if descending into my soul;
and my heart poured itself out
like a fountain of holiness,
for in peace did I approach Him,
and the foundations of my being
were upheld through His guiding will.

Note: the words, "to be inwardly upright" is literally, "to stand on my own feet" but this is a metaphor for the ability to consciously maintain one's ego-sense or awareness of self, in the presence of sublime Powers.[24]

That this Ode is derived from an initiate, from someone who underwent a very high spiritual experience, as part of the substantial esoteric-mystical Mystery cultures in the Hellenistic world, is evident when it is contemplated with spiritual-esoteric awareness. Consider my version, "*And like the descending dew materializing, from my mouth words emerged, as if descending into my soul*". The usual versions have verbatim the abrupt, enigmatic Syriac, "*my mouth was opened like a cloud of dew*" (R. Harris, J. Charlesworth, M. Lattke, H. Grimme). The meaning which lies behind this is obscure to modern scholars, for it derives from the holistic-spiritual understanding of antiquity.

Here I can only give a brief note about the scientifically mysterious nature of dew. Dew forms every morning and evening between 9-10am, and then between 9-10pm, at local time, around the Earth, (it may not be noticed, depending on local weather). This simple everyday rhythmical phenomenon is not scientifically explainable. But as the great Johann Wolfgang von Goethe intuited, the answer is found when one realizes

---

[24] If the original was in Greek, (which is quite likely) then it probably contained the verb istaemi (ἵστημι) which is used in just this way.

that the planet is alive through activity of its life-forces.[25]

So, dew subtly condenses in the air and settles onto the ground, from out of an invisible energy-field which has its own Circadian rhythms; that is, dew is formed by the life-forces of mother Earth. Whereas by contrast, rain emerges from visible physical clouds.

The word 'dew' as the materializing of a life-force which induces moisture, extending around the globe in a layer high in the atmosphere, also has this meaning in Scripture. In Genesis, (27:28) "Therefore the Elohim give thee of the dew of the firmament..." (that is, rain also condenses out of the ether, but then forms a physical cloud), and in Zechariah (8:12) "and the heavens (*firmament*) shall give of their dew..."[26] It is of course natural to think of the originating matrix of dew, a field of life-force, in terms of an invisible 'cloud'.

But following on from this dynamic, the word dew was also used to refer to spiritual emanations from a Divine being, descending and emerging into the consciousness of an initiate. This is found already in the preceding ode, (35): "*The dew of the Lord, in quietness he distilled (this) upon me*", (this is yet another expression in need of clarification). This same usage is also found in another initiatory text, called *2 Baruch*, "...and then healing shall descend in dew..." (73:2)

A similar usage occurs in a primary Manichaean text "...He established Dwellings of Life and set up living images in them, which never perish: he evoked Clouds of Brightness, from which descend dew and life..."[27] Here the expression "Clouds of Brightness" is better rendered as "radiant fields of ethereal energy", since visible moisture-bearing clouds as such are not meant.

---

[25] My *Rudolf Steiner Handbook*, provides research into this and other related phenomena, from a 'Goetheanistic' assessment of middle and upper atmosphere Aeronomical studies.

[26] In both these texts the word for heaven or firmament is 'shamayim' (שָׁמַיִם), and not one of the words that mean a cloud usually ('anan' or 'ab').

[27] *Manichaean Psalm-Book*, Pt.2, edit. C.R.C. p. 208, Allberry, Kohlhammer Vlg, Stuttgart, 1938.

A further example of this usage of dew as a pointer towards an emerging of something from an invisible spiritual-ethereal source, occurs in Psalm 110:

"... on the Day of thy Empowerment
Like dew from the womb of the morning
Shalt Thou receive thy people..."   (Author's translation).

Another example is from Clement of Alexandria: "...indeed 'the Sun of Righteousness' who drives his chariot over all, traversing across all humanity equally, resembling the Father, who causes his sun to rise upon all human beings and distills the dew of truth...."[28]

So the poet of Ode 36 is saying "*And like the descending dew materializing, from my mouth, words emerged, as if descending into my soul*", whereas the literal meaning "and my mouth opened like a cloud of dew" is not comprehensible.

Hence Ode 36 is indicating that this initiate in spiritual realms, experienced his faculty of speech stirring – but as inwardly resonating, or 'intoning', not becoming audible sounds carried on the physical breath-stream. So here speech is being spoken forth 'mentally' in high spiritual realms.

The Son of Man
This phrase needs to be understood, because it has an important place in the teachings of Jesus; and it occurs in this Ode. This phrase has remained a riddle to theologians, and it will continue to be obscure until it is contemplated from a spiritual-esoteric viewpoint. It was often used to mean simply a human being, in the Hebrew Scriptures, but it was also used in an esoteric sense.

The Son of Man, when it occurs in an esoteric context, refers to a person who developed themselves up to a high state of spirituality; i.e., someone who could be described as a seer or an initiate. Rudolf Steiner

---

[28] In his *Exhortations to Non-Christians*, Chapt. 11 "...ὁ γὰρ τὰ πάντα καθιππεύων δικαιοσύνης ἥλιος ἐπ' ἴσης περιπολεῖ τὴν ἀνθρωπότητα τὸν πατέρα καὶ καταψεκάζει τὴν δρόσον τῆς ἀληθείας."

explained that the term The Son of Man refers to that state of higher sanctification wherein the soul has overcome all of its unspiritual or base qualities, and has now attained to clairvoyant cognizing, appearing as a radiant form. Steiner calls this state of spirituality, 'the Spiritual-self'.[29]

In the Book of Ezekiel the seer is addressed by deity some 90 times as "The Son of Man", and these do appear to refer to the esoteric meaning. In the Christian Scriptures it is used by Jesus as an esoteric term, but in a complex manner. At times it refers to himself, but other times, it does not directly refer to him.

Yet each time that it seems to refer to Jesus, there is also the implication that it also refers to human beings in general; that is, to people, once a high spiritual state is achieved. This complex double nuance is the result of an intention to veil the deeper meaning of this phrase, and yet to also indicate that a deeper, transcendent reality is being brought to the attention of the listener.

Jesus usually refrained from designating himself as the Messiah, so the term is only rarely a title he directly wished to publicly apply to himself. Also, scholars are aware that this term was never a title for the Messiah in Jewish Scriptures. When the meaning of this term is understood from spiritual-esoteric insights, then a very significant aspect to the Gospel message is perceived, one which was previously unknown.

A significant indicator of 'The Son of Man' being an initiatory term, is in Mark 8:31 and Luke 9:22. When Jesus used it there in conversation with the disciples, they showed no surprise and needed no explanation of its meaning. There is the same dynamic with expressions in the Gospel of John, "The Lamb of God', used by the Baptist in reference to the cosmic Christ, and the word 'Logos'; both of these words assume that the readers (or listeners) already knew what these esoteric terms meant.

This term is indirectly referred to in the Book of Daniel, where from a clairvoyant, initiatory experience, this seer describes a mysterious, unexplained figure;

---

[29] GA 123, lect., 11 Sept. 1910.

> Dan 7:9 "As I looked, thrones were set in place, and the Ancient of Days took his seat. His clothing was as white as snow; the hair of his head was white like wool. His throne was flaming with fire, and ....."

Here there is a spirit being who is not called the 'Son of Man', but "The Ancient of Days"; a term which is not explained. However, another similar reference, including both of these figures, indicates that these two beings are interlinked. This occurs in an esoteric text which dates to shortly before the time of Christ, *The Book of Enoch* (46:1-3). As mentioned earlier, this book was probably written (at least in part) by the leader of the Essenes.

"And there I saw One who had a 'head of days',
and his head was white like wool,
and with him was another being whose countenance
had the appearance of a man,
and whose face was full of graciousness,
like the holy Angels
and I asked the Angel who accompanied me,
and who showed me all the hidden things,
about that Son of Man, who he was,
and whence he was....
and he answered me and said,
this is the Son of Man who has righteousness
with whom righteousness dwells....

The figure with the 'head of days' (a phrase that means 'very ancient') is known as The Ancient of Days. The reason for this seer describing the interweaving of The Son of Man with The Ancient of Days is not clarified, but it is to some extent explained through another seer, the prophet Ezekiel. In the *Book of Ezekiel* (1:26) there is a detailed description of God enthroned amidst the four 'apocalyptic animals. The seer describes part of the figure seen in his vision as looking like 'glowing metal'.

Next he refers to the 'the Glory of God' (Jahve) appearing above a throne of sapphire, and then of this same deity, who is radiant with glory, Ezekiel writes, "high above, on the throne, was a figure **like that of a man**." (emphasis mine, AA)

So here is a reference to the god Jahve as The Ancient of Days, but yet manifesting a human quality. This brief comment reveals that there is an aspect of God which has a similarity to the human being. Understood with spiritual insight, Ezekiel is conveying here through his seership, that Jahve is the archetype of the future perfected human being, known as The Son of Man, (or on an even higher level, The Son of God.)

The Son of Man is a term which refers to both the spiritual aspect of the human being and the divine reality from which this higher spiritual quality derives. (This spiritual aspect can also be called the Spiritual-self.) But though the text from Ezekiel refers to Jahve, the highest of these Elohim, the cosmic Christ, is also an integral part of the divine milieu from which the Spiritual-self or Son of Man derives. This situation is shown in the following passage from the Gospel of John, but only when its hidden layer of meaning is perceived.

In v. 8:28 Jesus said, Whenever you have exalted the Son of Man, then you will know that[30] **I am the I am** {in you}; also {you will now experience} "from myself I do nothing, but only as the Father taught me". These things I speak, and moreover, the One having sent me, is with me. He has not left me alone, for I always do that which is pleasing to Him.

See the Commentary on 8:28 for more about this. For more about what 'the Father' refers to, see Section Six, "A deeper understanding of the concept of 'God'. Here we learn that the sanctified person, who attains to The Son of Man state, then experiences their 'I' as an expression of the Christ. (The 'I' or ego here means our sense of self.)

Thereby the sublime meaning of the words spoken to Moses from the burning bush become an experiential reality to the initiate. The name of God as given in Exodus (3:13-14) is in Hebrew, 'ehyeh asher ehyeh'

---

[30] In the NIV Bible, the word "that" has been inserted, although it is not there in the Greek.

translated in the NIV as, "I AM that I AM". But as I have shown elsewhere,[31] the words can also be translated as,
" I, God, am the eternal 'I' (of you). "

That is, Christ-Jahve is saying in a veiled manner to Moses, that unknown to our earthly ego, the (germinal) eternal 'I' in which our human sense of self is enveloped, has its origin in the Divine. These words from Exodus are further explored in the Commentary, with the various relevant verses.

I am the 'I am': ego eimi
Before considering The Son of Man further, it is necessary to return to the phrase "I am the I am." The Greek, ego eimi, (ἐγώ εἰμι) is a core phrase in the Gospel, of huge importance to the message of Christ. However, its vital, profound esoteric meaning is not perceived in theology. As a result it is translated in most Bibles as "I am he", which is usually missing the point of what Jesus is stating.

As a result, theologians remain uncertain as to what some extremely important words of Christ in the Gospel actually mean. They are aware that this Greek phrase may be an equivalent to the famous Hebrew phrase where God tells Moses His name, which is usually translated as "I am that I am", but which as noted above, means, "I am the 'I am' (in you)'.

The Greek phrase, 'ego eimi' can be used as an equivalent to the Hebrew "I am the I am", and in the Gospel precisely this meaning is often meant (the 'I' I am).[32] So it is used by Christ as the equivalent of the Hebrew name of God, but from the viewpoint that the Hebrew name is understood more esoterically as, 'I am at the core of your sense of self'. This insight unlocks the veiled initiatory meaning in the words of Christ,

---

[31] In *Rudolf Steiner's Esoteric Christianity in the Grail painting by Anna May.*
[32] Technically, the word ego (ἐγώ) has the quality in these verses of a noun; i.e., as a *substantive* pronoun τό ἐγώ, but with the definite article being anarthrous, as befits its role in this context.

allowing various verses in the Gospel to be translated correctly, (such as John 6:20 and 8:24).

There is yet another place where the term The Son of Man is used in a manner which has been very difficult for theological studies to comprehend. It is the use of this term by Jesus in reference to some disciples seeing The Son of Man before they die. His words about this, (Matt. 16:28, Mk. 9:1 and Lk. 9:27) have never been deciphered; the theological attempts have resulted in many theories. Matt. 16:28 has,

> "Truly I say to you, some who are standing here will not taste death before they see The Son of Man coming in his kingdom."

Theologians have thought that this may refer to the Transfiguration, or the second Coming of Jesus or the establishing of the church, the Pentecost event or the Resurrection of Jesus.

But when assessed by the Initiatory Quest approach, the meaning of this saying is seen as highly esoteric, and fully embedded within its context, and not a separate segment ('pericope') that has been placed awkwardly here. For it is taking up and continuing the theme of several preceding verses. These verses are about arising above the normal earthly persona or self. Verse 28 is then pointing to The Son of Man state as an initiatory stage which some of the more advanced disciples shall individually achieve, before their life ends.

Returning now to the *Odes of Solomon*, we are reading in Ode 36 of the stages in the path of initiation, wherein this Essene is advancing from a 'Son of Man' to a 'Son of God'. Insight into these terms is given by Rudolf Steiner who taught that when the phrase 'The Son of Man' is used in an esoteric context, it refers to a stage of high spirituality or initiation wherein the capacity for spiritual insights, for (clairvoyant) intuitive cognizing, has been attained; but to the degree that the eternal 'Spiritual-self' has also started to become present in the person (in the 'I'). It becomes clear that the writer of the Ode is describing becoming elevated to a higher spiritual rank; this could be called a 'Life-spirit' initiate or 'Son of God" (see next page),

"....and, because I was a Son of Man,
I was named 'The Illumined One',
The Son of God,
as I gave praise, amidst the Praising Ones."

The context of Ode 36 is decidedly that of the initiatory quest. We now need to understand the phrase 'The Son of God".

The Son of God is a term which is usually associated with Jesus, but it has various meanings in the Bible and in esoteric apocryphal literature. On a general religious-spiritual level, it implies that a person is blessed by influences from the Divine. So in Jewish literature, various kings of Israel were referred to as a Son of God; and so too in ancient Egyptian and other cultures, the ruler was likened to a son of God (whichever deity it may have been).

But on an esoteric level, it was used to indicate that a person was regarded as a highly advanced initiate. King Solomon is referred to as a Son of God in this sense, and not so much because he was king, but because he was an illumined sage. Two revered men in the Hebrew Scriptures, Jacob and Joseph, are also each referred to as a Son of God, in non-canonical texts. A short mystical text, *Joseph and Asenath*, (6:6) describes Joseph as a Son of God. Also *The Prayer of Joseph*, surviving only as a few fragments, refers to the patriarch Jacob, as a Son of God.

When used in an esoteric context, The Son of God refers to a higher stage of spirituality than 'The Son of Man'. According to Rudolf Steiner, this title refers to a person who has achieved not only the Spiritual-self, but who has also undergone such spiritual development that even their life-forces are permeated by divine energies. He explains that as a soul becomes sanctified, the life-forces which maintain our body, and underlie reproduction, etc, may also be permeated by divine energies. This higher state of the life-forces is called the Life-spirit.

Such sanctified people have remarkable healing powers bestowed upon them. Steiner also describes that this term indicates an advanced state of spirituality in which the Spirit descends down towards an initiate, permeating him or her.[33] But this occurs from the viewpoint that this Spirit is both the source of, and brings to the initiate, the spiritual qualities from which all three aspects of the human spirit is formed.

The three aspects are: Wisdom, developed by purity of heart and by spiritualizing thinking. Secondly, Beauty in the sense of enhanced life-forces which confer powerful healing capacities and artistic ability.

Thirdly, Love or 'agape' which is a deep capacity for love; a love which envelops the will, not just the emotions. This third state enables intuitive powers of perception which have immense depth.

An extremely valuable, but almost unknown Gnostic text from about 300 CE, (it has not been translated into English until now), provides a crucial insight as to what 'The Son of God' status of an initiate means;

"The Son of God (initiate) may behold everything of their own soul becoming (re-)born as pure (sanctified) soul, so that this person may draw away from the realm "heimarmene", (and thus enter) into a bodiless (not-reincarnating) state."[34]

That is, the soul who is a 'Son of God' is now so highly spiritualized that such an initiate need not return to the Earth, but may remain in lofty blessed realms.[35] To the Gnostics, Heimarmene is a relatively high spiritual realm, but it is also the realm in which the soul has to prepare for re-birth.[36] So Ode 36 provides valuable insight into what was once a widespread and highly respected, if discreet, initiatory striving which formed the very life-blood of the spiritual-esoteric culture. It was from within this culture that Jesus carried out his mission, with the help of the Essenes.

---

[33] Ref. 29.
[34] From the Greek of Zosimus Panopolitanos, (translated the author); Greek text in *Hermetica*, Vol. 4, edit. Walter Scott.)
[35] This high stage is similar to the Indian concept of 'avatars'.
[36] This viewpoint has strong affinity to the Oriental wisdom of the avatars or initiates who remain in high spiritual realms.

Ode 42
This Ode is another indicator of substantial esoteric initiation experiences of the Hellenistic Age, the literary records of which circulated in groups associated with the Essenes, and thus close to Jesus. The Ode is about a descent into the Underworld, where the souls of the Dead are encountered. This was referred to in Greek texts as the 'katabasis' experience; and accounts of such experiences are widespread and well attested in the literature of many earlier cultures.

The initiates of ancient times, referred to as 'heroes', had to undertake a journey into the realm of the Dead. There they would encounter souls existing in gloomy darkened realms, who would ask for help from the initiate, or perhaps provide some information about other-worldly beings or dynamics. The Biblical story of Jonah being swallowed up by a whale is just such an episode, but presented in a veiled manner (see below for more about this).

However, Ode 42 is one of three Odes that are seen as evidence by some scholars that these texts are from a Christian writer, and refer to Jesus. In my view and that of many other scholars, this is erroneous. It is more likely that a Christian writer may have altered some of these poems, adding some Christian elements.

One reason for people concluding that this Ode is referring to Jesus is that it includes as a major theme, the 'katabasis' experience. This theme is included in the Christian Scriptures; it eventually became known as "The Harrowing of Hell". This is a misnomer, as the word Greek word is 'Hades' which is the Underworld or the Soul-world, and not the horrendous realm of 'Hell', which in Greek is called Tartaros.

It refers to the descent of Jesus, (in his soul-body) into the Underworld whilst his physical body is in the grave. There in the Underworld, the mighty Christ-power brings light to deceased souls, opening up a pathway out of the darkened Soul-realms.

When this Ode 42 is translated with a conviction that it has a Christian origin, it can appear to be referring to the 'Harrowing of Hades', by Jesus. It is a long poem, so we won't be examining it here in detail, but the last few verses, in the version by Charlesworth, are sufficient to show how this scholar views it as a Christian text:

v.15 And those who had died ran towards me; and they cried out and said, Son of God, have pity on us.
v.16 And deal with us according to your kindness, and bring us out of the bonds of darkness.
v. 17 And open for us the door by which we may come out to you; for we perceived that our death does not touch you.
v.18 May we also be saved with you, because you are our Saviour.
v.19 Then I heard their voice, and placed their faith in my heart.
v.20 And I placed my name upon their head, because they are free and they are mine.

As noted above, the reference to "The Son of God" does not always refer to Jesus. Also, the last verse (v.20) can be understood to be saying that an unknown initiate put his name upon the souls, as proof, to the Rulers of these realms, that these souls may be released from the dark Underworld. So they 'belong' to this initiate, in the sense of being protected by him. The translation by German scholar Grimm shows this conclusion,

"I drew my name upon their head, as {evidence that} they are free* and they are mine."[37]
(*That is, free to leave the darkness)

Also, in regard to verse 17, other scholars view this verse not as meaning, "open the door by which we may come out **to you**", but instead,
"...open the door by which we can come out **with you**.."[38]
or, "open the door **through which** we are **to go out**"[39]

---

[37] In his German, "Da hörte ich ihre Stimme und zeichnete meinen Namen auf ihr Haupt, (zum Beweis) daß sie frei waren und mir angehörten."
[38] S. Zimmer and M. Mattison's translation, *The Odes of Solomon, the Nuhra version.* www.academia.edu

or, "open the door so that we may go out through this **towards you.**"[40]

Additionally, two points in these verses directly echo teachings found in the *Book of Sirach*, written about 185 BCE; a non-canonical book which was however treasured by the Essenes; fragments of it were found at Qumran. This book is one of only three non-canonical Hebrew texts in the library at Qumran.[41]

"Also withhold not kindness from the Dead' (7:33) and "Mourn for the Dead for his light has failed" (22:11)

So these verses of the Ode can also be translated as the experiences of an Essene initiate in the Underworld,

v.15 And those who had died ran towards me; and they cried out and said, Son of God (*high initiate*), have pity on us.
v.16 And deal with us according to your kindness, and bring us out of the bonds of darkness.
v. 17 And open the door through which we are to go out; for we perceived that our death(-state) does not touch you.
v.18 May we also be redeemed with you, because you are our Redeemer.
v.19 Then I heard their voice, and placed their faith in my heart (*i.e., I viewed their conviction and hope, as to my ability, sincerely*).
v.20 I drew my name upon their head, as {evidence that} they are free, and they are mine.

The Katabasis journey to the Underworld
It was understood in antiquity that an initiate could carry out assistance to souls immersed in the darkness of the Netherworld. Once it is conceded that the term

---

[39] J. Flemming and A. Harnack's translation, in *Jüdisch-Christlich Psalmbuch..* "...und öffne die Tür, durch die wir hinausgehen sollen..." Leipzig, 1910.
[40] J. Labourt and P. Batiffol "...et ouvres-nous la porte, pour que elle nous sortions vers toi." *Les Odes de Salomon Texte*, in Revue Biblique Vol.8 No.1 (Janvier 1911).
[41] They are Sirach, Tobit and the Epistle of Jeremiah.

'The Son of God' can refer to an initiate, not only to Jesus, these alternative renderings are evidence that this Ode is about the achievements of a high initiate, (not Jesus), amongst the souls of the dead in the Underworld.

There was a supportive cultural context for this view in the Hebrew culture; firstly many non-canonical Hebrew texts refer to the journey into spirit realms by initiates such as Enoch. Secondly in the Hebrew Bible itself there is an account of a similar initiatory descent into Sheol or the Underworld, by the seer Jonah. To those with awareness of such esoteric topics, this Jonah incident has long been recognized as an initiatory experience. In the words that Jonah speaks whilst in his experience, in his prayer to God for help, there are some esoteric references, carefully intermingled with more normal imagery:

"...From the depths of Sheol, I called for help, and you listened to my cry. You hurled me into the deep, into the very heart of the seas, and the currents swirled about me; all your waves and breakers swept over me...in the troughs of mountains I was sinking into a realm whose bars would hold me forever. But you brought my life up from the pit, O Lord my God."   (Book of Jonah 2:2-6)

Whilst these words are not firm proof of a 'katabasis', they are highly suggestive of this. The most obvious indication of a 'katabasis' experience here is that the realm where the 'whale' is taking Jonah is described as the Realm of the Dead, 'Sheol'.

A poem written in the 6th Century CE, apparently by King Urien Rheged, ruler of Cumbria, shows that he regards this episode of Jonah as actually an initiatory descent into the Underworld, the realm of the Dead. King Urien was a prominent figure in the mystical traditions of his times. He was the patron of the initiate bard Taliesin, who was probably in residence at his court.

In one line of his poem, he asks the potent question, "Who brought Jonah out of Kyd?". The term Kyd is short for Kyridwen or Keridwen; this is the Celtic name for the

Realm of the Dead and its spirits, and also for the goddess ruling this realm.[42]

Additional cultural support for the conclusion that this was such a journey is the achievement of an initiate most likely an Essene, and not Jesus, is found in very early Christian esoteric, non-canonical texts which declare that such a journey into the Underworld was part of the initiatory capabilities of the Disciples of Jesus. Clement of Alexandria refers to the teachings of an ancient text, *The Shepherd of Hermas*, as validating this idea. He writes,

"Hermas says, that the apostles and teachers, who had preached the name of the Son of God, and who had fallen asleep in power and by faith, had preached to those (Christians) who had fallen asleep (and were in the Underworld), before they themselves died."[43]

Clement is referring to Hermas, Similitude 9, where the writer reports that a guiding Angel, who had the appearance of a shepherd, declared to him that,

"...the apostles and teachers, who had preached the name of the Son of God, dying after they had received his faith and power, preached to those souls who were dead before themselves..."[44]

Hermas is said to have been the brother of a certain Pius, Bishop of Rome, and the text is dated to about 150 CE. This book was esteemed by various church fathers including Origenes, and was read in churches, and a copy of it was attached to some ancient 'New Testament' manuscripts, such as the great Codex Sinaiticus.

So, both Hebrew and early Christian texts provide evidence for the understanding in the cultural context of the Odes of Solomon, that initiates, not only the Saviour, had the ability to journey to the realm of the Dead. Moreover, in the first line of this Ode, the initiate

---

[42] E. Davies, *The Mythology and Rites of the British Druids*, J. Booth, London, 1809, p. 409.
[43] *Stromateis*, Bk. 2:9 and Bk. 6:6.
[44] Hermas, *Similitudes* (9:157-58).

declares that he is stretching out his hands to approach "his Lord"; it is questionable to assign such an expression uniquely to Jesus, for the stretching out and raising of the hands was a recognized body-gesture of priests and priestesses in times of prayer.

There are many other initiatory references in these Odes, such as,

"And I took off the darkness and clothed myself with light. And my soul acquired limbs free from illness, affliction or pain...and I was clothed with the covering of thy spirit, and thou didst remove from me my covering of skin..." (Odes 22 and 25)

This initiate is declaring they are now capable of existing consciously in their soul-body. In summary, what is so striking here is that the 'hero' or initiate in this katabasis journey was seen as capable of raying out light to the souls of the Dead. This feature is perhaps the most striking of the various expressions of initiation; it is an ability which may not have been attained by all initiates or 'heroes'.

We have already noted that the Ode reflects points in the *Book of Sirach*, which was valued by the Essenes. Their scrolls reveal a strong focus on Sheol, that is the gloomy after-life circumstances of the Dead, who exist in a dark realm, which was also called 'the pit'. The theme in Ode 42, that help can be given to souls of the Dead by God (or an agent of God) in Sheol, is echoed in the scrolls, which reveal the Essenes' concern about this,

"I belonged to death because of my sins, and my iniquities had sold me to Sheol..."[45]

"He will deliver my soul from the Pit and direct my steps to the (rightful) Way."[46]

"...and how the Dead shall groan on account of all (*evil deeds?*)....(but) the dark places shall be made light because of Your abundance...."[47]

---

[45] Psalm 11PQS, p. 19 *The Dead Sea Scrolls*, Vermes, Penguin,1987.

[46] DSS, 1QS Vermes, p.79.

If the Christian elements are recognized as coincidental or as later additions, the dating of these poems could be put back to some decades BCE, or to early in the first century CE. In any event they are striking evidence for initiatory experiences occurring in the cultural landscape of the world in which Jesus was working. These were experiences which were attractive to the early Christians, since these odes were integrated into the early church's religious life.

Veiled esoteric words
It is important to note that in ancient times, initiatory experiences and knowledge were kept secret. Various everyday Greek words were selected as names of spiritual beings and other initiatory subjects; this enabled communications about esoteric matters to be veiled. But this also meant that a sentence could become ambiguous; and such communications in Hellenistic literature, when read by modern humanistic theologians, would very often be misunderstood. The nine ranks of divine beings have names such as 'Powers' or 'Mights' or 'Thrones'; yet the Greek words for these deities are also used in the everyday sense.

The important esoteric term, 'The Son of Man', used to designate a certain stage of initiatory spirituality, also means in Hebrew simply a human being, the offspring of another human being.

So part of the challenge of translating this Gospel has been to detect when the esoteric usage of a word is meant. Likewise when a verb is used for seership or higher consciousness experiences, this needs to be acknowledged (see Section 7 for more about this).

---

[47] DSS *Fragments* 4Q416,418; *The Dead Sea Scrolls Uncovered*, Eisenman & Wise, 1992.

Section 3

Various ranks of spiritual beings
In the Hellenistic Age, Scriptural texts and other esoteric writings which appear to derive from the Mysteries, are based on the premise that people can develop higher faculties of cognition, and through this, can perceive various ranks of spiritual beings. These deities became known as the ranks of 'divine Hierarchies'. (These are actual experienced spiritual entities, not social-theoretical constructs).

In Biblical literature various such deities are mentioned as a straightforward, unquestioned fact, because in antiquity it was accepted that seers and sages have this level of perception, and do perceive such deities. So there are no attempts in the Jewish Bible, nor in the Christian Scriptures, to persuade the reader that these deities exist. It was an accepted fact.

Many modern theologians pass over references to these beings in the Christian Scriptures, as this is not a concept that resonates with them, for it is not compatible with humanistic views. Such scholars will argue that the references to ranks of divine beings in a well-defined nine-fold form, first occurred in the 5th century in Greek texts named as the writings of Dionysos the Areopagite, a Christian figure of the first century.

The Book of Acts (17:34) describes that Dionysos was a first century student of St. Paul. According to Rudolf Steiner, Dionysos was instructed by Paul in the esoteric Judaic-Christian wisdom.[48] The texts bearing his name are regarded as a product of the 5th century, because of the style of the Greek text. As I wrote in *The Hellenistic Mysteries and Christianity*, there is therefore linguistically little support for identifying these texts about the Hierarchies, such as *The Divine Names,* as having been written by Dionysos the Areopagite.

However, dating texts from esoteric circles is prone to errors, because it was a tradition in such circles to transmit their treasured wisdom in an oral way for

---

[48] GA 103, lect., 20 May 1908.

centuries, only committing them to a written form much later. This becomes a source of error when assessing the age of the text. At the time the material is finally written down, the linguistic idiom of that century would naturally be used. Secondly, during the centuries that it was orally transmitted, there may well be some absorption of semantics and of concepts from the various eras through which it passed.

But significantly, a little-known esoteric text from the early centuries of Christianity, *The Testament of Adam*, establishes that in the early centuries of Christianity, nine ranks of divine beings, from Angels up to the Seraphine (or Seraphim) were known, and were an accepted part of the religious view on the cosmos. The date of this text is debated; but a number of scholars assign it to the 3rd century CE. It then pre-dates the manuscript with the name of Dionysus the Areopagite by about 200 years, but in my view it derives from the first century, with antecedents going back earlier.

These nine hierarchies are also mentioned in other early Christian texts, such as *The Cave of Treasures* and the *Book of the Bee*. However, these texts are usually dated to the 4th or 5th centuries AD. But again they may incorporate material from the 2nd century.

In addition, various Church Fathers formed their own lists of divine beings, which were similar to those passed down over the centuries in the name of Dionysos. St. Paul mentions some of these deities, in Eph.1:21 and in Col. 1:16. He also refers to fallen or malignant beings amongst the Hierarchies. That these lofty deities are cognized only through a higher consciousness empowered through a high spirituality, meant that there is very little mention of them outside of the more mystical Jewish or Christian texts, and these writings were discreetly circulated.

Often the ancient Christian writers affirmed the existence of knowledge of the ranks of hierarchies, which was kept away from public access. But these writers used the word 'Angel' for any of the ranks of hierarchical beings; so this can be confusing. For example, the early church writer, Athenagoras (in the

2nd. century CE), when explaining Christianity to the Roman Caesars, writes that,

> "Nor is our teaching, in what relates to divine reality, confined only to these points (i.*e., the Father, Son and Holy Spirit, just mentioned*); but we recognize also a multitude of spiritual beings who are 'ministers', whom....God...appointed, through the (agency of) the Logos, to their several places (in the cosmos)."[49]

But Athenagoras then says not a word more about the Hierarchies. The 'ministers' refer to various of the divine Hierarchies; the usual translations call them Angels. But this term here obviously refers to various ranks of deities. Origenes makes it fully clear that this word Angel, (which also means 'messenger' in Greek) can often mean various of the hierarchical beings, far above the rank of Angels, "These spirit mights who serve God, are the messengers ('angels') of God, and they consist of, on the one hand, certain Dominions, or Thrones or Principalities or Powers...."[50]

In addition, a Bishop Ignatius (ca. AD 120) in a letter to the church at Tralles, written when on his way to Rome, as a prisoner in chains, tells them,

"I myself, who, although in chains, am indeed able to comprehend heavenly things, with regard to the different ranks of spiritual beings, and the nature of the ruling deities.[51] In regard to this, things visible and invisible, I am already indeed a student."[52]

---

[49] *Writings of Athenagoras*, p.386, T. & T. Clarke, 1868.

[50] Origenes, *Commentary on John*, Bk. 10. #269

[51] Or, possibly: "the ranks of the Angels and the Hierarchy of the Principalities" (*Apostolic Fathers*, M. Holmes, Baker Books, Grand Rapid, 1999, p.163).

[52] "I am already indeed a student." Translated as "I am not yet a disciple" in *Apostolic Fathers*, (Holmes), reading 'ου' as οὐ (a negating adverb) and transferring it from 2 lines earlier. Since the original text had no accidences, as these generally appeared about 600 AD, I surmise it was intended to be οὖ or οὐ(ς). Otherwise it disconnects to the line above, 'Bear with

This is a rare glimpse into esoteric-initiatory strivings being discreetly carried out by an early Christian leader. He says nothing else about his endeavours to gain cognition of the various deities and realms. Apart from St. Paul, these beings are mentioned by name in early esoteric writings which pre-date the time of Jesus; in particular the Book of Enoch, and the Slavonic Book of Enoch.[53]

In modern times, Rudolf Steiner attained the higher spiritual consciousness capable of perceiving the various divine beings in the cosmos. In many lectures, he spoke from direct experience of the significance for humanity of these ranks of beings, or 'Hierarchies'. He gave a title to each rank of these beings, which points to the influence which each rank has exerted upon humanity during its evolving.

Included in this Section is a list of these spiritual beings and how often they are mentioned in the Bible. Most cultures from ancient times were informed about various kinds of deities, and their stories or religious texts convey in a simplified language, what the initiated priestesses or priests experienced of these beings.

That the existence of these ranks of beings has been widely ignored in theology, has impoverished the Christian religion, and resulted in divine phenomena, or higher human consciousness states, being ascribed to 'God', instead to whichever rank of these divinities are actually involved in this. In this regard, *The Testament of Abraham* for example states that:

Angels are intrusted with the watching over of human beings.

Archangels have the care all that is living; implying where life-forces are active behind matter.

---

me, in case I say things that are too esoteric for you'. There are various versions of the Greek text extant, Holmes follows Migne (*Patrol. Grae.* Tome 5, p.680 #92) with 'οὐ', but he deviates often from the Migne edition elsewhere.

[53] However, some scholars consider, regarding the Slavonic Enoch, that a later Christian writer possibly added some material.

Archai or Principalities have a responsibility for the Earth's meteorological energies.
The Powers have a primary role with light as it appears from the Sun, Moon and stars....

These comments, though brief, are an invaluable testimonial to the awareness of these hierarchies amongst the early Christians. The teachings about the hierarchies preserved from Dionysos the Areopagite are much less specific, and more theological-philosophical in tone. It has probably been subject to editorial activity carried out in an increasingly hostile world.

Pre-existence and Post-existence
Another context in which the Gospels were written, is one in which the soul is comprehended as a reality in its own right. Hence it was not considered the by-product of bodily electrical impulses and chemical nerve processes. As such, the soul comes into the body from spiritual realms, and after death, it returns to these realms, and undergoes a journey into ever higher realms.

Scholars are aware that it is, and has been for some millennia, a core perspective in spiritual literature, that the soul undergoes 'transmigration', that is, it eventually returns to the Earth for another life. This concept, which is now known as 'reincarnation', is famously not part of Christian theological beliefs. The view has long existed that it contradicts or invalidates the concept of Salvation by Christ.

However, the concept of Salvation and the idea of repeated earth-lives, is not seen as incompatible, when viewed with an esoteric perspective. To explore this, it is necessary firstly to make an historical survey into the topic of reincarnation in Biblical literature. We need to briefly discuss: was 'reincarnation' or the similar concept of 'transmigration', once an accepted part of Christian beliefs. Did it once have a place in theological views of the early Church Fathers? From this, two major questions arise. If it is regarded as a valid possibility, how can this be brought into harmony with Christianity? If is not valid, but widely accepted, why was it not opposed by Jesus?

This theme is highly controversial for various reasons: one is a disappointing quality of research by prejudiced writers which has distorted understanding of core texts from the early days of the church. This is due to a highly subjective mindset which has been allowed to colour the debate. This occurs from both sides.

Such subjectivity occurs from those who feel that to affirm the idea of reincarnation as compatible with Christianity is to undermine the sacred truths of the Gospels. It also occurs with those who feel that reincarnation and therefore 'karma' are self-evident from the experience of life itself, and that it is vital to incorporate this into Christianity. Instead of a detailed presentation of the arguments for and against reincarnation with regard to Christianity, I shall endeavour to provide some clarity by firstly pointing out that virtually all 'New Age' books which argue that reincarnation was definitely part of the early church, are unfortunately misleading.

Reincarnation, transmigration and the Bible
These books often provide false quotes from early Christian authorities. For example, it can be declared that:
A: Justin Martyr "affirmed many earth-lives as a reality" – but Justin never did this in any of his writings. He once presented this idea as valid – but not from himself, he was representing the teachings of Plato, and then arguing against this, in an imaginary dialogue.
B: that St. Gregory of Nyssa "affirmed many earth-lives, for the soul to be purified" – but Gregory never did in any of his writings. This assertion is simply untrue.
C: that St. Jerome "affirmed many earth-lives, to a certain Avitus" (in letter no. 124) – yes, Jerome did, **but** he was quoting a passage from Origenes, and was then strongly condemning it.

Various other famous early Christian authorities can be cited by New Age writers as teaching this idea; but these writers give no reference as to when and where this was allegedly said by church leaders. The fact is that nowhere in the teachings of any notable Church Father is this concept ever taught.

The Nine Hierarchies

Biblical name	R. Steiner's term	Meaning of name

The highest group: the First Hierarchy, are:

Seraphim[54]	Seraphim	inflaming, noble (Hebrew)
Cherubim	Cherubim	grasping (Hebrew)[55]
Thrones	Thrones	throne, seat (Greek: *Thronoi*) (2x in NT)

The middle group, the Second Hierarchy are:

Dominions	Spirits of Wisdom	dominion Greek: *Kyriotaetes* (4x in NT)
Mights	Spirits of Movement	inherent power Greek: *Dynameis* (3x in NT)
Powers	Spirits of Form	active power Greek: *Exousiai* (7x in NT)

The lower group, the Third Hierarchy are:

Principalities	Spirits of Personality or Primal Beginnings	beginning, origin Greek: *Archai* (8x in NT)
Archangels	Spirits of Fire	chief of the angels Greek: *Archangeloi* (2x in NT)
Angels	Spirits of Twilight	messenger Greek: *Angeloi*

---

[54] In the plural they are more correctly, the Cherubine and Seraphine.

[55] The references to Cherubim & Seraphim in the Bible can refer to lesser beings, but these names have been used for the two highest ranks.

But a special mention should be made of the brilliant and esoterically informed Origenes, for he is represented in New Age books as affirming reincarnation. To summarize the situation here, I conclude – along with many scholars – that Origenes very probably did accept reincarnation, but proof of this is very difficult to provide.

He avoided directly stating this, and sometimes he was alluding to the soul going on into some other realm of being (technically, this is 'transmigration'), not coming back to the Earth (i.e., reincarnation). But in his *Commentary on the Gospel of John*, when writing about the Baptist and Elijah (in Bk.6) it is obvious that he wishes to let this concept be presented, as one who supports it, and yet not openly reveal his agreement.

Secondly, as with any person ahead of their time, Origenes' work was met with confusion. His texts were therefore at times condemned as heretical, or copied in haste, in a somewhat abbreviated or inaccurate manner. Sometimes they were translated into Latin improperly, because the translator, to avoid serious consequences to himself for making available 'heretical' notions, omitted some of the text or 'watered-down' some passages.

As a result in one place, Origenes is discussing the fate of the soul, when he states that he shall cease from further exploration of the topic, in case he "enters into the wrong doctrine of reincarnation". This is a very obscure comment, which can be interpreted as either for, or against, reincarnation. In other places he apparently condemns reincarnation as false, yet in various places his arguments closely and logically imply that it is true.

There is however, one text where Origenes is clearly confirming reincarnation; but it is not from a specific, identifiable book written by him. It is quoted by St. Jerome in a letter written about AD 404 (to Avitus mentioned above).[56] But this text was obtained by Jerome from an unknown source, and may not be genuine. Such sources need not be invalid; they are known as 'catenae' and occur in regard to other early

---

[56] The reference is in sections 7 and 15 of letter #124.

church fathers. They are 'lost' texts, preserved only in the writings of other church fathers, often in the margins of their manuscripts.

But since the above text quoted by Jerome is a 'catenae' text, academics consider that it may not actually be from Origenes, and so it is usually ignored. I am inclined to regard it as a valid text, showing that Origenes did accept reincarnation; but no proof of this conclusion is available, except the general trend in his identifiable writings. A similar situation applies to remarks from Theophilus, Patriarch of Alexandria around 400 CE. He too states that Origenes taught reincarnation, which Theophilus then condemns. But his alleged comments are also without any evidence, and were made in highly politically charged circumstances.

Now, the literature from the other side of the argument, against the idea of reincarnation, also suffers from problems. Texts which do point towards a figure in the Biblical world as accepting reincarnation are misinterpreted to avoid this conclusion. But on a logical and intuitive level, those who argue against reincarnation are left with only weak alternatives.

People can point to horrific circumstances that can destroy our lives and our hopes, or to exceptional abilities existing in a person, or to wonderful opportunities that open up to someone, and denied to someone else. If reincarnation is not accepted, then such human circumstances must derive from either chance, or because God had 'pre-destined' these things to occur.

These alternative solutions are deeply unsatisfactory to many people. For a discerning view of life usually concludes that events and abilities have a cause; a cause that is the natural metamorphosis of dynamics entered into in a past life, not laid down by a divine decree. This leads to the conclusion that the abilities of this current life must also have a cause, and this can only be found in a past lifetime. The apparent conflict between this concept and Christianity is discussed below.

Repeated lives on Earth: the cultural context of Jesus
Historically, this concept was very widespread at the time of Christ and well known in the Jewish and Greek

Hellenistic world, as well as in the Celtic peoples of Europe, where Christianity would soon be encountered. It was not a prominent, publicly advocated truth; rather, it was present as an undercurrent. It was nevertheless, a significant feature in the cultural-religious life of the time of Jesus.

For example, in a mystical text in the Apocrypha, *The Wisdom of Solomon*, the writer speaks of himself as a soul who had been pre-existing, and thereby implying a past life which produced good karma for this life:

"As a child I was born to excellence, and (so) a noble soul fell to my lot; or rather, I myself was noble and therefore I entered into an unblemished body..."

These thoughts today are rejected as a form of prejudice in regard to physical infirmity, but it still serves as an example of the acceptance of reincarnation and karma amongst Hellenistic people. It is relevant here to note that Origenes states that the concept of reincarnation had been held for many centuries by the Jews, hence they asked the Baptist if he were Elijah. Origenes also taught that the idea of reincarnation "was part of the secret teachings of the Jews".[57]

These words of Origenes are shown to be correct by a prominent and esoterically informed Jewish sage, a writer of many metaphysical treatises, Philo Judaeus (20 BCE - CE 50). Philo was a contemporary of Jesus, but lived in Alexandria, in Egypt, (and hence was not aware of Jesus). He wrote openly of the pre-existence of souls, of existence in spirit realms and also of reincarnation. In his treatise *On Dreams*, he is writing about many souls being in spirit realms, apparently not far from the Earth. He then comments,

"Now of these many souls, on the one hand some indeed descend, to be bound to mortal bodies, but others ascend. The number of (this latter group of) souls, and the timing of their ascending, is determined according to their inherent nature. (Whereas) the former group of souls yearn for mortal life, and eagerly turn back again

---

[57] Origenes, *The Commentary on John*, Bk. 6, #73.

towards it (to be reincarnated).... whereas the latter souls view this as foolishness and as a prison..."⁵⁸

(trans. A.A.)

Moreover, there are the references affirming reincarnation in the writings of Josephus (37-100 CE), another very prominent Jewish scholar, a famous historian. He gives advice about the fate of the deceased, which demonstrates that reincarnation was indeed part of his religious worldview. In his *Wars of the Jews*, (b.j.3.372-74) he states with regard to deceased virtuous people, that they are allotted a place in Heaven; but then later,

"....at the turning-point of the Age, pious souls are again put into a new body".⁵⁹

"the turning-point of the Age": this refers to a time-cycle of some kind. It is not clear as what cosmic-spiritual cycle is meant here, but his words demonstrate that in esoteric groups within Judaism, there was knowledge about the spiritual context and cosmic cycles underlying the soul's existence after death, and when it is to time to reincarnate.

Some scholars, to whom reincarnation is not an acceptable concept, have sought to interpret these words of Josephus to mean that good souls are given a new 'replacement' body of a celestial-physical kind suitable for existence in Paradise, and not on the Earth. The basis for this interpretation is that the Pharisees believed in a universal Resurrection of humanity from the Dead, which results in people at some future time existing in this celestial-physical existence in Paradise.

But Josephus here emphasizes that souls are **once again** given a **physical** body.⁶⁰ In other words, to

---

⁵⁸ Philo, *On Dreams*, Bk.1: 138-39.

⁵⁹ "a *new* body" literally, "into a *replacement dwelling*". (ἀντ{ι}-ενοικίζονται: not a 'counter' body, but a replacement body.) The Greek: ἔνθεν ἐκ περιτροπῆς αἰώνων ἁγνοῖς πάλιν ἀντενοικίζονται σώμασιν.

⁶⁰ Josephus goes on to say that bad souls stay in the darkness of Hades, but we note that he says Hades (ᾅδης) which is **not** Hell. For Hell is Tartarus in Greek, so the bad souls are only

Josephus, there is no inconsistency in his worldview: the souls incarnate again and again, until at some future Age there shall be a climactic Day of Judgement.
In addition, in his treatise *Against Apion*, (2.218) because of the wars and civil commotion causing many causalities at the time, Josephus again writes about the fate of souls after death. This time he states that if a person dies through noble actions then,

"...the soul comes into earthly being again, at the completed cycle, to then receive a better earthly life.[61]

Now, Josephus was also a Pharisee, therefore it is quite possible that other members of the Sanhedrin at the time of Jesus, and presumably long before, also held this view.
"soul comes into earthly being": There was no verb in the Greek language for 'reincarnated' (just as the English language did not have this word, until 1828). The Greek verbal context used here, is how in ancient Greek a writer says, 'reincarnated'. It is based on the verb in Biblical language for being 'incarnated'. The same word is translated in the King James Bible as, "begotten". Also, the Greek word used for 'better life' here is 'bion' (βίον) which specifically refers only to earthly existence, and not to existence in a spirit realm.

But another text, an extremely remarkable, obscure, highly esoteric document, preserved in a Coptic manuscript, contains statements from Jesus, as the Risen Saviour, which specifically teach reincarnation. This is the fascinating *Pistis Sophia*, wherein the risen Jesus is recorded as speaking to his disciples in private sessions, about higher realms and their beings.[62] This is

---

placed in a darker part of the soul-realm. There is possibly the implication that these souls may later be re-born.

[61] The Greek ...γενέσθαι τε πάλιν καὶ βίον ἀμείνω λαβεῖν ἐκ περιτροπῆς. "at the completed cycle": literally, 'out of the turning-point', (or turning around, or circuit). Translated by Whiston as, "at a 'certain revolution of things'..."

[62] Chapters 110-112 refer to the discarnate soul being cast into a body again. This immensely interesting papyrus is somewhat obscure and being highly esoteric is not considered

further evidence that to some early Christians, reincarnation was an accepted and core truth, taught by Jesus.

Why was this topic not mentioned in the Gospels?
The most significant point about the concept of reincarnation and the teachings of Jesus is this: since it was a wide spread well-known idea, and regarded as a core truth of human existence by some highly regarded Jews and Greeks, as well as many 'Gnostic Christians' - the silence from Jesus and from St. Paul on this subject is very significant.

In view of just how widespread was awareness of, or belief in, reincarnation, it must be said about the Gospels and the idea of repeated Earth lives, that a conspicuous silence was maintained about this very significant idea. This silence is all the more important and enigmatic to those people to whom it is a true concept.

If the idea of reincarnation is a direct threat to, and incompatible with, the Gospel message, as those people think who are opposed to this idea, why did not Jesus or Paul warn against it? Was there not a moral necessity to make such a warning?

Nowhere in the Gospels is reincarnation specifically identified and declared to be a false, harmful belief. Nowhere in the Gospels is it specifically identified and declared to be true. There are various Biblical texts which have been used to oppose the idea of reincarnation, but none of them actually specifically declare reincarnation to be false.

For example, in the *Epistle of the Hebrews* it is declared that "we only die once"; but this cannot be used as the basis of an argument here. For this text is simply saying that just as human beings die once in their life, so too did the sacrifice of Christ occur but once. (Heb. 9:27) So the writer of Hebrews is simply pointing out that we only die once, in a lifetime.

---

as relevant to Christian theological studies. This is partly because it is dated to the 3rd or 4th centuries; but I regard it as primarily a valid document of the first century, although the current manuscript itself is of a much later date.

In essence, the opposition to the idea of reincarnation comes from its apparent incompatibility with the doctrine of the resurrection of human beings at the 'end of time', bringing Salvation to humanity, and that no ongoing further efforts are needed for a spiritual validity, since Christ has redeemed humanity, (see below for comments about this topic).

The most insightful explanation of this enigma that I have encountered was given by Rudolf Steiner. He explains that Jesus wished to avoid this aspect of human existence in his teachings, because the times were changing, so it was not appropriate to emphasize this concept. People were moving into a more individuated sense of self, away from the extended family-group feeling; and this change in the sense of self, is directly affected by the idea of repeated earth-lives. An impulse towards a strong self-awareness is weakened by immersion in the idea of many lives, and journeying through associated spiritual realms.

Christianity is the religion of the individual, of the personal self. Jesus was appealing to the core of our inner self – what are doing with your life, in terms of ethics? Although Christianity is very much about the human community, and caring for each other, its teachings are an appeal to the individual to develop a personally derived morality within, for which a strong sense of selfhood is needed. This is the only basis possible for a spiritual human being of the future, and for a caring community life.

According to Rudolf Steiner this subtle change and development in human consciousness, towards a strong awareness of self, was why Jesus avoided reference to the concept of repeated earth lives.[63] For freedom from an externally implied sense of self, and freedom from an externally imposed code of ethics, can only be attained in the confines of an individuated self-sense. This is the reason for these words of Jesus:

"If anyone comes to me and does not inwardly reject his father and mother, his wife and children, his brothers

---

[63] In various lectures, e.g., GA 131, lect., 14 Oct. 1911.

and sister, yes, even his own life – he cannot be my disciple." (Lk. 14:26)

(These words are usually very poorly translated as, "hate father and mother...").[64] So here Christ is declaring that unless you inwardly reject mother and father and other family members, **as the basis of what you feel yourself to be,** (in a deeper sense) then you can have no part of Him. For any such higher persona, or 'I', is what the Christ-light bestows upon us. So Jesus is simply pointing out that a blood-related link to someone needs to be on a lower level of priority, in regard to one's own sense of self.

Salvation and karma
In the light of the above thoughts, the idea 'Christ has saved us' or 'Christ has brought Salvation' needs to be re-examined. This was a concept developed when Christianity was new, hence over the past 2,000 year phase humanism gradually became predominant, and esoteric, cosmic perspectives on life were not so welcome.

From an esoteric Christian viewpoint, Salvation is seen as the outcome of the deed of the cosmic Christ (also known as the great 'solar Logos' or 'sun-god Christ', see below) through the death and resurrection of Jesus. This has made possible the spiritual perfecting of human beings, over the course of time. It has disempowered to a substantial degree, the influences of the malignant powers. As a result, in life after life, the soul can find the impulse to make the ethical decision, and to avoid the wrong way of being.

But this deed of Christ has not obliterated the ability of the individual to make his or her own decision. Individuals can still maintain their freedom, and make deeply unethical decisions, which shall affect their karma. But such cosmic perspectives were not part of the Christian world-view in the past, as we noted above. So this fuller understanding of life in a spiritual context

---

[64] The Greek verb here (miseoe - μισέω) can mean to hate, but it also means to abhor or dislike. There is here perhaps typical Semitic hyperbole.

could not be taught, nor comprehended, if this were taught. The message had to be adapted to the needs and demands of the times.

The dynamics and structure of Creation and of the human being, upon which the esoteric Gospel teachings are based.

There were various mystical groups of the Hellenistic Age, to whom the cosmos was a many-sided reality. This context is an integral part of the culture and thought-world of the time of Jesus. To such groups, the cosmos consists not only of the physical-mineral realm, but also of life-forces which maintain life in all living beings. Then above this realm of life-forces or 'ethereal energies' is a series of seven realms in which the so-called Dead exist.

This could be called the Soul-world, and it was viewed in Hellenistic times as sevenfold. Its seven realms are identified in Hellenistic texts with the seven planetary spheres of the Ptolemaic solar system. These spheres are thought of as spiritual realms, in which various ranks of deities manifest.

In addition, zodiacal influences were prominent in Hellenistic spiritual systems, in both Greek and Jewish cultures. In the Bible, the number twelve and seven are both prominent; especially striking is the selection of twelve tribes and twelve disciples. This may be viewed as a direct indication of the actual presence of an underlying zodiacal influence in the fabric of Israel's tribes and in the disciples of Jesus.

To the Greeks and Romans, the highest aspect of 'the Divine' was in fact a trinity of leading deities. But in addition the concept of 'God' was understood as the "twelve-fold divine gods" (hoi doedeka theoi – οἱ δώδεκα θεοί). So this phrase became a standard, common expression throughout the Hellenistic world; as scholars noted, "it designated the unity and totality of the gods who ruled creation."[65] Therefore, in contrast to the traditional theological approach, whenever a Gospel text appears to be referring to either planetary or zodiacal

---

[65] As noted in the *Theologisches Wörterbuch*, (*Theological Dictionary*) vols. 1-13, edit. Kittel, vol. 3, p.57, article 'θέος'.

themes, this shall be noted and explored in the commentary for that verse.

With regard to the number seven, various documents in extra-Biblical Hellenistic literature refer to the existence of seven realms where the Dead exist. Beyond the sevenfold 'soul-realms', there are also higher spiritual realms, such as the realm of Plato's Archetypal Idea; but little was written about these higher realms.

The human being is viewed as having in addition to the physical body, a life-force field permeating the body; and the air was viewed as permeated by this 'ether' energy.

The soul itself is experienced as triune. There are three words for the triune qualities of our soul in the Hebrew Bible, but they are expressed in just one generic word in modern languages, such as 'soul' or 'mind'.

The emotions and desires are one specific aspect. If the mind was referred to as a general attitude tinged with feeling, or if emotions are directly mentioned, the word 'Nephesch' was used for this in the Hebrew Bible. For example, in Psalm 43,5 "Why art thou cast down, O my soul?"

Whereas when the more logical, rational mind was the focus, the word 'Ruach' was used, as in these two examples:

"...the Pharaoh's soul was hardened." (Deut 2:30.)

"A wise man knows the thoughts that come to his soul, but the fool utters all his soul." (Prov. 29:11)

(Ruach was also used when referring to intelligence in a broad sense; so it was used of spiritual entities or the intentions of God.)

Additionally, a third word was reserved for a third faculty of the soul; a capacity for cognition which is beyond logic, and best defined as intuitive insight, bordering on spiritual cognizing. In the Hebrew Bible the word 'Neschamah' was used for this. But this third faculty is only rarely experienced by most people, and hence it occurs very rarely in the Hebrew Scriptures. When it does occur with regard to the soul, it refers to a deeply spiritual aspect of the soul. This is demonstrated for example in these words,

"The soul of the human being is the lamp of the Lord, shining into his innermost being." (Prov. 20: 27)

"It is the soul of the human being which is the spirit of the Most High, this gives a person spiritual insights." (Job 32.8)

There were parallels in Greek to at least two of these terms. Aristotle used 'Orektikon' when he was referring to the 'desire-soul', and 'Kinektikon' when referring to the logical, intellectual mind. Greek texts of an esoteric kind also have nouns that are not in common use today, such as 'soul-body' and 'spirit-body'. The Gospel translations offered in this book incorporate awareness of the subtle and complex nuances of language, and the mystical-esoteric context of the life of Jesus, as noted above.

Section 4

The cosmic nature of Christ

The religious texts of Christianity contain statements that are extremely striking, in that they imply that the central being in Christianity has a supreme importance. For example, in the Gospel of St. John, in 6:51, it is (apparently) Jesus who says,

> "I am the living bread that came down from heaven. If anyone eats of this bread, he will live forever. This bread is my flesh, which I will give for the life of the world."

This, and other passages, give the impression that the speaker is more than a mortal human being. It requires the speaker of these words to have a more than human status to substantiate such a potent claim. Such words also imply that the speaker has a very important role in the ongoing future of humanity. The implication of Origenes' writings, and of certain verses in the Gospels, are that statements such as these in 6:51 derive from the fact that a divine being, not only a human being, is involved.

And when this is understood, the relation of Jesus to the Divine can be much more clearly grasped. To make this distinction may well have an impact which is unwelcome to those who are committed Christians. For this brings complexity and hence confusion into a personal, sacred space of the soul. However, once these additional features of divine realities are grasped, then the feelings of reverence re-emerge, but now integrated with a much more empowered understanding of Christianity.

A statement from Rudolf Steiner, which has the quality of a Zen Buddhist koan, provides a hint of what this initiate understands Christianity to be,

> "Christianity began as a religion, but is greater than all religions, including Christianity."[66]

---

[66] GA 97, lect., 17 March, 1907.

In other words, what we know (or, don't really know) as Christianity is in fact something else, something which transcends the formal structure of a religion. The words in v. 6:51 point to a veiled cosmic facet of Christianity. The essential message of esoteric Christianity is that the death and resurrection of Christ have a pivotal role in a vast process, unfolding throughout long Ages, through which humanity is being offered the possibility of achieving a wonderful future goal: the Spiritual-self, rather than the normal earthly personality.

According to Steiner, humanity has been developing on Earth ever more as to its consciousness qualities, through a series of Ages or time-cycles. During this evolutionary process humanity descends down from non-material realms into the physical, material Earth, through many lifetimes.

Jesus or Christ ?
In Christian theology there is a lack of clarity regarding the nature of Jesus and of God. To Origenes and Rudolf Steiner, there is a sublime cosmic deity overshadowing Jesus, and that this deity may be called the 'cosmic Christ'. A deity is a different kind of entity to a human, even the most sacred human being. However, it is also understood that the person Jesus, after the Baptism in the River Jordan, became eternally united to this cosmic deity, becoming the archetype of what future humanity is to inwardly move towards.

To Rudolf Steiner, Jesus was of immense sanctity. He taught that for a person to be Christian, she or he needs to consciously make a sincere inner decision to be someone who regards Jesus Christ as their Saviour. But he also pointed out that awareness of the cosmic nature of 'Christ' is crucial to achieve a consciously spiritual-insightful comprehension of Christian truth. As a result, the words 'Saviour' and 'Salvation' take on a much clearer and more specific meaning, as will become clear in the new translation of the Gospel.

There exists a sublime spiritual being; the so-called 'cosmic Christ'. But already here some confusion occurs, because the term 'Christ' is a Greek term which translates a Hebrew word for 'Messiah', which refers to a human being who is anointed, thereby becoming the vessel of the 'Divine'. Technically, in the old Hebrew world, there were many 'Messiahs', because the term referred to all those who were anointed by priests as agents of God, such as their kings.

In Christian theology, Jesus is understood to be 'Christ', in that he was anointed directly by God, in a spiritual sense, thereby extending this idea of being a vessel of the divine, up to its highest level. But in addition, Christian theologians regard Jesus as an aspect of God. This idea needs to be clarified, for the use of the word 'Christ' both for the human Messiah and for a deity has led to confusion.

This confusion is embodied in the view that Jesus is also the Logos or Word, mentioned in the Prologue of St. John's Gospel. Then the confusion here is compounded by concluding that the Logos is an aspect of God, and not a specific, separate deity. Theologians have reached their conclusion by thinking that when Jesus is referred to as "The Son of God" he must be a direct offspring of God. This problem was exacerbated when the phrase 'The Son of God' was thought to refer to the Logos. Both of the conclusions are regarded as erroneous in esoteric Christianity, and will now be explored.

Indications of a 'cosmic' Christ

In esoteric terms, the word 'Christ' refers, in a formal usage, to the cosmic being who came upon (or 'anointed') Jesus at the Baptism in the Jordan River. So the person known as 'Jesus Christ' is a being consisting of the man Jesus, and also of the deity, the Christ being, who became present within him, as from the Baptism in the Jordan. This viewpoint of two distinct, but deeply interlinked entities being involved, was held by some Christians in the early church, but later was condemned as a heresy.[67]

The implication of the Book of Genesis is that originally humanity existed in a non-material state, a

---

[67] Associated with Adoptionism, identified as starting with Theodotus in AD 190, is one form of this perspective; and Monophysitism (associated with Eutyches (378-454) is another, and Apollinarianism (Syria 4th cent.) is another.

kind of Paradise. But in this state, humanity was not endowed with a sense of self-hood. The descent of souls into the 'incarnate' state of living in a flesh body made possible the development of an ego or sense of self, but this process of being within the physical world, was also inherently a process which would bring about a spirit-deserted materialism and ego-centric sensuality, and thus a potential for evil in the human being.

This change in humanity's existence is what the expression, the 'Fall of Man' means, when esoterically viewed. Then the reference to Eve tempting Adam does not refer to a woman, but to everyone's capacity in primordial times for sentiency, and thus our feelings and desires.

To enable humanity to have the needed spiritual capacity to conquer the lower qualities and to bring to birth the 'Higher-self', the cosmic Christ descended to the Earth, to sacrificially carry out a deed, through Jesus of Nazareth, intended to bring about the reversal of this cosmic process. This deed of Christ can be regarded as a sublime manifestation of the love of the Father-God for humanity.

The events on Golgotha hill
This deed started at the Baptism in the Jordan, through which the deity, the cosmic Christ, united spiritually to the soul of Jesus and to the life-forces (or etheric body) of Jesus. In addition, this cosmic being also permeated the energy template sustaining the physical body of Jesus.

This process was achieved by the sacrificial death on the cross; and then fully completed by the mysterious events of the Resurrection. Rudolf Steiner refers to these events as 'the Mystery of Golgotha'. He was thereby alluding to the initiation processes carried out in the ancient Mysteries, in which the Higher-self of the acolyte was brought into being. His point here is that the coming of the Christ to the Earth was a parallel event, except that it was on a planetary scale.

In addition to the Resurrection bringing the opportunity for the life-forces and soul of human beings to be spiritualized, there were also spiritual energies permeating Jesus which maintain the underlying energetic structure of the physical body. Thus through the events which led to the death and resurrection of Jesus, the human soul, and its life-forces (or etheric energies) were rescued from an inner withering and darkening. But there was also the renewal given to the bodily aspect of the human being; (not the protoplasm, but the underlying forces of the physical body). For this reason the bodily resurrection of Jesus is a theme included in the Gospels.

Steiner gives a very insightful explanation of this enigmatic theme.[68] It refers to the rescuing of the tenuous physical energy-field, which underlies the physical body. This archetype of the body will be needed forever, and is actually a separate thing from the protoplasm or flesh which fills it out in varying ways, in the different evolutionary phases.

The process of Jesus being over-shadowed by the sublime deity, the cosmic Christ, allowed this cosmic deity to speak to humanity, through Jesus. But more important than his teachings are the deeds which he carried out, especially that of permeating the planet with His (or more accurately, Its) own divine spiritual light. Before considering the deeds of Christ, the absence of the Nativity stories need to be noted. That an account of the birth of Jesus is omitted in this Gospel is a unique aspect, but this allows it to start with the Logos.

The events of the conception and birth of Jesus, such as the rejoicing of the Angels and the visit of the Magi, are two of the prominent features of the Nativity in the synoptic gospels. The birth of Jesus is given prominence, because this emphasizes the uniquely holy nature of the child; the only 'unfallen' soul in humanity. It was this exceptional inner goodness which enabled Jesus to be the vessel of the Christ.

This understanding is affirmed in the Gospel of John, but it is approached from a deeper, wider perspective, in which the involvement of the Logos or cosmic Christ is seen as central, and vital for humanity's spiritual future.

---

[68] Mentioned throughout lectures in GA 131.

As the vessel of a deity so near to God, Jesus embodied in his actions a selfless love, and his teaching about love was unique. As with many other founders of a religion, he taught people to forgive their friends and family for any wrongs they may have done, and to love their neighbours.

In addition however, Jesus taught people to love their enemies, that is to refrain from developing hatred and revengeful desires, and to bring active good-will towards them. This state of deep goodness is known as 'agape' in Christianity. Such actions by human beings today are an expression of the influence of Christ, active in the soul as a kind of enhanced conscience. So the events occurring on Golgotha hill at Jerusalem are understood to result in a permeation of the aura of the Earth with sublime spiritual energies. As Jesus died on the cross, the great deity illumining him, the cosmic Christ, merged its own divine life-forces and soul with the soul of our planet, with mother Earth. This is the most sacred and most important event in the lifespan of the planet.

This event resulted in a radiant spiritual light permanently imbuing our planet. Rudolf Steiner describes how this event can be seen by the modern initiate. If from a position far out in space, the seer gazes down to the Earth, but then goes back to the time when the Crucifixion occurred, a golden light in the shape of a star, is seen arising in the distant Earth's own aura.[69]

So the term 'the cosmic Christ' refers to a divine being who united to the Earth-soul. The key dates in the life of Jesus are a matter of dispute; some scholars, including Steiner, date the crucifixion as occurring on the 3rd April, AD 33. He describes how this permeation of our planet by the cosmic Christ, the 'Christ-light' has made accessible to all human beings the spiritual matrix of spirituality, or the 'Spiritual-self' (or a Son of Man).

In addition, the light is also the source of a future higher level of spirituality, referred to by Steiner as the 'Life-spirit' (or a Son of God). As noted earlier, he

---

[69] GA 103, lect., 26 May, 1908.

explains in regard to the Life-spirit, that as a soul becomes sanctified, the life-forces which maintain our body, and underlie reproduction, etc, may also be permeated by divine energies.

This allows the person to attain remarkable healing powers and artistic abilities, and to ray out into the environment influences which bring about harmony and* healing to the world; this is the 'Life-Spirit' or Son of God state. There is evidence of a 'cosmic' Christ in the Christian Scriptures; these will now be discussed. This topic is related to the idea of the 'pre-existence of Jesus'.

There are several places in the Gospels where, in a discreet manner, the words or deeds of the Messiah are those of a high deity, not of a man. In fact, of that deity who is referred to as 'God' in the Book of Genesis, Chapt.1. The term for God here is 'the Elohim', a plural word; the cosmic Christ is the leader of these deities, according to Rudolf Steiner.[70] Whereas, from chapter Two in Genesis onwards, it is primarily not the Christ, but Jahve, another of these deities, who is referred to when, the word 'God' or 'the Lord' is mentioned. See Section 6 where these passages are discussed.

The cosmic Christ and Jesus in the Gospel of John
The report about the Last Supper in John's Gospel occupies five chapters, whereas the report in Mark's Gospel occupies just eight verses, and Matthew uses thirteen verses. John's report culminates in the 17th chapter, with the 'Prayer of the High Priest', wherein startling passages occur. For although the reader assumes that Jesus is always speaking, sometimes the cosmic Christ itself is speaking through Jesus, as a more specifically, separate being.

In the address given at the Last Supper, in Chapter 17, there is an especially startling example of this. Verse two in this majestic, profound chapter, has statements about how it is God's intention, through Christ, that people receive "eternal life".

---

[70] GA 103, in various lectures.

What is 'eternal life'?
This core term is more understandable, and more accurately translated as 'aeonic existence'. In other words, the phrase actually means after death, human beings may have conscious existence (or 'life') in the divine worlds, called 'the aeons' in Hellenistic times. This state may also be attained before death in special instances. This concept is of huge significance; there are references to attaining such transcendent high spirituality in Buddhism and Hinduism, for example. Such a deep term can be much more profoundly understood once the structure of the cosmos and of the human being is known.

But 'eternal life' stands as a viable term without acquiring such knowledge, as one's heart can sense its meaning. However, when one knows that there exists divine realms (called aeons) beyond the Soul-world, and that deep meditative practice and spiritual study can bring about some resonance in the human consciousness with these higher realms, then this term 'eternal life' grows ever more meaningful.

The entire purpose one could say, of the creating of humanity is that people attain to this high consciousness in the future, and thereby to an eternal sense of self. The term is further discussed under v. 3:15.

Then in verse three, words occur which have deeply perplexed theologians down through the centuries, as they are truly startling, and for which these scholars could not find a satisfactory explanation. In the NIV version these are,

John 17:3 Now this is eternal life: that they may know you the only true God, and Jesus Christ, whom you have sent.

In my translation:

17:3 And this is the aeonic existence: that they cognize You {as} the only true God, and Jesus, the Anointed One {as} the one You sent forth. [71]

At first, it seems that here Jesus is referring **to himself by his own name** - but this is extremely unlikely, in this context, or in any context. The name "Jesus Christ" means "Jesus, the Anointed One" which means, 'the Messiah'. The Aramaic equivalent of this phrase was used in Palestine and beyond, and would have been used of Jesus by his contemporaries who were discussing him. Only gradually, as the Gospel message was spread via the Greek language, was the Greek term "Christ" used instead of 'Anointed One' or 'Messiah'.

Over some decades this expression, "Jesus, the Anointed One" (the Messiah), became fixed into a kind of set name, "Jesus Christ". But these words recorded in the Gospel were spoken before that happened; the famous term, "Jesus Christ" had not yet historically come into being. This happened primarily only decades later, as the Christian religion was forming.

So, here we have the speaker naming a person called 'Jesus', who is defined as the Messiah, therefore one may conclude that the speaker in this verse **is not Jesus**, because a person does not normally refer to themselves by their own name. Scholars have noticed this startling fact, and are perplexed by this sentence; some have suggested that these words come from the writer of the Gospel, and **not from Jesus**.

I have concluded from a study of the Greek text that the speaker is the cosmic Christ, (understood as being present within Jesus, as alluded to already by the Baptist when he proclaimed the "Lamb of God").

Here is a passage **wherein actually the cosmic Christ is speaking, and who names Jesus as a separate being, as the Messiah.** A divine being is declaring that to attain an empowered consciousness in divine realms (to have 'eternal life'), human beings need to have some inner unity with, or intuitive awareness of, the spiritual

---

[71] The Greek here is: αὕτη δέ ἐστιν ἡ αἰώνιος ζωή ἵνα γινώσκωσιν σὲ τὸν μόνον ἀληθινὸν θεὸν καὶ ὃν ἀπέστειλας Ἰησοῦν Χριστόν

reality, or God; and they also need an awareness of Jesus as the Messiah, as the vessel of God. But see v. 17:3 for further discussion of this topic.

It has been noted that theologians had concluded that 'Jesus was/is God'. But the word God is in itself a term which is not specific, and actually can be inclusive of the activity of many divine beings. Lacking awareness of this, theological conclusions about what 'God' was, accelerated the non-understanding of the highly esoteric, transcendent reality of the cosmic Christ. Consequently, there was no chance of this sentence in v.17:3 being understood as involving the man Jesus and also a deity. In fact for many centuries, in their confusion, Church Fathers interpreted the sentence to mean,

> This is eternal life; that they may know You and Jesus Christ, whom You have sent: the only true God.

In other words, God and Jesus are here defined as the same being. This way of interpreting the Greek is not in accordance with the grammar, and is derived from a powerful wish to be faithful to the understanding that Jesus is God, a concept which is foundational for many Christians. Yet this interpretation still does not answer the query why someone (i.e., Jesus) would refer to himself as if he were not that same person.

Section 5

The cosmic Christ and the Sun

We have been discovering that there is a cosmic aspect to 'Christ'; the question now is, what does this mean ? In the writings of Origenes and Steiner, 'Christ' is the highest of the deities known as Powers (or Exousiai), in the language of Paul. Although there is a still higher aspect to Christ, as this same term can be applied to the great Logos in the Trinity (see next Section.)

So in esoteric Christian thought, the Elohim are understood to be deities in the 'Sun-sphere'. So Christ is understood as the 'Sun-god Christ'; the leading deity in the Sun-sphere (in the sense of the 'planetary spheres' of the ancient Ptolemaic solar system. What evidence is there for this conclusion?

One can begin by noting that when the list of nine ranks of divine beings are placed onto the Ptolemaic planetary spheres, the Powers have the Sun-sphere as their location. They are the fourth rank of deities, after Angels (Moon), Archangels (Venus) and Principalities (Mercury). One recalls that this list of nine ranks is found already in the very old 'Testament of Adam' (at least 2nd century CE) and with Dionysius the Areopagite (1st century CE, but extant in a 5th century document).

But are the Powers the same as the Elohim? If so, then Christ, as the highest of the Powers, is a Sun-deity. We will consider two examples from the Gospels which subtly indicate that Christ is a solar deity. But first, we note that the letters 'el' (as in Elohim) denote a deity in many ancient Near Eastern languages; El was the name of the highest god of the Sabeans, and was a Sun-god.[72]

But since the esoteric truths, with their more cosmic nature, were kept private, there are no direct statements in the Hebrew Scriptures identifying the Elohim as from the Sun-sphere. However, such deeper truths at times are less veiled. One such example is in the book of the Psalms; indeed many deep initiatory truths are to be found there. Psalm 19 is especially relevant here, as it

---

[72] As shown by J. Fürst, in his *Hebräisches und Chaldäisches Handwörterbuch über das Alte Testament*.

directly implies that Yahweh, and thereby also Christ, is a deity whose location is in the Sun-sphere.

Psalm 19
This Psalm begins with a reference to a core esoteric theme: the interconnectedness of the human being and the planetary system. Here I can only make a brief mention of the complex Hebrew text, but first this Psalm in the King James version,

> The heavens declare the glory of God
> And the firmament showeth his handiwork.
> Day unto day uttereth speech
> And night unto night showeth knowledge.
> There is no speech nor language where their voice is not heard.
> Their music rays out through all the Earth,
> And their words unto the end of the world.
> In them he hath set a tabernacle for the Sun.

The beautiful poetic verse is actually about the planetary spheres, and the powerful esoteric truth that human language arises from the influence of the planets in the soul-body. But it is the last line which is so important regarding the Sun, the normal translation is, as above:
"In them he hath set a tabernacle for the Sun".
But there are two small prefixes in the Hebrew here, which can mean 'among' or 'in', etc. So the last line can also be:
"*Among* them he hath set his tabernacle *in* the Sun."
A remarkable statement, which specifically places the location of God in the Sun-sphere. This is not some strange interpretation which disregards the grammar and the context; for this is how Jewish scholars themselves long ago understood the text, when they made the Septuagint:

"He put his tabernacle in the Sun".[73]

---

[73] Septuagint Ps. 18, v. 4 : ἐν τῷ ἡλίῳ ἔθετο τὸ σκήνωμα αὐτοῦ. G. Lamsa also translated the verse this way, from an Aramaic version.

This then is my translation:

> The Heavens* declare the glory of God,
> (*planetary spheres)
> And the Firmament reveals his efficacy,
> For speech arises from within each day,
> And inner knowing arises from within each night.
> There is no speech, nor language, where the
> voice of the planetary spheres is not heard.
> And their resonance encompasses all the globe;
> Among these influences, God has set up
> his tabernacle in the Sun.

So here is strong support for identifying the Elohim as divine beings whose location is in the Sun-sphere; and who were later known as the Powers. That the esoteric message here is somewhat veiled is to be expected; especially as the Hebrews were not to be focused on the cosmos, and thereby worshipping planetary deities; but they were to focus on their own inner nature, and how the commands of God should be resonating in their souls.

Regarding the cosmic Christ as the great Sun-god, there is a passage in the Gospel of John which hints at this. It is in 9:5, where the healing of the man born blind is recorded. Before the healing Christ speaks; and announces that he is 'the light of the world'. In the NIV, it translated as,
"While I am in the world, I am the light of the world."
In the NRSV it is,
" As long as I am in the world, I am the light of the world."
But the text can be understood as saying that each and every time it occurs that 'Christ' is in the world, this same being is the source of illumination for the planet. Because the Greek word used here can mean "whensoever' not just 'when'; so 'every time that such and such happens'. Thus, verse 16 can also be translated as,

"Every time it is the case that I am in the world, I am the world's light".

Since Jesus was only once in the world, these words are indicating that it is the Sun-god Christ speaking here, who illumines the world in a recurring manner, each morning. That this is the case, becomes clearer when one notes the context of these words. A man who was born blind is about to be given his sight, so he is someone who has never seen the sunlight; for when we see something, we are seeing the sunlight reflected off objects.

The solar influence is intensified here, when Christ declares that the healing can only come about if it is done before the Sun sets. (See Appendix 5 for more about this verse.)

In the Gospel of Luke there is also a veiled reference to the Christ as the Sun-god. At the beginning of his Gospel, St. Luke gives, by freely utilizing texts from the Hebrew Scriptures, a veiled indication as the cosmic aspect of the Messiah. He quotes from the Hebrew Scriptures which prophesy the coming of the 'Messiah' to people existing in darkness. It is a well-known and beautifully poetic passage. But unknown to the majority of scholars, it conceals a profoundly cosmic truth. We recall here that it is usual for passages with an initiatory meaning to be convoluted and grammatically difficult. The NIV renders this passage as,

"Salvation (is coming) because of the tender mercy of our God, by which the rising sun will come to us from Heaven, to shine upon those living in darkness and in the shadow of death, to guide our feet into the path of peace." (1:78-79)

This lovely passage is seen as referring to Jesus, who is poetically described as 'the rising Sun'. It may be considered simply as a fine piece of poetry, as are the texts of the Hebrew Scriptures from which it is taken, (Psalm 107:10,14 and Isaiah 9:2; 59:9-10). But by varying the Hebrew text, St. Luke allows it to discreetly refer to a mission of the cosmic Christ, involving the dead. The accepted translations miss various fine points of grammar, which veil a message which, when perceived, directly reveal an initiatory message.

But when the Greek text here is carefully examined using the Initiatory Quest approach, Luke is actually indicating that the cosmic Christ is to bring an empowering light to the souls in the Underworld,

Salvation {is coming} ...
through the fervent compassion of our God,
by which a Dawning-Radiance from the heights of Heaven shall make visitation to us,
in order to dynamically appear (hence to give light)
to the people in the oceanic Netherworld darkness
and languishing disempowered in death's Shade –
     (i.e., in the shadowy 'soul-body')
in order to guide our feet into the path of peace.

These words in Luke are only correctly interpreted, in terms of their grammar, when one understands that he is alluding to the cosmic Christ as the great leader of the Elohim, whose location is the Sun-sphere, hence they are in effect, sun-gods. See Appendix 5 for more about this verse.

Origenes and the two aspects of the Logos and Christ

Origenes is regarded widely as one of the two or three most brilliant theologians in Christendom. He had the capacity to discern that there is an esoteric aspect to the Gospels; he became deeply revered and very influential. There is an extremely significant text from Origenes which refers specifically to the Logos as a term for two distinct beings; both of whom are referred to as 'Christ'. But the surviving texts of Origenes as handed down to us, are not in the best condition. For example, words that help to connect one thought to the next can be missing.

In two paragraphs (291,292) from his *Commentary on the Gospel of John*, we find reference to a cosmic dimension to Christ, and to the fact that there are two divine-spiritual beings to whom this name 'Christ' can be applied. He had been writing about the Logos, as referred to in the Prologue of St. John. He understands this Logos to be the primal wisdom of God, because he believes that this Logos, who is also referred to as

'Christ', is inspired by the ineffable wisdom of God. Origenes means here the primal uncaused Godhead, sometimes defined as the 'Weltengrund'. This German term means the basis of, or the foundational element of, creation. So this is the *primal* Logos; it is part of the high Trinity of deities.

Then Origenes continues on, writing that there is **another** 'Christ' or Logos deity, who is the highest or most evolved of a particular rank of divine hierarchical beings. He writes that this high deity is part of a group of powerful spiritual beings, referred to in the Old Testament as "The Sabaoth", or "The (mighty) Hosts of God". Origenes refers to these Hosts as belonging to a rank of beings identified as 'Mights' or 'Powers'.[74] So these deities are obviously not as high as the primal Logos he had been writing about a few minutes earlier. For the 'Powers' belong within the nine ranks of spirits. Yet, Origenes does refer to the leader of these beings not only as the 'Logos' but also as 'the Christ'.

One can then conclude that *this* Christ-being is "the *solar* Logos". For, as noted in Section 4, the Powers or Elohim are regarded esoterically as deities whose primary sphere of activity is the Sun-sphere. So, this 'Logos' is the Sun-god Christ, but from the aspect of its divine out-raying thoughts and intentions.

The full text of his difficult Greek text and an English translation is available in Appendix 2, where it is also carefully assessed. In summary, the leader of the Powers (or Exousiai) – the Sun-god Christ – could be called the solar Logos. Whilst the high, primal Logos is the ineffable, divine, out-raying second aspect of the primal Trinity.

The nature of the Logos
Rudolf Steiner views the primal Logos as part of a triune Godhead, which has an existence or consciousness beyond that of the nine ranks of deities, 'the

---

[74] *Commentary on St. John*, Bk.1:1, 214/215, It is not fully clear which rank of deities these beings are, because earlier, Origenes referred to these powerful Hosts by saying, "in addition to the Thrones, Dominions...Powers....there are besides other deities, less familiar to us, i.e., the Sabaoth."

Hierarchies'. These spirits are active as instruments of the triune Godhead. His understanding of The relationship of the Logos to the Father-God is presented in brief notes, taken down from a lecture in the summer of 1903,[75]

"The relation of the Father-God to the Logos or Son is similar to when we stand in front of a mirror and undertake to pass over (in our mind) from our actual life into this reflection of us. The surrendering or 'passing over' of existence is the first, primal sacrifice; this is the deed of the Father-God. The Logos is exactly the same as the Father-God, except only that he, the Logos, has received his existence from a sacrifice.....the nature of the Logos consists in this: that it reflects the inner nature of the Father-God, back to the Father-God."

"Thus the consciousness of the Logos, who had received his own existence from the Father-God, is a reflecting-back to the Father-God of that existence which he had received from the Father-God."

Jesus as a person permeated by the 'Christ-Logos'

Rudolf Steiner concluded that the Logos permeated not only the spirit and soul and life-forces of Jesus, but also the physical body of Jesus.[76] That is, energies from the great Sun-god permeated even the skeleton, and within this deity is the primal Logos, whose energies are subtly active in the forming of the physical world. So there is no 'docetic' viewpoint here; i.e., not an attitude which denies a connection between the Logos and the physical body of Jesus.

Actively present in the being of Jesus was the solar Logos and, present within this deity, raying-in from afar, is the high, primal Logos.[77] But the human person, Jesus, is not the primal Logos. The misunderstanding that the human Jesus is also the primal Logos, who then somehow 'shrank down' to be conceived by Mary, is not

---

[75] Published in GA 89, p. 231.

[76] He taught this on various occasions, e.g., GA 244, p. 265.

[77] This dual presence in Jesus is indicated in the *Last Supper* painting by Leonardo da Vinci. (My book, *Rudolf Steiner on Leonardo's Last Supper* provides contemplations on this.

regarded as a viable viewpoint, to esoteric insight. The various passages in the New Testament which have been used as evidence of this theory are discussed in detail in the commentary on the Prologue of St. John's Gospel.

Life contrasted with 'Eternal Life'
Among the crucial core themes in the Gospel of John, is 'eternal life' and 'life'. The first term is used by Christ in connection with the human being, indicating that the higher sense of self has an inner connection to Christ. A deep engagement with these verses confirms that our sense of 'I' is the focus here. Once a deep spirituality develops, then the human 'I' becomes a receptacle for Christ.

This term in Greek is 'zoeae aioenios' (ζωή αἰώνιος) which does not really mean a never-ending life, but rather having an existence in high spiritual realms (which is beyond past, present and future). The word 'aioenios' is often misunderstood as meaning 'eternal' in the sense of never-ending. But its core meaning is that of high spirit realms, although generally this esoteric nuance is not discussed by theologians. This term is discussed in the Commentary with every verse in the Gospel where it occurs.

Whereas the term 'life' is used at times to mean something else than 'eternal life' or just every day existence. This other, unusual, meaning is in this verse, 5:26, "For as the Father has life in himself, so he has granted the Son also to have life in himself."
Since 'the Son', i.e., Jesus is already alive, the term 'life' here, and in other similar verses, 'life' means an ongoing existence into an ever higher reality that never ends.

Section 6

An expanded understanding of the concept of 'God'.
An especially insightful view of the concept of 'God' is provided through the initiatory consciousness of Rudolf Steiner. The first step to gaining a meaningful view of 'God' from such esoteric insight is to overcome the view of God as 'almighty'.

This adjective is found in translations of the Hebrew Scriptures about 48 times, and about 10 times in the Christian Scriptures (all but one in the Book of Revelation). But the translations are regrettable, for the original Hebrew and Greek words do not mean this. It is this description of God as 'almighty' that has become a primary force motivating so many people to reject the religion of Christianity.

One only has to acknowledge the, at times, horrendous life-circumstances which can inflict intense suffering, to see why so many people have turned away from a religion which refers to God as 'almighty'. In rejecting this actually misguided view, such people are paradoxically, aligning themselves to the true nature of God and of Christianity.

The Hebrew and Greek terms actually mean something like 'grand', 'great' or 'powerful', but never 'almighty'. The Greek word, 'pantokrator', is found only in one New Testament text (2Cor. 6:18), and there it is a quote from the Hebrew Scriptures. In non-Christian Greek literature, it is used for such deities as Hermes and Isis, and the Egyptian deity Serapis; none of these were considered to be the great uncaused Godhead.

The Hebrew word involved is 'shaddai', and it is of unknown origin and hence unknown meaning, in a precise sense. But we can know from its context, that it obviously means, 'very grand', or 'more powerful' or possibly, 'more bountiful', just as it does, in a Greek translation, for Serapis and Isis, etc.[78]

It was so used by early Christian writers also. In particular, the Apostolic Fathers; but they did not declare this word to mean 'almighty'. They were in

---

[78] In the Greek, κοσμοκράτωρ, in the Hebrew, שַׁדַּי.

effect echoing the Hebrew Scriptures; sometimes directly quoting from the Prophets (e.g., 1Clement: Epist. to Romans, 56:6.)[79]

The interpretation of these terms to mean 'almighty' probably first occurs in the works of the church father, Augustine of Hippo. As noted earlier, it is regrettable that the NIV, which has many valuable features, has mistakenly inserted the word 'almighty' some 270 times in the Old Testament to replace the previous correct phrase, 'Lord of Hosts' (sometimes referred to as 'God Sabaoth'). The Lord of Hosts refers to the actuality in spirit realms of God (either Jahve or the Elohim in general) having a 'host' of deities of lesser rank, helping them.

Here it is relevant to note that there are different terms in the Hebrew Bible for 'God': Elohim and El Elyon and Jahve, for example. The 'Elohim' is a plural noun, and refers to a group of seven sublime deities of especial importance to humanity; they are of the rank of Powers.

The cosmic Christ or solar Logos belongs to this rank of beings, as noted above. Furthermore Jahve or Jehovah - usually translated in English Bibles as The LORD or as JHVH - is a different deity. This great being is also one of the leading Powers, and is active together with the 'cosmic Christ' in creating and guiding humanity. The ancient Hebrews were guided by this deity in their task of preparing for the Messiah.

In teaching about the nature of God, meaning the high uncaused Godhead, Rudolf Steiner points to the existence of three great spiritual realities, namely Wisdom, Power and Love.[80] He explains that God cannot be all-wise, as that would prevent humanity attaining to true freedom, because God can only know all things if the decisions that are as yet unborn in the human soul were also known in advance.

He further explains, from his experience of the spiritual realms and its deities, that God refrains from being an all-powerful (almighty) ruler, as that would also

---

[79] An excellent survey of this usage is in Aune's *Revelation 1-5"* in the Word Biblical Commentary, p.59.
[80] "Love and its meaning in the world" 17th Dec. 12 (GA 143).

prevent human freedom. That is, such a condition prevailing in 'God' would prevent humanity from manifesting its own will. The implication here is that whatever spiritual being this term 'God' may refer to, it is beyond 'almighty', see below for more about the uncaused Godhead or 'Weltengrund'. The nature of God is far more sophisticated than this projection of human values, hopes and anxieties onto a Creator.

But over many centuries, influenced by Augustine's narrow view of 'God', scholars in recent times, in translating ancient Christian writings that pre-dated Augustine, imposed this erroneous meaning back onto these earlier Greek texts. For example, Clement of Alexandria (155-220 AD) is represented in modern languages as referring to 'Almighty God' whenever he uses the word 'pantocrator'.[81]

The word 'God' is invested with different meanings, by many groups; it is also used in the Bible to refer to different beings. Before considering this, we note that 'God' in its deepest meaning, refers to a sublime being, evolved far beyond all nine hierarchies. Little can be said from earthly intelligence about such a being.

As noted earlier, the scholarly term 'Weltengrund' is used for such an 'ultimate', primal foundation of the All. This term means something like, 'the cosmos-foundation' or 'cosmos-fundament' or 'basis of creation', or 'substratum of being'. It is commonly found in learned theological and philosophical works of 18th and 19th centuries. But Steiner gives a profoundly deeper understanding of this term,

> "The Weltengrund (God) has fully poured out Himself into the (multi-layered) cosmos. He has not withdrawn from it in order to guide it from **outside**. Rather He impels it from within; so He has not withheld Himself from it. The highest mode of His manifestation within the reality of

---

[81] Clement, *The Miscellanies*, Bk. 6: 5, "…by which the Almighty is glorified among the Greeks…." The Ante-Nicene Greek Library, translations of the Church Fathers, vol. 12, *Clement of Alexandria* Vol. 2, Edinburgh, 1882, p. 327.

normal existence is ***thinking*** and through this factor, the human personality.

Thus if God has goals, then they are identical with the goals that human beings set for themselves, for He exists within these. But this does not occur through the human being trying to investigate one or other 'command' from this Regent of the cosmos, and acting according to such a perceived goal.

It - the active involvement of God - occurs through the human being acting from his or her own understanding. For this Regent of the Cosmos is living **within** these human beings. He does not exist as Will somewhere **outside** of the human being, for he has forgone such a Will of his own, in order to make everything dependent upon the Will of the human being." [82]

In another lecture he presents further profound insights about Deity,

"Evolution is to keep on occurring, because God, in infinite Love to all of his separate parts,[83] wants to make **these** perfect, just as he himself is. This was a free decision not a necessity; it was a sacrifice. Through this decision we have a development of the separate parts of God up to Godliness. Through your inner work, the possibility for perfection which is already within you, comes into manifestation."[84]

He once commented that people don't observe why it is that he himself refers so seldom to 'God'. He notes that "this is because no human concept can truly encompass *That* in which we actively live, and have our existence."[85] He also pointed out the use of this word is so often

---

[82] "*Outlines of a Theory of Epistemology of the Goethean World-view*" page 125 (German edition), in the chapter, *Human freedom.*
[83] This in German is „einzelnen Gliedern".
[84] Archive document from 19th Jan. 1905.
[85] From GA 152, lect., 20 May, 1913.

misguided, because divine intervention in human life, and inner sustenance for humanity, comes in the first instance, from the nine ranks of hierarchical deities, not from the Weltengrund. But since awareness of these nine ranks of beings was removed from a large part of Christendom, people only had the word 'God' to use.

The different meanings of 'God' in the Gospels

A: Jahve or Jehovah
Sometimes Jehovah (JHVH) is meant, as for example in, Matt. 15:3-4:
> Jesus replied, "And why do you break the command of God for the sake of your tradition? For God said, 'Honor your father and mother'.

Lk. 2:22,
> When the time of their purification according to the Law of Moses had been completed, Joseph and Mary took him to Jerusalem to present him to the Lord God.

and 4:8,
> Jesus answered, "It is written: 'Worship the Lord your God and serve him only.'

Obviously, in these quotes from the Hebrew Testament, 'God' means specifically JHVH.

B: Both Jehovah and the Christ.
Sometimes 'God' means both Jahve and Christ. We note again that JHVH is one of the Elohim, whilst Christ is the highest of the Elohim (or Exousiai). This usage occurs for example in Mk.10:6,
> But at the beginning of creation God made them male and female.

and also in Mk.12:26,
> Now about the dead rising – have you not read in the book of Moses, in the account of the (*burning*) bush, how God said to him, 'I am the God of Abraham, the God of Isaac, and the God of Jacob'.

Note that in this last verse, these words to Moses were spoken by Jahve, but the leader of the Elohim, the Christ, also can be thought of as present in this moment, there is an interweaving between these two deities. Such an interweaving exists also between Jesus and the cosmic Christ who, through Jesus, is quoting to the crowd words which itself had spoken to Moses long ago, and who was referred as 'God'. Note too that 'God' in these verses does not refer to the 'Weltengrund' in the sense of the primal Godhead.[86]

C: God or 'the Father' as a general divine being-ness
It is also the case that 'God' can refer to the actions and influences from various of the divine hierarchies. Rudolf Steiner taught that the term 'the Father' was often used amongst the mystae (i.e., those people involved in the Mysteries) to mean not a specific deity, but a confluence of various divine beings and their influences, from which the human soul was created.

Brief notes from a 1904 lecture report, "the various spiritual developmental streams (of creativity) interweave with each other, and these are at different stages of spiritual achievement...these streams (of divine creativity, which are beyond space and time), this perfect origin of all beings, esoteric Christian knowledge calls 'the Father'."[87]

So then the word 'God' or 'the Father' in the Gospels can mean in effect, 'general divine being-ness'. As in Matt. 5:8, which in the usual versions is like this,

> Blessed are the pure in the heart, for they will see God.

As I have shown elsewhere, this usual translation of the Beatitude is incorrect, if here the term 'God' (in Greek 'theos' – θεος) means the 'Weltengrund' or primal Godhead.[88] For such 'seeing' is and will remain, impossible, as the Gospel of John (1:18) in the Prologue declares, "no-one has ever spiritually-clairvoyantly seen God", meaning the primal Godhead.

But sanctification, a high purity of soul, does bring spiritual perception of divine realities. At its highest

---

[86] But in existential terms to Moses, the great Elohim were the 'Weltengrund'; they were a sublime and lofty reality.
[87] Mss. archive lecture notes of 12th Aug. 1904.
[88] See my *Blessed: Rudolf Steiner on the Beatitudes.*

level, this spiritual perceiving could extend as far as cognizing one's own eternal 'Higher-self' as an expression of divine beings.

The same word for God, *theos*, also means any deity or god. It has meant this from the ancient Greek of Homer (about 750 BC), through to the Hellenistic Age, with Plato etc, and on into the time of Jesus, and beyond. So the Beatitude is correctly translated like this,

> "Blessed are those pure as to the heart, for they shall spiritually perceive divine being-ness."[89]

Another example of this usage appears to be:
> "And when you stand praying, if you hold anything against anyone, forgive him, so that your Father in heaven may forgive you your sins." (Mk.11:25)

There are about ten places in the Gospel of John where Jesus refers to 'the Father' and not to 'my Father', such 3:35, 4:21,23, 5:19-26, 36. It is not always clear whether the reference in such verses is to "divine being-ness" or to a specific deity (see below).

D: God the Father, as a specific being

A core lesson embedded in the Gospels for human beings, through the use of the word 'God' or 'Father' by Jesus, is that all human beings may start to awaken to the potent idea, to the awed feeling, that the core of their consciousness has a divine origin. In other words, a sublime deity has called human beings into existence.

Not that such awareness by the soul then directly identifies the human being with the Father-God – as we are in our current earthly, imperfect persona, but it turns our awareness in this direction. This outcome of the teachings of Jesus, and his way of referring to 'God' was in great contrast to the understanding and attitudes current in the time of Jesus. For then people of different ethnicities thought of themselves as part of an ancestral

---

[89] Ref. 88

patriarchal spirit, or simply as servants of various lesser deities.[90]

It is an extraordinary and joyous message of the Gospels that there is, in a germinal sense, a link between the human being and 'God'. That Christ has such profound love for human beings, and underwent a sacrificial death from out of this love, is the other aspect to these 'glad tidings'. The germinal sense can become a very real truth as the human being sets out to develop her or his spiritual potential

The implications of the above view of 'God' as a word which could be applied to various divine realities may not be welcome at first, in terms of prayer. But it does eventually enable a clearer understanding of prayer and of our relationship the Divine, to be achieved. This is actually of great help to meditation and prayer.

---

[90] 'The Father', if used as a title for one specific deity, is referring to the most sublime of the sublime 'Thrones', according to Steiner. It was these deities who 'in the Beginning" (in the 1st Age) rayed forth, as vessels of the primal Logos, the germinal 'divine spark' (the Atma) of the human spirit.

Section 7

Identifying the other meaning of 'faith': the ability to be spiritually-holistically discerning

Faith (in Greek, pistis)
The experience of 'faith' is central to a religious attitude and way of life. But today for many non-religious people, it is a negative term, for it is seen as an attitude which arises when a person ignores scientific knowledge and their own logical thinking, to remain loyal to religious ideas.

However before we explore this word, it is important to note that the 'faith' which many religious people have, can be a valid and noble state of soul, which does not retreat into illogical or absurd beliefs. This best form of traditional 'faith' is an inner sensing of the right-ness of a Biblical statement. This deeper form of religious faith is similar to a spiritual ability inherent in some people to directly cognize divine-spiritual reality. But such deeper 'faith' is obviously still not the same as this direct spiritual cognizing capacity, which progresses into seership.

Here we are concerned with identifying a second meaning of faith. This is a spiritual-intuitive ability; and this is implied in the Gospels, but has been mistakenly thought of as 'faith' in the traditional sense. There is a second meaning to the word 'faith', as used in the Gospels, which has no connection to the age-old religious understanding of this word.

This second meaning is about the ability to perceive (by the mind, not the senses) subtle non-physical realities behind the sensory world. In other words, the ability to have an intuitive, almost psychic, sensing of a spiritual presence (or of life-forces) that one is encountering.

Very important texts exist showing awareness amongst esoterically informed people of the time of Jesus, that there is a second meaning to the Greek word for 'faith' (pistis), namely an intuitive-spiritual sensing ability. These texts are preserved in several passages of a book by an early Christian sage, Flavius Clement of

Alexandria (3rd century AD), called *Stromata* (or *The Miscellanies*). The first passage occurs in Bk. 2:2,3 and involves reports about the views of three esoterically oriented Christians from the 2nd and 3rd centuries: Theophrastos, Basilides and Valentinos. We shall consider first what Clement reports, disapprovingly, of Theophrastos.

This theme has to do with epistemology, that is, with cognition, or the process of cognizing. This means registering and assessing what one perceives through the mind, although these three texts are about a specifically spiritual approach to cognizing. With Theophrastos it is about inner soul processes, including spiritual or intuitive consciousness. The following statements from these three people, are about how we cognize things, especially things in the inner landscape of the mind. These inner realities can be perceived as a flash of insight, which is almost clairvoyance.

Theophrastos
As Clement reports,

> Theophrastos says, mental perceiving[91] is the beginning of 'faith', for from this perceiving derives the beginnings of the inward debate of the soul[92], and *then* the understanding (of what we perceive) occurs; this understanding is what we call 'faith'.[93]

These words are referring to a spiritual cognizing, or an intuitive 'thinking' beyond normal logical, intellectual processes. Such cognizing is what we could today refer to as intuitive awareness, or a flash of insight. So

---

[91] The Greek word, aisthaesin (αἴσθησιν) was often used to refer to mental or spiritual perceptions.

[92] The Greek term is 'logos' (λογός), which I have translated as 'inward debate of the soul', for in classical Greek this is a recognized, major meaning of this word. (Meaning #4 in the entry, λογός, in Liddell-Scott's *Greek-English Dictionary*).

[93] The Greek of Clement: Θεόφραστος δὲ τὴν αἴσθησιν ἀρχὴν εἶναι πιστεώς φησν· ἀπὸ γὰρ ταύτης ἀι ἀρχαὶ πρὸς τὸν λόγον τὸν ἐν ἡμιν καὶ τὴν διάνοιαν ἐκτείνονται.

Theophrastos is saying that the soul can experience, if not a clairvoyant image, at least a flash of inner understanding or an intuition, and as a result, our mind, perhaps semi-consciously, engages with this, trying to become clearer about it.

Then the third step occurs, which is when our intellect does comprehend it: this, Theophrastos says, is 'faith'. So faith in this second sense, starts with an intuitive or psychic perceiving of a spiritual truth or reality, a religious idea or text.

Basilides

Then Clement provides in the next chapter, (Bk.2:3) some words from the early Christian esotericist Basilides, which are exceptionally important for confirming the existence – in the Gospels – of a second meaning of the word, 'faith' (i.e., pistis). Understanding of this second meaning is needed to fully grasp some incidents in the Gospels. Clement's Greek here is complex grammatically and in parts somewhat ambiguous.

Other translations do not seem to convey the full meaning of this passage. I have taken care to include the full nuances of the Greek text, and some additional explanatory words have been added to make the meaning clearer; these are placed in brackets,

> In this matter (of faith) the people around Basilides think that faith is inherent (in the soul), and indeed even to this extent, regarding the selecting action[94] (by 'faith'): that such (intuitive) 'selecting' provides a foundation which enables demonstrable, spiritual knowledge to be encountered[95], and which is later intellectually grasped.[96]

---

[94] The word 'choice' or 'selection' (eklogaes - ἐκλογης) used by this thinker in this context, as reported by Clement, is a term for specifically selecting something; Clement himself uses a different word for 'choice', just one page earlier (proaireo - προαιρεω) which implies to choose as a personal preference.

[95] Normally the verb here, 'heurisko' (ευρισκω) is translated as 'discovers', but it also means, 'to get (for oneself) or 'to fetch'

We note that the nature of this second type of 'faith' is specifically defined by Basilides as occurring through 'selection' or 'choice';[97] this is a very significant part of his statement. For this use of the word 'choice' by Basilides implies that what he is calling 'faith', in this second sense, is an intuitive process.

In fact, he is implying that **the insight itself is choosing or selecting us**, because the Greek word for 'choice' used here suggests a selecting process which occurs from unknown sources. So it is not a matter of personal rational preference, it is not worked out intellectually. It 'happens' to us, from the intuitive part of our soul.

This is actually how the process of having an intuitive insight occurs in us: it is not intellectually planned, it just happens (or it doesn't). In fact, the ancient Greek word for 'selection' or 'choice' used here became the basis of another word[98], which was used for the imprecise, and somewhat random action, of 'estimating' a quantity of rural produce and other goods.[99]

So this first part of the statement from Basilides is not about a religious conviction. Rather it is about the unacknowledged, second meaning of pistis: **an intuitive cognizing, almost a seership, or psychic cognizing ability**. This is precisely what Clement is reporting here: that these Gnostic thinkers or esoterically aware Christians, define pistis (or 'faith') as an inherent intuitive ability, through which a spiritual reality is encountered in our mind.

---

or 'to bring about', especially in Classical Greek, which was Clement's preferred literary mode.

[96] The Greek of Clement:'Ἐνταῦθα φυσικὴν ἡγοῦνται τὴν πίστιν οἱ ἀμοι τν Βασιλείδην, καθὸ καὶ ἐπι τῆς ἐκλογῆς τάττουσιν αὐτήν, τὰ μαθήματα ἀναποδείκτως εὑρίσκουσαν καταλήψει νοητικῇ.

[97] In the Greek, eklogaes - ἐκλογῆς.

[98] In the Greek, *eklogistikos* - ἐκλογιστίκος.

[99] The mainstream interpretation of these words about Basilides by Clement is unsatisfactory. For this interprets the words of Basilides as saying that 'faith' discovers substantial spiritual knowledge, and indeed through intellectual comprehension – but without any demonstrable evidence for this knowledge.

Our mind then experiences insights about it. Just think how significant is this new understanding when the word 'faith' is found in the Gospels. How this changes the meaning of the famous words of Jesus, such as "O ye of little faith."

This intuitive ability occurs when the soul itself, is making efforts towards a contemplative-meditative state. It is then is enabled to become a receptacle for higher insights. The choice of this insight is made by something higher than our normal mind; it is not an academic, intellectual process. It has its origin in a spiritual intuitive capacity.

Valentinos
Then Clement provides (Bk.2:3) some words from the controversial esoteric Gnostic-Christian thinker, Valentinos which are a valuable witness to an understanding of a subtle spiritual cognizing process,

> Now, in fact Valentinos and his followers, assign **faith** (*in the traditional, first sense*) to us, the 'simple ones'. But as for themselves – they, the Saved Ones – their given condition is **Gnosis** (*spiritual cognizing*). This is because of their superior advantage, coming from an inherent, germinal faculty (*of cognition*) existing as a predisposition in them. They say this (*Gnosis*) state of theirs is as distant from 'faith', as the spiritual-body is from the soul-body.[100]

Here we see that the view of Valentinos does not re-define 'faith', rather it leaves as it is usually understood, and instead introduces the idea of a highly intuitive, almost clairvoyant, faculty of discerning.

So Valentinos presents faith, as do the other Gnostics, as a spiritual seeing or a semi-psychic ability. This view is echoed in the works of Rudolf Steiner,

---

[100] The Greek of Clement; οἱ δὲ ἀπὸ Οὐαλεντίνου τὴν μὲν πίστιν τοῖς ἁπλοῖς ἀπονείμαντες ἡμῖν, αὐτοῖς δὲ τὴν γνῶσιν τοῖς φύσει σῳζομένοις κατὰ τὴν τοῦ διαφέροντος πλεονεξίαν σπέρματος ἐνυπάρχειν βούλονται, μακρῷ δὴ κεχωρισμένην.

"Faith as it originally was understood, referred to the quality of not weakening the inherent spiritual reality of something that we encounter, {especially for the first time}, by that which we ourselves are..."[101]

In other words, when we first encounter a significant, 'spiritually charged' person or reality, our cognizing should intuit this spiritual presence; and not be blinded by our habitual, matter-oriented consciousness.

So there is an esoteric view of faith as an intuitive, almost clairvoyant, cognizing ability existing in the highest part of the soul, which derives from the human spirit. The human spirit is a higher part of our nature than the soul, and has its own 'spiritual-body'.

The use of the word 'faith' by Jesus can at times refer to having a perceptive, intuitive sensitivity, tending towards a spiritual-psychic power of cognizing. Summing up, when in the Gospels the call is made to 'have faith', this can mean faith in the accustomed sense. Or, it can mean on the esoteric level, an intuitive, almost psychic perception, an incipient clairvoyance, which reveals the spiritual aspect of something.

Only when this second meaning of 'pistis' is realized, can Gospel accounts of some incidents communicate their intended message. (In the extraordinary esoteric Coptic manuscript, the Pistis Sophia, the word pistis is also translated erroneously as 'faith' when it means intuitive discerning, see Appendix 3.)

A new look at the word '**FAITHFUL**' (**Pistos**)
We have demonstrated that the Greek word translated as 'faith' (pistis), actually has a second meaning. This second meaning of 'faith' implies that people can be either less aware, or more aware, of subtle spiritual influences or qualities in something or someone which they are perceiving.

Another key Greek word related to 'pistis', is 'pistos', which has always been translated as 'faithful' or 'trustworthy'. But just as pistis has a second, subtle, and very significant meaning, so too does pistos. Various

---

[101] R Steiner, Lect., 7 Dec. 1905; in G/A 54 (untranslated).

Greek writers outside of the Scriptures, used pistos to mean *a discerning perception* or *accurate cognizing* – and as shall be shown, this is what it often means in the Gospels.

Homer used it in the Iliad, (3:269) describing the votive offerings made by Agamemnon to Zeus, in conjunction with a solemn oath, as 'pistos': meaning '*trustworthy*', or '*correct*'.[102] But this in turn implies that the hero's mind was acutely perceptive; it was this capacity which led him to make the correct choice of a votive offering in a dramatic scene. So Agamemnon displayed **discernment** as he assessed his situation.

This usage occurred long before the time of Jesus, but this same meaning of 'pistos' of being perceptive, or accurately discerning, remained in the Greek consciousness beyond even the lifetime of Philo of Judea, who lived at the same time as Jesus, and wrote many mystical treatises.

Philo used the word 'pistos' to mean a distinct *trustworthiness of perception*, when describing the words of God as reported by prophets in the Jewish Scriptures, declaring that what God says is especially trustworthy, being derived from divine discernment.[103] In addition, in his essay *On Drunkenness* Philo refers to the eyes as more trustworthy (pistos) than the ears, as regards their perceiving (not more 'faithful' in a religious sense).[104]

The well-known writer Lucian of Samosata (2nd century CE), used a word derived from pistos, 'pistoeteos' (πίστωτέος) to declare that something had been affirmed as correct, true or accurate.[105] This is also the case with the renowned physician Galen (2nd century CE), when referring to a definite diagnosis, he called it a 'pistos' diagnosis. This means 'an accurate' diagnosis, not a 'loyal, faithful' diagnosis; so here too

---

[102] In Homer's Greek, ὅρκια πιστός.

[103] In *The sacrifices of Cain and Abel* (para. 93).

[104] Here he uses the word 'pistotera' (πιστοτέρα), which is derived from 'pistos'.

[105] Lucian Hist. *Conscr. 60*, as noted in Liddell & Scott *Greek-English Dictionary*, entry, πιστ-ωτεος.

'pistos' implies accurate, very discerning perception (of a patient's symptoms).[106]

These examples of the usage of pistos show that this word can also mean a very perceptive cognizing or discerning assessment of any given situation, and not only 'faithful' or 'loyal'. When translating the Gospels, this second meaning has to be kept in mind, and accurately represented in translation.

Faith and faithful, believing and belief
Summarizing the above, we see that 'pistis' and 'pistos' are usually translated as 'faith' or 'faithful' or 'belief' or 'believing/loyal'. But in the Gospels these words can also mean 'higher, psychic discernment'; that is, intuitively cognizing or accurately perceiving. As a consequence of this, the associated verb, pisteuoe (πιστεύω), usually translated as 'believe', can also mean 'to discern intuitively' or 'to cognize spiritually'.

Whenever these Greek terms are used in the Gospels, if this other meaning is meant, then the centuries-old view of a Gospel text has to radically change. Such changes in the meaning of a Gospel passage will be noted, wherever this is relevant.

Seership, spiritual beholding, clairvoyance
A regrettable aspect of the journey of Christianity through humanism has been that the vibrant, all-enveloping role of spiritual beings and seership in the life and times of Jesus has been neglected.

Whenever in the Bible we read of someone talking with, or seeing, a divine being, or a demon or a deceased soul, this means that such a person is clairvoyant, which can also be referred to as having 'spiritual perception' or 'seership'.

So when a demoniac refers to Jesus as The Son of God, this is an example of seership, on the part of a non-human entity. When Jesus is recorded as knowing the inner thoughts of a person this too, is seership. Thus when Mary beheld the Archangel Gabriel at the

---

[106] Galenus, *9:857*, in Liddell & Scott; entry, krithaenai pistos - κριθῆναι πιστός.

Annunciation, or when Zechariah, the father of John the Baptist, saw this same divine being, this requires seership or clairvoyance.

When, as reported in the Book of Acts (5:1), St. Peter knew that a new convert to the church, Ananias, had sold some land, but secretly kept back some of the money for himself, that ability was from seership or clairvoyance.

Such seership was fully known to, and acknowledged by, the early Christians, (and people generally) in the Hellenistic Age. Thus when St. Peter is miraculously released from a jail and comes to a safe house, and the maid reports to the people inside that Peter is at the door, the people, not believing that anyone could escape from such a place, decided that the maid had just (clairvoyantly) seen the Guardian Angel of Peter (Acts 12:15).

Consequently, the Greek language has a number of verbs for a variety of cognition faculties of the soul; that is, for spiritual abilities we inherently possess, but seldom awaken. These are in effect, clairvoyant cognizing or higher consciousness states, in a deeper sense. The traditional approach to translating these words has been to ignore these actual meanings, and to replace them with an everyday nuance.

In my translation of this Gospel, whenever a verb is used which refers to direct spiritual seership or subtle insights or psychic experiences, this is made clear – especially when the subject of the verb (the thing seen) is itself not a physical, material entity.

Furthermore, there is also the phenomenon of a human soul or a non-human spirit speaking through a human being. We noted above that demons speak through a person who is possessed. This is also the case with the high initiate Elijah, who was present in the soul of John the Baptist. For we can surmise that words from the Baptist were at times, words from Elijah; and also that the Baptist has an enhanced perception of divine realities, subtly helped by Elijah's indwelling presence.

Section 8

Codex Bezae: the most valuable ancient text of the Gospels, preserving early and esoteric teachings

Overview

There are four major ancient manuscripts which contain the complete Bible, (or did once contain this, as some pages or verses may now be missing). They are in the codex format, that is, they are written as separate leaves or pages, on papyrus or animal skin, and stitched together in a book format (not in papyrus rolls). These are, codex Vaticanus, Sinaiticus, Alexandrinus and Ephraemi Syri.

These were written in the 4th or 5th centuries, being copied from earlier manuscripts, which have perished. In addition, there are two substantial papyrus manuscripts of New Testament texts; papyrus 66 and 75 (these also have some missing sections). These date from early to late 2nd century, some 200 years before the above codices, and hence they are of exceptional value.

Very important amongst the major manuscripts is codex Bezae, copied in the 5th century; it never contained the entire Bible.[107] It now contains the four Gospels and the Book of Acts, but very probably had two more New Testament texts. But this codex is different to the others, for it records many verses in the Gospels and Acts which are quite different from the versions preserved in other manuscripts.

The early history of this codex is unknown. But it appears that sometime early in the second century, an excellent copy of the Gospels and Acts was made.[108] It is my conclusion that this was done by a Christian who

---

[107] Also called Bezae Cantabrgiensis, the latter word meaning 'of Cambridge'.

[108] F. Scrivener, *Codex Bezae Cantabrigiensis*, "to the time of Origenes (AD 220-230) or earlier" p. xvii. R. Harris, *Codex Bezae*, "at least by the third century... very ancient," p.51; G. Rudberg, *Neutestamentlicher Text und Nomina Sacra*, "the second century" ...

was sympathetic to, perhaps a member of, an esoteric Christian group. Over the centuries, this early document was no doubt subject to copying, and thereby to scribal errors and alterations. Then in the 5th or 6th century a copy of this modified text was made, and became what we now know as codex Bezae. It was firstly a Greek text, but at some point, a Latin version of the Gospels and Acts were added.

To have different versions of Gospel texts is itself interesting but these Bezae variations are often of high value. When this codex is examined with awareness of the esoteric aspect of Christianity, further significant features emerge. There are some verses in this codex which are especially valuable, as they more accurately and thus more meaningfully, present the Gospel message. But moreover, in codex Bezae there are texts with esoteric or initiatory meanings. As a result, codex Bezae contains teachings of Jesus which are otherwise unknown.

Codex Bezae came to the notice of scholars in 1546 when the Bishop of Clermont in France brought it to the Council of Trent. In 1562 a prominent Protestant reformer from Geneva, Theodore Beza, the successor to Calvin, obtained it, probably by force during religious strife, from the monastery of St. Irenaeus at Lyons. In 1581 Beza gave it to the University of Cambridge, presumably to safeguard from religious disputes in Europe.

That this codex is of high quality is indicated by the fact that the predecessor to what is now this codex, was esteemed by Clement of Alexandria and his student, the great Origenes (who also used codex Vaticanus), and somewhat later, in the 4th century, the scholar Eusebius also used this. These prominent scholars in their commentaries of the New Testament quoted from codex Bezae, or more accurately, from its antecedent.[109]

However it is also true that this codex has been subject to editorial activity over several centuries, such as impromptu alterations by scribes who were copying

---

[109] A. Souter, *The Text and Canon of the New Testament*, revised edition 1954, ps. 76,77.

it. As Souter mentions, about eleven scribes have left their imprint upon the codex.[110] Some of their work was of poor quality (see below). In essence, codex Bezae contains:

A: Variations of the usual words in many verses. Some of these variations are insignificant; but others provide a clearer understanding of the relevant verse. A specialist in Aramaic texts has stated "...codex Bezae has preserved the nuances of the original Aramaic text in the Greek translation, better than any other manuscript".[111] This opinion is based on the conclusion that the Gospels were originally written down in Aramaic (or remembered in Aramaic) and then translated by the evangelist into Greek.

This view may well be only partially correct, as some or indeed many of the verses may have been spoken by Jesus in Greek, for example. But the point remains valid that the Bezae Greek text is the text most capable of being translated back into Aramaic sentences which flow properly and convey a clear meaning.

B: Deeply significant variations from the usual words and also additional text to Gospel verses; these present an esoteric viewpoint of the Gospel message. These are all identified in the Commentary (see below).

C: Hierophantic sayings preserved nowhere else
(see below)

D: The episode about the woman taken in adultery and Jesus writing in the ground.
This famous episode was placed only in the Bezae version of the Gospel of John. It was inserted into chapter 8, and was thereby preserved for posterity by its inclusion in codex Bezae (though it was later copied into other versions of the New Testament, some centuries later). This episode is a vital part of esoteric Christianity, for it conveys, but also veils, extremely important initiatory truths. This episode's veiled initiatory message is discussed under 8:1-12.

---

[110] A. Souter, *The Text and Canon* .....p. 26.
[111] M. Black, *An Aramaic Approach to the Gospels*, p. 53.

The decision by the compiler of the original version of this codex to insert this episode, despite it probably not being in the original Gospel text, reveals that the compiler had the capacity to access, and make copies of, esoteric material circulating amongst early Christian groups which contain esoteric truths of Christianity.

B: **Deeply significant variations**
There are many of these; the following sample from the Gospel of Luke illustrates this valuable feature of the codex. This example also serves to demonstrate the affinity of the compiler of codex Bezae with the esoteric initiatory groups in early Christian circles.

In Lk. 3:22, as the Holy Spirit descends upon Jesus at the Baptism, Gospel texts usually state "And a voice from Heaven came, "You are my son, with you I am well pleased." But here Bezae records, "You are my son, this day I have begotten you." Though both versions are valid statements of a spiritual event, that of Bezae has a more esoteric significance, namely that Jesus has now become 'spiritually born' to an even higher level, the result of the Divine merging into his soul and spirit.

It is also reported by the church father Epiphanius that the unusual, somewhat esoterically inclined Ebionite sect used a similar text to that which became codex Bezae. So again this version of the Gospel (and Acts) is seen as valued by people with an esoteric view of the Christian message. Another example of additional esoterically deeper material is that which was added to John 6:56,

Just as the Father is in me, I also am in the Father. Very truly, I say to you, if you do not receive the body of The Son of Man as the bread of life, you do not have life within him.

This follows a variation to the earlier verse (v. 6:54) in which Christ, through Jesus, normally says "unless you *eat* the flesh of the Son of Man..." This verse is famously puzzling (even disquieting) to many Christians. But in Bezae this verse is "unless you *receive* (take up) the flesh of the Son of Man..." not 'eat' the flesh. The same variation is in the above additional material added to verse 6:56, where the word 'receive' is recorded, not eat, (see under v.6:56b)

These Bezae variations from the usual text are the most accurate versions, for they reflect awareness of the deeper cosmic message here. This message concerns the absorption by human beings of the divine 'soul-substances' of the cosmic Christ. (This theme is discussed in detail in the relevant chapter)

We note that here is also a very prominent core theme in the Gospel, of 'life'; but life as something which God bestows, which is not simply about being 'alive' on the Earth. This verse, (and many similar), is in fact referring to a different theme than the well-known topic of receiving 'eternal life' from Christ, although these two themes are obviously interlinked. See Section 6, where these two themes were discussed.

C: Hierophantic sayings preserved nowhere else

A hierophantic saying of Jesus can scarcely be acknowledged in the prevailing humanistic approach to the Gospels. But to the early Christians, to those who were esoterically aware, such sayings were a deeply treasured, sacred heritage of the life and work of Jesus.

A hierophantic saying refers to words spoken by a high initiate to acolytes in a Mystery Centre. Such words convey, in a somewhat veiled form, profound spiritual truths, and often demand that the acolyte raises the consciousness to a level beyond logical thinking. An historically known example, but a very dramatic one, comes from the Mysteries of Demeter.

A Christian writer from the 3rd century, Hippolytos, reports that in the Mysteries of Eleusis, a loud triumphant cry resounded from the guiding hierophant at the crucial moment of initiation, as the acolyte was awakened out of a kind of sleep,

"Noble Brimo has begotten the holy boy, Brimos {her son}!

Hippolytos then comments that these hierophantic words mean that "the strong goddess has brought forth the strong."[112] Brimos, as the name of her 'son', is not really a name, but a way of describing the qualities of the person now initiated. It is a way of saying that the acolyte had become like unto the goddess.

So, in a loud triumphant cry, the hierophant is announcing that the great Earth goddess, Demeter, has brought to birth in an initiate, their Higher-self, and that this self is symbiotically linked to the goddess. Such hierophantic sayings, but of a more contemplative, instructional kind, were given by Jesus to those of his followers who were on the initiatory path.

The Gospel of Thomas presents many examples of such hierophantic sayings. His so-called 'Gospel' is really a collection of sayings of Jesus, the majority of which are hierophantic in nature. I regard them as valid words of Jesus. At least 90 of the 114 sayings are of the initiatory type, that is, they are statements which were intended only for his more advanced followers.

There are two types of such initiatory esoteric sayings in the Gospel of Thomas. The first category consists of about 24 sayings, which are also found 'reflected' in the Gospels. That is, they are recorded there for the wider community, but in a gentler, that is, less esoteric, and less confronting, form.

This leaves about 70 of these initiatory esoteric sayings which are not reflected in the Gospels, (not hinted at in the public Scriptures). I have concluded that these are profoundly esoteric and for use of those on the initiatory path. That is, they were specifically formulated by Jesus, both during his life, and later as the Risen Saviour, in the manner of a hierophant in the Mysteries, seeking to help his disciples or students on the path to initiation. This is why this collection by Thomas is given the sub-title "*These are the secret words which the Living Jesus spoke...*"

If my view is valid, that these sayings are hierophantic, then there are many examples from the collection by Thomas which can confirm that Jesus gave truly initiatory instructions. This is seen in saying 72 for example:

---

[112] Hippolytus, *The Refutation of all Heresies*, B. 5 #40.

> A man said to Jesus, "Tell my brethren to divide my father's possession with me". Jesus said to him, "O man, who made me a divider? I am not a divider, am I ?"

Now, in the Gospel of St. Luke, an associated, but far less profound, saying is to be found, 12:13-15:
> Someone in the crowd said to him, "Teacher, tell my brother to divide the inheritance with me."
> Jesus replied, "Man, who appointed me a judge or an arbiter between you?"
> Then he said to them, "Watch out! Be on your guard against all kinds of greed; a man's life does not consist in the abundance of his possessions."

Here we experience an ethical lesson from Jesus about greed, and that Jesus is not be used as a judge or authority regarding financial or other disagreements between people. This incident is a gentle version of a profoundly potent, deeply esoteric teaching for his disciples and other close students, communicated in a private session, and preserved in saying 72.

But in the initiatory saying, the "I" is the central theme. For saying 72 is one of only eight in the collection by Thomas in which Jesus refers to his own 'I' or self as a manifestation of the cosmic Christ. In these 8 sayings, Jesus uses the equivalent to our little word 'I', or 'I myself'.[113]

In translations of other sayings in this collection by Thomas, "I" may appear often, but in these additional sayings, this little word is only implied; it is not actually there. It is included as part of a Coptic verb, so such expressions as, "I say", I guard", etc, actually don't have the separate word "I".

Saying 72 communicates a truly humbling, yet also exalted, meaning. That the human "I", if it is the higher Self, the 'Spiritual-self', actually comes from the cosmic Christ. So saying 72 is declaring:

---

[113] These are 13, 43, 77, 114, and especially 30, 61, 72 and 108, where the Coptic words expressing the sense of "I, I am, I myself" (anok or soop) occur, suggesting a potently enhanced self-sense.

> "The I-sense that I am, is not a divider, is it?"

That is:

> "If I (Christ) am in you, then the sense of "I" which you experience in yourself, is not egoistic, is it?

The word 'divider' here means egoist, a self-centred anti-social person. In other words, Christ is saying here; if your sense of self, your "I", is not limited to an earthly personality, but has a spiritual quality, that is, if I (Christ) am in you, in the veiled core your own self – which you vaguely sense as the 'I' – if My presence is in you, contributing to your higher-self, then the 'I' which you experience, is not a divider, not an egoist, is it? It has not become a divider, a self-centred ego, has it?

Now, in the Gospel of Luke, chapter six, the incident occurs where the disciples pick and eat some grains in the fields on the Sabbath. Codex Bezae has a very significant contribution to this incident. The Pharisees object to this harvesting work happening on the Sabbath, to which Jesus replies in a potent statement which has a deeply esoteric implication:
"The Son of Man is Lord of the Sabbath".

To theologians these words mean that Jesus is above the rules given in the Mosaic Law. But to the esoterically aware reader, it is signifying in addition, that once an acolyte attains to the Spiritual-self (The Son of Man), an inner link to the Divine is established for that person.

This initiatory state enables one's own volition or will to carry out actions which are directly inspired by the Divine, and these actions may violate culturally established religious rules. For example, working on the Sabbath was strictly forbidden under the Law.

But in codex Bezae, this incident is followed by these hierophantic words,

> "On the same day, Jesus seeing someone working on the Sabbath, says to him, 'Man – if you know what you are doing, you are blessed; but if you do not know, you are accursed, and a transgressor of the Law'.

These words preserve an invaluable hierophantic teaching of Jesus; that is, Jesus is here educating those followers who are capable of rising to spiritual understanding which transcends their own cultural taboos and attitudes. He is saying to them:

"Man, if you are working on the Sabbath, yet in doing this, if you are carrying out actions which your awakened higher 'I' specifically perceives to be in harmony with Divine purpose, then you are an initiated person; divine wisdom is present in you (you are 'blessed'). You can set your own 'rules of conduct' in full accordance with Divine reality, from an inner intuitive perceiving."

"But if you are not someone who has attained to this high stage, then you are being active without regard to what the spiritual guidelines for your culture have decreed is wholesome (so you are ethically darkened, or 'accursed'). For you are breaking the rules established for us by Moses, with God's inspiration."

Anyone working on the Sabbath would be severely punished by the Sanhedrin, so these words of Jesus are revolutionary.

CODEX BEZAE A sample page from the 1864 edition of this ancient codex. Written about AD 500, copied from a much earlier text. On the left is the Greek, on the right is a Latin version.

	152	ΚΑΤ ΙΩΑΝ		SEC IOHAN
		αγιασον αυτουσ εν τη αληθεια	XVII 17	sanctifica eos in ueritate
		ο λογοσ ο σοσ αληθεια εστιν καθωσ εμε	18	uerbum tuum ueritas est sicut me
		απεστειλασ εισ τουτον τον κοσμον καγω		misisti in hunc mundum et ego
		απεστειλα αυτουσ εισ τουτον τον κοσμον		misi eos in hunc mundum
		και ὑπερ αυτων εγω αγιαζω εμαυτον	19	et pro eis ego sanctifico me ipsum
		ϊνα ωσιν και αυτοι ηγιασμενοι		ut sint et ipsi sanctificati
		εν αληθεια ου περι τουτων δε ερωτω	20	in ueritate nunc autem propter istos rogo
		μονον αλλα και περι των πιστευοντων		solum sed et pro his qui credituri sunt
		δια του λογου αυτων εισ εμε ϊνα παντεσ	21	per uerbum eorum in me ut omnes
		εν ωσιν καθωσ συ πατηρ εν εμοι		unum sint sicut tu pater in me
		καγω εν σοι ϊνα και αυτοι εν ημειν ωσιν		et ego in te ut et ipsi in nouis sint
		ϊνα ο κοσμοσ πιστευση οτι συ με		ut hic mundus credat quoniam tu me
		απεστειλασ καγω την δοξαν ην	22	misisti et ego gloriam quam
		εδωκασ μοι δεδωκα αυτοισ ϊνα ωσιν το εν		dedisti mihi dedi eis ut sint unum
		καθωσ ημεισ εν συ εν εμοι καγω εν αυτωσ	23	sicut nos unum tu in me et ego in eis
		ϊνα ωσιν τετελιωμενοι		ut sint perfecti consummati
		εισ το εν ϊνα γεινωσκη ο κοσμοσ		in unum ut cognoscat mundus
		οτι συ με απεστειλασ και ηγαπησα αυτουσ		quoniam tu me misisti et dilexi eos
		καθωσ συ με ηγαπησασ		sicut tu me dilexisti
		πατερ ο δεδωκασ μοι θελω ϊνα οπου ειμι εγω	24	pater quod mihi dedis uolo ut ubi ego sum
		κακεινοι ωσιν μετ εμου ϊνα θεωρωσι		et illi sint mecum ut aspiciant
		την δοξαν ην δεδωκασ μοι οτι ηγαπησασ με		gloriam quam mihi dedisti quia dilexisti me
ρνδ	:	προ καταβοληϲ κοσμον : πατερ δικαιε	25	ante constitutionem mundi · pater sancte
		ο κοσμοσ τουτοσ σε ουκ εγνω εγω δε σε		mundus hic te non cognouit ego autem te
		εγνωκα και ουτοι εγνωσαν		cognoui et isti cognouerunt
ρνε	:	οτι συ με απεστειλασ : και εγνωρισα	26	quoniam tu me misisti et manifestaui
		αυτοισ το ονομα σου και γνωρισω		eis nomen tuum et manifestabo
		ϊνα η αγαπη η ηγαπησασ με εν αυτοισ η		ut caritas quam dilexisti me in eis sit
		καγω εν αυτοισ		et ego in illis
ρνϛ	:	ταυτα ειπων ο ιησ εξηλθεν συν τοισ	XVIII. 1	haec cum dixisset ihs exiit simul cum
		μαθηταισ αυτου περαν του χειμαρρου		discipulis suis trans torrentem
		του κεδρου οπου ην κηποσ εισ ον εισηλθεν		cedri ubi erat hortus in quem introibit
ρνζ	:	αυτοσ και οι μαθηται αυτου : ηδει δε και	2	ipse et discipuli eius sciebat autem et
			(Fol. 167 b.)	(Fol. 168 a.)

CAPP. XVII. 17—XVIII. 2.

Some of the more accurate texts
There are too many superior texts in codex Bezae to be given here, they are all noted in the Commentary, but some may be noted now. All of these examples are fully dealt with in the Commentary.

5:20 the relation of God the Son
"the Father loves the Son": here Bezae has 'agape', others have the 'phileo' (to be fond of) which falls short of the truth of the bond between these two divinities.

5:32 Knowing that God's testimony is valid:
"and you know that God's testimony is valid": Bezae (and Sinaiticus) has correctly, 'you know'; others have "I know that God's testimony is valid" which is not a viable statement in the context.

6:11 The Feeding of the 5,000:
"he gave this to the disciples, then these disciples gave this to the reclining people": only Bezae records these additional words which establish that the disciples were directly involved in this spiritual process.

6:53 consuming the Son of Man
"you receive the 'flesh' of the Son of Man" only Bezae has 'receive' not 'eat'; a much more accurate version.

12:50 What is the nature of God's commands?
"And I know that his eternal command is life..." or, more clearly translated, "And I know that his command - intoning in spirit realms - is life..." But other versions have the obscure, "And I know that his command is eternal life", which most scholars agree only has meaning if other words are supplied.

Finally this crucial example, from chapter 21,
21:22 Jesus says to him, "If I will that he remains *in this same manner*, until I am reappearing, what is that to you; you, follow me !" The words in italics are only preserved by Bezae; and they make a major difference to the meaning of this mysterious verse. They indicate a subtle, behind the scenes, influence of Lazaros for many centuries (explained in the commentary for 21:22)

Editorial alterations to the codex

Codex Bezae also has various defects; but these are primarily due to later editorial revisions, noted above. One such activity concerns the two different lists of ancestors of Jesus, given in the Gospels of Luke and Matthew. The logical explanation of two different sequences of ancestors being listed, is that two different individuals are being discussed.

Since this solution has always been unacceptable to the church authorities, these two lists have always posed a problem. So one later editor of codex Bezae actually altered the list of ancestors of Jesus in one Gospel to make it compatible to some extent with the other list. This is utterly inappropriate editorial mischief, but a little reflection reveals that this does not discredit the codex itself.

Another kind of inappropriate editing occurred later in its history, when a Latin version of the Gospels and Acts was added side by side to the Greek. In Lk. 23:53 in Bezae, these words were added, "and after Jesus had been laid there (in the tomb), he (Joseph of Arimathea) placed over the tomb a stone which twenty men could scarcely roll."

Rendel Harris concludes that this is the result of a Latin editor's decision to insert into the Latin version some words borrowed from Homer, about a rock placed over a cave so heavy that some 22 wagons could not move it (Odyssey 9:240). The editor translated Homer's words into Latin,[114] but then he had to add into the Greek version of the Gospel, a Greek translation of his Latin addition, to disguise his editorial work.

Such improper editing alerts the reader to be aware that there may be other inappropriate editing. So care is needed when working with this codex. But it preserves immensely valuable, genuine Gospel passages which are not preserved anywhere else.

---

[114] J. R. Harris, *Codex Bezae*, 1893, p. 47.

Notes about the Translation of the Gospel of John
In the following chapter, I have endeavoured to convey in translation the sense of immediacy which is in the Greek narrative. This Gospel was written in the present tense, as if the writer is seeing the events unfold before his eyes. As discussed in the Commentary (The Source of the Gospel) this style is called 'the historic present'. For the reader, this style has a wonderful effect: one feels as if transported back to the very time of Jesus.

This Gospel is more a series of 'episodes' like living cameos of key incidents that occurred, and not so much a chronological account of the three years. The evangelist was writing down events which he was remembering or experiencing through his seership.

The Gospel of John starts with a striking poetic, cosmic Prologue. His presentation of the Christian reality commences with a reference to a sublime lofty deity, the Logos. This word is usually translated in Bibles as 'word', but here I am leaving it as Logos, because 'word' is too limited. As noted in Part One, Section 5, to the ancient Greeks 'Logos' meant thoughts and intentions which, deriving from high deities, stream out across the cosmos. But in particular the Greeks thought of that sublime deity or deities from whose creativity the cosmos arose or is being nurtured.

That there are two deities each called a Logos, derives from the awareness of these ancient initiates of the central role in creation of the leader of the spirits in the Sun-sphere, the 'solar Logos'; but also of the central role the sublime primal Logos had in bringing about Creation in 'the Beginning'. The Gospel uses it this same way; it starts with alluding to the primal Logos, and then moves to the solar Logos, the cosmic Christ.

Leaving out all references to the Nativity, to biographical details of the human Messiah, this Gospel presents a 'cosmic' Christianity. Its Prologue presents an historical perspective, commencing with indications about remote primordial times in humanity's development and moves forward to less remote Ages.

Part Two of this book follows; Chapter One has the Gospel itself, in a new translation. Chapter Two contains the Commentary; this gives the reason for some verses being translated in a different way to the customary versions and also discusses any veiled esoteric meaning in the verses.

The Author of the Gospel

The authorship of this Gospel is disputed; a number of scholars including myself, have concluded that the author cannot be the Apostle John, and is actually Lazaros, the disciple "whom the Lord loved." There are a number of very substantial reasons for this conclusion, which are examined in the Commentary. Lazaros is mentioned only in this Gospel, from which we learn that he lived in the village of Bethany, with his two sisters, and was a disciple 'beloved of the Lord'.

He was resurrected from a death-state, which is regarded as the greatest miracle recorded in the Gospels. In Chapter Two, there is an extensive section presenting the reasons as to why Lazaros is viewed as the author of this Gospel, and more about Lazaros generally is given in the Commentary on relevant verses.

Concerning the words, 'the Jews' in this Gospel

Some scholars have concluded that in this Gospel there is an 'anti-Jewish' tone. I do not share this view, for Lazaros himself and his siblings were Jews, as was Jesus; and furthermore, Lazaros was a respected and prominent member of the Jewish community in Jerusalem. But I note that there is a significant problem in one of the three ways that the term 'the Jews' is used here.

His Gospel was not written out of antagonism towards the Jewish people; that would be towards himself, his own family and his own community. Lazaros in his Gospel refers to "the Jews" in three distinct ways. One of which has had a very bad outcome for Jews over the centuries.

A: this group consists of normal and acceptable use of these words, in a text designed for primarily non-Jews; e.g., "the festival of the Jews", or 'the earthenware used by the Jews for cleansing…"
B: in about a dozen places he refers to "the Jews" when there appears to be no need to do this; for example,

when Jesus was speaking to people inside the temple, or at a sacred Jewish festival, it is obviously the case that all the people there are Jews, like himself. The reason for this is to emphasize to his Hellenistic (non-Jewish) readers that the world-saving Messiah arose out of Judaism. But in these cases 'the Jews' may be replaced with 'the crowd' or 'the people', etc, in my translation, as it is in various Bibles.

C: this group is used in circumstances where Jesus was being rejected or attacked. But regrettably, it is very clear that in these verses, Lazaros means by 'the Jews' some of the **religious authorities** of his own people (primarily, the Sanhedrin). The antagonism towards Jesus was not from all of the Sanhedrin, but probably from the majority. In some cases, an unruly mob, which was stirred up by the Sanhedrin, displays antagonism.
But the scribe used by Lazaros failed to make this clear, so this group of references implies, to those who have not read all of this Gospel, a negative attitude towards Jesus from all of the Jewish community. Centuries later, this had the result in the minds of the Christians, of blaming the entire Jewish community for the hostility towards Jesus. But, as Lazaros obviously knew, this was not the case. Indeed he reports in various verses, that many of the Jewish people were positive towards Jesus.

Consequently, I have, in common with many versions of the Gospels, changed the phrase 'the Jews' in these approximately 20 instances, to "the Jewish leaders" or "the Sanhedrin"; meaning the majority of these influential people.

That Lazaros has a positive and healthy attitude towards his own people, and a high opinion of the Jewish religion, is established by various verses. In particular, he records Jesus saying to the Samaritan woman, "...for salvation is from the Jews." (4:22)
But it remains regrettable that he used the phrase, 'the Jews' instead of "the Sanhedrin" when Jesus was facing hostile actions, because it is misleading about the situation. And historically, this feature of the Gospel later fed the vile anti-Jewish actions that, from time to

time occurred amongst Christians over the past two millennia.

What is a Gospel ?
The word 'Gospel' means 'good news' and comes from Old English. It is a translation of the Greek 'euangel' (mistakenly transcribed as 'evangel'). The Greek 'euangel' has an exoteric and an esoteric meaning; just as Power and Might and Dominion all have normal exoteric meanings but are also used as names of divine beings.
'eu'   = fine, ideal, good, morally good
'angel' = messenger, message, news, tidings
So 'eu-angel' (evangel) is "good news"
But 'eu' can be used to signify a higher thing = 'spiritual', 'divine'.
and likewise 'angel' can be used to signify a higher thing = an Angel, or other divine beings
To these people 'euangel' (or evangel),i.e., 'Gospel', meant as Rudolf Steiner concluded,

a divine message – i.e., influence – from spirit realms, becoming active amongst human beings.[115]

This is what 'Gospel' really means; and applies to pre-Christian spiritual influences. Hence it was the case that before Christian times, a priest of the goddess Hera was called an 'evangelis', (actually 'euangelis') and various Hellenistic priests were called 'evangelistaes' (actually' 'euangelistaes'). For they represented and manifested a divine, holy influence from spirit realms which was seeking to become effective amongst their people.

So the 'Gospel' of Jesus Christ is that especial holy influence from spiritual realms which derives from the cosmic Christ, and which is embodied in the words and actions and being of Jesus.

The traditional view that Jesus is the Logos
As we noted in Chapter One, mainstream theologians have the view that the Logos of the Prologue is actually referring to Jesus. They point to various verses in the

---
[115] GA 139, lect., 15 Sept. 1912.

same Gospel, which to a non-esoteric mindset, seem to identify Jesus with the Logos. But to the Initiatory Quest analytical pathway, these verses are not seen as supportive of this view. My different approach to those verses will be discussed in the relevant chapters of the Gospel.[116] See Appendix 4 for my assessment of the various Scripture passages which are used as evidence that Jesus is (apparently) the Logos.

Note: about the word 'Amen'.
There are many times when Jesus begins a solemn sentence saying, with the Hebrew words, "Amen, amen...", such as in 6:26. I have translated this, as do many versions with, "Very truly, I say to you...'. But it is important to note that the word 'Amen' has an esoteric, deeper meaning than simply 'truly'. It can be identified as a Hebrew word, meaning, 'so it is' or 'truly'. But it may have entered the Hebrew language directly from an Egyptian term invoking God; scholars are not in consensus about this possibility.

For 'Amen' is the name of the primordial God in Egypt, in the initiatory wisdom developed at Heliopolis; this site is the most ancient and most significant centre of ancient Egyptian initiation wisdom. Amen is that deity associated with the creation of the world, whose name means, "what is hidden" or "what cannot be seen". The god Amen - both his name (or inner essence), and his appearance - are described in Egyptian texts as "hidden to gods and to human beings"; he is also referred to as 'eternal".[117]

Also, 'Amen' occurs several times in the deeply esoteric Book of Revelation, which is also written by Lazaros-John.[118] On one occasion in *Revelation* (3:14) Jesus speaks of the 'intonings' of 'the Amen'. In addition to this, the same portrayal of 'the Amen' as a deity of unfathomable depths is found in the highly esoteric

---

[116] These passages are: verses 5:23, 8:58, 10.30 and 20:28.
[117] See E.A. Wallis-Budge, *The Gods of the Egyptians*, Vol. 2.
[118] Revelation is an initiatory book, its meaning veiled without esoteric insights. This apparently inferior 'dreadful' Greek is in fact the opposite; a masterly text enclosing multi-level meanings.

ancient 'Pistis Sophia' text. However when Jesus uses 'Amen' in the Gospel of John, he speaks it twice, to emphasize the profound truth which he is about to speak.

So 'Amen, amen' is said in order to affirm the validity and importance of the words Jesus is about to declare; these two words invoke a divine being or divine 'being-ness'. According to Rudolf Steiner, there is also the nuance in 'Amen' of affirming that the truth about to be spoken is directly linked to the end-point of the purpose of creating humanity by God, in the first place, long Ages ago.[119]

The term 'Christ' as Messiah

Whenever the term 'Christ' appears in the Gospels it is actually a Greek term used by the evangelists to translate the Hebrew word for the long-awaited 'Messiah'. Messiah meant someone who was anointed by diviner powers.

This causes confusion, because what the word 'Christ' now means, and has meant ever since the Resurrection, has become totally linked with the person whom we know as Jesus – his words, his deeds, his ministry on Earth. But during the three years when he was being encountered by people, all of that was not yet fully known; it was being experienced day by day.

So, the word 'Christ' in the Gospels refers to the expected Messiah, not to the now well-known, revealed, person and personality of Jesus.

---

[119] In GA 104, p. 94 and 104a, p. 51. He also mentions that it is of similar meaning as the 'Aum' in esoteric Hinduism.

PART TWO

Chapter One

The Gospel of John: Translation

The Prologue vs.1-18:
1:1 In the Beginning was the Logos, and the Logos was inwardly with God, and a god was the Logos.
1:2 This being was in the Beginning, inwardly with God.
1:3 All things through it were created, and without the Logos was created not even one thing that has been created.[1]
1:4 In the Logos was life, and then the life was the light of human beings.
1:5 And the Light shone in the darkness, and is shining, but the darkness does not perceive it, and has not conquered it.
1:6 There arose a man, who was sent forth from God, his name: John.
1:7 He came to witness, that he might testify concerning that Light, so that through him all people might discern the Light.[2]
1:8 He himself was not the Light; he came so that he might testify to this Light.
1:9 This was the true Light, which illumines every person; it was coming into the world.
1:10 The Logos was in the world, and though the world was made by it, the world did not cognize it.
1:11 The Logos permeated its own creation, but its own especial creations – human beings – did not receive it unto themselves.

---

[1] Logos is called the neuter 'it' as we don't think of deities as gender-based, and the Light (a neutral word in Greek) is now the form of the Logos.

[2] The 'Light' is the Logos' radiance, 'light' is the human soul.

1:12 Yet those who did so receive the Logos – those who perceived its true being – these were empowered through it to become 'children of God'.
1:13 Those begotten, not from the blood, nor from the will of the flesh, nor the will of a male, but from God.
1:14 Thus the Logos became flesh, and dwelt amongst us: and we beheld its splendour, that of the Uniquely-begotten from the Father, full of Grace and Truth.
1:15 John testifies concerning this being. He cried out, loudly saying, 'This was the being of whom I said, 'That one who is coming after me, came into existence before me; for prior to me, this being existed.'
1:16 Consequently, from its fullness we all have received indeed Grace after Grace.
1:17 Since the Law was given through Moses, Grace and Truth manifested through Jesus Christ.
1:18 No one has ever spiritually beheld God; however that deity, uniquely-created, who is close to the Father, it has revealed the nature of God.

(From verse 19 on, the Gospel takes up the contemporary course of events in the life of Jesus.)

1:19: Now this is John's testimony when the Jewish authorities in Jerusalem sent priests and Levites, in order to ask him, 'Who are you'?
1:20: He then solemnly declared, thus did not deny, but solemnly declared that, "I – I'm not the Messiah".
1:21: They asked him, "Then who are you? Are you Elijah?" And then he said, "I am not." Are you the prophet? Then he replied, "No."
1:22: So they said to him, "Who are you – that we may give an answer to those who sent us. What do you say about yourself?
1:23: He said,

I, a voice crying out in the desolate place:
'Make straight the path of the Divine Being !'
just as the prophet Isaiah said.

1:24: Now among those who had been sent there were some of the Pharisees,

1:25: who questioned him, "Why do you baptize, if you are not the Messiah, nor Elijah, nor the Prophet?"

1:26: "I, I baptize in water," John replied, "but among you is present One you do not perceive,

1:27: He is the one who is coming after me, the straps of whose sandals I am not worthy to untie."

1:28: This all happened at Bethany on the other side of the Jordan, where John was baptizing.

1:29 The next day John saw Jesus coming towards him and said, "Behold, the Lamb of God, who takes away the sin of the world !

1:30 It is with regard to this Being[3] that I said, "after me comes a man who is before me, because he existed prior to me".

1:31 I myself did not know this Being, but I came with water baptizing, so that this Being might be revealed to Israel.

1:32 And then John testified saying, 'I beheld the spirit[4] emerging gradually[5] taking on a dove-like appearance, and this remained around him'.

1:33 And yet, I did not know this Being,[6] but the One who sent me to baptize in water, that One said to me, 'The person around whom you see the spirit arising, and remaining nearby, this is he who shall baptise with the Holy Spirit'.

1:34 I have seen, and so I do testify, that this man is the Chosen One of God.

---

[3] That is, the Lamb of God.

[4] The 'Spirit' : the highest divine spiritual element in Jesus.

[5] That is, from the soul-spiritual element (aura) of Jesus.

[6] "this being": the Baptist knew Jesus well, so the Lamb of God (or, 'the cosmic Christ') is meant.

1:35: The next day, John was again present there, with two of his disciples.

1:36: And having observed with seership the spiritual ambience encompassing Jesus, John exclaims, "Behold, the Lamb of God!"

1:37: And the two disciples heard him speaking, so they then followed Jesus.

1:38: Jesus, in turning around, then saw them following; he says to them, "What do you seek?" They said to him, "Rabbi" - which when translated, means 'Teacher' - "where is your dwelling place?"

1:39: He says to them, "Approach me in spirit, and perceive with seership." So then they drew near, and spiritually beheld where he abides. And then they dwelt with him for that day; it was about the tenth hour.

1:40: Andrew, Simon Peter's brother, was one of the two who heard what John had said, and who had followed Jesus.

1:41: Thereupon Andrew firstly found his brother Simon and tells him, "We have found the Messiah" (that is, the Christ).

1:42: And he brought him to Jesus. Jesus gazed at him with seership and said, "You are Simon, son of John. You shall be called Cephas" (which, when translated, is Peter).

1:43: The next day Jesus decided to leave for Galilee. Finding Philip; he said to him, "Follow me."

1:44: Philip, like Andrew and Peter, was from the town of Bethsaida.

1:45: Philip found Nathanael and told him, 'The person about whom Moses wrote in the Law, and the prophets also spoke of, we have found: Jesus, the son of Joseph, the one from Nazareth."

1:46: Then Nathanael asked, "Can anything good come from Nazareth?" Philip says to him, "Come and see."

1:47: Jesus saw Nathanael approaching, and said of

him, "Behold, a true Israelite, in whom there is nothing false."
1:48: "How do you know me?" Nathanael asked. Jesus answered, saying to him, "Before Philip called you here, I saw you, while you were under the fig tree."
1:49: Then Nathanael declared, "Rabbi, you are the Son of God; you are the King of Israel."
1:50: Jesus said, "You believe because I told you I saw you underneath the fig tree? You shall see greater things than that."
1:51 He says to Nathanael, "Very truly, I say to you (ye), you (ye) shall see Heaven open, and the Angels of God ascending and descending on the Son of Man.

(Note: the archaic word 'ye' is shown here, and in some following verses, to show that, in mid-sentence, no longer is one person (Nathanael) referred to, but many people are.

CHAPTER TWO

The Marriage of Cana
2:1 On the third day, a wedding occurred in Cana of Galilee; and the mother of Jesus was there.
2:2 and Jesus was invited to the wedding, and his disciples also.
2:3 But wine was not there; the mother of Jesus says to him, "They have no wine".
2:4 Jesus says to her, "Dear lady, this concern of yours is not really for me to attend to. My time has not yet arrived – but, I shall assist."
2:5 His mother says to the servants, "Do whatever he tells you to do".
2:6 Nearby stood six stone water jars, the kind used

by the Jews for ceremonial washing, each holding from twenty to thirty gallons.

2:7 Jesus said to them, "Draw up fresh spring water and fill the jars"; so they filled them up to the brim.

2:8 Then he told them, "Now pour some water out and carry it to the master of the banquet." They did so,

2:9 and the master of the banquet tasted the water which had become wine. The master of the banquet did not know where it comes from, though the servants who had drawn the water knew. The master of the banquet called the bridegroom aside

2:10 and said, "Everyone brings out the choice wine first and then the cheaper wine, after the guests have had too much to drink; but you have saved the best until now."

2:11 This, the first of his signs, Jesus carried out at Cana in Galilee. He thus revealed his radiant power; and his disciples spiritually perceived this regarding him.

2:12 After this he went down to Capernaum with his mother and brothers and his disciples. There they stayed for a few days.

2:13 When it was almost time for the Jewish Passover, Jesus went up to Jerusalem.

2:14 In the temple courts he found men selling cattle, sheep and doves, and others sitting at tables exchanging money.

2:15 So he made a scourge out of rushes, and drove all from the temple area, both sheep and cattle; he scattered the coins of the money changers and overturned their tables.

2:16 To those who sold doves he said, "Get these out of here ! How dare you turn my Father's house into a market !"

2:17 His disciples remembered that it is written: "Zeal for your house will consume me."

2:18 Then the Jews demanded of him, "What miraculous sign can you show us as proof of your authority to do all this?"
2:19 Jesus answered them, "Destroy this temple, and I will raise it again in three days."
2: 20 They replied, "It has taken forty-six years to build this temple, and you are going to raise it in three days?"
2:21 But the temple he had spoken of was his body.
2:22: After he was raised from the dead, his disciples recalled what he had said. Then they believed the Scripture and the words that Jesus had spoken.
2:23: Now while he was in the Jerusalems[7] at the Passover during the Feast, many people saw the miraculous signs he was doing, and intuitively discerned his divine nature.
2:24: But Jesus would not entrust himself to them, for he knew all people.
2:25: He did not need a person's testimony about human nature, for he knew what was in a human being.

CHAPTER THREE

Nicodemus comes to Jesus
(Note: the archaic word 'ye' is used, when in mid-sentence, not one, but many people are referred to. And 'thee' is used if only one person is being addressed, and then suddenly, many are addressed.)

3:1 There was a man of the Pharisees, named Nicodemus, a member of the Jewish ruling council.
3:2 He came to Jesus during the night-time and said, "Rabbi, we know you are a teacher who has come from God. For no one could perform the miraculous

---

[7] The name Jerusalem here is plural (see Commentary).

signs you are doing if God were not with him."

3:3 Jesus responded, "Very truly, I say to you, no one can see the Kingdom of God unless he is born again."

3:4 "Nicodemus says to him, "How can a man be born when he is old?" "Surely he cannot enter a second time into his mother's womb to be born."

3:5 Jesus answered, "Very truly, I say to you, no one can enter the Kingdom of God unless he is born of water and of spirit.

3:6 Flesh gives birth to flesh, but the Spirit gives birth to spirit.

3:7 You (thou) should not be surprised at my saying, 'You (ye) must be born again.'

3:8 The wind blows wherever it pleases. You (ye) hear its sound, but you (ye) cannot tell where it comes from or where it is going. So it is with everyone born of the Spirit."

3:9 "Nicodemus responded and said to him, "How can this be?"

3:10 Jesus answered and said to him, "You are Israel's teacher, yet you do not understand these things?

3:11 "I tell you (thee) the truth, we speak of what we know, and we testify to what we have seen, but still you (ye) do not accept our testimony."

3:12 "I have spoken to you (thee) of earthly things and you (ye) do not believe; how then will you (ye) believe if I speak of heavenly things?"

3:13 No one has ever gone into Heaven except the one who came from Heaven – The Son of Man.

3:14 Just as Moses lifted up the serpent in the desert, so the Son of Man must be lifted up,

3:15 so that everyone who believes in him may have eternal life.

Or:

3:15 so that everyone who spiritually perceives it,[8] may have eternal life."[9]

3:16 For God so loved the world that he gave the uniquely created Son, that whoever believes in him shall not perish, but have eternal life.

3:17 For God did not send his Son into the world to condemn the world, but to save the world through him.

3:18 Whoever believes in him is not condemned, but whoever does not believe, is condemned already, because he or she has not spiritually discerned the nature of God's uniquely-begotten Son.

3:19 This is the judging process: light has come into the world, but people were inwardly at one with darkness rather than with the light, because their deeds were base.

3:20 Everyone who does base things hates the light, and will not approach the light, for fear that their deeds will be exposed.

3:21 But whoever lives by the truth comes into the light, so that it may be seen plainly that what they have done, has been done through God.

3:22 After this, Jesus and his disciples went out into the Judean countryside, where he spent some time with them, and baptized.

3:23 Now John also was baptizing at Aenon near Salim, because water was plentiful there, and people were constantly arriving to be baptized.

3:24 (This was before John was put in prison.)

3:25 An argument developed between some of John's disciples and a certain Jew, over the matter of ceremonial washing (that is, baptism).

3:26 They came to John and said to him, "Rabbi, that man who was with you on the other side of the Jordan – the one you testified about – he is baptizing, and everyone is going to him."

---

[8] Perceives the Son of Man state as a specific spiritual reality.
[9] 'Eternal life": a conscious existence in spirit realms.

3:27 To this John replied, "A man can receive only what is given him from Heaven.
3:28 You yourselves can testify that I said, 'I am not the Christ, but am sent ahead of him.'
3:29 The one who has the company of the bride is the bridegroom. The friend who attends the bridegroom waits and listens for him, and is full of joy when he hears the bridegroom's voice. That joy is mine, and it is now complete.
3:30 He must increase; I must decrease.
3:31 The one who comes from above is above all; the one who is from the earth belongs to the earth, and speaks as one from the earth. The one who comes from Heaven is above all.
3:32 He testifies to what he has seen and heard, but no-one accepts his testimony.
3:33 The person who has accepted it, has attested to the reality of God.
3:34 For the one whom God has sent, speaks the words from God: moreover, God gives forth the Spirit without measure.[10]
3:35 The Father loves (agape) the Son and has placed everything in his hand.
3:36 Whoever believes in the Son has eternal life, but whoever rejects the Son will not experience eternal life, for God's wrath remains on him or her.

CHAPTER FOUR

The Samaritan Woman
4:1 The Pharisees heard that Jesus was gaining and baptizing more disciples than John,

---

[10] Or; "the Divine gives forth the Spirit without metrical structure".

4:2 although in fact it was not Jesus who baptized, but his disciples.

4:3 When the Lord learned of this, he left Judea and went back once more to Galilee.

4:4 Now he had to go through Samaria.

4:5 So he came to a town in Samaria called Sychar, near the plot of ground Jacob had given to his son Joseph.

4:6 Jacob's well was there, and Jesus, tired as he was from the journey, sat down by the well. It was about the sixth hour.

4:7 When a Samaritan woman came to draw water, Jesus said to her, "Will you give me a drink?"

4:8 (His disciples had gone into the town to buy food.)

4:9 The Samaritan woman said to him, "You are a Jew and I am a Samaritan woman. How can you ask me for a drink?" (For Jews do not associate with Samaritans.)

4:10 Jesus answered her, "If you knew the gift of God and who it is that asks you for a drink, you would have asked him, and he would have given you living water."

4:11 "Sir," the woman said, "you have nothing to draw with and the well is deep. Where can you get this living water?

4:12 Are you greater than our father Jacob, who gave us the well and drank from it himself, as did also his sons and his flocks and herds?"

4:13 Jesus answered, "Everyone who drinks this water will be thirsty again,

4:14 but whoever drinks the water I give him will never thirst. Indeed, the water I myself give him will become in him a spring of water, welling up to eternal life."

4:15 The woman said to him, "Sir, give me this water so that I won't get thirsty and have to keep on coming here to draw water."

4:16 He told her, "Go, call your husband and come

back."

4:17 "I have no husband," she replied. Jesus said to her, "You have rightly said that you have no husband.

4:18 The fact is, you have had five husbands, and the man you now have is not your husband. What you have just said is quite true."

4:19 "Sir", the woman said, "I can see that you are a prophet."

4:20 Our fathers worshiped on this mountain, but you Jews claim that the place where we must worship is in Jerusalem."

4:21 Jesus declared, "Believe me, woman, a time is coming when you will worship the Father neither on this mountain nor in Jerusalem.

4:22 You Samaritans worship what you do not know; we worship what we do know, for salvation is from the Jews.

4:23 Yet a time is coming, and has now come, when the true worshipers will worship the Father in spirit and truth, for they are the kind of worshipers the Father seeks.

4:24 God is spirit, and his worshipers must worship in spirit and in truth."

4:25 The woman said, "I know that the Messiah (called the Anointed) is coming. When he comes, he will explain everything to us."

4:26 Then Jesus says, "I, who speak to you, I am he."

4:27 Just then his disciples returned and were surprised to find him talking with a woman. But no one asked, "What do you want?" or "Why are you talking with her?"

4:28 Then, leaving her water jar, the woman went back to the town and said to the people,

4:29 "Come, see a man who told me everything I ever did. Could this be the Christ ?"

4:30 They came out of the town and made their way toward him.

4:31 Meanwhile his disciples urged him, "Rabbi, eat

something."

4:32 But he said to them, "I have food to eat that you know nothing about."

4:33 Then his disciples said to each other, "Could someone have brought him food?"

4:34 My food, said Jesus, is to do the will of him who sent me and to bring his work to perfect completion.

4:35 Do you not say, 'Four months more and then the harvest'? But now, I am telling you: raise your vision and behold the spirit realms, for they are radiant, ready for harvest.

4:36 Even now the reaper draws his wages, even now he harvests the crop for eternal life, so that the sower and the reaper may be glad together.

4:37 Thus the saying 'One sows and another reaps' is true.

4:38 I sent you to reap what you have not worked for. Others have done the hard work, and you have reaped the benefits of their labour."

4:39 Many of the Samaritans from that town believed in him because of the woman's testimony, "He told me everything I ever did."

4:40 So when the Samaritans came to him, they urged him to stay with them, and he stayed two days.

4:41 And because of his words many more became believers.

4:42 They said to the woman, "We no longer believe just because of what you said; now we have heard for ourselves, and we know that this man really is the Saviour of the world."

4:43 After the two days he left for Galilee.

4:44 (Now Jesus himself had pointed out that a prophet has no honor in his own country.)

4:45 When he arrived in Galilee, the Galileans welcomed him. They had seen all that he had done in Jerusalem at the Passover Feast, for they also had been there.

4:46 Once more he visited Cana in Galilee, where he had turned the water into wine. And there was a royal official whose son lay sick at Capernaum.

4:47 When this man heard that Jesus had arrived in Galilee from Judea, he went to him and begged him to come and heal his son, who was close to death.

4:48 "Unless you people see miraculous signs and wonders," Jesus told him, "you will never believe."

4:49 The royal official said, "Sir, come down before my child dies."

4:50 Jesus replied, "You may go. Your son will live." The man believed the words that Jesus had said to him, and departed.

4:51 While he was still on the way, his servants met him with the news that his boy was living.

4:52 When he inquired as to the time when his son began to recover, they then said to him "The fever left him yesterday, at the seventh hour."

4:53 Then the father realized that this was the exact time at which Jesus had said to him, "Your son will live." So he and all of his household believed.

4:54 This was the second miraculous sign that Jesus performed, having come from Judea to Galilee.

CHAPTER FIVE

Jesus heals the crippled man at Bethesda

5:1 Some time later, Jesus went up to Jerusalem for a feast of the Jews.

5:2 Now there is in Jerusalem near the Sheep Gate a pool which in Aramaic is called Bethesda, and which is surrounded by five covered colonnades.

5:3 Here a great number of disabled people used to wait – the blind, the lame, and the paralyzed, waiting for the water to be disturbed.

5:4 They waited for the moving of the waters.

From time to time an Angel would descend and cause the waters to stir. The first person to get into the pool after such a disturbance would be healed.[11]

5:5 One person who was there, had been an invalid for thirty-eight years.

5:6 When Jesus saw him lying there and spiritually perceived that he had been in this condition for a long time, he asked him, "Do you want to get well?"

5:7 "Sir," the crippled man replied, "I have no one to help me into the pool, when the water is stirred up. While I am trying to get in, someone else goes down there ahead of me."

5:8 Then Jesus said to him, "Get up ! Pick up your mat and walk."

5:9 At once the man was cured; he picked up his mat and walked. The day on which this took place was a Sabbath,

5:10 and so the Jewish authorities said to the man who had been healed, "It is the Sabbath; the law forbids you to carry your mat."

5:11 But he replied, "The man who made me well, said to me, 'Pick up your mat and walk.' "

5:12 So they asked him, "Who is this fellow who told you to pick it up and walk?"

5:13 The man who was healed had no idea who it was, for Jesus had slipped away into the crowd that was there.

5:14 Later Jesus found him at the temple and said to him, "Look, you have become healthy. Stop sinning or something worse may happen to you."

5:15 The man went away and told the people that it was Jesus who had made him well.

5:16 So, because Jesus was doing these things on the Sabbath, the Jewish authorities persecuted him.

5:17 Jesus responded to them saying, "My Father is

---

[11] This verse was not in the Gospel, but added from an unknown source; not in Bezae nor the best early manuscripts, but it provides necessary background information.

ceaselessly active and thus am I also."

5:18 For this reason the Jewish leaders tried all the harder to kill him; not only was he breaking the Sabbath, but he was even calling God his own Father, making himself equal with God.

5:19 Jesus responded to them saying: "Very truly, I say to you, the Son can do nothing by himself; he can do only what he perceives his Father doing, because whatever the Father does, the Son also does.

5:20 For the Father loves (agape) the Son and makes known to him all that he does. He shall make known to him even greater things than these, that you may be filled with wonder.

5:21 For just as the Father raises the dead and gives them life, even so the Son gives (eternal) life to whomever he wishes to give it.

5:22 Moreover, the Father judges no one, but has entrusted all judgement to the Son,

5:23 that all may honour the Son, just as they honor the Father. He who does not honour the Son does not honour the Father who sent him.

5:24 "Very truly, I say to you that whoever accepts my teachings, and so believes Him who sent me, has eternal life and shall not be condemned; that person has crossed over from death to life.

5:25 "Very truly, I say to you that a time is coming and has now arrived, when the dead will hear the voice of The Son of God, and those who hear shall live.

5:26 For as the Father has (eternal) life in himself, so he has granted the Son to have life in himself.

5:27 And he has given him authority to bring about assessment of people, because he is The Son of Man.

5:28 "Do not be amazed at this, for a time is coming when all who are deceased will hear his voice –

5:29 and come forth – those who have done good, shall rise to live, and those who have done evil, shall rise to be condemned.

5:30 By myself I can do nothing; I judge only as I hear, and my judgement is just, for I seek not to please myself, but Him who sent me.

Jesus answers the Pharisees

5:31 "If I testify about myself, my testimony is not valid.

5:32 There is another who testifies in my favor, and you know that his testimony about me is valid.

5:33 "You have sent a deputation to John and he has testified to the truth.

5:34 Not that I accept human testimony; but I mention this so that you may be saved.

5:35 John was a lamp that burned and gave light, and you chose for a time to enjoy his light.

5:36 I have testimony weightier than that of John. For the very work that the Father has given me to finish, and which I am doing, testifies that the Father has sent me.

5:37 So the Father who sent me has himself testified concerning me. You have never heard his voice nor seen his form,

5:38 thus what rays forth from him does not live in you, for you do not believe the One he sent.

5:39 You diligently study the Scriptures because you think that by them you possess eternal life. These are the Scriptures that testify about me,

5:40 yet you refuse to come to me, to have (eternal) life.

5:41 "I do not accept praise from people,

5:42 but I know you. I know that you do not have the love of God in your hearts.

5:43 I have come imbued with the might of the Father, and you do not accept me; but if someone else comes on the basis of his own authority, you will accept him.

5:44 How can you believe, if you accept praise from one another, yet make no effort to obtain the praise that comes from the only God[12] ?

5:45 "But do not think I will accuse you before the Father. Your accuser is Moses, on whom your hopes are set.

5:46 If you believed Moses, you would believe me, for he wrote about me.

5:47 But since you do not believe what he wrote, how are you going to believe what I say?"

CHAPTER SIX

The Feeding of the Five Thousand

6:1 After these things, Jesus crossed over to the eastern side of the Sea of Galilee (that is, the Sea of Tiberias),

6:2 and a great crowd of people followed him, because they saw the wonders he was performing, healing the sick.

6:3 Then Jesus went up into a mountain, and he was seated there with his disciples.

6:4 It was about the time of the Jewish Passover Festival.

6:5 Then, having raised his vision, and having seen that a great crowd is coming towards him, he says to Philip, "From where may we buy bread so that these people can eat?"

6:6 But he was saying this, testing him, for he himself knew what he was about to do.

6:7 Philip answered him, "Six months' wages could not buy enough bread for each of them to receive a little."

6:8 One of the disciples, Andrew, the brother of Simon Peter, says to him,

6:9 There is a young boy here who has five barley loaves and two fish; but what are they among so many?

---

[12] "only God": i.e., the only deity that Jews should worship.

6:10 Jesus said, "Get the people to recline". Now there was much grass in that place, therefore the people reclined: there were about 5,000 in all.
6:11 Then Jesus took the loaves, and having given thanks, he gave this to the disciples, then these gave this to the reclining people, as also with the fish, as much as they wanted.
6:12 And when they were satiated, he tells his disciples, "Gather up the fragments left over, so that nothing may be lost".
6:13 So they gathered these up, and they filled twelve baskets with fragments which were left over from the barley loaves.
6:14 When the people saw the wonder he performed, they were saying, 'Surely this person is truly the prophet – the one who is coming into the world".
6:15 When Jesus perceived that they are about to approach and seize him, to make him king, he again departed into the mountain alone.

The next section has two levels of meaning, and is therefore given here in two versions.

    Walking on the Sea of Galilee
Verses 6:16-21   The surface level
6:16 Then, as evening came, his disciples went down to the sea.
6:17 then, having embarked into a boat, they were going across the sea towards Capernaum, but darkness had already fallen, and Jesus had not yet come to them
6:18 and the sea was being agitated by a strong wind
6:19 However, having rowed about 3 or 4 miles, they see Jesus walking about on the sea, and approaching near to the boat, and they were afraid.
6:20 But he says, "It is I; don't be afraid."
6:21 They were then willing to take him into the boat, and immediately the boat reached the land

towards which they were going.

6:16-21 : The Initiatory Quest level
(Learning to be in the 'I am' in spirit realms.
The sea is the soul-world, the boat is their soul.)

6:16 When evening came, his disciples entered into the Soul-world.
6:17 then, having embarked in the 'soul boat', they were going westwards across this realm, but darkness had already fallen, and Jesus had not yet come to them.
6:18 And the Soul-world was being agitated by lower soul qualities.
6:19 However, having moved deep into this realm, they perceive the spirit of Jesus is there, away in the distance, yet as if near to the 'soul boat'; and so they were afraid.
6:20 But he says, "I am the I AM in you"; do not have fear."
6:21 They were thus willing to receive him into their 'soul boat', and immediately their soul reached that secure sense of 'I' within this realm, towards which they were striving.

6:22 On the next day, the crowd that had stayed across on the eastern side of the sea, saw that there had only been one boat there. They also saw that Jesus had not been aboard the boat in which his disciples had departed.
6:23 Other boats came from Tiberias near to the place where they had eaten the bread, after the Lord had given thanks.
6:24 But when the crowds saw that neither Jesus nor the disciples were there [on the eastern shore], they embarked into these boats and sailed back to Capernaum, seeking Jesus.
6:25 And having found him, they said to him,

"Rabbi, when did you appear here?"

6:26 Jesus answered them and said, "Very truly, I tell you that you are seeking me, not because you saw wonders performed, but because you were able to eat all that you needed of the loaves.

6:27 Do not make effort for food that is perishing, but for the food remaining for eternal existence, which The Son of Man shall give to you. For within him, the Father – God himself – has imprinted his own being.

6:28 They therefore said to Him, "What must we do to carry out the works of God?"

6:29 Jesus answered and said to them, "This is the manifestation of God in you: when you perceive with discernment the One whom He has sent."

6:30 So they then said to Him, What wonders will you do for us to see, that we may truly perceive you? What wonders are you doing?

6:31 Our ancestors ate manna in the wilderness; as it is written, "He gave them bread from Heaven to eat."

6:32 Then Jesus said to them, "Very truly, I say to you, it was not Moses who gave you bread from Heaven, but my Father, who gives you the true bread from Heaven."

6:33 For the bread of God is that which comes down from Heaven and gives life to the world.

6:34 So they said to Him, "Lord, give us this bread, always."

6:35 Jesus said to them, "I myself am the bread of life; whoever comes to me shall never be hungry, and whoever believes in me, shall never thirst again.

6:36 However, I said to you that, you have been in my presence, but you do not believe.

6:37 Everyone whom the Father gives to me, shall come to me, and those coming to me, I shall never drive away.

6:38 For I have descended from Heaven, not to do

my own will, but to do the will of Him who sent me.

6:39 And this is the will of Him who sent me, that I should lose nothing of what has been given to me, but raise it up on the Last Day.

6:40 For this is the will of my Father, that everyone experiencing inwardly the Son, and believing in him, may have eternal life, and I shall raise that person up on the Last Day."

6:41 The crowd began to complain about him because he said, "I myself am the bread of life, which has come down from Heaven".

6:42 So they were saying, "Is not this Jesus, the son of Joseph, whose father and mother we know"? How then can he say, "I have come down from Heaven"?

6:43 Jesus responded and said, "Don't grumble amongst yourselves."

6:44 No-one can approach me unless drawn to me by the Father; and I shall raise up that person on the Last Day.

6:45 It has been written in the Prophets, "And they shall all be taught by God." (Isa. 54:13) Everyone having heard from the Father, and having learnt, comes to me."

6:46 Not that the Father has been spiritually seen by anyone, except the One who is from God; this One has seen the Father.

6:47 "Very truly, I say to you, whoever is spiritually perceptive has eternal life."[13]

The Bread of Life

6:48 "I myself am the bread of life."

6:49 Your fathers ate manna in the wilderness and (eventually) died.

6:50 This is the bread which is coming down from Heaven, so that anyone may eat of it, and not die.

---

[13] That is, regarding the Son.

6:51 I myself am the living bread which has come down from Heaven; if anyone eats of this bread they shall live forever. And the bread which I shall give for the life of the world, is my 'flesh'.

6:52 The crowd then disputed with each other, saying, 'How is this man able to give us his flesh to eat?

6:53 So Jesus said to them, "Very truly, I say to you, unless you receive the 'flesh' of the Son of Man and press out his 'blood', you do not have life in yourselves.[14]

6:54 The person nourished by the life-force of its body and drinking in the vitality of its 'blood' has eternal life; and I shall raise up that person on the Last Day.

6:55 For my 'flesh' is true food and my 'blood' is true drink.

6:56 The person nourished by the life-force of my 'body' and drinking in the vitality of my 'blood' abides in me, and I in that person.

6:56b (This verse is found only in codex Bezae)
Just as the Father is in me, I also am in the Father. Very truly, I say to you, if you do not receive the body of The Son of Man as the bread of life, you do not have life within him.

6:57 Just as the living Father sent me, and I live because of the Father, so also the person nourished by me – that very person, shall live because of me.

6:58 This is the bread descended from Heaven, which is not like that which your ancestors ate, and then later died. For the person being nourished by this bread shall live forever.

6:59 These things he said while teaching in the synagogue in Capernaum.

6:60 Then many of the disciples, having heard this,

---

[14] The Greek here is 'to press out', not to 'drink', and refers to accessing the divine life-forces of the Christ.

said, 'This is a hard saying, who can accept it' ?

6:61 Jesus, knowing in himself that the disciples were complaining about this said, "Does this offend you?"

6:62 What if you were to spiritually behold the Son of Man ascending back to where he was at first?"

6:63 It is the spirit which bestows life; the flesh is of no value."

6:64 But there are some among you who do not perceive." (For from the beginning Jesus had known who would not be spiritually perceptive, and thus who would betray him.)

6:65 And he said, "For this reason I have told you that no-one is able to come to me, unless it has been granted by the Father."

6:66 Because of this, many disciples turned back and no longer went about with him.

6:67 Then Jesus said to the Twelve, "Surely, you do not want to go away?

6:68 Simon Peter answered, "Lord, to whom can we go? You have the words of eternal life."

6:69 We have perceived you truly, and hence we know that you are the Holy One of God."

6:70 Jesus answered them, "Did I not choose you, the Twelve; yet one of you is a devil?"

6:71 He was speaking of Judas, son of Simon Iscariot, for he, one of The Twelve, was soon to betray him.

CHAPTER SEVEN

7:1 And after these things, Jesus went about in Galilee, for he did not want to go about in Judea, because the Jewish authorities were wanting to kill him.

7:2 Now the Jewish festival of Booths was near.

7:3 So his brothers said to him, "Depart from here and go into Judea so that your disciples will see the wonders you are doing.

7:4 For no-one who wants to be widely known, does anything in secret. Since you are doing these wonders, show yourself to the world."

7:5 For even his own brothers did not believe in him.

7:6 So Jesus said, "The right moment for me has not arrived, but the time for your actions is always here.

7:7 The world cannot hate you, but it hates me because I testify about it, that its works are evil."

7:8 You go the festival, I am not going up to this festival just now for my time has not yet fully arrived."

7:9 And having said these things, he remained in Galilee.

7:10 But after his brothers had gone to the festival, he then also went, not in a public way, but discreetly.

7:11 However the people were looking for him at the festival, and asking, "Where is that man?"

7:12 And hushed words were spoken about him among the crowds. Some were saying, "He is a good man", others were saying, "No, he deceives the people".

7:13 However, no-one was speaking openly about him, for fear of the Jewish authorities.

7:14 About the middle of the feast time, Jesus went up to the temple and was teaching.

7:15 So the people were marvelling, saying, "How does this man have such learning, when he has never been instructed?"

7:16 Then in response, Jesus answered, saying, "My teaching is not mine, but is from the One who sent me.

7:17 If anyone wants to do the will of Him, they shall know whether my teaching is of God or whether I am speaking from myself.

7:18 The person speaking from their own self, seeks their own spiritual empowerment, but a person who seeks to spiritually empower the One who sent him – this person is genuine, and there is no unrighteousness in him."

7:19 Did not Moses give you the Law? Yet none of you keep the Law. Why are you seeking to kill me?"

7:20 The crowd answered, "You are demon-possessed. Who is seeking to kill you?"

7:21 Jesus responded, and said to them, " I have carried out a single wonder, and everyone was astonished, because of this.

7:22 Moses gave you the law of circumcision (yet it is not from Moses but the Patriarchs); so on a Sabbath, you may circumcise a person (if that is the stipulated eighth day).

7:23 If a boy receives circumcision on the Sabbath, in order that the law of Moses is not broken, why are you angry with me because a man's entire body was healed by me on the Sabbath?

7:24 Do not judge by appearances, but decide with right judgement.

7:25 Then some of the people from Jerusalem said, "Is this not the man whom they are trying to kill?

7:26 And, look – he is speaking openly and they are saying nothing to him. Perhaps the rulers really know that this man is the Christ?"

7:27 Yet we know where this man is from, but when the Messiah appears, no-one shall know where he is from.

7:28 Then Jesus cried out, as he was teaching in the temple saying, "You know me and you know where I am from. And yet it is not from my own decision that I have come here; the One who sent me, is trustworthy: but you do not know Him.
7:29 I know Him, because I am from Him, and it is that One who sent me.
7:30 Then they tried to arrest him, but no-one laid hands on him, because his hour had not yet arrived.
7:31 Yet many in the crowd believed in him and were saying, "When the Messiah comes, surely he will not do more wonders than this man has done?"
7:32 The Pharisees heard the crowd murmuring such things about him, so the chief priests and the Pharisees sent temple guards to arrest him.
7:33 Jesus then said, "I am with you for yet a little while, then I go away to the One having sent me.
7:34 You will seek me, but not find me, for where I am then, you are not able to come."
7:35 So the people then said to one another, where is this man about to journey to, that we will not find him? Surely not to the Dispersion among the Greeks, to teach the Greeks then?
7:36 What do his words mean, "You will seek me, but not find me, for where I am then, you are not able to come."
7:37 Now, on the last great day of the Feast, Jesus was standing, and he cried out saying, "If anyone thirsts, let him come to me, and drink."
7:38 "For that person, the one believing in me, streams of living water shall flow from his inner being, as the Scriptures indicate."
7:39 This he said about the spirit, which believers in him were soon to receive, for the Holy Spirit was not yet upon them, because Jesus was not yet glorified.
7:40 Some of the crowd, having heard these words, were saying, "Surely this is the Prophet".

7:41 Others were saying, "This man is the Christ"; but some were saying, "The Messiah does not come from Galilee, does he?"
7:42 "Has not the Scripture said that the Messiah is to be a descendant of David, and comes from Bethlehem, where David lived?"
7:43 So there was division in the crowd because of him.
7:44 Some were wanting to arrest him, but no-one laid their hands on him.
7:45 Then the temple guards went back to the chief priests and the Pharisees, who asked them, why they did not bring him.
7:46 The guards answered, "Never has anyone spoken like this".
7:47 Then the Pharisees replied, "Surely you have not been deceived as well, have you?"
7:48 None of the authorities believed in him, nor any of the Pharisees, have they?"
7:49 But this crowd, they don't know the Law, they are accursed."
7:50 Nicodemus, the one who had earlier gone to Jesus, said,
7:51 "Our law does not judge people without first giving them a hearing, to find out what he is doing, does it?"
7:52 They replied, "Surely you're not from Galilee are you? Search and you will find that no prophet is to arise from Galilee."
7:53 Then each of them went home.

CHAPTER EIGHT

The woman taken in adultery.
This deeply esoteric account was preserved only in codex Bezae.
8:1 Jesus went to the Mount of Olives
8:2 and early in the morning he came again to the temple and all the people were coming to him, and

having seated himself, he began to teach them.

8:3 Then the scribes and the Pharisees brought a woman who had been caught in adultery, and made her stand before all of them,

8:4 They said to Jesus, "Teacher, this women has been caught in the act of committing adultery,

8:5 Now, in the law, Moses commanded us to stone such women; so what do you say?"

8:6 However, this they were saying to test him, so that they might have some charge to bring against him. But Jesus stooped down and was drawing figures in the ground with his finger.[15]

8:7 When they kept on questioning him, he stood up and said to them, "Let the one among you who is without sin, be the first to throw a stone at her."

8:8 And again he stooped down and wrote in the ground.

8:9 When they heard this, they went away, one by one, beginning with the oldest; and Jesus was left there alone, and the woman being in the midst.

8:10 Jesus stood up and said to the woman, "Where are they? Has no-one condemned you?"

8:11 Then she said, "No-one, Lord." Jesus said, "Neither do I condemn you. Go your way, and from now on, do not sin again."

8:12 Jesus spoke to the people, saying, "I am the Light of the World, whoever follows me shall never walk in darkness, but will have the light of life."

8:13 So the Pharisees said him, "You are testifying on your own behalf, your testimony is [therefore] not valid."

8:14 Jesus responded and said, "Although I testify about myself, my testimony is valid, because I know where I have come from, and where I am

---

[15] In the dust on the temple paving.

going. But you do not know where I come from, nor where I am going."

8:15 You judge according to the manner of the flesh, I judge no-one.

8:16 Yet, even if I do judge, my assessment is valid, because it is not I alone who judge, but I and the Father who sent me.

8:17 Also in your law it is written that the testimony of two people is valid.

8:18 I myself testify on my own behalf, and also the Father who sent me, testifies on my behalf.

8:19 Then they said to him, "Where is your father?" Jesus answered, "You know neither me, nor my father. If you had known me, you would also have known my Father.

8:20 He spoke these words whilst teaching in the Treasury of the temple; but no-one arrested him, because his hour has not yet come.

8:21 Therefore he again said to them, I am leaving, and you will seek me, but you will die away in your sin.

8:22 So the people were saying, Surely he will not kill himself, although he says "Where I am going, you cannot come"?

8:23 So then he said to them, "You are from below, but I am from above; you are of this world, but not of this world am I.

8:24 "For this reason I said to you, that you will die in your sins, for if you do not inwardly discern that **I am the I am** – then you will die away in your sins."

8:25 They were saying to Jesus, "You, who are you?" Jesus said to them, "I am the One who, in fact since the Beginning, has been intoning to you."

8:26 "Many things about you I have to speak, and to judge, for indeed the One who sent me is Truth itself."

8:27 They did not know that Christ was speaking to them of the Father.

8:28 So Jesus said to them, Whenever you have

exalted The Son of Man, then you will know [16] **I am the I am** (in you); you will also know: 'from myself I do nothing, except as the Father taught me'.[17]

8:29 These things I speak, for the One who sent me is with me; he has not left me alone, for I always do that which is agreeable to Him.

8:30 As he was saying these things, many believed in him.

8:31 So Jesus said to the people who believed in him, if you abide within my words you are truly my disciples.

8:32 Then you will know the Truth, and the Truth shall set you free.

8:33 They answered him, saying, "We are descendants of Abraham, and have never been slaves of anyone. So how can you say that we can become free?"

8:34 Jesus answered them, "Very truly, I say to you that everyone existing within sin is enslaved.

8:35 Yet the slave does not remain in the household for ever, but the Son remains forever.

8:36 If therefore the Son frees you, then indeed you will truly be free people.

8:37 I know that you are the descendants of Abraham, yet you seek to kill me, because what is intoning in my words, has no effect on you.

8:38 Yet that which I have beheld in the presence of the Father, I speak; likewise you do that which you have heard from your father.

8:39 They responded to him saying, "Our father is Abraham." Jesus said to them, "If you are Abraham's children, you would do what Abraham did.

8:40 Yet now you are seeking to kill me, a man who

---

[16] In the NIV, the word "that" has been inserted, although it is not there in the Greek.

[17] See the Commentary about the difficulties here in the Greek.

has told you the truth which I heard from God: this is not what Abraham would not do.

8:41 You are doing the works of your own father. "We are not illegitimate children", they protested, "We have one father, and that is God."

8:42 Jesus said to them, If God were your father, you would have developed love (agape) for me, for I came forth from God. I have not come here on my own, but He sent me.

8:43 Why do you not comprehend what I am saying? Because your souls are deaf to my words.

8:44 You are from your father the Devil, and you wish to carry out the desires of your father. He was a murderer from the beginning and is not placed in the truth, because there is no truth in him. When he lies, he speaks from his own reality, because he is a liar, and the father of lies.

8:45 But because I speak the truth, you do not believe me.

8:46 Who among you convicts me of sin? If I speak the truth, why do you not believe me?

8:47 Whoever belongs to God, hears the words God says; therefore you do not hear, because you are not of God.

8:48 The Jewish leaders answered him, "Are we not right in saying that you are a Samaritan and have a demon?

8:49 Jesus answered, "I do not have a demon, but instead I honour my Father, and you dishonour me.

8:50 For I am not seeking spiritual empowerment of myself; but there is One who does require to be honoured, and he is the judge.

8:51 Very truly, I say to you, whoever keeps my words within their heart, shall never experience death (in the heavenly realms).

8:52 So then the Jewish leaders said to him, "Now we know that you have a demon, for Abraham died, and so did the prophets, and yet you declare that

"Whoever keeps my words within their heart, shall never experience death, in the heavenly realms."

8:53 So are you greater than our father Abraham, who died? The prophets also died. Who are you claiming to be?

8:54 Jesus answered, if I give divine empowerment to myself, such empowerment is nothing; it is my Father who empowers me – the One of whom you say, "He is our God".

8:55 But you have not known Him: however, I have known Him. If I were to say that I have not known Him, then I would be like you, a liar. But I know Him and I obey his word.

8:56 Abraham, your father, was glad that he could see my day, and he saw it and rejoiced.

8:57 The Jewish leaders therefore said to him, "You are not yet fifty years old, and yet you have seen Abraham?"

8:58 Jesus said to them, Very truly, I say to you: before Abraham existed, **I am the 'I am'**.

8:59 Then the crowd picked up stones to throw at him, but Jesus hid himself and went out of the temple.

CHAPTER NINE

9:1 As he walked along, Jesus saw a man who was blind from birth.

9:2 His disciples asked him, "Who sinned; this man, or his parents, that he was born blind?"

9:3 Jesus answered, "Neither this man, nor his parents have sinned, but this situation has arisen so that the actions of the Divine may become manifested in him."

9:4 It is necessary for us to carry out the actions of the One who sent me, whilst it is still daytime; for night is coming when none can exert their power.

9:5 Every time that I am in the world, I am the light of the world."

9:6 Having said these things, he spat upon the ground and made mud with the saliva and then spread this mud on the man's eyes,

9:7 and said to him, "Go ! Wash in the pool of Siloam ! (which translated, means 'sent'.)" So he went and washed and came back, able to see.

9:8 Therefore the neighbours and those who had seen him before as a beggar, began to ask, "Is this not the person who was sitting and begging?"

9:09 Some said, "It is he." others were saying "No, it is someone like him." He kept declaring, "I am that person."

9:10 So they were then saying to him, "Then how were your eyes opened ?"

9:11 He replied, "That man, the one called Jesus, made some mud and anointed my eyes, and said to me, "Go; wash in the pool of Siloam !" I went there, and washed, and received my sight."

9:12 They said to him, "Where is he?" He said, "I do not know".

9:13 They led the man who had been blind to the Pharisees.

9:14 Now it was a Sabbath day when Jesus had made the mud and opened his eyes.

9:15 Then the Pharisees also began to ask him how he had received his sight. He said to them, "He put mud on my eyes. Then I washed, and now I see."

9:16 So some of the Pharisees were saying, "This man (Jesus) is not from God, for he does not observe the Sabbath." But others were saying "How can a man who is a sinner perform such wonders?" So they were divided.

9:17 So they said again to the blind man, "What do you say about him? It was your eyes that he opened." He replied, "He is a prophet".

9:18 The Jewish authorities did not believe that he had been blind, and had then received his sight, until they called the parents of the man who had received his sight,

9:19 and asked them, "Is this your son who was born blind?" So how is it that he now sees?"

9:20 Then the parents answered, "We know that he is our son, and that he was born blind.

9:21 But we do not know how it is that he now sees. Ask him, he is of age. He will speak for himself."

9:22 The parents said these things because they were afraid of the Sanhedrin, which had already agreed that if anyone who acknowledged Jesus to be the Messiah, that person would be put out of the synagogue.

9:23 For this reason the parents said, "He is of age, ask him."

9:24 So for the second time, they called the man who had been blind, and said to him, "Give praise to God !" We know that this man (Jesus) is a sinner.

9:25 The blind man answered, "I do not know whether he is a sinner; one thing I know, I was blind but now I see.

9:26 They said to him, "What did he do to you? How did he open your eyes?"

9:27 He answered them, "I have told you already, but you would not listen. Why do you want to hear it again?" Do you also want to become his disciples?

9:28 So they reviled him, saying, "You are his disciple, but we are disciples of Moses."

9:29 We know that God has spoken to Moses, but as for this man, we do not where he comes from."

9:30 The man replied, saying to them "Here is an astonishing thing ! You do not know where he comes from, and yet he opened my eyes.

9:31 We know that God does not listen to sinners, but he does listen to one who worships him and obeys his will.

9:32 Never since the world began has it been heard that anyone opened the eyes of a person born blind.

9:33 If this man were not from God, he could do nothing."

9:34 They answered saying to him, "You were born entirely in sin, and are trying to teach us?" So they drove him out.

9:35 Jesus heard that they had driven him out, and having found him, said, "Do you believe in The Son of Man?"

9:36 Who is he, Lord?" the man asked. Tell me so that I may believe in him."

9:37 Jesus said, "You have (now) seen him; in fact he is the one speaking with you.

9:38 Then the man said, "Lord, I believe", and worshipped him.

9:39 "For judgement I have come into this world, so that the blind will see and those who see become blind."

9:40 Some Pharisees who were with him, heard him say this and asked, "What? Are we blind too?"

9:41 Jesus said, "If you were blind, you would not remain guilty of sin; but now that you claim that you can see, your guilt remains."

CHAPTER TEN

     The Good Shepherd

10:1 "Very truly, I say to you, anyone who does not enter the sheepfold by the gate, but climbs in another way, is a thief and a robber.

10:2 But the person entering by the gate is a shepherd of the sheep.

10:3 The gatekeeper opens the gate for him, and the sheep hear his voice. He calls his own sheep by name and leads them out.

10:4 When he has brought out all of his own, he goes ahead of them, and the sheep follow, because they know his voice.

10:5 A stranger they will not follow, but flee from him, because they do not know the stranger's voice."

10:6 Jesus used this figure of speech, but the Pharisees did not understand what it was that he was saying to them.

10:7 Therefore Jesus said again, "Very truly, I say to you, that I am the gate for the sheep."

10:8 "Those who have come before me are thieves and robbers, but the sheep have not listened to them."

10:9 "I am the gate, whoever enters through me will be saved. They will come in and go out, and find pastures."

10:10 "I am the good shepherd. The good shepherd lays down his life for the sheep."

10:11 "The thief comes only to steal and to kill and destroy. I have come that they may have life, and have it to the full."

10:12 "The hired hand is not the shepherd and does not own the sheep. So when he sees the wolf coming, he abandons the sheep and runs away. Then the wolf attacks the flock and scatters it."

10:13 "This man runs away because he is a hired

hand and cares nothing for the sheep."

10:14 "I am the good shepherd: I know my sheep and my sheep know me –

10:15 just as the Father knows me and I know the Father."

10:16 "I have other sheep that are not of this flock. I must bring them also. They too will listen to my voice, and there shall be one flock and one shepherd."

10:17 "The reason that my Father loves me (agape) is that I lay down my life – so that I may take it up again."

10:18 "No-one takes it from me, but I lay it down of my own accord. I have authority to lay it down and to take it up again. This command I received from my Father."

10:19 The people who heard these words were again divided.

10:20 Many of them said, "He is demon-possessed and out of his mind. Why listen to him?"

10:21 But others said, "These are not the sayings of a man possessed by a demon. Can a demon open the eyes of the blind?"

10:22 Then there came the Festival of Dedication at Jerusalem.

10:23 It was winter, and Jesus was in the temple courts, walking in Solomon's Colonnade.

10:24 The people who were there gathered around him, saying, "How long will you keep us in suspense?" If you are the Messiah, tell us plainly."

10:25 Jesus answered, "I did tell you, but you do not believe. The works I do, imbued with my Father's might, testify about me,

10:26 but you do not believe because you are not of my sheep.

10:27 My sheep hear my voice. I know them and they follow me.

10:28 I give them eternal life, so they shall never perish; no-one shall snatch them out of my hand,

10:29 My Father, the one who has given them to me, is greater than all; no-one can snatch them out of my Father's hand.
10:30 I and the Father are one.
10:31 Again those opposed to him picked up stones to stone him.
10:32 But Jesus said to them, "I have shown you many good works from the Father. For which of these do you stone me"?
10:33 "We are not stoning you for a good work," they replied, "but for blasphemy, because you, though only a human being, claim to be God."
10:34 Jesus answered, "Is it not written in your law, 'I said, you are gods'?"
10:35 If those to whom the word of God came were called 'gods' – and the Scripture cannot be annulled –
10:36 can you say that the one whom the Father has sanctified and sent into the world is blaspheming, because I said, "I am God's son"?
10:37 Do not believe me, unless I do the works of my Father.
10:38 But if I do them, even though you do not believe me, believe the works, so that you may know and understand that the Father is in me, and I am in the Father.
10:39 So they tried again to seize him, but he escaped their grasp.
10:40 Then Jesus went back across the Jordan again, to the place where John had been baptizing earlier, and he remained there,
10:41 and many people came to him and were saying, "Although John performed no wonders, yet everything that he said about this man was true."
10:42 And in that place many believed in Jesus.

CHAPTER 11

11:1 Now a certain man, named Lazaros was sick; he was from Bethany, the village of Mary and his sister Martha.

11:2 And, it was [this same] Mary, whose brother Lazaros now lay sick, who poured perfume on the Lord and wiped his feet with her hair.

11:3 So the sisters sent word to Jesus, "Lord, the one you love is sick."

11:4 Then, having heard this, Jesus said, "This sickness is not there so that death happens, but to make manifest the spiritual power of the Divine, for it shall result in the spiritual power of The Son of God becoming manifest.

11:5 Now, Jesus loved (agape) Martha and her sister and Lazaros.

11:6 Consequently[18], when he heard that Lazaros was sick, he stayed where he was for two more days.

11:7 Then after this time, he said to his disciples, "Let us go to Judea again."

11:8 "But his disciples said, "Rabbi, just a little while ago the crowd there tried to stone you, and yet you are going back?"

11:9 Jesus answered, "Are there not twelve hours of daylight? Those who walk around during the day do not stumble, because they see the light of this world.

11:10 But if anyone walks around during the night, they will stumble, because the light is not in the night."

11:11 He said these things, and after doing that, he says to them, "Lazaros, our friend, has fallen asleep, therefore I am going, so that I may awaken him."

11:12 Therefore the disciples said to him, "Lord if

---

[18] "Consequently": this indicates that there was an initiatory process underway.

he has fallen asleep, then he will be all right."

11:13 But Jesus had spoken about his death, however; the men supposed that he was speaking about the resting condition of sleep.

11:14 So therefore Jesus told them plainly, "Lazaros died."

11:15 And I rejoice on your behalf, because of this: that I was not present (when Lazaros died), so you may be spiritually discerning (when he is awakened); so now let us go to him.

11:16 Consequently Thomas, the disciple called 'Didymos' (which means 'the twin') said to the fellow-disciples, "Let us also go, so that we may die away and emerge[19] with him (Lazaros).

11:17 Therefore, when Jesus arrived, he ascertained that Lazaros had already been in the tomb for four days.

11:18 Now Bethany was near Jerusalem, some two miles away.

11:19 And many of the Jews had come to Martha and Mary to console them about their brother.

11:20 When Martha heard that Jesus was approaching, she went out and met him, while Mary stayed at home.

11:21 Martha said to Jesus, "Lord, if you had been here, my brother would not have died.

11:22 But even now I know that God will give you whatever you ask of him.

11:23 Jesus said to her, "Your brother shall rise again."

11:24 Martha said to him, " I know that he will rise again in the resurrection on the Last Day."

11:25 Jesus said to her, "I myself am the resurrection and the life." The person believing in me even though they die, they shall live.

11:26 and everyone who is living, and believing in

---

[19] The verb used here often means to die and to then emerge, as does a plant seed when placed in the soil.

me, shall never die (in spirit realms). Do you believe this?"

11:27 She said to him, "Yes, Lord, I myself have believed and do believe that you are the Messiah, the Son of God, the one coming into the world.

11:28 When she had said this, she went back and called her sister, Mary, and told her privately, "The Teacher is here and is calling for you."

11:29 When she heard that, Mary arose quickly and went to him.

11:30 Now Jesus had not yet arrived at the village, but was still at the place where Martha had met him.

11:31 When the Jews who had been with Mary in the house, comforting here, noticed how quickly she arose and went out, they followed her, supposing that she was going to the tomb, to mourn there.

11:32 When Mary reached the place where Jesus was, she fell at his feet and said, "Lord, if you had been here, my brother would not have died."

11:33 Therefore, when Jesus saw her weeping, and also her companions weeping, those who had accompanied her, Jesus' spirit was stirred, as if in anger,

11:34 and he said, "Where have you placed him?" They said to him, "Come and see."

11:35 Jesus wept.

11:36 So the crowd said, "See how he loved (phileo) him!"

11:37 But some of them said, "Could not he who opened the eyes of the blind man, have brought it about that this man did not die?"

11:38 So Jesus once again deeply stirred in himself, arrives at the tomb. It was a cave, and a stone was lying across the entrance.

11:39 Jesus says, "Take away the stone." Martha, the sister of the person having died, said, "Lord, there is already a stench, for it is now four days.

11:40 Jesus says to her, "Did I not tell you that if you believed you will behold the glory of God?"
11:41 So, they took away the stone, then Jesus lifted up his gaze, and said "Father, I thank you for having heard me,
11:42 I knew that you always hear me, but I have said this for the sake of the crowd standing here, so that they may believe that You sent me.
11:43 Then, having said these things, he cried out with a loud voice, "Lazaros, come out !"
11:44 Then the man who had died came out, his hands and feet bound with strips of cloth, and his face wrapped in a cloth. Jesus says to them, "Unbind him, and let him go."
11:45 Thus, many of the crowd, who had come with Mary, and who had seen what Jesus did, believed in him.
11:46 But some of the crowd went to the Pharisees and told them what Jesus had done.
11:47 Then the chief priests and the Pharisees called a meeting of the Sanhedrin. "What are we really accomplishing?" they asked. "Here is this man performing many wonders.
11:48 If we let him go on like this, everyone will believe in him, and then the Romans will come and take away both our temple and our nation.
11:49 Then one of them, Caiaphas by name, who was high priest that year, spoke up. "You don't know anything."
11:50 You do not realize that it is better for you that one man die for the people, than that the whole nation perish."
11:51 He did not say this on his own; but as high priest that year, he had prophesied that Jesus would die for the Jewish nation.
11:52 and not only for that nation, but also for the scattered children of God, to bring them together and make them one.
11:53 So from that day on, they plotted to take his

life.

11:54 Therefore Jesus no longer walked openly among the people, instead he went from there to a village in the region near the wilderness, called Ephraim. He remained there with his disciples.

11:55 Now the Passover of the Jews was near, and many went from the country up to Jerusalem to purify themselves.

11:56 They were looking for Jesus, and were asking one another, as they stood in the temple courts, "What do you think?" Surely he won't be coming to the festival ?"

11:57 Now the chief priests and the Pharisees had given orders that anyone who knew where Jesus was, should let them know, so that they might arrest him.

CHAPTER 12

12:1 Six days before the Passover festival, Jesus came to Bethany where Lazaros lived, whom Jesus had brought up from the Dead.

12:2 There they made a supper for him. Martha was serving, whilst Lazaros was among those reclining at the table with him.

12:3 Then Mary took about a pint of genuine nard, an expensive perfume; she anointed Jesus' feet and wiped them with her hair. And the house was filled with the fragrance of the perfume.

12:4 But Judas Iscariot, one of the disciples, (the one who intended to betray him) said,

12:5 "Why wasn't this perfume sold, for about a year's wages, and this money given to the poor?"

12:6 He did not say this because he cared about the poor, but because he was a thief; he kept the common purse and used to steal what was put into it.

12:7 But Jesus said, "Allow her to do this; for she has kept this perfume for the preparatory-day of my burial.
12:8 You will always have the poor with you, but you do not always have me.
12:9 Then a large crowd heard that he is there, so they arrived, not only because of Jesus, but also that they might see Lazaros, whom Jesus has raised from the dead.
12:10 So the chief priests discussed plans to kill Lazaros as well,
12:11 since it was because of him, many were leaving, giving allegiance to Jesus, and believing in him.
12:12 The next day, the large crowd that had come for the festival heard that Jesus was on his way to Jerusalem.
12:13 They took palm branches from the palm trees and went out to meet him, shouting,
"Hosanna !"
"Blessed is He who comes in the name of the Lord !"
"Blessed is the King of Israel !"

12:14 Jesus found a young donkey and sat on it, as it is written:
12:15 "Do not be afraid, Daughter of Zion;
Behold, your king is coming,
seated on a donkey's colt."
12:16 At first, his disciples did not understand these things. Only after Jesus was glorified, did they realize that these things had been written about him, and that these things had been done to him.
12:17 Now, the crowd that was with him when he called Lazaros from the tomb, and raised him from the dead, continued to spread the word.
12:18 It was also because Jesus has performed this wonder, that the crowd went out to meet him.
12:19 So the Pharisees then said to each other, "Look, this is getting you nowhere. See how the

world has gone after him."

20:20 Now, among those who went up to the temple to worship were some Greeks.

12:21 They came to Philip, who was from Bethsaida, and they were asking, saying, "Sir, we want to see Jesus."

12:22 Philip went and told Andrew, then Andrew and Philip went and informed Jesus.

12:23 Jesus then answered them, saying, "The hour has come for The Son of Man to be glorified.

12:24 Very truly, I say to you, unless a grain of wheat falls into the earth and dies away, it remains just a single grain, but if it dies away and re-emerges, it bears much fruit.

12:25 Those who are fond of their soul, nullify their soul; but those who are repulsed by their soul in this world, they shall preserve it for eternal life.

12:26 Whoever serves me, let them follow me, for where I will be, there shall my servant also be. Whoever serves me, the Father shall esteem in spirit.

12:27 Now my heart is troubled, so what should I say – Father save me from this hour ? No – because it is for this coming hour (of my death) that I came into the world.[20]

12:28 Father, make powerfully manifest your being now, with the radiant power which I had in your presence before the world was created. Then a voice came from Heaven, "I have manifested myself with power, and I will again so manifest myself."

12:29 Therefore the crowd, who had stood there and heard this, were saying, "It was thunder", others were saying, "An Angel has spoken to him".

12:30 Jesus responded, and said, "This voice has

---

[20] Here 'soul' refers to the unfallen, divine soul of Jesus, not to the fallen human soul of people, as in v.25.

happened not for my sake, but for your sake."

12:31 Now is judgement of this world; now the Ruler of this world will be cast out.

12:32 And I, when I am lifted up from the Earth, I shall draw all people to myself.

12:33 He said this to indicate what manner of death he was to die.

12:34 Then the crowd answered him, "We have heard from the law, that the Messiah remains forever. How can you say that it is necessary that The Son of Man be lifted up? Who is this Son of Man?"

12:35 Then Jesus said, "For a little while, the light is still among you. Walk while you have the light, in case the darkness overtakes you. For whoever walks in the dark, knows not where they are walking."

12:36 Perceive the light with discernment whilst you have the light, so that you may become sons of light. These things Jesus said, then having departed from them, he was hidden from them.

12:37: Although he had performed so many wonders in their presence, they did not believe in him,

12:38: So that the word of Isaiah the prophet, may be fulfilled, who said: (Isa.53:1) "Lord, who has believed our message and to whom has the arm of the Lord been revealed?"

12:39 Thus they were not able to believe, because again, Isaiah the prophet said, (Isa.6:10)

12:40 "He has blinded their eyes, and hardened their hearts, so that they might not perceive spiritually with their eyes, nor understand with their hearts, and consequently not change; otherwise I would heal them."

12:41 These things Isaiah said, because he saw the glory of the Christ and spoke about him.

12:42 Nevertheless, even many of the elders believed in him, but because of the Pharisees, did not acknowledge him, for fear that they would be put out of the synagogue.

12:43 For they loved praise from men more than they loved praise from God.[21]

12:44 For Jesus had proclaimed loudly, saying, "Whoever believes in me, does not believe in me, but rather, in the One who sent me."

12:45 For the person spiritually experiencing me, experiences spiritually the One who sent me.

12:46 I have come, as a light in the world, so that everyone believing in me, need not remain in the darkness.

12:47 And if anyone hears my words, but does not respond to them, I do not judge that person, for I did not come to judge the world, but to save the world.

12:49 For I do not speak from myself, but the One who sent me - the Father - he has given me a command as to what I may proclaim, and what I may speak.

12:50 And I know that his command - intoning in spirit realms - is life; so therefore what I speak, I speak just as the Father has given me.

CHAPTER 13

13:1 Shortly before the festival of the Passover, Jesus knew that the hour had arrived for him to depart from the world, and to go the Father. He had developed an inner union of spirit (agape) with the souls of his own, those in the world: with regard to the goal, he had inwardly united with them.

13:2 Then, the supper having begun, the Devil had already put into the heart of Judas, the son of

---

[21] "praise from.." or 'glory' from men and God.

Simon Iscariot, to betray him.

13:3 Jesus, knowing that the Father had given all things into his power, and that he had come from God, and was going to God,

13:4 rises from the supper table and puts aside his outer garment, and put a large towel around himself.

13:5 Then he pours water into a basin and began to wash the feet of the disciples, and to then wipe them with the towel which he had placed around his body.

13:6 Jesus then comes to Simon Peter, who says to him, "Lord, you are not going to wash my feet ? !"

13:7 Jesus replied and said to him, "You do not now realize what I am doing; but you will understand after these events."

13:8 Peter says to him, "Never will you wash my feet, ever !" Jesus replied to him, "Unless I wash you, you have no part of me."

13:9 Simon Peter says to him, "Not only the feet, but the hands and the head also !"

13:10 Jesus says to him, "The person who has bathed does not need to wash, except the feet, for he is entirely clean; and you (ye) are clean, although not all (of you).

13:11 For he knew the person betraying him; therefore he said, "not all are clean".

13:12 When he had finished washing their feet, he put his outer garment back on, and returned to his place. He said to them, "Do you understand what I have done to you?"

13:13 You call me 'Teacher' and 'Lord', and rightly so, for that is what I am.

13:14 If I, being the Lord and Teacher, have washed your feet, then how much more should you therefore wash one another's feet.

13:15 For I have set you an example, so that you may do as I have done to you.

13:16 Very truly, I say to you that a servant is not

greater than their master, nor is a messenger greater than the one who sent that person.

13:17 If you know these things, you are blessed if you do them.

13:18
I am not speaking about all of you; I know whom I have chosen. But it is to fulfil the Scripture, "The one who is eating my bread, has lifted up his heel against me."

(**13:18b: initiatory level**)
The one who is consuming living plant foods, is eating that which belongs to me, and those same persons are walking across me.[22]

13:19 I am telling you now, before it happens, so that when it does happen, you will perceive that I am he (the Messiah).

13:20 Very truly, I say to you, the person who receives whomever I may send, receives me; and whoever receives me, receives Him who sent me.

13:21 After he had said this, Jesus was troubled in spirit and testified, "Very truly, I tell you, one of you is going to betray me."

13:22 His disciples looked at one another, uncertain of whom he was speaking.

13:23 One of the disciples – the one whom Jesus loved – was reclining next to him,

13:24 Simon Peter therefore motioned to him to ask Jesus of whom he was speaking.

13:25 Having leaned back, this disciple who was thereby inclining on the chest of Jesus, says to him, "Lord, who is it?"

13:26 Jesus answered, "It is that one to whom I will then pass this piece of bread, after I have immersed it in the dish." Having therefore dipped the morsel in, he gives it to Judas, son of Simon

---

[22] See the Commentary about the veiled meaning in this verse.

Iscariot.

13:27 Then after (Judas received) the morsel, Satan entered into him. Therefore Jesus to him, "That which you are to do, do quickly".

13:28 Now, no-one reclining at the table knew why Jesus had said this to him.

13:29 Some were thinking, because Judas had the purse, that Jesus was telling him, "Buy what we need for the festival."

13:30 Then, having taken the morsel, that person went out immediately: and it was dark.

13:31 When Judas had gone out, Jesus says, "Now the Son of Man is as if empowered, and God is as if empowered in him."

13:32 If God is manifested with might in the Son of Man, then God shall empower The Son of Man in Himself; indeed God will immediately empower him.

13:33 Little children, I am with you only a little while longer; you will seek me, but as I said to the Pharisees and chief priests, this I now say to you: where I am going, you cannot come.

13:34 A new commandment I give to you: that you love (agape) one another, just as I myself have loved you – so that you then shall love one another.

13:35 By this everyone will know that you are my disciples: if you love one another.

13:36 Simon Peter asked him, "Lord, where are you going?" Jesus replied, "Where I am going you cannot now follow, accompanying me; but you will follow me later."[23]

13:37 Peter asked, "Lord, why can I not follow you? I will lay down my life for you."

13:38 Will you lay down your life for me? Very truly, I tell you, the rooster shall never crow, until you will have denied me three times.

---

[23] The additional words, "accompanying me" are in Bezae.

CHAPTER 14

14:1 Do not let your hearts be troubled. You believe in God, believe in me also.
14:2 In my Father's house there are many way-stations amidst permanent abodes. If that were not so, I would have told you, for I go to prepare a place for you.
14:3 And if I go to prepare a place for you, I shall come again and take you to myself, so that where I am, you may be also.
14:4 And you know the way to the place where I am going.
14:5 Thomas says to him, "Lord, we do not know where you are going. How can we know the way"?
14:6 Jesus says to him, "**The 'I' I am**, is the Way, and the Truth and the Life. No-one comes to the Father, except through me."
14:7 If you have known me, then you will also know the Father. From now on, you do know Him, for you have experienced Him.
14:8 Philip says to him, "Lord, show us the Father and that is enough for us."
14:9 Jesus says to him, "Have I been with you for such a long time and you still do not know me?" Whoever has spiritually perceived me, has perceived the Father spiritually.
14:10 "Do you (ye) not believe that I am in the Father, and that the Father is in me?"
14:11 Believe me that I am in the Father and the Father is in me; or if you (ye) just cannot, then believe from the evidence of the wonders themselves.
14:12 Very truly, I say to you, that the one who believes in me, will also do the wonders that I do, and shall do even greater things than these, because I am going to the Father.
14:13 And I shall do whatever you ask in my name,

so that the Father is more manifest (in humanity).

14:14 If you ask me for anything, in my name, I will do it.

14:15 If you love (agape) me, keep my commands.

14:16 And I will ask the Father, and he will give you another Paraclete,[24] so that there shall remain forever with you, the Spirit of Truth,

14:17 which the world cannot receive, because it neither perceives this being, nor knows it. But you know it, because it abides with you; and it will be in you.

14:18 I will not leave you as orphans; I will come to you.

14:19 Before long, the world will not see me any more, but you will see me. Because I live, you will also live.[25]

14:20 On that day you will realize that I am in my Father, and you are in me, and I am in you.

14:21 Whoever has received my commandments and keeps them, that person is the one who loves (agape) me. The one who has love for me, will be loved (agape) by my Father, and I too, will love them, and make myself perceptible to them.

14:22 Then Judas, (not Judas Iscariot) said, "But Lord, why do you intend to manifest yourself to us, and not to the world?"

14:23 Jesus replied, saying "If anyone loves (agape) me, he will live within my teachings, then my Father will love them, and we shall come to that person and abide with them.

14:24 Anyone who does not love (agape) me, will not live within my teachings; indeed the word which you hear is not mine, but is of the Father, who sent me.

14:25 I have said these things to you, while I am still

---

[24] The Paraclete is a comforter, or an advisor, and more besides, see Commentary.

[25] That is, live in the spirit.

with you.

14:26 But the Paraclete, the Holy Spirit, whom the Father will send in my name, will teach you all things, and will remind you of everything which I have said to you.

14:27 Peace I leave with you; my peace I give you. I do not give to you as the world gives. Do not let your hearts be troubled; and do not be afraid.

14:28 You have heard me say to you, "I am going away and I am coming back to you". If you loved me, you would be glad that I am going to the Father, because the Father is greater than I.

14:29 I have told you now, before it happens, so that when it does happen, you may believe.

14:30 I shall not say much more to you, for the Prince of this world is approaching; but he has nothing to discover in me.

14:31 But so that the world may know that I love (agape) the Father, and I do just as the Father has commanded me – arise, let us set out.

CHAPTER 15

15:1 I myself am the true vine, and my Father is the vine grower.

15:2 Every branch in me not bearing fruit he removes, and every branch bearing fruit he prunes, so that it bears much fruit.

15:3 You are already clean because of the word which I have spoken to you.

15:4 Remain in me, and I in you. Just as the branch is not able to bear fruit by itself, unless it remains on the vine, neither can you, unless you remain in me.

15:5 I am the vine, you are the branches, those who abide in me, and I in them, bear much fruit, because separated from me you can do nothing.

15:6 Unless a person remains in me, that person is cast out, like the branch, and withers; such branches are gathered up and cast into the fire, and burned.

15:7 If you remain in me, and my words abide in you, ask for whatever you wish, and it will be done for you.

15:8 By this shall my Father become powerfully manifest in humanity: that you bear much fruit, and become my disciples.

15:9 As the Father has love (agape) with me, so have I loved you: remain in this love of mine.

15:10 If you keep my commands, you shall remain in my love, just as I have kept the command of my Father, and remain in his love.

15:11 These things I have spoken to you, that my joy may be in you, and that your joy may be complete.

15:12 This is my command: that you manifest love (agape) between each other, just as I have loved you.

15:13 No-one has greater love (agape) than this; that they lay down their soul for the sake of their friends.

15:14 You are my friends if you do what I command you.

15:16 I do not call you servants any longer, because the servant does not know what the master is doing. But I have called you friends, because I have made known to you everything which I have heard from my Father.

15:17 I am giving you these commands so that you may love (agape) one another.

15:18 If the world hates you, be mindful that it hated me before it hated you.

15:19 If you belonged to the world, the world would have liked you as its own. Because you are not of the world, I have chosen you out of the world – therefore the world hates you.

15:20 Remember the saying which I told you, 'A servant is not greater than his master.' If they persecuted me, they will persecute you. But if they kept true to my word, they shall also keep true to yours.

15:21 But those who will persecute you, do so because of my name, because they do not know the One who sent me.

15:22 If I had not come and spoken to them, they would not have sin; but now they have no excuse for their sin.

15:23 The one who hates me, hates my Father.

15:24 If I had not done the wonders amongst them, which no-one else did, they would not have sin.

15:25 But this was to fulfil the word that is written in their law, "They hated me without any cause".

15:26 When the Paraclete comes, the Spirit of Truth, whom I will send to you from the Father, who derives from the Father, that one will testify on my behalf.

15:27 You also are to testify, because you have been with me since the beginning.

CHAPTER 16

16:1 All this I have told you, so that you do not fall away.

16:2 They will put you out of the synagogue; in fact, the time is coming when those who kill you will presume that they are serving God.

16:3 And these things they will do, because they have not known the Father or me.

16:4 Therefore these things I have spoken to you so that when their time comes, you may remember that I warned you about them. I did not say these things to you from the beginning because I was with you.

16:5 But now I am going to him who sent me. None of you asks me, "Where are you going?"

16:6 But because I have said these things, sorrow has filled your heart.

16:7 But truly do I say to you, it is better for you that I am departing, for if I do not go away, the Paraclete will not come to you. But if I am departing, I will send him to you.

16:8 When he comes here, he will expose the failings of the world, as regards sin and righteousness and judgement.

16:9 Concerning sin, in that people do not intuitively discern my nature.

16:10 and concerning righteousness, because I am going to the Father, where you can no longer see me.

16:11 and concerning discernment, because the Ruler of this world has been judged.[26]

16:12 I have much more to say to you, more than you can now bear,

16:13 but when he comes, the Spirit of Truth, he will guide you into every truth. He shall not speak on his own, he shall speak only what he hears, and he will tell you of things that are yet to come.

16:14 And he shall make powerfully manifest my being, because what he shall make known, he shall receive from me.

16:15 All that belongs to the Father is mine. For this reason I said that the Paraclete shall receive what is mine and declare it to you.

16:16 A little while and you will no longer see me, then again a little while, and you will see me.

16:17 Then some of his disciples said to one

---

[26] Vs. 16:8 to 11 have very deep and relevant meanings to people seeking the spirit: see Commentary.

another, "What does he mean by saying, 'A little while and you will no longer see me, then again a little while, and you will see me', and 'because I am going to the Father?

16:18 Therefore they kept asking, "What does he mean by 'a little while'?

16:19 Jesus knew that they were wanting to ask him about this, so he said to them, "Are you asking among yourselves about this, what I meant when I said, "A little while and you will no longer see me, then again a little while and you will see me"?

16:20 Very truly, I say to you, you will weep and mourn, but the world shall rejoice; you will grieve, but your grief shall turn into joy.

16:21 A woman giving birth has suffering, but when her baby is born, she forgets the suffering because of her joy that a child is born into the world.

16:22 So, soon you shall have pain, but I will see you again and you will then rejoice, and no-one will take away your joy.

16:23 On that day you will not ask anything of me. Very truly, whatever you ask the Father in my name, he will give to you.

16:24 Until now, you have not asked for anything in my name, but ask and you will receive, that your joy may be complete.

16:25 I have said these things to you in figures of speech. The hour is coming when I shall no longer speak to you in figures of speech, for I shall tell you plainly of the Father.

16:26 On that day, you will ask in my name. I do not say to you that I will ask the Father on your behalf,

16:27 because the Father himself loves (phileo) you, because you have loved (phileo) me, and have perceived that I came from God.[27]

16:28 I came from the Father, and entered the world; I am leaving the world and going back to the Father.

16:29 His disciples are saying; "See, now you are speaking plainly, no longer in parables !"

16:30 Now we know that you know all things and that you have no need for anyone to question you. By this, we believe that you came forth from God.

16:31 Jesus answered them, "Do you now believe?"

16:32 Behold – the hour is coming, and has now arrived, when you will be scattered, each to his home, and you will leave me alone, yet I am not alone because the Father is with me.

16:33 These things I have spoken, so that in me you may have peace. In the world you face persecution; but have courage, be cheerful; I have conquered the world.

CHAPTER 17

The Prayer of the High Priest

17:1 "After Jesus said these things, he directed his perception spiritually to Heaven and said: "Father, the hour has come. Make powerfully manifest your Son, that your Son may manifest you with might,

17:2 since you gave to him power over all flesh, in order that all those which You have given to him, may have eternal life (aeonic existence)."

17:3 And this is eternal life: that they cognize You {as} the only true God, and {that they cognize} Jesus, the Anointed One {as} the one You sent

---

[27] Here 'liking' (phileo) is used, not agape: see Commentary.

forth into this world.

17:4 I manifested the power of your being on the Earth by completing the work which you gave to me, work intended for me.

17:5 And now Father, let my being be powerfully manifested with the radiant splendour which I had with you, before the world was created.

17:6 I manifested your very being to the people whom you gave me out of the world. They were yours and you gave them to me, and they have retained that which intoned forth from you.

17:7 Now they know that everything whatsoever you have given me, is from you,

17:8 for the words which you intoned to me, I entrusted to them; and they perceived truly that I came forth from you, and they believed that you sent me.

17:9 I am asking on their behalf; I am not asking on behalf of all people, but on behalf of the ones you gave to me, because they are yours.

17:10 All mine are yours, and yours are mine; and I was manifested powerfully in them.

17:11 Yet no longer am I in the world, but they are in the world, and I am coming to you. No longer am I in the world; yet in the world I am. Holy Father, keep them in your name, as I kept them in your name when I was with them – those whom you have given to me – so that they may be as one, as we are one.

17:12 When I was with them – those which you gave to me – I kept them in your name; and I kept watch so none of them perished, except the son of perdition, that the Scripture might be fulfilled.

17:13 And now I am coming to you, so I speak these things in the world, that my joy may be fulfilled in themselves.

17:14 I have given them your word, so the world has hated them, because they do not belong to the world, just as I do not belong to the world.

17:15 I do not ask that you take them out of the world, but that you keep them from the evil one.
17:16 They are not of this world, just as I am not of this world.
17:17 Sanctify them in the Truth; your word is Truth.
17:18 As you have sent them into this world, so have I sent them into this world.
17:19 And for their sake I am sanctifying myself, so that they may also be sanctified in Truth.
17:20 I ask not only on behalf of these, but also on behalf of those who will believe in me through their word,
17:21 that they may all be one. As you, Father are in me and I am in you, may they also be in us, so that the world may believe that you sent me.
17:22 The spiritual empowerment which you have given to me, I have given to them, so that they may be one, just as we are one.
17:23 I am in them, and you are in me, that they may become completely one, so that the world will know that you did send me, and that you shall then love (agape) them, even as you have loved me.
17:24 Father, I desire also that those, whom you have given me, may be with me where I shall be, so that they may behold the radiant splendour which you have bestowed on me, because you have loved me before the foundation of the world.
17:25 Righteous Father, this world does not know you, but I knew you, and these men know that you sent me.
17:26 I made known your very being to them, and I shall continue to make it known, so that the love (agape) with which you have loved me, may be in them, and I in them.

CHAPTER 18

18:1 Having said these things, Jesus went out with his disciples and crossed the Kidron Valley, where there was a garden; he and his disciples went into it.
18:2 Now Judas, who betrayed him, also knew the place, because Jesus had often gathered there with his disciples.
18:3 So Judas came to the grove, guiding a detachment of soldiers and some servants from the chief priests and Pharisees. They were carrying torches, lanterns and weapons.
18:4 Then Jesus, knowing all that was going to happen to him, went out and asked them, "Who is it you are seeking?"
18:5 "Jesus the Nazarene," they replied. "I am he," Jesus said. Judas the traitor was standing there with them.
18:6 When Jesus said, "I am he," they drew back and fell to the ground.
18:7 Again he asked them, "Who is it you are seeking?" And they said, "Jesus the Nazarene."
18:8 "I told you that I am he," Jesus answered. "If you are looking for me, then let these men go away."
18:9 This happened so that the words he had spoken would be fulfilled: "I have not lost anyone of those whom you gave me."
18:10 Then Simon Peter, who had a sword, drew it and struck the high priest's servant, cutting off his right ear. The servant's name was Malchus.
18:11 So Jesus said to Peter, "Put your sword away! Should I not drink the cup the Father has given me?"
18:12 Then the detachment of soldiers with its commander and the Jewish officials, arrested Jesus, and bound him,

18:13 and brought him first to Annas, who was the father-in-law of Caiaphas, the high priest that year.
18:14 Caiaphas was the one who had advised the Sanhedrin that it would be good if one man died for the people.
18:15 Simon Peter and another disciple were following Jesus. Because this disciple was known to the high priest, he went with Jesus into the high priest's courtyard,
18:16 but Peter had to wait outside at the door. Then the other disciple, who was known to the high priest, came back, spoke to the girl on duty there and brought Peter in.
18:17 "You are not one of his disciples, are you?" the girl at the door asked Peter. He replied, "I am not."
18:18 It was cold, and the servants and officials stood around a fire they had made to keep warm. Peter also was standing with them, warming himself.
18:19 Meanwhile, the high priest questioned Jesus about his disciples and his teaching.
18:20 "I have spoken openly to the world," Jesus replied. "I always taught in synagogues or at the temple, where all the Jews come together. I said nothing in secret.
18:21 Why question me? Ask those who heard me. Surely they know what I said."
18:22 When Jesus said this, one of the officials nearby struck him in the face. "Is this the way you answer the high priest?" he demanded.
18:23 "If I said something wrong," Jesus replied, "testify as to what is wrong. But if I spoke the truth, why did you strike me?"
18:24 Then Annas sent him, still bound, to Caiaphas the high priest.
18:25 As Simon Peter stood warming himself, he was asked, "You are not one of his disciples, are you?" He denied it, saying, "I am not."

18:26 One of the high priest's servants, a relative of the man whose ear Peter had cut off, challenged him, "Didn't I see you with him in the garden?"
18:27 Again Peter denied it, and at that moment a rooster began to crow.
18:28 Then the Jewish leaders led Jesus from Caiaphas to the palace of the Roman governor. By now it was early morning, and to avoid ceremonial uncleanness the Jews did not enter the palace, as they wanted to be able to eat the Passover.
18:29 So Pilate came out to them and asked, "What charges are you bringing against this man?"
18:30 "If this man were not a criminal," they replied, "we would not have handed him over to you."
18:31 Pilate said, "Take him yourselves and judge him by your own law." "But we are not permitted to execute anyone," the Jewish leaders objected.
18:32 This happened so that the words Jesus had spoken indicating the kind of death he was going to die would be fulfilled.
18:33 Pilate then went back inside the palace, summoned Jesus and asked him, "Are you the king of the Jews?"
18:34 "Are you saying this from him (Caiaphas)," Jesus asked, "or did others talk with you about me?"
18:35 "Am I a Jew?" Pilate replied. "It was your people and your chief priests who handed you over to me. What is it you have done?"
18:36 Jesus said, "My kingdom is not of this world. If it were, my followers would have fought to prevent my arrest by the Sanhedrin. But in fact my kingdom is not of this place."
18:37 "So, you are a king?" said Pilate. Jesus answered, "You are saying I am a king. In fact, for this reason I was born, and for this I came into the world, to testify to the Truth. All those who are of the Truth, hear my voice."
18:38 "What is truth?" Pilate asked. With this, he went

out again to the crowd and said, "I find no basis for a charge against him.

18:39 But it is your custom for me to release to you one prisoner, at the time of the Passover. Do you want me to release 'the king of the Jews'?"

18:40 They shouted back, "Not, not this man ! Instead, Barabbas !" But Barabbas had taken part in a rebellion.

CHAPTER 19

19:1 Then Pilate took Jesus and ordered him flogged.

19:2 The soldiers twisted together a crown of thorns and put it on his head. They clothed him in a purple robe.

19:3 They went up to him again and again, saying, "Hail, king of the Jews!" And they struck him in the face.

19:4 Once more Pilate came out and said to the crowd, "Look, I am bringing him out to you to let you know that I find no case against him."

19:5 When Jesus came out wearing the crown of thorns and the purple robe, Pilate said to them, "Here is the man !"

19:6 As soon as the chief priests and their officials saw him, they shouted, "Crucify him! Crucify him!" But Pilate answered, "You take him and crucify him. As for me, I find no basis for a charge against him."

19:7 The Jewish leaders insisted, "We have a law, and according to that law he must die, because he claimed to be The Son of God."

19:8 When Pilate heard this, he was even more afraid,

19:9 and he went back inside the palace. "Where do you come from?" he asked Jesus, but Jesus gave him no answer.

19:10 "Do you refuse to speak to me?" Pilate said. "Don't you realize I have power either to free you or to crucify you?"

19:11 Jesus answered, "You would have no power over me if it were not given to you from above. Therefore the one who handed me over to you is guilty of a greater sin."

19:12 From then on, Pilate tried to set Jesus free, but the crowd kept shouting, "If you let this man go, you are no friend of Caesar. Anyone who claims to be a king opposes Caesar."

19:13 When Pilate heard this, he brought Jesus out and sat down on the judge's seat at a place known as the Stone Pavement (which in Aramaic is Gabbatha).

19:14 It was the day of Preparation for the Passover, about the sixth hour. "Here is your king," Pilate said to the crowd.

19:15 But they shouted, "Take him away! Take him away! Crucify him!" "Shall I crucify your king?" Pilate asked. "We have no king but Caesar," the chief priests answered.

19:16 Finally Pilate handed him over to them to be crucified. So the soldiers took charge of Jesus.

19:17 Carrying his own cross, he went out to the Place of the Skull (which in Aramaic is called Golgotha).

19:18 Here they crucified him, and with him two others – one on each side and Jesus in the middle.

19:19 Pilate had a notice prepared and fastened to the cross. It read: JESUS THE NAZARENE THE KING OF THE JEWS

19:20 Many of Jewish people read this sign, for the place where Jesus was crucified was near the city, and the sign was written in Aramaic, Latin and Greek.

19:21 So the chief priests protested to Pilate, "Do not write 'The King of the Jews,' but that this man claimed to be king of the Jews."

19:22 Pilate answered, "What I have written, I have written."

19:23 When the soldiers crucified Jesus, they took his cloaks,[28] dividing it into four segments, one for each of them, and also his tunic. Now, this tunic was woven as a seamless garment, from the top downwards, in one piece.

19:24 Therefore they said to each other "Let us not tear it. May divine will determine, regarding this garment, whose it shall be". This happened that the scripture might be fulfilled which said, "They divided my garments among them and cast lots for my clothing." So this is what the soldiers did.

19:25 Near the cross of Jesus stood his mother, and his mother's sister, Mary – the wife of Clopas – and Mary Magdalene.

19:26 When Jesus saw his mother there, and the disciple whom he loved, standing nearby, he said to his mother, "Dear woman, here is your son,"

19:27 and to the disciple, "Here is your mother." From that time on, this disciple took her into his home.

19:28 Later, knowing that all was now completed, and so that the Scripture would be fulfilled, Jesus said, "I am thirsty."

19:29 A jar of cheap wine was there, so they soaked a sponge in it, put the sponge on a stalk of the hyssop plant, and lifted it to Jesus' lips.

19:30 When he had received the drink, Jesus said, "It is finished." With that, he bowed his head and gave up his spirit.

19:31 Now it was the day of Preparation, and the next day was to be a special Sabbath. Because the Jewish leaders did not want the bodies left on the crosses during the Sabbath, they asked Pilate to have the legs broken and the bodies taken down.

---

[28] It is called plural 'cloaks' although in fact a single cloak; this shows it has a very potent significance, see Commentary.

19:32 The soldiers therefore came and broke the legs of the first man who had been crucified with Jesus, and then those of the other.
19:33 But when they came to Jesus and found that he was already dead, they did not break his legs.
19:34 Instead, one of the soldiers pierced Jesus' side with a spear, bringing forth a sudden flow of blood and water.
19:35 The man who saw it has given testimony, and his testimony is true. He knows that he tells the truth, and he testifies so that you also may believe.
19:36 These things happened so that the Scripture would be fulfilled: "Not one of his bones will be broken,"
19:37 and, as another scripture says, "They will look on the one they have pierced."
19:38 Later, Joseph of Arimathea asked Pilate for the body of Jesus. Now Joseph was a disciple of Jesus, but secretly, because he feared the Jewish leaders. With Pilate's permission, he came and took the body away.
19:39 He was accompanied by Nicodemus, the man who earlier had visited Jesus at night. Nicodemus brought a mixture of myrrh and aloes, weighing about seventy-five pounds.
19:40 Taking Jesus' body, the two of them wrapped it with the spices, in strips of linen. This was in accordance with Jewish burial customs.
19:41 At the place where Jesus was crucified, there was a garden, and in the garden was a new tomb, in which no-one had ever been placed.
19:42 Because it was the Jewish Day of Preparation and since the tomb was nearby, they laid Jesus there.

CHAPTER 20
The Resurrection

20:1 Early on the first day of the festival week, while it was still dark, Mary Magdalene went to the tomb and saw that the stone had been removed from the entrance.
20:2 So she went running to Simon Peter and to the other disciple, the one Jesus loved, and said, "They have taken the Lord out of the tomb, and we don't know where they have put him!"
20:3 So Peter and the other disciple set out, going towards the tomb.
20:4 Both were running, but the other disciple outran Peter and reached the tomb first.
20:5 He bent down to look in and saw the strips of linen lying there, but he did not go in.
20:6 Then Simon Peter, who was behind him, arrived and went into the tomb. He saw the strips of linen lying there,
20:7 as well as the cloth that had been around Jesus' head. The cloth was folded up by itself, separate from the linen.
20:8 So then the other disciple, who had reached the tomb first, also went inside. He saw and perceived intuitively (the situation).
20:9 (For as yet they did not understand from Scripture that Jesus had to rise from the dead.)
20:10 Then the disciples returned to their homes.
20:11 But Mary had stood outside the tomb, weeping. As she wept, she bent over to look into the tomb;
20:12 And she sees two Angels in white, seated where the body of Jesus had been laid; one at the head, the other at the feet.
20:13 And they say to her, "Woman, why do you cry?" She said to them, "They have taken my Lord, and I do not where they have placed him."
20:14 When she had said this, she turned around,

and she sees Jesus there; but she did not know that it was Jesus.

20:15 Jesus says to her, "Woman, why are you crying? Whom are you looking for?" Supposing him to be the gardener, she says to him, "Sir, if you have removed him, tell me where you have placed him, and I will take him away."

20:16 Jesus says to her, "Mary." Her awareness changed, she says in Hebrew, "Rabbouni !" which means 'Teacher'.

20:17 Jesus says to her, "Don't hold onto me, as I have not yet ascended to the Father. But, go to the brothers and say to them, 'I am ascending to my Father and your Father; to my God and your God'."

20:18 Mary Magdalene departs and reports to his disciples, that she had seen the Lord. And she revealed to them what he had said to her.

20:19 Then, in the early evening of that day, the first day of the week, when the doors of the house where the disciples met were locked, for fear the Jewish leaders, Jesus appeared, and was present amongst them, and says to them, "Peace be with you".

20:20 After he said this, he showed them the hands and the feet, and his side. So then the disciples rejoiced at having seen the Lord.

20:21 So Jesus said again to them, "Peace be with you." As the Father has sent me, so do I send you."

20:22 Having said this, he breathed upon them and said, "Receive the Holy Spirit !"

20:23 Those whose sins you forgive, they are removed; if you retain the sins of anyone, they are retained.

20:24 But Thomas, one of the twelve, the one called the Twin, was not with them, when Jesus appeared.

20:25 So the other disciples told him, "We have beheld the Lord." But Thomas said to them,

"Unless I see in his hands, the mark of the nails – and put my finger in the mark of the nails, and my hand in his side, I will not believe."

20:26 After eight days, his disciples were again in the house, but Thomas was with them, and Jesus appears – the doors having been shut – and was there in the midst of them – and he says, "Peace be with you".

20:27 Then he says to Thomas: "Bring over here your finger ! And now behold my hands ! And bring over your hand and put it into my side. And so, do not be non-perceiving, but be truly perceptive !"

20:28 Thomas answered Jesus, and said to him, "My Lord and my God !"

20:29 Jesus says to him, "You have beheld me, and you believe; blessed are those who believe, yet have not seen.

20:30 Indeed Jesus also carried out many other wonders in the presence of his disciples, which are not written in this book.

20:31 But these things have been written that you may come to know that Jesus is the Messiah, the Son of God; and that, in so believing, you may have eternal life, through the divine power of his being.

CHAPTER 21

(An initiatory lesson)

21:1 After these things Jesus appeared to his disciples, by the Sea of Tiberias. He manifested in this way:

21:2 there were gathered together, Simon Peter and Thomas, the one called Didymos, and Nathanael from Cana of Galilee, and the sons of Zebedee and two other of his disciples.

21:3 Simon Peter says to them, "I'm going fishing". They say to him, "We are coming with you. They went out and embarked into the boat, but in that night they took hold of nothing.[29]

21:4 Early in the morning, Jesus appeared and was present on the shore, and yet even so, the disciples did not realize that it was Jesus.

21:5 However, Jesus called out to them, 'You children, you certainly don't have any prepared fish provisions, do you? They replied, "None."

21:6 He said to them, Throw the net to the right sides of the boat,[30] and you shall encounter {this}. Therefore they cast it out {in this way}, and then they were no longer strong enough to draw it in, because of the multitude of fishes.

21:7 Consequently the disciple, that one whom Jesus loved, says to Peter; "It is the Lord !" Simon, thus, Peter, having heard that it was the Lord, girded himself around with the outer garment, for he was semi-clothed, and cast himself into the sea.

21:8 The other disciples followed in the small boat, towing the net of fish, for they were not far from the shore, about 200 hundred cubits.

21:9 When therefore they had disembarked on to the land, they see a charcoal fire laid, with a meal of fish provisions lying upon {it}, and a bread-loaf.

21:10 Jesus says to them, "Bring forth from the fish provisions which you have just now taken hold of."[31]

21:11 Consequently, Peter went up, and dragged the net, full of large fish onto the land -153; and though there were so many, the net was not torn.

21:12 Jesus says to them, "Come, have the morning meal". But not one of the disciples dared

---

[29] "took hold of" : not the right verb for catching fish; it refers to the soul absorbing spiritual influences, see Commentary.

[30] 'Sides' is plural; see Commentary about this.

[31] "fish-foodstuff": Jesus has redefined the 'fish' as foodstuff, see Commentary.

to directly enquire, "Who are you?" – because they knew that it was the Lord.

21:13 Jesus approaches them, and takes the bread, blesses it, and gives this to them, as also the fish-provisions.

21:14 This was already the third time that Jesus appeared to the disciples, after he was raised from the dead.

21:15 Then, after they had eaten, Jesus said to Simon Peter, "Simon, son of John, do you love (agape) me, more than these?" He says to him, "Yes, Lord, You know that I love (phileo) you." Jesus said, "Feed my sheep."

21:16 Again Jesus said, "Simon, son of John, do you love (agape) me?" He answered, "Yes, Lord, you know that I love you (phileo)." Jesus said, "Take care of my sheep."

21:17 The third time he said to him, "Simon son of John, do you love (phileo) me?" Peter was hurt because Jesus asked him the third time, "Do you love (phileo) me?" He said, "Lord, you know all things; you know that I love (phileo) you." Jesus said, "Feed my sheep".

21:18 Very truly, I tell you, when you were young, you used to fasten your own belt, and to go wherever you wished, but when you grow old, you shall stretch out your hands and someone else shall fasten a belt around you, and others shall take you where you do not wish to go.

21:19 This he said, to indicate the kind of death by which Peter would make powerfully manifest the Divine. After this, he said, "Follow me".

21:20 So Peter, changed inwardly, directs his attention to the disciple following them, he whom Jesus loved; the one who had reclined next to Jesus at the supper, and said, 'Lord, who is the one betraying you ?'

21:21 Then, having seen spiritually this person, Peter says to Jesus, "Lord, what about this man?"

21:22 Jesus says to him, "If I will that he remains in this same manner, until I am appearing, what is that to you? You, follow me !"

21:23 So word went out into the community, that this disciple would not die; yet Jesus did not say that he would not die, but "If I will that he remains in this same manner, until I reappear, what is that to you"?

21:24 This is the disciple who is testifying to these things, and the one who has written them; and we know that his testimony is true.

21:25 But there are also many other things which Jesus did, which if they were written down, I suppose that the world itself could not contain the books which would be written.

****

PART 2

Chapter Two

The Gospel of John: Commentary

Introductory notes
Before discussing the verses, the authorship of this Gospel needs to be examined. As mentioned earlier, I have concluded that the author was Lazaros, as have some other scholars. The reasons for concluding that the author was Lazaros, fall into three categories.

One is that key events in the life of Jesus, to which the Apostle John was a witness, are ignored in the fourth Gospel. Another is that this Gospel - as I hope to demonstrate in my translation and commentary - contains immensely deep esoteric material which only a person with a deep initiatory level of spiritual insights could attain. This perspective is based on the view that the Awakening of Lazaros, described in Chapter 12, was a kind of initiation experience, which gave him direct perception of high spiritual aspects of Christ (see below).

Thirdly, biographical information about the Apostle John, son of Zebedee, and Lazaros from the Gospels and *The Book of Acts* describe historical incidents from which it is demonstrated to my satisfaction that the Apostle John could not have written this Gospel.

1: There is no mention at all of the following key events in the life of the Apostle John:
The Transfiguration, Jesus praying in the Garden of Gethsemane, and the miracle which brought back to life the daughter of Jairus. We need to note that the author of the Gospel stipulates that he was a witness and writes of what he witnessed. Yet these events in the life of the Apostle John are omitted in the fourth Gospel.

Some argue that the Apostle John omitted these because there were many other incidents to include; but this is unconvincing in view of just how very significant these incidents were. But there are other potent episodes which were ignored. Among these is the

rebuke of John and Andrew by Jesus when they suggested using occult powers to destroy a village, "When the disciples James and John saw this, they asked, "Lord, do you want us to call fire down from heaven to destroy them?" But Jesus turned and rebuked them..." (Lk 9:54) Also ignored is the request of James and John, "Let one of us sit at your right and the other at your left in your glory." (Mk. 10:37) Finally, the following crucial task, which Jesus given to Peter and John is ignored,
"Then came the Day of Unleavened Bread on which the Passover lamb had to be sacrificed. Jesus sent Peter and John saying, "Go and make preparations for us to eat the Passover." (Lk. 22:7,8)

The list of crucial incidents in the life of the Apostle John which are ignored in the fourth Gospel are simply too central to be omitted, if this Apostle were the author.

2: The author of the Gospel is identified as "the disciple whom the Lord loves." This is made clear in the last chapter of the fourth Gospel, "Peter turned and saw that the disciple 'whom Jesus loved' was following them." (Jn.21: 21)
Then a few verses later,
"This is the disciple who testifies to these things and who wrote them down. We know that his testimony is true." (Jn. 21:24)

So the author of the fourth Gospel is the disciple 'whom Jesus loved' and this person also calls himself 'the other disciple'. The Apostle John, son of Zebedee, was never defined as 'the disciple whom Jesus loved'. The only disciple given this status was Lazaros (19:26, 21:7). So here is a clear indication that the Apostle John was not the author of this Gospel.

The second sentence "We know that his testimony is true" does not cancel the declaration that Lazaros is the 'beloved disciple'. It is evidence either that a student of Lazaros brought the Gospel to a close, or that Lazaros. presents himself there as a dual reality, in a similar way that Jesus twice did (see Commentary).

One notes again that in addition to being called "the disciple whom Jesus loved" Lazaros is also called "the other disciple". This leads on to further evidence that Lazaros wrote the fourth Gospel, and this evidence to myself and other scholars, seems to be irrefutable (see point 3).

3: The author of the fourth Gospel relates how, when Jesus was arrested and taken to the high priest's house, Peter and "another disciple" (i.e., Lazaros) followed. Peter had to wait outside, because he was a commoner, but this 'other disciple' was allowed to enter that house "because he was known to the high priest":

"Simon Peter and another disciple were following Jesus. Because this disciple was known to the high priest, he went with Jesus into the high priest's courtyard, but Peter had to wait outside at the door."(Jn. 18:15,16)

Later, after the Resurrection, word was spreading that the Risen Jesus had been seen. Intense interest was developing in regard to this, in Jerusalem and elsewhere. The same Sanhedrin high priests (Caiaphas and Annas) who had interrogated Jesus, ordered that Peter and John, son of Zebedee, be brought to them for interrogation.

These Sanhedrin members met Peter and John for the first time, and discovered that they were uneducated ordinary men, whom however when speaking, had a remarkable power in their words,

"When they saw the courage of Peter and John and realized that they were unschooled, ordinary men, they were astonished and they took note that these men had been with Jesus." (4:13)

It is confirmed from this that these Jewish authorities, Caiaphas and Annas, were indeed meeting John for the first time. So we have proof that the author of the fourth Gospel - a disciple who was 'beloved of the Lord' and also referred to as 'the other disciple' - was not, and could not be, the Apostle John. Because the author of this Gospel was well-known to Caiaphas and Annas; whereas the Apostle John was unknown to them, and did not have the privileged social status that gave him access to the house of the high priest. Whereas Lazaros did have this social status.

It is true that Mark and Luke report that at the Last Supper, the twelve were with Jesus, but this does not actually exclude others also being there. That the beloved disciple, i.e., Lazaros, not the Apostle John, was present at the cross on Golgotha, is affirmed by Mark (14:50) as he reports all twelve disciples fled when Jesus was arrested,[120] but this fleeing excludes Lazaros, since he was not one of the twelve.

So the question arises, why did not early church tradition confirm that Lazaros wrote the fourth Gospel, but instead reported that 'John' wrote it? Could it be that Lazaros also had the name 'John'? Could it be that 'John' was, apart being a common personal name, also a sacred name?

The sacred name of God, as experienced by the ancient Hebrews (never to be used in common speech) was primarily formed of the vowels, 'IOA'. From these vowels the word 'Adonai' was formed, as a way to speak the name of God without speaking the forbidden actual name. This fact of i,a,o as the core vowels in the name of God, was already confirmed by various scholars in antiquity.[121]

The IOA vowels in a name
The name 'John' (in Greek) has three vowels, i,a,o which

---

[120] Keener *Gospel of John*, prefers that it was the Apostle John who was there, because he "could have crept back" to be a witness.

[121] The ancient Greek historian Diodorus Siculus, writing in 384 AD (*Works 1:94*), "The Jews ascribed his laws (i.e., the 10 Commandments) as derived from the God who is invoked as "IOA". Flavius Clement also indicates this in his *Stromata V.6:34*, where he states that the high priests at the Jewish temple were called "Iaou" (in his Greek, "λέγεται δέ Ιαοῦ).

The 5th century Greek theologian states that the title for people working as adjunct helpers in the Jewish Temple "were referred to as Nethinim, which means gift of IAO". (*Quaest in 1. paral.*, section 9).

also form a key part of the name of God; so the bestowing of the name John, if done as a ritual re-naming, is affirming that this person's soul is in harmony with, or sanctified by, God. For in Greek, the name John simply has the letter 'n' added twice to these three vowels, plus a short ending, such as 'aes', depending on the grammatical context of the sentence:

"Ioann-aes" – Ἰωανν-ης.

Rudolf Steiner reports that Lazaros became known as 'Lazaros-John' after being awakened from a death-like sleep of three days, by Jesus; an event which was in effect an initiation process.[122] Is there any supportive evidence for such conferring of 'John' onto a person?

Ritual re-namings

Indications occur in the Gospels of a name being used for its esoteric meaning, namely a person in whom the Divine was present. Theologians can overlook that ritualistic re-naming in response to spiritual influences, was a very common process with ancient peoples still capable of seership, and is still practiced today amongst some indigenous peoples. A person can be re-named in response to their perceived relationship to a spirit being, or to an ancestor, etc.

One example of this in the Gospels appears to be that of St. Mark, who is several times referred to as "John Mark", but the most significant example concerns Simon Peter. Firstly Jesus bestows an epithet on the disciple Simon, namely, 'Peter', for he was actually called Simon, although he later became known to us as St. Peter. The Aramaic word for 'Peter' appears never to have been used as a personal name amongst the Hebrews. It means either 'stone' or 'rock' and its meaning regarding Simon is not clearly specified by Jesus. But his words indicate that it was an epithet given to him on a special ritual re-naming occasion by Jesus, to indicate that he was to become a foundational force in the building up of the Christian church.

On other occasions, Jesus refers to Simon as Simon, not Peter. As befits this esoteric Gospel, Lazaros

---

[122] In GA 94, lect., 19 Feb. 1906, and various other lectures.

includes this epithet 17 times; but Mark never uses it, Luke and Matthew use it only once each. Many Christians in the early years found this esoteric epithet unfamiliar or puzzling, hence Simon is often called Simon, not Peter, in the Book of Acts (10:5, 18 etc.)

Then twice in the Gospel of John, at crucial moments for Simon, Jesus himself re-names him as the "son of John". This is another esoteric epithet. These are 'ritual' re-namings, intended to reveal and affirm his closeness to 'God', to help him achieve spiritual success in the challenges on his apostolic path. (See at Jn. 1:42 and 21:15-17)

These three re-namings are not due to Jesus wanting to formally identify the name of Peter's father, precisely at the moment when Peter's own specific 'ego' or selfhood is facing a major challenge.

Such a legalistic and blood-lineage motivation behind a 'naming', is fully irrelevant to, and also deeply alien to, both the view of Jesus on familial connections, and to the intense spiritual challenges occurring on these two occasions. Christians were to rise above defining their own self or 'I' as part of a family.

The third example where St. Peter is re-named, is in Matthew's Gospel (16: 17). By doing this, Jesus intends to both reveal and to affirm to Simon Peter, the especial spiritual influences active in his soul. He has a resonance in his soul of 'the divine', that is, of the IOA, hence the name 'John' was added, at least in that especial moment.

Another very striking example of naming someone 'John', occurred with John the Baptist. The Archangel Gabriel commanded Zechariah, the father of the Baptist, to give the baby the name 'John' (Lk.1:13). That the Baptist was to be named 'John' is an affirmation that his soul had divine influences and qualities within it, for such a naming was fully alien to that family, as there was no earlier male with that name.

I have accepted Rudolf Steiner's view that Lazaros wrote the fourth Gospel, but it bears the name 'John', because Lazaros was known as 'Lazaros-John' after his awakening or initiation. This is because he had achieved a closeness to 'God', that is, he had attained to a higher, sanctified consciousness. Steiner explains that these vowels, for sacred purposes, were experienced as embodying these qualities:

i embodies the striving towards God or a deity
a embodies the sublime nature of deity
o embodies a comprehending, coming near to God [123]

This would explain the confusion about the authorship; for early church fathers reported that this Gospel was written by 'John'. These people either did not know that John was the sacred initiation name for Lazaros, or they felt it was not right to declare this openly. So people in the early centuries of the church, in saying that 'John' wrote this Gospel, created confusion which lives on in the modern era.

Gaining understanding of this situation, helps to show the reason why this Gospel is the deepest of the four. For Lazaros-John was the author, and he was 'beloved of the Lord'. This is a veiled statement used in initiatory circles to signify that the core spiritual nature of the acolyte's being - his or her volition or will, not only thinking and emotions - was so sanctified, that their soul and spirit had attained harmony with the deity involved.

In the case of Lazaros, it is in harmony with Jesus Christ himself. Consequently, Lazaros was a vessel of the Christ-being; and hence his Gospel has remained the least understood, when assessed from a humanistic viewpoint. As shall become clear, the resurrection of Lazaros as described in the middle of this Gospel, was in effect, an initiation process. From the resulting high initiatory consciousness, Lazaros was able to perceive the presence of the primal Logos and the solar Logos, both overshadowing and permeating Jesus.

The source of the Gospel

The sources of the four Gospels are not fully clear; there are several likely sources, and the theme is complicated by specific editorial activity of the Evangelists. There is the personal involvement in the life of Jesus of a Gospel

---

[123] GA 265, p. 215 (German edition).

writer, who consequently had his own memories of events.

But there were also sayings of Jesus, generally known in the community; these could be integrated into a narrative. Any notes taken down of such words by the Evangelist, or by close friends, could also be consulted. Some of these may have been written in Aramaic, and then translated by the Evangelist into Greek, leading to some interesting 'Aramaisms' (Greek terms in the Gospels which show an Aramaic origin).

Also, there were surely spiritual visions which had the effect of enhancing the memories of events; these visionary moments being inspired into the Gospel writers by Jesus. Rudolf Steiner spoke of this as the 'Resurrection memory"; and this is alluded to in the Gospels when we are told that only after the Resurrection or after Pentecost did the full significance of words of Jesus become clear to them; after the pentecostal Spirit descended upon them.

There is also another source of a Gospel which can't be discussed in detail here, that Gospel writers each had their link to one of four prominent cosmic-spiritual influences. Awareness of this faded out early in the Church's history, but has remained for posterity in artistic form, with the symbols of eagle, lion, bull and Angel (or a human being in its higher potential). These four symbols relate to four cardinal zodiacal influences (Scorpio, Leo, Taurus and Aquarius) as seen by the seer Ezekiel (Chapt.1). These four also correlate to the fourfold-ness of creation and hence of human nature (body, life-force, soul and ego/sense of self).

But the origin of the Gospel of Lazaros-John has a unique element amongst its sources. This is the profound initiatory insights and visionary (or clairvoyant) consciousness of that disciple who was an initiate. He had been initiated by Jesus, as indicated in Chapter Eleven. For Lazaros had not simply been near death and then revived by Jesus to return to his normal functionality and persona, but he had been undergoing a classical age-old initiation experience, in a new way.

He became re-born, awakened to a new and much higher state of spirituality, his sanctified consciousness flowering into an empowered seership. Just before Jesus departed for Bethany to awaken Lazaros, he explained to his Disciples what was going to happen.

Although the reader gains the impression that Jesus affirms that Lazaros "is dead" they were aware that the term 'death' here meant a death-like sleep. But the usual translations do not reflect the spiritual-esoteric nuances in the account in Chapter 11. For example, after Jesus says that Lazaros is so-called 'dead', he declares his intention to 'awaken' him, rather than restore Lazaros to life.

Thomas then suggests "Let us also go, that we may die with him". But unlike modern languages, the Greek verb here which means to die, also extends to include arising as if re-born into life again. This is because in the Hellenistic Age, the view was that when a person dies, they are re-awakened, in the Soul-world (known as Hades).

Consequently, this verb was used of putting a plant seed into the ground, to die, in order that it may 'arise' as a new plant. So in fact though Thomas says, 'to die', the verb used includes a re-birth or arising of new life, after death. "Let us also go, that we may wither away as a seed does, to then be re-born, on a higher level". For this is what the initiation 'sleep' offered to acolytes in the Mysteries. (This theme is further discussed in the Commentary for chapter 11.)

With this lofty origin, the Gospel focuses not so much on the actual physical historical events of those years, but the higher spiritual dynamics that were present behind the life of Jesus. In particular it focuses on cosmic processes that were occurring through the presence of the cosmic Christ in Jesus.

It is important to note that since this Gospel was written from an initiatory seership, it is not so much a chronological account of the three years, as a series of 'episodes' like living cameos, of key incidents that occurred. In addition, it also provides veiled descriptions of profound spiritual dynamics which are crucially important to humanity's existence.

The Historic Present
As mentioned in Part One, Section 8, the type of narrative used in the Gospel is called the 'historic present'. The reader can gain the impression that, as a result of Lazaros seeing in visionary form the events and the inner dynamics in the life of Jesus, he writes in a way which is telling the reader what is happening as he is seeing it.

It is as if all the scenes are still occurring in spirit, which a seer with a deep reverence for the Gospel could still access, given an enhanced clairvoyance, and nearness to Christ Jesus. My translation keeps this wonderful narrative form wherever it occurs in the Gospel.

The initiatory experience
It is helpful here to consider some of the very rare, brief glimpses given into what the initiation process bestowed upon the acolytes in the ancient Mysteries. The first example comes from ancient Egypt; a lofty initiatory experience testified to by the pharaoh Thothmes III himself (about 1450 BCE), as recorded on a stele,

> I stood in the northern colonnaded hall
> as Amun appeared out of the holiness of
> his realm
> His beauty made heaven and earth festive
> and great wonders began, for his radiance,
> in the eyes of the high priests, was like that of
> the dawn.
> The serving priests gave praise to him, ...
> For me he opened the portals of heaven,
> he opened the door of his sanctuary.[124]
> I soared up to heaven like a divine falcon
> and beheld his secret image in heaven.
> I prayed to his majesty...
> I saw the forms of his realms
> on his secret pathways to Heaven.[125]

---

[124] The Egyptian hieroglyph here '*pr*' is often better translated not as 'horizon', but in its other meanings; here, it seems to means 'sanctuary' and then (second last line) 'realms'.

Here we see quite clearly that the ancient Egyptians indeed had initiatory Mysteries, and that their rulers, the Pharaohs, were given admittance to them. Even if one dismisses this entire text as a politically motivated account by the Pharaoh, it remains proof that in this culture the process of being initiated was a known and venerated reality.

Another example also derives from ancient Egypt, but is preserved in ancient Greek, in texts known as *The Hermetica*. This consists of hundreds of pages of esoteric initiatory teachings, which starts with an acolyte describing how a spiritual being appeared to him, to guide him into higher spheres and educate him about those realms,

"Once it happened that when I had begun to think about existence, my thoughts have soared high, whilst my bodily senses had been put under restraint by sleep - yet not such sleep as that of people who have been weighed down by fullness of food or bodily weariness - my mind saw a Being of vast and boundless magnitude coming to me, this called upon me by name.... His name, he said, was Poimandres...and he said to me, "What do you wish to see and hear and to learn about and to know by your consciousness ?"

" ...I wish to know the things that are, to understand their nature and to achieve knowledge of God"... "I shall teach you", said this Being...suddenly everything changed, and opened out in a quick moment...I beheld a boundless vista, everything was now light, a mild and joyous light; I marvelled as I beheld this ……..then I saw that the light now consisted of innumerable spiritual Powers and had become an ordered world, but a world without bounds. This I saw in my consciousness, perceiving it by means of the (hierophantic) word which Poimandres had just spoken. My son, he said, you have seen within your mind, your mental cognizing, the

---

[125] Original text translated in *Urkunden der 18. Dynastie Erster Band*, edit. K.Sethe, Leipzig, J. Hinrichs'sche Buchhandlung 1906; German version in Jan Assmann / M.Bommas, edits, *Ägyptische Mysterien?* W. Fink Verlag, Munich 2002.

Archetypal Form which is the beginning of all things, and is without limit...."[126]

A few brief examples of what the higher consciousness of an initiated person experienced are found in the writings of the Essenes. For example, in the Dead Sea Scrolls are such lines (or fragments of lines) as these,

"The words of the book that the (Archangel) Michael spoke to the Angels of God [after he had ascended to the highest heaven]. He said, "I found troops of fire there...there were nine mountains ..I beheld Gabriel the (arch-)Angel...I said to him...."   (4Q554)
"I saw Watchers in my vision, in the dream-vision. Two beings were fighting over me, saying....and building a great contest over me. I asked them "Who are you, that you are thus empowered over me?" They answered me, "We have been empowered and rule over all mankind. Which of us do you choose to rule you?" (4Q543, 545-548) The fragments in the papyrus go on to indicate that the initiate has to choose between the 'Prince of Darkness' and a great being of Light. Only brief texts exist which report initiatory experiences, because it was forbidden to communicate anything about these to the general populace. In addition, some of reports are not genuinely first-hand accounts, but artificial, pious texts, perhaps built on genuine earlier experiences, and written in a generic style to expound various religious eschatological beliefs in Judaism.

However the great Jewish esoteric scholar Philo Judaeus, reported very factually about the reality of initiation.... "It is not lawful to speak of the sacred mysteries to the uninitiated...it is not lawful to divulge the sacred mysteries to the uninitiated until they are purified by a perfect purification....to do this violates the privileges belonging to the priesthood."[127]

---

[126] *The Hermetica*, Book 1, (page 1) Ἑρμοῦ τρισμεγίστου Ποιμανδρης.

[127] His words reported by John of Damascene, in *The Works of Philo*, trans. C.D. Yonge, ps. 881, 885.

One of the most revealing statements about initiation as a cultural reality, is attributed to a Greek writer called Themistios, writing about 350 AD. By this time the Mysteries were losing their authority and power, and as a result, confidential information was being made public,

"The soul at death has the same experience as those who are being initiated into the Great Mysteries... at first one wanders, and wearily hurries to and fro, and journeys with suspicion through the dark, as if not initiated. Then come all the terrors, before the final initiation: shuddering, trembling, amazement.

Then one is impacted by a marvellous light, and one is received into pure regions and meadows, with voices and dances and the majesty of holy sounds and shapes. Being amongst these, he who has fulfilled initiation, wanders free, released and bearing his crown, joins in the divine communion, and consorts with pure and holy men." [128]

The legend of Cyprian and Justina
The next text about initiation is a pious Christian work of fiction called the *Legend of Cyprian and Justina*. The account existed in various versions dating from about CE 250 to CE 350, and texts survive in three separate documents. It is designed to persuade people of the superiority of Christianity over the old esoteric wisdom and practices.

But these texts in reporting, with disapproval, on the esoteric beliefs of the man Cyprian, actually preserved for posterity rare glimpses into the highly esoteric knowledge and experiences of people initiated in the Mysteries. In about AD 450 a Byzantine Christian empress, called Eudocia, wrote a very long poem based on these documents. This story is entirely fictional, but it is based on real knowledge as to the experiences occurring to those who were initiated in the Mysteries.

---

[128] Published in *Themistius: on Aristotle On the Soul*, R. Todd (trans.), 1996.

"And 20 years of age was I, when I journeyed to Egypt... I went to Memphis, where I learned of things by nature far beyond the earthly. I learnt of the {ethereal} terrestrial forces, how they combine with each other, and of the remote {i.e., planetary} spirits – their intelligence and names, and with what planet they are associated. I learnt the laws that govern these spirits, and what are their tasks. How they flee from darkness and yet dwell in darknesses."

"I was man of 30 years now as I left the land of Egypt and guided my path to the ancient city of the Chaldeans. Here I wanted to learn how the heavens revolve, and also the pathways of the stars. There I learnt about the stars; their associations one with another, the astrological houses to which they belong."

"And I learnt too how, impelled by love, lofty spirit beings gather and create within rays of light....sages taught me of these things.... I then came to {the Mystery centre at} Elis, and later I came to Sparta and saw the clumsy idol, made of wood, of Artemis Tauropolos. And thus I learnt diverse properties of matter, the nature of metals, and of {gem}stones....."[129]

It is interesting to compare this extract from the poem, with the same episode about Memphis, which I have translated from the much older, original Greek text,

"After these things, when I was twenty years old, I came to Egypt, to Memphis, and there in the initiatory sanctuaries, I took up an {initiatory} ordeal about the spirit beings who are located in the spheres surrounding the Earth. {I learnt} about in what place {in the celestial spheres} they ward off evil..... I learnt of amulets and of {esoteric} images – and the script of the cosmos – and of earthly myths..."[130]

We see how this text is presented by the ruling church authority, as a self-evident presentation that the

---

[129] From a German translation of the poem by Eudocia by F. Gregorovius, in *Athenais*, F. A. Brockhaus, 1882.

[130] Greek text of the official 'Confession of Cyprian" in Migne: Patrologia vol. CCX (V) METANOIA TOU AGIOU KUPRIANOU, pages 296 – 329.

Mysteries could bestow an initiatory higher consciousness upon the acolytes. In view of the above rare glimpses into the actual experiences of divine realms and beings, bestowed upon the initiated acolyte, we can conclude that what Lazaros underwent in his initiatory experience, guided by Jesus himself, would have been a sublime, almost overwhelming experience. And in view of the prohibition against public disclosure, it is not surprising that the Gospel draws a veil over what Lazaros experienced, so that this was not described in his Gospel.

Commentary

Chapter 1

The cosmic nature of the Prologue

The Prologue is implying that a high divine being, the Logos, is associated in some way with the man Jesus. Therefore the mission of Jesus, culminating in his death and Resurrection, and then the Ascension, involves this sublime deity. When contemplated with the Initiatory Quest approach, the Prologue's verses reveal truths which are incompatible with the non-esoteric views accepted by the Church for many centuries. As noted in Part One, Section 4, 'Logos' is a term which, in addition to various literary meanings in normal Greek, such as 'word' or 'reason', also had an esoteric meaning in Hellenistic literature.

In this usage, it referred to a high deity or god; thus a god or deity separate from the one, true, 'only God'. In common with various other scholars, I have concluded that it is better to leave the Greek word 'Logos' untranslated, and not render it as 'word', for this everyday term is misleading here; it reduces the status of the deity involved to that of a resonance, a proclamation.

Theologians understand the word 'Logos' in accordance with a humanistic viewpoint, in which it is not a specific being, but an aspect of God. The first two verses of the Prologue show why it can be controversial:

1 In the beginning was the Logos, and the Logos was inwardly with God, and a god was the Logos.
2 This being, it was, in the beginning, inwardly with God.

The Book of Genesis records that 'God', i.e., the Elohim, made Creation, and then, as from chapter two, it proceeds to focus more on Jahve. Whereas the Prologue starts by considering Creation from an even higher perspective. The term Logos, as noted in Part One, Section 4, can apply to either the highest of the Elohim (the 'solar' Logos) or to the great primal Logos, who is beyond the Powers (Elohim), for it is part of the primal Trinity. To spiritual-esoteric understanding this in turn implies that the term 'a God' (in Greek 'theos' - θεος) as regards the Logos, is not referring to the Elohim, but to a much higher divinity – part of the actual Godhead or highest aspect of a Trinity of sublime deities.

In most translations, verse 1:2 is translated as, "...and the Logos was God", and not "...was a god", for the very potent reason that, if the verse is saying that the Logos is a separate deity, then the especial focus in Christianity on "God" – a unique, only God – appeared to be threatened. But this idea concerns a very complex theme, which cannot be discussed here; except to note that the Bible itself alludes to various divine-spiritual beings.

The wish to avoid declaring the Logos to be a specific separate deity became ever more pressing due to the lack of esoteric knowledge in humanistic theology. People were concerned that this Gospel, if its 'Logos' were a separate deity, appeared to put into question the required monotheism.[131] This attitude appears to be the result of a misunderstanding.

Early esoterically informed Christians were aware of nine ranks of divine beings of ever-higher splendour, called the 'divine Hierarchies' as we noted in Part One, Section 5. The Church fathers, as from the 5th century, were disinclined to acknowledge these ranks of hierarchical beings; so knowledge of, and an intuitive sense for, the hierarchies faded.

This resulted in some concern about the Logos of John's Gospel as a distinct being. But just as a reference to a second deity occurs in the Prologue, so too, in the opening words of the Book of Genesis, which the

---

[131] In terms of grammar, the definite article, ('the'), is not in the verse. If it were there, this would mean, 'the Logos was (the) God', but 'the' is not there. So the indefinite article, ('a'), can be assumed, and this means, 'the logos is a god'. But that brings in polytheism, therefore, the definite article ('the') is always assumed by scholars to be what is meant. This is valid in terms of grammar, because in such a context, the word 'the' can be missing and yet still implied. Then what was meant here would be, '*the Logos was God (himself)*'. So the Greek phrase is ambiguous.

Prologue of John echoes, there is a veiled reference to 'God' as a number of creator-beings, not a single deity.

For the first words in the Bible, "In the Beginning, God created Heaven and Earth..." contains a Hebrew noun translated as 'God', but it is in the plural - the 'Elohim'.[132] However, as the verb 'created' used here is singular, this phrase is seen in theology as an example of the 'royal plural'.[133] But there are many scholars who understand this sentence in Genesis to refer the 'Elohim' as a real plural, the singular verb being used here exactly as we use it when referring to a multitude of people, e.g., the crowd *was* getting impatient.

This view is supported by the occurrence of at least nine other verses in the Old Testament where 'God' is plural, and where the 'royal plural' suggestion cannot be applied. Moreover, with regard to the New Testament, St. Paul himself also acknowledges divine beings as realities, on several occasions. He does this directly in a letter to the people at Corinth (1Cor. 8:5), even though he then attempts to direct the people's attention away from these deities and towards the idea of a Deity greater than these beings.[134]

So returning now to the Prologue, both translations are grammatically possible - "was God" or "was a god" - but the accepted version, "and the Logos was God", is the version that most Bibles use.[135] However, once the

---

[132] The words, "In the Beginning, God created Heaven and Earth" (Be'Reshith bara Elohim.... בְּרֵאשִׁית בָּרָא אֱלֹהִים) refer to 'God' in the plural - the 'Elohim'. There is a singular form of Elohim, (eloah – הוֹלאָ) which is not used here.

[133] As when a Monarch could say, "We are not pleased."

[134] Paul does not treat them as figments of pagan fantasy; he specifically refers to various divine beings or gods; such as Principalities, Powers and Dominions.

[135] Technical grammatical note: as Wallace (*Greek Grammar beyond the Basics,* 1996) demonstrates, the view of some scholars that the version, "the Logos was a god" is definitely grammatically wrong, it is itself an error. For, the idea that the word theos (θεος) here, is the only pre-verbal, anarthrous, predicative nominative in this Gospel, and therefore suspect, is factually incorrect, for there are others.

Prologue is understood in its context, on a more spiritually informed level, then the version presented here, "and a god was the Logos" is seen as a viable version. This will become clear below.

Theologians understand the Logos in terms of Old Testament references to the 'Word of God', such as in Genesis, when God spoke, and the world came into being. But then to these theologians, this 'Word' still has to be a part of God; as a result, complex, tangled reasoning has been applied to this problem. For the version, "the Logos was God", results in inconsistent ideas – as is the case with many other transcendent themes in the Gospels when approached without esoteric insight.

Theology has to grapple with the problem caused by not acknowledging that the Logos is a separate deity. This has led to such conclusions as, 'we have the divine paradox: that the Logos is not God and yet is God'. Or as the Athanasian Creed states, 'The Logos existed from all eternity, distinct from the Father, and yet is equal to the Father, neither confounding the persons, nor dividing the substance'. Yet, the insights of Origenes about the Logos had already resolved this confusion:
"This 'Son of God' is nothing other than a (*specific, separate*) deity in whom is present the wisdom and creative power of God; the uncaused Logos, referred to as 'the demiurgos'....a deity having real being-ness."[136]

(trans. A.A.)

But these wise words were later rejected, and much of Origenes' brilliant teachings were lost or destroyed. Awareness of the vastness of the cosmos, with its various divine realms and multitudes of divine beings, was phased out during the course of Christianity's history. Rudolf Steiner explains that this assisted the individuation process occurring amongst the souls who were born into the Christian world; that is, the arising of an individual "I-sense".

---

[136] These words are preserved in the 'Catenae' or annotations in the margins of ancient church documents; "ὁ δὲ τοῦ Θεοῦ υἱὸς οὐκ ἄλλος ὢν ἢ σοφίας καὶ τεκνης δημιουργός εἰκότως λόγος ὀνομαζεται....ὑπάρχων" (E. Klostermann, *Origeneswerke Matthäus-erklärung*).

For psychologically, the birth of the ego or the feeling of being a self, a separate definable person, was coming about in the Hellenistic Age more strongly than in earlier Ages. As noted in Part One, Section 3, this new phase required a feeling of isolation from an all-embracing spiritual milieu, and also from awareness of, or belief in, repeated earth-lives.

But consequently, we now exist in an emptied-out world-view wherein consciousness of the divine hierarchical beings and of the cosmic nature of the Christ, has died away. This now impedes efforts to achieve a renewed, meaningful relationship to the enfilled, living cosmos.

The emptying-out from the Christian worldview of the existence of the nine ranks of divine beings, with their increasingly higher levels of cosmic consciousness, means that theologians have no knowledge of the structure of the cosmos spiritually, and similarly they have little knowledge of the complex structure of the human being soul and spirit.

Theologians have concluded that John borrowed the concept of 'Logos' from the Hellenistic world. Lazaros-John was of course aware of the Logos concept from Hellenistic associates and their literature, but he also surely had knowledge of the Essenes' esoteric teachings, and his own experience of the Logos and of other divine beings, through his initiatory seership – brought about through his initiation by Jesus himself, referred to as the Awakening of Lazaros, which is reported in his own Gospel. The high, primal Logos is part of a triune Godhead, which has an existence or consciousness beyond that of the nine ranks of spirits; but these act as instruments of the Godhead.

We noted in Part One, Section 5, that there are two deities called 'the Logos', and either of these may be referred to as 'the cosmic Christ'. One deity is part of the Godhead, in the remote Trinity, who brought forth Creation as we experience it.

Whereas, the other is the 'solar Logos' or the 'Christ' of the sun-sphere; the leader of the Powers. This same deity is also called 'the Sun-god Christ'. We saw in Part One, Section 5, how in his commentary on the Gospel of

John, Origenes demonstrates that these 'Logoi' are separate, distinct deities.

The Prologue to the Gospel of John refers firstly to the primal Logos, but then later alludes to the solar Logos. Elsewhere in this Gospel there are some veiled references to this solar Logos or 'Sun-god Christ'. See Appendix 5 for Biblical texts that allude to Christ as a cosmic being from the Sun-sphere.

In a similar way to the Hellenistic initiates, Lazaros-John understood the primal Logos as an immensely high deity, permeating Creation in a subtle way. One may conclude that Lazaros-John experienced the Christ (the solar Logos or great Sun-god) as the matrix of the human soul, and as a divine being seeking to impel human beings towards spirituality.[137] In addition, both of these divine realities were experienced by him as drawing nearer to humanity through the crucial sacrificial deeds of the Messiah, Jesus.

However, to Lazaros the quality of the Logos which he primarily experiences and wishes to emphasize in his Gospel, is that of the divine 'Fiat': the 'word' which created the world, rather than the specific aspects that Hellenistic initiates focussed on. Their focus was the intelligence of the Logos, and how it has been involved in a complex interweaving with many hierarchical beings during the course of the Earth's existence.

Lazaros experienced the Logos as the underlying spiritual deity which is seeking to become realized within human beings as the core of their spiritual nature; and above all, as a spiritual presence which is uniquely connected to Jesus. See Appendix 4 again for a discussion of those verses which are understood to show that Jesus is the Logos.

---

[137] Both of these deities and their connection to humanity are alluded to in Leonardo's painting; the *Last Supper*. See my *Rudolf Steiner on Leonardo's Last Supper*.

Verses 1 and 2 have already been discussed to some extent in the Introduction. This Gospel omits the Nativity stories, and other biographical notes about the human vessel of the cosmic Christ, as given in the Synoptic Gospels. Likewise at the Last Supper, it omits the sharing of the bread and wine – the sacred core of the ritual offered by churches. This is because this Gospel has its emphasis on the cosmic Christ, as the source of the teachings of Jesus, and also as permeating the body, soul and spirit of Jesus.

1:1 In the Beginning was the Logos, and the Logos was inwardly with God, and a god was the Logos.

Verse 1 heralds the cosmic perspective which is the core feature of this Gospel, namely that 'the Christ' is a cosmic being, the Logos; the primal Logos, a deity having its own distinct identity and part of the ineffable Trinity. There is also, as discussed earlier, the great Sun-god Christ or the 'solar Logos', but this deity is not meant in v.1.

1: 2 This being was, in the Beginning, inwardly with God.

This verse refers to the relationship of the Logos to the uncaused God, declaring that the Logos is 'pros' (πρὸς) God. This little word has several meanings, such as 'from', 'near' and 'towards'; its specific meaning here is not so directly applicable; it has to be intuited. Contemplation on this text reveals, as many theologians conclude, that there is an 'interweaving' of the consciousness of the Logos, who is part of the triune Godhead, with that of God. ('God' here does not refer to Jahve, but to the uncaused 'Weltengrund' or foundational being-ness of creation).[138]

---

[138] The ending of Verse 2 is ambiguous in Greek, so theologians are not agreed as to where it ends. But many theologians conclude that it ends with, "that has been created." Having the full stop after 'created', allows verse 4 to start with "In him was life..." which is the correct start of verse 4, as the next verses make clear.

Of profound significance here is that a Gospel which presents the events in the ministry of Jesus, starts out with contemplative, historically oriented references to the sublime Logos. This implies that the highest divine beings in the cosmos (since the Logos is close to the Father-God) are associated with the man Jesus. But the Prologue, in referring to the Logos, gradually changes from the primal Logos to the solar Logos. This will be pointed out in the commentary. So the Prologue is a meditative text not about the over-shadowing of a person by an Angel or Archangel – such as occurred with initiates of ancient times. It is about a more sublime reality.

1:3 All things through it were created, and without the Logos was created not even one thing that has been created.

The Logos in Greek is a masculine noun, but since we don't think of a remote sublime deity as having gender, 'it' is a more appropriate term here; this also helps to distinguish this deity from the man, Jesus. The verse emphasizes that the primal Logos brought forth Creation, but as the agent of the uncaused God, the foremost of the triune Godhead. It is also alluding to the first evolutionary Age, when Creation began to exist in a rudimentary form as an Idea, which was descending down towards, but not yet reaching, a physical state.

1:4 In the Logos was life, and then the life was the light of human beings.

This tells us that verse 4 is about the next part of a process which follows on from verses 2 and 3. As Rudolf Steiner explains, these verses are very brief meditative, cosmological statements indicating that the Logos was the actual guiding, creative force in humanity's development. He taught his students that Creation has proceeded through four vast 'Ages' or developmental-evolutionary periods. Brief references to these four Ages occur in ancient Greek and Hindu literature.

In the first Age, we were created as intangible, tenuous physical forms. Then, in the second, this primordial physicality became animated, for in the primal Logos "was life". There was a vast outpouring of life-forces through what would become the solar system. This was achieved by various divine beings, but ultimately this 'life' was derived from the primal Logos. We gained 'life'; that is, life-forces permeated our tenuous invisible, delicate physical form. These next words, "then the life was (*became*) the light of human beings" refer to the third phase (or aeon).

For in this third Age, a faint primitive sentiency or 'soul-quality' was rayed forth by hierarchical beings and permeated the human being. Again this divine creativity, from which the human soul has its origin, had its origin in the Logos.

As a result, our nature expanded from just physicality and life-forces, to having a primitive soul capacity. So the human being was now illumined by an awareness, by feelings; the 'light' of consciousness arose. This light was a dim reflection of the divine Light of the Logos. We can conclude that to the seers of ancient times, any entity with a soul has a living, scintillating radiance. These several processes in remote Ages, were undertaken by hierarchical deities, but guided by the Logos.

1:5 And the Light shone in the darkness, and is shining, but the darkness does not perceive it, and has not conquered it.

Using 'it' for the Light is correct because now the light is in effect the form that the Logos takes on, bestowing again a neutral quality on the Logos. The word 'Light' now refers to the high spiritual radiance of the Logos, and is spelt with a capital letter, to distinguish it from the much lesser radiance of the human soul. (Although this primitive soul radiance could be seen as having its origin – many stages removed – from the Logos.)

So this next stage occurred in remote times, however, the Greek verb is in the present tense (phainei – φαίνει), and there are no records of any variations to this verb in the oldest manuscripts. So verse 5 does say "the light is shining", yet the process started in the past, so the present dynamic had its origin in the past. Many scholars have concluded that the past has to be implied, as well as the present; see Appendix 6 for examples of their conclusions.[139] For the Prologue moves subtly from the past, when the world was created, on into the present tense, in the next verses (see below).

This moving from the past into the present, indicates that the Greek past tense here is a 'gnomic present'. This term simply means that this shining was experienced by Lazaros as a general, timeless fact. It obviously commenced in the past (in the 3rd evolutionary phase or aeon) but is still occurring today.

The 'gnomic' condition of a verb in ancient Greek creates a kind of timeless situation. This feature allows the Gospel writer his wide survey of the ongoing evolving of humanity, starting from the remote past, but flowing on into the present. Likewise, the verb used for "perceive it" is also used in a timeless manner, embracing both the past and the present.[140]

The relevance of this for human beings today is that we have gained a sense of having a personal existence; but our consciousness, our cognizing, is primarily earth-oriented, so we do not have perception of the spiritual. Into this situation, the Logos, permeating the being of Jesus, appears in the world. So this 'unawareness of the Light' has its most immediate, and for this Gospel writer, most critical, phase when the source of this 'light' – the Logos – came to the Earth by permeating the being of Jesus at the Baptism in the Jordan, and then undergoing the events on Golgotha hill.

Yet, Lazaros-John still does not mention the name of the Messiah, nor his role in his present day (i.e., in the

---

[139] In his formal translation of this verse, Rudolf Steiner presents this verse as in the past tense: "The Light shone in the darkness, but the darkness did not grasp it". But, when encouraging his audiences understanding of the Prologue, he treats this verse as in the present tense, and translates it: "the light is shining in the darkness…"

[140] katalambanoe (καταλαμβάνω) this is the 'gnomic aorist' condition.

lifetime of Lazaros). In fact, Jesus is not specified until v.17. However, John the Baptist is both named and referred to several times early in this Prologue, showing again the focus for Lazaros being here firstly the historical sequence of events, and then the importance of the spiritual influences active from within the Baptist, preparing the way for the Messiah.

To emphasize the herald of the Messiah was especially important to Lazaros-John; and this is part of his underlying historical approach to the coming of Jesus. The verses so far point to deeds which brought the cosmic Christ-Logos into the sphere of the Earth, permeating the planet's aura, and hence near to the human soul. However, this light remains imperceptible to most people.

But now another vital point needs to be mentioned again, since 'light' is a prominent feature of the Prologue: the difference between 'light' and 'Light'. It was noted above in v. 4, that 'light' is mentioned, but as of v. 5, it is spelt 'Light'. This is because in the remote past, (the 3rd Age) from the impulse of the Logos, a primitive soul quality is bestowed upon human beings, creating radiance within the human being, to the eye of a seer.

But the reference to 'Light' in all succeeding verses is to the sublime radiance of the Logos (either the primal Logos or the solar Logos). This difference needs to be kept in mind, even though Lazaros does not make a definitive statement about two different kinds of light. This is because within the human being there is also present, but as only a small germinal seed-spark, this divine Light, this spark from the primal Logos; indeed the normal, somewhat tainted, 'soul-light' is a fallen version of this divine Light.

But in practical terms, the Light of the two Logos deities, from which the hierarchical beings gain their sublime splendour, and which enables advanced human beings to become enlightened sages, may not be identified with the general soul-light ('auric radiance') of the human being. The radiance of the Logos in its nature, is a much higher light; it is truly 'spirit' deriving from more sublime realms than that of the soul.

Complex nuances in this Gospel are present in v. 5, for it has two meanings. The verb (katalambanoe - καταλαμβάνω) although translated as 'to perceive it' can also mean 'to grasp', or 'seize it', in the destructive sense of defeating or conquering it. This other level of meaning alludes to the antagonism towards the divine radiance by the urges and impulses inherent in the primordial 'Earth-soul'. Whereas on the other level, "to perceive it", refers specifically to the unawareness by humanity of spiritual light in general, in Ages which are not so remote in time.

1:6 There arose a man, who was sent from God, his name: 'John'.
The verse emphasizes that this man was specifically sent into incarnation on the Earth at the will of 'God'. Codex Bezae records that John was 'sent by the Lord"; and this may be the more correct text; it is difficult to determine which version is right.

"arose": it is literally, "there came into existence".

But that a divine purpose was behind the incarnation of the Baptist is affirmed by the report in Luke's Gospel of the divine intervention, through Archangel Gabriel, in the life of John's parents, Zechariah and Anna. The result of this was that a couple, who were far past the age of parenting, conceived a child; then, they are commanded to give their baby the name 'John'.

The name John was given to him to signify that high spiritual powers would be manifesting through him. The Greek here in v. 6, signifies all this by very abruptly stating "...his name: John."[141] In the Hellenistic world,

---

141

The Greek text here in most ancient texts is abrupt, (onoma autoe Ioeannaes - ὄνομα αὐτῷ 'Ιωάννης) and this may mean, "the name (given) to him John", but it is more likely "the name of him, John", if grammatically here is a rare "dative of sphere", hence "*of* him" and not "(*given*) *to* him". That this more emphatic phrase is intended, is affirmed by codex Bezae which says, "aen honoma autoe Ioeannaen - ἦν ὄνομα αὐτῷ · ἰωάννην" ; "his name was: John". A pause is placed before "John" to create a significant emphasis on this name.

words used in everyday settings could also be used for esoteric purposes.

The IOA: likewise the name 'John' also had an esoteric usage, this is because its three vowels are IOA, and these are the same vowels in the name Jehovah, as noted in the Introduction.

1:7 He came to witness, that he might testify concerning that Light, so that through him all people might discern the Light.

The verse is usually, "so that through him all people might *believe*", which is correct to the Greek, but there is also present here, the nuance of cognizing or discerning: 'so that through him all people might *discern* it'. For the verb, (pisteuoe - πιστεύω) is related to the word 'pistis', which as shown in Part One, Section 7, does not only mean faith or belief, it can also mean an intuitive, discerning cognizing.

1:8: He himself was not the Light; he came so that he might testify to this Light.

On the esoteric level, it is significant that the verse declares that the Baptist was not the light, because the reader, in contemplating these words, is directed towards the presence of a divine being permeating John the Baptist. This is because since John is a human, he cannot be confused with an actual supernal radiance.

The term 'Light' in the Prologue has been referring to the sublime spirit radiance of a high deity, a Logos. Now on this deeper level, the verse is indicating that the words spoken, apparently by the Baptist, are actually those of a radiant spiritual being. In this connection we can refer to the famous prophetic words in the Book of Malachi (3:1) "See, I will send my Messenger, who will prepare the way before me..." Whilst on the surface this is referring to the Baptist as a human messenger, the Hebrew word here for 'Messenger' can refer to an Angel, who would speak through John. In fact, in the Hebrew

Scriptures, the word used by Malachi for an 'Angel' does at times refer to divine beings higher than Angels.[142]

It was used for the Archangel Gabriel (Dan. 8:15), and even for God himself, (Hosea 12:5 and Gen. 48:12). In the case of the Baptist, to the eye of the seer other sources of radiance also enveloped the Baptist, including the spirit of the great initiate Elijah.

So the Prologue here is making the point firstly, that there is a radiant glow around the Baptist, but secondly that this radiance, whether from an Angel or other beings, does not compare to the radiance of the Logos.

1: 9 This was the true Light, which illumines every person; it was coming into the world.

We have noted that some of the verses have two meanings; two separate messages are being presented. Consequently, this verse can also be translated as:

"This is the true Light, the Light which illumines every person who is coming into the world."

In this version, the focus is on the past, and declares that the Logos has an inner connection to every human being - even though it is in a germinal, slumbering state. With this verse, the Prologue begins to indirectly allude to the mission of Jesus, for he is to become the vessel of the Logos.

1:10 The Logos was in the world, and though the world was made by it, the world did not cognize it.

In most translations, this verse starts with "He was in the world...", and indeed 'Logos' is masculine, but as noted for v.5, the neutral word 'it' is preferred, since to modern minds, deities are regarded as neutral, that is, gender-free. Using 'it' also clarifies that the Logos is meant throughout these verses, not the man Jesus. As a human, Jesus did not, and could not, issue forth the divine 'Fiat' or creative impulse from which the cosmos

---

[142] The Hebrew term is 'Malak' (מַלְאָךְ) and is also used for "the Angel of the Countenance of God" (Isa. 63:9).

has its origin. This verse, like verses 1-9, is referring to the Logos.

The traditional view, which sees the verse as referring to Jesus, was formed as knowledge faded away of divine-spiritual beings in the cosmos, and of how these deities can permeate the soul of a chosen human being. As from the Baptism in the Jordan, the solar Logos permeated Jesus, and within this, the primal Logos has its presence. This Logos is part of the sublime Trinity: it is not the same entity as the human, Jesus.

In my translation, the usual expression "the world was made by it..." is replaced by "was made by the Logos". This is to demonstrate that the Logos is referred to here, and not a human. This translation also reduces the very frequent use of the word "it" in these verses, and keeps the reader aware that the verse is about the Logos, not a man.

A glimpse of this deeper and wider meaning is echoed in the words of a notable mainstream scholar, who declares, "it is impossible to refer these words (v.10) simply to (the historical presence of the Word in) Jesus".[143]

1:11 The Logos permeated its own creation, but its own especial creations – human beings – did not receive it unto themselves.

The usual rendering (e.g., KJ, NIV) is simply, 'He came to that which was his own, but his own did not receive him.' Whereas my version is truer to the Greek text, which refers to two distinct parts of Creation, not just one. The differences between these usual versions and to mine, need to be briefly noted.

A: "permeated", the verb here (erchomai - ἔρχομαι) often means, 'approach' or 'come (to)', but 'went to' is also one of its meanings. The Greek therefore can be either 'came to' or 'went into'.[144] When the verse is translated with this latter meaning, it is declaring in effect, that the Logos 'went to' creation – declaring the inherent permeating of creation by the Logos. Whereas "the

---

[143] B. F. Westcott, *The Gospel of St. John*, p. 9.
[144] The Greek is 'eis aelthen' (ἐις.... ηλθεν).

Logos *came to* its creations" implies that a visitor came from outside creation. That the Logos permeated creation is a deeply true and ancient concept; it is found in Plato's works and in the *Hermetica* and elsewhere. In these Hellenistic texts, what is called the 'World-soul' is in effect the solar Logos.

B: "its own creation", the Greek literally says at first, "things which were its own"; and here a neutral word for "its own" is used (ta idia - τά ἴδια). Most scholars agree that this refers to the world, and all that is therein, which was created by the Logos.

C: "human souls – its especial creations", then the Greek uses a different plural word for the second "its own", which is now masculine (hoi idioi - ὁι ἴδιοι). Scholars agree that this word refers to human beings (males being the prioritized gender in the Hellenistic Hebraic world). The human life-wave is of especial significance to the Logos, to God, because eventually human beings shall bring the Divine consciously into expression in a sanctified soul, their true spirit nature.

Already the emergence of the faculty of speech in the soul is an echo of the Logos, the 'divine Word'. So two distinct parts of Creation are mentioned in this verse: nature and humanity. Human beings are also the creation, very intentionally, of the Logos; so we are "its own especial creations".[145]

D: 'receive it unto themselves', many versions just have 'receive it', but the verb also means 'to take something into oneself' especially if it is about accepting and being

---

[145] In fact, it is a core Christian teaching that we are the most important creations of the Word. Human beings are the especial creation and concern of God and therefore the Logos, too. This is why human souls are called "its own (creations)", for the Logos has been the creator, via the hierarchical deities, over Ages, of the human soul. Note too, that although the verse states that human beings did not receive the Logos, this blunt statement, though correct to the Greek, is not meant literally; it expresses a mood, not a precise factual circumstance. For the next verse tells us that some human beings did in fact inwardly perceive the Logos, and therefore took it unto themselves.

influenced by esoteric wisdom or initiatory experiences.[146] So the meaning here is that most human beings did not receive the Logos into their soul. That is, generally, people remained earthly, and did not enable their spiritual potential to come into being – this is the transformative outcome of absorbing the divine radiance of the Logos.[147]

1:12 Yet those who did so receive the Logos – those who discerned its true being – these were empowered through it to become 'children of God'.

In the NIV version this verse is:
"Yet to all who received him, to those who believed in his name, he gave the right to become children of God."
Variations from the NIV, in my translation are:
"its": instead of 'him', the pronoun is masculine, but using 'it' again reminds the reader that the Logos is meant.
'discerned': instead of 'believe in his name', the verb here is from the word 'pistis', which as noted in Chapter One, can also mean 'perceptively discerned' not only 'believed in'.
'did so receive': the verb means 'to receive' or 'to take to oneself', and relates to the receiving of the Logos into their soul in verse 11.
'its being": instead of 'its name'. The expression 'name' no longer has any real meaning to us. In ancient times, 'name' signified the core nature and power of a being.
'empowered through it': that is, it gave the power, which in this context is more correct than 'he gave the right'.[148]

---

[146] Bauer, *Greek-English Lexicon*...παραλανβάνω 2:γ, p. 619.

[147] The verb is used in this way elsewhere. For example, in Matt.14:3 "Joseph, son of David, do not be afraid to take Mary unto thyself as your wife". And in John 14.20 "And if I go and prepare a place for you, I will come back and take you unto me, that you also may be where I am".

[148] Technical grammar note: the verb, didoemi (δίδωμι) here is functioning in a passive manner in the 'middle voice', but in the aorist form. So the Logos is exerting an influence upon the recipient (the initiate) through the latter's efforts, and to the 'benefit' of the Logos.

The process is brought about and empowered precisely by, the presence of the divine light within the soul.

In Part One, Section 6, it was noted that the word 'God' is often a term which 'stands in' for various divine beings and spiritual influences. It is used in a cultural context wherein sadly, knowledge of the various ranks of hierarchical beings has been lost. Consequently, 'children of God', means 'children of spiritual realms', or those whose soul and spirit derive directly from divine beings. So the above translation,
"these were empowered through it, to become children of God," means:
"these were empowered through it, to become children of divine beings."

This means that influences streamed into these initiates from divine beings dwelling in those realms. In a unique contribution to the study the Prologue, in his lectures on this Gospel, Rudolf Steiner explains that this verse is a reference to the spiritual leaders of humanity in remote Ages, long before the advent of Jesus. Knowledge of these ancient epochs has been lost to historians, but recent archaeological research is indicating that there is a basis to this idea of lost ancient civilizations.[149]

Many ancient civilizations had sacred centres for initiation and spiritual research, which became known as 'the Mysteries'. These Mysteries in such ancient civilizations offered a spiritual self-development process which allowed souls to achieve a permeation by higher spiritual influences.

---

[149] The verse is referring to the initiates of remote times. An Egyptian priest, Manetho (3rd century BC), from the significant initiatory site Heliopolis, wrote in his *History of Egypt,* about the existence of pre-Flood civilisations extending back about 20,000 years. His account is today considered legendary, but it is reasonable to view the core of his chronology as having a factual basis. He writes that semi-gods, and semi-divine 'priest kings' were the rulers of civilizations, many millennia before the time of the building of the Great Pyramid (about 2,900 BC, by pharaoh Khufu or Cheops).

Such spiritual influences, existing within several of the divine hierarchical deities, are the origin of the 'human spirit', in the first instance. This can be called the Spiritual-self, when achieved by the person; meaning that the emotions, thinking and volition have all been ennobled. This Spiritual-self can be viewed as deriving ultimately from the Logos, and hence from God: this is the exalted perspective within the Prologue.

A brief text suggesting a similar understanding as to how the sublime light of the Logos is held by lesser divine beings, and then rayed forth into the human being, surfaced in the ninth century. This occurred when a senior prelate, Patriarch Photius (AD 810-89), speaking at a church Council, quoted a text from Clement of Alexandria. Photius was presenting it as an example of what the Church should condemn; see Appendix 7 about this.

1:13 Those begotten, not from the blood, nor the will of the flesh, nor the will of a male, but from God. [150]

When understood esoterically, the term 'virgin birth', is relevant here. It refers to the process of attaining the Spiritual-self. For then the 'substance' of the otherwise only germinal human spirit, derives from the higher spiritual realms; one could say, from the Christ-Logos.[151] There is nothing in this higher human quality from the parents, or from an earthly soul-quality, so it is pure or virginal.[152]

1: 14 Thus the Logos became flesh, and dwelt amongst us: and we beheld its splendour, that of the Uniquely-begotten from the Father, full of Grace and Truth.

---

[150] The reference to 'male' points to the inappropriate dominance over women by the menfolk.

[151] The human spirit to the seer has its own radiance, separate from the soul; it envelops the advanced soul as a spiritual-aura.

[152] The Greek here has the unusual expression "from the bloods"; see under 2:23 where other examples of making a very significant object into a plural object occurs, to indicate its high importance.

'Thus', instead of the usual 'And'; a grammatically valid and significant variation here, showing that this verse is taking further the consequences of verse 13, of the ancient initiates being spiritually re-born; achieving the 'Son of God' state. We noted earlier that this title refers to a person who has achieved not only the Spiritual-self, but also has undergone such spiritual development that their life-forces also are permeated by divine energies; this can be regarded as 'the Life-spirit.

Consequently, they attain remarkable healing powers, for now the life-forces have been permeated by the solar Logos (the cosmic Christ) and thus radiate forth life itself.

The verse has 'Father' instead of 'God'. Rudolf Steiner concludes that this is because 'God', as used in vs. 1 and 2, refers to the uncaused Godhead, whereas 'Father' refers to the reflection of this Godhead within the Hierarchies.[153] Both terms are used by Lazaros in this verse because both Logoi - the solar Logos (or cosmic Christ), and the great primal Logos - are the focus here.

The implication of the Prologue is that both the cosmic Christ (or solar Logos) and the primal Logos were enveloping and permeating Jesus, and thereby were united to the Earth and humanity.[154]

It is the misunderstanding of this verse above all others in the Prologue, which resulted in the age-old view that Jesus is also a deity, i.e., the Logos. This is because theologians for many centuries have regarded this verse, which refers to the Logos, as referring to Jesus. This situation developed because, already from their reading of other verses, Jesus in their view, is the Logos. As noted in Part One, Section 4, awareness of the difference

---

[153] According to Rudolf Steiner, the 'Father' refers especially to the Thrones. This is because when the humanity was created (in the 'first aeon) this occurred through the Thrones (but considered as vessels of the Logos and God).

[154] The term, 'Father-God' is a later theological term which is not focused on precisely which rank of Being is meant, but rather on the intense, will-impelled creativity which was associated with male power, rather than the more inward, nurturing qualities of women.

between the cosmic Christ and the man Jesus was lost early in the church's history; as a result, this core truth was soon regarded as a serious heresy.

A similar blurring of Christian esoteric awareness occurred when the Roman church began in the 4th and 5th centuries to enforce the view that on Jan. 6th the church is to celebrate the visit of the Three Kings to the Jesus Child, and not, as was the custom, the descent of a cosmic Christ reality upon Jesus at the Baptism in the Jordan. For example, Pope Leo (440-81) wrote to bishops in Sicily (letter 18), commanding that on Jan. 6th they celebrate only the visit of the Three Kings to the Jesus Child.[155]

As noted for verse 12, in ancient times there were exalted souls, called initiates, in whom the Logos-light was present. This verse likewise continues this same theme of the Logos becoming awakened within these initiates in earlier Ages.[156] In remote antiquity the cultural guidance provided by these high souls had been profoundly important and deeply revered. In contrast to mainstream historians, this belief exists in some ancient wisdom traditions, implying that notable civilizations flourished 10,000 to 20,000 years ago. This Age of the 'semi-gods' has faded from memory; hence in mainstream Christianity, awareness of such exalted persons and of the guidance they provided in antiquity, is negligible. But evidence of such ancient civilizations is gradually gaining interest from academia.

However, it is the case that in the Hellenistic Age, such advanced souls were known. These people are referred to in mystical Jewish texts, as "Sons of Man", or at an even higher level of attainment, as "Sons of God". To spiritual awareness, the meaning of "the Logos becoming flesh" in v. 14, is that a spiritual influence, derived in the final analysis from the Logos, had permeated the more spiritualized human beings in antiquity, giving rise to their Spiritual-self. This interpretation means that the high status of 'a Son of

---

[155] Augustine of Hippo emphasized the same, relatively trivial theme (Sermons 199-204).

[156] As Steiner concluded in *The Gospel of John*, lect. 22nd May 1908; GA 103.

God' was achieved by these initiated people in ages now long past.

But the concept of such saintly persons with miraculous powers, including a healing capacity, was very much alive also in the Hellenistic Age. One such person, who was approximately contemporary to Jesus, was Apollonios of Tyana who was reputed to have a miraculous power of healing, and of distant-visions and of teleportation; he was venerated widely, especially because of his wisdom and saintly nature.[157]

As with other verses in the Prologue, the primary meaning here is about the Logos, but it is so written that it alludes to Jesus also. The verse is ambiguous because the Logos was permeating Jesus, and because Lazaros-John seeks to both provide an historical perspective, and also point towards the role of Jesus in bringing the Logos to the Earth. It incorporates two meanings; the primary one as given above, and yet also alluding to Jesus as the vessel of the Logos.

It is this secondary meaning which has predominated in religious thought in church history. So the NIV version is also correct, but by having 'his' and not 'its', the translation misses the primary message,

> 14: The Word became flesh and made his dwelling among us. We have seen his glory, the glory of the One and Only who came from the Father, full of Grace and truth.

Consequently, the interpretation of this verse by theologians is that this verse is about Jesus only, and not the Logos; and indeed a Jesus who, though identical to the sublime Logos, became a human baby. To esoteric knowledge, this view is seen as an error.

The understanding here of the NIV translators is that the Logos (Word) is the same entity as Jesus, whose birth therefore brought about the literal incarnation of God himself in the baby Jesus. Furthermore, because the

---

[157] An epigram dedicated to Apollonios in Cicilia is discussed in *New Documents Illustrating Early Christianity*, edit. G. Horsley, 1978, vol. 3, p.49-50.

Logos was (mis-)understood as an integral part of God, then Jesus is also literally God.

Thus the above version "we have seen **his** glory" (Jesus' glory, not the Logos' glory), became the only acceptable view. However, to the Initiatory Quest approach, the 'incarnation' of the Logos occurred at the Baptism in the Jordan River, as discussed in Part One, Section 4. Now, to establish the basis of the insights incorporated in my translation here, this key verse needs to be assessed in detail. But before this, the word 'Glory' needs to be explored.

Glory
This word is 'doxa' in Greek (δόξα) and is another of those terms which have become in need of regaining a meaningful quality. It has three meanings:
A: Magnificence, radiance, radiant-splendour, majesty, and 'glory' in the sense of a holy, empowered, divine qualities of a deity (or initiate).
B: Honour, praise, high social standing, (and therefore 'glory' in a secular sense).
C: Semblance (i.e., illusion) or appearance, opinion
D: Ideas (rarely found).
Here are some examples of A, B and C,
A: we beheld the 'glory' of the Logos (Jn 1:14)
B: you seek 'glory' from people, not God (Jn. 5:28)
C: not even Solomon in all his glory (Matt.6:29)[158]

The usual interpretation of v. 14, which regards this verse as referring to Jesus as a deity (the Logos), obscures the meaning of the verse. Here is again my translation:

1:14 Thus the Logos became flesh, and dwelt amongst us: we have beheld its splendour, that of the Uniquely-begotten from the Father, full of Grace and Truth.

---

[158] A similar situation occurs in the Hebrew (with the word 'tiphereth') in Isaiah 10:12. In the KJV, "I will punish the stout heart of the King of Assyria, and the glory of his high looks." But in the NIV, to reflect directly this third meaning of 'glory', the word is translated as 'haughty'': "I will punish the king of Assyria for the willful pride of his heart and the haughty look in his eyes."

* "Uniquely-begotten from the Father"
From the earlier verses of the Prologue, we learn that everything was created by the Logos, except it itself was created in some unique, mysterious manner, by the Father. This does not appear applicable to Jesus, as no Biblical references to Jesus specify that he was created (not conceived) in a manner different to that of other human beings.

* 'it (or he) dwelt amongst us'
The unusual verb used here actually means, 'to tabernacle', that is, to create a temporary dwelling. This is vitally applicable to the Logos becoming present in the soul and spirit of holy initiates, who eventually left the Earth; but it is only vaguely relevant to Jesus, in so far as he had resided in Palestine.

* was enveloped in a 'splendour' or Glory, which people with seership (clairvoyantly) saw. Again, this is not really applicable to Jesus, who was described only once in a similar manner. This was at the Transfiguration, but then he was seen by just three disciples. Lazaros-John was not among them, he did not see the transfigured Jesus (it was Peter, as well as James and John, sons of Zebedee, who did).

So the Gospel writer, if he is including himself here as a witness, has to be referring to events other than the Transfiguration. But there are no such events recorded. If such a 'beholding' refers to Jesus, in general terms, this could only be an inner sensing of a divine quality within the love and wisdom of Jesus, but this is not what is implied here: rather a direct beholding (i.e., clairvoyantly) of a supernal cosmic radiance.

In addition, this 'beholding of glory' can suggest a larger number of people, and be referring to a widely known, and accepted, historical incident, or indeed, incidents. This is compatible with the wider community beholding initiates in whom the light of the solar Logos was present, in times when people still possessed some clairvoyance.

There is a nuance here that this occurred in various cultures, over some centuries, long ago. To Initiatory Quest critical analysis, it is clear that the 'splendour' or 'glory' referred to here, is about the radiance belonging to a deity. Finally we note these points:

* the verse starts by specifically saying that the Logos became flesh, not the man Jesus.
* Later, verse 16 speaks of humanity receiving spiritual gifts from the "fullness" of **this same entity**. The concept of 'fullness' refers more naturally to a deity, than to a human being. Esoterically viewed, it is less applicable to a human being, even Jesus; in this case, it is referring to the solar Logos or leader of the Powers.

Rudolf Steiner concluded that here, "fullness" or in Greek, 'Pleroma', refers to the harmonious interweaving of "the Elohim", that is the group of Powers, led by their leader, the cosmic 'Christ'.[159] It is this divine host of beings who are referred to in Genesis, (1:1), "In the Beginning the Elohim created Heaven and Earth".

Grace

Rudolf Steiner offers an esoterically nuanced explanation of Grace, explaining Grace as a spiritual state which transcends wisdom or enlightenment. When Grace is present, the human being has the ability through their life-energies (or life-force) to enhance their compassion, making it into a tangible power.[160] This is a power to miraculously heal, or to uplift the subtle 'qualities' of the area where they are living, bringing blessings to the inhabitants. (See v. 16 where Grace has an historical meaning referring back to ancient times.)

Truth

Lazaros here is referring to wisdom; or 'enlightenment' as this soul-state is called in Buddhism and Hinduism. For it is from the influence of the solar Logos, or cosmic Christ, in the soul that spirituality develops; and the first fruit of this is wisdom, or knowing the Truth. He does not use the word 'sophia' at all in the Gospel. Instead, for wisdom, he uses 'alaetheia' (ἀλήθεια) which is translated as 'truth', but encompasses the meaning of 'wisdom'. The closeness of these two words 'truth' and

---

[159] GA 103, lect. 22 May, 1908.
[160] GA 266a, p. 46 and elsewhere in his Complete Works.

'wisdom' is shown in the initiatory text, the Hermetica, "the person who philosophizes to the highest level, will learn where Truth is, and what this is."[161]

1:15 John testifies concerning this same being. He cried out, loudly saying, 'This was the being of whom I said, 'That one who is coming after me, came into existence before me; for prior to me, this being existed.

This verse may appear to refer primarily to Jesus, however it is referring to the Logos. (Although there is here a secondary allusion to the future appearing of Jesus.) Here it is probably neither the personality of the Baptist, nor the spirit of the high initiate Elijah speaking. For over-shadowing John was an angelic being, as Malachi prophesied, (see v. 8). The prophet Isaiah also made a similar declaration, see v. 23. The above words, although from the Baptist physically, are derived from the Angel.

This view is not an odd interpretation of the verse. For we have here the same dynamic as in the Jewish Scriptures when often, God spoke through a prophet. A prophet's words are very firmly regarded as the words of God: this is in fact why the Bible is regarded as "God's word". Through this age-old religious concept, many of the Jewish people listening, would have regarded these words as not from the personality of John, but from the inspiring spirit of Elijah.

"for prior to me, this being existed": The reference here, to someone existing prior to someone else, is understood in theology as referring to Jesus having existed before the Baptist, or as being superior to the Baptist (as the Greek is ambiguous). But from an esoteric view, one relates this text to the prophecy that an Angelic being would appear and precede the advent of the Christ (the solar Logos), to help prepare its way.

Here this Angel is saying that prior to itself coming into existence, the cosmic Sun-god Christ (the solar-Logos) had already long been in existence. The Christ is a much

---

[161] *Hermetica, Stobaei* vol. 1 p.390   ὁ δὲ (ἄκρως) θιλοσοθῶν (μαφ)ησεται καὶ ποῦ ἐστιν ἡ ἀλήθεια καὶ τίς ἐκείνη.

more empowered deity than an Angel, having risen to its higher rank in remote aeons.[162] Therefore the cosmic Christ shall bring much greater spiritual healing and light to the Earth.

Yet, the theological conclusion that this verse is referring to Jesus is also relevant, for the Prologue wishes to interweave the mission of the Messiah with the ancient but ongoing influence of the Logos. Lazaros intended to subtly allude to the imminent, soul-saving outcome of this ancient sacrifice, through Jesus.

Note: v. 15 and v. 30. "This *was* the being of whom I said": yet in verse 30, similar words of the Baptist occur, but they are now present tense, "This *is* the being I meant when I said..." The reason for the past tense here is that the Angel is looking back to the manifestation of the Logos in initiates of ancient civilizations: precisely the theme of v.14.[163] Whereas in v. 30, the Baptist (or Elijah) is speaking of an immediate, present-day event.

1:16 Consequently, from its fullness we all have received indeed Grace after Grace.

These words are not from the Baptist, but from Lazaros.

"from *its* fullness we all have received indeed Grace..." and not as in the usual versions, "from the fullness of *his* Grace..."

The giver here is the Logos, not a human being. This term normally refers to events occurring in historical or recent times, wherein divine spiritual qualities are bestowed specifically upon a person who has developed towards the Spiritual-self, and then lifts the human spirit even higher. Here Grace is referring to a sequence of events already occurring in remote Ages, which had

---

[162] The established view that the words refer to Jesus, implies that to God, one's age – or earlier time of creation – is the basis of valuing two human beings. However, the reader of the Gospels has learnt that the Baptist was older, for he was born, or created, before Jesus was. But this problematic chronology is irrelevant for those who think of Jesus as God.

[163] Theologians generally conclude that in v.15, the Baptist is looking back in memory, from his work of baptising, to a time a few days ago when apparently he saw Jesus in the vicinity.

the effect of ennobling, in an over-all sense, what were then primitive human beings (see below).

"Grace after Grace": more precisely it is 'Grace subsequent to Grace'; this phrase has remained unclear to scholars. The NIV version is similar to mine: "...Grace in place of Grace already given..."

The meaning is clearer if the vast historical perspective which underlies the Prologue is considered. Then the bestowing of high spiritual qualities or Grace is presented as occurring throughout the course of humanity's existence, ever since remote Ages. Grace was again and again rayed-forth into the emerging, primordial human soul, but without humanity being conscious of it.

This verse reflects the historical-evolutionary nature of the Prologue. Grace was repeatedly bestowed by the Christ from a high spirit realm in order to moderate the influences of malignant beings on human beings in its long and arduous journey upon the Earth.[164] That is, Grace was constantly rayed forth to moderate the degrading influence of lower, malignant spirits upon the soul of human beings existing down in the turbulent darkened world of matter. This verse could perhaps be applicable to the Messiah, but only weakly so.

"we all": the verse is about all of humanity, across long Ages. But scholars note that 'the inclusion of the word 'all' appears to place us in new company".[165] However, because the underlying large historical perspective in the Prologue was not seen as applicable here, these words were mis-interpreted as referring more personally to people who were either all disciples, or were the prophets of old, or are the future apostolic church.

"thus": because the cosmic Christ existed long ages before the Angels, and continually rayed-forth Grace (as

---

[164] This realm is understood esoterically to be the Sun-sphere; meaning the sphere formed by the orbital path of Sun around the Earth (in the Ptolemaic view) but on a spiritual level.

[165] Westcott, *The Gospel of St. John*, p.14.

spiritual light) it came about that humanity received Grace repeatedly, since remote ages.
"fullness": this refers to the solar Logos, as discussed in v. 14.

1:17 Since the Law was given through Moses, Grace and Truth manifested through Jesus Christ.

This is the first time in the Prologue that the Messiah is named, and yet here the focus is a retrospective one, looking back to the role of the Messiah (who at this stage in the Gospel has not yet been presented). Leaving the bestowal of Grace after Grace of ancient times, the role of Jesus is now in the foreground. We are told that Moses had brought the Law, but much more was needed by humanity: Grace and Truth (or spiritual wisdom) were needed. It was through Jesus, as the vessel of the Logos, that this was now about to be achieved.
'Since the Law' instead of '*For* the Law ..." The Greek is ambiguous here, but "Since the Law..." keeps the historical continuity of the narrative intact, as well as the intention to emphasize the uniqueness of Jesus Christ.
"manifested through": usually, 'came' through; but the verb here, ginomai' (γίνομαι) means to beget, to come into existence, to happen, or to occur. It only rarely means to arrive or come. Through the Messiah, the Grace which had been rayed forth in primeval Ages, was to be manifested on the Earth through Jesus.

1:18 No one has ever spiritually beheld God, however that deity, uniquely-created, who is close to the Father, it has revealed the nature of God."

"revealed": in addition to meaning in everyday use, 'to explain' or 'make known' something, the Greek verb here (exaegeisthai – ἐξηγεῖσθαι) was used in the Mysteries for the revealing or unveiling of a deity's nature to acolytes. This is exactly what is meant here: the Logos, by its presence within the Spiritual-self in the earlier initiates, directly discloses the nature of God to these sages, who would in turn attempt to communicate this to their people.

"that deity uniquely-created": not 'that uniquely-created son" even though this version is still used in some older versions.

This verse creates serious problems for theology which, unaware that the Logos is a specific deity, views this verse as referring solely to the man, Jesus. In fact, in one later manuscript, from the 5th century (the Alexandrinus Codex), the correct word 'deity' (theos - θεος) was erroneously replaced with 'son' (huios - υιος).

As the earlier esoteric perspective faded out, this stepping-down of the meaning to a humanistic level became widely appealing and persisted up to the 20th century. Then, modern discoveries of very early papyrus texts of the Gospels brought final confirmation that 'deity' is the correct word, not 'son'. One of these reliable ancient texts is papyrus 75, which as we noted in earlier, has a superior system of punctuation and has a more decisive assessment of a passage in chapter 8 of this Gospel, about 'The Son of Man'. [166]

But as a result of this confused history, some translations are still adhering to the traditional Greek text, which is now known to be erroneous; see Appendix 8 about this. However, in view of the complex nature of spiritual realities, these words are also indirectly alluding to Jesus, since the Gospel writer intends to direct the reader's attention to Jesus, as the chalice and mediator of the Logos.

Reviewing the Prologue

The Prologue has several key features:

* The Nativity is not referred to, because the role of the cosmic Christ is predominant; whether the primal Logos or the leader of the Powers or Elohim (the solar logos).

* Underlying the Prologue is a long-term historical perspective, as well as the intention to point to a cosmic aspect of Christ. Humanity's development is surveyed, during which the text moves between the past and present, so it alludes at times to Jesus. In addition, the connection of Jesus with the primal Logos of the triune

---

[166] The other manuscript is Papyrus 66 (ca. AD 150) in *The Complete Text of the Earliest NT Manuscripts*, edit. Comfort & Barrett, 1999.

Godhead, and of the solar Logos (or leader of the Elohim) is alluded to.

* The roles of John the Baptist, and the Angel above him, as preparers for the advent of the Christ, are emphasized.

* The role of Jesus is directly indicated in verse 9, but he is not named until verse 17; however, his role is alluded to in several other verses. These verses subtly interweave two messages, the crucial significance of the Logos to humanity's evolving, and how the sacrifice of Jesus enables divine influences to envelop the Earth, providing a pathway for human beings to spirituality.

Appendix 9 has notes on Rudolf Steiner's interpretation of v. 14 which makes use of the old, venerated, but incorrect, Greek text. Appendix 10 presents his interpretation of v.18, using the traditional, alternative Greek text.

The Prologue to the Gospel of John

PAST primal Logos	**1** In the Beginning was the Logos, and the Logos was inwardly with God, and a divine being was the Logos.
PAST primal Logos	**2** This being, it was, in the Beginning, inwardly with God.
PAST 1st Age Primal Logos	**3** All things through it were created, and without the Logos was created not even one thing, that has been created.
PAST 2nd Age to 3rd Age. From primal Logos to solar Logos	**4** In the Logos was life, and then the life was the light of human beings.
PAST into PRESENT 3rd Age to 4th Age solar Logos	**5** And the Light shone in the darkness, and is shining; the darkness does not perceive it, and has not conquered it.
PRESENT	**6** There arose a man, who was sent forth from God, his name: John.
PRESENT	**7** He came to witness, that he might testify concerning that Light, so that through him all people might discern the light.

8 He himself was not the Light; he came as a witness to this Light.

| | PRESENT |

9 This was the true Light which illumines every person; it was coming into the world.

| | PRESENT
The solar Logos
(alludes to the
later role
of Jesus) |

10 The Logos was in the world and though the world was made by it, the world did not cognize it.

| | PAST
The solar Logos |

11 The Logos permeated its own creation, but its own especial creations – human beings – did not acknowledge it.

| | RECENT PAST
Solar Logos
As from the Age
when humans
became egoic |

12 Yet those who acknowledged the Logos – those who perceived its true being – these were empowered through it to become 'children of God'.

| | RECENT PAST
The Logos in
initiates of
antiquity |

13 Those begotten, not from the blood, nor from the will of the flesh, nor the will of a male, but from God.

| | RECENT PAST
(birth of the
eternal self in
the initiates) |

RECENT PAST initiates of antiquity	**14** Thus the Logos became flesh, and dwelt amongst us: and we beheld its manifested splendour, the splendour of the Uniquely-begotten from the Father, full of Grace and Truth.
PAST into the PRESENT, the Angel in John, about the cosmic Christ, i.e., solar Logos	**15** John testifies concerning the Logos. He cried out loudly, saying, "This was the being of whom I said, 'The one who is coming after me, came into existence before me; for prior to me, this being existed.' "
PAST into PRESENT the solar Logos	**16** Consequently, from its fullness, we have all received indeed Grace after Grace.
PAST & PRESENT	**17** Since the Law was given through Moses, Grace and Truth came from Jesus Christ.
PAST & PRESENT (alluding also to Jesus)	**18** No one has ever spiritually beheld God; however that deity, uniquely-created, who is close to the Father, it has revealed the nature of God.

Chapter 1: 19 - 28
(From v. 19 that the Gospel takes up the contemporary course of events in the life of Jesus.)
1:19 Now this is John's testimony when the Jewish authorities in Jerusalem sent priests and Levites, in order to ask him, 'who are you'?

This verse prepares the reader for significant words coming from the mouth of the Baptist, yet originating with the Angel who hovered above him (or 'over-lighted' him).

1: 20 He then solemnly declared, thus he did not deny, but solemnly declared that, "I – I'm not the Messiah".

In this verse the response of the Baptist is a forcible assertion, declared three times, that he is not the Messiah. However, in some translations his answer is abbreviated to: "He did not fail to confess, but confessed freely..." Many versions also render the next part as:
   "He answered, and said, I am not the Christ".
But in the dialogue of verses 20-23, the word "I" is deliberately emphasized. Theologians note the unusual emphasis placed upon the 'I' in these verses; but can be unsure as to why this is done, "This emphatic personal pronoun is a marked feature in John's speech (here)."[167]

In verse 20 we have a dense sentence which emphasizes the individual 'I'; it is literally, "*I, not am I the Messiah*".[168] This emphatic phrase enables the contemplative reader to intuit a deep truth. The human sense of 'I' is a crucial concern to the cosmic Christ, and to the Angel inspiring the Baptist, who voices the condition and perspective of the 'I' in contemporary people.

The core mission of the Christ is to bestow upon humanity the possibility for a true, eternal self. Whereas the angelic herald does not possess this capacity, a fact

---

[167] For example, L. Morris, *The Gospel according to John*, NICNT, 1995, p.117.
[168] The Greek is: Εγώ οὐκ εἰμὶ ὁ Χριστός. The traditional, "Received Text' has less accurate Greek; οὐκ εἰμι Ἐγὼ ὁ Χριστός which has the same meaning, but is clumsy.

which the angelic herald wishes to emphasize. The second reason for the emphasis upon the ego becomes clear with v. 23.

1:21 They asked him, "Then who are you? Are you Elijah?" And then he said, "I am not". Are you the prophet? Then he replied, "No."

Again, there is emphasis on the 'I', that is, on his own core spiritual nature, but in a mood of humility, being so far below the cosmic Christ, the great archetype of the higher "I".

"I am not": there is emphasis in the Greek which is literally, "Not am I" which puts 'not' first, thus emphasizing the 'I'.

But just before that, the speaker denies being Elijah (re-appeared), an event which people were anticipating. To resolve this riddle, we need to briefly clarify the context. Jesus himself declared that the Baptist is Elijah, reappeared; and as the Gospels indicate, an aspect of the spirit of Elijah was present in John the Baptist. (So it is not a case of reincarnation in the full sense, but it is in an unusual, partial sense; hence Jesus did declare that John was, in effect, Elijah.)

Therefore, it is striking that the speaker in the dialogue with the Pharisees denies that he is Elijah. The reason for this is already indicated above: that it is the Angel above John who is now speaking, and not the person John, nor Elijah, although the presence of the great initiate Elijah was always there.

Also note that the 'reappearance' of Elijah did not necessarily imply a reincarnation to all Jewish people at this time. For many had concluded that Elijah never died, because the end of Elijah's time on the Earth is described as an ascension into a fiery chariot; therefore, some people thought Elijah could return in a bodily form.

The Angel above the Baptist also had to deny being 'the prophet' – but this is anyway a question caused by a widespread misunderstanding. Some people thought that another great prophet had been foretold by Moses, (in Deut 18:15). But Moses was referring to the Messiah.

1:22 So they said to him, "Who are you – that we may give an answer to those who sent us. What do you say about yourself?

The question by the deputation from Jerusalem, in asking about 'the self' of the Baptist, invokes an answer which points to the core dilemma arising for the individual person, for their self-sense.

1:23 He said,
 I, a voice crying out in the desolate place,
 'Make straight the path of the Divine Being !',
 just as the prophet Isaiah said.

The cultural context, and surface meaning here is, that John was a desert-dweller and was on a mission to prepare people for the work of Jesus; and people did come out to the desert to see him. Consequently, he is 'a voice in the (literal) desert'.

But on the esoteric level, much more is signified in this remarkable answer. The questioners in asking the Baptist pointedly about 'himself', invoke a response in which the Angel's intentions are interwoven with the Baptist's own self.

The answer is actually not a personal, self-affirming nor a self-defending one; it has an impersonal quality. As Myer noted, "John is divesting himself of every personal characteristic".[169] Although it appears that the word 'I' is referring to the Baptist, his answer, inspired by the Angel, is describing with startling clarity, the condition of the 'I' of the people of his times everywhere. A common translation is, "I am a voice crying out..." But here the word 'am' has been added, giving a personal nuance, but there is no 'am' in the Greek text. The answer is referring to, and directly defining, the core dynamic of the ego or 'I'.

The second reason for the emphasis placed upon the ego, as noted already in v. 21, is now unveiled. The Greek word for 'desert' also means 'a desolate place', and as Rudolf Steiner noted, this term can be applied to the soul-state of people in the Hellenistic Age, wherein

---

[169] H.A.W. Meyer, *Handbook to the Gospel of John*, 1881, p.107.

the earlier holistic sense of life was fading. It was used in this metaphorical way by the Essenes, who referred to Jerusalem as 'a desert', or place of inner desolation.[170]

So now, in an oracular manner, the core dynamic of the human being is declared. For the Pharisees and for all people of those times, there is a subtly desolate situation of increasing self-awareness within, but decreasing awareness of spiritual realities without.

Compared to the more holistic, more spiritually sensitive consciousness of earlier millennia, people of the Grecian world for some centuries had been entering a 'spiritual desert' in which both religious convictions and spiritual cognizing were fading.

As such, these people were a herald of the Age of Materialism which would emerge in Renaissance Europe and England, and become global in modern times, bringing widespread social alienation and environmental indifference. Thus the individuated human being in that Age was in a state of inner desolation, having lost the previous holistic consciousness of ancient times. This condition was noted by those who still retained a sense for the spiritual. The writer of *The Wisdom of Solomon*, writing in the first century BCE, notes,

"These people said to themselves in their deluded way, when a person reaches the end of life, there is no solution, for no-one was ever known to return from the grave...our intelligence is kept alive by the beating of the heart.... and when that stops, our existence will disperse like empty air."[171]

When one knows of the intense focus in earlier times, on the existence of the soul after death, these new materialistic convictions, echoed by the writer of the *Wisdom of Solomon* are highly significant. The sense of self or personal 'I', which was destined to emerge and strengthen in our modern times, though vital to humanity's development, is a two-edged sword. If the 'I' or sense of self is not spiritualized, the future will be

---

[170] DSS, the War Rule, 1QM:2.
[171] Extracted from *The Wisdom of Solomon*, 2:1-4, New English Bible version.

bleak, because then the potently anti-social, ego-centric personalities will predominate. Here is v. 22 again:

"So they said to him, "Who are you – that we may give an answer to those who sent us. What do you say about yourself ?"

Then the answer comes:
"I, a voice crying out in the desolate place..."

This is how the Baptist experienced people's situation to be, and this was also as the Angel would have perceived the human soul's condition to be, when surveyed from its own loftier perspective. Before examining further the gradual historical change in consciousness, we note that most translations then have, 'Make straight the path of the Lord', translating the Greek word here, 'Kyrios' (κύριος) as 'Lord'. Again on the non-esoteric level, 'Lord' is fully correct, and completes the idea of the Baptist preparing for Jesus.

But I have chosen:
'Make straight the path of the divine Being'.

The Greek word, 'Kyrios' was not only used to refer to God or to Christ. It was also used for a person's guardian, or their trustee, or for any powerful person, and also for a deity. It was also used for any person or a spiritual being who was regarded as important in a social setting.

Using this meaning, the verse is now referring to what one could describe as the 'Higher-self' of the human being; in other words, to the as yet unrealized, spiritual potential, the 'divine spark' within us. By the 'Higher-self' we mean that in exceptional people, or in exceptional circumstances, human beings can manifest a magnificently ethical, selfless wisdom and love. It is this which can be viewed as the true, ethical self. Here in the words of the verse, this is viewed as the 'lord' over the soul. But this 'divine spark' is to be understood as interwoven with the Christ.

Consequently, where Isaiah declared that people should '*prepare* the path of the divine Being', the Gospel text has instead used the verb 'to make straight' the path. This change emphasizes the inner life; that is, the soul is to assist the emerging of its higher qualities empowered from the entangled, darkened lower soul qualities.

The oracular answer, from the Baptist and his inspiring Angel, indicates that only by striving to open up an inner pathway which enables the presence of the higher 'I' to emerge in the personality, can humanity have a worthwhile future. This higher ego is what the word 'Kyrios' is pointing to here. This is also what lies behind the famous admonishing words, "Repent (*undergo an inner development*) for the heavenly realms are drawing near" (Matt. 3:2).

It was the intention of Christ that, from the deeds on Golgotha hill, the higher-I could emerge over some millennia, from the otherwise precariously self-focussed state of the personal ego-sense. So the call of the Baptist and the Angel is,

"Make straight (*i.e., facilitate*) the emergence of the higher ego from your personality – for the Messiah is coming, from whose divine nature this same human Higher-self derives."

1:24 Now among those who had been sent there were some of the Pharisees,

This verse needs no commentary, although there are some text variations.[172]

1:25 who questioned him, 'Why do you baptize, if you are not the Messiah, nor Elijah, nor the Prophet?'

The question makes evident that the Pharisees were incensed at the insult implied to them. Normally only converts to Judaism were required to be baptised for soul cleansing. To the Pharisees, this is something which

---

[172] The Greek manuscripts here vary, some have "and those who had been sent were Pharisees", or "the priests and Levites had been sent by the Pharisees".. but these are very unlikely, since 'priests and Levites' implies that these men were not Pharisees; and the Pharisees were not authorized to command such persons.

only the Messiah or Elijah could demand of them. But other people had realised that the Baptist had a special power. The baptism process helped them to perceive just how much more they needed to strive towards a higher state.

1:26 "I, I baptize in water", John replied, "but among you is present One you do not perceive,"

In earlier verses the Angel has spoken from its viewpoint, emphasizing its task, and implying that the 'I' of the human being is specifically the focus of the Angel's interest. Now the Baptist speaks from his own acute self-awareness; he is also emphasizing his inferiority to Jesus.

"...is present One you do not perceive": the Baptist is alluding to the presence of the Messiah, the bearer of the cosmic Christ, but whose existence is not perceptible without seership or at least the psychic-intuitive cognizing that a successful baptism should bestow, a process in which most Pharisees presumably had little interest. Such intuitive cognizing is, as we have noted, 'faith' in its alternative meaning.

Many have felt that with these words, the Baptist has not in fact really answered the question. But he has answered it; this verse has to be contemplated together with v. 27 to fully see his answer.

1:27 He is the one who is coming after me; the straps of whose sandals I am not worthy to untie.

The answer in v. 26 is spoken with awareness of the primary spiritual dynamic of the times. This dynamic was generally beyond the capacity of the Pharisees to intuit. It is saying that: I, the Baptist, am attempting to bring at least some people up to enhanced awareness, not only about their own core soul challenges, but also to realize that the time is at hand, when the Messiah is to appear. For the person immersed by the Baptist could also sense the approach of the Messiah; they knew, a crucial time in their history is coming.

The Baptist's answer is also saying the following; what I am doing is of minor importance, it is only a preparatory work, compared to what the Messiah shall achieve. Compared to the Messiah, I am a mere lowly servant, for the Christ shall both demand of people, and also offer to humanity, something much greater.

1:28 This all happened at Bethany on the other side of the Jordan, where John was baptizing.

The actual location of the site is unclear. Origenes could find no reference to a town called Bethany in the area, and suggested a place called Bethabara.

1:29 The next day John saw Jesus coming towards him and said, "Behold, the Lamb of God, who takes away the sin of the world !

To describe the action of 'the Lamb of God', the Baptist used a verb (airoe - αἴρω) which has a substantial meaning: 'to take up and to carry away' (the sin of the world). The word 'sin' here is singular, so it is not a matter of immoral actions being forgiven individually, as an 'inner' private process.

Rather, it was an 'outer' process, whereby the cosmic Christ takes hold of the dark cloud of lower qualities in the general sphere of the planet - the combined 'sins' of people - and removes this from creation. Here 'sin' or unethical behaviour is seen as a disturbing influence in the cosmos.

The Lamb of God: this phrase remains a riddle until esoteric insights arise. One conclusion is that the Hebrew sages, in coining this phrase, were thinking of the Passover lamb. Whilst this lamb is certainly relevant, it is not a full explanation, as that lamb was not thought of as "taking off and away the sin of the world".[173]

---

[173] This lamb sacrifice was instituted to remind the Israelites of the Exodus from Egypt, about 1300 BC, when various plagues were sent upon the Egyptians, to punish the Pharaoh for not letting the Israelites depart. The blood of a lamb was smeared above the entrances to houses of the Hebrew tribespeople, to protect them from the last and worst of these disasters.

This phrase also indirectly alludes to Jesus, as the vessel of the cosmic Christ or Lamb of God; who shall also be sacrificing himself to help humanity. However, one notes that in Israel the concept of a self-sacrificing Messiah was not prevalent in his lifetime, and the sacrifice on Golgotha hill was still three years in the future.

1:30 It is with regard to this Being that I said, after me comes a man who is before me, because he existed prior to me.

"with regard to this Being": here the Baptist continues to speak about the deity, the Lamb of God. The Greek word here (houtos - ουτος) means 'this (same) one' and so it can be understood as applying to either the man Jesus or the deity. Although he is pointing to Jesus, this is because Jesus is the vessel of this deity. For here he is not referring to the man Jesus, but referring back to v. 29.

For the Baptist, when pointing towards Jesus, adds the special phrase, "it was **with regard to** this Being that I said...." So it was not directly Jesus that he was referring to; he had mentioned Jesus, because Jesus was the vessel of the Lamb of God.

So it is both valid and more accurate grammatically, to interpret his words as applying to the cosmic Christ (the Lamb of God) and not to Jesus - especially as in the next verse the Baptist declares that he does not know the being involved; so it cannot refer to Jesus, since the Baptist knew Jesus well, since childhood.

1:31 I myself did not know this Being, but I came baptizing in water, so that this Being might be revealed to Israel.

"I myself did not know this Being": the Greek word (auton - αυτον) means 'him' and is usually applied to Jesus, but it also applies to the Lamb of God, since 'lamb' is masculine. So following on from v. 30, the Baptist is still referring to the deity, not the human vessel thereof. Hence as with v. 30, the Baptist knew

Jesus, so these words are referring to the Lamb of God.[174]

The baptism by John was not needed to enable Jesus to be made manifest to people in Israel; he would be making himself known all over the Holy Lands. But people needed some assistance to help them discern that the Lamb of God, who is the source of spiritual renewal of the human soul, was soon to be among them.

A premonition of this is what the baptism by John could bring about, for he possessed a divine power which induced in the soul of those he baptized, a brief moment of spiritual awareness about their life. The implication of v.31 is that the people who were baptised had a realisation that the Messiah, as the vessel of 'God' (the cosmic Christ or the Lamb of God) was soon to appear.

That the Baptist required people to make efforts towards spiritual development before the baptism, to help them have this moment of awareness, is indicated by the records made by Flavius Josephus, the ancient Jewish historian; "the Baptist....commanded the Jews to exercise virtue...and then come to baptism". [175]

"in water baptizing": The role of water in this baptism is strongly emphasized in Greek; it literally states, "in water baptizing" instead of simply "baptizing in water".

1:32 John then testified saying that, 'I beheld the Spirit emerging gradually, taking on a dove-like appearance, and this remained around him.

This is different to the usual versions, such as the NIV: "Then John gave this testimony: I saw the Spirit come down from heaven as a dove and remain on him."

But this is the surface level of the verse. For the Greek has unusual features, and from this, it appears that there is an esoteric narrative here, behind the apparent meaning. Steiner refers to this, and the Greek text is

---

[174] Lacking this perspective, theologians have been struggling to account for the Baptist saying that he did not know Jesus, when he obviously knew Jesus well.

[175] Josephus, *Antiquities*, Bk.18; chapt. 5, para 2.

supportive of his view. The veiled esoteric meaning is about the opposite dynamic to the descent the Spirit upon Jesus, as reported in the synoptic Gospels. They report that 'Heaven opened' and a 'voice from Heaven' was heard. That these two features are absent here, points to a different message. There is also a third point which will be noted below.

The lack of these two features suggests that this Gospel is subtly referring to an *ascent* of high spiritual 'substance' from Jesus, which remained around him, to become the chalice for the Holy Spirit.

According to Rudolf Steiner, who affirmed that the Divine indeed descended upon Jesus at the Baptism, this Johannine account is not referring to a divine element **descending** – that was understood – but to high human spirituality **emerging** and slightly arising, from the soul and spirit of Jesus, to become a vessel of the Divine.[176]

This verse is a continuation of v. 31; the Baptist is now narrating how, with his seership he had never before perceived the Lamb of God (the cosmic Christ); but as reported in the next verse his Angel required him to recognize that Jesus would be the chosen vessel of the Spirit. So the Baptist's seership now reveals a striking spiritual phenomenon around Jesus.

Verse 32 records the Baptist perceived a spirit-form take shape, as especially holy soul qualities of Jesus emerge, and coalesce around him into approximately a dove shape. Engagement with the Greek text using the Initiatory Quest approach, supports this view. For example:

A: The Baptism of Jesus in the Jordan is nowhere mentioned in this Gospel. So there was no need to refer to the Spirit descending.

B: Since there is no account of the descent of the Holy Spirit, this Gospel, unlike the other Gospels, omits any mention that "the heavens opened up"; a phrase which allows the Divine to come out, and descend to the Earth.

---

[176] "…in the imaginative (*spirit*) form of a white dove…a spiritual element appears, as it releases itself ….and rises up (*to be a vessel of the descending Spirit*)", GA 112, *The Gospel of St. John* lecture cycle, lect., 3. July, 1909.

C: "emerging gradually from out of spirit": that is, out of the spiritual aura of Jesus. The verb used for 'descending', also has a second, quite different meaning: to gradually attain to a condition or state of being or accomplishment.[177]

D: This group of verses is emphasizing that the Lamb of God is now drawing near to humanity, and this is occurring via Jesus. In v. 32, the task of Jesus to be a vessel of the Holy Spirit is pointed to, by alluding to the gathering together, emerging and arising of his finest soul-forces, to become a receptacle for the Holy Spirit.

E: "emerging gradually (out of the soul of Jesus)": instead of the usual translation, "descending from Heaven". We have seen that 'descending' is not the only meaning of the verb. In addition, although the word 'ouranos' (οὐρανός) very often means 'Heaven', it also means the personal soul (or spirit) of a human being, so it means 'spirit-reality' in a general sense.

This word was also used to refer to the finer regions of the soul-world, (the realm of the blessed Dead), and to high spirit realms.[178] Importantly it was also used for the soul (or aura) of the human being, as a microcosm of Creation.[179] This is the intended meaning of verse 32.

The verb for 'seeing' used here is theaomai - Θεάομαι, which is often defined in Gospel commentaries as referring only to physical seeing. But in fact it is also used in this Gospel and elsewhere for clairvoyance, that is to cognizing spiritually. For example, in the Prologue, (1:14) people saw clairvoyantly the splendour of the Logos. In Acts (1:11) the disciples saw clairvoyantly Jesus as a being of soul and spirit ascend into Heaven.[180]

---

[177] Liddell & Scott, Greek-English Lexicon entry, καταβαίνω, p. 884.

[178] Kittel, *Theologisches Wörterbuch.* vol 5, p. 497, German edition.

[179] For example by Philo Judaeus in Op. Mundi (*On the Creation)* para. 82.

[180] Some other usages for higher cognizing are, in 1 Jn. 4:12, "no-one has ever (clairvoyantly) seen God"; and in the *Hermetica*, with expressions such as, to see with the "eye of the mind" (190:86) and to "behold God" (418:4), and to "see the soul" (196:22).

Here in v. 32 the Baptist through his seership, saw the spiritual qualities of Jesus emerging as a vessel for the Divine. So the verse is in effect saying:

"I clairvoyantly beheld the Spirit, from out of the spiritual matrix {*of Jesus' own being*}, gradually emerging and taking on a dove-like appearance, and this form remained, {*hovering*} around him."

The implication of these words is that the Divine within Jesus' soul emerged to hover around and above him, forming itself into a vessel for the Christ-spirit that was soon to be permeating Him.

The third point in verses 32 and 33 supportive of this more esoteric narrative, is that the spirit (in dove-like shape) was said to 'remain near him'. But this is not consistent with the normal understanding of the 'descent of the Spirit'. Even though such understanding is of necessity vague, it is assumed that such a descending holy Spirit would fully merge with its human vessel.

So it would not be seen clairvoyantly as a separate entity, hovering permanently near by, or just above. This is not how the divine aspect of Jesus is understood. Yet this 'remaining nearby' is emphasized as being an ongoing condition in the Gospel (for as Westcott notes, this is because the verb is in its 'finite' form). So the report in this Gospel is about a different phenomenon.

Namely, that the especially spiritual qualities of Jesus arise and form a chalice, for the time when the Spirit descends. One has to note that this does not prevent the Spirit – the Lamb of God or the cosmic Christ – also gradually permeating all of Jesus' being; thus merging with him, in the normally understood sense.

1:33 And yet, I did not know this Being, but the One who sent me to baptize in water, that One said to me, 'The person around whom you see the spirit arising, and remaining nearby, this is he who shall baptise with the Holy Spirit'.

The Baptist himself certainly knew Jesus, and had known him since childhood, so here he is referring back to the theme of the Lamb of God (the cosmic Christ). The Baptist then confirms that what his seership revealed – as noted in v. 32 – had been revealed to him earlier by another spiritual experience. It was either his inspiring Angel or the spirit of Elijah who informed him of this phenomenon, which results in a dove-like form.

It was this guidance that helped the Baptist to realize that the deity descending to merge with Jesus, would need a special human being – someone whose holiness would be capable of forming what would be a dove-like chalice, for the presence of 'God', i.e., the cosmic Christ or Logos. One notes here how this Gospel is presenting the reality of life for John the Baptist, in his role as Herald of Christ.

That the Baptism in the Jordan is omitted in this Gospel has caused much consternation over the centuries. Some have concluded that it is simply regarded by the Gospel writer as a given fact. But the reason that Lazaros did not refer to this descent of a divine spirit upon Jesus is because he was focusing more on the experiences of the Baptist as the Herald of the Messiah; in particular, on the Baptist perceiving the capacity of Jesus to become a chalice for the Spirit.

1:34 I have seen, and so I do testify, that this man is the Chosen One of God.

Following on from seeing this dove-like chalice form around Jesus, the Baptist then affirms that Jesus is the vessel chosen by 'God' to be the cosmic Christ. The ancient Greek versions are not in agreement; most say 'Son of God', but some others of high reliability have, 'Chosen One of God', and this is more consistent with v. 33.

1:35 The next day, John was again present there, with two of his disciples.

As we later learn, one of these is Andrew; the other unnamed one is generally understood to be Lazaros.

1:36 And having observed with seership the spiritual ambience encompassing Jesus, John exclaims, "Behold, the Lamb of God !"

Two levels of meaning have been interwoven from v. 36 to v. 39. On the surface level, this text says, "when John saw Jesus walking past"; but it appears that there is a more esoteric level here. One can conclude that the Baptist is clairvoyantly observing Jesus, for the verb here 'emblepoe' (ἐμβλέπω) like its associated verb 'blepoe' (βλέπω) can be used for seership.[181]

But emblepoe means to gaze more intently at something than 'blepoe', and such gazing can be with the soul: "...let us gaze at the Maker of the world, see him in our mind....look with eyes of the soul on his patient will."[182]

This meaning of the verb suggests that the Baptist observed far more than a 'walking around' of Jesus. In fact, although the word here (peripateoe - περιπατέω) does often mean 'a walking around', it also means 'the attendant circumstances' of someone or something; that can be the inner life-reality of a person.[183]

As a result of directing his 'eye of the soul' to the soul-spirit reality of Jesus, the Baptist proclaims that the cosmic Christ is present and active within the soul-spirit of Jesus; within the dove-like chalice that hovers close to Jesus.

1:37 And the two disciples heard him speaking, so they then followed Jesus.
The words from the Baptist were a spontaneous exclamation, not directed to his disciples. But such is the impact of the words uttered by him, that the two disciples leave him, to follow Jesus.

1:38 Jesus, in turning around, then saw them following; he says to them, "What do you seek?" They

---

[181] An isolated sentence (epigram 7669) probably from Plato speaks of seeing (blepoe) from Heaven the higher-self (called a star) of a human being: "would that I had been created as Heaven itself, that I might look at thee (my star) with the many starry eyes of Heaven." (The rumour from Aristippos, that this epigram has a different meaning, can be ignored.)
[182] 1 Clement:19 (eyes of the soul - ὄμμασιν τῆς ψυχῆς) in *The Apostolic Fathers*, referred to in Bauer, *Greek-English Lexicon*, entry ἐμβλέπω, p. 254.
[183] Bauer, *Greek English Lexicon*, περιπατέω (2β), p. 649b.

said to him, "Rabbi" – which when translated, means 'Teacher' – "where is your dwelling place?"

Note that the surface level of translation starts to lose its coherency, for the disciples do not really answer the question of Jesus. Instead according to the usual view, we apparently read in this Gospel, with its grand cosmic message, that these two disciples simply want to know where Jesus, who is an itinerant preacher, lodges. This wish, it is said, was perhaps arising not from curiosity; perhaps it was from a wish to talk in private with him. But to me this is an unconvincing suggestion, for private words can be exchanged on the path in the countryside.

However, the disciples are having their first direct encounter with the Messiah, the man through whom the cosmic Christ, 'the Lamb of God' is soon to commence his ministry. My translation presents this sacred, esoteric level of meaning. They yearn to know of, and to enter into, that location in spiritual realms where the Messiah spiritually abides, i.e., where his consciousness has its presence.

That is, these two men wish to truly know the spiritual reality of their new Master, and especially since they realize that he is the vessel of the cosmic Christ. For, as we noted earlier, the Baptist was an esoterically awakened person, a Nazirite, and his disciples were very likely either Nazirites or Essenes (perhaps informally).

As noted in the Introduction, the specific idea of the soul having a dwelling-place in spiritual realms after death (and even during earthly life, if an initiate) was a prominent theme in the Essene community. The same idea occurs in the Transfiguration scene, where St. Peter feels the urge to create a habitation for the divine spiritual persons he is seeing, to dwell in.

The question, 'where do you abide?' refers to 'location', and this can include spiritual location; for the Greek word 'menoe' is used precisely with this meaning by Lazaros later in his Gospel. In 14:23, Jesus refers to humanity existing with God in the future: "...and we will come to our Father and make our home (or location) with him." Here we are told that true Christians shall have a place, a spiritual location where God is to be found.[184] The same Greek word and the same yearning are present in chapter 14, as here in v. 38.

1:39 He says to them, "Approach me in spirit, and perceive with seership." So then they drew near, and spiritually beheld where he abides. And then they dwelt with him for that day; it was about the tenth hour.

The usual version, "Come and see..." is grammatically valid, but gives only the surface meaning. For the verb 'to come' can also mean 'to spiritually approach'. Moreover, the verb here 'to see' is very often used for clairvoyant cognizing. (Note that in v. 46 the expression 'Come and see" also occurs, but there it refers only to a physical meeting of Jesus by Nathanael. The same verb for 'see' is used, but in a very different form, which refers to a purely physical event.)[185]

The surface meaning in the usual version reports that they stayed at his lodgings for that day, "because it was about 4pm". This is a very substantial indicator of an esoteric message here, because the weakness in the surface level is striking. The disciples cannot have stayed for the whole day as reported, because they didn't get there until 4 pm; and the Jewish day finishes at sunset.[186]

---

[184] In v. 38 the verb 'menoe' (μενω) is used, and in 14:23 the noun 'monae' (μονή) is used, which derives from the verb.

[185] Technically in grammatical terms, in v. 39 the verbal form is 'opsesthoe' (ὄψεσθω) which is 'transitive' that is the beholding is to be directed over to something (i.e., Jesus) and this will be to the benefit of the disciples (the Middle voice). But in v. 46 the form is 'ide' (ἴδε) which is intransitive and means only 'just look', so the seeing is an action within the disciples, it does not flow over to a specific object. This is reinforced by the insular, 'particle' status of this word.

[186] To resolve this defect, some scholars conclude that the time of day was 10 am; they argue that here instead of the usual from sunrise to sunrise system, the legalistic Roman time-system of midnight to midnight was used, But all other Gospel time references follow the usual sunrise system.

This weakness is a pointer to the deeper meaning, which is revealed in the phrase, 'the 'tenth hour'. The number ten signifies spiritual completeness and triumph; for example, there are 10 Commandments, and in Genesis, when God is bringing about Creation, he gives 10 directives.

Hence, the 'tenth hour' here means that the disciples have achieved, for a while, through their spiritual-clairvoyant cognition, access to the 'habitation' of the Messiah, in higher realms. The word for 'day' often means a period of time, as it does here, and not an actual day.

So, the verse is saying this: He says to them, "Approach me in spirit, and perceive with seership." So then they (in their souls) drew near, and spiritually beheld where Jesus abides in spirit realms. And so their souls dwelt for a while with him; for it was about the tenth hour. That is, these two disciples attained their goal, the number ten signifies this.

A passage in Origenes' *Commentary on St. John* shows that he had a similar interpretation; "...when Jesus says to them, "Approach" he is perhaps encouraging them in regard to an active (spiritual) life; and by saying 'Behold with seership", he is indicating that such beholding will occur for those who are seeking this - subsequent to them successfully completing their spiritual development; this seership shall occur in the (spiritual) dwelling-place of Jesus."[187]

1:40 Andrew, Simon Peter's brother, was one of the two who heard what John the Baptist had said and who had followed Jesus.

Andrew is called the brother of 'Simon Peter' before Jesus has bestowed the epithet 'Peter' upon Simon. It is

---

[187] ΟΙΓΕΝΟΥΣ, ΤΩΝ ΕΙΣ ΤΟ ΚΑΤΑ ΙΩΑΝΝΗΝ ΕΥΑΓΓΕΛΙΟΝ ΕΞΗΓΤΙΚΩΝ (Origenes, *Commentary on the Gospel of John*) Bk.2, #219. Unfortunately the key Greek term, 'opsesthe' (ὄψεσθε) i.e., 'seership', is often translated as 'contemplation' or 'speculation'.

a characteristic of the Gospel to give the reader a clearer perspective on a character or a location, by mentioning a noted feature of that person or place.

But notice too that as from this verse, the 'other disciple' disappears from the narrative. The writer of this Gospel never mentions himself (until in the very last verses, and still without giving his name), yet gives such precise information about times of day, and movements of people in a locality.

Many scholars have concluded, as I have, that this all indicates someone who is personally seeing these events. At the end of his Gospel the evangelist emphasizes that he was a witness. On this basis, the author would normally be named, since an un-named witness is an oddity. The fact that he is not named, is itself more evidence that Lazaros-John is the author, as noted in the Introduction.

1:41 Thereupon Andrew firstly found his brother Simon and tells him, 'We have found the Messiah' (that is, the Christ).

The word 'we' refers apparently to Andrew and the un-named disciple who were followers of the Baptist, and who then followed Jesus.

"Andrew firstly found": the Greek here is ambiguous, it could mean, that the first one to find Simon Peter was Andrew, but most translators agree with the above version.[188]

---

[188] Technically, the word proeton (πρῶτον) is understood here by me, and most translators, to mean 'firstly'. This is an adverbial usage of this word, and it is used in this way in the Gospel about seven other times. Other possibilities are that Andrew found Peter before Lazaros did, or he found Peter before he found anyone else.

The un-named disciple
Many theologians have concluded that it is likely that this man was "the Beloved Disciple", but they remain uncertain just who this disciple was. This train of thought could have led them to 'Lazaros-John', except that the church had not queried whether Lazaros had the additional name John bestowed upon him.

So theologians remain undecided, but conclude that this unnamed disciple, if he is also the 'beloved disciple' could not be St. John, the brother of James, for that particular 'John' has not yet met Jesus.[189] This situation is in itself an indicator that Lazaros-John is the un-named disciple.

"...the Messiah": Many theologians find it inconsistent or puzzling that these two disciples identify Jesus as the Messiah, so early in the three years. But in v. 36 the Baptist's words informed them that Jesus was the bearer of the cosmic Christ, and in v. 39 they perceived, through seership, the lofty spiritual status of Jesus.

"We have found": the emphasis is on the verb 'found', the Greek sense is therefore more accurately translated as "*Found* have we the Messiah..."

1:42 And he brought him to Jesus. Jesus gazed at him with seership and said, "You are Simon, son of John. You shall be called Cephas" (which, when translated, is Peter).

"with seership": not just 'intently gazed', for the verb here is also used of 'the eyes of the soul'; a phrase which can include clairvoyant perceiving.[190]

"You are...son of John": this is a 'ritual re-naming'. Jesus intends to both reveal and to affirm to Simon, the especial spiritual influences active in his soul. He has a resonance in his soul of 'the divine', that is, of the IOA, hence the name 'John' was later added, as noted earlier.

---

[189] Ref. 11.

[190] As with v. 36, the verb (emblepoe - ἐμβλέπω) is used here. It was used in this way by Philo in *De Sobrietate* and by an early church father in "*1 Clement*".

1:43 The next day Jesus decided to leave for Galilee. Finding Philip, he said to him, Follow me.
1:44 Philip, like Andrew and Peter, was from the town of Bethsaida.

No commentary is necessary for these verses.

1:45 Philip found Nathanael and told him, 'We have found the person about whom Moses wrote in the Law, and the prophets also spoke of – Jesus, the son of Joseph, the one from Nazareth.

These words are hugely significant for the esoteric aspect of the life of Jesus. As was noted in Chapter One, this tells us that Nathanael was esoterically aware, and hence an Essene or perhaps a Nazaritic Essene, for he knew the Nazaritic-Essene colony of Nazareth. Consequently, he had access to this secluded Nazarene colony; and whilst there, he had already met, or heard about, Joseph.

1:46 Then Nathanael asked, "Can anything good come from Nazareth?" Philip says to him, "Come and see".

This famously dismissive query of Nathanael has remained an enigma to theologians. But the reason for Nathanael's doubt is indicated in the interaction of Jesus with the Nazarenes, when he returned to this colony as an adult, and as the Messiah. For on one occasion, after a short positive response to Jesus, the Nazarenes quickly became dangerously hostile (Lk.4:14-30). On another occasion (Matt13: 53-57, Mk 6:1-6) it is reported that Jesus was astonished at their lack of spiritual discernment.

The saintly Nathanael was aware of the imperfect social-spiritual reality of the idealistic Essene-Nazaritic people in Nazareth. His seership had made more obvious to him the lack of a sincere spirituality, in a deeper esoteric sense, amongst these people. This falling away of a colony, into a sectarian, rigidified state, or into a casual flippant attitude towards previous core principles of the original impulse, is a common social phenomenon affecting religious-esoteric groups.

1:47 Jesus saw Nathanael approaching, and said of him, "Behold, a true Israelite, in whom there is nothing false."

An esoteric explanation for this verse was given by Rudolf Steiner, which is discussed in conjunction with the next verse.

1:48 "How do you know me?" Nathanael asked. Jesus answered, saying to him, "Before Philip called you here, I saw you while you were under the fig tree."

The response from Nathanael is not immodest; he is confirming his specific degree of initiation, or higher consciousness. Steiner's view is that if one is called a "true Israelite" or a "true Egyptian", etc, this was a veiled way of confirming that the person in question has attained to that high level of consciousness which bestows communion with one's 'Folk-spirit'.[191]

Such a guiding national spirit is mentioned in the Hebrew Scriptures, where each nation or ethnic group has its own 'Folk-spirit'. In the *Book of Daniel* reference is made the guiding Spirit of several nations; the word is usually translated as a "Prince" of that nation.[192]

Such a person, from the viewpoint of their guiding Folk-spirit, has attained an enhanced cognizing, which enables them to commune with this Folk-spirit. That seer is then able to intuit and advocate the intentions of their Folk-spirit.

This veiled esoteric message is confirmed in the answer from Jesus, about perceiving Nathanael whilst he was 'under the fig-tree'. This is another veiled esoteric phrase and refers to a core spiritual dynamic known in many other civilizations of the ancient world. As noted in Part One, Section 1, this phrase refers to the esoteric meditative work in which the effort is made to develop a higher consciousness.

So here Jesus is telling the highly spiritual Nathanael, that when he was in a higher consciousness (meditative-

---

[191] GA 103, lect., 23 May, 1908.
[192] *Daniel*, 10:13, 20.21 &12:1. to Rudolf Steiner the Folk-spirit is a spirit being of the rank of Archangel.

seership) state, Jesus perceived him. His especially radiant soul was prominent to the seership of Jesus, even from a distance. It is for this reason that the otherwise inexplicable, deeply reverential response, was spontaneously made by Nathanael to Jesus (in v.49).

1:49 Then Nathanael declared, "Rabbi, you are the Son of God; you are the King of Israel."

Nathanael's seership has enabled him to perceive to some extent, the sublime spiritual reality of the cosmic Christ, or the 'Lamb of God', enveloping Jesus. Also, he had just been told by Philip, that Jesus was the Messiah, the vessel of the 'cosmic Christ'. Then he is given a startling glimpse into the exalted seership of the Messiah. (Regarding: 'The Son of God' see verse 51.)

1:50 Jesus said, "You believe because I told you I saw you underneath the fig tree? You shall see greater things than that."

Again Jesus refers to 'the' fig-tree instead of 'a' fig-tree; this phrase can be seen as referring to not just an actual tree, but to something else. The most persuasive interpretation that I have found of this is in the work of Rudolf Steiner, who taught that it refers to the blossoming of a higher cognizing (clairvoyance) of this acolyte.[193] The soul now has its 'eyes' opened, and actively cognizing into spirit realms; these 'eyes' are well known in Oriental wisdom.[194] Also, this second time, Jesus says *'underneath'* the fig-tree, not simply 'under', thereby emphasizing the state of Nathanael being immersed in his higher cognizing or seership.

1:51 He says to Nathanael, "Very truly, I say to you (ye), you (ye) shall see Heaven open, and the Angels of God ascending and descending on The Son of Man."

---

[193] GA 139, Lect., 22 Sept., 1912.
[194] The statues of Buddha with an unusual form on his forehead refers to this. The fig was chosen because of its 'inflorescence' or presence of a flower inside its fruit; the fruit signifying the life-forces of the initiate.

The archaic English plural word 'ye' is used here, otherwise the reader cannot know what Jesus is speaking about. For although in v. 50 he was addressing Nathanael, now in v. 51, he refers to a number of people. So, the words of Jesus are about not only Nathanael, but also a number of other people who are known to him. These companions on his esoteric path – Essenes or Nazirites – they also shall see the glorious sight of Angels interweaving with 'The Son of Man'.

The Son of Man: This expression occurs in the Bible and in associated mystical literature, but its usage is complex and derives in part from esoteric knowledge, so its meaning is often disputed. It was discussed in Part One, Section 2. It can be used to mean simply a human being, but it is also used to refer to an initiate. That is, those who have attained to the eternal Spiritual-self.

The Son of God is a term with various meanings in Biblical literature; but it generally implies that a person is blessed by influences from the Divine. When used in an esoteric context, it refers to a higher stage of spirituality than 'The Son of Man'. This was discussed in Part One, Section 2 as a term used for the advanced state of having the Spirit descending down towards an initiate, permeating him or her.

"Angels of God ascending and descending": this phrase appears to refer to experiences accessible to esoterically developed disciples whose seership is quite advanced. They would have the capacity to behold the divine-spiritual influences interweaving in the aura of the Messiah, Jesus. It may also be pointing to the future experience for sanctified disciples, of beholding angelic beings within and around their own, now sanctified, soul and spirit.

Chapter 2

The Miracle at Cana
This well-known episode has remained mysterious to many people; some have found it confronting because it appears to show that Jesus approved of alcohol. Others find it enigmatic because of the numbers involved, and because the mother of Jesus is not named as 'Mary'.

I have found the most satisfactory solution to understanding it is to see it as having two aspects. One aspect is to view the numbers as relating to seven historical Ages of humanity. The second aspect is that alcohol has a function in humanity, which however, has a time limit (it is to end in the 6th Age).

In the esoteric-mystical literature of the Jewish people, history was viewed as occurring in seven stages; echoing the seven days of Creation in the Book of Genesis. This view of history as unfolding over seven Ages is briefly mentioned in the *Zohar* (Vayera 119a) and in the *Talmud* (Sanhedrin 97a). It also occurs in the *Testament of Abraham*, written about AD 100 (para. 19), and in the *Book of Enoch* (93:3-8.) Christian scholars took up the idea, starting with Augustine of Hippo, and was echoed by Bede and others. Rudolf Steiner had a similar view, but starting with civilisations re-emerging after the Great Flood; the Greco-Latin era being the 4th Age.

Then one notes that alcohol is the only toxic liquid allowed as part of human foodstuffs, and it can of course, bring about a coarsened, degraded state. But it also effectively prevents the emergence of higher, spiritualized consciousness. This same conviction was shared by various ancient esoterically oriented religious groups; the Nazarites for instance, were forbidden to consume alcohol.

The key to this episode in the Gospel, as Rudolf Steiner sees it, is that earlier humanity had an holistic consciousness, a psychic-intuitive capacity, and hence a strong focus on religion and reverence for various deities. This perspective on earlier humanity is now often affirmed by researchers; but the striking point Steiner made is that the holistic awareness of antiquity had to gradually close down, to allow a more earth-aware consciousness to arise – and from this, a much stronger sense of a personal 'I' to arise than had been the case in earlier times.[195]

There has to be a strong sense of being a separate individual, before any such individuated 'self' can be spiritualized. He concluded that alcohol has the effect of closing down the old holistic consciousness. But by the 6th Age, the re-emergence of the earlier spiritual, holistic awareness is to occur; then the 'role' of alcohol shall no longer be relevant. Already in our own current time (called the 5th Age), souls who wish to strive towards higher consciousness, feel that alcohol is counter-productive to their personal goals, both in terms of consciousness and of health.[196]

The Dionysian priests in antiquity had a similar perspective on the changing needs of human consciousness, and interesting depictions of the effects of alcohol were found in a Dionysian temple in the ruins of Pompeii. One scene depicts an image of a kind of ugly 'lower-self' reflected in the wine goblet, as a man drinks from it; as if to say that your lower earth-bound self will arise and you must deal with it.

2:1 On the third day, a wedding occurred in Cana of Galilee; and the mother of Jesus was there.

When an initiatory meaning is being presented, it is veiled within a surface level of meaning. So a Scriptural passage can have two or more layers of meaning within it. There was no doubt a wedding, and Mary was no doubt there. But an esoterically insightful engagement with this passage can point out substantial indicators of a deeper meaning. The 'third day' here is alluding to the 3rd Age, which is when the Israelites entered history,

---

[195] GA 123, lect., 23 May, 1908.

[196] Relevant to this concept is the medical fact that alcohol within a few minutes of being ingested goes, contrary to non-toxic liquids, straight through to the brain, where fine frontal lobe cells are dissolved by it. It is through this part of the brain that our higher, finer intelligence comes to expression. It is also where the Buddhists locate the 'third eye', said to be the non-physical organ of spiritual seership.

separating off from the Egyptian empire, to pioneer a new way of connecting human souls to the Divine, and to prepare for the coming of the Messiah.

The expression, the 'Mother of Jesus' is very striking, as this Gospel is always emphatic about naming people, so this not naming of Mary veils a deep meaning. It appears that on the deeper level, this expression refers not to a woman, but to the cosmic 'soul' from which all human beings draw their souls – but on a higher level. This feminine entity is a kind of matrix of the soul of every person in its original, 'unfallen' state, not the less-than-perfect, soul qualities of 'fallen' humanity.

This 'soul-entity' is personified here. As we noted earlier, that such a high cosmic perspective is embedded in the words of this Gospel is due to Lazaros-John having become an initiated disciple.

2:2 and Jesus was invited to the wedding, and his disciples also.

The verb here ('invited') is in the singular only; this is a very striking feature, because it is ungrammatical; it should be in the plural. This indicates that the invitation applies above all to Jesus, with the (plural) disciples there only as a secondary subject. For they are to be witnesses of the power of the Christ-reality, not agents thereof.

2:3 But wine was not there; the mother of Jesus says to him, 'They have no wine'.

Translations such as, "When the wine was gone", or "they have no more wine", whilst somewhat accurate, ignore the subtle nuance in the Greek, which states abruptly that wine "was lacking".[197] So it does not emphasize that earlier there had been some wine, which had been consumed. But on the surface level, one would not necessarily consider this subtle point; so a reader would assume that all the earlier wine had been consumed.

---

[197] The participle here is from the verb 'hustereo' (ὑστερέω) which means 'to lack', especially here in the active voice.

However, this unusual situation was noticed long ago, and in one early text (Codex Sinaiticus, 4th cent.) a scribe added the words, "because the wine for the wedding feast has been consumed". Two other Latin manuscripts (5th and 8th cents.) added: "It came about that, because of the great crowd of those who had been invited, all the wine was finished".[198]

2:4 Jesus says to her, "Dear lady, this concern of yours is not really for me to deal with. My time has not yet arrived – but I shall assist."

The words of Jesus here have been a confronting enigma to theologians.
"Dear lady": the Greek word here was wrongly interpreted for centuries as harsh, but this word is actually a respectful term. However, it is not how either a Jewish or a Roman man addressed his mother; he would always say 'mother', almost never 'dear lady'. This is already a strong indicator of the second deeper level of meaning.
"this concern of yours..." here the Greek uses an Aramaic idiom, and as with all idioms, there is not one 'correct' set of words to translate it, because it expresses a mood.

The mood of an idiom can be translated accurately, but there are many different choices of words to do that. The mood here is one of giving consent reluctantly to help in a task which is not related to yourself:
"You are pointing out to me a problem, for which you are wanting my help – but I am not interested in assisting here, because this matter has little to do with my goals, or my abilities. However, nevertheless, I shall help you."

On the deeper level, the Christ, in communing with the matrix of the human soul – on its original, pure, higher level – is affirming her perception that alcohol is indeed necessary, and will be needed for some Ages, but that by the 6th Age, this 'earth oriented' type of self-consciousness should be over. Only then can the light from Christ arise fully in large numbers of people.

---

[198] Metzger, *Textual Commentary on the Greek New Testament*, 1994, p.172.

Already in that 4th Age (the Greco-Latin time), those who were anticipating the future, by striving to achieve a higher state, avoided alcohol. As noted above, the Nazirites were such people, (as were the Essenes so far as can be known, from the scanty data available).[199]

So, in an affirmation of the insights motivating the earlier Dionysian priests, Christ ensured that wine would be present; but he himself is waiting for the time when people shall feel no need for alcohol. It is for this reason that the narrative does not emphasize the miracle – none of the guests at the wedding were even aware of such a thing happening. (There are vaguely similar features in the Dionysian cult: this god causes three empty jars to become filled with wine overnight, and on a festival day, a fountain in a temple flows with wine, not water.)[200]

On the surface level, it was about Jesus being helpful to a wedding party; and it was very helpful, for serious consequences awaited anyone who had insufficient wine at a Jewish wedding. It could even result in legal action.

On the deeper level, it is indicating that Christ, a cosmic deity, was supporting the reality that alcohol would be needed by the human race for some millennia. For this is a pre-condition for the eventual arising, in the 6th Age, of ethical spiritually conscious individuals. That is when the bridegroom – the ego or self – shall meet the bride, the Spiritual-self. But this 'soul wedding' has not yet happened, hence the bride is entirely absent from the narrative.

2:5 His mother says to the servants, "Do whatever he tells you to do".

On the surface level, the mother of Jesus, as a guest, gives orders to the servants of the household: socially, a possible, but unlikely situation in that culture. On the

---

[199] Though references to drinking of 'wine' occurs in 1 or 2 sentences in the Dead Sea Scrolls, the word used there was 'tirosh' (תִּירוֹשׁ), (e.g., in 4Q251, Frag. 5) which was used of fresh grape juice (e.g. Isaiah 65:8) as well as of wine.

[200] As noted by Beasley-Murray in *John*, in the Biblical Word Commentary, 1999, p. 35.

deeper level, our higher soul qualities, represented by a matrix-like figure, is entreating cooperative assistance from the cosmic Christ, on behalf of human beings. Christ did not reject this, but affirmed and supported the needs of human beings, as perceived by the matrix of the higher human soul. However, the influence of Christ would be not be fully empowered until the 6th Age arrives.

2:6 Nearby stood six stone water jars, the kind used by the Jews for ceremonial washing, each holding from twenty to thirty gallons.

The number six alludes to the view that in the Sixth Age no more wine would be needed. The size of these jars – their capacity is difficult to accurately estimate, estimates vary, but it was perhaps about 120 gallons (400 litres) – represents a very large amount of wine, more than would be needed at a wedding.

This large quantity indicates that wine would be available in abundance for humanity in general, throughout several Ages. The variation in sizes of the stone jars alludes to the varying amount of alcohol that the various Ages may or may not require.

2:7 Jesus said to them, Draw up fresh spring water and fill the jars; so they filled them up to the brim.

The verb here refers to drawing up living, fresh water, not ladling water into the stone jars from some other larger water container.

2:8 Then he told them, "Now pour some water out and carry it to the master of the banquet." They did so,

Once the six jars were filled, the servants then had to pour out some of that water which had become wine, and carry it to the master of the banquet.
"master of the banquet": here the surface meaning becomes less coherent, for several reasons. At such a wedding, there might be a toast-master who was chosen from amongst honoured guests, and who is in charge of the drinking and toasting. There is also a kind of head-waiter, usually one of the servants, who has to ensure

that the tables and utensils are furnished appropriate to the occasion, and the food and wine is made available as required.

This head-waiter cannot, nor would not, summon the bridegroom, nor insult the bridegroom about the quality of the wine. Whereas the toast-master does not sample the food nor the wine to ensure its quality; nor would he insult or query the judgement of the bridegroom.[201] But in this narrative, the "master of the banquet" does sample the wine and does in effect, insult the bridegroom.

These points indicate that the "master of the banquet" represents, on the deeper level, not a person, but is a personification of a spiritual reality monitoring humanity's consciousness processes over the Ages; an influence regulating the cultural integrating of alcohol into society.

A further pointer to a hidden meaning is linked to the underlying human reality that the soul has three aspects to it: thinking, emotions and will. The Greek term for a "master of the banquet" (architriklinos - ἀρχιτρικλινος) means the ruler of the 'threefold-couch'. A three-fold couch referred to a banquet-seat. Such a person had the task of arranging three couches, on each of which three persons could recline at the table, when guests came to the house. In the Gospel, this 'toast-master' could have simply been called a "sumposia-archos" meaning "ruler of the banquet", but he was not given that title.[202]

Then, to further emphasize the triune aspect, this term occurs three times in just two verses. This is a literary device which is not seen by the commentators, so many translations delete one of these terms.[203] But this triune term was chosen to allude to the nurturing of the triune human soul. The master of the threefold-

---

[201] Information about these wedding procedures is reported by many Commentaries on this Gospel, e.g., Westcott, Bernard, Barrett, Keener.

[202] This term (συμποσίαρξης) already occurred in "Sirach" (32:1), from ca. 180 BC, "If you are appointed banquet-master, do not exalt yourself".

[203] Prof. Myer described it as "superfluous repetition" and as being probably parenthetical, *John*, Vol.1, p. 145.

couch represents a being who supervises the life circumstances of humanity: that is, the traditions around alcohol consumption.

2:9 and the master of the banquet tasted the water which had become wine. The master of the banquet did not know where it comes from, though the servants who had drawn the water knew. The master of the banquet called the bridegroom aside …

"did not know where it comes from". Usually translated as, "did not know where it *came* from". However, the present tense is there in the Greek, and though this can refer back to the past, it is more likely to be a normal present tense. It is then a further example of the living 'narrative style', mentioned in Chapter One, which puts the reader vividly inside the dynamics the life of Jesus, as if it were a current event.

This verse refers to the surface meaning, adding essential details about the miracle. But, as we noted above, it is very significant that the miracle made no impact upon anyone at the feast, for it was not witnessed by anyone, including the master of the banquet. We can assume that the servants knew, but they have no role in the narrative otherwise.

2:10 and said, 'Everyone brings out the choice wine first and then the cheaper wine, after the guests have had too much to drink; but you have saved the best until now'.

There are two meanings in this episode: the social surface meaning, and the deeper spiritual dynamic. On the social level, the wine had all been consumed, so more was needed, as the consequences of not having enough wine at a wedding in those days was serious. So Jesus assists, even though the impact of alcohol on the soul meant that for him, it was not something to encourage. This means that on the surface level, the admiration of the master of the banquet is triggered by the superiority of the wine which Christ has miraculously wrought, compared to usual wine.

On the deeper level, a dialogue is occurring between the cosmic Christ and another high being, in a spiritual context. It appears to indicate that, on this esoteric level, this dialogue is referring to the future, to the sixth Age, when the 'drink' which shall be produced by Christ is not wine, but something much more satisfying to the soul than alcohol.

This 'drink' is the 'living water' mentioned as a core gift to humanity by Christ in later chapters of the Gospel, such as in the dialogue with the Samaritan woman. This why in 2:7, a verb is used which means that fresh spring water is what the 'wine' is made from, not from water already stored up in some other container.

2:11 This, the first of his signs, Jesus carried out at Cana in Galilee. He thus revealed his radiant power; and his disciples spiritually perceived this in regard to him.

"the first of his signs": the word 'signs' is best understood as an indicator pointing to the majestic power of the cosmic Christ, but discreetly active in the larger, historical development of humanity, (apart from the transformation of water into wine here, which was not noticed by the guests).

"disciples spiritually perceived this regarding him": this is preferred over the usual "and his disciples believed in him", because his disciples already believed in Jesus, having personally heard from the Baptist that he was the vessel of the Lamb of God. As we noted earlier, the verb to believe or to have faith, also means to be perceptive, to perceive in an intuitive, discerning way.

So, the small number of disciples present, now inwardly perceived that, through Jesus the mighty Lamb of God was manifesting and active. The task here being to ensure that although alcohol was necessary, by the future 6th Age alcohol shall no longer be part of life. Then, a higher consciousness shall be attained, enabling human beings to become aligned to the Christ reality. (Only a handful of disciples were there, as most of the twelve had not yet received the 'call' from Jesus.)

"thus revealed ...at Cana in Galilee": the region of Galilee is strongly emphasized. That the location is in Galilee is mentioned in the first and in the last verses; so this feature 'envelops' the episode with a specific locality. Rudolf Steiner's insights here are helpful, adding a profound dimension to the episode.[204] He mentions that this region was one where there was an intermingling of different ethnic groups, and therefore of different religious groups. Consequently, Isaiah referred to this area as "Galilee of the Gentiles" (9:1).

The cultural-historical background is that when the Hebrews first entered Palestine, about 1,400 BCE, the three tribes who settled in the main part of Galilee were unable to drive out the inhabitants; consequently, Galilee became an area with a mixture of peoples.[205]

Then in the 8th century BCE, an Assyrian conqueror deported many Galileans to Assyria, and some Assyrians settled into the area. Also by the time of Jesus, Galilee was bordered by many 'Gentile' cities, and there were also Galilean cities around the shores of the Sea of Galilee inhabited by Greek people. There were also extensive Roman garrisons; the area became a Roman province in 63 BCE.

Moreover, the main trade route from Egypt to Mesopotamia, the 'Via Maris', went through lower Galilee. Although this route avoided main population centres, it enabled nomadic traders to travel extensively within Galilee, which was interlaced with many walking tracks.

In addition, commercial traders were present, because building materials needed in Israel for temples and palaces, etc, had to be obtained by trading agricultural produce. These trade arrangements took place in Galilee, for it was phenomenally productive in such agricultural goods as olive oil, figs and wheat.

It is very likely that most Galileans were Jewish, but as a result of these historical events, some people in Galilee were from 'mixed marriages', and thus had become less bound by specific ethnic-religious customs.

---

[204] GA 103, lect., 23 May, 1908.
[205] The tribes were Asher, Zebulon and Napthali (1 Judg.1:30-33).

The actual percentage of non-Jewish inhabitants, and the degree to which their religious or cultural practices were prominent is unknown, and is the subject of academic debate. But the bonds that held people together into an ethnic group, were weaker there than in Judea. The choice of Galilee then for the miracle of Cana, is alluding to the human situation wherein interaction between people, including bonds of personal love, could often rise above ethnic and religious customs and traditions.

These simple beginnings of an 'inner freedom', allude to a later universal love which Christ was seeking to develop in the soul, beyond familial or ethnic or religious bounds. Such inner freedom is a characteristic of the Spiritual-self, for in this the Holy Spirit is present.

2:12 After this he went down to Capernaum with his mother and brothers and his disciples. There they stayed for a few days.

This verse has a transitional role. Jesus goes to Capernaum which is soon to become his new place of residence, and many important episodes of the three years shall occur here. We learn that his siblings and mother go with him away from Cana, as they later urged Jesus to attend a festival in Jerusalem (7:3). It is possible that his siblings didn't stay in Capernaum, as they seldom appear in the narrative thereafter.

Jesus in effect separates from the place of his upbringing (Nazareth). He now becomes a public figure, his ministry begins, and the conflict between his spiritual reality – the vessel of the Christ – and the Jewish religious establishment becomes immediately apparent.

2:13 When it was almost time for the Jewish Passover, Jesus went up to Jerusalem.
2:14 In the temple courts he found men selling cattle, sheep and doves, and others sitting at tables exchanging money.
2:15 So he made a scourge out of rushes, and drove all from the temple area, both sheep and cattle; he scattered the coins of the money changers and

overturned their tables.

This event in the Temple is not an example of Jesus 'losing his temper'; he was in control of himself, but was manifesting the 'divine wrath' that deities also manifest; various references to this in regard to Jahve occur in the Scriptures.

So the 'scourge' was a harmless thing made by binding together plant rushes, which were there in abundance, as bedding for the cattle. But it no doubt contributed a dramatic element to the actions of Jesus. It was really the power of the Divine overshadowing Jesus which made the traders somewhat compliant, rather than seeking to physically restrain Jesus.

2:16 To those who sold doves he said, "Get these out of here ! How dare you turn my Father's house into a market !"
2:17 His disciples remembered that it is written: "Zeal for your house will consume me."

These words are from Psalm 69, and refer to how the complete dedication of Jesus to the will of the Father will be the entire motivation of his life; and eventually cause him to be arrested and executed.

2:18 Then the Jews demanded of him, "What miraculous sign can you show us as proof of your authority to do all this?"
2:19 Jesus answered them, "Destroy this temple, and I will raise it again in three days."
2: 20 They replied, "It has taken forty-six years to build this temple, and you are going to raise it in three days?"
2:21 But the temple he had spoken of was his body.

Verses 2:13 - 21
These verses present the scene wherein Jesus drives the money-changers out of the temple, and also demands that the many animals brought there to be slaughtered as a sacrifice at the Passover, are removed. Money-changing here means to exchange any coins with images of Caesar on them, for coins that had no such imagery, because any such were seen by Jews as idolatrous. This money exchanging work was very profitable.

The synoptic Gospels present this scene as occurring at the end stage of the ministry of Jesus, but Lazaros places it here at the beginning. Unless two such events happened, it occurs in this Gospel now to highlight the potent antagonism that the religious establishment would continually manifest towards the teachings and spiritual reality of Jesus.

Lazaros was known to, and socially accepted by, the Sanhedrin, as shown in the Gospel. For after the arrest of Jesus, Lazaros was allowed to enter the home of the high priest Caiaphas, where Jesus has been taken under orders of this authority. Such entry was only possible "because this disciple was known to the high priest..." (Jn. 18:15).[206]

When the crowd wanted to see a demonstration of spiritual power, as evidence that Jesus was divinely permitted to intervene in the Temple activities, Jesus replies "Destroy this temple, and I will raise it again in three days." By this he is not declaring that he can rebuild the huge and sumptuous Temple in three days.

He is saying in a veiled way, that there shall be a rejection of his message, followed by the execution of himself. Later on, aggressive opposition to Roman rule from the Jews will result in the Romans destroying the temple and wreaking devastation upon Judea. But also, three days after his death, the Messiah shall arise, resurrected, in a new kind of body.

---

[206] As noted earlier, I conclude that the 'Beloved Disciple' is Lazaros-John. An early Bishop of Ephesos, Polycrates (130-196 CE), records that the 'Beloved Disciple' was a member of an aristocratic family in Jerusalem, was a priest and hence wore the sacerdotal plate.

When speaking of 'the temple' arising after three days Jesus uses the word 'naos' which refers to the inner sanctuary of the temple, not 'hieros' which means the outer Courts. This points to the truth that Paul declared in Romans, "the body is the temple of God". But now it takes on new and more profound meaning, for as the Christ-force renews humanity, this is making possible that the divine – the Spiritual-self – can find a home in the living human being.

So a temple, an inner sanctuary for the Divine, shall thereby exist. One can extend this understanding into the idea that the church – or all truly Christ-aligned souls, regardless of their religion – shall become the new temple for the Divine. A verse in Matthew's Gospel 12:6 alludes to this, "I tell you that one greater than the temple is here."

The period of three days alludes to the interval between the Crucifixion and Resurrection. Thus it also alludes to the special 'sign' that the crowd wanted: the sign of Jonah being three days in the Underworld, symbolized by a whale. (The three days with Jesus being counted as including part of Friday, Saturday and Sunday, but not all of those days.)

2:22 After he was raised from the dead, his disciples recalled what he had said. Then they believed the Scripture and the words that Jesus had spoken."

This verse is not from a later editorial action, as some think; it is affirming a significant experience in the lives of the disciples. For they gained much clearer insights into the significance of the life of Jesus after the Resurrection. It is likely that the Risen Jesus was then assisting them spiritually to attain this clarity.

2:23 Now while he was in the Jerusalems at the Passover during the Feast, many people saw the miraculous signs he was doing, and intuitively discerned his divine nature.

The ritualistically plural nature of singular objects
'the Jerusalems: the text actually has 'the Jerusalems': this is the first of several remarkable instances where in

this Gospel, the city of Jerusalem is referred to as a plural city. This unusual feature occurs in the New Testament about 20 times, and is used for places and things which have a strong spiritual resonance or significance to the writer or speaker.

So a sacred festival can be plural (Jh.10:22, Mk.14:1) and the 'bosom of father Abraham' is literally in the plural (Lk.16:33), as are the East and West when great apocalyptic events are involved (Mt. 8:11). Likewise the 'Holy of Holies' in the Temple, and a heavenly 'sanctuary' are in the plural (Heb. 8:2, 9:3).

With regard to Jerusalem, my research shows that it is identified as plural when the evangelist is affirming the esoteric idea of a spiritual counterpart to Jerusalem, located above the earthly city, so to speak. Origenes also interprets the plural word in this way, "Perhaps the Jerusalem above" is what is meant, into which the Lord shall (later) ascend.[207]

This idea was committed to writing in several initiatory non-canonical inter-testamental texts. In *4 Ezra*, (10:47,49) the seer speaks of a 'heavenly model' of Jerusalem, which is imbued with the 'Shekinah', or divine glory. In *Two Enoch*, one reads of Enoch (55:2) ascending after death "to the uppermost Jerusalem" and in *Sirach* (24) the reader is informed that the earthly Jerusalem is paralleled by "the Jerusalem that is above".

These statements are affirmed in *Hebrews* 12:22, in a reference to Mount Zion. Mount Zion is a substitute name for Jerusalem, its sacred core; Zion itself being an acropolis section of the city. The writer of Hebrews refers to the heavenly counterpart of Jerusalem or 'Mount Zion',
"But you have come to Mount Zion, to the heavenly Jerusalem, the city of the living God. You have come to thousands upon thousands of angels in joyful assembly...."

By a careful reading of the use of the name Jerusalem, I have found that that all the evangelists are affirming this esoteric viewpoint. For every time they are recording that someone has simply entered or departed

---

[207] *Commentary on John*, Bk. 10 #182.

from this city, as part of a journey, its name is in the singular. But otherwise, whenever significant actions occur involving Jerusalem, the city is a 'double city', e.g., A: when a person is carrying out a significant activity within Jerusalem, such as when Jesus is preaching there (Jn. 2:23), or when people are worshipping there (Jn. 4:20).
B: or when a decisive action which originates from Jerusalem occurs, such as when Teachers of the Law left Jerusalem to seek out and confront Jesus (Mk.3:22).

In these situations, Jerusalem is referred to as 'the Jerusalems'.[208] A striking example of this subtle point is shown in two closely following verses: John 5:1 (a journey report) and then 5:2 (a healing miracle),

> Jn. 5:1 Some time later, Jesus went up into **Jerusalem**[209] for a feast of the Jews.
> 5:2 Now, in **'the Jerusalems'**,[210] there is near the Sheep Gate, a pool, which in Aramaic is called Bethesda and....Jesus saw him lying there...

Although this is ignored in translations, the evangelists take very seriously the conviction that spiritual activities in Jerusalem involve an interaction with spiritual beings and influences located in a holy site. A site which is not on the Earth physically, but existing in an ethereal-spiritual continuum above the earthly city.

Again v. **2:23 Now while he was in 'the Jerusalems' at the Passover during the Feast, many people saw the miraculous signs he was doing, and intuitively discerned his divine nature.**

"the miraculous signs he was doing": the Gospel does not give any reports of such miracles, but we are to assume that these did occur in this festival week.

---

[208] In the Greek: 'the teachers of the Law left the Jerusalems' is ...καὶ οἱ γραμματεῖς οἱ ἀπὸ ῾Ιεροσολύμενων καταβαντες .....)

[209] In the Greek: *eis Jerosolumena* - εἰς Ἱεροσόλυμενα)
[210] In the Greek, *en tois Jerosolumois* - ἐν τοῖς Ἱεροσολύμοις)

"...and intuitively discerned his divine nature": instead of the usual 'and believed in His name", because as noted earlier, this traditional phrase no longer conveys much meaning.

2:24 But Jesus would not entrust himself to them, for he knew all people.
2:25 He did not need a person's testimony about human nature, for he knew what was in a human being.

These two verses are quite clear, showing that, at the start of his public ministry, Jesus was not intending to encourage a widespread popular response, with all the problems which that would create.

Chapter 3

Nicodemus comes to Jesus
Verse 3:1 There was a man of the Pharisees, named Nicodemus, a member of the Jewish ruling council.

"There was a man of the Pharisees": the Greek here is unusually laboured, as various scholars have noted. It could have simply said: "A Pharisee, named Nicodemus..." Instead it is at pains to define the visitor to Jesus as firstly, a human being, and secondly a Pharisee, and thirdly a learned teacher (or a highly placed senior figure). The reason for this becomes clear when verse 2 is considered.

3:2 He came to Jesus during the night-time and said, "Rabbi, we know you are a teacher who has come from God. For no one could perform the miraculous signs you are doing if God were not with him."

That Nicodemus came to Jesus "during the night-time" very probably refers to a 'soul-encounter' occurring in the spirit, and not a discreet physical visit. This more esoteric narrative is of the same kind as the episode from Chapter One, when John the Baptist beheld the Saviour with seership, (1:36, 37):
"And having observed with seership the spiritual environs encompassing Jesus, the Baptist exclaims (to himself), "Behold, the Lamb of God !"
    Here Nicodemus is inwardly impelled to encounter the Saviour, whilst in a dream state or perhaps during a quiet, contemplative time. The souls of various people and spiritual beings were no doubt also drawn to encounter Jesus. What lives in the soul of any entity resonated clearly to the immensely high seership of the Saviour. He perceives the wrestling going on in the soul of Nicodemus, who is intrigued and inspired by what he senses about Jesus.

3:3 Jesus responded, "Very truly, I say to you, no one can see the kingdom of God unless he is born again."

Though Nicodemus has not actually formulated any questions, Jesus brings a response to his inner questioning, correcting the confusion in the Sanhedrin's expectation of the future for humanity and the role of the Messiah. For their understanding was that the Messiah would have a direct political impact in the world, punishing evil-doers and ushering in a new glorious earthly world.

Jesus points out that human beings shall attain to the 'Son of Man' state (the Spiritual-self) only through taking on an arduous process, and in terms of humanity in general, only after a long evolutionary journey.

3:4 Nicodemus says to him, "How can a man be born when he is old?". "Surely he cannot enter a second time into his mother's womb to be born."

The objection of Nicodemus appears foolish, but it probably comes from the rabbinic tradition of 'mental dueling' which seeks to provoke a more detailed answer by an exaggerated response.

3:5 Jesus answered, "Very truly, I say to you, no one can enter the kingdom of God unless he is born of water and of spirit."

This answer from Jesus has remained an enigma, for it concerns deeply esoteric and transcendent matters, hence it actually starts with "Amen, amen", which as noted, I have always translated as "Very truly". This expression was discussed in Part One, Section 2. The exact meaning of the word Amen is unknown, but it is a way of emphasizing the importance of what follows, for usually in Jewish usage it occurred at the end of a sentence, not the beginning. The synoptic Gospels only have a single 'amen'. The double 'amen' occurs very rarely, apart from in this Gospel, in a few Psalms and in the Dead Sea Scrolls.

In the work of Rudolf Steiner, Jesus' answer is seen as alluding to esoteric knowledge. He explains that it has two meanings. Jesus does not say that we must be born of "The Spirit", but simply 'of spirit'.[211] On one level, the answer is referring to a vast evolutionary process, wherein humanity came into earthly existence, on the Earth, when it was an airy-watery planet. Very primitive animals and proto-humans started out in an aquatic environment, gradually developing lungs and living on dry land, as the planet became drier and more dense. So we were 'born of water'; emerging out of a primordial aqueous environment.

According to the general perspective of Rudolf Steiner's cosmology, in the course of future Ages, humanity shall become ever less in need of a physical body and become spiritual beings, existing in a non-physical state. In that condition, consciousness shall naturally perceive and resonate with, divine reality. People shall then "enter the kingdom of God". So then we shall arise from a physical state into a non-material, spiritual condition.

On another level, the answer relates to initiatory knowledge of the various levels in the structure of the cosmos. In this situation, 'water' is a symbol of the Soul-world, so then 'spirit' alludes to a realm higher than the Soul-world. This is understood to be a realm where divine beings form the thoughts of Creation, in all its details, from which the multitude of life-forms on the Earth derive. This is the realm that Plato refers to as the realm of archetypal Ideas. For consciousness to be able to function in these realms, a higher level of spiritual cognition is required than for the Soul-world; the initiate is then within the being of God.

3:6: Flesh gives birth to flesh, but the Spirit gives birth to spirit.

The meaning of this verse is quite clear.

3:7 You (thou) should not be surprised at my saying, 'You (ye) must be born again'.

The archaic words 'thee' and 'ye' are used to show that Jesus at first addresses Nicodemus, but then refers to

---

[211] The Greek "...καὶ πηεύματος" it is not "καὶ του πνεύματος."

many people; presumably, at least initially, the Sanhedrin in general. Jesus here is admonishing Nicodemus, pointing out that he and others should have knowledge of the various realms of the cosmos. (Perhaps also knowledge of the future of the Earth and humanity.) For knowledge of lower and higher spirit realms, including realms beyond the seven 'Soul-worlds', were a part of the inner esoteric tradition of Judaism.[212]

3:8 The wind blows wherever it pleases. You (ye) hear its sound, but you (ye) cannot tell where it comes from or where it is going. So it is with everyone born of the spirit.

This poignant verse is an admonishing observation on the inner blindness of the human being. The word for 'wind' in Greek is 'pneuma' (πνεῦμα) and it is also used for spirit. Thus the first sentence in the reply from Jesus relates to, and enriches, the second sentence. (So the word 'sound' here can also mean 'voice'.)

The meaning is, human beings can only perceive the nature of the winds on a superficial level; and it is the same with regard to the real intentions, the living pulse, of the spirit. In particular this applies to the intentions of initiates, or the 'Sons of Man' in whom the spirit has been born.

3:9 Nicodemus responded and said to him, "How can this be?"
3:10 Jesus answered and said to him, "You are Israel's teacher, yet do you not understand these things?"

In these two verses the inappropriate ignorance of Nicodemus about becoming re-born spiritually, is again shown and remarked upon.

3:11 "I tell you (thee) the truth, we speak of what we know, and we testify to what we have seen, but still you (ye) do not accept our testimony."

---

[212] Such realms are mentioned in *The Book of Enoch*, and the *Book of the Secrets of Enoch*.

Once again Jesus is addressing his remarks initially to Nicodemus, but then to many Jewish people. But more significant is that Jesus now speaks of himself in the plural: "*we* speak of what *we* know, and *we* testify to what *we* have seen." Many scholars conclude that it cannot be explained.[213] I have concluded that Jesus here is educating Nicodemus about the nature of a Son of Man initiate. For his words appear to echo his teachings just before the Marriage in Cana to Nathanael and hence to others known to Nathanael:

He says to Nathanael, "Very truly, I say to you (ye), you (ye) shall see heaven open, and the angels of God ascending and descending on The Son of Man." (1:51)

So as with Nicodemus, Jesus is not speaking as a normal human being, but as the vessel of the Divine, as a Son of Man; but in his case not simply as that, but as the great archetypal Son of Man. Nicodemus is being informed that a person attaining The Son of Man state does not exist in isolation, but in a continual interweaving of their self-awareness with the intentions and actions of divine beings.

3:12 I have spoken to you (thee) of earthly things and you (ye) do not believe; how then will you (ye) believe if I speak of heavenly things?

Once again many people are soon addressed, although initially Jesus is speaking only to Nicodemus.

3:13 No one has ever gone into heaven except the one who came from heaven – The Son of Man.

This verse confirms the reference to The Son of Man state, in v. 11. Following on from v. 5 ('one cannot enter the Kingdom of Heaven unless one is born of water and of spirit') Nicodemus is being told that the human being

---

[213] Morris, "it is curious"; Westcott, 'it is remarkable'. Some conclude that Jesus is including the disciples, or the Spirit in general, or simply emphasizing his own self, as is sometimes done by anyone in speaking or writing, to politely de-emphasize their own self.

long ago descended into earthly existence, but each person has always been linked with a Spiritual-self potential (i.e., The Son of Man) which exists, up in high spiritual realms.

Hence one can conclude from this viewpoint, that in the course of Earth's evolution, the higher nature of the soul may emerge as a reality for the individual, and then humanity shall exist in spiritual realms. In other words, if the human soul had not become an earthly reality, it could not have become a self-aware entity; it is on this basis that in future ages, the soul eventually becomes spiritualized.

3:14 Just as Moses lifted up the serpent in the desert, so the Son of Man must be lifted up, (Num.21:5)

Here the dual nature of The Son of Man idea emerges. In this verse we are told that for the human being to ascend into the spiritual state of existence, the Spiritual-self (or The Son of Man) has to be developed. But it is a core Gospel truth that the process of spiritual development involves the Christ.

The source of the holiness which forms the Spiritual-self derives from the Christ, as does the wish to attain this. This is made clear in the next verse; and in this way these two verses interweave these two interconnected meanings.

The reference which Jesus makes here to an action of Moses, is deeply esoteric. Rudolf Steiner explains that in the secret language of the initiates a 'serpent' referred to human beings who had overcome the influence of the lower qualities in the soul.[214] The sages of olden times chose the word serpent partly because of the deeply esoteric story in the *Book of Genesis*, about the 'Fall of Man' brought about by the Devil, who is called 'that old serpent'.

Their reasoning was that, if a person becomes holy, i.e., an initiate, then they have only attained that ennobled status because they encountered their lower qualities, and worked to overcome them. If the 'old

---

[214] GA 103, lect., 25 May, 1908; GA 34, p. 38; GA 97, lect., 4 April, 1906.

serpent' had not placed those qualities in the soul of primordial humanity, then the state of sanctification would not have been attained.

So Moses was reminding his people of this dynamic, indicating that a high level of godliness can be attained, once the old serpent influences are overcome. He did this by elevating a symbol of a serpent. It is presumably the case that many of his people would not have understood the symbol, but even so, been affected by it.[215]

3:15 ...so that everyone who believes in him may have eternal life.

This verse follows on from v. 14, and has two meanings within it. On the level of referring to Jesus, the above translation is quite clear. Namely that historically, Jesus, as the archetypal Son of Man, must undergo a 'lifting up' onto a cross, that is, he must be sacrificed, for humanity to succeed in attaining its future goal.

So firstly, everyone who believes in this proclamation of the saving of humanity by Christ can find their way to 'eternal life' that is, eternal existence in divine realms.[216] This powerful Gospel message is of enormous significance. But secondly, this verse continues the dual meaning placed within v. 14, and therefore can be equally well translated as,

3:15 ...so that everyone who spiritually perceives it, may have eternal life.

Now the verse is referring to The Son of Man or the Spiritual-self, as a potential in everyone, implying that

---

[215] An elevated serpent is a metaphor of the initiate, for such a person has ennobled or elevated the influences which derived from lower beings, symbolized as serpents. The majority of the Israelites may have taken note of the message in this unusual symbol in a semi-conscious way.

[216] The word 'him' and 'it' is the same word in the Greek (αὐτό), whether referring to a neuter or masculine thing. The verb 'to believe' (πιστύειν) can also mean 'to perceptively discern' as shown earlier.

those who seek a high spirituality shall perceive their divine potential. The soul would then seek to bring this potential into reality. This stage of higher consciousness brings 'eternal life'.

Eternal Life
What does this term, 'eternal life' really mean? As we noted in Part One, Section 4, this term in Greek is 'zoeae aioenios' (ζωή αἰωνίος) which does not mean a never-ending life, but having an existence in high spiritual realms (which is beyond past, present and future). The word 'aioenios' is commonly misunderstood as never-ending or eternal. But its core meaning refers to high spirit realms, although this esoteric nuance is not discussed by theologians. It could be translated as 'aeonic existence'.

An example of not acknowledging the core meaning of this word is found in a translation of a section of a non-canonical esoteric text, known as *4 Ezra* which is contemporaneous with the Christian Gospels, dating from ca. 70-80 AD. It has a remarkable verse, (9:18) imbued with transcendental spirituality, in which God speaks to the seer. It was translated by a mainstream Bible scholar as,

"For there was a time in the *eternal Ages* (αἰῶνα - aioena) when I prepared for those who now exist - before they had come into being - a world wherein they might dwell..."[217]

This is a very imperfect rendering. It is more accurately translated as,

"For there was an occasion, in the spiritual realms, when there was prepared by me, for those who now exist - before they were created - a spiritual realm in which they may have abode...."   (trans. A.A.)

It is the same with the phrase 'eternal life' (zoeae aioenios); it is not about eternity as such, but about high spirit realms. So verse 3:15, wherein the great central

---

[217] G.H. Box, *The Ezra-Apocalypse*, 1912, p. 207.

gift of Christ to humanity is declared, is more correctly translated as, "...that everyone who spiritually perceives it, may have aeonic consciousness." (That is, empowered consciousness in spiritual realms.)

3:16 For God so loved the world that he gave the uniquely created Son, that whoever believes in him shall not perish, but have eternal life.

"He gave *the* uniquely created Son": usually "*his* only son". But the most reliable Greek texts say "the Son", not "...his Son".

"eternal life": that is, consciousness in high spiritual realms; 'aeonic consciousness'.

Two profound questions arise here: What does it mean, that Jesus is "the son of God", and what kind of 'love' is meant here? It was discussed earlier that the expression "The Son of God", was used in esoteric circles to refer to an initiate who achieved especially high spirituality. This usage occurs in the Prologue, verse 12; "these were empowered through it to become children of God". It was also used in a religious-political way in various cultures to convey the conviction that a king or revered sage was linked to the deity of that cult or nation. With Jesus, it was used in a related, yet unique, way.

Why is Jesus called The Son of God ?
To get clarity about this, we need to note as discussed earlier, that the word 'God' has various meanings in the Bible, and in the Hellenistic world. The Greek word 'theos', is defined today in dictionaries as meaning 'God'. However, in the Hellenistic Age this word often applied to various deities, especially the highest of the Greek pantheon, Zeus.

But it was also used in a generic way; it then referred to various divine beings interacting with each other; so a 'divine being-ness' was meant. It was also used for the cosmos or Creation itself (as a result, Creation was viewed as divinely permeated), and often this usage alluded to twelve zodiacal forces sustaining Creation. As we noted earlier (Part One, Section 3) the more holistic consciousness of earlier peoples resulted in the influences of the zodiac becoming a primary factor in their view of Creation.

In the Gospels, the meaning of this phrase, 'The Son of God' when used of Jesus, is not explained in an esoteric sense. The Gospel texts have 'theos', but since this word has several meanings, it is not a word which is self-explanatory; that is, to what kind of 'divine-ness' does it refer?

My conclusion is that 'God' in this phrase refers to the cosmic Christ, for this deity, (along with the others of the Elohim in Genesis 1:1) is 'God' to the Hebrew people. However, Jahve can also be called 'God' or "The Lord" in the Bible, but as noted earlier, this deity is also one of the Elohim.

The perception underlying the statements that Jesus is 'The Son of God' – which started with proclamation of the Archangel Gabriel to Mary (Lk. 1:32), has its basis in this; that Jesus is the only 'unfallen' human being in the human life-wave. In his soul and spirit there is nothing of a lower self or qualities derived malignant beings; so he is therefore derived solely from 'God'. The actual meaning here of God is a deep theme, which requires contemplation, since this word has various meanings.

Jesus is unique in the human life-wave, for the rest of humanity has some of its nature derived from fallen beings. Hence from the perspective of great initiates known as The Sons of God, Jesus is the archetypal Son of God, and the fountain of this high spirituality for everyone else.

Verse 16 is a core verse, succinctly proclaiming the essence of the Gospel message. Believing in Jesus, that is, in his significance as the portal to the Divine, and as the archetype of the future redeemed human being, is essential. For this is the soul-state which bestows eternal life, after a contemplative encounter with the Gospels, whether sustained by an inner conviction, or a discerning perception. This opens the portal to developing The Son of Man, or the Spiritual-self.

A primary feature of Steiner's Christology is that at the Resurrection when the cosmic Christ permanently united with Jesus, Jesus became the first 'perfected', or divine, human being. To take an example from music; just as many tuning forks do begin to resound when, near to them, one larger tuning fork is sounding, so too can humanity now become a truly spiritual reality, because the archetype of a godly human being has now been created.

Here the message is resounding that "God is love" and that Jesus is the selfless, sacrificial, vessel of that love. So what is meant by 'love' here?

Love and Agape

Whereas modern English has but one word for 'love', the ancient Greek language had four verbs for what we today call love. One of these is 'phileoe' (φιλέω) which means 'to like' someone as a friend; another word is 'eros' (ἔρος) which refers to passions and sensual affection. A third verb is stergoe (στέργω) which means the affection felt between family members. But the fourth verb is 'agapaoe' (ἀγαπάω), from which the noun 'agape' (ἀγάπη) was derived.

This word appears in the Septuagint, the Greek translation of the Hebrew Scriptures, in about 300 BCE. There it was often used for the three kinds of love, as well as in just a few instances, for the fourth kind, agape; a holy, selfless love, including the love of God for humanity. There are some 25 usages of 'agape' in the Septuagint, of which about 6 are referring to an 'agape' love as a divine good-will between two entities. One of these was about two people (2Sam.1:26), one was the initiate Elijah towards people (Sirach 48:11) otherwise, it was about God and another entity, usually a prophet or Israel itself.

Outside this Hellenistic Biblical text, it was hardly ever used before the time of Jesus. But when this word was used by Jesus it meant an 'inner union' of one's deepest soul layer (the will or volition) with a deity, or with the core of another person.

This deepest layer of our consciousness is our volition or will; for this is a more potent capacity than our thinking or emotions. It is also more veiled, because much of our will lies in the subconscious.

Agape is the kind of love which actually arises from a 'will-unity' which becomes good-will towards the other. But such an inner union with another entity, of our will, this core part of our nature, is not so subject to the ebb and flow of emotions; that is, of liking and disliking. To reverse this will-embedded state is a major effort, unlike *eros* (sensual-romantic love) or *phileo* (liking friends) and *stergo* (family affection); for a person can reverse or alter these feelings fairly easily.

But agape, which arises as a blessing of the spirit in response to our endeavours, is the condition of the will, of the core of our consciousness. But here is the potent situation; such an inner unity can be a state which is either a malignant, or a highly spiritual, condition of inner unity. This fact is understandable from a spiritual approach to psychology, and is also confirmed from words of Jesus. In v. 19 he presented agape in this light (see below), regarding the malignant state of un-spiritual people. That is, of those who have brought about an inner union – an alignment of their will – to malignant beings.

But in its positive mode, which is how it is nearly always used in the Gospels, agape is a selfless, deep, good-will arising in the core of the soul, in our volition or will, rather than only in the emotions. So this is then a quality which can be defined as 'love', but it is quite different to the three other forms of love. It is a condition that requires a truly selfless, spiritual nature, because such higher will qualities in humanity have a divine origin, and draw this forth in the soul. So it is, as noted above, a spiritual gift to the aspiring soul.

It is the message of Jesus that this 'love' or deep-seated good-will is what God has for humanity, and this loving good-will is what a human being should bring to deity, and also to one's fellow human beings.

It was used by the early Christians in other situations, such as the selfless love of a parent for a child, the love that would lead a human being to sacrifice their life for another. Both of these usages required in reality a profound inner unity to exist between the two beings in question.

So agape, in its moral use, is best understood as meaning 'good-will' in the profound sense of a selfless love, deriving from an unshakeable inner union. Jesus used this word to inspire his disciples and all Christians to become people manifesting this kind of love.[218] So from then on, Christians began to refer not only to spiritual 'loving', but also to such love as a specific 'object', a specific reality. So it expanded from being a verb to a noun. (Outside Christian literature, it was later rarely used in this way; just once by Philo (in *Deus*.69) and it occurs in one non-Christian Greek inscription, from the 3rd century AD).

3:17 For God did not send his Son into the world to condemn the world, but to save the world through him.

This is one of many verses in which the cosmic importance of the Christ-reality is proclaimed, an importance that points to a cosmic being, a deity, striving for a joyous future outcome for humanity. Through the ongoing love and deeds of the risen Jesus, the cosmic Christ and the primal Logos can exert an influence in humanity's ongoing evolving.

3:18 Whoever believes in him is not condemned, but whoever does not believe, is condemned already because he or she has not spiritually discerned the nature of God's uniquely-begotten Son.

"discerned the spiritual reality of": instead of the usual 'believed in his name', because as noted earlier, the usual literal translation of this ancient expression seldom conveys its intended meaning today.

This verse points to a dynamic enveloping human existence, wherein the soul-state of a person, or of a community, whatever state that may be, invokes a corresponding response from the cosmos. Those who discern in the course of any lifetime on Earth, the uniquely important significance of the Christ – these people can, through this 'faith', that is through a discerning perception, be saved from drifting towards a meaningless, or even malignant, future.

The Gospel here is teaching that the opposite dynamic applies to those who lack this capacity for discernment.

---

[218] As established in the article, "ἀγάπαω" in *Theologisches Wörterbuch zum Neuen Testament*, erster Bd, edit. G Kittel.

Yet it is, and will remain, the loving intention of the Christ that such an incapacity is healed.

3:19 This is the judging process: light has come into the world, but people were inwardly at one (agape) with darkness rather than the light, because their deeds were base.

The NRSV and NIV have, "this is the judgement", which is unfortunate, as the verse is about a gradual process, invoked by the person's way of being, interacting with a cosmos which has specific dynamics built into it; not a cold judgement or verdict.
"inwardly at one with darkness": this is usually "loved the darkness", but as noted above, the word for agape can be used also for an unethical state, and this was used here. So Jesus is pointing out that people who are not ethical have an inner unity of their will with evil, and such a debased state is obviously not 'love'. This verse shows clearly that 'agape' means 'an inner union', which can be either highly spiritual or quite evil.

However, the use of the word agape in the Gospels for evil, can never be translated as 'love' in any sense. It follows then that 'agape' itself is not correctly translated as 'love', but as 'an inner union', with the understanding that if agape is used in its positive sense, then a noble, selfless love encompassing more than the emotions, is very much present.

The understanding of 'love' in the Gospels, when it is from God or from Jesus, or from people towards God or Jesus, transcends 'phileo'. It is much deeper than this; it refers to the deepest level of the soul, as noted earlier. St. Paul describes this so well in 1Cor. 13:2-4.

3:20 Everyone who does base things hates the light, and will not approach the light, for fear that their deeds will be exposed.
3:21 But whoever lives by the truth comes into the light, so that it may be seen plainly that what they have done, has been done through God.

These two verses need no especial commentary.

3:22 After this, Jesus and his disciples went out into the Judean countryside, where he spent some time with them, and baptized.

In chapter 4:3, we are told that actually Jesus himself did not baptize, but rather it was his disciples. So then Lazaros is saying here that the spiritual power of Jesus was pervading the baptisms, but only the disciples carried them out.[219]

3:23 Now John also was baptizing at Aenon near Salim, because water was plentiful there, and people were constantly arriving to be baptized.
3:24 (This was before John was put in prison.)
3:25 An argument developed between some of John's disciples and a certain Jew, over the matter of ceremonial washing (that is, baptism).
3:26 They came to John the Baptist and said to him, "Rabbi, that man who was with you on the other side of the Jordan – the one you testified about – he is baptizing, and everyone is going to him."

These four verses show that there was some rivalry felt by followers of the Baptist, regarding Jesus.

3:27 To this John replied, "A man can receive only what is given him from heaven."

The Baptist is calmly reminding his followers that, regardless of whatever kind of baptism a person undergoes, the blessing that follows for that person depends upon their capacity to receive spiritual influences, and the capacity of the baptizer to transfer spiritual blessings to the person in the water.

3:28 You yourselves can testify that I said, 'I am not the Christ, but am sent ahead of him.'

---

[219] F. Godet also concluded this: "the inner deed belonged to him, the external performing of the baptism was undertaken by his Disciples." (Das innere Thun gehörte ihm an, die äusserliche Verrichtung geschah durch seine Jünger: *Das inner Tun gehörte ihm an; die äusserliche Verrichtung geschah durch seine Jünger*, (*Kommentar zu dem Evangelium Johannes*, 1903, p.170)

The Baptist reminds his followers that he is very clear about himself being a lesser person than the Messiah.

3:29 The one who has the company of the bride is the bridegroom. The friend who attends the bridegroom waits and listens for him, and is full of joy when he hears the bridegroom's voice. That joy is mine, and it is now complete.

The perfect selflessness of the Baptist is clear.
"have the company of": the verb here (exoe - ἔχω) has many nuances, including, to have, to be in the company of, to hold, to have the benefits of.

3:30 "He must increase; I must decrease."

The words here relate to a flourishing growth and a decline in growth. This nuance in the Greek words here refer to a spiritual influence becoming more powerful, whilst the other preparatory influence, from the Baptist, weakens. For now the impetus towards an individuated and inherently moral sense of I' is present. The verses 31 - 36 are spoken by the Baptist and refer to both Jesus and to those who speak from spiritual inspiration.

3:31 The one who comes from above, is above all; the one who is from the earth belongs to the earth, and speaks as one from the earth. The one who comes from heaven is above all.

This verse can be read as applying to both Jesus and to other human souls who achieve a high spirituality.

3:32 He testifies to what he has seen and heard, but no one accepts his testimony.

This verse refers equally to Jesus, and to other human beings who have attained some experiences from higher realms, and wishes to speak about them. Such a person will find that only the few, those who have some spiritual perception or awareness, will comprehend what they report.
3:33 The person who has received it, has attested to the reality of God.

"the reality of God": or, **"the reality of the Divine"**. Usually translated as "that God is true". This is an expression which follows the Greek literally, but its meaning is obscure, which has led to much scholarly debate. I conclude that what is meant is that the reality, the real existence of, the Divine is powerfully attested to by the oratory of inspired vessels of the Divine: the spiritual sages or prophets of earlier times.[220]

"attested to": literally means 'has set his seal upon", it also occurs v. 6:27.

3:34 For the one whom God has sent, speaks the words from God: moreover, God gives forth the Spirit without measure.
or
For the one whom God has sent, speaks the words from the Divine: moreover, the Divine gives forth the Spirit without metrical structure.

Here on the level of referring to Jesus, and interpreting 'metrou' as meaning 'in abundance', the Baptist proclaims that God inspires Jesus in abundance, not in a meagre way. But this is a somewhat unnecessary statement regarding Jesus. However, on the level regarding a spiritual human being who speaks forth from spiritual awareness, the term "without measure" has a different and more significant meaning. For this now refers to the actual metrical structure or 'measure' of a sentence.[221]

---

[220] L. Morris, *Gospel accord. to John*, p. 217, referencing M. Black, *An Aramaic approach to the Gospels,* but in fact, Black does not refer to this verse there. In view of the obscurity of the Greek (if one takes 'true' in a literal sense) it has been argued that the Aramaic words for 'true' and for 'sent' are very similar, and if this Gospel were, at least in part, translated into Greek from some Aramaic notes, then such a mistake is easily made: "God has sent him"). But this theory supposes that a student of Lazaros made this translation incorrectly, and Lazaros never revised the work of this student.

[221] Rudolf Steiner has pointed this out, in the context of a more detailed esoteric commentary; in GA 103, chapter 5.

The Greek word here (metrou – μέτρου) has this second meaning. A sentence usually is formed in accordance with laws of grammar and has it own 'melody'. In addition, a poem may have a definite metre, giving it a particular 'pulse', or rhythm, etc. But when a spiritual person is inspired to speak from 'the spirit' (and the Greek word 'theos' also means the Divine or the spirit, not only God) their words may well be mantric; an inspired, oratorical mystical/mantric speaking, not following the accepted metrical structure of language.

3:35 The Father loves (agape) the Son and has placed everything in his hand.

"loves the Son": i.e., God is inwardly at one with Jesus and with those who attain to The Son of Man stage. This verse continues the two levels of meaning; one regarding Jesus, the other, the attainment of the Spiritual-self or The Son of Man.

3:36 Whoever believes in the Son has eternal life, but whoever rejects the Son will not experience eternal life, for God's wrath remains on them.

As with v. 35, this continues the two levels of meaning. On the level of the individual person seeking spirituality, it reads,
"Whoever discerns spiritually the Spiritual-self, (and then seeks to become that), attains to 'eternal life'.

But it is crucial to discern that "*for God's wrath remains on him or her*" is not to be thought of in terms of a vengeful God waiting to punish us. It means that the distressing reality of earthly life, with its suffering, diseases and crimes, are the inevitable outcome of humanity having a lower-self (or 'fallen' state). The troubles and diseases that pursue humanity are understood as the expression of the negative influences invoked by the normal soul-state, and which are an integral part of earthly life. This outcome is the expression of dynamics underlying the cosmos.

However, it is also true that JHVH has brought punishment upon the Hebrews at times, when they failed to remain in reverence to him and to be obedient to his guidance. But this verse is about dynamics involving higher deities, or more complex spiritual dynamics, wherein a specific punishment by one specific deity is not the theme.

Chapter 4
The Samaritan Woman

4:1 The Pharisees heard that Jesus was gaining and baptizing more disciples than John,
4:2 although in fact it was not Jesus who baptized, but his disciples.
4:3 When the Lord learned of this, he left Judea and went back once more to Galilee.
4:4 Now he had to go through Samaria.
4:5 So he came to a town in Samaria called Sychar, near the plot of ground Jacob had given to his son Joseph.
4:6 Jacob's well was there, and Jesus, tired as he was from the journey, sat down by the well. It was about the sixth hour.
4:7 When a Samaritan woman came to draw water, Jesus said to her, "Will you give me a drink?"
4:8 (His disciples had gone into the town to buy food.)
4:9 The Samaritan woman said to him, "You are a Jew and I am a Samaritan woman. How can you ask me for a drink?" (For Jews do not associate with Samaritans.)[222]
4:10 Jesus answered her, "If you knew the gift of God and who it is that asks you for a drink, you would have asked him and he would have given you living water."
4:11 "Sir," the woman said, "you have nothing to draw with and the well is deep. Where can you get this living water?
4:12 Are you greater than our father Jacob, who gave us the well and drank from it himself, as did also his sons and his flocks and herds?"
4:13 Jesus answered, "Everyone who drinks this water will be thirsty again,
4:14 but whoever drinks the water I give him will never thirst. Indeed, the water I myself give him will become in him a spring of water, welling up to eternal life."

---

[222] This sentence is not in codex Bezae nor codex Sinaiticus, and was probably added by a scribe in later centuries.

4:15 The woman said to him, "Sir, give me this water so that I won't get thirsty and have to keep on coming here to draw water."

4:16 He told her, "Go, call your husband and come back."

4:17 "I have no husband," she replied. Jesus said to her, "You have rightly said that you have no husband.

4:18 The fact is, you have had five husbands, and the man you now have is not your husband. What you have just said is quite true."

4:19 "Sir", the woman said, "I can see that you are a prophet."

Commentary on verses 4:1-19

There are two levels of meaning within this incident; one is the religious-cultural interaction of Jesus with a Samaritan woman. The other concerns a major theme in this Gospel: the flow of history, viewed as a sequence of Ages through which humanity is journeying, and the influence of the Christ-reality in these epochs. In Chapter two, with the Marriage of Cana, there were the six water jugs; here in Chapter four, there are in effect, five plus one husbands, and in Chapter five, the covered pool at Bethsaida, has five porticoes plus one extra space where Jesus is located.

These are all discreetly devoted to the same theme: the relation of Christ to humanity throughout history, culminating in a future sixth Age. This is why scholars have noted various puzzling features to the story of the Samaritan woman, which have remained unresolved.

On the esoteric level, one takes note that the woman goes out to a distant place to get water, but the well is very deep, yet normally the site of any town was chosen because water was available at that site. She went out at "the 6th hour", which means midday; this hottest part of the day is not the time to carry water. Then when she realizes that she is now near to a source of 'living water', she cannot directly receive this. That is, not until the nature of the influences she has partnered with, becomes clear.

There are two distinct spiritual messages in the meeting with the Samaritan woman. One is that the well is Jacob's well, whose children formed the ancestors of the twelve tribes of Israel. But Christ is offering water to someone who is not an Israelite. He is offering something beyond the hallowed traditions of the Hebrew people, and beyond the spiritual foundations of Israel. So the message here is that a source of spiritual advancement will be available to all human beings.

The second message in this story, as Rudolf Steiner concluded, is that this woman is a symbol of the individual soul, and that she needs to present herself to the Christ-power as united with her true partner – the Higher-self.[223] Only then can the soul receive the 'living water'. For none of the five aspects of human nature which she was closely linked to, in the course of five Ages, are the true ones. And her current, 'informal partner' is also not the real one.

Hence in 4:17 Jesus said to her, "You have rightly said that you have no husband." On the esoteric level this dialogue is between the human soul on its arduous journey, seeking its true partner, and the Christ, who affirms that the soul has indeed not yet found its higher spiritual reality; its true partner.

Therefore in v.5, the Christ admonishes the soul (woman) saying that it (she) should have asked him for living water, and intimates that the Christ has been intoning to the human soul through out the Ages. In actual earthly life, never would a woman, especially from Samaria, ask this of an unknown Jewish male.

Living water is a term deeply embedded in Jewish literature, including Essene texts from Qumran, as a symbol of deity or divine being-ness in general. The five aspects of the human being alluded to here are: the physical corporeal nature, a life-force, the 'soul' in a basic sense, and then our sentiency (i.e., our awareness of the environment and emotional responses to this.) Finally, somewhat higher, is the logical mind, and there is also an even higher, but less common, intuitive capacity.

But only when the soul merges with a further aspect of itself, a sixth aspect, shall she have found her true

---

[223] GA 103, lect., 23 May, 1908.

'partner' – this is the Spiritual-self, or The Son of Man stage. Underlying this esoteric perspective is the spiritual view of the flow of history. The sixth 'husband', which is only germinal now, shall emerge in its full power in a future sixth Age. Just as, in the preceding Marriage of Cana episode, (which is interlinked with this episode), we noted that the custom of drinking alcohol is to fade out, in a future sixth Age.

In the meantime, the everyday sense of self, which is an imperfect reflection of the Higher-self, is what the soul has as its friend: "and the man you currently have is not your husband". (Likewise in Chapter five, the Gospel points to the Christ bringing healing to humanity only in the sixth section of the pool at Bethesda.)

Verse 14: "the water I myself give them": codex Bezae has this more emphatic version;[224] usually it is "the water I give them...". Verse 15 is another indicator of the deeper layer of meaning (...give me to drink so that I won't get thirsty and have to keep coming here to draw water.). This is not a flippant remark, but derives from the human soul sensing what the Christ could bestow.

For the well is near a village called Sychar; such a place is otherwise not mentioned in the Bible. This name is probably symbolic, for scholars report that it appears to mean either 'drunken town' or 'lying town'; thereby alluding to unsatisfactory sources of 'soul-vitality' that the somewhat self-centred, illusory self seeks.

John 4:20 - 30
4:20 Our fathers worshiped on this mountain, but you Jews claim that the place where we must worship is in Jerusalem."
4:21 Jesus declared, "Believe me, woman, a time is coming when you will worship the Father neither on this mountain nor in Jerusalem.
4:22 You Samaritans worship what you do not know; we worship what we do know, for salvation is from the Jews.

---

[224] "alla to hudoer ho egoe autoe" - ἀλλα τὸ ὕδωρ ὁ ἐγω δώσω αὐτῷ

4:23 Yet a time is coming and has now come when the true worshipers will worship the Father in spirit and truth, for they are the kind of worshipers the Father seeks.
4:24 God is spirit, and his worshipers must worship in spirit and in truth."
4:25 The woman said, "I know that the Messiah (called the Anointed) is coming. When he comes, he will explain everything to us."

"The Messiah": usually, 'Messiah' or 'a Messiah'; but 'the' is also possible, and here it is the most likely meaning.[225]

4:26 Then Jesus says, "I, who speak to you, I am he."
4:27 Just then his disciples returned and were surprised to find him talking with a woman. But no one asked, "What do you want?" or "Why are you talking with her?"
4:28 Then, leaving her water jar, the woman went back to the town and said to the people,
4:29 "Come, see a man who told me everything I ever did. Could this be the Christ?"
4:30 They came out of the town and made their way toward him.

These verses are quite clear, with no second layer of meaning veiled within them, but various notable cultural-religious points. These include that Jesus spoke to a woman outside of his home, (forbidden for a man to do at that time) and that Samaritans were open to hearing from Jesus.

Verses 4:31 - 42

4:31 Meanwhile his disciples urged him, "Rabbi, eat something."
4:32 But he said to them, "I have food to eat that you know nothing about."
4:33 Then his disciples said to each other, "Could someone have brought him food?"

---

[225] The word 'the' is often omitted before a very important noun in biblical Greek.

4:34 "My food," said Jesus, "is to do the will of him who sent me and to bring his work to perfect completion."

The earlier verses were about the 'living water' or inexhaustible fountain of life-forces which the cosmic Christ can bestow upon those who seek spirituality; especially upon the soul that unites with the sixth aspect, the higher spiritual potential, rather than the five lesser aspects of our being. Whereas vs. 31 to 34 are about an opposite dynamic, yet one which is linked to the first. That is, how the attainment of a high spirituality by human souls, such as The Son of Man, and The Son of God stages, in response to the influence of the Christ, actually 'ray back' inner nourishment to the Christ.[226]

4:35 Do you not say, 'Four months more and then the harvest'? But now I am telling you: raise your vision and behold the spirit realms, for they are radiant, ready for harvest.
4:36 Even now the reaper draws his wages, even now he harvests the crop for eternal life, so that the sower and the reaper may be glad together.
4:37 Thus the saying 'One sows and another reaps' is true.
4:38 I sent you to reap what you have not worked for. Others have done the hard work, and you have reaped the benefits of their labour."
4:39 Many of the Samaritans from that town believed in him because of the woman's testimony, "He told me everything I ever did."
4:40 So when the Samaritans came to him, they urged him to stay with them, and he stayed two days.
4:41 And because of his words many more became believers.
4:42 They said to the woman, "We no longer believe just because of what you said; now we have heard for

---

[226] Rudolf Steiner emphasized that as human beings achieve these higher stages, the divine beings who have worked to nurture the human soul over long Ages, are themselves enriched inwardly.

ourselves, and we know that this man really is the Saviour of the world."[227]

Commentary on verses 4: 31-42

These verses weave esoteric truths into the historical-physical encounter with the Samaritan, to indicate that the attainment of spiritual enlightenment by human souls, is an 'inner food' for the Christ. That the Samaritan woman is receptive, and her community shall also be receptive, is what provides nourishment to the Christ.

Verse 35 discreetly points to this veiled message, but the usual translations do not indicate this, "...now I tell you, open your eyes and behold the fields, for they are ready for harvest." This is correct for the surface level, but one notes that the reference to the fields being white or radiant is often omitted in Bibles, for this word doesn't naturally belong there; it refers to the esoteric level of meaning. My version allows the hidden layer to be discerned:

"...now I tell you, raise your vision and behold the spirit realms, for they are radiant, ready for harvest."

The word for 'fields' also means 'realms' or 'regions'; however since the disciples are to use their clairvoyance, these abodes or realms are spiritual, not earthly things.[228] The reference to being 'radiant' alludes to souls observed in their spirit regions; these now have a glowing radiance to them, which is a sign of spirituality.

The usual version has "open your eyes and look..." but the Greek text has 'raise your eyes', and the verb for 'behold' is 'theaomai' (θεάωμαι), which was used for clairvoyant perceiving as well as physical gazing, as noted earlier. The remainder of this section refers to the work of achieving a 'spiritual harvest' of redeemed souls.

---

[227] Codex Bezae in v. 42 has a slight variation here, which may be the correct text: '...because of what you reported, for in this very place we have heard, and thus know that this person is truly the Saviour of the world, the Messiah."

[228] The word here (choera - χωρά) is used of spiritual regions by Philo, for example; in *De Cherubim* 2, #49.

4:43 After the two days he left for Galilee.
4:44 (Now Jesus himself had pointed out that a prophet has no honour in his own country.)
4:45 When he arrived in Galilee, the Galileans welcomed him. They had seen all that he had done in Jerusalem at the Passover Feast, for they also had been there.
4:46 Once more he visited Cana in Galilee, where he had turned the water into wine. And there was a royal official whose son lay sick at Capernaum.
4:47 When this man heard that Jesus had arrived in Galilee from Judea, he went to him and begged him to come and heal his son, who was close to death.
4:48 "Unless you people see miraculous signs and wonders," Jesus told him, "you will never believe."
4:49 The royal official said, "Sir, come down before my child dies."
4:50 Jesus replied, "You may go. Your son will live." The man believed the words that Jesus had said to him and departed.
4:51 While he was still on the way, his servants met him with the news that his boy was living.
4:52 When he inquired as to the time when his son began to recover, they then said to him, "The fever left him yesterday, at the seventh hour."
4:53 Then the father realized that this was the exact time at which Jesus had said to him, "Your son will live." So he and all of his household believed.
4:54 This was the second miraculous sign that Jesus performed, having come from Judea to Galilee.

Commentary on verses 4: 43 - 54
These verses appear to have no veiled levels. The time given, "the seventh hour" probably refers to the servants informing the father on the next day, as he was nearing Capernaum, that his son had improved at 1 pm, on the day before.

Chapter 5
Healing of the man disabled for 38 years

5:1 Some time later, Jesus went up to Jerusalem for a feast of the Jews.

5:2 Now there is in Jerusalem near the Sheep Gate a pool which in Aramaic is called Bethesda and which is surrounded by five covered colonnades.

5:3 Here a great number of disabled people used to wait – the blind, the lame, and the paralyzed, waiting for the water to be disturbed.

5:4 They waited for a disturbance of the waters. From time to time an Angel would descend and cause the waters to stir. The first person to get into pool after such a disturbance, would be healed.

5:5 One person who was there, had been an invalid for thirty-eight years.

5:6 When Jesus saw him lying there, and spiritually perceived that he had been in this condition for a long time, he asked him, "Do you want to get well?"

5:7 "Sir," the invalid replied, "I have no one to help me into the pool, when the water is stirred up. While I am trying to get in, someone else goes down there, ahead of me."

5:8 Then Jesus said to him, "Get up ! Pick up your mat and walk."

5:9 At once the man was cured; he picked up his mat and walked. The day on which this took place was a Sabbath,

5:10 and so the Jewish authorities said to the man who had been healed, "It is the Sabbath; the law forbids you to carry your mat."

5:11 But he replied, "The man who made me well, said to me, 'Pick up your mat and walk.' "

5:12 So they asked him, "Who is this fellow who told you to pick it up and walk?"

5:13 The man who was healed had no idea who it was, for Jesus had slipped away into the crowd that was there.

5:14 Later Jesus found him at the temple and said to him, "Look, you have become healthy. Stop sinning or something worse may happen to you."

5:15 The man went away and told the people that it was Jesus who had made him well.

Commentary on verses 5: 1-15
As noted earlier, this is another incident with the feature of 'five plus one'. For there are five colonnades - plus the area where Jesus is, making a sixth area. It is in the sixth area that the healing occurs.

Verse 5:3
"...waiting for the water to be disturbed."
This additional phrase is in codex Bezae, and I conclude that it is an original part of this verse.[229]

Verse 5:4
The validity of this verse is doubted, because it appears to be a later addition, as it is not in the most reliable early versions of the Gospel, including codex Bezae. It also contains various words that appear nowhere else in this Gospel. However it is valid to include it, because regardless of the actual author, it belongs here in terms of the cultural-religious context.

It makes verses 3 and 7 much more meaningful: "...I have no one to help me into the pool, *when the water is stirred up...*" One may assume that it was for this reason that it was included in several early versions, though these are not of the highest reliability.[230]

Most people today are unaware that in Jesus' time, it was the very widespread belief, in the Middle East (and in many other parts of the world) that springs were often inhabited by water-spirits with healing powers, or else by malignant entities. This understanding remained alive right into the 20th century.

A medical doctor, T. Canaan, after a lifetime of work in Palestine, recorded in 1922, that he knew of 125 springs which were regarded as 'inhabited' in this sense;

---

[229] The Grk. here is "ἐκδεχομένων τήν τοῦ ὕδατος κινήσιν."
[230] These are *Codex Alexandrinus* (5th cent.), Syr[p] (ca. 300 CE), Syr[pal] (ca. 450 CE) and Co[bo] (ca. 250 CE).

each spring had a specific entity.[231] People today may dismiss this viewpoint, and no doubt superstition has played a role in humanity's earlier view of nature. But these old, holistic views can also have a certain validity in them, deriving as they do from the ancient, natural psychic perception of earlier times.[232]

Also relevant here is the fact that several serpent carvings of the cult of Aesclepius, the god of healing, were found by archaeologists, showing that this Greek cult of healing was practised at the pool of Bethesda.

Verse 4 tells us that the waters in the pool were irregularly stirred up, and that this was understood in those times as due to the actions of a spirit-being who bestowed healing on people. Today, this is viewed as the result of the impact of further water being released into the pool from a second northern pool, which was larger, and acted as reservoir for this southern one.

However, owing to these pools being built-over quite a long time ago, any such physical mechanism cannot be tested. Whether the Bethesda pool had a healing spirit or not, the actions of Jesus were undertaken without regard for this phenomenon.

5:6 "When Jesus saw him lying there and inwardly perceived that he had been in this condition for a long time, he asked him, "Do you want to get well?"

The question from Jesus is rhetorical; designed to instill in the sufferer an awareness that he could be healed; and indeed through Jesus. It also implies that through Jesus, such healing is in fact about to occur, yet the disabled man does not perceive this. His hope is on the power that suddenly brings a disturbance in the pool.

---

[231] T. Canaan, "*Haunted Springs and Water Demons in Palestine*" Journal of the Palestine Oriental Society, 1 (1922) 23.

[232] My essay, *The nature and origin of 'the Dreaming'* presents evidence of the reality behind the old holistic-psychic worldview of earlier people, and includes the official Swedish Birth & Death Registry, of several centuries ago, reporting that hundreds of men died through cognizing of mesmerizing seductive water-sprites. Official records of the same cause of death were also made in Palestine, as T. Canaan reports.

5:8 "Then Jesus said to him, Get up ! Pick up your mat and walk."

The abruptness of these words reflects the lack of an intuitive discernment, (or 'faith' in the esoteric sense) on the part of the sufferer. A strong command had to be given to have the right effect on him.

5:14 Later Jesus found him at the temple and said to him, "Look, you have become healthy. Stop sinning or something worse may happen to you."

These words have a mysterious quality, because they are alluding to a larger, cosmic aspect of the Christ's healing powers for humanity. The man has been crippled for 38 years, and consequently it is unlikely that he has been regularly 'sinning' in a way that would be viewed as a cause of his crippled state; it would seem that any such unethical behaviour must have been undertaken over 38 years ago.

Now also, the healing occurs in the sixth area, beyond the five colonnades, just as the Samaritan woman is needing her sixth partner, who shall finally be her true 'husband'. Likewise the need for the wine of Cana shall peter out in the sixth Age. So on this esoteric level, the power of the Christ shall be able to permeate and thus heal the 'fallen' human soul in the sixth Age.[233] This view makes sense of the otherwise very odd admonition that the sufferer should stop sinning or worse shall befall him. An explanation for this admonition is that, this is what Christ shall intone to human souls in the 6th Age.

5:16 So, because Jesus was doing these things on the Sabbath, the Jewish authorities persecuted him.
5:17 Jesus responded to them saying, "My Father is ceaselessly active and thus am I also."
5:18 For this reason the Jewish leaders tried all the harder to kill him; not only was he breaking the

---

[233] Awareness of this flow of past history into the future, is the great 'signature' of the Book of Revelation, the other text from Lazaros.

Sabbath, but he was even calling God his own Father, making himself equal with God.

5:19 Jesus responded to them saying: "Very truly, I say to you, the Son can do nothing by himself; he can do only what he perceives his Father doing, because whatever the Father does, the Son also does.

5:20 For the Father loves (agape) the Son and makes known to him all that he does. He shall make known to him even greater things than these, that you may be filled with wonder.

5:21 For just as the Father raises the dead and gives them life, even so the Son gives (eternal) life to whomever he wishes to give it.

5:22 Moreover, the Father judges no one, but has entrusted all judgement to the Son,

5:23 that all may honour the Son, just as they honor the Father. He who does not honour the Son does not honour the Father who sent him.

Most of the verses in this group are clear as to their meaning, although so central and so deep is their meaning that they call upon the reader to engage in a contemplative way with them. But the more complex verses in this group will now be discussed.

5:17 "Jesus said to them, My Father is ceaselessly active and thus I am also."
The Sanhedrin demanded that Jesus refrain from any work, including miracles, on the Sabbath. Jesus replies that God does not give himself times of rest, but is continuously active in his creating, so too Jesus is always ready to carry out his tasks.

5:20 For the Father loves (agape) the Son and makes known to him all that he does. He shall make known to him even greater things than these, that you may be filled with wonder.

In most Greek versions, the word 'love' here is 'phileo' (fondness). But in Codex Bezae, the verb 'agapaeoe' is used here, which refers to 'agape'. I have used this version. This codex has very old and deeply valid material in it; scholars have concluded that some of the verses have their origin in the texts or oral traditions of the first century. As noted earlier, agape refers to an inner union of the deep core of the soul (the will) to another being, and this is the kind of inner connection which Jesus has to God.

But if here the correct word were 'phileo', which has more the nuance of liking, of friendship, then since Jesus is addressing a crowd, he may be wishing to convey a sense of the father God having a warm, affectionate rapport with a son, rather than a deep cosmic statement about the inner union of the Father-God to the Logos (as in v.3:16).

5:21 "For just as the Father raises the dead and gives them life, even so the Son gives (eternal) life to whomever he wishes to give it."

These are deep core teachings, which are not explained directly. That the Father "raises the dead" may refer to the ability given to the human soul, after the death of the body, to become once again self-aware, and hence cognizing (without the sensory organs or brain) in spiritual realms. If 'the dead' means unspiritual souls, it refers to the bestowal of a higher, eternal spiritual consciousness.

That the Son 'gives eternal life' refers to various aspects of the divine power in Christ. One of these is to lift the soul up and out of literal death (as shown in the Gospel accounts of the raising of the dead). Another is to enable a sense of purpose to arise, which urges the soul to develop a higher level of spirituality. Another aspect is to bring the already spiritualized human being, who has a deep inner attunement to Christ, up to a state wherein an empowered and ennobled sense of self can conquer their 'deadness' or 'lower self' qualities.

5:22 Moreover, the Father judges no one, but has entrusted all judgement to the Son,
5:23 that all may honour the Son, just as they honour the Father. He who does not honour the Son does not honour the Father who sent him.

This is again a vast topic, which concerns the future path for human souls in a large cosmic context; perhaps after death and on in far future times. The associated theme of 'the Son' judging or not judging is subtle, see below, v. 27.

5:24 "Very truly, I say to you that whoever accepts my teachings, and so believes Him who sent me, has eternal life and shall not be condemned; that person has crossed over from death to life.

"accepts my teachings": this phrase brings out the meaning of the idiomatic actual text "hears my word".
"and so believes him": usually, "and believes him" but this leaves out the consequence of accepting Jesus' words, which is expressed in the Greek connecting word here, 'kai'.

5:25 "Very truly, I say to you that a time is coming and has now arrived, when the dead will hear the voice of the Son of God, and those who hear shall live.
5:26 For as the Father has (eternal) life in himself, so he has granted the Son to have life in himself.

"have (eternal) life in himself": this means, 'For as the Father has a source of inexhaustible, eternal life in himself, so he has granted the Son to have a source of inexhaustible life in himself.'
"the dead will hear": again 'the dead' may refer to 'fallen' souls who now, if they are discerning, receive an eternal, ongoing life.

To the Initiatory Quest interpretive approach, this verse is indicating that the divine life-forces inherent in the Father-God are interwoven with the very being of the Jesus Christ. It is from these life-forces that the earthly world derives its much lesser life-forces (known in the Orient as Ch'i or prana).

5:27 And he has given him authority to bring about assessment of people, because he is The Son of Man.
5:28 "Do not be amazed at this, for a time is coming when all who are deceased will hear his voice –

5:29 and come forth – those who have done good, shall rise to live, and those who have done evil, shall rise to be condemned.
5:30 By myself I can do nothing; I judge only as I hear, and my judgement is just, for I seek not to please myself but Him who sent me.

Most of these verses have just one level of meaning, and don't require a commentary, except for verses 25 and 28 which are more complex.

5:25 "Very truly, a time is coming and has now arrived, when the dead will hear the voice of the Son of God and those who hear shall live."

"shall live": vs. 25 and 29 both are referring to living on in the far future as part of a living, multi-layered cosmos. So v. 29 continues the theme of v.25, as noted above. There are several implications in these colossal statements; one is that 'the dead' is figurative and refers to incarnate people, who have not found a link to the Christ, but live within a materialistic worldview. Another implication concerns those souls whose bodies have died, and who now exist in the soul-realm, but who brought very little inner light with them over into this realm of the Dead.

These people shall hear the Saviour's intonings, and responding to him, find that both their inner selves and their pathway are illumined. This task of Christ is confirmed in the Gospels and Epistles, from which it soon became known as the "Harrowing of Hades". This deed of Christ within the Soul-world for the dead, was proclaimed as a major task of the Messiah by Luke, early in his Gospel, (1:78-79). This theme is deepened in 14:2, where 'the many mansions in my Father's house' theme occurs.

5:27 And he has given him authority to bring about assessment of people, because he is The Son of Man.
This verse identifies 'the Son' of v. 22 as 'The Son of Man', an entity which here is distinct from the person Jesus, as such. So it is referring to the Spiritual-self or

Son of Man state, which humanity can achieve (and of which Jesus is the perfect archetype).

"...bring about assessment..." usually, "to execute judgement" or "authority to judge". But as 3.17 states, "For God did not send his Son into the world to judge the world, but to save the world through him." Scholars have noted these two statements, which appear to be inconsistent: the Son is 'to judge the world', and yet, he is not to judge the world.

By having "...bring about assessment..." - which is fully correct to the Greek verb - instead of 'judging', the answer to the apparent inconsistency is emerging. Namely, as people attain to the Spiritual-self, the qualities in their soul respond to the dynamics prevailing in the cosmos. The lower ones invoke a certain response, the better qualities invoke a different response. But see also under v. 8:16 and v. 12:47.

5:28 Do not be amazed at this, for a time is coming when all who are deceased will hear his voice,
Verses 27 and 28 form a unity; usually verse 28 is translated poorly as, "Do not be amazed at this, for a time is coming when *all in their graves* will hear his voice", but this phrase (in italics) is a Semitic idiom, which is very confusing if taken literally. My translation seeks to clarify what is really meant (see below).

Also verses 28 and 29 are interlinked:
5:29 and come forth - those who have done good, shall rise to live, and those who have done evil shall rise to be condemned.

Before vs. 28 and 29 can be understood, the expression "in their graves" needs clarity, otherwise this verse appears to have a disturbingly materialistic quality. The solution here is that, from v. 19 to v. 47, Jesus is speaking to his opponents, the Pharisees. So he is adapting his words to their mindset, in two ways.

Firstly, alluding to their view of the future of humanity: namely that a great Messiah shall appear one day, and a dramatic event occurs - the dead who have been in their tombs and graves, shall then arise, in renewed bodies, and enter a judgement process. The evil-doers to a terrible Netherworld and good souls to a wonderful Paradise world.[234]

Secondly, in referring to the dead as remaining "in their graves" Jesus is not meaning at all that the dead lie inside their graves for millennia, as if their soul is part of their physical body. This is not his meaning; he is using a well-known Hebrew figure of speech.

For Jesus is here using a poetic word for the grave (Sheol), which in fact means the Soul-world. The actual word for a real grave is 'qeber', which was not used here. For it was known to the Pharisees that the soul or soul-body is a separate reality, which leaves the earthly body to dwell in the Soul-world (called 'Sheol' in Hebrew) at death. It was an idiom amongst the Hebrews to refer to the souls who have 'crossed over' into Sheol as being 'in their graves'. This occurs for example, in the Psalms:

"I am set apart with the dead, like the slain who lie in the grave, whom you remember no more, who are cut off from your care. You have put me in the lowest pit, in the darkest depths." (Ps. 88:5,6)

Here one notes that the poet is feeling as if he is deceased, 'like the slain who lie the grave', but this actually means existing in the Soul-world. In fact, in his case, he is in 'the pit', which is the realm below Sheol, (a hellish place known as Gehenna).

This same metaphor which describes existence in Sheol as 'being in the grave', is used in Psalm 49:14, "Like sheep they are destined for the grave..." But the word used for 'grave' here is again Sheol, the realm of the Dead. This same metaphor of 'grave' as a way of referring to the soul-realm, is used again in the next line, (Psalm 49:15), "But God will redeem my life from the grave; he will surely take me to himself." The Hebrew word for 'grave' here is also Sheol.

---

[234] This is mentioned or alluded to in various Jewish texts; but especially in the *Psalms of Solomon* (3, 13, 14 & 15), in *The Apocrypha and Pseudepigrapha of the Old Testament*, edit. Charles.

Jesus answers the Pharisees
5:31 If I testify about myself, my testimony is not valid.
5:32 There is another who testifies in my favor, and you know that his testimony about me is valid.

Usually this is "There is another who testifies in my favor, and I know that his testimony about me is valid." However not only codex Bezae but also codex Sinaiticus record "*you* know" (oidate - οἴδατε) not "I know"; these two codices confer significant authority to this version.

It has been assumed that the other entity referred to here - "there is *another*" - is God, but I conclude it is John the Baptist. Because firstly, in the next verse Jesus notes that not long before, the Sanhedrin had sent a deputation to query the Baptist about these matters, and he had testified the Messiah was among them. Then in v. 36 Jesus declares that he has weightier testimony than that of the Baptist; namely his miraculous deeds.

Furthermore, if Jesus were referring to God in v. 32, he is unlikely to state that he believes that God's testimony is true (i.e., valid). For to all Jews, and especially in regard to Jesus, this was a given fact, a sacred truth; to state that this is the case, appears unnecessary. If Jesus is referring to the Baptist in v. 32, then it is the crowd that needs to be urged to acknowledge that this is valid testimony; Jesus' his own view about the Baptist is less significant to the crowd.

Then in v. 36 Jesus declares that, in regard to another witness which testifies to him, there is the reality that he has a capacity to perform miraculous deeds. It is not God who is his witness, but his power of working wonders, which is given by God.

5:33 You have sent a deputation to John and he has testified to the truth.
5:34 Not that I accept human testimony; but I mention this, so that you may be saved.
5:35 John was a lamp that burned and gave light, and you chose for a time to enjoy his light.
5:36 I have testimony weightier than that of John. For the very work that the Father has given me to finish,

and which I am doing, testifies that the Father has sent me.
5:37 So the Father who sent me has himself testified concerning me. You have never heard his voice nor seen his form,
5:38 thus what rays forth from him does not live in you, for you do not believe the One he sent.

5:37: Here Jesus is affirming that he is experientially aware that God has sent him to the Earth, whereas in v. 32 he is confirming to the crowd that they are aware of the testimony spoken by the Baptist.

"So the Father who sent me": usually "*and* the Father who sent me", but this leaves confusion as to what testimony is being referred to here. By starting with 'And', the solution is often seen in the words of the Prophets of olden times; but with "So the Father who..." it is simply that, as in v.36, the deeds of Jesus - an expression of God - are themselves the testimony. In addition, the usual version also disconnects the two sections of v.37, and leaves v.38 floating, without any connection to v. 37.

Whereas with "*So* the Father who sent me..." v. 37 is declaring that the crowd has not had any direct perceiving of God, unlike Jesus. Nor have they taken up his teachings, and therefore what emanates from God as spiritual goodness and insights, is not in them.

v. 38 "what rays forth": usually, "his word" (i.e., the word of God). Here the term, 'word' (of God) means the subtle intuitive awareness existing in one's own soul, as to how to conduct oneself morally in the moment.

5:39 You diligently study the Scriptures because you think that by them you possess eternal life. These are the Scriptures that testify about me,
5:40 yet you refuse to come to me, to have (eternal) life.

These two verses confirm the interpretation given here of vs. 37 and 38. The study of the Scriptures by the Sanhedrin is of limited use if they cannot perceive the divine reality enveloping Jesus.

5:41 I do not accept praise from people,
5:42 but I know you. I know that you do not have the love of God in your hearts.
5:43 I have come, imbued with the might of the Father, and you do not accept me; but if someone else comes on the basis of his own authority, you will accept him.

"the might of the Father": literally, "in my Father's name". The term 'name' meant in those days, the core quality and inherent power or significance of gods or spirits or significant people. So when used by Jesus in this way, it means that Jesus was permeated, and empowered spiritually, by the being of the Father; he was a vessel of Divine reality.
"his own authority": literally, "in his own name".

5:44 How can you believe, if you accept praise from one another, yet make no effort to obtain the praise that comes from the only God?
5:45 But do not think I will accuse you before the Father. Your accuser is Moses, on whom your hopes are set.
5:46 If you believed Moses, you would believe me, for he wrote about me.
5:47 But since you do not believe what he wrote, how are you going to believe what I say?"

Commentary Chapter 5: 41-47
These verses in this group are clear as to their meaning, except v. 44, which needs a brief comment.

5:44 "only God": this phrase is a set phrase in Judaism, and means the only deity that Jews should worship; although 'God" in the Hebrew Scriptures, esoterically understood, can be either JHVH or the entire group of the Elohim.

So these verses continue the theme of earlier verses, namely that within the Christ, the Father has a presence. In terms of an esoteric view of these verses, the message here is that efficacious within Jesus is the cosmic Christ (the solar Logos) and actively present within this deity is the Father. (Mystical literature of all Ages allude to an

interlinking of divine influences in spirit realms.) As noted in Part One, Section Six, 'the Father' can refer to either the highest of the exalted Thrones, or the interweaving of various high deities. This is where the expression, "Jesus is the Christ" needs to be discussed again. Towards the end of this Gospel, these words occur,
"But these words are written that you may believe that Jesus is the Christ, the Son of God, and that by believing you may have life in his name."

When it is said that 'Jesus is the Christ' this means that the man Jesus is the 'anointed one'. To the Hebrews, an important person, usually a king, had to be anointed, before being empowered to serve the will of JHVH thereby becoming "a messiah" since 'messiah' meant 'anointed person'.

But the prophets had foreseen that one day there would appear a person who was to be anointed in such a special, sacred event that God himself became deeply united to that person; so he became not simply a Messiah, but "The Messiah".

The word 'Christ' was used in the Greek to translate the Hebrew word for that unique and holy man who was anointed to this sublime degree. So, Jesus is the anointed one, The Messiah, because he is that human being who was selected to be the unique vessel of the Divine.

Chapter Six

The Feeding of the Five Thousand
This is a well-known incident, reported in all four Gospels. From the perspective of the Initiatory Quest approach, it involves both a physical-historical miracle and also an activity of the Sun-god Christ, who now specifically involves the disciples as part of their initiatory training. This activity concerns a cosmic aspect to the 'Salvation' of humanity; so some introductory comments are needed here.

Such a miraculous multiplying of food is not unique in the Bible. The Jewish Scriptures report on several instances of this wrought by the initiate Elisha (2 Kings: 4). He multiplied olive oil for a poor widow, her nearly empty oil jar filling up many other jars (probably several dozen) which she could then sell. More relevant to the Gospel account, he also multiplied 20 loaves of bread (with some sheaves of grain) sufficient to feed 100 men.

The esoteric message within the account of this event will be discussed after the later segments of the chapter are considered. This is where we learn that human beings have to actually absorb qualities from Christ into their own soul and their own germinal spiritual nature. This is essential in order to achieve a spirituality which grants 'Salvation', that is, which over lifetimes leads to the ascending pathway of future blessedness.

6:1 After these things, Jesus crossed over to the eastern side of the Sea of Galilee (that is, the Sea of Tiberias),

Although Jesus had the mission of preaching to all of Israel, there is here perhaps a suggestion that there was no compelling reason for Jesus to journey to the eastern side of the sea. The region of Gaulanitis was on the very edge of Galilee and was sparsely populated, with non-Jewish ethnicities predominating. The words "to the eastern side" have been added by me, to make clearer the various crossings which soon occur over the sea (vs. 16 to 26). But going eastwards is going towards the Sun (which in springtime, is now growing in power (see v. 4). These verses do present physical events; but in addition, crossing a lake or a sea also alludes to crossing a threshold between the physical and the spiritual worlds.

6:2 and a great crowd of people followed him because they saw the wonders he was performing, healing the sick.

Actual physical crowds of people decide to cross the sea to be near to Jesus.

6:3 Then Jesus went up into a mountain, and he was seated there with his disciples.

The phrase "to go up the mountain' is a veiled reference, used amongst people on the initiatory quest, for entering into a higher consciousness state. Scholars have noted that here the expression '*the* mountain' is unusual, as there is not one specific, mountain on the eastern shore of the lake of Galilee. There are various hills in this area which rise up from an elevated plateau, and all are technically mountains, when measured from sea level.

The disciples also undertook to enter into a higher consciousness; that Jesus 'sat down' indicates that he was now preparing to instruct them in initiatory matters, as their spiritual teacher.

6:4 It was about the time of the Jewish Passover Festival.

This festival occurs at the first Full Moon after the spring equinox, and thereby points to the Sun; for now the influence of the Sun is growing stronger over the hemisphere. The Sun will rise higher in the sky than the Moon, until the autumn equinox. So the events of the miraculous feeding are connected to the vitality of the springtime Sun; which means, on a spiritual level, to the cosmic Christ, the Sun-god.

6:5 Then, having raised his vision, and having seen that a great crowd is coming towards him, he says to Philip, "From where may we buy bread so that these people can eat"?

The phrase, 'to raise one's vision' (literally, 'to lift up the eyes') alludes to clairvoyantly cognizing. So on the esoteric level, Jesus beholds many souls in spiritual realms. There is the implication here, that if you 'lift up your eyes' in a physical sense, when seated on a mountain, you would be gazing up into the atmosphere. Any souls seen then will be in spiritual realms, high above the Earth. Yet, because this episode interweaves physical-historical with events in spiritual realms, it also refers to actual crowds of people following Jesus.

In asking Philip where to buy bread, the focus is back onto the physical. Now the crowd is the actual people who had been following Jesus, and they probably numbered in the many hundreds. (The number 5,000 refers to spiritual dynamics and will be discussed later.)

The account of the Feeding of the 5,000 contains a veiled level of meaning, alluding to a central activity on behalf of humanity by the cosmic Christ. This event is recorded as a miraculous physical occasion, but veiled inside the narrative is a second layer of meaning, revealing the challenges facing the disciples in their initiatory quest to be actively mediating to human beings, cosmic influences radiating out from the Christ. This remarkable implication becomes clearer when the next section is contemplated, that of the 'walking on the water'.

6:6 But he was saying this, testing him, for he himself knew what he was about to do.
6:7 Philip answered him, "Six months' wages could not buy enough bread for each of them to receive a little."
6:8 One of the disciples, Andrew, the brother of Simon Peter, says to him,
6:9 "There is a young boy here who has five barley loaves and two fish; but what are they among so many?"

These four verses are clear descriptions of actual events. From verse 9 through to verse 13, the cosmic aspect of the Christ is being hinted at; the solar Logos, the leader of the Powers. There are also subtle references to the relationship of the sun to the zodiac. For the two fishes can be a symbol of Pisces, the fishes; the Sun had only recently entered the constellation of Pisces, which is a major reason for fish becoming a symbol of Christianity. The twelve baskets of crumbs (v.13) represent spiritual influences from the Sun but spread throughout the zodiac. One recalls how widespread and central was the reverence for 'the twelve deities' throughout the Hellenistic Age.

Jesus, as the vessel of the Christ or solar Logos (called the Lamb of God by the Baptist), is testing his disciples as to a profound dynamic; a truly core aspect of the relationship of humanity to the solar Logos (or in simpler terms, 'the cosmic Christ'). Namely, that of nourishing the soul and the germinal spirit of each human being, so that the Spiritual-self may arise. This is a theme which is abruptly emphasized later in this same chapter, and will be discussed in some detail below.

6:10 Jesus said, "Get the people to recline." Now there was much grass in that place, therefore the people reclined: there were about 5,000 in all.

The verb used here means 'to recline', not to sit, and this suggests participation at a festive or sacred meal event, as the Hellenistic people reclined on lounges at the table, rather than being on a chair. The number of people, as noted earlier, like that of the other multiplying of food, which involved 4,000 people, has a cosmic significance (see below). That there was 'much grass' can be seen as alluding to a non-physical realm in creation, that of life-forces, since plants can signify life-forces.

6:11 Then Jesus took the loaves, and having given thanks, he gave this to the disciples, then these disciples gave this to the reclining people, likewise with the fish, as much as they wanted.

A significant point here is that Jesus did not break the bread into pieces; the absence of this practical action allows the process to involve something other than physical food. For on the esoteric level, it is the cosmic Christ, the great Sun-god, who is nurturing the people, and therefore not with physical bread, but with soul qualities and life-forces (see below). One recalls here that v. 1 begins by alluding to the East, thus to the Sun.

The above version is taken from codex Bezae, which uniquely includes the additional words, "...he gave this to the disciples, then these disciples gave this to the reclining people..."[235] This indicates that the disciples were involved, mediating the spiritual light of Christ into human souls, as an initiatory 'training experience'.

6:12 And when they were satiated, he tells his disciples, "Gather up the fragments left over, so that nothing may be lost".
6:13: So they gathered these up, and they filled twelve baskets with fragments which were left over from the barley loaves.

These two verses indicate that the disciples have a relationship to the zodiac: the zodiac forces mediated to the soul by the spiritual aspect of the Sun. This is a conclusion that many spiritually oriented Bible students have reached. Those people in the initiatory movements of the Hellenistic Jewish and Christian worlds, shared the widespread, common view of their times, that twelve zodiacal influences are deeply and vitally important, as core spiritual influences operative behind the existence of Creation, and also of Israel itself.

This is seen in the writings of Philo Judaeus (1st century) and in the writings of Clement of Alexandria, (2nd century). Both these men comment on the mysterious objects attached to the garment worn by the high priest of Israel.

This garment had the Thummin, an object which had twelve jewels set in it, in four rows of three. The sacred garment was adorned with this breastplate, of twelve gemstones, and it also had a pouch in it, where two small objects were kept; together these were known as the Urim and Thummin. These two objects are described in the Bible as being used by the priests to actually ascertain the will of God. Clement comments on this saying that,

---

[235] Bezae, 6:11 "καὶ ἔδωκεν τοῖς μαθηταῖς οἱ δὲ μαθηταί ..."

> 'the twelve stones, set in four rows on the breastplate, display for us the zodiac circle, according to the four solstice and equinoctial points of the year.'[236] (trans. A.A.)

From this comment we see that to Clement, the sacred gemstone arrangements, enabling the High Priest to commune with God, were actually symbols of the twelve zodiac signs of the zodiac. He makes no reference to the twelve tribes of Israel and the zodiac, but it is widely held in both early Jewish and Christian literature, that they were associated with the zodiac.

Also, Philo Judaeus, who wrote on many spiritual and religious themes in the years AD 30-45, views the zodiac as the basis of the Urim and Thummin breastplate of the Hebrew High Priest;

> "...the twelve stones on the breast {plate}, arranged in four rows, each of three stones. What else are these than signifiers of the circle of the zodiac? And indeed this zodiac is divided into four parts, each with three signs; these divisions setting up the seasons of spring, summer, autumn, winter; the four turning points (solstices and equinoxes)...'[237] (trans. A.A.)

That the twelve disciples are associated with the zodiac is alluded to in Leonardo da Vinci's masterpiece, *The Last Supper*. But there appear to be no actual statements to this effect in any surviving early Christian or Gnostic texts. However, we can conclude that the disciples'

---

[236] In Clement's Greek: οἱ δὲ ἐπὶ τῷ στήθει τέτραχα τεταγμένοι δώδεκα τὸν ζῳδιακόν διαγράφουσιν ἡμῖν κύκλον κατὰ τὰς τέσσαρας τοῦ ἔτους τροπάς. (*Miscellanies*, Bk.5:6)

[237] The Greek of Philo: ἔπειθ' οἱ κατὰ τὰ στέρνα δώδεκα λίθοι ταῖς χρόαις οὐχ ὅμοιοι διανεμηθέτες εἰς τέσσαρας στοίχους ἐκ τριῶν ἑτέρου δεῖγματ' εἰσὶν ἢ τοῦ ζῳδιακου κύκλου; καὶ γάρ οὗτος τετραχῆ διανεμηθεὶς ἐκ τριῶν ζῳδίων τας ἐτησίους ὥρας ἀποτελεῖ ἔαρ θέρος μετόπωρον χειμῶνα τροπας τέσσαρας.
(*On Special Laws* I:87)

actions here allude to the interaction of the Sun with the zodiac (see below).

6:14 When the people saw the wonder he performed, they were saying, "Surely this person is truly the prophet – the one who is coming into the world."
6:15 When Jesus perceived that they are about to approach and seize him, to make him king, he again departed into the mountain alone.

These two verses bring the focus back to physical events, and refer to the reaction of the crowd, presumably of many hundreds, who were miraculously fed by Jesus. When the remaining verses in this Chapter have been discussed, then the Feeding of the Five Thousand will be explored further.

6: 16 – 25 Walking on the Sea of Galilee
The text of this well-known episode has two layers of meaning; on the historical, physical level it records an actual miracle. But within the Greek text another veiled meaning is communicated; this concerns the challenge for the disciples to maintain their own consciousness whilst in the spiritual realms. This is a crucial stage of spiritual development and a highly esoteric matter, which was kept confidential for millennia.

There are however poetic texts in the Judaic-Christian world which refer to this initiatory challenge. The account of Jonah, which was noted earlier, is directly relevant here, once its esoteric nature is seen: "…The engulfing waters threatened me, the Deep surrounded me…" This reference to waters trying to engulf a person, as a metaphor of the soul being assailed by potent spirit forces in itself or from spirit beings, also occurs in Psalm 69 and unlike Jonah, there is no mention of the writer perhaps being in a physical ocean,

"..deliver me from those who hate me,
from the deep waters,
do not let the flood waters engulf me,
or Sheol close its mouth around me.."

But there exists a clearer reference to the experience of an initiate rising above the supra-physical level of cognition, and entering into the soul-world. This text from the Dead Sea Scrolls, refers to experiencing threatening waters, and a roaring whirlwind. It is in the "Thanksgiving Scroll", written by an unknown Essene,

"....The torrents of Satan have encompassed my soul,
Leaving me without deliverance....
There is no calm in the whirlwind,
That I may restore my soul,
No path that I may straighten my way
On the face of the waters,
The deeps resound to my groaning,
and my soul has journeyed
to the gates of death..."   (1QH)

Also amongst *The Odes to Solomon* is a reference to waters, symbolizing spiritual powers which can engulf the acolyte seeking higher consciousness. This text is usually dated to after the time of Jesus, but it may derive from an earlier Essene text which later had been edited by Christians, who incorporated allusions to Gospel accounts of the walking on the water by Jesus,

Great rivers are the power of the Lord....
They are more swift than lightning ...
and those who cross them in faith
are not disturbed....   (Ode 39)

But what is especially interesting here, is that ancient Egyptian texts exist in which the journey of the soul after death in the Soul-world is described with parallel references to the threat of being engulfed in the 'waters' of the Soul-world. However, help is available to the soul regarding the threatening 'waters' in this other-worldly journey, by becoming permeated with the spiritual rays of the sun-god Ra-Osiris, (in his form of the god Shu).

We note that the Egyptian sun-god is viewed in esoteric understanding as the equivalent of the Sun-god Christ, experienced in the millennia before the time of Jesus by initiates (not only in Egypt, but in various lands). The following words are in *The Book of the Dead* (Chapt. 63),

"..the blossoms of Shu (the sun-god) shall be in me ....
I am the being who is never over-whelmed in the waters...
I am he who is never over-whelmed in the waters...."[238]

That the next verses in the Gospel are about the same age-old initiatory challenge, on a veiled level, will become evident.

Verses 6:16-21   Surface level
Walking on the Sea of Galilee
6:16 Then, as evening came, his disciples went down to the sea.
6:17 then, having embarked into a boat, they were going across the sea towards Capernaum, but darkness had already fallen, and Jesus had not yet come to them
6:18 and the sea was being agitated by a strong wind.
6:19 However, having rowed about 3 or 4 miles, they see Jesus walking about on the sea, and approaching near to the boat, and they were afraid.
6:20 But he says, "It is I; don't be afraid."
6:21 They were then willing to take him into the boat, and immediately the boat reached the land towards which they were going.

Commentary: vs. 16-21   The Surface level
As evening came the disciples wished to sail westwards, back to Capernaum. But although darkness came, Jesus, whom they were apparently expecting to see by now, perhaps on the seashore, had not appeared, but a strong wind caused high waves. However, as they were about halfway across the sea, they see Jesus walking on the water and approaching near to their boat. They became afraid, but Jesus identifies himself, and they wanted

---

[238] Much is written in popular books about the Egyptian gods especially Horus, in relation to Jesus and the Gospels, most of which has no factual basis.

then to take him onboard. Immediately, the boat reaches the shore.

That there is a much deeper narrative here is shown by the dream-like sequence at the end: as they became willing to receive Jesus, the boat is instantly (i.e., impossibly) at the shore. Note also how the disciples were expecting Jesus, even though they were in the middle of the sea, yet no mention of a planned meeting was made in earlier verses. These are indicators of the initiatory level.

Translation vs. 6:16-21   The Initiatory Quest level
Learning to be within the sense of 'I' in spirit realms; the sea is the Soul-world, the boat is the soul or soul body.

6:16 When evening came, his disciples entered the Soul-world.
6:17 then, having embarked in a 'soul boat', they were going westwards across this realm, but darkness had already fallen, and Jesus had not yet come to them.
6:18 And the Soul-world was being agitated by lower soul qualities.
6:19 However, having moved deep into this realm, they perceive the spirit of Jesus is there, away in the distance, yet as if near to the soul boat, and so they were afraid.
6:20 But he declares, "I am the I AM in you; do not have fear."
6:21 They were thus willing to receive him into their soul boat, and their soul immediately reached that secure sense of 'I' towards which they were striving.

Commentary vs. 16-21 the Initiatory level
6:16 **When evening came, his disciples entered the Soul-world.**

As evening came, the disciples prepared to enter into a spiritual state of consciousness in the Soul-world.

6:17 **then, having embarked in the soul boat, they were going westwards across that realm, but darkness had already fallen, and Jesus had not yet come to them.**

Going to the West alludes to entering the Soul-world which is also the realm of the Dead (in many cultures). Entering into the Soul-world through meditation, they were soon in darkened environs, and Jesus had not as yet drawn near to assist them.

6:18 and the Soul-world was being agitated by lower soul-qualities.
The elemental forces in the Soul-world respond to unspiritual qualities in the soul, in the form of what is the equivalent of powerful winds.[239]

6:19 However, having moved far into the Soul-world, their souls perceive the spirit of Jesus is there, away in the distance, yet as if he were near to the soul boat; and so they were afraid.

They are fully within the Soul-world when Jesus assists them to perceive him spiritually. The verb here, theoereoe (θεωρεω) rarely means to simply 'see'; it means 'to experience', 'to gaze upon', and 'to clairvoyantly see'. The resplendent auric glow of the soul-body and spirit-body of Jesus is perceived, whilst he is in a distant place. However, such an unexpected visionary experience probably gave the impression that what the disciples saw was quite near, and hence startling.

Although the usual translation is that Jesus was "coming near the boat", the verb here is ginomai (γίνομαι) which usually means 'to be created, 'to occur', 'to come into existence', 'to exist', although it can sometimes mean 'to come to a place'.[240]

6:20 But he says, I am the I AM; do not have fear.

In everyday social discourse the Greek phrase, 'ego eimi' means "It's me !" and this fits in well with the surface level of meaning here. But as noted earlier, this same

---

[239] An identical dynamic is presented in Goethe's '*The Fairy tale of the Green Snake and the Beautiful Lily*'.
[240] There are several other instances where scholars have concluded that 'ginomai' has to mean 'to come', although it actually means 'to be' (e.g., Acts 20:16, 21:17 & 25.15)

phrase is alluding to the phrase used by God to Moses, from the burning bush, as various scholars have noted, such as Abbott and Bernard.

But furthermore, this phrase implies that the highest, still germinal ego-sense, or sanctified sense of self, which people may attain on the initiatory path, is actually derived from God (which here means Jahve and also the cosmic Christ).

So when used by Jesus here and in other places, unless it is a simple emphatic way of saying "it's me", it is an affirmation of the presence of the cosmic Christ within the higher 'I'. So, to counter their uncertainty and fear, Christ proclaims this through Jesus, and thereby makes this even more actual for the disciples. He is saying in effect,

"I am the 'I am' in you; feel this and do not have fear."

To the disciples, this call admonishes and encourages them: "Within your sense of self, perceive me ! I have chosen you, and I am within you." For the twelve were developing 'The Son of Man' or Spiritual-self, and it is this which has its origin in Christ Jesus. Thus, as the ancient Egyptian initiates said of the good soul after death or in initiation, "the blossoms of Shu, the sun-god, these are in me".[241]

6:21 They were thus willing to receive him into the soul boat, and immediately the soul boat reached the secure sense of 'I' within this realm towards which they were striving.

As soon as the disciples were capable of perceiving the Christ within their own consciousness, helped by the rays from the Christ-light, they were secure in their souls. They were being supported in their efforts to cognize beyond the physical sensory organs. Their soul boat, (known as 'the bark of the soul', in the Egyptian Book of the Dead) was safely at the shore.

---

[241] The *Egyptian Book of the Dead*, chapt. 114, p.220, trans. Wallis-Budge.

"reached the shore": their sense of self or self-consciousness was now firmly attained by the inner presence of the Christ.

6:22 On the next day, the crowd that had stayed across on the eastern side of the sea, saw that there had only been one boat there. They also saw that Jesus had not been aboard the boat in which his disciples had departed.
6:23 Other boats came from Tiberias, near to the place where they had eaten the bread, after the Lord had given thanks.

The directions of these journeys are:
From Tiberias = going eastward, from the western side of the sea
From near 'the place' = going westward, from the eastern shore

6:24 But when the crowds saw that neither Jesus nor the disciples were there (on the eastern shore), they embarked into these boats and sailed back to Capernaum, seeking Jesus.
6:25 And having encountered him, they said to him, "Rabbi, when did you appear here?"

Verses 6:22-24 These verses are grammatically complex, and, as scholars comment, are somewhat cumbersome in the Greek. The reason for this is that they veil an extension of the initiatory message in vs. 16-21, of souls experiencing Christ on a spiritual level. On the surface level, they narrate how the crowds managed to follow Jesus back to the western shore of the sea. But it is these multiple crossings 'over the sea' which also allude to entering into a higher consciousness state. In fact in these verses,

from west to east go:
-Jesus and the disciples
-The crowd of some hundreds
-Another group in boats the next day from Tiberias

And from east to west go:
-The disciples at night

-The crowd seeking Jesus
-(and Jesus himself, somehow)

To unveil what these verses are presenting, it is helpful to start with v. 25, with their question which has puzzled scholars for centuries; asking When? not How? ("Rabbi, *when* did you appear here?). Theologians have concluded this question arose perhaps because there were no other boats, and it also appears that Jesus, if walking around the seashore from east to west, would have involved too long a time-span.

These verses can be seen as narrating physical incidents, as in the usual translations: "And having found him, they said to him, "Rabbi, when did you get here?" But as in my translation, the crowd 'encountered' him, or indeed 'clairvoyantly perceived' him, as the verb here heuriskoe (εὑρίσκω) also means to mentally perceive, rather than to see something physically. So when they perceived Jesus, they asked him,
"When did you *appear* here (or manifest here), for the verb 'ginomai' (γίνομαι) means exactly this. It only rarely means 'to arrive'; it means to beget, to come into existence, to happen, or to occur. So now these verses are depicting what happened, perhaps subconsciously, in the souls of the multitude who had experienced the cosmic Christ nurturing their soul.

These souls, on the esoteric level of the verses, are in the spirit and are enquiring when did the Messiah become a spiritual presence, spiritually, in the Earth's soul-being.[242] Something impelled them to "cross over the sea", going westwards, which is the direction of the realm of the Dead, the Soul-world. So their souls were journeying (not in a conscious manner) in the Soul-world in the search for the Messiah.

In verse 23 the phrase, "after the Lord had given thanks" occurs: this reminder is not strictly necessary, but it emphasizes firstly, that the miraculous feeding occurred because the inner spiritual process which

---

[242] Paul would also later spiritually perceive Jesus, but by then the Messiah would, as the Risen Lord, have attained an even higher level of being.

Jesus had undertaken, had invoked the power of the Christ. Secondly, it reminds the reader that the incident with the crowd is interwoven within a purely spiritual dynamic; something which Jesus then confirms in v. 26.

6:26 Jesus answered them and said, Very truly, I tell you that you are seeking me, not because you saw wonders performed, but because you were able to eat all that you needed of the loaves.

Jesus here is alluding to the large crowd being drawn to seek him, not because of having earlier witnessed a miracle, but because they were aware that their souls had been filled with inner substance, helping them to combat a feeling of inner emptiness. When he says "...able to eat all that you needed of the loaves", this is not referring to a desire for food.

6:27 Do not make effort for food that is perishing, but for the food remaining for eternal existence, which The Son of Man shall give to you. For within him, the Father – God himself – has imprinted His own being.

Here the scene of action, whilst still in the realms of spirit, is moving back to include the physical crowd.
"has imprinted His own being": usually, 'For on him the Father has placed his seal'. This usual version is also correct, for the verb here (sfragizoe – σφραγιζω) in most cases means 'to attest' or 'to certify' or 'to set one's seal'.

But in esoteric contexts it is used when a spiritual entity imprints its own nature into another being or into a spirit-talisman, (as a bronze stamp into soft wax).[243] So, 'The Son of Man' here means Jesus, but also Jesus as the doorway to, and the archetype of, our Spiritual-self.
"food remaining for eternal existence": this is a crucial statement, referring to that spiritual 'substance' which maintains and nourishes the Spiritual-self, especially in the future when humanity will be existing in supra-physical realms. (This is further discussed under v. 48.)

---

[243] For example in the Pistis Sophia, an ancient Coptic work wherein the deeply esoteric teachings of the Risen Jesus are preserved, though mixed with other Gnostic material.

6: 28 They therefore said to Him, "What must we do to carry out the works of God?"
6:29 Jesus answered and said to them, "this is the manifestation of God in you: when you perceive with discernment the One whom He has sent.

"the manifestation of God in you": usually, "This is the work of God." The Greek word here can mean either 'work' or 'manifestation'; but with the questioners it meant those works or actions which Jewish Scriptures have decreed shall bring the blessings of God. Since this is not what Jesus meant, but something more profound, he uses the other meaning of the same word in a way which powerfully makes his point.

The 'inner work' which the spiritually seeking souls have to undertake is not connected to the external duties of a truly religious person, but has to do with the Divine becoming awakened in oneself, manifesting in oneself; thus one's self becomes more spiritually perceptive, because the Divine is awakening in the soul.

"...you perceive with discernment the One...", usually, 'that you believe in the One whom He has sent.' But as noted earlier, the word 'believe' (in the Greek, pistis) can also mean 'truly perceptive' or 'intuitively cognizing'.

6:30 So they then said to Him, "What wonders will you do for us to see, that we may truly perceive you? What wonders are you doing?"
6:31 Our ancestors ate manna in the wilderness; as it is written, "He gave them bread from Heaven to eat."

The crowd has taken up the earlier references to food (and eternal 'food'). Various answers have been proposed as to why this challenge was put to Jesus, considering that he had just recently multiplied bread for hundreds; i.e., for this same crowd, most of whom were no doubt present at the events on the eastern side of the sea.

I conclude that, triggered by the earlier references from Jesus to food, these people sensed in a semi-conscious manner, that some kind of divine 'soul-feeding' had indeed occurred. So they challenged Jesus to exceed the wonder of the mysterious manna that came to the Israelites under guidance of Moses, in their emigration from Egypt.

6:32 Then Jesus said to them, "Very truly, I say to you, it was not Moses who gave you bread from Heaven, but my Father, who gives you the true bread from Heaven."
6:33 For the bread of God is that which comes down from Heaven and gives life to the world.

Manna is the mysterious food which kept the twelve tribes alive during their time in the desert in the Exodus from Egypt, under the guidance of Moses. But the crowd is told that such manna is not on the same level as 'the true bread', for this bestows life on creation. These words point to the life-forces behind the material world, which sustains its existence.

6:34 So they said to Him, "Lord give us this bread, always."

Just as the Samaritan woman wanted to have the 'Water of Life' to avoid carrying water again, the crowd here seems to have only a rudimentary grasp of the words of Jesus. And yet they address him as 'Lord' – a rare event, which indicates high esteem. These verses, on to the end of this chapter, contain teachings about the 'bread of life'. As these verses are explored, the esoteric significance of 'the bread of life' and its connection with the miraculous feeding of the 5,000 will become clearer.

6:35 Jesus said to them, "I myself am the bread of life; whoever comes to me shall never be hungry, and whoever believes in me, shall never thirst again."

The special expression 'ego eimi' is used here, and would have been understood as an emphatic phrase ("I myself"). But as we have noted earlier, this phrase also carries the esoteric meaning of: "The 'I' that *I am*....(is the bread of life). So there is here a nuance of the higher 'I' or higher self (The Son of Man), which derives from Christ, is the bread of life. That is, the person who seeks a higher spiritual state, can find their Spiritual-self developing (called 'The Son of Man'). Within this sanctified consciousness lives a spiritual radiance from Jesus Christ, so that the 'I' becomes a manifestation of the Christ.

Attaining to that exalted state means to exist within divine energies which are nourishing oneself eternally. But in addition, as the archetypal Son of Man, Jesus is also the portal to attaining this higher 'I'. (See under v. 48.)

6:36 However, I said to you that, you have been in my presence, but you do not believe.

On some occasion not recorded, the people were told that they have failed the challenge, so far, of discerning the nature of Jesus, and thus believing in him. So one may conclude that Jesus is anticipating that in a future time, humanity shall be able to have an intuitive perception of the reality of Jesus as the vessel of the cosmic Christ; and perhaps also of the Son of Man state.[244]

6:37 Everyone whom the Father gives to me, shall come to me, and those coming to me, I shall never drive away .

"never drive away": This phrase is a 'litotes'; a literary device which presents as null and void an action or an idea, in order to powerfully confirm that the opposite thing is true. So Jesus is saying, 'I shall indeed always welcome those who come to me'.

6:38 For I have descended from Heaven, not to do my own will, but to do the will of Him who sent me.
6:39 And this is the will of Him who sent me, that I should lose nothing of what has been given to me, but raise it up on the Last Day.

These two verses declare profound cosmic truths for contemplation, but they need little commentary except

---

[244] This verse has a variant form: "...that you have seen me and yet you do not believe", most scholars view the word 'me' as a later addition.

to note that the phrase "the Last Day" is unique to this Gospel, and appears to refer to the prophecy about the End-times in Isaiah (2:2) and Micah (4:1), when the Messiah appears, and judges the world.

6:40 For this is the will of my Father, that everyone experiencing inwardly the Son, and believing in him, may have eternal life, and I shall raise that person up on the Last Day.

"experiencing inwardly": this expresses the meaning of the verse. For here the verb (theoereoe – θεωρέω) usually means to gaze at, or to clairvoyantly see; but these meanings, as scholars acknowledge, don't relate to the sentence. The verb also means 'to experience' something, therefore some versions are: "to look to the Son" (NIV), or "look upon" (NEB). Both of these have to mean, an inner experience of souls living long after the first century. As Alford explains, it means "the awakening of attention, preparatory to faith".[245]
"the Son..." this phrase is ambiguous, and forms both a contrast to, and a close connection with, Jesus. Jesus is referring to The Son of Man potential in everyone. Notice how these words, "I shall raise up that person who cognizes the Son of Man..." seems to suggest that The Son of Man which Jesus is referring to here, is both himself, as well as the Spiritual-self or Son of Man, as a potential, slumbering in the human soul. Furthermore, Jesus is also this Son of Man in every person, in an over-arching, archetypal sense.

6:41 The crowd began to complain about him because he said, "I myself am the bread of life, which has come down from Heaven".

In addition to the confusion that the crowd felt when faced with such a claim, the veiled other meaning: "the 'I' I am" is the bread of life" would have intensified the discomfort to those who were not perceptive. For Christ was indicating to them that their own potential Higher-self (The Son of Man) is the eternal nourishment for

---

[245] *The Greek Testament*, p.763.

their spirit; but he is also teaching that this quality comes from him. The meaning of 'the bread of life' will be discussed with v. 48.

6:42 So they were saying, "Is not this Jesus, the son of Joseph, whose father and mother we know? How then can he say, "I have come down from Heaven?"

This indicates firstly, that some of the crowd were part of, or sympathetic to, Essene-Nazaritic groups, and thus familiar with the reclusive Nazareth community. Secondly, that the crowds had not been intuitively perceptive as regards the figure of Jesus; they had not sensed the radiant presence of 'God' (i.e., the great cosmic Christ-being) around and above Jesus.

6:43 Jesus responded and said, "Don't grumble amongst yourselves.
6:44 No-one can approach me unless drawn to me by the Father; and I shall raise up that person on the Last Day.

Here the reader again encounters a depth and a vastness, a solemnity and yet also a joyous promise, in this 'cosmic' Gospel. These verses respond to the dissatisfaction of the crowd by further alluding to even more profound realities. Firstly, that the Christ-presence is within (and beyond) Jesus, and that therefore the Father-God is also interwoven within the being of Jesus. Secondly, that the Father is also present within the Christ (the highest of the Powers or Elohim).

6:45 It has been written in the Prophets, 'And they shall all be taught by God' (Isa. 54:13). **Everyone having heard from the Father, and having learnt, comes to me.**

The original meaning of this quotation from the Hebrew Scriptures is that God (i.e., Jahve) shall endeavour to inspire understanding of his will in the hearts and minds of the Hebrew people.

    The meaning of the word 'Father' is uncertain; possibly it is Jahve, as Jesus is addressing fellow Jews who are probably in the majority. But he may be speaking in a wider sense. As noted in Chapter One, 'the Father' is also a term which refers to various divine beings, whose many interweaving influences were experienced by early initiates as if deriving from one source. The message here is that a person can perceive insights into the significance of Christ, through an insightful awareness blessed by the Divine.

6:46 Not that the Father has been spiritually seen by anyone, except the One who is from God; this One has seen the Father.

Although people may receive insights from the spirit concerning the Messiah, this does not imply a seership which can bestow clairvoyant perceiving of God. Such pinnacle of seership (or higher consciousness) is limited to one entity - to that entity who is directly derived from God. These words surely apply to Jesus, but don't specify that Jesus is meant; so possibly other people who attain to The Son of Man state, may also be included.

6:47 Very truly, I say to you, whoever is spiritually perceptive has eternal life.

Usually translated as, "Truly, I say to you, whoever believes, has eternal life." This is also valid, but it appears to be a less emphatic statement.
"spiritually perceptive": that is, regarding the Son.
In 17:3 the attainment of 'eternal life' - conscious existence in higher divine realms - is specifically defined as the result of 'insightful discernment' or 'intuitive perceiving' bordering on seership. To achieve this eternal life, the soul, in experiencing the message and nature of Jesus, has to intuitively discern that he is indeed the Messiah; and secondly there is a similar challenge for people with regard to becoming aware of God, or the origin of their own spirit.[246]

The verb 'to cognize' here (ginoeskoe - γινώσκω) is used by Jesus when referring to perceiving spiritual realities

---

[246] How a spiritually aspiring, but not yet clairvoyant soul, can cognize deity, is discussed with v. 17:3.

(which occurs via the soul, not the sensory organs), as in Matt. 13:11 and Mk. 8:10 and other places. In the verse here, 6:47, the word 'pistis' (which can mean 'believing') means the same kind of higher cognizing as in 17:3, which is almost seership. (As discussed in Chapter One, pistis also means this, not only 'to believe'.)

6:48 I myself am the bread of life.

"I myself am the bread of life": but this verse is closely linked to v. 47 "...whoever is perceptive spiritually has eternal life" because it can be interpreted as "*The 'I' I am, is the bread of life.*" If someone on the initiatory quest has a spiritually perceptive awareness, and develops The Son of Man or Spiritual-self, then their 'I' will be interwoven with the Christ, and then this 'I' shall then become the bread of life. So the 'I' of any person which has the Christ within itself, shall become this mysterious 'bread of life'.

The above view, that v. 48 in addition to referring to Christ, also is implying that the Spiritual-self or higher 'I' is the bread of life, is affirmed by the words of Christ in vs. 50-51, wherein this same bread is referred to very impersonally as "this" ("*this* is the bread"); it is not referred to as 'me' or "I".

What is the Bread of Life ?

Before considering the next verses, the meaning of 'the bread of life' needs to be examined; this phrase is already alluded to in verse 35 (and basically in v.41) Ancient Jewish texts had presented the idea that spiritual wisdom is like food for the soul; the soul develops a higher spirituality if it is 'fed' by contemplating the Divine.[247]

But the Gospel is not referring to this, nor to manna. As noted with v. 35, the bread of life is a spiritual 'substance' which maintains and nourishes the Spiritual-self. This substance is the actual matrix of The Son of Man or the Spiritual-self; so attaining this stage of spirituality consequently invokes this spiritual food. But

---

[247] The Book of Sirach (15:3) and Philo (*On Creation,* 56:158 & *Allegorical Interpretations* III, 56:162).

anyone who attains to 'The Son of Man' state attains to eternal life.[248]

In verse 48, we learn that this inner food is conveyed to us by Jesus, but comes from the cosmic Christ. However, the central promise or gift to humanity from Christ is "eternal life". So the bread of life is that spiritual substance from which the Spiritual-self (or The Son of Man) derives, and this is what flows to the human being from Jesus Christ, and it is this which confers 'eternal life'.

Paul endeavoured to convey this same message when he taught that the first or rudimentary state of the primitive human being was the 'soul-body' (the 'psyche-ikon'); the imperfect soul.[249] But in the future course of humanity's evolving, the 'spirit-body' would be developed (the 'pneuma-ikon'); the perfected actual spiritual-body or spiritual aura (in 1 Cor. 15:44-45).[250]

6:49 Your fathers ate manna in the wilderness and (eventually) died.
6:50 This is the bread which is coming down from Heaven, so that anyone may eat of it and not die.

Here Christ is emphasizing the difference between the famous manna and the bread of life.

6:51 I myself am the living bread which has come down from Heaven; if anyone eats of this bread they shall live forever. And the bread which I shall give for the life of the world, is my flesh.

---

[248] This phrase means being conscious in spiritual realms or the aeons, both whilst still in the body and after the death of the body.

[249] The 'soul-body' is often unfortunately translated as 'natural body'.

[250] Rudolf Steiner taught that the 'spirit-body' has the same three primary dynamics of the soul (soul-body); i.e., thinking, emotions and will, but these have been ennobled, suffused with holy qualities from divine spirit realms, becoming eternal. It is 'soul-body' (ψυχικόν), not 'natural-body'.

This 'bread of life' is the higher-self or The Son of Man (or Spiritual-self); a message repeated and elaborated on in the following verses.

6:52 The crowd then disputed with each other, saying, 'How is this man able to give us his flesh to eat?

The crowd badly misunderstood the words in v.51 "...and the bread which I shall give, for the life of the world, is my flesh." For actual physical flesh and blood is not meant, it is a very obvious metaphor; there is no question of devout people consuming the flesh of someone.

6:53 So Jesus said to them, "Very truly, I say to you unless you receive the flesh of the Son of Man and press out its blood, you do not have life in yourselves.

"receive the flesh": recorded in codex Bezae, this is a better, less literal version, than the majority of ancient texts "unless you *eat* of the flesh".
"and press out its 'blood'": usually this is "...and drink his blood". But the verb here means 'to extract' or 'press out', not to drink. As such, in everyday life it alludes to grape juice (or olive oil, although this is not actually a drink.) So here it refers to the human soul extracting and absorbing into itself the life-renewing vitality of the cosmic Christ, by a consciously spirit-oriented way of life.

6:54 The person nourished by the life-force of its body and drinking in the vitality of its blood has eternal life; and I shall raise that person on the Last Day.

"its body....its blood": usually 'my body....my blood'; but codex Bezae records 'its body' and 'its blood' (See below).
This verse is a statement of huge significance, and is commonly translated poorly, as "the people who eat my flesh and drink my blood have eternal life." The somewhat grotesque nuance in this usual version has made it very well-known, but also perplexing, or even disagreeable.

A: "*The person nourished by the life-force of its 'body'* ": this is more accurate and more appropriate than the usual versions of 'eating my flesh', for the verb used here (troegein – τρωγειν) nearly always meant the consuming of plant food, not meat. It would be several centuries after Jesus before it became commonly used for eating meat. So in the time of Jesus it was very rarely, if ever, be used for eating human flesh, theoretically or metaphorically.

So in this verse there is a contradiction: a verb used almost always for eating of fruit and vegetables, is now apparently referring to eating flesh, indeed human flesh. This is signalling a veiled initiatory meaning. For those with spiritual awareness, it is directing our attention to the Earth's life-forces. For the world's flora is a manifestation of the planet's life-forces, and hence are used as a symbol of these.[251]

Therefore the word 'body' does not refer to a human body, and cannot refer to any flesh body, since Jesus shall soon be deceased, and The Son of Man is not a physical bodily entity.

B: "*....drinking in the vitality of its 'blood'...*" instead of "drinking my blood". Firstly, the verb here (pinoe - πινω) does not only mean 'to drink'; it also means 'to soak up', or 'to absorb', as when the dry land absorbs the rain. Secondly, the word for 'blood' (aima - αιμα) can also mean 'an inner vitality' (e.g., with Aristotle) or 'grape juice' or other liquids which have similarities in colour, etc, to blood.[252] The *Book of Sirach* (39:26) describes literal grape juice as the 'blood of the grapes".[253]

So just as with 'flesh', actual human blood is obviously not meant here, but rather a flowing, pulsing enlivening vitality. In the Hellenistic Age it was understood that our vitality (or life-force) exists in the

---

[251] One can see this in Celtic art, for example; the Celts retained a perception of ethereal energies longer than other European peoples.
[252] It was so used from Timotheus Lyricus (340 BCE) through to Proclus (CE 450).
[253] When this text of Sirach was put into the Greek Septuagint.

bloodstream; "the vitality of the human being traverses the arteries in the bloodstream".[254]

So neither of these phrases refer to Jesus, but to the cosmic Christ, as well as to the Spiritual-self, and therefore not any human body. As noted in Chapter One, Christ became not only the source of a redeeming spirituality for humanity, as a result of the Resurrection, but also the source of life-renewing vitality for our planet; one could say, Christ became the in-dwelling spiritual light of the Earth.

Another indicator that the above veiled references to 'flesh' and 'blood', are actually to spiritual realities, is found when Christ refers to 'eating the flesh of the Son of Man' in verses 49,50,51 and 53; for here the normal verb 'to eat' (phagein – φαγεῖν) is used. So the message is still symbolic, but is teaching that people may eat, i.e., take into themselves, their own germinal higher qualities (The Son of Man).

But when the eating of the 'flesh' of Christ is referred to, in verses 54,55,56,57 and 58, then the very rare verb for digesting plant food (troegein) is used. So this is a subtle indicator that people are to be nourished in their life-forces on a high spiritual level, by absorbing divine, 'un-fallen' life-forces from the Christ. These life-forces imbue our consciousness, as it becomes spiritualized, with vitality for eternity.[255]

In summary: the usual version would be more appropriately translated as: "The person nourished by

---

[254] In the *Hermetica*, #196:1.

[255] Only very few usages of 'troegein' are known in ancient Greek literature era. One is from Demosthenes, (300 BCE) in *On the False Embassy* about a woman eating food; his words are translated as her 'eating dessert', not a meat dish. Polybius, *Histories* (Bk 31:23,9 150 BCE); where the phrase "two brothers in feasting" (δύο τρώγομεν ἀδελφοί) occurs, which probably refers to both meat and vegetable food. Thirdly, Plutarch, (CE 80) *Moralia* 613b, refers to Orestes eating with the Athenian legislators (the Thesmothetai) but this very probably refers to a formal 'banquet' which actually meant in those days, a modest occasion with mainly plant-derived delicacies on offer, and a lot of wine.

my body's life-force and drinking in the vitality of my 'blood' has eternal life." But it is still more correctly translated as above, where the words 'my body' are replaced with 'its body'. This version is preserved in codex Bezae, and has the great superiority of showing that Christ is referring to the spiritual substances of The Son of Man or the Spiritual-self, not of a flesh and blood person. With this insight it is then understood that the cosmic Christ is speaking here, and speaking in a symbolic way, using a metaphor, to help communicate the meaning.

"and I shall raise that person on the Last Day": this additional sentence is only in codex Bezae, and emphasizes that to develop the Spiritual-self is crucial for it enables Christ to grant entry into the wonderful future that he is nurturing for humanity.

6:55 For my flesh is true food and my blood is true drink.[256]

Here the verse declares that the origin of The Son of Man (or the Spiritual-self) is Christ, so he uses 'my body' and 'my blood' instead of 'its body' or 'its blood'.

6:56 The person nourished by the life-force of my body and drinking in the vitality of my blood abides in me, and I in that person.

This verse re-states the earlier verses, but with a focus on Christ as the source of the Spiritual-self.

6:56b: (This verse is found only in codex Bezae)
Just as the Father is in me, I also am in the Father. Very truly, I say to you, if you do not receive the body of The Son of Man as the bread of life, you do not have life within him.

This verse is referring both to the Christ as the archetype of the Spiritual-self and to the Spiritual-self potential which every person can develop. (Most scholars dismiss this 6:56b text as a pious addition, added by a later scribe.)

---

[256] Codex Bezae omits "and my 'blood".

6:57 Just as the living Father sent me, and I live because of the Father, so also the person nourished by me – that very person – shall live because of me.

Here the rare verb for consuming plant foods, 'troegein', is again used, so the powerful message is that those persons whose life-forces can be imbued with the divine life-forces of the Christ, shall have an eternal existence. Here again is presented the uniqueness of, and vital importance of, the cosmic Christ reality. The Gospel of Lazaros-John, (and the three synoptic Gospels) were regarded with deep reverence already in the first decades of the Christian church. One reason for this was that the implication of this verse was discerned, even if these deeper aspects were not seen in their full esoteric meaning.

6:58 This is the bread descended from Heaven, which is not like that which your ancestors ate, and then later died. For the person being nourished by this bread shall live forever.

"live forever": that is, shall exist in higher (eternal) realms of spirit.

6:59 These things he said while teaching in the Synagogue in Capernaum.
6:60 Then many of the disciples, having heard this, said "This is a hard saying, who can accept it?"
6:61 Jesus, knowing in himself that the disciples were complaining about this said, "Does this offend you?"

These three powerful verses are clear as to their meaning.

6:62 "What if you were to spiritually behold the Son of Man ascending back to where he was at first?"

This is a verse with a veiled initiatory meaning, so scholars have struggled to explain it. Some have suggested that the 'raising up' refers to the Ascension of Jesus, or even the raising up of Jesus onto the cross (and then his Resurrection). More convincing is what arises from the Initiatory Quest critical interpretative approach.

For then this verse indicates that the crowd is not perceiving Jesus in a discerning way; they are not intuiting that the Divine (or 'God') is present within Jesus and speaking through him. Nor do they perceive that the Christ is, at times, referring to their own potential to develop The Son of Man or Spiritual-self; whilst at other times he is indicating that The Son of Man derives from himself.

So the crowd is then challenged with the question, how perceptive would they be, if they were to clairvoyantly witness the coming into existence of The Son of Man in themselves or in someone else – obviously a sanctified person. Once The Son of Man stage is attained, then this new Higher-self is on the path back to the heavenly realms, where it shall have an eternal existence.

However, that a person may attain to this stage is the outcome of what Christ has brought down as a possibility to the earthly world. So a clairvoyant perceiving (it could not be seen by physical vision) of the Ascension is also implied in this verse, even if only indirectly.[257]

6:63 It is the spirit which bestows life; the flesh is of no value.

That is, the flesh is powerless to bestow an eternal existence. The inherent opposition of the earthly world and earthly ego-sense, to that of the divine realms and the Spiritual-self consciousness, is here strongly expressed; it was already a nuance in v. 62. It also confirms that the reference to eating 'flesh' in the earlier verses is entirely a metaphor; actual flesh is not meant. Much of what verses 48-63 are saying was presented in

---

[257] The non-esoteric theological viewpoint had already emerged by the 4th century, when St. Cyril of Alexandria (CE 378-444) wrote: "the Son of Man ascending back, refers to the Ascension, at which event the disciples shall see Jesus in a physical body, somehow ennobled, flying up to heaven". (*Commentary John*, Jn.6:62, para. 550).

v. 47: "Very truly, I say to you, whoever is perceptive spiritually (regarding the Son) has eternal life."

The message of this verse, and the above verses in general, is that the Messiah has descended to the Earth, to bring about such ennobling of the spiritual dynamics of humanity, as to enable the initiatory quest to succeed. **That is, to assist us in the search for a deeper meaning in life and a higher spirituality in oneself.**

A glimpse into this mission of Jesus was more esoterically presented for those on the quest for initiation, in a valuable hymn-like Gnostic text which survived the antagonism of the increasingly humanistic church. An unknown Gnostic sage wrote these inspiring words from a higher (clairvoyant) experience of Jesus, sensing how he was compassionately gazing down on humanity, prior to his incarnation. Here is an extract of a text known as the Naasseni Psalm (see Appendix 11 for more about this text),

...Jesus said, "Behold, O Father,
how this being (upon the Earth)
The victim and target of all evil
Wanders, far from your breath.
It seeks to flee the bitter Chaos,
Not sensing how to pass through,
Bearing with me the Seals (of the Mysteries)
I shall descend,
Every Aeon I shall traverse,
All Mysteries I shall unveil,
and reveal the forms of the Gods.
The deep secrets of the Path of Holiness
I shall bestow on you:
Gnosis it is now called. (Trans. A.A.)

To carry "the Seals of the Mysteries" means Jesus has the spiritual essence of the higher realms within himself, and shall thereby be enabled to initiate his disciples, giving them a consciousness of these higher realms.

6:64 But there are some among you who do not perceive with discernment. (For from the beginning

Jesus had known who would not be spiritually perceptive, and thus who would betray him.)

The presence of evil in the world of humanity, and the resulting lack of perceptive cognizing with regard to the spirit, is pointed out.

6:65 And he said, "For this reason I have told you that no-one is able to come to me, unless it has been granted by the Father."
6:66 Because of this, many disciples turned back and no longer went about with him.

These two verses emphasize the difficulty felt by many who had wanted to be disciples, when faced with such cosmic realities. It was a struggle for these people to discern, even faintly, the presence of 'God' speaking through Jesus; that is, the cosmic Christ, the great 'solar Logos'. (The cosmic Christ is the highest of the Elohim).

The emphasis here is also that influences from the 'Father God' are inherently interwoven within the being of Christ. Furthermore, for such 'faith' to occur with a follower of Jesus – such really intuitive cognizing – some influences from the Father God need to be present. This occurs in a subtle semi-conscious way, for our will or volition is primarily veiled, so our intuitive responses or decisions often cannot be intellectually registered.

6:67 Then Jesus said to the twelve, "Surely, you do not want to go away?
6:68 Simon Peter answered, "Lord, to whom can we go? You have the words of eternal life.
6:69 We have perceived you truly, and so have understood that you are the Holy One of God."

These three verses are quite clear. Usually v. 69 starts with "we believe..." or "have come to believe". But here again we encounter 'pistis'; and its other meaning 'discerning perception' is more correct. This makes it clear that Peter is declaring that the disciples have understood who Jesus is, on the basis of an intuitive-spiritual perception of his nature.

6:70 Jesus answered them, "Did I not choose you, the twelve; yet one of you is a devil?"
6:71 He was speaking of Judas, son of Simon Iscariot, for he, one of the twelve, was soon to betray him.

These two verses not only usher in the solemn nuance of evil, of hostility towards Jesus, they also allude to the unwelcome truth that evil is inherent in creation. For Jesus himself had to choose Judas, so that evil would be present in his inner circle, and ensure that the betrayal of the Messiah took place.

The core theme of Chapter Six – human beings absorbing from the cosmic Christ the essence of their newly coalescing spirituality – is a profound and central theme in this Gospel. It is also the underlying reality in the church sacrament of the Eucharist (or holy Mass). In this Gospel it comes powerfully to the fore, but on a cosmic level.

Therefore the offering of the bread and grape juice within a religious sacrament is not a theme in the Gospel of John. The teaching that people must absorb the life-force in the flesh and drink in the vitality of the blood of Christ to be saved, is remarkable, but without knowledge of the cosmic aspect to Christ, remain enigmatic and confronting.

These initiatory teachings also imply that such absorbing of the spiritual substances of the cosmic Christ can be achieved by an inner spiritual path, and does not require participation in a formal sacrament provided by the church.

CHAPTER 7

7:1 And after these things, Jesus went about in Galilee, for he did not want to go about in Judea, because the Jewish authorities were wanting to kill him.
7:2 Now the Jewish festival of Booths was near.
7:3 So his brothers said to him, "Depart from here and go into Judea, so that your disciples will see the wonders you are doing.
7:4 For no-one who wants to be widely known, does anything in secret. Since you are doing these wonders, show yourself to the world."
7:5 For even his own brothers did not believe in him.
7:6 So Jesus said, "The right moment for me has not arrived, but the time for your actions is always here.
7:7 The world cannot hate you, but it hates me because I testify about it, that its works are evil."
7:8 You go the festival, I am not going up to this festival just now, for my time has not yet fully arrived."
7:9 And having said these things, he remained in Galilee.

Commentary: This group of verses is quite clear, with just a few points to be noted.

7:3 "So his brothers said to him, "Depart..."
It is understood that Mary had more children, after the return from the flight to Egypt, and settling into Nazareth.

7:4 "no-one who wants to be widely known..." It appears that these comments are of a negative kind; indicating doubt about Jesus from his brothers.

7:6 "The right moment for me..." The Greek word 'kairos', means simply that it is not yet the opportune time to join the festival; for 'kairos', means the appropriate moment, not a specific hour decreed by destiny.

7:8 In ancient documents, there are two versions of this verse. One has "....I am not going up to this festival for my time has not yet arrived...." The other version has "I am not going *just now* to the festival for my...." The first version leaves a problem, as Jesus does in fact go to the festival. The second version resolves this problem, and is found in a very early Papyrus (#66, from ca. 150 CE) and many other versions; this papyrus gives some authority to the second version.

But the first version is in the very important codex Bezae; so it is highly probable that the first version is the correct one. This implies that it was in the manner Jesus spoke these words, in the tone he used, that he was wanting to still leave open the possibility of going sometime, saying in effect, "You all go, I'm not ready right now", because he knew it was better not to go with his brothers.

Also in **7:8** "You go the festival..." This again demonstrates that these brothers were not supportive of Jesus, or not socially identified as such, otherwise they would also be in danger.

7:10 But after his brothers had gone to the festival, he then also went, not in a public way, but discreetly.
7:11 However the people were looking for him at the festival, and asking, "Where is that man?"
7:12 And hushed words were spoken about him among the crowds. Some were saying, "He is a good man", others were saying, "No, he deceives the people'
7:13 However, no-one was speaking openly about him, for fear of the Jewish authorities.
7:14 About the middle of the feast time, Jesus went up to the temple and was teaching.
7:15 So the people were marveling, saying, How does this man have such learning, when he has never been instructed?
7:16 Then in response, Jesus answered saying, "My teaching is not mine, but is from the One who sent me.
7:17 If anyone wants to do the will of Him, they shall know whether my teaching is of God or whether I am speaking from myself.
7:18 The person speaking from their own self, seeks their own spiritual empowerment, but a person who seeks to spiritually empower the One who sent him –

this person is genuine, and there is no unrighteousness in him.
7:19 Did not Moses give you the Law? Yet none of you keep the Law. Why are you seeking to kill me?"

This group of verses is quite clear; Jesus now steps fully into the public domain, and has to face increasing antagonism from the religious authorities.
With v. 7:15 Jesus was explaining the Scriptures, and yet he had never been to any training school for Rabbis. This meant that he had no socially approved right to expound the Holy Scriptures.
Also with v. 18, "spiritually empower" is usually 'seeking glory', but this traditional expression does not convey the meaning of the verse.

7:20 The crowd answered, "You are demon-possessed. Who is seeking to kill you?"
7:21 Jesus responded, and said to them, "I have carried out a single wonder, and everyone was astonished, because of this."

Jesus ignores the crowd's insulting comments and refers to his healing of the blind man at Bethesda. It appears that the crowd was astonished that this healing was carried out on the Sabbath (see 5:1-10).

7:22 Moses gave you the law of circumcision (yet it is not from Moses but the Patriarchs); so on a Sabbath, you may circumcise a person (if that is the stipulated eighth day).
7:23 If a boy receives circumcision on the Sabbath, in order that the law of Moses is not broken, why are you angry with me because a man's entire body was healed by me on the Sabbath?[258]

---

[258] The Greek text is unclear: it is either, as above,
A: "7:22 Moses gave you [the law of] circumcision..."
   Or, as in some Bibles,
B: (the end of 7:22 comes into 7:23): "Because of this, Moses gave you circumcision..."
Scholars are divided as to which is correct. If "B" is correct, then what "this" refers to, is quite unclear. It may then mean: *Moses gave you the law of circumcision in order that a*

353

7:24 Do not judge by appearances, but decide with right judgement.

Here Jesus is urging the crowd to discern the inherent morality of his actions, beyond the mere 'letter of the Mosaic Law'.

**7:25 Then some of the people from Jerusalem said, "Is this not the man whom they are trying to kill?
7:26 And, look – he is speaking openly and they are saying nothing to him. Perhaps the rulers really know that this man is the Christ?
7:27 Yet we know where this man is from, but when the Messiah appears, no-one shall know where he is from.
7:28 Then Jesus cried out, as he was teaching in the temple saying, "You know me and you know where I am from. And yet it is not from my own decision that I have come here; the One who sent me, is trustworthy but you do not know him.
7:29 I know Him, because I am from Him, and it is that One who sent me.
7:30 Then they tried to arrest him, but no-one laid hands on him, because his hour had not yet arrived.**

The crowd had correctly understood that Jesus was referring to God, but among the crowd were some Pharisees who concluded that Jesus was equating himself with God, or at least, as very close to God, and to them this was blasphemy.
Also in v. 27, "no-one shall know where he is from..." this idea that the family or locale of the Messiah would be unknown, was a view developed by the Rabbis.
In v. 28: "is trustworthy": literally, "is true", which today conveys very little meaning. Here the word 'true' appears to means that God is the most genuine source

---

precedent exists for breaking the law of the Sabbath. Or, *Moses gave you the law of circumcision to serve as a prototype of the complete renewal of human nature, which Jesus then accomplishes.*[258]
But I conclude that both these two options are unlikely, and that 'A' is correct.

from which a prophet (or the Messiah) can declare spiritual truths.

And v. 30: "his hour had not yet arrived". This refers to the time when Jesus was to be handed over to the Sanhedrin, and then executed.

7:31 Yet many in the crowd believed in him and were saying, "When the Messiah comes, surely he will not do more wonders than this man has done?
7:32 The Pharisees heard the crowd murmuring such things about him, so the chief priests and the Pharisees sent temple guards to arrest him.

The Pharisees were alarmed that people were starting to view Jesus as the Messiah, and so with permission of their superiors, the chief priests, some temple guards were sent to arrest Jesus.

7:33 Jesus then said, "I am with you for yet a little while, then I go away to the One having sent me.
7:34 You will seek me, but not find me, for where I am then, you are not able to come.

Unperturbed, but with grave authority, Jesus responds to the attempt to arrest him; knowing that a specific time was appointed for his death and Resurrection.

7:35 So the people then said to one another, where is this man about to journey to, that we will not find him? Surely not to the Dispersion among the Greeks, to teach the Greeks then?

That a possible relocation of Jesus to Greek cities is mentioned indicates that a substantial number of Jewish people were living in Grecian towns.

7:36 What do his words mean, "You will seek me, but not find me, for where I am then, you are not able to come."

This is a rare occasion when the words of Jesus are repeated exactly by a crowd; this is indicating how powerful was the impact made by these potent words on their soul.

7:37 Now, on the last, great day of the Feast, Jesus was standing, and he cried out saying, "If anyone thirsts, let him come to me, and drink."

The Feast was "The Festival of Booths"; knowledge of this is essential to understand the power of what is presented in v. 37. The Festival was celebrated for a week; it was both a merry harvest festival and a joyous festival of spiritual triumph. The term 'booths' referred to the stipulation that when the people came to Jerusalem for the week, they had to make for themselves 'booths' from branches of trees. This was to directly symbolize that they were enveloped within a living, vital embrace of God, despite a fading, withering natural world.

Thus during this autumn festival, the community resided inside living houses, made from the leaves and branches "of splendid trees", including the myrtle tree, the foliage of which is fragrant. The theme of the temple services concerned the many blessings Jahve-God had bestowed on the Israelites, and especially his triumphant powers which, for example, had guided the Israelites out of Egypt and safely across the desert.

Eventually, a significant symbolic water ritual was added. On the second day of the festival, four oil lamps were ignited, in large golden lamp stands, in an outer section of the temple, the Court of the Women. Then in this court, dancers, holding flaming torches, danced to the accompaniment of music. The next morning and for the remaining mornings of the week, a priest brought water in a golden pitcher and poured it into the hollow altar, while the congregation, accompanied by flute music, sang triumphant songs.

Water is a symbol of the soul, and the intention of this festival was to direct the community's awareness toward the potential in the soul for spiritual triumph, for spiritual renewal, when the blessings of the Divine are invoked into the soul.

7:38 For that person, the one believing in me, streams of living water shall flow from his inner being, as the Scriptures indicate.

On the last day of the festival, no water was brought to the community, making the words of Christ especially potent. In addition, instead of being seated, as all Rabbis were when teaching, Jesus stood up to make the dramatic proclamation. In the Greek it is not simply 'the one believing in me' but emphatically, 'that very person' believing in me, shall experience what the Scriptures prophesy as a blessedness for future people.[259]

Verse 38 is sometimes revised, to imply that it is from Christ that the symbolic living water flows, and not from the spiritual person. But when speaking to the Samaritan woman (in 4:13) Jesus states that such inner renewal arises from within the redeemed soul, once the Christ power has blessed that person.

7:39 This he said about the spirit, which believers in him were soon to receive, for the Holy Spirit was not yet upon them, because Jesus was not yet glorified'.

His words were in effect, prophetic.
"for the Holy Spirit was not yet upon them": these words are only found in Codex Bezae. Most ancient texts have briefer comments, e.g., "for there was no spirit as yet."
'glorified': this means he was not yet permanently raised to a state of higher, divine empowerment, because the Resurrection had not occurred.

7:40 Some of the crowd, having heard these words, were saying, "Surely this is the Prophet".
7:41 Others were saying, "This man is the Christ", but some were saying, "The Messiah does not come from Galilee, does he?"
7:42 Has not the Scripture said that the Messiah is to be a descendant of David, and comes from Bethlehem, where David lived?
7:43 So there was division in the crowd because of him.
7:44 Some were wanting to arrest him, but no-one laid their hands on him.

---

[259] Technically, there is here an anacoluthon, formed by the *nominative absolute* case being used (ho pisteuoen - ὁ πιστεύων) instead of 'tou pisteuontos' (τοῦ πιστεύοντος).

7:45 Then the temple guards went back to the chief priests and the Pharisees, who asked them, why they did not bring him.
7:46 The guards answered, "Never has anyone spoken like this".
7:47 Then the Pharisees replied, "Surely you have not been deceived as well, have you?"
7:48 None of the authorities believed in him, nor any of the Pharisees, have they?"
7:49 But this crowd, they don't know the Law, they are accursed."
7:50 Nicodemus, the one who had earlier gone to Jesus, said,
7:51 "Our law does not judge people without first giving them a hearing, to find out what he is doing, does it?"
7:52 They replied, "Surely you're not from Galilee are you? Search and you will find that no prophet is to arise from Galilee."
 7:53 Then each of them went home.

One sees a positive attitude of Nicodemus and the incorrect view of the Pharisees about Galilee. For the prophet Jonah came from there, and it is possible that Hosea also was a Galilean.[260]

---

[260] Bernard, *A Critical and Exegetical commentary on the Gospel according to St. John*, p. 289.

CHAPTER 8

This episode is significant on several levels, not only sociologically, but also from its esoteric content. It is however absent from all ancient versions of the New Testament – with the sole exception of Codex Bezae (from where it spread to various other, later versions). As with other differing verses in this codex, the origin of this episode goes right back into the early years of Christianity.

It is referred to in the "Apostolic Constitutions", a collection of procedural church documents, which date from the second century. As Meyer notes, this episode (or 'pericope') has its origin in the Apostolic Age just decades after the Resurrection, and it was somehow inserted into the Gospel of John, late in the 2nd century, or early in the 3rd century.[261]

Six other finely written versions of the Gospels ('uncials') from the 6-9th centuries have included it, as did some 300 other versions, written in a more fluid, lower-case style ('minuscules').

It was very likely not part of this Gospel originally, but it is nevertheless a striking example of the deep initiation secrets of esoteric Christianity, most which have been lost. We can be grateful to the unknown, esoterically informed person who inserted it here, making codex Bezae so valuable.

(The woman taken in adultery)
8:1 Jesus went to the Mount of Olives
8:2 and early in the morning he came again to the temple and all the people were coming to him, and having seated himself, he began to teach them.
8:3 Then the scribes and the Pharisees brought a woman who had been caught in adultery, and made her stand before all of them,
8:4 they said to Jesus, "Teacher, this women has been caught in the act of committing adultery.
8:5 Now, in the law, Moses commanded us to stone such women; so what do you say?"

---

[261] H.A.W. Meyer, *The Gospel of John*, vol 2, p.1.

8:6 However, this they were saying to test him, so that they might have some charge to bring against him. But Jesus stooped down and was drawing figures in the ground with his finger.

That is, he was drawing in the dust on the paving stones of the temple court.

8:7 When they kept on questioning him, he stood up and said to them, "Let the one among you who is without sin, be the first to throw a stone at her."
8:8 And again he stooped down and wrote in the ground.
8:9 When they heard this, they went away, one by one, beginning with the oldest; and Jesus was left there alone, and the woman being in the midst.
8:10 Jesus stood up and said to the woman, "Where are they? Has no-one condemned you?"
8:11 Then she said, "No-one, Lord." Jesus said, "Neither do I condemn you. Go your way, and from now on, do not sin again."

On a social level, this episode speaks of the support by Jesus for a woman who was being used callously as bait for political intrigue (the man is allowed to go free). Also, since v. 9 can be translated as, "and the woman being in the middle", this episode shows the support for women by Jesus in a male-dominated society. For with this translation, she is alone "in the middle" of the temple courtyard surrounded by her accusers. But she is rescued from men who were soon impelled to find their conscience, which defeated their own malignant plans.

v.11: the word 'sin' can invoke antagonism, as the religious usage of this word is often resented. It is important to note that in Greek, 'sin' is harmatia (ἁμαρτία) which originally meant 'failing to meet one's mark', as in archery, for example. Gradually this word was applied to human ethics; so when a person acted in an anti-social way, he or she became a 'harmatia' person.

That is, their actions were, ideally viewed, intended to be moral actually, but their lower self came into expression and so they carried out an anti-social deed.

Their will or intentions 'missed the mark' of what ideally their inner being would have liked to do.

Now, this episode communicates on the initiatory level, in a veiled manner, a deeply esoteric aspect of cosmic Christianity. In v. 6 "....was drawing figures in the ground with his finger." The verb here is used for drawing diagrams or graphics, not for writing words. However, in v. 8 a different version of the verb is used, which means 'to write'; this implies that some words were also then written.

The most satisfactory commentary on this episode, on the esoteric level, was given by Rudolf Steiner, from his seership and scholarship. He points out that inside the Earth are elemental energies which from time to time manifest in earthquakes or volcanic eruptions. In the religious and esoteric Hellenistic cultural streams, the interior of the Earth was a sinister place; on a spiritual, not a geological, level. It was to realms deep down beneath the ground that the souls of the Dead who had committed many sins descended.

As noted in chapter Two, the Earth is a living being, with both soul-dynamics and a complex life-force body. There is a vital, linking connection between the Earth and the human soul. The Earth's energies are impacted by the inner life of humans; it is harmed by sensual desires and malignant thoughts. This is where 'sin' makes an objective, tangible impact on the environs.

A profound observation by Rudolf Steiner is that the scene of Christ drawing images in the ground can therefore become a meditation on firstly, the cosmic Christ (or solar Logos) confirming and contemplating that people are inscribing karmically into the Earth-soul the dynamic inherent in whatever they do.

Secondly, this writing on the ground signifies that Christ is contemplating how he may help to bring back harmony to the 'Earth-soul', and also give insights to human beings, as to how their actions will impact their karma.

Jesus was tracing out profoundly powerful symbolic imagery or sigils which 'spoke' to the Earth's soul and which also had a resonance with its life-forces. Christ was in some way thereby assisting the Earth-soul in regard to the impact of the sensuality of the woman and her partner.[262]

Indicative of the veiled initiatory message are the mysterious words in v. 9. Her accusers have departed, and she is left there with Jesus, "...the woman being in the midst." (As noted above, it can also mean "in the middle".) But now on the esoteric level: in 'the midst' of what? The answer is not given, it has to be sought by a spiritual intuitive process.

The woman is in the midst of a highly potent field of spiritual activity, brought about by a process wherein Christ has been contemplating, and seeking to moderate, the impact of her – and her partner's – lower impulses on the Earth's soul. He was also seeking to awaken her conscience, but especially that of her accusers. Since it is a core theme of this Gospel that the cosmic Christ is to become the guiding spirit of our planet, this initiatory scene (or cameo) has direct relevance to the concerns of the Christ.[263]

8:12 Jesus spoke to the people, saying, "I am the Light of the World, whoever follows me shall never walk in darkness, but will have the light of life."

"I am the Light of the World"

Before considering this well-known phrase, we note that in Part One, Section 4, the evidence for the cosmic nature of 'Christ' was presented, together with the perspective that this deity is the highest of the Sun-spirits or Powers. This Sun-god can also be understood as the 'solar Logos'; and as a deity, it far transcends the human life-wave.

However, at the Resurrection, this sublime deity became in effect the spiritual 'self' of Jesus. In chapter Nine of the Gospel there is another statement from the Christ which points to his status as the great Sun-god

---

[262] GA 94, p.287 (German edition): GA 155, p. 88 (German edition).

[263] Rudolf Steiner taught his students that the sigils, so drawn, had the power to help make effective the Grace of Christ in the people there, i.e., cause his intentions to stir their conscience.

(this was discussed in chapter Five, and will be examined further in chapter Nine). Many texts from ancient times speak of the reverence of the Sun-gods, but texts discussing the Sun as a multi-level celestial body are very rare. That is, texts describing the Sun as an en-souled being, as is our planet (but on a much lesser level). The most explicit such text was written about CE 300 by the Emperor Julian the Apostate.

His treatise is an invaluable record of how initiates in earlier Ages understood and experienced the spiritual levels of the Sun. His treatise discusses various levels of the Sun, and was written in reverence of the Sun-god, whom he called 'king Helios'. His words convey something of what the ancient initiates perceived regarding the 'spiritual Sun', and therefore of the Sun-gods; that is, their crucial role in the existence of humanity.

Modern science sees all of the planets as created by the Sun, (that is, cast out of the Sun). But ancient priesthoods had a more comprehensive view of this, and revered the Sun-gods as the creators of humanity, in that humanity became the primary life-wave formed on the Earth, once it was cast out of the central solar body. The paradox with Emperor Julian is, that he revered the leading solar deity of Hellenistic religions, but was unaware that the Gospels indicate that the cosmic Christ is that same deity. The following sentences from his treatise are about the physical Sun:

"....king Helios has the power to make visible all things in creation...this is done by the {physically} visible disk of Helios... in this world of our evolving. For the region of the Earth contains being in a state of becoming." [264]   (trans. A.A.)

Note: "our evolving" is literally, "our becoming".
The next sentences are about the 'soul' of the Sun; the level where many spiritual beings exist:

"The creative power of the sun-god Helios enables him to sustain the cosmos; creating the form and personality

---

[264] Julian the Apostate, ΕΙΣ ΤΟΝ ΒΑΣΙΛΕΑ ΗΛΙΟΝ ΠΡΟΣ ΣΑΛΛΟΥΣΤΙΟΝ (*To King Helios, for Sallust*) in *The Works of Emperor Julian* The Loeb Classical Library, ps. 367,385.

of the solar spirits. In the teachings of the Phoenicians, the rays of {spiritual sun-}light, everywhere diffused around us, are the undefiled incarnations of pure spiritual-beingness." (trans. A.A.)

Note: "pure spiritual-being", this is literally 'pure Nous" (καθαροῦ νοῦς), Nous being the term in Classical Greek for the consciousness of divine beings. The next sentences are about a third aspect: the actual spiritual level of the Sun, beyond the soul level,

"An......activity of the sun-god is his empowered raying-forth of divine goodness amongst the gods and non-material forms." (trans. A.A.)

So, just as the physical sunlight rays forth, suffusing the entire solar system, so too the sublime spirituality of the Sun-spirits (the Elohim of Genesis) envelops the solar system, infusing all spirits with its goodness. This third level of being refers to a much higher level of spiritual existence than that of 'soul'. This level is called 'devachanic' in theosophical and anthroposophical literature.
"divine goodness": the Greek phrase can also mean divine beauty.
"raying-forth": literally, 'distributing amongst"
"non-material forms": this means lesser entities, various spirits, who are not embodied in matter, but are lower than gods.

The Gospels do not openly identify 'Christ' as the great Sun-god, the leader of the Powers, instead, as noted in chapter Five, his solar nature is discreetly alluded to. In Luke (1:79) this is strongly indicated, as it is in Chapter 9 of John's Gospel. The above view of the Sun-god or the solar Logos (the leader of the Elohim), as a source of radiance, which is at the same time a source of goodness (i.e., holiness) echoes what is said in the Prologue, ""This was the true Light, which illumines every person; it was coming into the world." (v.9).

There are also many references to Christ in older Christian religious texts as possessing a solar quality; these are not mentioned here, as most of these appear to be poetic statements, and not intended to be declarations of spiritual fact. Those that are relevant were quoted in Chapter Five.

"I am the Light of the World": There is a second meaning in this verse, because the phrase, 'ego eimi' is used. On this level, we are told that "The 'I' which I am, is the light of the world; so whoever follows in the path of Christ shall never walk in darkness..." The Christ radiance shall be within, in the Spiritual-self.

The "Light of Life"

This is an uncommon phrase, rarely used; but it is in the Dead Sea Scrolls (1QS:3). The community is told that by achieving spirituality they shall be able to contemplate 'the light of life'.[265] In the Initiatory Quest pathway, 'the life' is understood as eternal higher consciousness, itself interwoven with an inexhaustible source of self-renewing vitality and healing power which the cosmic Christ-life bestows. The 'light' is understood to be the joyous radiance which such sublime spiritual consciousness naturally rays forth.

8:13 So the Pharisees said him, "You are testifying on your own behalf, (therefore) your testimony is not valid."
8:14 Jesus responded and said, "Although I testify about myself, my testimony is valid, because I know where I have come from, and where I am going. But you do not know where I come from, nor where I am going."
8:15 You judge according to the manner of the flesh, I judge no-one.
8:16 Yet, even if I do judge, my assessment is valid, because it is not I alone who judge, but I and the Father who sent me.
8:17 Also in your own law it is written that the testimony of two people is valid.

---

[265] In *Jesus Christ Sun of God*, D. Fideler, relying on a paraphrased partial English translation of the text, states that Helios is called the 'Light of Life' in Orphic Hymn 8:18, but these words are not in the original Greek text of that hymn.

"your own law": this phrase emphasizes to his critics a particular point which exists in the Law of Moses: in that same Law which Jesus often affirms, and sometimes re-interprets in challenging ways.

8:18 I myself testify on my own behalf, and also the Father who sent me, testifies on my behalf.
8:19 Then they said to him, "Where is your father?" Jesus answered, "You know neither me, nor my Father. If you had known me, you would also have known my Father.
8:20 He spoke these words whilst teaching in the Treasury of the temple; but no-one arrested him, because his hour had not yet come.

This group of verses is quite clear, showing the persistent lack of discernment or intuitive perception by the crowd. Verse 8:16 needs some comments. Jesus declares that any judgement he makes, is in fact carried out in conjunction with the Father (see v.26).

8:21 Therefore he again said to them, I am leaving, and you will seek me, but you will die away in your sin.

An immensely deep statement which remains veiled without knowledge of the experience that souls undergo in the after-life. According to Rudolf Steiner, existence in the Soul-realms, without an inner link to the cosmic Christ, or solar Logos, causes a lack of vitality and integrity in the consciousness of the souls who are journeying through there.[266]

8:22 So the people were saying, Surely he will not kill himself, although he says, "Where I am going, you cannot come?"
8:23 So then he said to them, "You are from below, but I am from above; you are of this world, but not of this world am I.
8:24 "For this reason I said to you, that you will die away in your sins, for if you do not inwardly discern

---

[266] See the basic texts of Rudolf Steiner for more about this; especially his "Theosophy".

that *I am the 'I am'* – then you will die away in your sins."

These three verses continue the theme of v.21.

8:24: the phrase here, "*if you do not inwardly discern that I am the 'I am'*" is not discerned by humanistic scholarship, so this verse remains deeply perplexing to them.[267] Hence it is usually translated as, "you would die in your sins, if you do not believe *that I am he*", meaning the Saviour. But scholars are aware that this version is invalidated by the grammar involved here; it still does convey a meaning however, but not the intended, esoteric meaning.

The esoteric level of this verse remains veiled until the crucial and potent truth is perceived that the cosmic Christ is the deity from whom the real, the non-illusory self or 'I' derives; the Spiritual-self or The Son of Man. This level of meaning has intimations of less-than-ideal conditions arising for the un-spiritual soul in the Soul-world after death. In the next verse, the cosmic Christ speaks even more powerfully, resulting in a verse that has remained unclear until the Initiatory Quest method is used.

8:25 They were saying to Jesus, "You, who are you?" Jesus said to them, "I am the One who, since the Beginning, has been intoning to you."

Most theologians agree that there is a disrespectful mood in the question from the crowd. But the meaning of the latter part of this verse remained unknown. Many different translations have been made in an effort to find some meaning, but these are not generally accepted. Many scholars conclude that the meaning is unknown (see Appendix 12).

However with the Initiatory Quest approach, a profound meaning emerges. It becomes clear that it is the cosmic Christ, through Jesus, who is speaking here, declaring that it has been intoning voiceless words of

---

[267] Barrett for example, was baffled, and concluded that "It is impossible to supply the missing word here... but it probably is saying that Jesus is equal to God." *Gospel accord. to John*, p.282.

cosmic resonance into the human soul, since primordial times, across the Ages of humanity's development.

"intones": the verb here (laleoe – λαλέω) can mean 'to speak', but also to 'intone', to 'resound', etc. For example, it was used in classical Greek for such expressions as, 'winged utterances', 'the murmuring of the aspen trees', and 'musical tones'.[268] That my translation correlates to the intended meaning, is supported by the conclusion from various scholars that one feasible translation is "(I am) from the beginning what I am telling you".[269]

My version is also supported by verses in the Prologue (1:5) "And the Light shone in the darkness, and is shining, but the darkness does not perceive it" and 1:12 "Yet those who acknowledged the Logos - those who discerned its presence - these were empowered through it to become 'children of God'." These ancient Initiates perceived the 'intonings' of the solar Logos. (See Appendix 12 for more about the confusion around this verse).

8:26 Many things about you I have to speak, and to judge, for indeed the One who sent me is Truth itself.

"truth itself": literally, 'he who sent me is true': as with 7:28, the word 'true' here appears to mean that the Messiah is able to claim authority from God - the truest, or most genuine, source of wisdom. And because the Divine is the source of the wisdom of the Messiah, it follows that Christ has much to communicate to human beings, to help them find their path in life, and Christ also is rightfully empowered to judge or assess a person's nature, in terms of ethics, on their path to sanctification.

8:27 They did not know that Christ was speaking to them of the Father.

---

[268] In Greek respectively, πτέρυγες λαλοι, λαλος κερκις, αὐλῷ λαλέω.
[269] Metzger, *A textual Commentary on the Greek NT*, p.191.

8:28 So Jesus said to them,[270] **Whenever you have exalted The Son of Man, then you will know I am the I am (in you); you will also know, 'from myself I do nothing, except as the Father taught me'.**

In most translations, this verse reads very differently; for there are some complex textual problems here; see Appendix 13.

8:29 These things I speak, for the One who sent me is with me; he has not left me alone, for I always do that which is agreeable to Him.

Here, what the crowd was told in v. 25 is again referred to, as the Christ 'intones' or speaks of immense truths about the human spirit. He is saying in effect "*these transcendent truths, almost beyond earthly languages to convey, is what I am 'speaking' to your soul, and these I inwardly hear from the Father*".

8:30 As he was saying these things, many believed in him.
8:31 So Jesus said to the people who believed in him, if you abide within my words, you are truly my disciples.

"abide within my words": usually, "remain in my word": here 'words' mean both the spoken teachings and the subtle non-verbalized spiritual influence of Jesus. If the soul contemplates and lives within what Jesus has spoken, then one remains inwardly in harmony with him.

8:32 Then you will know the truth, and the truth shall set you free.

A commentary on this famous sentence could fill a book; here one can briefly note that the spiritual seeker who is aligned to the Christ (the solar Logos) has a new power of cognizing (i.e., of perceiving and then assessing) whatever they encounter. This power enables

---

[270] In the NIV Bible, the word "that" has been inserted, although it is not there in the Greek.

them to avoid an un-grounded, naïve, self-indulgent mind-set which cannot properly relate spiritual truths of existence to the reality of human life.

It also enables them on the other hand, to avoid a subtly self-willed hunger for dominance and power, fuelled by clever but shallow thinking. In the middle between these two extremes, lives the Truth; and such a mindset or consciousness, gives access to high spiritual realms.

8:33 They answered him, saying, "We are descendants of Abraham, and have never been slaves of anyone. So how can you say that we can become free?"
8:34 Jesus answered them, Very truly, I say to you that everyone existing within sin is enslaved.

The theme in these three verses is about the core ethical dilemma facing humanity: living one's life in an unethical or immoral state is un-freedom. Whereas freedom is the condition of being inherently ethical, in which doing the moral thing is undertaken from an inner 'decision' which transcends both emotion and intellect, and arises as an intuitive act of will.

It is an act which does not seek to obey, as in a reflex action, parental or religious guidelines; it is simply what one is, deep within.[271] (Wise parental and religious education may have contributed, in years gone by, towards developing this inner ethical state.)

On this point the great codex Bezae is again important; it has, as above, "...everyone existing within sin is enslaved." But most other ancient texts have, "everyone existing within sin is enslaved *to sin*." In its brevity, the briefer Bezae version conveys the message more wisely and more powerfully.

8:35 Yet the slave does not remain in the household forever, but the Son remains forever.
8:36 If therefore the Son frees you, then indeed you will truly be free people.

---

[271] Rudolf Steiner's *The Philosophy of Freedom*, is a valuable study of this view of freedom and consciousness.

In these verses 'the Son' is deliberately ambiguous; referring to both The Son of Man (or the Spiritual-self) and to the Christ, who is the archetype of, and the mediator of, this state of blessedness. If you become a Son of Man, then you of course remain eternally in that exalted state, whereas unredeemed soul qualities have only a limited future.

8:37 I know that you are the descendants of Abraham, yet you seek to kill me, because what is intoning in my words has no effect on you.

"what is intoning in my words to you": usually, 'my word has no place in you...'.

8:38 Yet that which I have beheld in the presence of the Father, I speak; likewise you do that which you have heard from your father.

Here the crowd is told, even though their descent from Abraham is acknowledged, that they (that section of the crowd which was hostile) are unreceptive to the teachings and the spiritual influences of the Messiah. Then these people are potently contrasted to Jesus; he who responds to Divine will, and they who have the Devil as the 'father' of their urges.

8:39 They responded to him saying, "Our father is Abraham." Jesus said to them, "If you are Abraham's children, you would do what Abraham did."
8:40 Yet now you are seeking to kill me, a man who has told you the truth which I heard from God: this is not what Abraham would not do.
8:41 You are doing the works of your own father. "We are not illegitimate children", they protested, "we have one father, and that is God."
8:42 Jesus said to them, If God were your father, you would have developed love (agape) for me, for I came forth from God. I have not come here on my own, but He sent me.

These four verses are quite clear.

8:43 Why do you not comprehend what I am saying? Because your souls are deaf to my words.

"Because your souls are deaf to my words": literally, "because you can not hear (the meaning of) my words". Morris renders it, "because you cannot comprehend my thought", since 'my words' ('logos') here does include the meaning of 'thought' not only audible speech.

8:44 You are from your father the Devil, and you wish to carry out the desires of your father. He was a murderer from the beginning and is not placed in the truth, because there is no truth in him. When he lies, he speaks from his own reality, because he is a liar, and the father of lies.

Jesus is declaring that the spiritual influence of those seeking to kill him, is from the Devil; he is not declaring that they, as a section of the Jewish people of the city, are created by the Devil. He spoke in the same direct manner to Peter, called him "Satan" when Peter rebuked Jesus (Mk.8:33) for saying that he must one day be killed. Jesus did not mean that Peter was Satan, but was in that moment deaf to what Jesus was teaching, and thereby seeking to hinder the mission of Jesus, Peter had been influenced by a malignant entity.

8:45 But because I speak the truth, you do not believe me.
8:46 Who among you convicts me of sin? If I speak the truth, why do you not believe me?
8:47 Whoever belongs to God, hears the words God says; therefore because you are not of God, you do not hear.

Verses 8:43-47 The meaning of this group is clear.

8:48 The Jewish leaders answered him, "Are we not right in saying that you are a Samaritan and have a demon?
8:49 Jesus answered, "I do not have a demon, but instead I honour my Father, and you dishonour me.
8:50 For I am not seeking spiritual empowerment of myself; but there is One who does require to be honoured, and he is the judge.

For a Jew to call another Jew 'a Samaritan' was a potent way to insult that person, given the hostility and bitter contempt that prevailed between these two groups. Jesus points out firstly, that as a vessel of the Christ, selflessness is the core quality of his being and way of life; and secondly, his aim is to empower God, by bringing the divine to birth within the human being. He is not seeking his own self-empowerment.

"empowering of myself": usually is translated as 'glory', but God does not seek to be 'glorified' in the sense of being praised, which is the context here. Rather the Divine seeks to become realized or awakened within the aspiring human soul.

8:51 Very truly, I say to you, whoever keeps my words within their heart, shall never experience death (in the heavenly realms).

"keeps my words within their heart": literally, 'keeps my word'; an expression which is not so meaningful today. This is another expression of the truly deep, cosmic aspect of the Christ; it concerns the degree and quality of self-awareness after death, and is made clearer in v. 11:25.

8:52 So then the Jewish leaders said to him, "Now we know that you have a demon, for Abraham died, and so did the prophets, and yet you declare "whoever keeps my words within their heart, shall never experience death, in the heavenly realms."

This verse emphasizes the initiatory quest in a very potent manner. This quest has a focus on what kind of consciousness the acolyte shall achieve in spiritual realms, after the death of the body.

8:53 So are you greater than our father Abraham, who died? The prophets also died. Who are you claiming to be?
8:54 Jesus answered, if I give divine empowerment to myself, that empowerment is nothing; it is my Father who empowers me – the One of whom you say, "He is our God".

8:55 But you have not known Him: however, I have known Him. If I were to say that I have not known Him, then I would be like you, a liar. But I know Him and I obey his word.

In these three verses it is obvious that the hostile section of the crowd cannot grasp that, Jesus is intimating that in the words he utters, the cosmic Christ directly speaks, or indirectly manifests. The emphasis here is that 'God' is the source of whatever spiritual empowerment or authority is in the Messiah.

8:56 Abraham, your father, was glad that he could see my day, and he saw it and rejoiced.
8:57 The Jewish leaders therefore said to him, "You are not yet fifty years old, and yet you have seen Abraham?"
8:58 Jesus said to them, Very truly, I say to you:
before Abraham existed, I am the 'I am'.

Here is another of the rare occasions when the cosmic Christ speaks of the awe-inspiring primary truth which is the core message of the Gospel. For these words are directly reflecting the name of God as spoken to Moses, but which also identify 'God' (the cosmic Christ) as the origin and source of humanity's Higher-self or eternal 'I'. The crowd does sense that this is somehow implied in these words, but fails to perceive that there is no blasphemy here with this speaker, for with him it is the truth. That is, here the cosmic Christ is speaking through Jesus.

8:59 Then the crowd picked up stones to throw at him, but Jesus hid himself and went out of the temple.

CHAPTER 9

**9:1 As he walked along, Jesus saw a man who was blind from birth.
9:2 His disciples asked him, "Who sinned; this man, or his parents, that he was born blind?"**

Theologians have concluded that this question is based on four possible scenarios:

A: that this person sinned in a past life. Dismissed by some theologians, because possible references to reincarnation are seen as not compatible with Christian theology. But many scholars have concluded that this is in fact the concept underlying the question. As shown earlier, the concept of reincarnation was known and accepted in various groups in the time of Jesus.

B: that his parents sinned whilst he was in the womb. Some Rabbis did have this view, but to most commentators and myself, this is not a viable concept. Importantly, this has to be ignored, because Christ declares that his parents did not sin.

C: that God especially arranged his blindness and his encounter with Jesus, so that the compassion of God could be made manifest. An interpretation accepted by many, but also rejected by many.

D: that God pre-arranged his blindness because of a sin that he would commit as an adult. Likewise a theory rejected by many. However, the timing of the blind man's life circumstances can be viewed as divinely inspired.

I reject scenarios B, C and D, as do many scholars. Thus scenario 'A' remains, and needs discussion. That a past life is a possible reason behind this question has been noted by scholars in recent times.[272] Even though 'A' is apparently rejected by Christ (in the next verse), Rudolf Steiner taught that this view 'A' holds the answer. He points out that, in precise terms, the current personality

---

[272] For example, Morris, *Gospel John*, p.425, Westcott, *St. John*, p.144, Plummer, *St. John*, p. 204.

is not actually the person who commits 'sins' in a past life; it was the previous personality (see next verse).[273]

9:3 Jesus answered, "Neither this man, nor his parents have sinned, but this situation has arisen so that the actions of the Divine may become manifested in him."

Here Christ is not saying that the man was born blind so that the compassion of God could be made manifest. Rather, that the negative karma of a past life brought about his blindness, but then the timing and context of the blind man's life was pre-arranged, to allow him the privilege of encountering and being healed by the Christ. Through this healing miracle, the power of the Christ would become manifested to all.

But the words "so that the actions of the Divine may become manifested in him" alludes to complex spiritual processes. For those higher powers who oversee humanity's karma were involved, as the Christ would be acting in harmony with their tasks, not ignoring the dynamics underlying the 'tapestry of destiny', even if fate or karma was not to be part of his teachings.

This incident also serves as an example of how, to bring about healing, the Sun-god would imbue earthly substance with solar life-forces from within his own being and from the Sun, (which was only possible because it has not yet set). This incident is also an indicator that soon the great solar Logos will become the indwelling spirit of the Earth (see under v. 13:18).

He shall then seek to imbue earthly life with a divine quality in many ways; whether 'en-gracing' human consciousness or nurturing the planet's own life-forces. So here the solar Logos is permeating earthly soil with his divine healing energies; this can be seen as preparation for this future phase.

9:4 It is necessary for us to carry out the actions of the One who sent me, whilst it is still daytime; for night is coming when none can exert their power.

---

[273] GA 112, lect., 2. July 1909.

"necessary for us..." the various deities involved (see below) need to access the solar energies from which light derives, to re-configure the internal structure of the eyes. Some ancient texts have "necessary for *me*..." Scholars are divided as to which one is correct. However, the first version appears to be the most authentic, as it is in codex Bezae, and other versions, (such as codex Vaticanus and the early papyri #66 and #75).

So, "it is necessary *for us* to carry out the actions..." here the cosmic Christ is referring to its own actions, as well as those of Jesus, and very likely also of the (germinal) Higher-self of the blind man. These would all be exerting their influences together, to make possible a remarkable healing miracle.

9:5 Every time that I am in the world, I am the light of the world.

Not, "*When* I'm in the world..." but "*whensoever*", or 'every time that it is the case' as scholars have observed.[274] As noted in Part One, Section 4, (*References to a cosmic Christ*) this key verse is hinting that every time the sun is visible (rises above the eastern horizon), it gives light to the world; these words also indicate that Christ is the solar deity.

9:6 Having said these things, he spat upon the ground and made mud with the saliva and then spread this mud on the man's eyes.
9:7 and said to him, "Go ! Wash in the pool of Siloam ! (which translated, means 'sent')." So he went and washed and came back, able to see.

The instructions from Jesus are very strong; two quite separate commands are given, one after the other, "Go ! Wash !"[275] The instructions given about washing are ambiguous in Greek; either he was to wash his body in the pool, or just wash his eyes. That "he came back" is also unclear; he did not go back to Jesus, however v. 8 infers that he 'came back' to his home.

---

[274] Westcott, *St. John*, p.144, Plummer, *St. John*, p.205
[275] These are technically 'asyndetic imperatives' as Barrett points out, *Gospel John*, p. 297.

"sent": the name of the pool might have spiritual significance. The water flowing to the pool came from or was 'sent' from, a source known as the Fountain of the Virgin; the reason for this name is unknown. It is unlikely that this played a role in the choice of pool by Jesus, since poetic references to 'virgin' in the Jewish Scriptures refer to Israel or to a city, not to any spirit being, or mystical entity.[276]

It might be that 'sent' indicates that if the man had not believed in the power of Jesus, who 'sent' him to the pool, and thus did not go there, his eyes would not have been healed.

9:8 Therefore the neighbours and those who had seen him before as a beggar, began to ask, "Is this not the person who was sitting and begging?"
9:9 Some said, "It is he." Others were saying, "No, it is someone like him." He kept declaring, "I am that person."
9:10 So they were saying to him, "Then how were your eyes opened?"
9:11 He replied, "That man, the one called Jesus, made some mud and anointed my eyes, and said to me, "Go; wash in the pool of Siloam !" I went there, and washed, and received my sight."
9:12 They said to him, "Where is he?" He said, "I do not know".
9:13 They led the man who had been blind to the Pharisees.
9:14 Now it was a Sabbath day when Jesus had made the mud and opened his eyes.
9:15 Then the Pharisees also began to ask him how he had received his sight. He said to them, "He put mud on my eyes. Then I washed, and now I see."
9:16 So some of the Pharisees were saying, "This man (Jesus) is not from God, for he does not observe the Sabbath." But others were saying, "How can a man who is a sinner perform such wonders?" So they were divided.

---

[276] See, J. Schmitt, "*The Virgin of Israel...*" in The Catholic Biblical Quarterly; jstor.org.stable/43718279

9:17 So they said again to the blind man, "What do you say about him? It was your eyes that he opened." He replied, "He is a prophet".

9:18 The Jewish authorities did not believe that he had been blind, and had then received his sight, until they called the parents of the man who had received his sight,

9:19 and asked them, "Is this your son who was born blind?" So how is it that he now sees?"

9:20 Then the parents answered, " We know that he is our son, and that he was born blind."

9:21 But we do not know how it is that he now sees. Ask him, he is of age. He will speak for himself."

9:22 The parents said these things because they were afraid of the Sanhedrin, which had already agreed that if anyone acknowledged Jesus to be the Messiah, that person would be put out of the synagogue.

9:23 For this reason the parents said, "He is of age, ask him."

9:24 So for the second time, they called the man who had been blind, and said to him, "Give praise to God !" We know that this man (Jesus) is a sinner.

9:25 The blind man answered, "I do not know whether he is a sinner; one thing I know, I was blind but now I see.

9:26 They said to him, "What did he do to you? How did he open your eyes?"

9:27 He answered them, "I have told you already, but you would not listen. Why do you want to hear it again?" Do you also want to become his disciples?

9:28 So they reviled him, saying, "You are his disciple, but we are disciples of Moses."

9:29 We know that God has spoken to Moses, but as for this man, we do not where he comes from."

9:30 The man replied, saying to them "Here is an astonishing thing ! You do not know where he comes from, and yet he opened my eyes.

9:31 We know that God does not listen to sinners, but he does listen to one who worships him and obeys his will.

9:32 Never since the world began has it been heard that anyone opened the eyes of a person born blind.

9:33 If this man were not from God, he could do nothing."

9:34 They answered, saying to him, "You were born entirely in sin, and are trying to teach us?" So they drove him out.

Verses 9:8 – 9:34 These verses are quite clear, and primarily highlight the hostility of the Sanhedrin to Jesus, and also that the blind man can now see, but the Sanhedrin remain blind.

Note that v.24 "give praise to God" was a stock phrase by which the Pharisees meant that the person being questioned must speak truthfully.

9:35 Jesus heard that they had driven him out, and having found him, said, "Do you believe in The Son of Man?"

9:36 Who is he, Lord?" the man asked. "Tell me, so that I may believe in him."

9:37 Jesus said, "You have (now) seen him; in fact he is the one speaking with you.

9:38 Then the man said, "Lord, I believe", and worshipped him.

In these four verses, Jesus is bringing to the attention of the formerly blind man, the initiatory stage of the Spiritual-self or The Son of Man. He is also declaring that he, Jesus, is the archetype and fountain of this blessed state of spirituality. This was a priceless gift to someone whose bodily infirmity would have excluded him from most opportunities to learn about the teachings of his religion.

Moreover, very few people were informed directly by Jesus of his exalted status. Some lesser manuscripts have "Son of God" here, but Christ is seeking to help the man to intuitively discern the presence of the Spiritual-self or Son of Man; for him to cognize the even higher Son of God condition would have been too demanding a challenge.

9:39 For judgement I have come into this world, so that the blind will see and those who see become blind.

"the blind will see": those who have no awareness of, nor inner perception of, spiritual-religious truths, shall now perceive these truths.

"those who see, become blind": some others are to become aware that their mental grasp of spiritual-religious truths is negligible; so they are to realize that in this regard, they are blind.

9:40 Some Pharisees who were with him, heard him say this and asked, "What? Are we blind too?"
9:41 Jesus said, "If you were blind, you would not remain guilty of sin; but now that you claim that you can see, your guilt remains."

CHAPTER 10

10:1 Very truly, I say to you, anyone who does not enter the sheepfold by the gate, but climbs in another way, is a thief and a robber.
10:2 But the person entering by the gate is a shepherd of the sheep.
10:3 The gatekeeper opens the gate for him, and the sheep hear his voice. He calls his own sheep by name and leads them out.
10:4 When he has brought out all of his own, he goes ahead of them, and the sheep follow because they know his voice.
10:5 A stranger they will not follow, but flee from him, because they do not know the stranger's voice.
10:6 Jesus used this figure of speech, but the Pharisees did not understand what it was that he was saying to them.
10:7 Therefore Jesus said again, "Very truly, I say to you, that I am the gate for the sheep."

The meaning of these seven verses is seen after v. 8 is understood. The 'figure of speech' is referring to the use of a parable, to veil what he wished to reveal.

10:8 Those who have come before me are thieves and robbers, but the sheep have not listened to them.

This verse is referring to initiatory themes, and as such, it remains an enigma to theologians, to whom it appears to be unjustifiably harsh.[277] Scholars suggest that the false shepherds are either:
A: the Pharisees (but this would ignore the noble Pharisees).
B: Some false Jewish Messiahs *before* Jesus (but there are virtually no such persons).

---

[277] One outcome of the widespread confusion about v. 8 was that Bernard (*Gospel according to John*, ICC, vol.1), in view of the apparent harshness, concluded that verses 1 to 18 should be placed after v. 19. There, amidst the verses full of hostility from the Pharisees, v. 8, it does not feel so harsh. But this suggestion is not a valid solution.

C: The kings of Israel, who were referred to as shepherds of their people; many of these were castigated by the prophets, such as in Ezekiel 34. But king David is amongst these, and he was sent by God as Ezekiel declared. So this option is also unlikely to be valid.

D: The Devil and his agents (scholars with this view refer to 'the Fall of Man' from the Garden of Eden).

I conclude that option "D" is nearest to what is meant. For here the great Christ-spirit (the Solar Logos) is speaking, who then declares (v.9) that "I am the gate; whoever enters through me will be saved." These words lift the level of activity implied in v.8 to that of an interaction between deities.

This is demonstrated by passages in Scripture and in esoteric Jewish apocryphal texts. Firstly, in the Gospels, Jesus is twice recorded as indicating that his God-given power has a primary task in battling against the power of evil:

John 12:31 "Now has come judgement of this world; now the Ruler of this World shall be driven out."

Luke 10:12 "I watched Satan fall from Heaven like a flash of lightning."

Moreover, even a brief glimpse into the esoteric wisdom of initiatory groups in Judaism shows just how central to their world-view was the existence of fallen spirits, and their influence on human souls. They were aware of a long-term battle of Jahve-God (and thus the cosmic Christ) against the 'Prince of the Air' (Lucifer), as well as the 'Prince of Darkness', down inside the Earth, called Beliar (or Satan).

The Dead Sea Scrolls refer to Beliar and his fallen Angels; and esoteric texts called *The Testament of the 12 Patriarchs*, written about a century before Jesus, mention a future battle against these fallen spirits as a core task of the coming Messiah. For example, *The Testament of Levi* (19:1) calls upon the Israelites to choose between Beliar and God: "...choose therefore for yourselves either the light or the darkness; the Law of the Lord or the works of Beliar."

The *Testament of Zebulon* declares that the Messiah "...shall redeem all the captivity of the sons of men from

Beliar." (9:8) The *Testament of Dan* (5:10/6:1) alludes to the descent into Hades of the Messiah to conquer Beliar.[278]

So the Prince of the Air is to be fought against, as declared in Colossians (2:14) as well as 1 Peter (3:18), and also the dark Beliar or Satan, down in Tartaros, is to be conquered. The influence of these fallen spirits upon humanity must be negated by the Messiah. So it appears that v. 8 is referring to these fallen spirits, and not to the Pharisees nor to earlier kings of Israel, as such; but some of these could still be included, as agents of these spirits. This understanding is supported by Clement of Alexandria, "the Devil is called a thief and a robber, having mixed false prophets with true prophets, as tares are mixed with wheat grains."[279]

So, in v. 8, Christ is referring to these fallen spirits as false shepherds, that is as spirits seeking to 'harvest' human souls, and to lead them into a future condition of servitude. Both of these groups gain access to the soul in a discreet, veiled manner (i.e., they sneak over the wall of the sheep fold).

The Temptation of Jesus by the Devil is a dramatic example of Scripture showing the intention within fallen spirits to take over human souls. Their true intentions are usually deeply hidden.

Rudolf Steiner's perspective is that there are two distinct groups of 'fallen spirits', which, behind the veil of material substance, are active in the souls of human beings. Their human targets are kept unaware of the deeply unethical, anti-social and ultimately self-destructive nature of the urges instilled in them, until it is almost too strong to be resisted.[280]

They constantly seek to turn human consciousness to directions that are harmful to the welfare of the soul, and which would eventually lead to alienation from the wonderful future which the sacrifice of the cosmic

---

[278] *The Testaments of the 12 Patriarchs*, in *Pseudepigrapha*, edit. R.H. Charles.
[279] Clement, *Miscellanies*, chapter 17.
[280] GA 13; *An Outline of Esoteric Science*.

Christ has made possible for humanity.²⁸¹ The one group uses naïve selfishness, unrealistic ideals and sensuality; the other uses a hardened, self-seeking will and empty, spirit-denying intellectuality. The selflessness and good-will to all, which flows into the soul from the cosmic Christ, and from Jesus Christ, is the opposite of these influences, and is protection against them.

10:9 I am the gate, whoever enters through me will be saved. They will come in and go out, and find pastures.
10:10 I am the good shepherd. The good shepherd lays down his life for the sheep.
10:11 The thief comes only to steal and to kill and destroy. I have come that they may have life, and have it to the full.
10:12 The hired hand is not the shepherd, and does not own the sheep. So when he sees the wolf coming, he abandons the sheep and runs away. Then the wolf attacks the flock and scatters it.
10:13 This man runs away because he is a hired hand and cares nothing for the sheep.
10:14 I am the good shepherd: I know my sheep and my sheep know me –
10:15 just as the Father knows me and I know the Father.
10:16 I have other sheep that are not of this flock. I must bring them also. They too will listen to my voice, and there shall be one flock and one shepherd.
10:17 The reason that my Father loves (agape) me is that I lay down my life – so that I may take it up again.
10:18 No-one takes it from me, but I lay it down of my own accord. I have authority to lay it down and to

---

[281] These he identifies as the hosts of the Devil (called 'Lucifer') and the hosts of Satan (called 'Ahriman'); teaching that these two terms refer to two different entities. One influences the desires/emotions, the other our thinking and will (see my *Rudolf Steiner Handbook* for more about this topic.)

take it up again. This command I received from my Father.

10:19 The people who heard these words were again divided.

10:20 Many of them said, "He is demon-possessed and is out of his mind. Why listen to him?"

10:21 But others said, "These are not the sayings of a man possessed by a demon. Can a demon open the eyes of the blind?"

The meaning of this group of verses is quite clear; except with v. 16, who the "other sheep not of this flock" are, is not explained. It no doubt refers to the Gentiles; but it might also have a wider perspective, such as including the souls of the Dead.

10:22 Then there came the Festival of Dedication at Jerusalem.

10:23 It was winter, and Jesus was in the temple courts, walking in Solomon's Colonnade.

10:24 The people who were there gathered around him, saying, "How long will you keep us in suspense?" If you are the Messiah, tell us plainly."

10:25 Jesus answered, "I did tell you, but you do not believe. The works I do, imbued with my Father's might, testify about me,

"imbued with my Father's might": literally, "in my Father's name", which as noted for 5:43, is a phrase meaning that Jesus was permeated by, and empowered spiritually, by the being of the Father

10:26 but you do not believe because you are not of my sheep.

10:27 My sheep hear my voice. I know them and they follow me.

10:28 I give them eternal life, so they shall never perish; no-one shall snatch them out of my hand,

10:29 My Father, the one who has given them to me, is greater than all; no-one can snatch them out of my Father's hand.

10:30 I and the Father are one.

10:31 Again those opposed to him picked up stones to stone him.
10:32 But Jesus said to them, "I have shown you many good works from the Father. For which of these do you stone me"?
10:33 "We are not stoning you for a good work," they replied, "but for blasphemy, because you, though only a human being, claim to be God."
10:34 Jesus answered, "Is it not written in your law, 'I said, you are gods'?"
10:35 If those to whom the word of God came, were called 'gods' – and the Scripture cannot be annulled –
10:36 can you say that the one whom the Father has sanctified and sent into the world is blaspheming, because I said, "I am God's son"?

The argument put forward here by Jesus in his dialogue with the hostile crowd is significant as it refers to an intriguing passage in Psalm 82. Like so much in the Hebrew Scriptures, the Psalms often have a veiled initiatory meaning which is hard to understand with humanistic attitudes.

This Psalm starts with a declaration of divine realities; the Elohim are in their spiritual realms, and are amongst various other deities, carrying out the task of assessing or judging the various elements of creation:
"The Elohim are placed in the Divine convocation, making judgement, amongst the other gods."

The Psalmist-seer then refers to the authorities of Israel ruling in a derelict, malignant way, and pleads for them to help the needy, rescuing them from their oppression.

He finishes this section referring to an esoteric truth; that the interior of the Earth is disturbed ("its foundations are shaking") by the impact of this evil resonating deep down below. Then the Psalmist pronounces words of JHVH,
"I have said that you (ye) are gods and sons of the Most
   High (El-yon)".
This pronouncement apparently occurred at some unspecified point in time; unless what is meant is an subtle 'intoning' to the souls of humans in spiritual realms or in the physical world.

Then the Psalmist or JHVH declares that these malignant rulers shall encounter death in the way that normal folk do. But in calling them 'gods' these people and therefore all other human beings, are being defined as potential deities; that is, as having a 'divine spark' which can transform the person into 'a Son of Man'. The Psalm is declaring that the divine potential in the unethical rulers shall not become empowered; hence their personalities shall not have a share in eternal life.[282]

"blaspheming": in v. 30 Jesus has declared himself to be 'at one' with the Father, but he had not actually spoken the name of God, which is the only ground for a charge of blasphemy.[283] This shows how strong was the hostility of the crowd.

10:37 Do not believe me, unless I do the works of my Father.
10:38 But if I do them, even though you do not believe me, believe the works, so that you may know and understand that the Father is in me, and I am in the Father.
10:39 So they tried again to seize him, but he escaped their grasp.
10:40 Then Jesus went back across the Jordan again, to the place where John had been baptizing earlier, and he remained there,
10:41 and many people came to him and were saying, "Although John performed no wonders, yet everything that he said about this man was true."
10:42 And in that place many believed in Jesus.

The meaning of this group of verses is quite clear.

---

[282] The humanistic interpretation is that the entire Psalm is about the authorities (judges or kings), for the word 'gods' refers to human judges, who are indeed called 'gods' but that this is simply shorthand for "you are vessels of God, so you are agents of God's will".

[283] Barrett, *The Gospel according to John*, p. 318.

CHAPTER 11

The Awakening of Lazaros

This episode is central to the Gospel, and in terms of the Initiatory Quest approach, the narrative is understood to be a veiled report of an initiatory event. Consequently there are numerous unusual features to the Greek text. In the process of commenting on these features, discreet references to initiatory processes placed in the text, will be encountered. Here Lazaros is writing as a spectator about his own initiation. He does this from his memory as well as his spiritual capacity to see, in a panorama of visions, the events in the life of Jesus.

What Lazaros underwent was an illness which could have resulted in his death. A severe illness has the effect of separating a person from their body; and if such a person has the cognitional ability to perceive where they are then placed, he or she could experience supra-physical realms of spirit.

But thirdly, in that Lazaros was a close disciple of Jesus, one can conclude that his soul was helped, so that death was prevented, and he was given the capacity to perceive in realms of spirit, and to remember those experiences, once he was back in his body.

One reason that we can view the Lazaros incident in this way, is that the Greek text has a second layer of meaning in it, which indicates that the Lazaros episode became in effect, informally an initiatory three-day sleep. To translate the Greek text giving the impression of an illness from which Lazaros is saved, is to offer a text which presents the surface level only. Such a translation ignores the odd nuances which the surface level has to have in it to embed, but veil, the esoteric level.

Another basis for this viewpoint is the presentation by Rudolf Steiner of his research into this incident; in his lectures on this Gospel, he describes the episode as an initiation process. Before examining the verses in the Gospel, it is necessary to provide a brief over-view of the context here.

With regard to a three-day initiatory sleep, there are very few written references to this process, because the old initiatory processes were kept confidential. But references to a descent into the Underworld (the realm of the Dead) is a specific feature of the spiritual practices undertaken by initiates in the various cultures in antiquity, including early and Classical Greek civilisations, through into the Hellenistic era. Such a descent was called a katabasis, and is similar to the three-day initiation sleep.

It was believed that during this descent the acolyte would enter into the Underworld, and gain an objective view of his or her own un-spiritual qualities, and their connection to the various beings and influences in the cosmos. Then later in this process, the acolyte could ascend up, to directly see the deity of their religion. (These deities are not the high Father-God of which it is truly said that no person has ever seen Him.)

For example, at the oracle of Trophonius, situated at Lebadea, it was widely understood that such a descent in one's 'soul-body' into the Netherworld, was the means by which the priests or priestesses acquired the wisdom that was needed to guide their people. Quite a number of semi-legendary early initiates, referred to as 'heroes' undertook this initiatory process.

Such heroes include Musaios and Eumolpos, and the famous Hercules, all of whom were initiated at Eleusis. And reports circulated to the effect that the great sage Pythagoras went through this process, too. However, in the old myths and sagas, such a descent is presented in a simplified and discreet way, because it was forbidden to mention the secrets of the initiatory process.

Also, in texts from Celtic Britain, from old Wales, centuries after the Gospels were written, there are references to the three-day initiatory 'sleep'; especially in the collection known as the *Myvyrian Archaiology*. Since the Celts were in Britain long before the Hellenistic Age, these reports probably have their origin from a time before the Gospels.

The story of Jonah's three-day journey inside a 'whale' in the sea, was understood in mystical circles of old Celtic Britain to be actually a Biblical version of the age-old three-day initiation 'sleep' of the ancient Mysteries. This is shown in a poem apparently written by King Urien Rheged, ruler of Cumbria, in the 6th Century AD. King Urien was a prominent person in the initiatory tradition of his times. He was the patron of the initiate bard Taliesin, who was probably in residence at his court. In one line of his poem, he asks the potent question, **"Who brought Jonah out of Kyd**?"[284] The term Kyd is an abbreviation of Kyridwen or Keridwen; this is the Celtic name for the realm of the Dead and its spirits, and also for the goddess ruling this realm.

The three-day journey in the Soul-world resembled to some extent the first stages of the journey of the deceased; ancient literature refers to these initiates (heroes) as going to the realm of the Dead, so it is quite likely that this three-day 'sleep' was referred to as a 'dying'.

The acolyte was placed in a sarcophagus in a remote sacred site, and for three days journeyed through the Soul-world before being awakened, on the fourth day, by the guiding hierophant. At least four of these initiation sarcophagi still exist; in an ancient mystery Centre in Rhodope (Bulgaria), inside the Great Pyramid, at the Externsteine (Germany) and deep underneath the Giza plateau.[285]

The verses in chapter 11 can now be considered, and gradually their veiled message emerges. Lazaros is to undergo a similar experience to the central initiation rite offered to acolytes for millennia in Mystery Centres throughout the ancient world.

11:1 Now a certain man named Lazaros, was sick; he was from Bethany, the village of Mary and his sister Martha.

---

[284] Quoted by E. Davies in *The mythology and rites of the British Druids,* 1809, p.409.

[285] A contemplative study of these sites is available in my books under the name of Damien Pryor: *The Externsteine*, and *The Great Pyramid and the Sphinx.*

11:2 And, it was (this same) Mary, whose brother Lazaros now lay sick, who poured perfume on the Lord and wiped his feet with her hair.

This is another example of the Gospel mentioning an event which has not yet happened, before it happens. Most scholars agree that it is mentioned because the event is so well-known by the time the Gospel was written, it helps the reader to place the individual more clearly in their mind.

"Mary... poured perfume": that this Mary was not the same woman reported in Luke's Gospel (7:37-39) with the alabaster jar, is discussed at the end of chapter 19.

11:3 So the sisters sent word to Jesus, "Lord, the one you love is sick."

The sisters here used the verb 'phileo' which is a lesser form of love, akin to a warm liking. But the actual inner bond of love between Jesus and Lazaros (and his sisters) was 'agape', as v. 5 states. The sisters did not want to declare such a high and privileged initiatory reality, in a message being conveyed to Jesus by someone else.

We note that it was only after the life of Jesus that the lofty word 'agape' gradually became a more commonly used term. Morris objects that this disciple cannot be Lazaros because after this chapter his name never occurs again. But the reason for this is that, after he was initiated, Lazaros refrains from referring to himself, for two reasons. One is that a deep humility envelops such a Christ-initiate; all the more existentially felt by Lazaros, because he had received the initiatory name (Lazaros-John.)

11:4 Then having heard this, Jesus said, "This sickness is not there so that death happens, but to make manifest the spiritual power of the Divine, for it shall result in the spiritual power of The Son of God becoming manifest.

That Jesus did not go immediately to help Lazaros in his serious illness, is an indicator that Jesus is preparing to be involved in helping Lazaros on a different level. Verses 3 and 4 indicate that the outcome of this illness will be that the initiatory stage of The Son of God is achieved by Lazaros.

"so that death happens": as Morris points out, this is an unusual construction and means 'with a view to death' or the purpose of causing death. The implication here is that there is indeed a purpose here, but it is not death, rather, it is initiation.

11:5 Now, Jesus loved (agape) Martha and her sister and Lazaros.

This the second time that Lazaros is described as the disciple "whom the Lord loved". But now it is 'agape', a term which the Gospel writer, Lazaros, was well able to understand and use. It is this which has led many scholars, including myself, to conclude that the unnamed disciple mentioned later in this Gospel, and identified as "the other disciple', is in fact Lazaros (see also v. 12:17).

It is repeatedly said that Jesus had agape in regard to Lazaros. When an initiate (or Master) is specifically said to 'love' a student, this refers to 'agape', and signifies that the student has made considerable progress, enabling an inner attunement to develop between the two people on the deep level of the will.

Again, that Jesus did not directly go to help Lazaros, someone whom 'he loved', signifies that an unusual process is underway, and also that any such initiatory process is only possible because of the agape condition or inner closeness of the core of the soul of Lazaros with regard to Jesus.

11:6 Consequently, when he heard that Lazaros was sick, Jesus stayed where he was for two more days.

"Consequently": this word, omitted by the NIV, but rendered 'accordingly' in the NRSV, shows that Jesus, though knowing that Lazaros was ill, deliberately remained away from Bethany for two days (see below). This is another clear indicator of the unusual initiatory situation. There has to be a three-day interval for this initiatory process.

11:7 Then after this time, he said to his disciples, "Let us go to Judea again."
11:8 But his disciples said, "Rabbi, just a little while ago the crowd there tried to stone you, and yet you are going back?
11:9 Jesus answered, "Are there not twelve hours of daylight? Those who walk around during the day do not stumble, because they see the light of this world.
11:10 But if anyone walks around during the night, they will stumble, because the light is not in the night."

"light is not in the night": most ancient manuscripts have "because the light is not in *him*." But the invaluable codex Bezae has, as above, in the *night*; this will be discussed later, when vs. 9 and 10 are considered in more detail.

11:11 He said these things, and after doing that, he says to them, "Lazaros, our friend, has fallen asleep, therefore I am going, so that I may awaken him."

"our friend": this is a significant description of someone in the Gospel; it shows that Lazaros, although not one of the twelve disciples, is closely associated with them. No-one else is called a friend of the disciples.

"He said these things, *and after doing that...*" that is, after Jesus had spoken such words. It is a very significant feature in v. 11 that it emphasizes these apparently unnecessary words in vs. 9 and 10; words spoken prior to the declaration by Jesus that he shall go and awaken Lazaros. For this puts strong emphasis on those earlier strange words in vs. 9 and 10; namely about the twelve hours in the day. This is an indication that these words are alluding to an initiatory secret.

These words seem to be stating the obvious about traveling, but actually they are a veiled initiatory message. For if Jesus wished to say that there are many hours still left in the day, he could have simply said that. But in any case, the disciples are not concerned about how many daylight hours are left; they were worried about Jesus going into danger. Also, since lighting was not available in the countryside in those days, everyone knew that walking in the dark was unsafe.

Therefore theologians often conclude that vs. 9 and 10 are about making full use of your time, and also about having a spiritual intention in whatever journey you undertake, so that you always can 'see', or be aware of, what your plan is. When applied to the surface level of meaning, this viewpoint is not wrong, but a deep initiatory meaning is veiled here; this will be discussed at the end of the episode about Lazaros.

"may awaken him": this alludes to an initiatory event, otherwise Jesus would say, "that I may heal him".

11:12 Therefore the disciples said to him, "Lord, if he has fallen asleep, then he will be all right."
11:13 But Jesus had spoken about his death; however, the men supposed that he was speaking about the resting condition of sleep.

Here the word 'death' means a death-like condition which the three-day initiation process involved, since Jesus has already stated that Lazaros was not going to actually die. This is why the strange and cumbersome phrase "the resting condition of sleep" is used; this hints at a difference between resting more or less unconsciously in sleep, or being highly conscious whilst out of the body. The next verses confirm that Lazaros is not entering into actual terminal death; rather his sickness will result in him undergoing an initiatory process.

11:14 So therefore Jesus told them plainly, "Lazaros died."
11:15 And I rejoice on your behalf, because of this: that I was not present (when Lazaros died), so that you may be spiritually discerning, (when he is awakened); so now let us go to him.
11:16 Consequently Thomas, the disciple called 'Didymos' (which means 'the twin') said to the fellow-disciples, "Let us also go, so that we may die away and emerge, with him (Lazaros).

Verse 11.15: It has been an enigma for theologians that Jesus here is rejoicing; a widely-held view is that Jesus is delighted that the disciples shall soon witness a powerful miracle.

Verse 11.16: Most theologians interpret this to mean that Thomas is suggesting that the disciples should go and be prepared to die with Jesus. However, grammatically it can also mean that the disciples should go and die with Lazaros; and this is what is actually meant.[286]

"die": the verb is usually translated as, "that we may die with him", instead of "die away and emerge". But the verb here, apothneaskoe (ἀποθνήσκω), although used of actual death, comes from a cultural context wherein people had an awareness that the soul exists. So they were aware that the soul arises out of the death of the body, to find itself still existing, but now in the Soul-world. Therefore the Greek word for 'soul' (psyche - ψυχη) also meant 'butterfly': because the butterfly arises from the rigid pupa and, after unfolding its wings, then flies away – a similar process occurs for the soul after death.

So this same word was also used of putting seeds of grain into the ground, where they would decay (die) but later bring forth new life. When farmers used this verb saying that their seed shall now 'die', they were in effect saying that their seeds would decay, but then re-emerge as new sprouts.

Consequently, with this extended meaning in it, this verb was not only used of actual death, but also of an inner soul process, wherein one's normal personality fades away and a new, higher person emerges. St. Paul meant exactly this when he declared that, "I die daily" (1Cor. 15:31).

Most theologians are naturally unaware of the initiatory level of meaning here: that Thomas is referring with eager anticipation to spiritually dying and becoming re-born, as an initiate, together with Lazaros.

---

[286] Several scholars have concluded this; Meyer notes two such scholars: H. Grotius (*Annotationes im Novum Testamentus*), 1830; and H. Ewald, (*Die Johanneischen Schriften übersetzt und erklärt*), 1862.

Furthermore, the disciples could not go to Bethany to then literally die with Lazaros, because he was already dead, (apparently).

Verse 11:15: "may spiritually discern something": usually, "may believe" (in Jesus). But this usual meaning of the verb is less likely here, as the disciples already fully believe in him. This is all the more the case because the verb here, to spiritually discern, (or to believe) is an 'aorist' verb, so this process is just now about to occur; yet as just noted, the disciples definitely already believed in Jesus.

So here Jesus has just declared his joy that the disciples shall soon be perceiving spiritually a wonderful event (when Lazaros is initiated); he has no concern that they may all be killed in Jerusalem.

Jesus is rejoicing that the disciples may soon observe the initiatory awakening of Lazaros with a truly discerning gaze, which should strengthen into a real clairvoyance, whilst they are perceiving the event. When the Divine awakens within Lazaros, enabling him to attain the stage of The Son of God, this will result in divine influences enveloping Lazaros; an awe-inspiring experience for those who can perceive with higher cognitional powers (i.e., clairvoyance in a deeper sense).

Thomas has realized this situation, and he voices an optimistic yearning that the group may share in this attainment.[287] Morris comments that it is 'curious' that Thomas has the leading role here; but if the epithet 'twin' is meant as a zodiacal reference, then Thomas is a Gemini who voices a typically sanguine Gemini hope.[288]

It is significant that Thomas describes the twelve disciples as a unified group or 'fellow-disciples', the only occasion when this Greek term (summathaetais – συμμαθηταῖς) is used in the New Testament. Thomas is signifying that the disciples are spiritually forming into

---

[287] Rudolf Steiner taught that the word 'twin' also refers to the zodiacal Age of Gemini and how Thomas is linked to the initiation wisdom of that past Age, see my *Rudolf Steiner on Leonardo's Last Supper*.

[288] Rudolf Steiner takes this zodiacal link much further, but that is beyond the scope of this book (my *Rudolf Steiner on Leonardo's Last Supper*, comments on this.

a unified group, and inwardly belong together, as a new kind of higher community of esoterically awakened Christians. Possibly Thomas has intuited that after Lazaros is initiated, Lazaros then shall act as a spiritual inspirer for the disciples, unifying them even more closely.

We note also with v. 15 "Let us go to him" that Jesus here is inferring that Lazaros is **not** dead; for they are to go to encounter "him"; i.e., the person Lazaros, not a corpse.

11:17 Therefore, when Jesus arrived, he ascertained that Lazaros had already been in the tomb for four days.

"Therefore": another use of 'therefore' to signify that there was a specific purpose to the time delay which Jesus arranged. Both the NRSV and NIV omit this word.

11:18 Now Bethany was near Jerusalem, some two miles away.
11:19 And many of the Jews had come to Martha and Mary to console them about their brother.

That many people had traveled to Bethany from Jerusalem indicates that ancient church traditions about Lazaros are correct; that he was a prominent, wealthy, and highly respected man; a devout, religious person.

11:20 When Martha heard that Jesus was approaching, she went out and met him, while Mary stayed at home.
11:21 Martha said to Jesus, "Lord, if you had been here, my brother would not have died.
11:22 But even now I know that God will give you whatever you ask of him.
11:23 Jesus said to her, "Your brother shall rise again."
11:24 Martha said to him, " I know that he will rise again in the resurrection on the Last Day."
11:25 Jesus said to her, "I myself am the resurrection and the life." The person believing in me even though they die, they shall live.

11:26 and everyone who is living, and believing in me, shall never die (in spirit realms). Do you believe this?"

Jesus was aware that he was about to act as hierophant and give the command to Lazaros which would awaken him, bringing him back into his body. Lazaros is about to personally experience that the 'Christ-self' or The Son of God state arises within himself. This becomes possible if the soul is so spiritualized that the human spirit is able to emerge from dormancy into active existence, merging into the acolyte's 'I' or sense of self.

The Spiritual-self (Son of Man) and then the Son of God (or the Life-spirit) can be born within. The latter results in divinized life-forces, which leads to extraordinary healing powers; and a high cosmic-spiritual consciousness, as we noted with Ode of Solomon, no. 36.

Just prior to the epochal event of the awakening of Lazaros, the cosmic Christ speaks, declaring the above core Gospel truth: that the sense of 'I' which becomes transformed and sanctified, allowing these higher spiritual aspects of the human being to emerge in it, is taking its 'substance' from himself, the cosmic Christ.

So the person who achieves this after their death, shall have an aeonic consciousness (or 'eternal life'). And therefore, the living person also can be assured that, if their 'I' becomes sanctified, then they can achieve such an eternal, consciousness while still alive; as well as existing within this state, after the death of their body.

These statements, in their fullest meaning, are about a high initiatory attainment; but such attainments are a gradual process, so, on a more normal level of speaking, the statements in vs.25,26 are still offering a wondrous and inspiring way forward for all believers.

11:27 She said to him, "Yes, Lord, I myself have believed and do believe that you are the Messiah, the Son of God, the one coming into the world.

"I myself": not just "I"; the Greek presents her as speaking with personal emphasis.

"have believed and do believe": the Greek verb is a past tense: 'have believed', yet this is not meant to be understood as a past attitude; her belief is a long-term reality and continues on into the present.

It is a powerful manifestation of how early Christians viewed women as equally valid witnesses as males, that Martha declares that Jesus is the Messiah, the Son of God. (Later the first manifestation of the Risen Jesus was to a woman – an exceptional affirmation of womanhood in this male dominated culture.)

11:28 When she had said this, she went back and called her sister, Mary, and told her privately, "The Teacher is here and is calling for you."
11:29 When she heard that, Mary arose quickly and went to him.
11:30 Now Jesus had not yet arrived at the village, but was still at the place where Martha had met him.
11:31 When the Jews who had been with Mary in the house, comforting her, noticed how quickly she arose and went out, they followed her, supposing that she was going to the tomb, to mourn there.

In this group of verses we note that Jesus is wanting discretion from the two women; he does not want a crowd at the tomb. That is, after all, why he did not walk on to the village of Bethany and go straight to the tomb of Lazaros; instead he stayed away in some rural spot. Martha accordingly whispers to Mary to go and see him there. But Mary leaves the group of women in her house in a way which is too eager, stirring the interest of the group in her intentions. The presence of a large crowd at such a momentous time was not what Jesus wanted (v.33).

11:32 When Mary reached the place where Jesus was, she fell at his feet and said, "Lord, if you had been here, my brother would not have died."
11:33 Therefore, when Jesus saw her weeping, and also saw her companions weeping, those who had accompanied her, Jesus' spirit was stirred, as if in anger,

This group of verses is quite clear, except v.33, which needs some comment. It starts with 'therefore', as do vs.6 and 17, to signify a causative factor, namely the crowd was an unwanted factor to Jesus. The Greek text that I have used here is from the codex Bezae which makes it clear that the spirit of Jesus was strongly impacted by the situation and as a consequence, a mood of censure, almost of anger, arose in him.[289]

One reason for Jesus being displeased is, that Mary and Martha should have been more 'believing', i.e., more intuitively (psychically) perceptive as to the existence of, and presence of, divine powers in the Christ. But more problematic was that various people had followed them, and who would then gather outside the tomb of Lazaros. These were anguished and intrigued people, as well as some who were close to the Sanhedrin.

All of these factors were creating an atmosphere of distressed and negative energies. This is not helpful to the delicate and challenging action that Jesus had to soon perform, especially as some of this crowd were antagonistic towards him (v. 37). Moreover, as 12:7 makes clear, this crowd spread word of the event, creating a sensation, and this social upheaval was a major factor in the decision of the Sanhedrin to arrest Jesus.

A formal 'hierophantic' work of this kind was usually done in a strictly isolated and tranquil setting (a secret chamber in a temple completely hidden from the public). Acting now as a hierophant, in an informal setting, the task for Jesus was to bring Lazaros back into his body, and consolidate his new sanctified consciousness as an initiated 'Son of God', and awaken him.

11:34 and he said, "Where have you placed him?" They said to him, "Come and see."
11:35 Jesus wept.

The reason for Jesus being saddened is not stated, but it is not from grief over Lazaros, for he has not met his

---

[289] Other early manuscripts have complex grammatical problems, which have frustrated attempts to assess their meaning.

death; he will be emerging alive, after Jesus 'awakens' him (v.11:11). But since this verse 35 is included, and yet the reason for the sadness is not revealed in the Gospel, it is included here to encourage contemplation on this; in this way, it becomes a lesson in the mystery of death, since that is what the crowd understood the situation to involve.

Perhaps one reason for the divine sadness is that humanity is so unaware of the true nature of their soul imperfections (and the consequent impact of these on the life-forces); and unaware how these have caused disease and death. So people are burdened with potent barriers to finding the solution to their own difficulties. This situation is a major concern of Christ, since his core promise to humanity is 'eternal life'.

This poignant verse, 11:35, the shortest verse in the Christian Scriptures, echoes the initiatory insights of the Naasseni Gnostics, noted earlier,

"...Jesus said, "Behold, O Father,
how this being (upon the Earth)
The victim and target of all evil
Wanders, far from your breath.
It seeks to flee the bitter Chaos,
Not sensing how to pass through,
Therefore O Father send me....

11:36 So the crowd said, "See how he loved (phileo) him!"
11:37 But some of them said, "Could not he who opened the eyes of the blind man, have brought it about that this man did not die?"
11:38 Jesus, consequently once again deeply stirred in himself, arrives at the tomb. It was a cave, and a stone was lying across the entrance.
11:39 Jesus says, "Take away the stone." Martha, the sister of the person having died, said, "Lord, there is already a stench, for it is now four days."

Verses 36-39
v.36: the crowd misunderstood the sadness shown by Jesus

v.37: very likely spoken out of a critical, negative mood by people aligned with the Sanhedrin.

v. 38 "consequently": or 'therefore', as in vs. 6, 17 and 33; this again points out a cause behind something, here the displeasure the crowd was causing to Jesus, because of the negative factors this introduced. (All four instances omitted in the NIV.)

v.39 "sister of the person having 'died'...". The special verb teleoe (τελεω) was used here, which is not the usual verb for dying. It not only means to die but also, to be initiated. So the text can also be:

"...sister of the person having been **initiated**".

This is an example of the deliberately double-nuanced choice of words by Lazaros, to enable a veiled esoteric message to be woven into the narrative.

11:40 Jesus says to her, "Did I not tell you that if you believed, you would behold the glory of God?"
11:41 So, they took away the stone, then Jesus lifted up his gaze, and said "Father, I thank you for having heard me,
11:42 I knew that you always hear me, but I have said this for the sake of the crowd standing here, so that they may believe that You sent me.

As Origenes commented, "Jesus knew that he had been heard, because he saw clairvoyantly that the soul of Lazaros had been restored to his body, since he had been sent up into this, from the Soul-realm".[290]

11:43 Then, having said these things, he cried out with a loud voice, "Lazaros, come out !"
11:44 Then the man who had died came out, his hands and feet bound with strips of cloth, and his face wrapped in a cloth. Jesus says to them, "Unbind him, and let him go."

v. 44: "man who had died": the Greek word 'died' allows the kind of death to be either a literal death, or death in a figurative sense. The verb here (thnaeskoe - θνήσκω)

---

[290] The Soul-world, literally, "the domain of souls": tou choeriou toen psuchoen – τοῦ χωρίου τῶν ψυχῶν. Bk. 28, #43.

was used for either of these, and here it is possible that Lazaros did actually die from his illness, whilst he was in the Soul-world; but through the actions of Christ, his life-forces and soul were not irrevocably severed from his body.[291]

This situation of Lazaros having a greatly loosened connection of soul and life-forces to his body through his illness, was used by Christ to allow Lazaros to undergo, in a somewhat modified form, the ancient three-day initiation 'sleep'. Lazaros had to let his earthly persona die away, in order to be initiated, to become a vessel for his higher spiritual nature.

11:45 Thus, many of the crowd, who had come with Mary, and who had seen what Jesus did, believed in him.

Further evidence in verses 9 & 10 for the Awakening of Lazaros being an initiation experience.
The classical three-day initiatory sleep involved a 'soul journey' through various realms in the Soul-world. As the literature of antiquity shows, various Mystery Centres in antiquity offered this process, and one can assume that this included those of ancient Egypt. This journey into the Soul-world was called a 'katabasis' in Greek. But it is from Egypt that we possess the most comprehensive texts about such experiences; these are primarily contained in the so-called *Egyptian Book of the Dead.*

It is of course a question as to whether Jesus, in vs. 9 and 10, in referring to the initiatory experience of Lazaros, would be subtly making references to ancient Egyptian wisdom. That question will be addressed later, but a few relevant points on this question can already be noted here. The Book of Acts (7:22) relates that Moses was "learned in all the wisdom of the Egyptians".

---

[291] In Biblical terms, the 'silver cord' connecting body and soul was not severed, see Eccl. 12:6. This perspective may reduce the long-held veneration for Jesus' deed here as one which returned a dead person to life, but it may also deepen one's awe, considering the momentous nature of the initiatory deed,

Moses was ethnically a Hebrew, he had been brought up in Egypt in the royal household of the Pharaoh.

That Moses had been initiated in their Mysteries, and developed a high cosmic awareness or clairvoyant consciousness, was a widespread belief in antiquity. The underlying cosmological wisdom in the early chapters of Genesis derive ultimately from Moses.

It is no doubt true that such wisdom was handed down orally for centuries, and became subject to additional material and editorial action from later people. So the first five books of the Bible derived in essence from Moses, but were no doubt subject to some later editorial work.[292]

Although the spiritual wisdom of Moses was later specifically deepened through becoming the vessel of 'God' (of Jahve and Christ), nevertheless much of what he had learnt in Egypt would have formed a basis of his initiatory understanding. Consequently, many scholars have noted that the principal elements of the Creation narrative in Genesis are almost identical to those in the Egyptian (and Mesopotamian) Creation stories.

It is accepted too, that Psalm 104 has content almost identical to those in the great Hymn to the Sun from Akhenaton.[293] Also the names of at least three persons in the Hebrew Scriptures appear to derive from ancient Egyptian gods: Asenath (from Neith), Harnepher (from Horus) and Potiphera (from Re, the Sun god). Additionally, it is the case that an entire section in Proverbs (paragraph 22) is drawn from an ancient Egyptian text.[294]

So, now verses 11:9,10 again:

11:9 Jesus answered, "Are there not twelve hours of daylight. Those who walk around during the day do not stumble, because they see the light of this world.

---

[292] There are references to people or individuals who lived centuries after Moses, and the report of the death of Moses is in these books.

[293] This parallelism led Sigmund Freud to theorize that Moses and Akhenaton were the same person in his book, *The Man Moses and the monotheistic Religion,* 1939.

[294] See https://www.bibleodyssey.org/en/places for the specific details of these points.

11:10 But if anyone walks around during the night, they will stumble, because the light is not in the night."

It was noted earlier that theologians think that these verses might be about the need for sunlight when walking along in the countryside, and about the need for clear awareness of what your intentions are in life. But as Barrett notes, the words 'light' and 'hour' indicate that there is a more extensive meaning to these verses than simply the obvious one, about how long is the day.[295]

These verses appear to have a veiled message, reminiscent of ancient Egyptian initiatory teachings, about the journey through the Soul-world or 'Am-Tuat'. This journey is detailed in the *Book of the Am-Tuat* and the *Book of the Gates*; these texts and illustrations were put on tomb walls, presenting a journey through a realm which has 12 divisions or hours. These texts describe dynamics encountered by the Sun-god Re, or by a deceased person making this journey after the death of their body.

As the soul journeys through the twelve hours or divisions of the 'Tuat' the necessary source of spiritual light is present in each of these twelve areas, through various deities, including the Sun-god, who have that task. The light raying forth from these deities illumines the soul-body of the deceased (or the initiate). In fact, chapter 80 in *The Egyptian Book of the Dead* is entitled, "The Chapter of making the Transformation [of oneself] into the God who gives forth Light". The soul then declares, "I am (now) 'Hem-Nu', who rays forth light into the darkness."[296]

Such texts as these explain why the so-called *Book of the Dead* was actually called by the ancient Egyptians "The Chapters of Coming-forth by Day".[297] But towards the end-stage of the journey, an area of darkness is encountered and no help is available for the soul at that

---

[295] Barrett, *The Gospel according to John*, p. 325.
[296] E. A. Wallis-Budge, *The Book of the Dead*, London, 1969.
[297] There are many non-academic theories about this theme of the Bible and Egypt, which are often without any real basis.

time. The soul has to get through this darkness in order to find itself empowered and at peace, rejoicing in a radiant realm.

As the translator of the Egyptian texts comments, before the soul (or the Sun-god in its daily journey) can emerge from the Soul-world, "He must pass through a region...where the darkness becomes deeper and deeper..."[298] This is in the context of an arduous, challenging journey encountering both divine and malignant beings, in the strange Tuat realm.

Another ancient Egyptian funeral text is a prayer that appears directly relevant to vs. 9 and 10. The person is praying that an inner light may develop in their soul, to enable them, in their after-death journey, to be "walking in the night"; that is, to journey through the dark realms of the after-life,

"Let light be placed in my two eyes, that I may walk by (spiritual) night time, and also by (spiritual) day time; let me see the rays of the great god every (spiritual) day time".[299]

In summary, these initiatory texts from ancient Egypt are directly compatible with the words of Jesus in vs. 9 and 10. It appears likely that Jesus was indicating that, whilst Lazaros is out of his body in the Soul-world, the light of the Sun-god, i.e., Christ, is illumining the twelve realms he is journeying through. But he will need help for the latter stage of the journey, where an outer darkness prevails. So vs. 9 and 10 are saying in effect:

11:9 Jesus answered, "Are there not 12 light-filled divisions in the Soul-world, where souls are illumined by the spiritual Sun? Those who journey there do not stumble, because they see the (spirit) light of this realm.
11:10 But souls shall surely stumble in the 'night' division of the Soul-world, where the spiritual Sun does not shine – they shall lose their way, unless they are helped, because there is no light there."

---

[298] E.A. Wallis-Budge, *The Egyptian Heaven and Hell*, p.178.
[299] Wallis-Budge, *Book of the Dead*, Funeral text of Hertu, p. 689.

So when the disciples suggested that Jesus should not go to see Lazaros in Bethany, not far from Jerusalem, for fear of the Sanhedrin, he tells them that, nevertheless, he needs to help Lazaros in the darkened, last stage of his journey; and to bring him safely back into his body. That is why in v. 16, Thomas suggests that all the disciples should go along with Jesus, to share in this blessed stage of spiritual achievement.

There are further indicators of a deep, but veiled, link between the esoteric wisdom of the Hebrews and that of Egypt. In *The Book of Revelation*, (2:11) is the unusual phrase, "the second Death"; it also occurs in the *Egyptian Book of the Dead*. Chapter 135 refers to this, and chapter 175 is entitled, "*The Chapter of Not Dying a Second Time*'.[300] Otherwise this is a phrase which is very rarely found.

Also, one of two Egyptian terms for the Soul-world, 'Amenti' appears in the remarkable Pistis Sophia, which contains highly esoteric teachings from the risen Jesus Christ. Scholars date the document itself to about 400 CE. But I conclude, even though the document which has survived is from this later date, that the teachings contained in the Pistis Sophia go back to the time of Jesus. This conclusion is derived from the uniquely deep esoteric concepts presented in the manuscript. Also as noted earlier, the word 'Amen' may well have an Egyptian origin.

My suggestion that verses 9 and 10 contain a veiled reference to initiatory wisdom of the ancient Egyptians, implies that such esoteric knowledge was valued and kept secret amongst those early Christians who were aware of this. We have already noted earlier that both Clement and Origenes and others, confirm that esoteric wisdom of the early Christians existed, and was kept secret.

Further words from Clement of Alexandria demonstrate that this was done, and included ancient Egyptian initiatory wisdom. He twice makes a brief comment in

---

[300] References to a 'second death ' are also found in medieval Jewish literature, but these texts probably go back to the time of Jesus or earlier, and thereby confirm the existence of this concept as existing in Judaism as from Biblical times.

his 'outline of esoteric knowledge' book, *The Miscellanies*, that the Egyptians kept their esoteric wisdom away from the public in general.[301] This fact is also affirmed from various other sources; the extraordinary initiatory 'Hermetica' texts have their origin in Egyptian esoteric wisdom, even though preserved in ancient Greek, and various Gnostics affirmed that their wisdom derived from ancient Egyptian initiation knowledge.[302]

Clement comments that the twelve zodiac signs are the pathways of the soul out of earthly existence at death, up into heaven; and also they are the pathways of the incarnating soul.[303] This striking esoteric concept appears to have its origin in ancient Egyptian or Mesopotamian initiatory knowledge.

Yet these remarkable words are not given the slightest context or explanation, so one senses that Clement is briefly raising the veil on initiatory knowledge which was kept alive, but very confidential, amongst the early Christians.

This hidden aspect is all the more obvious when one compares Clement's book, *The Miscellanies* with his introductory book for enquirers into Christianity, *Exhortation to the Heathen*, where only at the end is there an indication of a private esoteric Christian initiatory pathway. We noted earlier this text in which Clement declares that there is Christian initiatory path, for which Christ is the hierophant.

11:46 But some of the crowd went to the Pharisees and told them what Jesus had done.

These people were presumably antagonistic to Jesus, and probably were those who had said, in a sarcastic tone, in v. 37, "Could not he who opened the eyes of the blind man, have brought it about that this man did not die?" Their negative response after witnessing the

---

[301] *Miscellanies*, Bk.5, chapt. 4, and Bk. 5, chapt. 7.
[302] In *Refutation of all Heresies* (Hippolytos) Bk.5; and in the treatise, "Asclepius 21-29" (#70) in the Nag Hammadi library.

[303] In Book 5, chapter 14.

awakening of Lazaros, and the response of the Pharisees, may have various causes (for example, v. 48 spells out a political concern). But it may also have been due to Jesus carrying out in public, against all the traditions around the Mysteries, an age-old highly secret initiation rite, although in a somewhat modified form.

11:47 Then the chief priests and the Pharisees called a meeting of the Sanhedrin. "What are we really accomplishing?" they asked. Here is this man performing many wonders.
11:48 If we let him go on like this, everyone will believe in him, and then the Romans will come and take away both our temple and our nation.
11:49 Then one of them, Caiaphas by name, who was high priest that year, spoke up. "You don't know anything.
11:50 You do not realize that it is better for you that one man die for the people, than that the whole nation perish."
11:51 He did not say this on his own; but as high priest that year, he had prophesied that Jesus would die for the Jewish nation.

"prophesied that Jesus would die": that is, his statements, apparently made earlier, that Jesus should and will die, are formally given the status of a divine prophecy because he was the high priest.
"that year": in that especially portentous year, as well as the other years in which he held that office.

11:52 and not only for that nation, but also for the scattered children of God, to bring them together, and make them one.

"make them one": this was a pretence, designed to give a veneer of justification to their hatred and intended murder of Jesus.

11:53 So from that day on, they plotted to take his life.
11:54 Therefore Jesus no longer walked openly among the people, instead he went from there to a village in the region near the wilderness, called Ephraim. He remained there with his disciples.

11:55 Now the Passover of the Jews was near, and many went from the country up to Jerusalem to purify themselves.
11:56 They were looking for Jesus, and were asking one another, as they stood in the temple courts, "What do you think?" Surely he won't be coming to the festival ?"
11:57 Now some of the chief priests and Pharisees had given orders that anyone who knew where Jesus was, should let them know, so that they might arrest him.

This group of verses presents the now decisive antagonism of the majority of the chief priests and the Pharisees towards Jesus; his life will soon come to an end. Some of the Sanhedrin, that is the leading authorities of the Jewish people, in Jerusalem, were well-disposed towards Jesus, but they were in the minority.

CHAPTER 12

From this chapter onwards, the Gospel presents the last week of Jesus' life and the significance of the events of Golgotha.

12:1 Six days before the Passover festival, Jesus came to Bethany where Lazaros lived, whom Jesus had raised up from the Dead.

"up from the Dead": The text here reports that Lazaros was brought up from the realm of the Dead, i.e., from being amongst those who were dead, not out of death itself.[304] For, the verse refers to 'the dead ones' (nekroen – νεκρῶν) and not 'from death' itself (thanatos – θάνατος). That is how the return to normal life was described for initiated souls in antiquity; they rose up from the Underworld, away from the realm of the Dead.

12:2 There they made a supper for him. Martha was serving, whilst Lazaros was among those reclining at the table with him.

"gave a supper": it is unclear whether the two sisters, or the general community, prepared the feast.

12:3 Then Mary took about a pint of genuine nard, an expensive perfume; she anointed Jesus' feet and then wiped them with her hair. And the house was filled with the fragrance of the perfume.

"wiped them with her hair": an exceptional action, indicating profound reverence, for usually only servants would have to wash their master's feet – a very lowly task. Mary had perceived the sublime spiritual power within Jesus that had healed and initiated Lazaros. (She was presumably unmarried, for a married woman's hair was always to be covered when in public.) One can

---

[304] Or being 'raised up' from, as the verb here has both meanings.

conclude that Mary did not 'wipe' away the perfume she had just applied; but simply removed any excess.[305]
"genuine nard": the word translated as 'genuine' is assumed to mean this, but it is actually unknown in all Greek literature.

12:4 But Judas Iscariot, one of the disciples (the one who intended to betray him) said,

"who intended to betray": following codex Bezae, instead of "was about to betray"; a minor correction, but one which points to an inherent tendency in Judas to betrayal of Jesus, through an inability to comprehend the real nature of his mission.

12:5 "Why wasn't this perfume sold, for about a year's wages, and this money given to the poor?"
12:6 He did not say this because he cared about the poor, but because he was a thief; he kept the common purse and used to steal what was put into it.[306]
12:7 But Jesus said, "Allow her to do this; for she has kept this perfume for the preparatory-day of my burial."

Mary has been anticipating the sacrificial death of the Master, and was intending to make her own contribution to the burial preparatory-day, which is when the corpse was anointed, prior to burial on the following day. (This verse is grammatically complex, see foot-note).[307]

---

[305] It is not helpful to understanding the presentation in this Gospel, to try to correlate this account with that of a similar scene in of the 'sinful woman' in Lk. 7.

[306] "to steal what was put into": hidden in here is an initiatory secret concerning the mysterious holy Grail; my "Rudolf Steiner on Leonardo's *Last Supper*" refers to this.

[307] There are difficulties with this sentence, leading to various versions, but my translation agrees with most official versions. Technically, it has a 'subjunctive' verb (taeraesae - τηρήσῃ) that seems to make Mary's actions not definite and to occur in the future. But many view it is an 'aorist subjunctive' case, which can be seen as a "periphrasis for the simple

12:8 You will always have the poor with you, but you do not always have me.

This verse is omitted in codex Bezae, but it is in nearly all other versions; whether this is a rare omission of a valid verse by the compiler of the codex Bezae, or whether its omission is accurate to the original Gospel, is difficult to assess.

12:9 Then a large crowd heard that he is there, so they arrived, not only because of Jesus, but also that they might see Lazaros, whom Jesus has raised from the dead.

Many early manuscripts have grammatical defects here, making any translation obscure; I have followed the Bezae codex, in which this verse is free of grammatical errors.

12:10 So the chief priests discussed plans to kill Lazaros as well,
12:11 since it was because of him, that many of the Jews were leaving, giving allegiance to Jesus, and believing in him.
12:12 The next day, the large crowd that had come for the festival, heard that Jesus was on his way to Jerusalem.
12:13 They took palm branches from the palm trees and went out to meet him, shouting,
     "Hosanna !"
"Blessed is He who comes in the name of the Lord !"
"Blessed is the King of Israel !"

"Hosanna": an ancient Hebrew expression apparently sung at the Festival of Tabernacles, which means literally, "Save (us) now (we pray) !" That Jesus was now

---

infinitive", of the 'purpose-result' type. This commonly follows the conjunction 'hina' (ἵνα) (Wallace, *Greek Grammar beyond the Basics ps.* 471-73). Such verbal forms are often the equivalent of 'future indicatives', as Robertson (*A Grammar of the Greek...* ps. 924-928) and also Moule (*Prolegomena* p.175) have pointed out.

at the peak of his social impact, intensified by his raising of Lazaros, becomes clear. Palm trees were a central motif in various ancient religions. They were depicted in Hebrew synagogues, and palm fronds were used, and are still used, in festivities in Judaism and in Christianity.

12:14 Jesus found a young donkey and sat on it, as it is written:
12:15 "Do not be afraid, Daughter of Zion;
 Behold, your king is coming,
 seated on a donkey's colt." (Zechariah 9:9)

To the Hebrews, entering a town on a horse was a statement of rulership, of power and of military intent. But on a donkey signified peace and humility.

12:16 At first, his disciples did not understand these things. Only after Jesus was glorified, did they realize that these things had been written about him, and that these things had been done to him.

The crowd was excitedly welcoming Jesus as their earthly king, having been so awed by the raising of Lazaros. The disciples did not immediately see a connection between Zechariah's prophecy and the entry of Jesus into Jerusalem.

The phrase "these things" occurs deliberately three times in these verses, to emphasize how significant were the events described here. As in v. 7:39 'glorified' means to be permanently raised to a state of higher, divine empowerment.

12:17 Now, the crowd that was with him when he called Lazaros from the tomb, and raised him from the dead, continued to spread the word.

This is the last time that Lazaros is mentioned by name. In chapter 11 and 12, Lazaros is mentioned as we learn about his awakening from a death-like state, or as reports are made of the social impact of this. As we noted for v.11:3, Morris objects, how can Lazaros also be 'the other disciple' – is it not strange to cease using his name, if he is also this person?[308]

To many, including myself, the answer to this feature of the Gospel is that, having been initiated by Jesus himself, Lazaros is now referred to in a very high, deferential manner, as 'the disciple whom the Lord loved". In an esoteric context, such a term can only be used of an acolyte after they have developed an 'agape' condition of a deep inner unity with their Master.

12:18 It was also because Jesus has performed this wonder, that the crowd went out to meet him.
12:19 So the Pharisees then said to each other, "Look, this is getting you nowhere. See how the world has gone after him."

These three verses (12:17,18,19) are emphasizing that the awakening of Lazaros made a powerful impression on the people of Judea. This impact is even more understandable when one realizes that a section of the populace had been involved with, or had some association with, the Essene-Nazaritic groups to whom the raising of Lazaros was clearly an astonishing hierophantic act, which had resulted in a new initiate.

12:20 Now, among those who went up to the temple to worship were some Greeks.
12:21 They came to Philip, who was from Bethsaida, and they were asking, saying, "Sir, we want to see Jesus."
12:22 Philip went and told Andrew, then Andrew and Philip went and informed Jesus.

"see Jesus": that is, to both experience being in his presence, and to speak with him. (The verb here in Classical Greek can mean to interview someone.) These three verses have an especially profound esoteric message. On a sociological level, one can conclude that this request from the Greek men is signifying that Christianity will spread into the Greek world, after the

---

[308] Morris, *Gospel According to John*, p. 478.

Resurrection, as the Jewish establishment spurns the new 'Jesus movement".

Also from the hesitancy of the disciples to introduce the Greeks to Jesus – as they were not Jews – we can also see here the radical implication for the Jewish establishment, that the Gospel shall soon be spreading to other ethnicities.

These Greeks were not Jews, yet they came in reverence to the Jewish temple. So they were perceptive souls, who were aware in some way, of the divine reality in Judaism; a reality which was now enveloping Jesus. Therefore they may have been involved with a cosmopolitan religious perspective nurtured in Grecian initiatory spirituality, such as the Eleusinian or Artemis Mysteries.

The sociological interpretation that these Greeks appeared now because the Gospel will soon spread to the Greeks, is without a firm basis, for actually the church did not spread just amongst the Greeks, but also amongst many other peoples. The appearance of these Greek men has a deeper meaning. The 'Hellenization' of much of the ancient world, through the conquests by Alexander the Great, had made the common Greek language into a universal language.

Thus Christian missionaries had a language available to them, which was known across the very many ethnicities in which they would be working in the centuries ahead. Their work would not be limited to the Greek people. So what is the significance of these Greeks appearing?

It was noted earlier that when the Jewish Scriptures refer to the 'princes' of various nations, this word really means the 'Folk-spirit' who subtly guides its populace. These Folk-spirits are defined as Archangels by Rudolf Steiner.[309] He taught his students that the Greek Folk-spirit surrendered its task of guiding and keeping coherent the Greek nation, in order to become the spiritual inspirer of Christianity, culturally across the world.

---

[309] GA 121, The Mission of the individual Folk-souls.

One could conclude that this is the deeper reason for the appearance of these Greek men at this point (and the decline of Greece politically). This event of the Greek Folk-spirit becoming the spiritual facilitator of Christianity, was intuited by the great German poet, Novalis (1772-1801), in his *Hymns to the Night*,

From a distant shore, born under the glad skies of Hellas, a singer came to Palestine and yielded all his heart to the wondrous child...
"Thou art the Youth who pondered above our gravestones, immersed in thought immense, a sign of solace in the dark of fears..." The singer journeyed on with joyousness to distant lands, his heart with dear love imbued, and poured it forth in fiery songs...so that a thousand hearts inclined to him, and the glad tidings sprang up, thousand-branching. Soon after that singer's departure, that precious life was a victim of the deep human fall....[310]

This mysterious 'singer' is in effect the Folk-spirit or 'genius' of the Grecian culture; it is from such a spiritual being that the language and ways of thinking of each folk receive their especial nuances.

12:23 Jesus then answered them, saying, "The hour has come for The Son of Man to be glorified."

To Jesus, these Greeks were a signifier that his earthly life will soon be over, and soon the Greek Folk-spirit shall nurture the spread of the Gospel message. They themselves were very probably aware of the age-old goal of the initiatory process offered by the Mysteries at their best: the birth of The Son of Man or the Spiritual-self.

So Jesus, as representative of, and source of, this sanctified ennobled human state, then speaks of several key events to be accomplished through his death and Resurrection. In particular, that he shall be elevated to an even higher state of spirituality ('glorified'), as the

---

[310] *Novalis, Werke, Tagebücher and Briefe*, Bk. 1, edit. R. Samuel, 1978. See, in English, *Novalis: Hymns to the Night and Other Selected Writings*, trans. C. Passage, 1960.

cosmic Christ permeates his being, for all eternity. Secondly, as a result of this deed, the goal of achieving The Son of Man shall become possible for all who so will.

12:24 Very truly, I say to you, unless a grain of wheat falls into the earth and dies away, it remains just a single grain, but if it dies away and re-emerges, it produces much fruit.

In this verse Jesus reveals in a veiled way, further secrets of the spiritual redemption of humanity. It is about what Rudolf Steiner's seership discerned as the 'multiplying' of the spiritual aspects of Jesus Christ. For Jesus will be permanently united to the cosmic Christ at the Resurrection, and then shall become the archetype and source of the redeemed, spiritualized human soul. Then those souls who seek spirituality shall have, as it were, a radiant light from the being of Christ Jesus incorporated into their own soul-body or even their spirit (i.e., spiritual-body).

12:25 Those who are fond of their soul, nullify their soul; but those who are repulsed by their soul in this world, they shall preserve it for eternal life.

In the usual versions, with 'hate their soul', this verse can be misunderstood to imply hating all of one's personality; this leads to an unhealthy distortion of what is meant. Below is the verse with some additional words to make its meaning clearer.

Those who are fond of their soul, nullify their fallen soul, in the spirit realms; but those who are repulsed by the lower qualities of their soul, as manifest in this world, shall become its custodian in a future aeonic existence.

The usual translations miss the esoteric depth of this verse: "Those who love their life will lose it, and those who hate their life in this world shall keep it for eternal life." For the verb here 'apollumi' (ἀπολλύμι) does not mean 'to lose' but to nullify or make void; and 'their life' is the Greek word 'psyche' (ψυχή) which means 'soul', not one's earthly life as such.

"preserve it": if there is antipathy to the ignoble qualities in one's personality, then one strives to ennoble the soul whilst alive. With the result that after death, the soul of that person is empowered, not disempowered, regarding the profound dynamics that envelop us in the spiritual realms.

The message here is clearer when considered with similar words from the Gospel of Matthew, (16:24-25). Just after the words about the cross, Jesus refers to the same demand, for those who seek spirituality, to rise above the fallen, earthly, illusory Self.

"Then Jesus said to his disciples, If anyone would come after me, he must disown himself and take up his cross and follow me.
For whoever wills to safely preserve his soul, shall nullify it, but whoever nullifies their soul for my sake, shall encounter it."

By clinging to an illusory self-centred consciousness with its many shallow interests and potential for unethical deeds, the opportunity to develop and spiritualize one's soul is neglected. But those who acknowledge the un-spiritual qualities in their earthly sense of self, can take steps towards developing and encountering a true, higher soul. In this sense the acolyte then 'encounters' their soul – its higher nature.

Both these verses are teaching about the need to overcome the illusory and ego-centric qualities of the normal soul, by bringing into existence a much deeper and nobler sense of self or 'I'. By contemplating profound spiritual truths, a higher, nobler consciousness develops, which is itself the expression of these truths, and these become the core of one's own new being.

12:26 Whoever serves me, let them follow me, for where I will be, there shall my servant also be. Whoever serves me, the Father shall esteem in spirit.

The spirit of the person who is truly following Christ shall then invoke the help of God, i.e., the dynamics arising from divine higher Powers, because the soul is now resonating with these holy influences. As a result, the sanctified soul is brought into the presence of the cosmic Christ.

12:27 Now my heart is troubled, so what should I say – Father save me from this hour? No – because it is for this coming hour (of my death) that I came into the world.

12:28 Father, make powerfully manifest your being now, with the radiant power which I had in your presence before the world was created. Then a voice came from Heaven, "I have manifested myself with power, and I will again so manifest myself."

Vs. 27 and 28 draw attention to a powerful manifesting of the Divine within Christ, and is thereby also an anticipation of the Resurrection.

"make powerfully manifest your being": usually, 'glorify your name'. But both 'name' and 'glorify' had deeper meanings in the Hellenistic Age than they have in the modern age. To 'glorify' is to make divine reality tangible in a powerful way; and 'name' meant the essential core nature of a person or a deity.

"which I had in your presence before the world was created": this in most translations is usually, just the short phrase "Father, glorify your name", without the additional words, "*with the radiant power which I had in your presence before the world was created*". These additional words are in codex Bezae.

They are an early expression of what occurs in more detail in chapter 17. It is also identifying the speaker not as Jesus, but as the cosmic Christ, who existed in remote Ages, prior the Earth being created. These additional words appear to be a valid original text, although preserved only in this codex.

Their validity is supported in that the words spoken by 'the voice from Heaven' refers to an earlier 'manifesting with power' followed by the declaration that there shall soon be another such manifestation: **Then a voice came from Heaven, "I have made**

manifest my being in power, and I will again manifest it."

But such a declaration is not meaningful as a response to the commonly used shorter version, "glorify your name", because this does not refer to any earlier time of already being 'glorified'.

"voice came from Heaven": this phenomenon is probably the same as a spiritual intoning heard by the prophets clairvoyantly, which was called the "bath-qôl" in Hebrew. This was well-known to the Hebrew people, as various instances of this are recorded in their Scripture.

12:29 Therefore the crowd, who had stood there and heard this, were saying, "It was thunder", others were saying, "An Angel has spoken to him".
12:30 Jesus responded, and said, "This voice has happened not for my sake, but for your sake."
12:31 Now is judgement of this world; now the Ruler of this world will be cast out.
12:32 And I, when I am lifted up from the Earth, I shall draw all people to myself.
12:33 He said this to indicate what manner of death he was to die.

"draw all people to me": codex Bezae and another codex record that Jesus said," draw *all things* to me". This is a more comprehensive declaration, but which of the two versions is the more accurate, is difficult to say.

On the religious-cultural level, these three verses are about the death of Jesus, whereby he is lifted up on a wooden cross, and also how, from reverence felt about this sacrificial death, people are drawn to Jesus. But this is not the full meaning, for on the initiatory level, these verses are subtly indicating a dynamic which the cosmic Christ shall be commencing at the Resurrection and Ascension': a dynamic of enormous significance.

Firstly, one notes that the verb here, 'to die' is the same used of Lazaros when he was being initiated (apothneaskoe - ἀποθνήσκω), which means a dying-away followed by arising into a new life. So Christ shall be dying, but then arising to a new, higher state of existence.

However, in this case, the verb is not implying that Jesus did not die; he did indeed die, but – the great core truth of the Gospels – he triumphed over the powers of death, and was thereby enabled to help bring 'eternal life' to those who follow him.

The implication here is that humanity in a future time-cycle shall move up into a state of existence beyond the physical-mineral realm. We will eventually be existing in a 'spirit-body', not a physical body, i.e., a 'body' formed of 'soul-substance'; and not even a soul-body as Paul indicates in Corinthians (1Cor.15:42-50). But as we noted earlier, humanity has exposure not only to one type of malignant beings whose influences harden the intellect and the will or volition, creating evil. The soul is also exposed to brightly flaming, extraordinarily attractive, wishes and yearnings which are subtly, but potently, self-centred.

A major concern of the religious life, as developed in various cultures, is to undertake prayer to avoid a future existence in some darkened, malignant state. But a second negative future threatens human souls; that of being attracted into a spiritual 'Paradise' existence, by a host of seductively appealing, but fallen, spirit beings. Such a prospect appeals to self-centred, indulgent desires and wishes; such a future state would be, as the old English maxim says, 'a fool's Paradise'.

In carrying out his intention of bringing Salvation to humanity, Christ is declaring that the Ruler of the World shall be defeated. This implies that the attraction of both these types of wrong pathways will be reduced; and entry to a wholesome and joyous kingdom will be made possible.

The Ruler of the World: the Greek has the word 'archon' which is a term used in esoteric initiatory wisdom of the Hellenistic Age to describe a ruling spirit power. This includes texts from Plato and the Hermetica literature (derived from Egypt) and from the Gnostics. But it is not limited to Gnostic-esoteric literature; it was also used in administrative documents for civil authorities, and for the Hebrew Scriptures when the word for 'authority' was translated from Hebrew into Greek. Just which malignant spirit is meant here, is not clear. One possibility is what Paul refers to as "...the Ruler of the Power of the Air" (Eph.2:2). This is where Paul allows a brief glimpse into deeply esoteric initiatory knowledge. For in the language of the Hellenistic Age, 'air' refers not only the Earth's air-layer, but also to subtle energies permeating the air, especially the regions above the tallest mountains. This area is what old texts refer to as 'the firmament'.

To initiation knowledge, this upper airy region, on a spiritual level, was filled with spirit beings, including human souls (those about to be born or those who are recently deceased). Pythagoras commented "all of the upper air region is filled with souls".[311] The *Ascension of Isaiah* (about 100 BCE, but re-worked perhaps as late as 100 CE) refers to the firmament as the region "where I saw Sammael and his hosts, and a great struggle taking place...there the Angels of Satan were envious of each other..." (7:9).

12:34 Then the crowd answered him, "We have heard from the law, that the Messiah remains forever. How can you say that it is necessary that The Son of Man be lifted up? Who is this Son of Man?"

"The Son of Man": this initiatory term was obviously only vaguely understood by the crowd.
The listeners believed that when the Messiah arrived, a kind of ever-lasting earthly Golden Age would be ushered in. But Christ is referring to spiritual processes; one of these is that he shall be firstly lifted up onto a cross, and secondly that he shall be 'glorified' or raised in a radiant manifestation of divine power, to a higher level of being. Thirdly, he is alluding to the need for all human beings who seek 'salvation' to attain to the Spiritual-self or Son of Man state.

12:35 Then Jesus said, "For a little while, the light is still among you. Walk while you have the light, in case the darkness overtakes you. For whoever walks in the dark, knows not where they are walking."

---

[311] Pythagoras (Diog. L. 8:32) quoted by T. Abbott, *Ephesians and Colossians*, 1897.

12:36 Perceive the light with discernment, whilst you have the light, so that you may become sons of light. These things Jesus said, then having departed from them, he was hidden from them.

If those who are devoted to Jesus and all which he represents, can attain to an intuitive cognizing when in his presence, they can invoke into their soul the Christ-radiance. It is from this that the Spiritual-self state or Son of Man state, derives.

12:37: Although he had performed so many wonders in their presence, they did not believe in him,
12:38: So that the word of Isaiah the prophet, may be fulfilled, who said: "Lord, who has believed our message and to whom has the arm of the Lord been revealed?" (Isa.53:1)
12:39 Thus they were not able to believe, because again, Isaiah the prophet said,
12:40 "He has blinded their eyes, and hardened their hearts, so that they might not perceive spiritually with their eyes, nor understand with their hearts, and consequently not change; otherwise I would heal them." (Isa.6:10)
12:41 These things Isaiah said, because he saw the glory of the Christ and spoke about him.

That people have become spiritually blind, and lacking 'faith', that is, lacking the ability to perceive in a spiritually discerning way, is a situation not imposed upon them 'from above', but invoked by themselves through pursuing a way of viewing the world which is not compatible with spiritual or religious truths.

12:42 Nevertheless, even many of the elders believed in him, but because of the Pharisees, did not acknowledge him, for fear that they would be put out of the synagogue.

These six verses show that, from his clairvoyant, prophetic faculties, Isaiah had fore-knowledge of the Christ. They also show that those who acknowledged Jesus as the vessel of the Christ risked being socially isolated and thereby financially ruined.

12:43 For they loved praise from men more than they loved praise from God.

"loved": the word 'love' here is 'agape', and hence refers to a deep bond and empathy for another, in one's core nature.
"than praise from God": this verse is usually "...than glory from God." The Greek word here is 'doxa', but here 'praise' seems to express the meaning more clearly than 'glory', unless the Pharisees were anticipating actual glory from God, occurring in some subtle sense.

12:44 For Jesus had proclaimed loudly, saying, "Whoever believes in me, does not believe in me, but rather, in the One who sent me."

In this verse, Jesus is not re-appearing before a crowd of people, making a specific speech, rather Lazaros is reporting key statements of what Jesus had said earlier.
"had proclaimed": here is the 'aorist' tense, which can mean a one-off event in the past, but can also mean, being fully completed in the past (the 'pluperfect' tense). This occurs elsewhere in John, e.g., 4:50 "...Jesus had said..." not "Jesus said".[312]
Verse 44 is providing a summary of the purpose of the public ministry of Jesus, which comes to an end here. The following chapters are about the end of his life, emphasizing the significance of his death and Resurrection.

---

[312] Technically this is where with an aorist verb, the 'antecedence' (the occurrence of the past) is fully in the past, ('had proclaimed', not simply 'proclaimed') but this fact was not emphasized to the Greek mind (Robertson, *Grammar*, ps. 840-842, and Bernard, Vol. 2 *John*, p. 163). Codex Bezae has here the imperfect tense, but not the 'aorist', so this version also means Jesus proclaimed in the past, but not so fully in the past; however it implies he did this on multiple occasions.

12:45 For the person spiritually experiencing me, experiences spiritually the One who sent me.

The verb here can mean either physical or clairvoyant perceiving; here spiritual seeing of Jesus is very likely what is meant. It is about seership, not seeing with physical eyes, because a divine being ('the One who sent me') cannot be physically seen.

12:46 I have come, as a light in the world, so that everyone believing in me, need not remain in the darkness.
12:47 And if anyone hears my words, but does not respond to them, I do not judge that person, for I did not come to judge the world, but to save the world.

The meaning of these two verses is clear.

12:49 For I do not speak from myself, but the One who sent me – the Father – he has given me a command as to what I may proclaim, and what I may speak.

Here two similar verbs occur, both can be understood to mean 'to say' or 'to speak'. The first verb (legoe – λέγω) is usually: speak, declare, or say. Whereas the second verb, 'I proclaim' (laleoe – λαλέω) can also mean this, but in addition it can mean to resound, or intone. So it includes uttering cosmic or spirit 'intonings' (as in 8:25) or hierophantic-mantric words (and also babble, hence it is used of glossalia or 'speaking in tongues'.)

12:50 And I know that his command – intoning in spirit realms – is life; so therefore what I speak, I speak just as the Father has given me.

The first section of this verse is translated in NRSV as:
"I know that his commandment is eternal life".
This is correct to the majority of ancient manuscripts. But it is often understood by scholars as needing some extras words, e.g., in the NIV: "I know that his command *leads to* eternal life". Or taken just as it is, scholars still interpret it in the same way as the NIV, without formally

adding extra words, but explaining that God's directives *are* what bestows eternal life.

My version of v. 50 is taken directly from codex Bezae; it says literally,

"I know that God's *eternal* word is life."[313]

But as noted before, 'eternal' (αἰώνιος - aioenios) in Greek, means of the aeons, or of the divine realms, the realms of spirit. So the verse is actually saying:

"I know that God's directive, of divine realms, is life."

The word 'intoning' I have added, since God's commands are naturally 'intoning' there; that is how Jesus perceives them.

I find this Bezae version a more convincing text, because God's command can only with difficulty be identified as 'eternal life' itself, for this is a promised characteristic of human beings; so, one has to supply some extra words.

Whereas, to say that God's directive, intoning through divine realms, **is life** is a clear and consistent statement. That is, where 'life' means the ongoing future existence of the Creation that shall eventually raise humanity up into higher realms. Such life is in effect the definition of God; of his will and core intention of seeking to let humanity spiritualize itself. This was discussed in Part One, Section 6.

This Bezae version is thereby consistent with v. 5:26 "For as the Father has (a source of) ongoing life in himself, so he has granted the Son to have (a source of) ongoing life in himself." I prefer the Bezae version, but it is unclear which of the two versions is the correct, original text. In either version, this verse emphasizes the interweaving of spiritual energies from the Father with that of Christ.

---

[313] Bezae text: οἶδα ὅτι ἡ ἐντολή αὐτοῦ αἰώνιος ἐστιν ζωή

CHAPTER 13

13:1 Shortly before the festival of the Passover, Jesus knew that the hour had arrived for him to depart from the world, and to go the Father. He had developed an inner union of spirit (agape) with the souls of his own, those in the world: with regard to the goal he had inwardly united with them.

"Shortly before": the question of just when the Last Supper occurred in relation to the official Passover Festival is shown with v.19:47. There are some difficulties in harmonizing the sequence of events in this Gospel with those of the Synoptics, but that is not a theme that needs to be explored, as this Gospel is presenting its own perspective.
"developed an inner union of spirit (agape) with the souls of his own: the usual versions are very different, being either,
"having loved his own...he loved them to the uttermost".
or,
"having loved his own...he loved them to the end".
The Greek text is ambiguous here, but both of these possibilities are less convincing compared to the third option, as given in my translation. As noted earlier, the word 'agape', means love which derives from an inner union at the core of each person. The core strand of the soul is the volition or will, the deeper intentions, not the emotions, although of course emotions are involved here too. In an initiatory context, this deep inner union is the prerequisite for the student (or mystae) to be assisted by the Master.

"the goal", instead of the usual, 'the end' or 'to the uttermost'. The word here is telos (τέλος) which can mean 'end' or 'the uttermost' as given in most translations; but it also means goal or attainment. This meaning of the word reflects its association with the verb teleiooe (τελείοω), which means 'to be initiated' (as well as to fulfill, or to attain). So this verse is about Jesus having brought about a deep inner union with his disciples, in order to assist them in their striving towards the Christian initiatory goal.

This goal is indicated at the end of this Gospel, where Jesus tells Peter, it is his will that Lazaros "abides here...until I am again perceived by human souls". In other words, for many centuries Lazaros, through developing ever more his initiatory state, is to remain, in some undisclosed manner, near to people living on the Earth, to provide inner guidance for them. (see under 21:23)

13:2 Then, the supper having begun, the Devil had already put into the heart of Judas, the son of Simon Iscariot, to betray him.

This verse points to the drama that is about to unfold, as the intense hostility of the 'Prince of the World' and his malignant hosts drive many of the Sanhedrin, who were already hostile from political-social reasons, to seek the death of Jesus. There are various disjointed versions of this verse; the above version is based on codex Bezae which has the clearest and most correct text for this verse.

13:3 Jesus, knowing that the Father had given all things into his power, and that he had come from God, and was going to God,
13:4 rises from the supper table and puts aside his outer garment, and put a large towel around himself.
13:5 Then he pours water into a basin and began to wash the feet of the disciples, and to then wipe them with the towel which he had placed around his body.

From these verses we learn that Jesus commenced a symbolic washing ritual. For an actual foot-washing procedure would start before the meal, and was such a lowly task that not even servants were required it do it, unless they were Gentiles, not Jews.[314] In such a practical cleansing act, the water was not kept in a basin, but poured from a pitcher onto the feet and then was caught in a basin.[315]

---

[314] G. Beasley-Murray, *John,* p.233.
[315] Bernard, *John,* p. 459. Normally the water was allowed to cascade down from the pitcher over the feet; and v.5 alludes

An actual hygienic cleansing foot-washing procedure, was carried out before a meal started; so this ritual of Jesus was not such, instead, it was a highly significant lesson in humility, which had two levels to it. There is an obvious ethical lesson about humility, but there is also a secret, initiatory level, which is a lesson about humility of a deeply esoteric nature (see below).

v.5 "pours water": normally in everyday feet-washing, water was allowed to cascade down from the pitcher over the dusty feet of a guest. Even though the ritual by Jesus was not an everyday cleaning of dusty feet, v.5 alludes to a cleaning action by using here the verb 'to throw' and hence 'to cascade' (balloe - βάλλω) not simply 'to pour'. After v. 16, the initiatory meaning of this ritual will be discussed.

13:6 Jesus then comes to Simon Peter, who says to him, "Lord, you are not going to wash my feet ?!"
13:7 Jesus replied and said to him, "You do not now realize what I am doing; but you will understand after these events."
13:8 Peter says to him, "Never will you wash my feet, ever !"
Jesus replied to him, "Unless I wash you, you have no part of me."
13:9 Simon Peter says to him, "Not only the feet, but the hands and the head also !"
13:10 Jesus says to him, "The person who has bathed does not need to wash, except the feet, for he is entirely clean; and you (ye) are clean, although not all (of you).

"you are clean": as noted earlier, the old word 'ye' is used to show when Jesus is suddenly referring to a number of people, even though he is initially speaking only to one person.

13:11 For Jesus knew the person betraying him; therefore he said, "not all are clean".

---

to this by using here the verb 'to throw' and hence 'to cascade' (balloe - βάλλω) not to simply pour.

The repeating in v.11 of words of Jesus, has an important function: it emphasizes that Jesus was fully aware of the malignant nature of Judas, but despite this, washed his feet also. This means that Judas was included in the process.

That Judas as a vessel of malignant spirits was included, signifies that the cosmic Christ has to include the factor of evil; for this is integral to life on Earth, and this is what Christ has to engage with. There is in this inclusive action, an indication that Christ shall seek to redeem such fallen spirits, in some distant time.
"For Jesus knew": from codex Bezae; usually "for he knew".

13:12 When he had finished washing their feet, he put his outer garment back on, and returned to his place. He said to them, "Do you understand what I have done to you?"
13:13 You call me 'Teacher' and 'Lord', and rightly so, for that is what I am.
13:14 If I, being the Lord and Teacher, have washed your feet, then how much more should you therefore wash one another's feet.
13:15 For I have set you an example, so that you may do as I have done to you.

Here one encounters a clear lesson in human social interaction. Verse 14, "how much more": this additional phrase is in codex Bezae.

13:16 Very truly, I say to you that a servant is not greater than their master, nor is a messenger greater than the one who sent that person.

These two similar statements are, on the surface, quite obvious, and hence irrelevant, for no-one disputes that a servant is lesser than a master. If these statements were reversed (the servant is greater than the master), then another lesson in humility or sensible social attitudes would be given. But they start with the solemn 'Very truly' indicating that an initiatory teaching is about to be given.

Rudolf Steiner's explanation of this verse is the most convincing that I have encountered. It is along these lines; firstly, a person (i.e., a soul) kneels before twelve people (i.e., their bodies).[316] To Hellenistic and later esoteric knowledge, the body has twelve parts to it, each a reflection of one part of the zodiac.

On this basis, an image arises of a soul kneeling in reverence before the divine cosmic wisdom which has designed and created the physical body (and manifested it by the zodiac; the vessel of the twelve-fold Godhead, revered in the Hellenistic Age).

Such divinely wrought perfection is sadly lacking in the soul however. With all of its lower desires, anti-social will, and empty vacuous thinking, the soul is distinctly inferior from this viewpoint, to the body, that is, to the wisdom underlying its design and functions. Awareness of this should inspire the person who is on the initiatory path to spirituality, to ennoble and purify their soul, to allow divine goodness to permeate it also.

Secondly, as a person moves towards initiatory consciousness, the inherent subtle egotism, or lack of humility in the soul, can become not weakened, but empowered, and lead to such pride that the Creator and all the other deities involved in creation are treated, semi-consciously, with a certain disdain.

The example of the various divine beings selflessly manifesting divine intentions, in service to the Uncaused Godhead, might be ignored, and replaced in the acolyte's soul with a veiled arrogance. But the messenger of the Divine, the person representing higher Powers, is definitely not superior to the Divine.

Contemplating these initiatory lessons can lead to the all-important question – what is my actual spiritual potential? That is, how do I myself become a vessel of the Divine, just as the body is permeated by divine wisdom raying in from the cosmos.

13:17 If you know these things, you are blessed if you do them.

---

[316] Lect. 26 June 1905 (archive document.)

This verse applies to the social lesson in humility, but it applies even more powerfully to the deeper, cosmically nuanced lessons in humility for those on the initiatory path.

13:18 the second part of this verse has two levels of meaning

      Surface level

I am not speaking about all of you; I know whom I have chosen. But it is to fulfil the Scripture, "The one who is eating my bread has lifted up his heel against me."

On the historical-social level, Jesus is saying that Judas, who is about to share a piece of dipped bread with Jesus, has decided to betray him to the Sanhedrin.

"lifted up his heel": this an old Hebrew expression for becoming hostile to someone.

But an in-depth study and contemplation of this verse following comments from Rudolf Steiner, reveals that it has a very complex grammatical structure, and this complexity is veiling an initiatory statement indicating that the cosmic Christ about to soon become the 'indwelling spirit' of our planet.

This hidden meaning in the latter section of the verse emerges when it is contemplated as an initiatory text. Then the following translation can be shown to be correct to the Greek,

Verse 13:18
The Initiatory level
The one who is consuming living plant food, is eating that which belongs to me, and those same persons are walking across me. (That is, across the surface of the Earth, which shall soon become my body)

These words were spoken not long before the events of Golgotha and are looking ahead in time to the momentous change in the Earth's spiritual reality, which occurs as a result of the Resurrection. The linguistic complexity of the verse is substantial, so the reader is referred to Appendix 15 for a detailed assessment of the verse, which demonstrates how the above translation is correct to the Greek.

The above meaning is not imposed onto the Greek, but is actually there, hidden inside the very subtle grammar used in this sentence. The sentence is especially veiled, as the meaning was apparently intended only for persons initiated into esoteric Christianity.

13:19 I am telling you now, before it happens, so that when it does happen, you will perceive that I am he (the Messiah).

This verse has the Greek phrase 'ego eimi' which can mean:
A: it's me !
B: I am he (the Messiah)
C: I am the *I-am* (in you)
Here it means B: you will realize that I am the Messiah

13:20 Very truly, I say to you, the person who receives whomever I may send, receives me; and whoever receives me, receives Him who sent me.
13:21 After he had said this, Jesus was troubled in spirit and testified, "Very truly, I tell you, one of you is going to betray me."
13:22 His disciples looked at one another, uncertain of whom he was speaking.
13:23 One of the disciples – the one whom Jesus loved – was reclining next to him,
13:24 Simon Peter therefore motioned to him to ask Jesus of whom he was speaking.

The key verse in this group is v. 23. The 'disciple whom Jesus loved' is understood to be Lazaros; as noted earlier, various scholars including myself, understand Lazaros to be the author of this Gospel. But substantial objections to this conclusion exist from other scholars. Their objections are derived principally from attempting to correlate the accounts in the Synoptic Gospels. Matthew and Mark both state that "Jesus and the Twelve" entered the Passover room; this would seem to effectively exclude Lazaros. However there is also an alternative possibility that Lazaros was somehow spiritually there (see below).

To seek to harmonize this Gospel's account with those of the synoptic Gospels, is not a fully valid approach. For this Gospel presents a profound perspective on the life of Jesus, in which the specific day-to-day details of his life are not the focus. It appears to have been written without seeking to harmonize its narration to the Synoptic accounts.

Even so, it is possible that the above words from Matthew and Mark do not fully exclude other persons, as they do not state "Jesus and the Twelve *only*...". Also Luke simply says that "Jesus entered with his apostles"; he does not stipulate exactly twelve. But these are weak arguments; the number twelve does appear to be correct. Otherwise, it would mean that Lazaros was seated next to Jesus, whilst John the Apostle was seated elsewhere. This is not impossible, but seems unlikely.

There is also the fact that the other Evangelists do not mention that Lazaros was present at the Last Supper. But they also omit any reference to the Raising of Lazaros, and they omit the Washing of the Feet incident. This implies that these Evangelists had the intention to omit references to Lazaros. On this basis, one could surmise that Lazaros was at the Last Supper, as an additional disciple.

The other possibility that explains the indicated presence of Lazaros is an entirely spiritual one, from Rudolf Steiner.[317] This explanation is similar to the phenomenon which we noted earlier, that within the persona of the Baptist, the lofty initiate Elijah was present. We also noted as a very significant point, that within Jesus, the cosmic Christ is present. With both of these examples, a dialogue occurred with the 'overshadowing' spiritual presence, rather than the human personality.

Did something similar happen between Lazaros and John the Apostle during the Last Supper? Lazaros had been through an initiation process. It is reported in Hellenistic literature that, during such a process, one is out of one's body and thereby enabled to cognize in

---

[317] From a conversation, reported in GA 264, p.239.

spiritual realms, being no longer cognizing via the body's sensory organs.

This indicates that Lazaros also was, in effect, capable of functioning out of his body, just as was St. Paul, who arose into what he termed 'the third Heaven' (2Cor.12:2); by which he meant a specific spirit realm.[318] It was believed by early Christians that the disciples possessed precisely such an ability, and actually used this to leave their body, and descend into the realm of the Dead, in their soul-body, to help the souls there.[319] This suggests that the Gospel account is based on a similar reality; that Lazaros too could be spiritually present beyond his body's limits. He could be present in the Last Supper room, and overshadowing John the Apostle.

However this riddle may be solved, it is the case that the Gospel records that Peter asked the 'beloved disciple' (i.e., Lazaros) to put the key question to Jesus about who was to betray him. Correlating this to the above two explanations, means that Peter's question was made either by addressing Lazaros who was physically there as a 13th person; or by Peter gazing at the Apostle John, but actually directing his query to Lazaros, whom he could perceive through his seership as a spiritual presence above John the Apostle.

13:25 Having leaned back, this disciple, who was thereby inclining on the chest of Jesus, says to him, "Lord, who is it?"

That Lazaros was near the chest of Jesus signifies that his soul, his heart, was in rapport with the heart of Jesus.[320]

---

[318] There are numerous inter-testamental Jewish texts in which an initiatory journey into various or all of the seven spirit realms known to these initiates, are recorded.

[319] Clement, in *Stromateis*, Bk. 6, Chapt. 6.

[320] This is the conclusion of Rudolf Steiner. That Lazaros was depicted in Leonardo's inspired painting, the *Last Supper*, as somewhat feminine, signifies that he had attained to the Spiritual-self stage, which was imaged in Renaissance times as 'the divine feminine'.

13:26 Jesus answered, "It is that one to whom I will then pass this piece of bread, after I have immersed it in the dish." Having therefore dipped the morsel in, he gives it to Judas, son of Simon Iscariot.

"pass this piece": usually 'give this piece', but the Bezae version has 'pass over to', or 'deliver to' (epidoemi - ἐπιδίδωμι).

"have dipped the morsel in": usually 'dipped it' (baptoe - βάπτω) but Bezae reports that it was a fuller dipping (enbaptizoe - ἐνβαπτιζω).

That Jesus includes Judas in the meal, by sharing a morsel with him, knowing that it was Judas who would soon betray him, is socially a very potent statement. For it was the firm custom of the Jews and many other ethnicities in the Hellenistic Age, that once you share an evening meal, you are being offered the hand of friendship, and so you are bound to refrain from any antagonism against your host, at least until sunrise.

But it is also a very potent gesture in terms of spiritual truths. For in delivering over to Judas the bread, he has been taken up into the divine reality and cosmic intentions of Jesus. Jesus is thereby acknowledging the role of evil as an integral part of earthly existence which has to be factored in, and worked with, in the endeavour to eventually disempower evil in the future.

A profound insight into this dynamic of working to turn the effects of evil into something positive, was achieved by the great Johann W. von Goethe, who in his play *Faust* has the character Mephistopheles state: "I am a part of that Power who constantly wills the evil, but constantly produces the Good."[321] The actions of Judas in all their reprehensible nature, set in motion the events which would lead to the death on Golgotha hill, and this in turn led to the Resurrection.

But the response of Jesus to this brutality, arising from his unconditional love, was to seek to ensure that humanity would find a way out of the evil side of

---

[321] *Faust*, lines 1336-7: „Ich bin ein Teil jener Kraft, die stets das Böse will, aber stets das Gute schafft."

human nature, and be redeemed. And this intention was triumphantly begun, in the Resurrection.

13:27 Then after (Judas received) the morsel, Satan entered into him. Therefore Jesus to him, "That which you are to do, do quickly".
13:28 Now, no-one reclining at the table knew why Jesus had said this to him.
13:29 Some were thinking, because Judas had the purse, that Jesus was telling him, "Buy what we need for the festival."
13:30 Then, having taken the morsel, that person went out immediately: and it was dark.

Judas departs to betray the Saviour to the Sanhedrin, impelled by the demonic entity now activated in him. In everyday terms, it was still before dawn, therefore dark. But in a masterly style, the Gospel also presents in these few words, the ominous strengthening of demonic influences, as hatred of the Messiah in malignant entities, senses an opportunity to destroy him.

However, in addition a further layer of malignancy pervaded that night, for it was believed in Judaism, that if anyone went out into the night before Passover Day dawned, demonic beings could possess that person. This idea goes back to the danger the Israelites faced in Egypt before the Exodus, on the night when the destroying Angel moved through villages and towns, to kill the first-born Egyptian children (Exod. 12:22).

13:31 When Judas had gone out, Jesus says, "Now the Son of Man is as if empowered, and God is as if empowered in him."

The verb here is usually translated as 'glorified', but this only faintly conveys the meaning, which is to be manifesting in an empowered manner. The verb is twice in the 'aorist' condition, and so it should actually be translated as a completed action, which implies the past tense, i.e., *Now the Son of Man has been glorified*. But this would be incorrect, as the Resurrection of Jesus has not yet occurred; so he cannot as yet be so empowered. The solution again here is that the verbs are 'gnomic' aorists, which means they refer to a condition beyond the flow of time.

So Jesus is saying that he, as the archetypal Son of Man, although not yet empowered in a new and high sense, can be regarded as so empowered, because nothing is more certain, more sure, than that the Resurrection shall occur, through which he shall be elevated to a new high status. His words also apply to the potential in humanity to attain to the Son of Man state. For the Resurrection shall indeed soon occur, because of what Judas is intending to do. The Resurrection shall bring about the gradual redemption of humanity, because it is already a reality, in the mind of God, or in realms of spirit. (See Appendix 15 for more about this timeless verbal state in 13:18).

13:32 If God is manifested with might in the Son of Man, then God shall empower The Son of Man in Himself; indeed God will immediately empower him.

This complex verse is declaring that, when Jesus as The Son of Man arises at the Resurrection, then God is 'glorified', that is, God will be manifesting spiritually within humanity in a more empowered way: Jesus is the 'first-fruits' of a new humanity. And also, as a natural response, The Son of Man (the Risen Saviour) shall manifest spiritually in an empowered way, within the being of God; and God shall ensure that this shall be the immediate outcome of the Resurrection.

13:33 Little children, I am with you only a little while longer; you will seek me, but as I said to the Pharisees and chief priests, this I now say to you: where I am going, you cannot come.

"as I said to the Pharisees...": Jesus had declared this to them in 7:34 and 8:21.

13:34 A new commandment I give to you: that you love (agape) one another, just as I myself have loved you – so that you then shall love one another.

"as I myself have loved" (or "as I also have loved..."): usually this is simply, "as I have loved..". The longer

version is that of codex Bezae, which enables a clearer understanding of the verse. The love here is 'agape', which, as noted earlier, is actually about attaining a goodness deep in the will, a condition which then allows a truly selfless love or good-will to form, bringing an inner union with another person.
Agape was discussed in regard to v. 3:16 (For God so loved the world..) and v. 5:20 (The Father loves the Son..."). The other prior examples about agape are in 8:42 and 11:05. As noted earlier, the noun 'agape' was very rare until the time of the Gospels, apart from a few instances in the Septuagint. Before the time of Jesus, there appears to be no record of people speaking of such a sublime state of truly selfless love manifesting outside of that love existing between divine beings, or of the love of a deity to an initiate in a Mystery Centre.

There is much debate as to what kind of 'new' love this commandment implies; but I conclude that it is not a new kind of love, but a new avenue for agape. It is about the disciples developing agape amongst themselves; they are to become a new vessel for agape, "that you then *love one another*". For they were already aware of this agape love from Jesus towards them. Now they are to attain to this with regard to each other, and help this develop between all those who soon shall become the Christian church.

So a momentous historical event is recorded in this verse wherein Jesus, himself the embodiment of unconditional love, requires his disciples to strive to attain this high state *as a dynamic between people*. His words took wings as Christianity was formed, and inspired vast numbers of people, even if the full character of agape, as something arising from the difficult challenge of ennobling the will (so much of which is veiled) was not always clear.

13:35 By this everyone will know that you are my disciples: if you love (agape) one another.
13:36 Simon Peter asked him, "Lord, where are you going?" Jesus replied, "Where I am going you cannot

now follow, accompanying me; but you will follow me later."[322]

13:37 Peter asked, "Lord, why can I not follow you? I will lay down my life for you."

13:38 Will you lay down your life for me? Very truly, I tell you, the rooster shall never crow, until you will have denied me three times.

V. 38: On the surface level, this prophecy about Peter's cowardice, when it occurs, graphically shows a weakness in human nature. But there is an initiatory level of meaning here as well. Rudolf Steiner explains, the startled crowing of a rooster at each sunrise is a living metaphor of the human being on the spiritual path, when that person awakens to the sheer greatness and majesty of the cosmic Christ, the great sun-god.[323]

Furthermore, the verse does not say, as most translations have, "before the rooster crows, you will deny me three times..." It has a much more emphatic tone, "the **rooster shall never crow until you** deny me three times".

The key to the initiatory wisdom in this episode is accessed through acquiring knowledge of the various Ages through which humanity has passed. In particular how, according to some ancient cosmologies and in the teachings of Rudolf Steiner, we have passed through three large developmental Ages, and are now in the fourth such Age.

So the lesson here in v. 38 is that long ago, during the first three vast evolutionary Ages, humanity manifested in lesser modes of being. The potential higher human self at first *slumbered* in the body, then *stirred* in the presence of its own life-forces and then was as if *dreaming* in the primordial soul. But after these three stages in its evolution, it awakens in fourth stage, as the 'I", the sense of self.

It is only in the fourth mode – the conscious earthly 'I' which is seeking spirituality – that the human being can acknowledge the Christ. On three occasions, i.e., in three lesser modes of evolutionary existence, the soul was

---

[322] The additional words, "accompanying me" are in Bezae.
[323] GA 93, p. 150.

enwrapped in something less than the 'I' with its higher potential, (in which the Christ may be perceived). This is why the odd phrase is used here, "the **rooster shall never crow until you** deny me three times." (See 18:27 for the Roman 3am trumpet call, known as a 'cock-crow'.) So this chapter ends with a veiled esoteric lesson woven around a cosmic view of Christ against the background of humanity's evolving.

CHAPTER 14

14:1 Do not let your hearts be troubled. You believe in God, believe in me also.
14:2 In my Father's house there are many way-stations amidst permanent abodes. If that were not so, I would have told you, for I go to prepare a place for you.

"way-stations amidst permanent abodes": the word here is monai (μοναι); it has puzzled scholars for centuries. It actually means two things, and they apparently contradict each other: permanent realms of habitation, and also temporary stop-over places. The context here is about the soul after death in realms of spirit, and the apparent contradiction is clarified in various Hellenistic initiatory texts, such as the *Hermetica*, Philo Judaeus, Origenes, Clement of Alexandria, and the *Sepher Zohar*.

The soul after the death of its body, finds itself on a journey through the 'planetary spheres'; this expression is derived from the geo-centric Ptolemaic solar system. In this widespread view of the Hellenistic Age, the orbital paths of the planets around the Earth are specific spheres, each of these realms are permanent abodes for various deities and lesser spirit beings.[324]

But in addition, the soul after death is drawn up through these spheres, remaining in the one or the other of these 'way-stations' for a while, before moving on towards every higher realms.

14:3 And if I go to prepare a place for you, I shall come again and take you to myself, so that where I am, you may be also.

"come again": different to v. 18, this alludes to when a disciple dies, Jesus shall meet that soul and lead it up to an exalted realm, which could be understood as the heavenly habitation of Jesus.

---

[324] In the work of Rudolf Steiner, this journey after death is extensively discussed.

14:4 And you know the way to the place where I am going.
14:5 Thomas says to him, "Lord, we do not know where you are going. How can we know the way"?
14:6 Jesus says to him, "The 'I' I am, is the Way, and the Truth and the Life. No-one comes to the Father, except through me."

Verse 6: Usually, "I am the way, and the truth and the life." This conventional translation has rich significance for many people. There is however, an esoteric level of meaning here also, which becomes visible when the Greek 'ego eimi' is understood as *the 'I' I am*, as in the above translation, just as it was in earlier verses (6:20, 8:28, 8:58, 11:25).

As scholars note, it is striking that the word 'the' is repeated in this verse three times; this in Greek, puts special emphasis upon the words 'way', 'truth', and 'life' pointing to these three nouns as having very substantial significance. This meaning is revealed in the initiatory quest approach, allowing the verse to reveal its profound, deeper meaning.

The sense of 'I' which is developing towards the Spiritual-self stage, will be imbued with 'the Christ-light'. Hence **'the way'** or the spiritualized will arises, bringing **inherently moral intentions** (or **volition**). Secondly also **'the truth'**, or the spiritualized, enlightened thinking arises, conferring **wisdom**.

Thirdly, one's **feelings and sentiency** are spiritualized, bringing purity and compassion. But these soul qualities impact on one's life-forces, and it this which brings **'the life'**; a blessed state wherein one's life-forces attain **healing powers**, through which the soul gains enhanced **artistic ability** (and appreciation).

"No-one comes to the Father": it is via these three modes of spirituality – the higher mode of will, thinking and feelings – that the soul develops its germinal Spiritual-self, and thereby draws near to the sphere of the Father, from whom the human spirit derives.

Note that Christ refers to "*the* Father", not '*my* Father'; this is because, as noted in chapter 6, the term 'the Father' can refer to a confluence of various divine beings and their influences, in sublime spirit realms from which all human souls were created.

14:7 If you have known me, then you will also know the Father. From now on, you do know Him, for you have experienced Him.

"experienced Him": usually, "have seen the Father", but no-one can see a deity physically. This requires seership, and indeed the verb here, 'horaoe' (ὁράω) is used for clairvoyance or seership, as well as for physical seeing. But even so, the meaning here is not that a clairvoyant beholding of the Father is achieved – that would be a very rare attainment.

If the meaning of the verb is regarded as 'seen', then that implies at most, an intuitive perceiving of the spiritual reality enveloping Jesus; since there is an interweaving of the Divine, with the soul and spirit of Jesus. And this can be validly said – but not regarding this verse. For that is what Jesus says in the next verse, when a direct clairvoyant seeing of the Father is requested.

So my version is the more accurate, because in the next verse Philip requests that Jesus shows them the Father; and then they will be convinced. Therefore 'to see' is not meant here, but the rare meaning of the verb is meant: to experience or to witness, something.

14:8 Philip says to him, "Lord, show us the Father and that is enough for us."

The subtle lesson of v. 7 has not been grasped by Philip; and it becomes clear that the disciples have not clairvoyantly seen the Father; they have had an inner experiencing of him.

14:9 Jesus says to him, "Have I been with you for such a long time and you still do not know me?" Whoever has spiritually perceived me, has perceived the Father spiritually.

So now, as they are yearning for a direct beholding of God, Jesus then tells them that, in a certain subtle sense, in beholding him, they have beheld the Father. As mentioned above, there is an interweaving of the Divine, with the soul and spirit of Jesus.

14:10 "Do you (thee) not believe that I am in the Father, and that the Father is in me?"
14:11 Believe me that I am in the Father and the Father is in me; or if you (ye) just cannot, then believe from the evidence of the wonders themselves.

In v. 10 Jesus is speaking to Philip, but in v. 11 he is speaking to all of the disciples.
"you just cannot": usually "if you cannot" as in many versions; however in Bezae it is stronger, "if you just cannot" (ei de maege – εἰ δὲ μηγε); and this additional emphasis seems justified here.

14:12 Very truly, I say to you, that the one who believes in me, will also do the wonders that I do, and shall do even greater things than these, because I am going to the Father.

The remarkable implication here is that in the future, human beings who achieve the Spiritual-self, shall have the power to perform even greater wonders – at least of certain category – than those of Jesus. This will be the result of Jesus ascending to the Father, for in some way, this shall assist human souls to progress spiritually.

This future achievement of human beings may also be caused by the evolutionary pathway of humanity spiralling ever higher upwards; so that a particular attainment in a previous Age is less than the same attainment, when it is achieved in a later Age.

14:13 And I shall do whatever you ask in my name, so that the Father is more manifest (in humanity).

"more manifest": usually 'glorified', but as noted for v. 1:31, the term 'glory' means to be more empowered and more radiantly manifesting.

14:14 If you ask me for anything, in my name, I will do it.
14:15 If you love (agape) me, keep my commands.

"keep my commands": an admonition, as per Bezae and many ancient manuscripts. Some manuscripts have, 'you will be keeping my commands' (as a natural consequence), which is a less challenging, and hence less convincing, prospect for the disciples.

14:16 And I will ask the Father, and he will give you another Paraclete, so that there shall remain forever with you, the Spirit of Truth,

"Paraclete": as with the term, 'Logos', the Greek word Paraclete has various meanings, so there is no one English word which does justice to it. It can mean: comforter, advocate, helper, guide and counsellor.

Here it is identified as the 'Spirit of Truth', implying that its influence shall provide accurate insights when the disciples are confronting difficult life-questions on their path of representing Christ and embodying his teachings. This term was soon to be most prominently used in regard to the Holy Spirit as that which came upon the disciples at Pentecost.

14:17 which the world cannot receive, because it neither perceives this being, nor knows it. But you know it, because it abides with you; and it will be in you.
14:18 I will not leave you as orphans; I will come to you.

That Jesus will be returning to his disciples, refers to him returning to their cognition, by being spiritually perceived by the disciples after the Resurrection and also at the day of Pentecost.

14:19 Before long, the world will not see me any more, but you will see me. Because I live, you will also live.

"will see me": re-stating the message of v.18, that the disciples shall have that seership or enhanced perceiving which will enable them to commune with the risen Jesus.
"you will also live": here 'to live' means to exist after death in spiritual realms, in an especially enhanced way.

14:20 On that day you will realize that I am in my Father, and you are in me, and I am in you.

"in the Father": this is a stupendous experience; to perceive that Messiah as an integral part of the transcendent Father-reality.
"that day": this appears to be not a specific calendar day, but whichever day it is for each individual, in which he or she encounters the risen Saviour in a deep meditative experience, or through seership.

14:21 Whoever has received my commandments and keeps them, that person is the one who loves (agape) me. The one who has love (agape) for me, will be loved by my Father, and I too, will love them, and make myself perceptible to them.

"has received my commandments": literally, "has my commandments"; this is a very brief phrase which may mean 'those in whose soul my commandments exist'. Adding 'receive' clarifies the meaning.
"make myself perceptible": the verb (emfanizoe - ἐμφανίζω) means to deliberately make oneself perceptible or visible to others. In other circumstances, a less dynamic word would be used, meaning to simply 'manifest' (φανερόω). This verse becomes deeper when the true nature of 'agape' is realized; it is an inner unity of being, a loving harmony between the volition or intentions of two entities. Because here 'agape' is so prominent, and is not so easy to understand, this verse is more clearly understood in a free rendering,

The one who has received my commandments and keeps them, is that person who has developed a love for me which arises from an inner unity of intention. To the one who has such inner union with me, my Father shall manifest that same love which arises from this inner unity of will, of intentions; and I too, will feel an inner union of will with them, and make myself visible to them.

14:22 Then Judas, (not Judas Iscariot) said, "But Lord, why do you intend to manifest yourself to us, and not to the world?"

14:23 Jesus replied, saying "If anyone loves (agape) me, their soul will live within my teachings, then my Father will love them, and we shall come to that person and abide with them.

"live within my teachings": literally, "will keep my word".

14:24 Anyone who does not love (agape) me, will not live within my teachings; indeed the word which you hear is not mine, but is of the Father, who sent me.

"live within my teachings": as with v. 23, literally "keep my word".
"will not live...": usually, 'does not live...', but here I am guided by codex Bezae, for its future-oriented text seems more correct, than the alternative 'does not live'.

**14:25 I have said these things to you, while I am still with you.
14:26 But the Paraclete, the Holy Spirit, whom the Father will send in my name, will teach you all things, and will remind you of everything which I have said to you.**

"in my name": that is, the Paraclete will be sent, imbued with the authority and will of Jesus. As the core founding group of the new humanity, the twelve disciples shall receive on Pentecost day such high spiritual influences that their Spiritual-self is born. In addition, a high deity, 'the Holy Spirit', who nurtures into ever higher spirituality this Spiritual-self, and strengthens its alignment with the cosmic Christ, shall form a specific link to these souls. Very little is said about the Holy Spirit in this Gospel, except that it is an advocate or comforter or counsellor.

14:27 Peace I leave with you; my peace I give you. I do not give to you as the world gives. Do not let your hearts be troubled; and do not be afraid.

"my peace": the world can grant some restfulness and inner peace at times, but from Christ comes the spiritual influences which help the soul to conquer the lower qualities. As this occurs, the Spiritual-self arises; it is this new blessed condition that confers true inner peace. The inner integrity of spirit, needed to conquer the ego-istic qualities, forms the basis for inner peace.

14:28 You have heard me say to you, "I am going away and I am coming back to you". If you loved me, you would be glad that I am going to the Father, because the Father is greater than I.
14:29 I have told you now, before it happens, so that when it does happen, you may believe.
14:30 I shall not say much more to you, for the Prince of this world is approaching; but he has nothing to discover in me.

V.29 "the Prince of this world": a term used to describe the Devil or Satan.
V. 30, "nothing to discover in me": usually, "nothing in me": this brief expression means that there is nothing in the soul-spirit of Jesus which belongs to the Devil. But codex Bezae, and a few later manuscripts, have an additional verb, 'to discover'. This creates a more likely meaning, i.e., that the Devil shall discover nothing in Jesus that resonates with him.

14:31 But so that the world may know that I love (agape) the Father, and I do just as the Father has commanded me – arise, let us set out.

This verse is ambiguous in Greek, and so various translations have resulted. I find the above version to be the most satisfactory, as do various scholars. Jesus is saying that in setting out into the pre-sunrise twilight, to encounter the temple guards and Judas, he is showing that he is obeying God's will. He is accepting the path to Golgotha.

CHAPTER 15

15:1 I myself am the true vine, and my Father is the vine grower.

"I myself am the true vine": the Greek is very emphatic, using "ego eimi"; this means in effect, "I, even I, am the true vine".

15:2 Every branch in me not bearing fruit he removes, and every branch bearing fruit he prunes, so that it bears much fruit.
15:3 You are already clean because of the word which I have spoken to you.

"clean": that is, purified of soul imperfections, jut a pruned branch becomes free of disease.

15:4 Remain in me, and I in you. Just as the branch is not able to bear fruit by itself, unless it remains on the vine, neither can you, unless you remain in me.

"because of the word:" 'word' here is an idiom for the teachings that Jesus has given.
"remains on the vine" and "remain in me": these verbs are not describing a simple present situation. They are declaring that the branch has to continue on, in the future, remaining as part of the vine, as a completed fact; and likewise the human being must continue on remaining within the Christ-reality, as a completed decision.[325]

---

[325] Technically, this 'futural' nuance is found in Bezae through its verbs having a 'aorist subjunctive' case; such a verbal condition is in effect functioning as a 'future indicative'. Other manuscripts have the simple present subjunctive (you would be remaining), which fail to present the meaning here. Morris states (*John*, p. 595) that it is only these two verbs and a verb in Lk. 13:3 in the entire New Testament which, as present-tense verbs, incorrectly follow 'unless' (ἐὰν μή). But codex Bezae's superior 'aorist' version should be followed; then these three ungrammatical instances are no longer there.

15:5 I am the vine, you are the branches, those who abide in me, and I in them, bear much fruit, because separated from me you can do nothing.

15:6 Unless a person remains in me, that person is cast out, like the branch, and withers; such branches are gathered up and cast into the fire, and burned.[326]

15:7 If you remain in me, and my words abide in you, ask for whatever you wish, and it will be done for you.

15:8 By this shall my Father become powerfully manifest in humanity: that you bear much fruit, and become my disciples.

15:8, "Father powerfully manifest....": usually, "my Father is glorified"; but this old expression fails to convey the profound meaning here. It is about the immanence of God; i.e., that God (or 'The Soul of the World') is present in a veiled way behind all Creation, and thus within humanity. But as newly sanctified souls arise (as initiates), in whom the Divine is awakened, then the Father becomes more dynamically present in humanity. God thereby becomes more dynamically active within human beings.

"and become my disciples": following Bezae, where the verb is 'aorist', so the event occurs once only and then the disciple remains in that blessed state for the future. Other versions have a simple future tense verb, "so shall you become my disciples".

15:9 As the Father has love (agape) with me, so have I loved you: remain in this love of mine.

As noted earlier, the word agape means an inner unity born of selfless love, into the level of the will, between two entities.

15:10 If you keep my commands, you shall remain in my love (agape), just as I have kept the command of my Father, and remain in his love.

---

[326] Technically 'gathered' (συνάγουσιν) and 'cast' (βάλλουσιν) are 'present active' cases, but here they are distinctly 'passive' verbs; Barrett concludes (*John*, p. 396), this is an indicator that they were translated from Aramaic or Hebrew notes.

15:11 These things I have spoken to you, that my joy may be in you, and that your joy may be complete.
15:12 This is my command: that you manifest love (agape) between each other, just as I have loved you.

This command repeats what was said in v. 13:34, that Christ seeks to enable people to achieve agape or a deep inner unity with each other, based on a selfless goodwill. This urging to find a selfless deep love for our fellow human beings is a core teaching in this Gospel.

15:13 No-one has greater love (agape) than this; that they lay down their soul for the sake of their friends.

The context here is the disciples learning to develop this highest form of love, which prior to Jesus was otherwise only briefly mentioned in earlier literature. In those instances, it was about a bond between a deity and an initiate (except, in a few rare instances, between people). What is meant is that one 'lays down', or subordinates, one's own persona with its subtle egotism, in regard to the needs and hopes of other people.

15:14 You are my friends if you do what I command you.
15:16 I do not call you servants any longer, because the servant does not know what the master is doing. But I have called you friends, because I have made known to you everything which I have heard from my Father.
15:17 I am giving you these commands so that you may love (agape) one another.
15:18 If the world hates you, be mindful that it hated me before it hated you.
15:19 If you belonged to the world, the world would have liked you, as its own. Because you are not of the world, I have chosen you out of the world – therefore the world hates you.
15:20 Remember the saying which I told you, "A servant is not greater than his master". If they persecuted me, they will persecute you. But if they kept true to my word, they shall also keep true to yours.

15:21 But those who will persecute you, do so because of my name, because they do not know the One who sent me.

"because of my name": as noted earlier, 'my name' means the spiritual might and authority and especial nature of a person or a deity; in this case, Jesus. His powerful reality was either not understandable or not perceptible to many people, who then reacted poorly.

15:22 If I had not come and spoken to them, they would not have sin; but now they have no excuse for their sin.
15:23 The one who hates me, hates my Father.
15:24 If I had not done the wonders amongst them, which no-one else did, they would not have sin.
15:25 But this was to fulfil the word that is written in their law, "They hated me without any cause".
15:26 When the Paraclete comes, the Spirit of Truth, whom I will send to you from the Father, who derives from the Father, that one will testify on my behalf.
15:27 You also are to testify, because you have been with me since the beginning.

CHAPTER 16

16:1 All this I have told you, so that you do not fall away.
16:2 They will put you out of the synagogue; in fact, the time is coming when those who kill you will presume that they are serving God.
16:3 And these things they shall do, because they have not known the Father or me.

"not known": meaning those who are hostile did not intuitively perceive the high spiritual nature of Jesus nor were they aware of the cosmic Christ enveloping him.[327]

16:4 Therefore these things I have spoken to you so that when their time comes, you may remember that I warned you about them. I did not say these things to you from the beginning because I was with you.
16:5 But now I am going to Him who sent me. None of you asks me, "Where are you going?"

"None of you asks": this appears to be a contradiction because earlier, Peter had asked about this (in 13:36):
Simon Peter asked him, "Lord, where are you going?" Jesus replied, "Where I am going you cannot now follow, accompanying me, but you will follow me later."
A clear answer to this contradiction is not available. But Jesus may be admonishing them here, in that they have not intuited that soon he will have departed. It is also the case that it has been some time since Jesus has specified that he is departing; that was in chapter 13:36 and 14:5.

But as various scholars conclude the solution may be that, in the earlier chapter Peter was enquiring from the impulsive viewpoint of 'you are *leaving* us, so can I *follow* you?' rather than, the contemplative 'to which sublime spirit realm are you going within the many-layered cosmos?

---

[327] John the Baptist called the cosmic Christ, the 'Lamb of God'.

16:6 But because I have said these things, sorrow has filled your heart.
16:7 But truly do I say to you, it is better for you that I am departing, for if I do not go away, the Paraclete will not come to you. But if I depart, I will send him to you.

Only after Jesus has arisen, as the first-fruit of the new sanctified humanity, will it be possible for him to begin the task of assisting humanity's spiritualization. Because he has then become Jesus Christ, that is, permanently part of a sublime cosmic deity.

Then he has the authority, and also has become the anticipatory model (archetype) of what we are to be in the far future. These two factors enable the sending of the Paraclete whose task is to help humanity move ever closer to the ideal, the archetype of which is Jesus Christ.

The above remarks derive from vs. 15:3,4, and 8 and reflect the view that Salvation can be understood in a more nuanced way. That the deed of Christ on Golgotha had provided the possibility for people to spiritualize (over life-times); but that it is possible for the soul to waver, even to fall away. So these verses indicate that there is an area of freedom here, showing that the final perfecting of souls is not 'automatically' guaranteed. (See the discussion in Part One, Section 3, on Salvation about this.)

16:8 When he comes here, he will expose the failings of the world, as regards sin and righteousness and judgement.
16:9 Concerning sin, in that people do not intuitively discern my nature.

"expose the failings": this phrase is complex in its nuance in Greek, and thus is translated in many ways. It is declaring that the Paraclete shall discreetly bring awareness to seeking human beings as to errors and limitations in our understanding of various deeper life-questions.

"intuitively discern my nature": this is to be preferred to the usual, "believe in me". The Greek does not say, 'believe me' which would be a justifiable demand; it literally says (in one meaning of the verb) 'believe *in* me"; which seems to miss the solemnity of the situation. In a more sophisticated meaning of the verb, it is about perception, not only belief. It is then referring to intuitive perceiving regarding the Messiah; the failing of the soul to discern the nature of Christ.

16:10 and concerning righteousness, because I am going to the Father, where you can no longer see me.

"righteousness": this word is rarely used outside of Biblical studies, and means in effect, a deep spirituality in which there is a reverence for holy wisdom, and then applying this to personal conduct. Here Jesus is pointing out that the subtle effect of the Paraclete's influence on our consciousness is, to make people conscious that, unless one attains high spirituality, the soul cannot perceive the realm of the Father.

The help of the Holy Spirit is given, to inspire effort towards the very demanding ideal of humanity becoming able to exist with the Saviour in high spirit realms, on into the far future, even when the Earth no longer exists.

16:11 and concerning discernment, because the ruler of this world has been judged.

"ruler": the word 'archon' is used, to specifically refer to a fallen spirit being.

"discernment": in the Greek, this word is usually translated 'judgement' as is also the last word. But it can also mean 'discernment', and this seems more meaningful here. That is, people have not shown discernment (and therefore judgement) in regard to the fallen spirit being, the 'archon', who maintains the fallen sinful nature, and instils a 'matter-bound' consciousness in the unawakened human soul. But Christ shall judge this entity and weaken its power; and so people are being admonished to strive for this discernment of the two adversarial influences. For the deed of Christ enables the striving soul to perceive the influences of the negative beings.

16:12 I have much more to say to you, more than you can now bear,
16:13 but when he comes, the Spirit of Truth, he will guide you into every truth. He shall not speak on his own, he shall speak only what he hears, and he will tell you of things that are yet to come.
16:14 And he shall make powerfully manifest my being, because what he shall make known, he shall receive from me.

"make powerfully manifest": this is preferred over the usual, 'will glorify me", as this tends to suggest bringing glory or praise to Jesus in an earthly, personal sense.

16:15 All that belongs to the Father is mine. For this reason I said that the Paraclete shall receive what is mine, and declare it to you.

The Paraclete hears from the Father the wisdom which he then seeks to communicate to human beings; but because Jesus is at one with Father, the wisdom given by the Paraclete can be experienced as coming from Jesus.

16:16 A little while and you will no longer see me, then again a little while, and you will see me.
16:17 Then some of his disciples said to one another, "What does he mean by saying, 'A little while and you will no longer see me, then again a little while, and you will see me', and 'because I am going to the Father?
16:18 Therefore they kept asking, "What does he mean by 'a little while'?
16:19 Jesus knew that they were wanting to ask him about this, so he said to them, "Are you asking among yourselves about this, what I meant when I said, "A little while and you will no longer see me, then again a little while and you will see me'?

This seeing and then not seeing, refers to the disappearing of Jesus at the Ascension, some 40 days after the Resurrection, and then the renewed perceiving of him, came 10 days later, at the Pentecost event.
This phrase, 'little while' is very emphasized. The most helpful answer to this emphasis I found from Rudolf

Steiner, who explains that, when the disciples' seership does lose sight of Jesus at the Ascension, they are plunged into immense grief.[328]

But it is through the effect of this grief on their souls, that an inner re-configuring of their consciousness occurred, and therefore their cognitional ability too; in other words, a higher seership arose. This was a crucial factor in making possible a full cognizing of the Holy Spirit at the Pentecost event; and from this Christianity was born.

16:20 Very truly, I say to you, you will weep and mourn, but the world shall rejoice; you will grieve, but your grief shall turn into joy.

The disciples' grief at the Ascension, when it seems that all connection to Jesus is lost as he fades from their limited seership, turns to joy at the Pentecost event. These words can also apply to the death on the cross followed by the reports of, and experiences of, the Resurrection of Jesus.

16:21 A woman giving birth has suffering, but when her baby is born, she forgets the suffering because of her joy that a child is born into the world.
16:22 So, soon you shall have pain, but I will see you again and you will then rejoice, and no-one will take away your joy.
16:23 On that day you will not ask anything of me. Very truly, whatever you ask the Father in my name, he will give to you.
16:24 Until now, you have not asked for anything in my name, but ask and you will receive, that your joy may be complete.

"in my name": this may not refer to asking by invoking the specific name of Jesus. It may refer to asking inwardly as a person with Christian initiation consciousness. That is, with an inner closeness (agape) to Jesus, whose spiritual qualities permeate the soul,

---

[328] GA 226, lect. 20 May, 1923.

and through this, a Christ-presence is interwoven with what they are asking for.

16:25 I have said these things to you in figures of speech. The hour is coming when I shall no longer speak to you in figures of speech, for I shall tell you plainly of the Father.
16:26 On that day, you will ask in my name. I do not say to you that I will ask the Father on your behalf,
16:27 because the Father himself loves (phileo) you, because you have loved (phileo) me, and have perceived that I came from God.

"love": here 'phileo' is used, not agape, because unlike Lazaros, the disciples had not as yet attained to the agape closeness to Jesus and therefore to 'God'. Hence God (meaning an aspect of the Divine) has an inner bond with these disciples, but not, as yet, the higher agape union.

In v.13:1 it was declared that Jesus had brought about an agape union with the disciples; but this was from Jesus towards them, it was not fully achieved by the disciples themselves, in regard to Jesus or to each other.

Jesus will not be asking God in regard to what the disciples are seeking, for they shall be able to pray to God directly, since they are close to Jesus, and he is at one with God.

16:28 I came from the Father, and entered the world; I am leaving the world and going back to the Father.
16:29 His disciples are saying; "See, now you are speaking plainly, no longer in parables !

"See"; the Greek here is 'ide' (ἴδε) which is a powerful emphatic. It can translated as 'Behold !', 'Look !' or 'See !'

16:30 Now we know that you know all things and that you have no need for anyone to question you. By this, we believe that you came forth from God.
16:31 Jesus answered them, "Do you now believe?"
16:32 Behold – the hour is coming, and has now arrived, when you will be scattered, each to his home, and you will leave me alone, yet I am not alone because the Father is with me.

16:33 These things I have spoken, so that in me you may have peace. In the world you face persecution; but have courage, be cheerful; I have conquered the world.

"peace": As with v. 14:27, peace refers to the new blessed condition that arises as the 'Son of Man' or Spiritual-self state is developed; it is this which confers true inner peace. It is from the Christ that this high spirituality has its origin.

CHAPTER 17

This chapter contains what is often referred to as 'The Prayer of the High Priest'; it is the deepest section of this Gospel. For it is here that the cosmic Christ speaks, directly referring to Jesus as a separate entity (see v. 3). This remarkable situation was noted already in Part One, Section 4.

As noted in earlier verses, a deity or semi-divine being does speak through a prophet, such as Elijah or an Angel speaking through the Baptist. This is a deep and core truth in the Hebrew Scriptures, where 'God' is understood to speak through the prophets. Moreover, as in many of the prophets, such as Jeremiah, (e.g., chapter six), at times it is clearly JHVH who is speaking, whilst at other times, it is the prophet speaking.

Yet in other verses, it appears that both JHVH and Jeremiah are speaking as one, as if their intentions and thereby their words, are interwoven. The same dynamic is occurring in the first verses of chapter 17; a deity is speaking – the cosmic Christ.

This chapter commences with profound words spoken by the Christ; that is, verses 1 to 5. Thereafter, from v.6, it is Jesus who is speaking. Although v. 1 does imply that it is Jesus speaking, the context of the first five verses reveals that we are to discern, as so often in earlier chapters, that through the mouth of Jesus, the Christ is speaking. Here, in vs. 1, 2 and 3 the Christ is speaking, but on behalf of Jesus.

17:1 "After Jesus said these things, he directed his perception spiritually to Heaven and said: "Father, the hour has come. Make powerfully manifest your Son, that your Son may manifest you with might,

Here a profound prayer begins, which reveals that there is a reciprocal interaction between spiritual beings. If the Son is powerfully active, then since the Father has endowed the Son with this power, the Father is also thus manifesting within the Son's power.

"Make powerfully manifest": usually, 'Glorify your Son', but as noted in earlier verses, this traditional phrase today does not always present the intended meaning.

17:2 since you gave to him power over all flesh, in order that all those which You have given to him, may have eternal life (aeonic existence)."

"all flesh": incarnate human beings, thus alluding to the fact that the Christ-power, active through Jesus, can ennoble both the soul and the physical body.
"that all those": meaning that portion of humanity actually given to Jesus. However, the word for 'people' is always masculine in Greek, yet it is striking that here this word is neutral, which is incorrect to the grammar of ancient Greek. So we may conclude that human souls are meant here, without regard for gender; thus humans as soul-beings from spiritual realms, where there is no gender.
"...all those which You have given to him, *may have* aeonic existence": this is the correct text, as preserved in Bezae.[329] This sentence has survived in various corrupted forms elsewhere.

17:3 And this is eternal life: that they cognize You as the only true God, and {that they cognize} Jesus, the Anointed One, as the one You sent forth into this world.

"Jesus the Anointed One": whereas most translations have 'Jesus Christ'. The reason for this difference is that, as noted at the beginning of this Commentary, the word 'Christ' appearing in the Gospels is actually a Greek way of expressing the Aramaic term for that man who would become the divinely anointed Messiah. It was only after the Resurrection that the set name 'Jesus Christ' would be become a formal term, linked to the person of Jesus.

So if the Aramaic term 'the Anointed One' is put in Greek here, or anywhere in the Gospels, it is actually not fully correct to how these words were used in the three years of Jesus' ministry. These points are known to

---

[329] other versions include these unnecessary clumsy additional words: "...all those which You have given to him, *he will give* aeonic existence *to them*". The NIV omits these words, as I have, and reads, "(so) that he might give eternal life to all those you have given him."

scholars, but since the tradition has become so firmly set, virtually all translations use the term 'Christ' instead of 'the Anointed One' throughout the four Gospels. Since it has become a set tradition, I have also often used the term 'Christ' throughout the Gospel: but not here.

This is because I do not share the reason why some translators specifically use the term 'Christ' here. Their reason for this is that they conclude this verse was added later by the Gospel's author as editor – writing when the name 'Jesus Christ' was already a firmly established title in the church.

So many scholars **do not think** that Jesus is speaking here; they have concluded that these words were **definitely not spoken by Jesus**. These scholars have decided that no-one spoke these words, but instead John, the Gospel writer, wrote these words down, using the set name, 'Jesus Christ', which he inserted into the Gospel, as an editor. The justifications for their views are unconvincing according to my research (see Appendix 16 for more about this).

"as": this connecting word is not in the Greek, but many scholars conclude that 'as' needs to be added twice, to make the meaning clear.
"into this world": these additional words occur in Bezae.
"cognize You": usually 'know You'; but 'cognize' or 'perceive' is what is meant here, for it is about what our consciousness perceives. If through contemplating sacred truths through spiritual effort, the Divine begins to be perceived with our mind (i.e., cognized), then that itself is an 'eternal' consciousness.
"the only true God": this is not to be taken literally, as there are many true or valid deities; it is an Aramaic idiom. It means that there is only one divine being from whom the human spirit derives; and this god is what the spiritually aspiring person needs to begin to perceive, at least to some degree.[330]

---

[330] This deity is, in Rudolf Steiner's teachings, the highest of the Thrones (who can be understood, in turn, as the vessel of the primal Godhead, who is beyond all nine hierarchies).

Reviewing the situation here: in this verse, we encounter the speaker referring to someone else – to Jesus – as the long awaited Messiah. I have concluded that the speaker is the cosmic Christ. For Jesus, like anyone else, would not refer to himself by his personal name, as if somehow he were not Jesus; and it is even less likely that he would use the formal Jewish designation 'Jesus the Anointed One" (Messiah) or the later Hellenistic title, Jesus Christ, when referring to himself.

In earlier chapters it had been noted that the cosmic Christ does speak through Jesus; such as in 8:57-58 "Before Abraham existed, I am the I am", and in 9:5 "Every time that it is the case that I am in the world, I am the world's light". However, some scholars have decided regarding this verse (17:3), because they don't factor in the role of a cosmic Christ, that it still must be Jesus speaking here, despite all the strangeness and awkwardness implied by this.

They explain this view by various proposals; such as, Jesus decided to use what would be his future name to instruct people in advance, as to how to think of him in the future (see Appendix 16).

"And this is eternal life": the cosmic Christ is declaring that to attain to 'aeonic existence', that is, to a spiritual consciousness which is in harmony with divine reality, a person needs to develop some higher perceiving which bestows awareness of God. But in addition, one must also realize that Jesus is the vessel of the Divine. This twofold requirement can be understood on ever higher levels.

The word 'God' here refers to the Father-God; that is, to a deity who is higher than the cosmic Christ. In his comments on this verse, Rudolf Steiner speaks about our sense of 'I' in relation to 'God', and tells his audience that the Mystery of Golgotha brings a new element to this age-old dynamic.[331]

He explains how here in this passage, people are being informed (by the cosmic Christ) that humanity now needs to feel in freedom, the 'Son-God' (meaning the cosmic Christ) in relation to their innermost 'I' – and

---

[331] Lect. 14th July 1923, GA 345.

not only to feel a link with the Father-God, which humanity in the old religions had been doing for millennia.

17:4 I manifested the power of your being on the Earth by completing the work which you gave to me, work intended for me.

Here the cosmic Christ speaks.
"manifested the power of your being": usually, 'glorified you'.

17:5 And now Father, let my being be powerfully manifested with the radiant splendour which I had with you, before the world was created.

Here again the cosmic Christ is speaking.
"my being powerfully manifest": usually, 'glorify me'.
"with the radiant splendour": usually, 'with the glory'. The word here 'doxa', usually translated as "glory", can mean either a radiance, or a powerful manifestation.
"before the world was *created*": the word 'created' is found in Bezae, which completes an otherwise very brief sentence.

The majestic cosmic tone of this chapter continues here, for it is the cosmic Christ who is speaking. There is nothing in Scripture that suggests that Jesus suffered a diminishing of his divine nature in the remote past. Hence this verse implies that the cosmic Christ long ago underwent, sacrificially, a diminishing of his original sublime condition.

This temporary reduction in his nature, was noted in Part One, Section 4, in regard to Rev.13:8 "...the Lamb who was slain from the foundation of the world". So in this verse 17:5, there is a veiled reference to an imminent event of far-reaching cosmic significance.

Namely, that The Lamb of God or the great sun-god Christ, at the Resurrection, will re-attain what it once forfeited in an act of sacrifice of huge importance. Rudolf Steiner taught that the cosmic Christ long ago declined to remain at its full spiritual status, which would have meant a path of spiritual progression vastly beyond the sphere of humanity.[332] So through sacrificing this potential, this sublime deity's pathway drew it closer to humanity. But v. 17:5 is saying that soon the Christ shall become again fully empowered; this is another aspect to the glory resonating from the Resurrection. Yet, through Jesus, the Christ-reality will be able to remain near to, and thus guide, humanity on its journey upwards.

17:6 I manifested your very being to the people whom you gave me out of the world. They were yours and you gave them to me, and they have retained that which intoned forth from you.

Here, and from this verse on, Jesus is speaking.
"your very being": usually 'your name', but here 'name' means the inherent core qualities of God, not any actual name, as we understand this word.
"that which intoned forth from you": usually, 'kept your word'. Here the Greek has 'logos', meaning spiritual 'words' or intonings which ray forth from God, and which transcend language as we know it.

The disciples have remained cognizant of, and devoted to, the 'intonings' of the Divine. This is what Jesus has been communicating to them, as verbal and the non-verbal teachings, because he is the vessel of God.

17:7 Now they know that everything whatsoever you have given me, is from you,
17:8 for the words which you intoned to me, I have entrusted to them; and they perceived truly that I came forth from you, and they believed that you sent me.

"intoned to me": usually, 'gave to me'.
"words": here the Greek does not have logos, but the usual term for any word, 'hraemata' (ῥήματα), which implies that what Jesus experienced was able to be verbally communicated in speech.

---

[332] GA 102, two lects. about primal Logos and the solar Logos: 27 Jan. and 24 Mar. 1908.

"they perceived truly": the disciples accepted that Jesus came from God; i.e., to their minds this concept was true. The verb here 'lambanoe' (λαμβάνω) is usually interpreted as 'receiving' the words of God. But here it refers to the disciples receiving the concept (i.e., perceiving in their minds) that Jesus came from God. Lazaros uses the same verb in this same way in 3:11 "... **but you people do not accept our testimony** (you do not mentally perceive it)".[333]

17:9 I am asking on their behalf; I am not asking on behalf of all people, but on behalf of the ones you gave to me, because they are yours.

"all people": literally the text has 'the world', but many scholars conclude, (e.g., Bernard, Godet, Steiner, Westcott) that this phrase means humanity in general, as the next section of the verse implies.

17:10 All mine are yours, and yours are mine; and my spirit has been powerfully manifested in them.

"my spirit powerfully manifested": this is a clearer way of communicating what the old traditional version means; 'I was glorified in them.'
Jesus was powerfully present and manifesting within the disciples, and this signifies that these souls shall have an on-going central role in humanity's future. This is indicated in the Book of Revelation (14:21) where we are told in a metaphor, that the names of the disciples are to be inscribed in the walls of the New Jerusalem.

17:11 Yet no longer am I in the world, but they are in the world, and I am coming to you. No longer am I in the world; yet in the world I am. Holy Father, keep them in your name, as I kept them in your name when

---

[333] Most versions have "they have received the words... *and know* in truth that I came from you..." But Codex Bezae omits the words in italics, as they are unnecessary, once the verb lambanoe is understood as meaning 'mentally perceiving' and refers to Jesus coming from God, not 'receiving' words of God.

I was with them – those whom you have given to me – so that they may be as one, as we are one.

"keep them....*those* whom you have given to me":
this is usually,
"**protect them...in that *name* which you have given me**". Scholars are aware that the grammar behind this usual version is dubious, so they are unsure whether that translation is really correct. This verse has an unusual grammatical feature, causing substantial confusion. Whereas the grammar behind the version presented here, is fully validated, as Bengel noted.[334]

The usual meaning is also not very convincing, in that it is not formally stated in the Gospel that God gave his name to Jesus. Whereas three times in preceding verses it is emphasized, as an important fact, that God has given souls into the care of Christ; once in v. 2, and twice in v. 6. Here there are also two additional sentences, which are preserved only in Bezae:

"**No longer am I in the world; yet in the world I am**":
this mysterious saying is unique to Bezae, but omitted from most translations. I have included it, as it appears to be a genuine hierophantic saying, in which Jesus is heralding his departure from the world, but also indicating that on a non-physical level, he is still, in some way, permanently part of humanity's sphere of existence. (See v. 12 for the other additional sentence.)

17:12 When I was with them – those which you gave to me – I kept them in your name; and I kept watch so

---

[334] The singular pronoun 'ho' (ὁ) in Bezae seems to require that this pronoun refers to 'name', not to 'many people'. But Lazaros does use it in a plural way; he does this undeniably, in v. 24 "those (ὅ) which you have given to me" and also in 1Jh. 5:4. Then there is no need to postulate that ὁ has been abbreviated from the plural οὕς. The unique text here in Bezae is superior to those of other versions, as Bengel notes (*New Testament Word Studies*, p. 705.) The objection that it cannot be the case that only Bezae is correct for this verse, is itself ignoring other places where Bezae is the only correct version.

none of them perished, except the son of perdition, that the Scripture might be fulfilled.

Verse 11 in the Bezae version contains a section which is also in v. 12; **"I kept them in your name - those whom you have given to me"**). Most scholars assume that in codex Bezae, an editor has added this to v. 11 arbitrarily, borrowing it from v. 12. But I regard these words as genuine, having a valid place in verse 11 as well as in v. 12, because they are about a theme so central to this last discourse made by Jesus before his arrest.

17:13 And now I am coming to you, so I speak these things in the world, that my joy may be fulfilled in themselves.
17:14 I have given them your word, so the world has hated them, because they do not belong to the world, just as I do not belong to the world.

"given them your word..."Jesus has imbued the disciples with the divine spiritual qualities of the Father.

17:15 I do not ask that you take them out of the world, but that you keep them from the evil one.
17:16 They are not of this world, just as I am not of this world.
17:17 Sanctify them in the Truth; your word is Truth.

"your word is Truth": 'word' here implies what intones forth from God, and that it is this which brings enlightenment, i.e., profound spiritual wisdom.

17:18 As you have sent them into this world, so have I sent them into this world.

Just as God sent the disciples to the Earth, to be incarnate beings, Jesus sent them out into the world, to proclaim the Gospel.
"this world": as in codex Bezae, (usually 'the world').

17:19 And for their sake I am sanctifying myself, so that they may also be sanctified in Truth.

"sanctifying myself": this means in effect, that Jesus shall *further* sanctify himself, in that he prepares to sacrifice his life, in service to the will of God, and the cosmic Christ. This process shall also sanctify him further in that he then becomes "Jesus Christ", i.e., Jesus the vessel of the cosmic Christ – no greater sanctification is possible.

17:20 I ask not only on behalf of these, but also on behalf of those who will believe in me through their word,
17:21 that they may all be one. As you, Father are in me and I am in you, may they also be in us, so that the world may believe that you sent me.
17:22 The spiritual empowerment which you have given to me, I have given to them, so that they may be one, just as we are one.

"spiritual empowerment": meaning 'the power to manifest spiritually'; usually 'Glory'. It is through an enhanced spiritual interweaving of soul to soul, that an inner union is formed amongst the disciples.

17:23 I am in them, and you are in me, that they may become completely one, so that the world will know that you did send me, and that you shall then love (agape) them, just as you loved me.

Another verse with the timeless nuance. That is, it looks ahead to the future when it will be true that God shall have made possible an enhancement of his love for them. As Jesus speaks these words, this love is a 'phileo' love (as noted in v. 16:27).

But the world shall find out that in later years the bond of love with the disciples will become one of agape. So here is a complex sentence, similar to v.13:31, where a future event is visualized as being already completed.

Reviewing the meaning of this verse:
Jesus declares that in the years after the Resurrection, people shall realize that God had sent him (a clear one-off event); and also people shall realize that through the

disciples' life and work, God by then, will have brought about a higher bond of love (agape) with these souls (an event which is completed yet ongoing, (so here the verb is a 'gnomic aorist' beyond the flow of time).

17:24 Father, I desire also that those, whom you have given me, may be with me where I shall be, so that they may behold the radiant splendour which you have bestowed on me, because you have loved me (agape) before the foundation of the world.

Jesus Christ, united to the cosmic Christ, shall be enveloped in splendour, radiant from the power and majesty emanating from the cosmic Christ. Jesus prays now that the disciples will be enabled to behold this, for in so doing, they shall experience a blessedness and also a fountain of love and wisdom that permeates and ennobles their spirits.

"loved me before...": God had love (agape) regarding Jesus, already long ago. This verse contrasts to v. 5, where as noted there, the deity, the cosmic Christ, is referring to having existed in a radiant empowered splendour, during a remote primordial phase of the world's evolving.

But here, in v. 24, it appears that it is Jesus speaking, who is referring to a much more recent phase of our history, when the Earth was in existence, but had not yet cooled and condensed into a stable, solid condition; the foundations of our world had not yet appeared. That is, Jesus is referring to an agape love between himself and God, whilst we were all existing in an ethereal, non-physical state of being.[335]

This alludes to what the book of Genesis mentions as 'Paradise', where humanity was located before the 'Fall of Man', that is, before the descent into a material-physical body. Because of this past agape between God

---

[335] As an important complement to scientific conclusions about the development of life on Earth, various religious and esoteric schools of thought, including Steiner, taught that humanity did already exist, as souls, but not as a physical 'incarnate' flesh and blood people, in these earlier Ages.

and Jesus, God has bestowed upon Jesus, during his life in Palestine, a gloriously radiant, blessed state of soul and spirit.

17:25 Righteous Father, this world does not know you, but I knew you, and these men know that you sent me.
17:26 I made known your very being to them, and I shall continue to make it known, so that the love (agape) with which you have loved me, may be in them, and I in them.

"your very being": as with v. 6, this is literally 'your name' and is usually translated as such.

CHAPTER 18

The perspective of Lazaros on the details of the arrest, trial and death of Jesus cannot be fully harmonized with the sequence of events portrayed in the three synoptic Gospels; so this theme will not be discussed here.

18:1 Having said these things, Jesus went out with his disciples and crossed the Kidron Valley, where there was a garden; he and his disciples went into it.
18:2 Now Judas, who betrayed him, also knew the place, because Jesus had often gathered there with his disciples.
18:3 So Judas came to the grove, guiding a detachment of soldiers and some servants from the chief priests and Pharisees. They were carrying torches, lanterns and weapons.

"torches': it was the Passover Full Moon, so bringing along torches shows how determined the Sanhedrin were to capture Jesus (if he retreated into some dark place.)

18:4 Then Jesus, knowing all that was going to happen to him, went out and asked them, "Who is it you are seeking?"
18:5 "Jesus the Nazarene," they replied. "I am he," Jesus said. Judas the traitor was standing there with them.

"I am he"; the Greek words here (ego eimi) have been discussed earlier. They can be simply an emphatic way of defining oneself, or a deeply esoteric declaration of Christ: "the 'I', I am". Here they are the former, yet even so, his words possessed a powerful resonance, since it is Jesus who says this to them; and because normally those who were to be arrested would seek to avoid capture.

18:6 When Jesus said, "I am he," they drew back and fell to the ground.
18:7 Again he asked them, "Who is it you are seeking?" And they said, "Jesus the Nazarene."

18:8 "I told you that I am he," Jesus answered. "If you are looking for me, then let these men go away."

18:9 This happened so that the words he had spoken would be fulfilled: "I have not lost anyone of those whom you gave me."

18:10 Then Simon Peter, who had a sword, drew it and struck the high priest's servant, cutting off his right ear. The servant's name was Malchus.

18:11 So Jesus said to Peter, "Put your sword away! Should I not drink the cup the Father has given me?"

18:12 Then the detachment of soldiers with its commander and the Jewish officials, arrested Jesus, and bound him,

18:13 and brought him first to Annas, who was the father-in-law of Caiaphas, the high priest that year.

18:14 Caiaphas was the one who had advised the Sanhedrin that it would be good if one man died for the people.

18:15 Simon Peter and another disciple were following Jesus. Because this disciple was known to the high priest, he went with Jesus into the high priest's courtyard,

18:16 but Peter had to wait outside at the door. The other disciple, who was known to the high priest, came back, spoke to the girl on duty there and brought Peter in.

"The other disciple": this was Lazaros. As noted earlier, it can not be John the Apostle, for amongst other reasons, he was unknown to the high priest. It has been conjectured that therefore, it was possibly Nicodemus or Joseph of Arimathea. The Gospels report that these two were secretly followers of Jesus, but out of fear of the Sanhedrin. So they would not have put themselves into danger at this very ominous time. Although the disciples had fled the scene when Jesus was arrested, Peter had regained his courage and followed behind; in this process he was joined by Lazaros.

18:17 "You are not one of his disciples, are you?" the girl at the door asked Peter. He replied, "I am not."

18:18 It was cold, and the servants and officials stood around a fire they had made to keep warm. Peter also was standing with them, warming himself.

Only in this Gospel is such coldness mentioned; otherwise scholars report that normally the nights are warm at the time of the Passover festival. So possibly the reference here to the cold is a signifier of malignant spirits, in whom a coldness exists, and which have taken hold of the hearts of those who have been planning to carry out their evil.[336]

18:19 Meanwhile, the high priest questioned Jesus about his disciples and his teaching.
18:20 "I have spoken openly to the world," Jesus replied. "I always taught in synagogues or at the temple, where all the Jews come together. I said nothing in secret.
18:21 Why question me? Ask those who heard me. Surely they know what I said."
18:22 When Jesus said this, one of the officials nearby struck him in the face. "Is this the way you answer the high priest?" he demanded.
18:23 "If I said something wrong," Jesus replied, "testify as to what is wrong. But if I spoke the truth, why did you strike me?"
18:24 Then Annas sent him, still bound, to Caiaphas the high priest.
18:25 As Simon Peter stood warming himself, he was asked, "You are not one of his disciples, are you?" He denied it, saying, "I am not."
18:26 One of the high priest's servants, a relative of the man whose ear Peter had cut off, challenged him, "Didn't I see you with him in the garden?"
18:27 Again Peter denied it, and at that moment a rooster began to crow.

"rooster began to crow": the profound esoteric meaning of this was discussed with verse 13:38. As noted there, a cosmic truth is manifesting in this call of the rooster, after Peter's three denials. Some have queried whether

---

[336] Westcott, *Gospel John*, p .256.

the sound was that of the Roman soldier's 3-am trumpet call, to signal the end of one 3-hour watch and the beginning of the next.

This call was known as the 'gullicinium' which means 'cock-crow', probably so named because about that time a rooster would often begin its crowing. It is also the case that the Jewish authorities disallowed keeping of poultry in Jerusalem, as recorded in the Mishna (baba Kamma vii7).

But this situation does not exclude that Peter heard an actual rooster, for two reasons. Another Mishnah tract (*Erubin*) records that there were in fact some poultry kept in households in Jerusalem. It is also possible that this rooster was in a property outside the city walls, and as the grand residence of Caiaphas was built on an elevated position, the cock crowing was audible to Peter.[337]

18:28 Then the Jewish authorities led Jesus from Caiaphas to the palace of the Roman governor. By now it was early morning, and to avoid ceremonial uncleanness the Jews did not enter the palace, as they wanted to be able to eat the Passover.
18:29 So Pilate came out to them and asked, "What charges are you bringing against this man?"
18:30 "If this man were not a criminal," they replied, "we would not have handed him over to you."
18:31 Pilate said, "Take him yourselves and judge him by your own law." "But we are not permitted to execute anyone," the Jewish leaders objected.
18:32 This happened so that the words Jesus had spoken indicating the kind of death he was going to die would be fulfilled.
18:33 Pilate then went back inside the palace, summoned Jesus and asked him, "Are you the king of the Jews?"
18:34 "Are you saying this from him (Caiaphas)," Jesus asked, "or did others talk with you about me?"

---

[337] This situation is pointed out in the *McClintock and Strong Biblical Cyclopaedia*, 1867 +.

"from him (Caipahas):" usually, 'from yourself', which is how some reliable manuscripts record this[338], and this may be the correct text. But codex Bezae (and Alexandrinus) has 'from himself', meaning Caiaphas. This seems more accurate, as it is most unlikely that Pilate, a non-Jew, would have ever thought this; and otherwise his question in v. 29 would be unnecessary. That Pilate asks this question confirms the obvious, that a few minutes earlier, the Sanhedrin had made this the basis of their action against Jesus.

18:35 "Am I a Jew?" Pilate replied. "It was your people and your chief priests who handed you over to me. What is it you have done?"

"Am I a Jew?": Pilate means that, although Caiaphas told him of the charge against Jesus, that he was pretending to be 'King of the Jews", he had no other conversations with Sanhedrin members about Jesus. Because as a Roman governor, Pilate did not socialize with the Jewish people. So he wants to know what actions, perhaps of a seditious nature, that Jesus may have been doing.

18:36 Jesus said, "My kingdom is not of this world. If it were of this world, my followers would have fought to prevent my arrest by the Sanhedrin. But in fact my kingdom is not of this place."

v.36 "in fact": the Greek word (nun – νῦν) also means 'as regards the present situation', the NRSV has, "as it is". Jesus makes it clear that he had not been involved in seditious political activity.

18:37 "So, you are a king?" said Pilate. Jesus answered, "You are saying I am a king. In fact, for this reason I was born, and for this I came into the world, to testify to the Truth. All those who are of the Truth, hear my voice."

"you": there appears to be some irony in these words of Pilate; for he has before him a disempowered man, who

---

[338] Papyrus 66, Sinaiticus, Vaticanus.

is despised by the Jewish leaders who are seeking his death; and who was not a political agitator.

"You are saying I am a king": Scholars agree that the reply Jesus gives to Pilate is somewhat obscure, as the Greek is ambiguous. It appears that Jesus is not wanting to directly affirm that he is a king - for Pilate would misunderstand the term - but nor does he want to deny this, because in a spiritual sense, it is true. So his answer is in effect,

"You are saying that I am a king."

Morris defines the mood of this answer very well, "I didn't say this, but if you put it that way, I can scarcely say no." If one enters into the brooding, malignant political-religious forces active around this trial and the hugely intense, but veiled, spiritual influences active behind the court of Pilate, and also leading to the impending death, this abrupt answer becomes understandable.

18:38 "What is truth?" Pilate asked. With this, he went out again to the crowd and said, "I find no basis for a charge against him.
18:39 But it is your custom for me to release to you one prisoner, at the time of the Passover. Do you want me to release 'the king of the Jews'?"
18:40 They shouted back, "Not, not this man ! Instead, Barabbas !" But Barabbas had taken part in a rebellion.

"Barabbas:" this name means 'son of the father', and as such, it presents a counter-type to Jesus, who is the 'son of the Father'.

CHAPTER 19

19:1 Then Pilate took Jesus and ordered him flogged.
19:2 The soldiers twisted together a crown of thorns and put it on his head. They clothed him in a purple robe.
19:3 They went up to him again and again, saying, "Hail, king of the Jews!" And they struck him in the face.
19:4 Once more Pilate came out and said to the crowd, "Look, I am bringing him out to you to let you know that I find no case against him."
19:5 When Jesus came out wearing the crown of thorns and the purple robe, Pilate said to them, "Here is the man !"

"Here is the man !": it appears that Pilate is presenting a person who has been flogged and tormented, as someone to feel pity for, in the hope that the anger against Jesus will subside. But it is also the case, as in v. 8, that Pilate was already afraid of allowing the execution of Jesus. This indicates that he had some intuitive sense that Jesus was not only innocent, but was someone to respect.

19:6 As soon as the chief priests and their officials saw him, they shouted, "Crucify him ! Crucify him !" But Pilate answered, "You take him and crucify him. As for me, I find no basis for a charge against him."

By his dismissive remarks, Pilate again shows his disdain for the hatred of Jesus coming from the crowd, since as he well knew, the Sanhedrin had no authority to execute anyone. To mock Jesus, the soldiers had put a purple robe on him; but this probably inflamed the hatred of the Sanhedrin even more, as purple was a colour reserved for rulers, senior military personnel and priestly dignitaries.

19:7 The Jewish leaders insisted, "We have a law, and according to that law he must die, because he claimed to be The Son of God."
19:8 When Pilate heard this, he was even more afraid,

"The Son of God": that Pilate was more afraid now of being involved in the killing of a highly ethical person, indicates that he may well have had knowledge of the esoteric teachings of the religions in the Hellenistic world. If so, he would known that the term 'The Son of God' referred to an initiate.

19:9 and he went back inside the palace. "Where do you come from?" he asked Jesus, but Jesus gave him no answer.
19:10 "Do you refuse to speak to me?" Pilate said. "Don't you realize I have power either to free you or to crucify you?"
19:11 Jesus answered, "You would have no power over me if it were not given to you from above. Therefore the one who handed me over to you is guilty of a greater sin."
19:12 From then on, Pilate tried to set Jesus free, but the crowd kept shouting, "If you let this man go, you are no friend of Caesar. Anyone who claims to be a king opposes Caesar."
19:13 When Pilate heard this, he brought Jesus out and sat down on the judge's seat at a place known as the Stone Pavement (which in Aramaic is Gabbatha).
19:14 It was the day of Preparation for the Passover, about the sixth hour. "Here is your king," Pilate said to the crowd.
19:15 But they shouted, "Take him away! Take him away! Crucify him!" "Shall I crucify your king?" Pilate asked. "We have no king but Caesar," the chief priests answered.
19:16 Finally Pilate handed him over to them to be crucified. So the soldiers took charge of Jesus.
19:17 Carrying his own cross, he went out to the Place of the Skull (which in Aramaic is called Golgotha).

17: "the Place of the Skull": the text here is so written, that instead of, 'the place of the Skull' it needs it be translated the 'Skull-Place'[339] putting the emphasis on

---

[339] Technically, as Morris points out, the pronoun is 'ho (ö) which is neuter, but it follows 'place' which is masculine, and hence should be 'hos' (ò). However skull is neuter, and

'skull'. Rudolf Steiner comments on this, that it is the earthly consciousness, enabled through the skull, (i.e., through the brain) which has brought about this 'earth-bound' state of the soul.[340] In other words, here another esoteric perspective is offered to the reader; our deadened 'anti-spiritual' thinking has brought about the death of the higher consciousness (Christ).[341]

19:18 Here they crucified him, and with him two others – one on each side and Jesus in the middle.
19:19 Pilate had a notice prepared and fastened to the cross. It read: JESUS THE NAZARENE THE KING OF THE JEWS
19:20 Many of the Jewish people read this sign, for the place where Jesus was crucified was near the city, and the sign was written in Aramaic, Latin and Greek.
19:21 So the chief priests protested to Pilate, "Do not write 'The King of the Jews,' but that this man claimed to be king of the Jews."
19:22 Pilate answered, "What I have written, I have written."
19:23 When the soldiers crucified Jesus, they took his cloaks*, dividing it into four segments, one for each of them, and also his tunic. Now, this tunic was woven as a seamless garment, from the top downwards, in one piece. {*although a single cloak}

It is here that a deep initiatory secret of esoteric Christianity has been veiled. For this verse in the light of the Initiatory Quest approach, reveals the following :
'his cloaks": his single cloak is put in the plural in Greek, to emphasize how important it is, on a spiritual level. For now the Gospel account is also alluding to the cosmic Christ, not the man Jesus. So the unitary (single)

---

therefore the pronoun is in effect referring back to skull, making it the primary word here, but 'skull' has to join up with 'place' for this to be grammatically viable.

[340] GA 175, p. 235.
[341] Perhaps an unconscious awareness of this has led to the skull of a skeleton symbolizing death, rather than the entire skeleton or its chest, etc.

garment is described as a fourfold 'plural garment' because this is now alluding to the Earth. The Earth is a single, living organism, but it was understood as having a fourfold nature, soon to be permeated by the cosmic Christ. These four natures encompass:
four life-waves: mineral, plant, animal and human
four elements: fire, air, water, earth
four elementary life-forces behind the four elements:
    warmth, airy, fluidic and solid[342]
four main landmasses of the planet as understood by
    the general populace in the Hellenistic world: Africa,
    Asia, Europe and India

To enter into the spiritual-esoteric lesson presented in this verse, it is important to bear in mind a central feature of Jewish esoteric literature, going back many centuries. An historical, factual event in Israel's history can be recorded in a way that encompasses spiritual truths.

Some examples are: the number forty is used in regard to an event, to signify a completion of a dynamic, without meaning to be historically accurate; thus the Hebrew people wander in the desert during the Exodus for forty years, and Moses stayed forty days and forty nights on the Mountain, and Jesus was in the wilderness for forty days.

More striking is in the Book of Joshua (10:12-13), which records that the sun and the moon stood still for a day above the valley of Ajalon. Both Joshua and Abraham fought against five kings; this is an initiatory narrative about overcoming the power of the five primary senses.

In our Gospel, a 'stalk' of hyssop is used, which is very unlikely because hyssop has no strong stalks, but its mention here brings in allusions to the original Passover. So too with this verse, it is now as if the reader is to view the episode of the cross and the role of the clothing, as a separate, veiled lesson about the cosmic aspect of Christianity.

---

[342] Greek Hellenistic esoteric literature refers to a kind of life-force or elemental energy behind the four states of matter (e.g., the Stobaei Hermetica; *Isis to Horus* #26.

"his tunic...seamless": this garment is here called a 'kiton' in Greek. This word 'kiton' was loosely used for several kinds of garments; it could be either the simple under-shirt worn by all men and women (the latter went down further, well below the knee). Or it could refer to a quite different garment, of very fine quality, and of full-length, going down to the ankles.

Such a fine quality seamless, long kiton, was woven on a special loom, and was identical to a 'stolae' (called in Latin, a stola); being a 'semi-outer' garment, for another garment was placed over it, functioning somewhat like a light coat or a shawl.

What Jesus was actually wearing under the usual robe, would have been the usual under-shirt, called a 'syndoen' (σινδών) and sometimes a kiton. But as noted above, small sections of the Gospel can be written so as to be symbolic of spiritual realities, and have no connection to the everyday real world. This literary device is a primary feature of the Hebrew Scriptures.

So now, just in this verse 19:23, we are presented with an imaginative scene; his garment now is to be thought of as a kiton; hence it would be highly valued by the soldiers. For it would be seamless, so it was a fine quality long kiton, not an everyday under-shirt. Such a garment is a tunic or stolae; it was a more valuable kind of 'inner' robe.

As an exercise in perceiving a spiritual dynamic, Jesus' inner garment is presented here as a seamless long kiton. This means moving the focus from Jesus and his clothing, to the link between the Earth and the cosmic Christ. It is a pointer to the cosmic Christ, who is to become the 'Earth-spirit' at the Resurrection, through the sacrificial death of Jesus.

This unified, seamless garment can be viewed as signifying the atmosphere of the Earth. As Rudolf Steiner commented, "the fine seamless tunic is the undividable atmosphere of the Earth....and the cloak which is divided into four parts, represents the four main landmasses {as thought of generally in that Age}."[343]

---

[343] GA 94, lecture of 6th Nov. 1906.

The Hellenistic world could view the atmosphere of the Earth as an indivisible enveloping cloak, for this is how the air appears to us all; whether above our local environs, or around the globe of the Earth. That the Earth was a round globe was accepted by some people as a fact already by 350 BC, from the work of Aristotle.

It was also long known as a fact to those initiated in the Mysteries; a work by Cicero, written about 50 BC, *The Dream of Scipio*, tells of an initiatory experience wherein the acolyte experiences the universe; seeing the Earth **as a globe**, amongst other planets, and with ice-bound areas at either pole.[344]

This view of the Earth as a globe was still held in the 3rd century, as shown in a mosaic, found in an underground tomb in Rome. Jesus, as the new sun-god, is holding the globe of the Earth in his hand.[345]

In other words, the initiated Lazaros in his Gospel, whilst referring to the physical garments on the body of the man Jesus now going to other people (soldiers), is also, for those readers with esoteric awareness, subtly pointing to the reverse dynamic happening, but on a cosmic scale.

The Earth, through the death of Jesus, is receiving the cosmic Christ into its indivisible atmosphere (or its aura), and into its fourfold nature. That this is the secret initiatory meaning here is confirmed by another discreet use of Greek grammar, in v. 24.

19:24 Therefore they said to each other "Let us not tear it. May divine will determine, regarding this garment, whose it shall be". This happened that the Scripture might be fulfilled which said, "They divided my garments among them and cast lots for my clothing." So this is what the soldiers did.

"May Divine Will determine": usually, "let us...cast lots for it". However this usual version is ignoring the fact

---

[344] *Somnium Scipionis*: "that globe which you see in the midst of the universe, which is called the Earth...ensouled by stars and constellations, themselves globular bodies".

[345] A restored version of this mosaic is in my *The Hellenistic Mysteries and Christianity*.

that the verb here 'lagchano' (λαγχάνω) does not ever mean to cast lots. It always means either,
A: 'to receive by divine will',
or B: for deities to cast the lot for humans.[346]
So again, this cosmic Gospel here is alluding to divine will active in the process which is soon to commence. This shall enable the great cosmic Christ to become the guiding spirit of the Earth.

19:25 Near the cross of Jesus stood his mother, and his mother's sister, Mary – the wife of Clopas – and Mary Magdalene.

Lazaros has presented here a spiritual-esoteric perspective, which was also historically true, in which three women are witnessing the death of Jesus, each of whom is named Mary. Before examining this further, it is important to recall that nowhere in this Gospel is the mother of Jesus ever named Mary. This fact was already noted in 2:1 in regard to the wedding at Cana. This enables 'her' to be both the actual historical mother, yet also the matrix of the Spiritual-self (or The Son of Man).

So, on one level there are three women near the cross, each of whom is named Mary; but since the mother of Jesus has not been given that name, the awkwardness of having two sisters, each named Mary, is not made so obvious here. But this unusual feature enables two significant truths to be communicated about Lazaros and this un-named Mary (see also next verse).[347]

Rudolf Steiner explained to his students, that one of the lessons interwoven in the narrative here, is that of these three feminine figures representing the three dynamics of the human soul, as presented in the Hebrew Scriptures[348] (see Part One, Section Three):

---

[346] As Plummer commented, "its use here, to mean 'to cast lots' (*apparently*, AA) is rare, if not unique." *St. John*, p. 330.
[347] It is unusual but not impossible, for two sisters to have the same name, plus an additional name, by which they are differentiated from each other.
[348] GA 100, lect., 20 Nov., 1907.

Mary, the mother of Jesus: the intuitive-spiritual consciousness (In Hebrew, Neschamah)
Mary of Cleophas: the intelligence, the rational mind (Ruach)
Mary Magdalene: the feelings or emotions (Nephesch)

The lesson here is that, the three primary qualities of the human soul are witnesses to the sacrifice of the Christ. A sacrifice undertaken to enable the soul to become spiritualized, to find a way out of the darkness of its earth-bound state. (See Appendix 18, for a note about Mary Magdalene.)

19:26 When Jesus saw his mother there, and the disciple whom he loved, standing nearby, he said to his mother, "Dear woman, here is your son,"
19:27 and to the disciple, "Here is your mother." From that time on, this disciple took her into his home.

On the historical, personal level, we experience that Jesus, in the very process of dying in agony, asks Lazaros to look after his mother; a very touching moment, and a profound lesson in loving kindness.

On the initiatory level, Jesus is undertaking yet another loving deed; purifying and ennobling the soul of Lazaros, to allow the Spiritual-self in him, to be enhanced further. For esoterically, the mother of Jesus can be viewed as the matrix of the Spiritual-self.[349] This divine reality is now indeed the 'mother' of Lazaros, for nothing that derives from the 'fallen' soul qualities are left in his soul. The 'mother' of his now even further sanctified soul, are those divine influences from which the Spiritual-self (or Son of Man) arises.

19:28 Later, knowing that all was now completed, and so that the Scripture would be fulfilled, Jesus said, "I am thirsty."

---

[349] This divine matrix of Jesus' own soul was referred to as the 'Sophia" in esoteric groups of his time; not a goddess, but a confluence of divine influences.

"thirsty": this appears to be a reference to Psalm 69, which alludes to an inner soul-thirst, which the Psalmist experienced in a 'dark night of the soul'.

19:29 A jar of cheap wine was there, so they soaked a sponge in it, put the sponge on a stalk of the hyssop plant, and lifted it to Jesus' lips.

"hyssop stalk: this short plant does not have strong stalks, so perhaps some other plant was used. As noted earlier, perhaps Lazaros is seeking to show parallels to the original Passover Lamb and the sacrifice of Jesus. In Exodus 12:22 it is recorded that on the night when the 'Destroying Angel' was to attack the first-born of the Egyptians, the blood of a lamb was to be daubed onto the entrance to dwellings of the Hebrews, to ensure that their children were unharmed. The blood was to be daubed on by using sprigs of hyssop leaves.

19:30 When he had received the drink, Jesus said, "It is finished." With that, he bowed his head and gave up his spirit.

"gave up his spirit": from these words many scholars including myself, conclude that Jesus voluntarily left his body. This he did after he perceived that some unspecified spiritual task or process was completed.

19:31 Now it was the day of Preparation, and the next day was to be a special Sabbath. Because the Jewish leaders did not want the bodies left on the crosses during the Sabbath, they asked Pilate to have the legs broken and the bodies taken down.

"special Sabbath": this expression is otherwise unknown in Jewish literature of the times; but it may mean that the first day of the Passover that year coincided with a Sabbath day.

19:32 The soldiers therefore came and broke the legs of the first man who had been crucified with Jesus, and then those of the other.
19:33 But when they came to Jesus and found that he was already dead, they did not break his legs.

See v.36 regarding 'did not break his legs".

19:34 Instead, one of the soldiers pierced Jesus' side with a spear, bringing forth a sudden flow of blood and water.

'blood and water": this reported gush of blood and water has remained an enigma. Whilst some medical experts do accept that this can happen to a corpse, most do not (it is possible with a living person, which is not the case here). My own conclusion is that this event did happen, but only because of the exceptional, indeed unique, circumstances here.

As noted with v. 30, Jesus' death did not occur because his body's vital organs ceased to function; instead, in some way unspecified, he willed his own death, and so his soul left his body, whose vital organs then began to die.

As a result of this, strange medical consequences would be invoked; this could explain the unusual flow. But this phenomenon of water and blood points to the inner significance of the death on the cross; for the blood may be seen as signifying the soul of the Christ, and the water as signifying his eternal life-forces.

Many times in the Gospel, water is used as a symbol of life eternal: so then this gush of blood and water from the side, pouring down onto the ground, alludes to the core esoteric truth of Christianity, as this Gospel discreetly indicates. Namely, that when these fluids gushed from the body of Jesus, the cosmic Christ, which had been permeating Jesus' body and soul, was released from that body, and enveloped the planet with its divine radiance.

19:35 The man who saw it has given testimony, and his testimony is true. He knows that he tells the truth, and he testifies so that you also may believe.

"the man": this third person phrase refers to the writer of the Gospel, who always keeps himself in the background, and whom I and others, understand to be Lazaros.

19:36 These things happened so that the Scripture would be fulfilled: "Not one of his bones will be broken,"

In the annual Passover festival, instituted many centuries before the Hellenistic Age, the sacrificial paschal lamb was not to have its bones broken.[350] So in that Jesus' bones were not harmed, his death demonstrates that he was, in some respects, the great Paschal Lamb.

Ever since the Israelites left Egypt, it had been stipulated that the lamb's bones must not be harmed. This was intended to signify a deeper aspect to the salvation of humanity through the future death of Jesus. This feature had to do with the reality underlying the physical body.

Rudolf Steiner's spiritual insight contributes to the understanding of the bones not being broken; a fact which obviously was of very substantial significance. In the commentary for chapter Four, it was noted that Steiner had concluded that the cosmic Christ also permeated the 'energy template' sustaining the physical body of Jesus (not the flesh). This is the underlying meaning of the bodily 'salvation' of humanity by Christ.

The soul and spirit of Jesus Christ is the perfected example, or archetype, of the future spiritualized humanity, from which the sanctified human being shall arise. But the redemption or salvation of humanity by Christ includes the body, not only the soul; that is, the 'energy template' of the body, not its flesh. However, this achievement required that the bones in the body of Jesus not be harmed.

At the Resurrection, not only the soul of Jesus, but also this body template, was permeated by divine influences. It thereby became a kind of archetype for the energetic template underlying the human physical body. The effect of creating this divine template meant that it could gradually redeem the physical body of human beings, by exerting an ennobling influence within it, making the physical flesh body less of an impediment to higher consciousness.

---

[350] Numbers, 19:12.

19:37 and, as another scripture says, "They will look on the one they have pierced."

There are scarcely any Biblical references to this piercing. Psalm 22:16 does refer to the hands and the feet being pierced, but not the side of the body.[351] This situation may indicate that a highly esoteric meaning may be veiled here.

**19:38 Later, Joseph of Arimathea asked Pilate for the body of Jesus. Now Joseph was a disciple of Jesus, but secretly, because he feared the Jewish leaders. With Pilate's permission, he came and took the body away.
19:39 He was accompanied by Nicodemus, the man who earlier had visited Jesus at night. Nicodemus brought a mixture of myrrh and aloes, weighing about seventy-five pounds.
19:40 Taking Jesus' body, the two of them wrapped it with the spices, in strips of linen. This was in accordance with Jewish burial customs.
19:41 At the place where Jesus was crucified, there was a garden, and in the garden was a new tomb, in which no-one had ever been placed.**

"no-one had ever been placed:" Contemplation on this verse gives rise to the thought that this phrase has a profound spiritual meaning, and is not just reporting on the past usage or non-usage of the tomb. It may be that 'tomb' here is a metaphor for the state in which the newly deceased find themselves.

Death, and our existence in the Soul-world thereafter, is obviously a deeply veiled and enigmatic part of human existence. The Bible gives only a few sparse, inconsistent indications as to what the soul undergoes when its body dies, and it finds itself in the Soul-world. However, various initiatory texts from the Hellenistic Jewish and Christian worlds do attempt to describe, even if only briefly, the trials, challenges and wondrous joys that can await the soul.

It may be the case that the enigma of death, the manifestation of life-destroying qualities in the human

---

[351] There is also an indirect reference in Zechariah (12:10).

soul, needed to be encountered by Jesus Christ, and that the opportunity for this to be done, occurred during the death on the cross. According to Rudolf Steiner's research, the divine beings have no experience of death; Christ had to learn about this from the human being.[352] His perspective is echoed by a brief passage in one of the remarkable Nag Hammadi texts, *The Dialogue of the Saviour*, dating from the 2nd century,
"Matthew said, 'Tell me, Lord, how the dead die, and how the living live?'
The Lord said, "You have asked for a word about that which the eye has not seen, nor have I heard about it – except from you......"

Like other such texts in this collection, this treatise contains what I believe to be genuine words of Jesus, but mixed in with inferior, speculative ideas. As noted in Part One, Section Eight, in reference to the *Gospel of Thomas*, some of the words of Jesus are hierophantic; these are words spoken for those on the initiatory path. The above extract is another example of such hierophantic words.

So on that fateful Saturday, Jesus was 'in a tomb in which no-one had ever been lain'; that is, he was in some process that the human mind can scarcely grasp. Jesus was undergoing an experience of what causes death in the human soul. This had to happen in order that the Christ might know in what way the soul could be granted, after the death of the body, an 'eternal life': a blessed and conscious existence in spiritual realms.

The Gospel and epistles do refer to another aspect of the tasks Jesus Christ was engaged in, after his death and before his Resurrection. As noted earlier, in Part One, Section Two, this was the so-called 'Harrowing of Hades". We commented then that in the Underworld, the mighty Christ-power imbuing Jesus brought light to deceased souls, opening up a pathway for them out of the darkened Soul-realm.

19:42 Because it was the Jewish Day of Preparation and since the tomb was nearby, they laid Jesus there.

---

[352] Indicated in GA 112, lect., 6 July 1909, and GA 108. p.300.

The dates and sequence of events involving Jesus, relative to the Passover festival that year, are shown in Appendix 17. In essence, this Gospel is saying that the day after Jesus was crucified, was the Passover Day (although it started at 6pm of the day of crucifixion). An actual slain lamb was the central part of the meal, to commemorate the protection given to the Israelites so that they may escape from Egypt.

Whilst Jesus, the instrument and vessel of the Lamb of God, lay in his grave, sacrificed in order that our planet may receive those divine influences whose powers are such, that the human soul and spirit can be freed from evil. In our times, it can appear that evil has increased, not decreased; but humanity can not really know what the future may bring, in the way of personal and planetary renewal.

CHAPTER 20

20:1 Early on the first day of the festival week, while it was still dark, Mary Magdalene went to the tomb and saw that the stone had been removed from the entrance.[353]
20:2 So she went running to Simon Peter and to the other disciple, the one Jesus loved, and said, "They have taken the Lord out of the tomb, and we don't know where they have put him!"

"to Peter and to the other..." the Greek indicates that these two men were in separate locations, but not far apart.
"the other disciple": this refers to Lazaros
"we don't know": the plural here implies that Mary Magdalene was with other women when she went to the tomb. When she is first mentioned in Luke's Gospel, she is referred to as "Mary, the Magdalene", and this appears to be emphasizing that she has a task similar to the tower of Magdola in Egypt that looks into the realm of the Dead. It is with the events of Golgotha involving death that Mary Magdalene is so involved. (See Appendix 18 for more about Mary Magdalene.)

20:3 So Peter and the other disciple set out, going towards the tomb.
20:4 Both were running, but the other disciple outran Peter and reached the tomb first.
20:5 He bent down to look in and saw the strips of linen lying there, but he did not go in.
20:6 Then Simon Peter, who was behind him, arrived and went into the tomb. He saw the strips of linen lying there,

---

[353] The Greek here actually says "on day one of the week, not "the first day"; this is not a usual Greek expression. But this also occurs in the synoptic Gospels, in regard to the Passover. It is derived from the Aramaic way of numbering the festival days; for the Festival of Passover, followed by the 7-day Festival of Unleavened Bread, so this event went for 8 days.

20:7 as well as the cloth that had been around Jesus' head. The cloth was folded up by itself, separate from the linen.

The way that the burial shroud and face covering were lying there, indicates that the body of Jesus somehow disappeared, yet leaving the cloth behind, unharmed.[354]

This disappearance of the body directly impacts on a very complex topic; that of the 'bodily resurrection' of Jesus. This was discussed in Part One, Section 4, and again in regard to v. 19:36. There the doctrine of the 'bodily resurrection' of Jesus was defined from an esoteric viewpoint.

It is understood as referring to the subtle ethereal 'energetic template' sustaining the body, being renewed and healed, not the flesh of the body. Consequently, whatever brought about the end of the flesh of Jesus' body, is not seen as so important.

At the death of Jesus on Golgotha hill, blood and water flowed from the wound made by the spear, and then went into the ground. This signified the release of the sacred spiritual reality permeating the body. The dual flow caused by the spear represents the process of the cosmic Christ permeating the earth; a powerful metaphor of a deep mystery.

20:8 So then the other disciple, who had reached the tomb first, also went inside. He saw and perceived intuitively (the situation).

"perceived intuitively": usually, 'believed'. Again the word 'pistis' is involved, and whilst 'he believed' is also accurate to the Greek, a discerning, intuitive perceiving

---

[354] Or perhaps the report is implying that whilst the body was somehow 'de-structured', spiritual beings took care of the cloth. This mystery has been intensified for many people by the Shroud of Turin, the authenticity of which is disputed. But the imprint on this cloth is suggestive of an energy being released, as the body disappeared, imprinting its image onto the cloth. The carbon-dating which produced a medieval origin is not crucial, if as suggested, it was based on a piece of the medieval cloth used for repairs.

is more likely. As the next verse states, the disciples had not understood that Jesus was to be resurrected. So Lazaros was spiritually discerning that an extraordinary mystery involving the Saviour - he who had declared that he was the source of eternal life - had occurred. In this moment Lazaros intuited that Jesus had overcome death, in some remarkable way.

20:9 (For as yet they did not understand from Scripture that Jesus had to rise from the dead.)
20:10 Then the disciples returned to their homes.
20:11 But Mary had stood outside the tomb, weeping. As she wept, she bent over to look into the tomb;
20:12 And she sees two Angels in white, seated where the body of Jesus had been laid; one at the head, the other at the feet.[355]
20:13 And they say to her, "Woman, why do you cry?" She said to them, "They have taken my Lord, and I do not where they have placed him."
20:14 When she had said this, she turned around, and she sees Jesus standing there; but she did not know that it was Jesus.

"did not know": various explanations have been made that Jesus, as the now resurrected Saviour, was not recognizable to Mary. For example, the dim early morning light is mentioned, but I find the explanation from Rudolf Steiner to be the most convincing. Namely that the 'body' of Jesus, was no longer a flesh and blood physical body, but was formed from life-forces. These energies were condensed sufficiently to be visible to those who had attained at least a limited clairvoyance or higher cognizing. So it had a different appearance to his flesh body. Many people have a capacity to see subtle energies in their environs; this was the case with those who saw the risen Jesus.

---

[355] The position of the two Angels may be not significant, but they do represent exactly ancient Egyptian scenes of the initiatory sleep (seeming death) of an acolyte, who is identified as a vessel of the sun-god Osiris (an aspect of Christ) and his triumphant awakening; the two goddesses Isis and Nephthys assume these positions, in grief.

Mary Magdalene obviously had a definite clairvoyant experience, or she could not have perceived the angelic beings. The resurrection body of Jesus was sufficiently dense to be touched and to move objects; the on-looker then assumes that it is a flesh and blood body.

20:15 Jesus says to her, "Woman, why are you crying? Whom are you looking for?" Supposing him to be the gardener, she says to him, "Sir, if you have removed him, tell me where you have placed him, and I will take him away."

Mary is distraught, doesn't directly answer the question; she does not identify who she looking for, and seems to imply that she could carry away the body of Jesus by herself.

20:16 Jesus says to her, "Mary." Her awareness changed, she says in Hebrew, "Rabbouni !" which means 'Teacher'.

"her awareness changed": or, her perception changed": usually, "turning around", which is a common meaning of the verb here, as used in v. 20:14.
But the verb, 'strephoe' (στρέφω) also means 'to be changed', 'to change inwardly', to change into', etc.
This other meaning is what is meant here. It is directly implied that Mary's awareness or perceiving was changed, for as the risen Saviour addresses her by name, his voice changes her perceiving, so she then can discern who this otherwise unrecognizable person really is.

Whereas, for Mary to 'turn herself around' in order to see Jesus again to speak to him, whilst she was in dialogue with him, suggests that even whilst questioning 'the gardener', she was looking around everywhere somewhat frantically in distress. This is possible, but it is unlikely, since she would know that the 'gardener' would not have just left the corpse on the ground somewhere. It is also unlikely, (but possible), that Jesus would have spoken his empowering word to her, even if she was looking frantically around.

"Rabbouni !": this is a Palestinian version of 'Rabbi', and some scholars say it means 'dear Master/Teacher'.

20:17 Jesus says to her, "Don't hold onto me, as I have not yet ascended to the Father. But, go to the brothers and say to them, 'I am ascending to my Father and your Father; to my God and your God'."

There are several profound esoteric themes in this verse. But first, only when one knows that in the culture at this time, the prevailing attitude was that women had no capacity to be a witness to anything of significance, does the experience of Mary Magdalene reveal its extraordinary social statement. If a Jewish man killed a person, and the crime was directly witnessed by one or more women, the criminal was not prosecuted, as the testimony of the women witnesses had no value in a court.

Yet now, through the specific intention of Jesus Christ, a woman was chosen to bear witness to what was, from the viewpoint of Christianity and of spiritual knowledge, the most significant event of all time.

Christianity, as a religious-social movement, came into being as a direct result of the witnesses to the risen Jesus, and the first such witness was the woman, Mary Magdalene. Her words prepared the men (the disciples) for the experience of seeing the risen Jesus themselves.

"go to *the* brothers": usually, 'my brothers"; but Bezae and many other manuscripts omit 'my'.[356]

"Don't hold onto me….not yet ascended to the Father": these words are indicating a process too profoundly transcendent to be explained to Mary. One may conclude that a process involving the ascent of Jesus to a high spiritual realm was needed, in order to somehow consolidate the unique 'body' he now had, and in which Jesus could soon manifest to other people. Direct and intense contact between a physical body and this remarkable, temporarily densified, 'resurrection body', of Jesus was harmful to this ethereal body, at least until it was consolidated, in higher realms.

---

[356] The official Aland Greek text (Novum, Testamentum Graece:28, fails to indicate that Bezae also omits this word.

Rudolf Steiner's research provides an esoteric perspective here. He concludes that this resurrection body was composed of the 'energy template', which exists behind every person's flesh body. But added to it were some ethereal energies, to make it perceptible to Mary and later, the disciples. It is from this renewed template that influences can stream forth, to heal the energetic template underlying everyone's body.

20:18 Mary Magdalene departs and reports to his disciples, that she had seen the Lord. And she revealed to them what he had said to her.

"reports": usually, 'tells'; but Bezae has the verb 'apangelloe' (ἀπαγγέλω) which means a more formal announcing of an event.
"his disciples': from Bezae, usually 'the disciples'.
"that *she* had seen": usually, "I have seen.." but codex Bezae has 'she had seen', which is more compatible to the rest of the verse, since it is a report from Lazaros.
"seen": the verb here 'horaoe' (ὁράω) is almost always used in this Gospel for clairvoyant perceiving.

20:19 Then, in the early evening of that day, the first day of the week, when the doors of the house where the disciples met were locked, for fear of the Jews, Jesus appeared, and was present amongst them, and says to them, "Peace be with you".

"appeared": usually translated as 'came', but Jesus directly manifested in the room, the physical doors being irrelevant. The resurrection body, being the energetic template with some added ethereal energies, was devoid of flesh and blood, and could thus move at will through solid doors, etc.

This is again a Sunday; and these two 'Sunday' experiences may have been a factor in the choice of Sunday by the emerging Christian church as their sacred day, as distinct from Saturday, the sacred day for Judaism.[357]

---

[357] As S. Bacchiocchi demonstrated in, *Anti-Judaism and the origin of Sunday*, 1975. In addition to the wish to be a separate entity from the Jewish community, I conclude that

"Peace be with you": As noted with 14:27, the giving of peace by the Risen Jesus means that through the Christ-spirituality enveloping him, the emerging of the Spiritual-self in the disciples is assisted; it is this new blessed condition that confers true inner peace. The inner strength of spirit, needed to conquer the egoistic qualities, forms the basis for such peace.

20:20 After he said this, he showed them the hands and the feet, and his side. So then the disciples rejoiced at having seen the Lord.

His new ethereal, quasi-physical body at this stage still had the marks on it from being crucified.

20:21 So Jesus said again to them, "Peace be with you. As the Father has sent me, so do I send you."

Soon Jesus shall send his disciples out into the world to spread the Gospel message.

20:22 Having said this, he breathed upon them and said, "Receive the Holy Spirit!"

It appears that this verse refers to a spiritual influence, similar to what shall take place at the Pentecost event.

20:23 Those whose sins you forgive, they are removed; if you retain the sins of anyone, they are retained.

"removed": usually, 'forgiven' as the same verb for 'forgive' is used here twice; the reason I have made this variation ('removed') with its second occurrence, is discussed below. The close followers of Jesus Christ who were gathered together on that occasion, receiving from the 'breath' of Jesus that holy influence, were given a special power.

To understand this remarkable gift, one needs to have a clear view of what the Gospel reports about

---

there was also, at some level, a sense of an inner unity between the Christ and Sunday. Whether people thought of the Sun imagery about Christ in Scripture, as just poetic, or as esoterically real.

'forgiveness of sin'. In chapter One, (1:29) we read of the Lamb of God who shall "take up and away" the sins of the world; not 'forgive' the sins. So in this account, 'sin' or unethical behaviour, was seen as a disturbing influence in the cosmos. This concept was widespread in ancient times, there was something 'objective' about unethical behaviour; it had a subtle impact on the world.

Forgiveness here does not mean that 'The Lamb of God' made the effort to not be offended in his own being, by some unethical behaviour. Rather, it was that the 'Earth-sphere' was impacted, and had to be cleansed of the impact of the sins.

Now, here near the end of the Gospel, we read of the 'forgiving' of sins of individuals, by the disciples. But the verb here, which is accurately translated as 'forgiving', literally means to 'take away' or 'remove' or 'let go away' of something. So, as in my translation , they 'removed' the sin. One sees that an objective quality to sin is also implied in the word itself.

For of the 14 times that Lazaros uses this verb, it always means 'to remove' in a normal sense (e.g., 4:3 "Jesus left Judea" or 16:28 "I am leaving the world"); and even here, where 'forgiveness' is clearly meant, this sense of 'removing' is still implied.

The forgiving of sins is usually presented as something which God does, after a person has acknowledged and confessed to them, as emphasized in the Lord's Prayer. Or it is presented as something which 'The Son of Man' does, who is at times identified with Jesus. But at other times, this title suggests a state of spirituality which sanctified or initiated persons attain.

It is then significant that here it is the disciples who are given this power of forgiveness, an action which suggests removal of the impact which unethical behaviour causes. But not its impact upon the world, as is implied with the Lamb of God, but its impact upon the person themselves (their inner or outer well-being).

Verse 20:23 again,
"Those who sins you forgive, they are removed; if you retain the sins of anyone, they are retained."
"they are retained": the above comments may clarify why the unusual word, 'retained' is used by Lazaros

here. It is because the un-forgiven 'sins' are still present or retained in the influence which that person has on the world around them. Otherwise the wording would be something like, "the person is still sinful".

This is a mysterious and deep topic; that the disciples attain a divine power which is usually associated with God. However, Jesus had earlier taught that The Son of Man also has this power, and since, as noted above, this phrase can refer to a spiritual status, one can assume that now the disciples have this status. (But this does not mean that later, when the Christian church has been established, that dignitaries in the church should claim this same power.)

20:24 But Thomas, one of the twelve, the one called the Twin, was not with them, when Jesus appeared.
20:25 So the other disciples told him, "We have beheld the Lord." But Thomas said to them, "Unless I see in his hands, the mark of the nails – and put my finger in the mark of the nails, and my hand in his side, I will not believe."

"We have beheld the Lord": again the verb here is horaoe (ὁράω) which is the primary verb used for clairvoyant perceiving in this Gospel (about 25 of the 28 occasions). So the implication here is that a form of slightly clairvoyant perceiving occurs for the disciples; which is what the disciples and Mary Magdalene had earlier experienced. But Thomas uses this same verb in its rare physical application (in this Gospel) of physical seeing, because he did not understand that the Risen Lord is no longer in a flesh and blood body.

20:26 After eight days, his disciples were again in the house, but Thomas was with them, and Jesus appears – the doors having been shut – and was there in the midst of them – and he says, "Peace be with you".
20:27 Then he says to Thomas: "Bring over here your finger ! And now, behold my hands ! And bring over your hand and put it into my side. And so, do not be non-perceiving, but be truly perceptive !"

This is a significant verse reporting on a crucial feature of the close interaction between a person and the Risen Jesus. Since the 'body' of Jesus is not a flesh and blood body, Thomas cannot actually get the 'proof' he wants; and yet he does get a finer proof. The Greek here has to convey all this. Jesus does this by using a verb 'pheroe' (φέρω) to convey a subtle message to the alert reader.

That is why he says, "Bring over here your finger", usually translated as 'put your finger"; yet the verb does not mean 'to put'. It can mean simply 'bring' or 'carry', but it also has another meaning: to let something 'be borne along', or 'brought forth', or 'moved along', or 'impelled along', by some subtle influence. In this usage it occurs in various ways in Greek secular literature and in Scripture:

of the wind, impelling clouds and boats along.[358]

of the Spirit surging through a house (Acts.2:2)

of the life-force in a seed bringing forth flower and grain (Jn. 15:14 and Mk.4:8)

when Christians are moved to speak by the Holy Spirit (2Pet.1:21)

Creation itself is being borne along and sustained by the Logos (Heb.1:3)

So this is not the appropriate verb for putting your hand out to touch something; as Morris comments, "this is not the verb we would expect for this kind of action".[359] There is a nuance in the words of Jesus here, of a life-force behind the muscles of the finger and hand, enabling motion: the verb is saying, "let your finger and hand *be carried along* to me". There is here a subtle indication of an impelling influence, moving the finger or hand toward Jesus.

Before contemplating further this nuance of the verse, note the very emphatic nature of his words to Thomas; Jesus uses the 'imperative' form of the verb; that is, he is ordering Thomas to do something. This forceful way of speaking is striking; Jesus is ordering Thomas to really intensely look at his hand: "**And behold my hands !**"

---

[358] Examples give in Bauer, *Greek-English Lexicon*, entry φέρω.
[359] Morris, *Gospel Accord. John*, p. 752.

Jesus is endeavouring to awaken in Thomas his intuitive discernment, which is a perceiving beyond matter; a spiritual seeing. There is then an initiatory dynamic here, of Jesus seeking to lift Thomas' cognizing up to the level of life-forces, for the body of Jesus is mainly composed of such energies.

This situation, that such an enhanced cognizing is necessary to see the risen Jesus, is not generally recognized. This has led to the view that "behold my hands !" means that Thomas should observe the *movements* of the hands of Jesus.[360] Therefore Morris comments "...we do not expect this word 'Behold' for the action of (looking at) the (moving) hands of Jesus".

But this interpretation is missing the point; it is erroneous.[361] For the next command makes it clear that Jesus is not saying 'look at how my hands are moving'. Jesus is wanting Thomas to become more perceptive of what kind of 'body' he now has; in other words, to really try to perceive with some seership, some holistic sensing, just what kind of reality is in front of him; …**"do not be non-perceiving, but be perceptive !"**

This is also a striking example of the second meaning of 'faith': here Thomas is to cognize beyond material substances.[362] So the lesson here from Jesus appears to be this:

"Try to sense the life-force that is animating your finger and hand; for on *that* level, is my new body to be experienced. You should be able, with enhanced perceiving, to sense when your own life-forces encounter my ethereal 'resurrection body'. And that is more significant proof of my existence, than physically touching wounds in a flesh and blood body."

As scholars note, Thomas does not actually touch the body of Jesus; for as he responds to the hierophantic urging of Jesus, his vision is enhanced, and he perceives the more-than-physical reality of the risen Saviour, and thus no longer seeks to touch a physical body.

---

[360] The Greek here: ide – ἴδε.
[361] Ref. 331.
[362] This same perspective was taught by R. Steiner (GA 244, p.253.)

20:28 Thomas answered Jesus, and said to him, "My Lord and my God !"

That Thomas exclaims in profound reverence, that Jesus is his "Lord and God" reveals firstly that he has perceived a spiritual power that has, amongst much else, created the 'resurrection body' of Jesus. Secondly, the phrase "my Lord and my God" is a Jewish expression of great reverence, in which the Hebrew words used are 'Jahve' (Lord) and 'Elohim' (God); it occurs for example in Psalm 35:23.

So this phrase is saying that a revered entity is 'God' whereby the worshiper emphasizes this by using not one, but the two most recognized names of God in the Hebrew Scriptures: Jahve and Elohim. So the exclamation of Thomas now, is saying that Jesus is the vessel of 'God'. (Barrett reports that this same phrase was also found in a Greek inscription in Egypt of 24 BCE, "To the god and Lord, Socnopaio"; and this same phrase was required to be used of the Emperor Domitian, CE 81-96.)

20:29 Jesus says to him, "You have beheld me, and you believe; blessed are those who believe, yet have not seen.

"beheld": that Thomas had to gain some slight seership to perceive the risen Saviour, is alluded to here, in that Jesus again uses the verb 'horaoe', (ὁράω) which is the primary verb for clairvoyance, rather than physical sense-based vision.

"and you believe": here Jesus is making a solemn statement and expanding on this to refer to other believers. Some scholars think that these words are actually a question, "...and you believe?" But there is no solid textual evidence for this, as the earliest manuscripts usually lacked a comprehensive system of punctuation. (Bezae and papyrus 66 and others, do not include question marks). But to myself and many other scholars, the solemnity of the pronouncement here excludes a rhetorical or ironical questioning of Thomas.

20:30 And indeed Jesus also carried out many other wonders in the presence of his disciples, which are not written in this book.
20:31 But these things have been written that you may come to know that Jesus is the Messiah, the Son of God; and that, in so believing, you may have eternal life, through the divine power of his being.

"through the divine power of his being": usually, 'in his name'; but as noted with v. 5:43 the term 'name' meant in those days, the core quality and inherent power and significance of a deity.

"may come to know": the verb used here occurs in two forms in various ancient manuscripts; in Bezae and several others, the verbal form here means that Lazaros is creating his Gospel to bring people who are not yet Christians, to a knowledge of the Christ reality: "that you may come to know". (The 'aorist subjunctive' form, but see below).

The verbal form in other manuscripts, differing only by one letter, means that Lazaros is directing his Gospel to those who are already Christians, seeking to consolidate their understanding: "that you may continue to know". (The 'present subjunctive' form.)[363]

Scholars are divided as to which version is correct. But I conclude, since Bezae is often superior in accuracy than other versions, that it has the correct version here also. This is especially affirmed, when one expands the definition of Lazaros' evangelistic purpose; that he was seeking to spread the Gospel message not only to non-Christians, but also to those who have some small acquaintance of the Gospel message, but are seeking a deeper grasp of it.

---

[363] Present subjunctive: pisteuaete - πιστεύητε
Aorist subjunctive: pisteusaete - πιστεύσητε

CHAPTER 21

This chapter is not part of the narrative of what occurred during the lifetime of Jesus; it is a purely transcendent, initiatory experience, added at the end of the Gospel, primarily because it provides valuable indicators for a future blossoming of Christianity. That is, when the initiatory dimension to the spiritual life and to Christianity, will be welcome. Naturally, the usual practice of veiling the deeper spiritual realities, as already encountered in this Gospel, is continued here.

As such, it presents a deeply esoteric spiritual training episode which, by its very nature, is far beyond everyday life. Since it has an esoteric meaning, it requires the Initiatory Quest approach, if it is to be understood. It remains enigmatic to the implicit humanistic focus underlying so much of our theology.

On the surface level, it is a story about a fishing trip, but many subtle points in the Greek, and some not so subtle, demonstrate that its main message is within the veiled esoteric level.

The following commentary is indebted to some brief remarks from Rudolf Steiner, whose seership and scholarship open a vastly different view on this enigmatic chapter. It is my hope that this esoteric viewpoint will be confirmed by my approach to the subtleties in the Greek narrative.

To understand the veiled teaching in this episode, some key esoteric cosmic concepts that underlie this, need to be mentioned. These tasks involve functioning in a meditative session, beyond the sense-world, hence in spirit realms, amidst divine beings.

To function, as a self-aware person in the realms of spirit, with the help of divine beings, was a well-established and revered aspect of the initiatory Hebrew world; many non-Biblical Hebrew and Greek texts still exist in which the acolyte reports on his attempt to properly cognize and understand transcendent realities. Earlier, we noted the Book of Enoch, and various Qumran texts, for example; as well as some from ancient Egypt and elsewhere.

It is this same age-old core challenge of the acolyte on the initiatory path, which this chapter 21 is presenting, but in the unique context of the risen Saviour guiding his disciples.

The commentary will attempt to unveil the lofty nature of the spiritual tasks awaiting those who become Christian initiates. The message of this last chapter is that the initiated Christian is enabled to experience and work with divine influences from the cosmic Christ that now envelop our planet. This requires seership or enhanced consciousness.

It was noted in 6:1-13, that the feeding of the 5,000 event was signifying that the disciples were being involved in an initiatory quest. They were to be actively mediating cosmic influences radiating out from the cosmic Christ, and from Jesus, to human beings. They had to learn how to nurture the human soul and spirit with cosmic Christ energies.

This is how the reality of the Resurrection is confirmed to those whose sanctified consciousness has been able to transcend the physical world. It is the presence of such spiritual influences which determine much of what happens in the human soul, and in the cultural life. In this chapter 21, this same process is the theme, but it is presented in a more detailed way than in Chapter Six.

The very transcendent concept here is that there are spiritual energies radiating out through the cosmos, which permeate the Earth-sphere. This concept affirms that a form of esoteric experience and knowledge similar to what is defined as 'Gnosticism', is an essential part of the Christian Gospels, and therefore has been interwoven, discreetly, into the Gospel texts. Such 'Gnosticism' in the sense of esoteric knowledge, had been a part of the Jewish tradition from long before the Hellenistic Age.

It is this dynamic which is of direct relevance to the cosmic Christ; his disciples are to learn how to assist in regulating and mediating these in-raying energies to humanity. This dynamic is the theme of this last chapter, but Lazaros has been careful to veil this in his narrative.

21:1 After these things Jesus appeared to his disciples, by the Sea of Tiberias. He manifested in this way:

"manifested": i.e., Jesus became perceptible to their seership.

Rudolf Steiner explains, that in this episode, Jesus Christ, as the vessel of the cosmic Christ, the great sun-god, manifested himself in the Soul-world (the sea) in such a way that the 'spiritual' sun influences were to be seen approaching from the direction of the constellation of Pisces. This was a new and significant dynamic for the Earth, as it was only a recent occurrence that the sun entered the constellation of Pisces, the Fishes (about 65 BC).[364] Therefore, one notes that with the miraculous feeding of people by Elijah with a few loaves, there is no mention of two fishes. To modern matter-focussed consciousness, this Sun-zodiac interaction is of very little interest or relevance to life, but it was not so in ancient times.[365]

21:2 there were gathered together, Simon Peter and Thomas, the one called Didymos, and Nathanael from Cana of Galilee, and the sons of Zebedee and two other of his disciples.

These disciples gathered for a probationary initiatory experience which arose through a meditative session. Simon Peter (who had been forgiven for his betrayal) and Thomas (who had made up for his lack of perception and his consequent doubt) and the initiate Nathanael (of Cana in Galilee) also James and John of Zebedee, and Lazarus-John and an unnamed person were there.

---

[364] Although in terms of zodiacal Ages, which appear to have been the cultural time-markers throughout Antiquity, the lifetime of Jesus was in the Age of Aries, the Lamb. These various astronomical-astrological factors were very likely why both a lamb and fish became symbols of Christianity.

[365] Those who explore gardening according to the position of the moon amongst the constellations, and animal life-cycles, are aware that definite influences become operative.

21:3 Simon Peter says to them, "I'm going fishing". They say to him, "we are coming with you. They went out and embarked into the boat, but in that night they took hold of nothing.

"took hold": the Greek word here 'episan' (ἐπίσαν) does not refer to 'catching' fish; for it means to seize, press, arrest, or apprehend, something.[366]

"fish": spiritual influences within the Soul-world, raying out from Pisces, and permeated by solar influences.

"but they took hold of nothing": it was possible, but not so common, that fishermen did not catch any fish in the actual sea of Tiberias, for it was teeming with fish. So the message in this verse is that their attempt to become perceptive of the spiritual influences failed.

"boat": this alludes to the soul-body; quite similar to the Egyptian Book of the Dead, and other literature.[367]

"*the* boat": this indicates a quite specific boat, but as scholars note, none was mentioned earlier. It alludes to the soul-body, indicating that this is the only 'vessel' in which one can cognize in the Soul-world.

So here on the initiatory level, Simon Peter says to the others, "I am now going to enter into the process of perceiving and absorbing Pisces influences, raying out towards us from the sun-god Christ, and mediated to humanity by Jesus." They said to him, "And we shall join with you in this attempt". They entered into a meditative state, in the attempt to attain the required seership or higher consciousness. But in that attempt, these acolytes were unable to take hold of these influences. Their souls failed to perceive and be permeated by, any streams of spiritual energy from the cosmic Christ. ('They took hold of no fish'.)

---

[366] The verbs for catching fish is alieuoe (ἁλιευω), or agreuoe (ἀγρεύω); but these verbs could also be used: 'to take' lambanoe (λαμβανω) or 'to take hold of' 'epilambanoe (ἐπιλαμβανω).

[367] Such as the Greek boat of Charon, the guide of the Dead as they leave the earthly realm.

21:4 Early in the morning, Jesus appeared and was present on the shore, and yet even so, the disciples did not realize that it was Jesus.

'the shore': signifies the definite, clearly aware consciousness, or 'I' state, which the advanced disciple has, whether in the body or out of the body. One is reminded here of the many initiatory out-of-body experiences of Hellenistic initiates, reported in the Apocryphal literature, and also of St. Paul whereby he entered into 'the third Heaven' (2Cor.12:2). The reference in the *Shepherd of Hermas* was noted earlier, that the disciples, like Jesus, went into the Soul-world to help the Dead (in Part One, Section 2).

"yet even so": the Greek 'mentoi' (μέντοι) is a strong expression, stronger than the usual 'but'.

21:4: paraphrased for the esoteric meaning
With dawn having arrived, the shared meditation session was about to end. Jesus was presenting himself to their consciousness, as their awareness of the spirit realm was integrated with the normal physical world. But surprisingly, the disciples had not realized that it was Jesus who was present and seeking to help them.

21:5 However, Jesus called out to them, 'You children, you certainly don't have any prepared fish provisions, do you? They replied, "None."

"prepared fish provisions": this is what the Greek word here, 'prosaphagion' (προσφάγιον) specifically means; it does not mean 'fish', freshly caught fish.[368] It is derived from the word 'opsov' (ὄψον) which means foodstuff or victuals made from preserved (salted) fish. So here already is an indicator of a veiled message, (of Piscean influences that are absorbable, or able to be assimilated, see below).

---

[368] More specifically it means; 1: a prepared dish of food, or 2: relish or dainties, often fish-based. (It can also mean, but only in Athens, fish itself).

"certainly don't": in Bezae, the question from Jesus is strongly phrased to the effect that they really have seized nothing, through the word 'maeti' (μήτι), not simply 'mae' (μή).

On the initiatory level, this 'fish provisions' represent a small quantum of solar influences coming from the cosmic Christ, interwoven with Piscean energies. The Saviour, as the hierophant of the disciples, is asking whether they have succeeded in encountering and taking hold of cosmic spiritual influences of the solar Logos (or cosmic Christ); these are influences which Jesus was endeavouring to make accessible to them.

"children": Jesus calls the disciples, 'children', as in v. 13:33. But here it refers to acolytes who are in training, and hence it implies 'apprentices', as Godet concludes.[369]

21:6 He said to them, Throw the net to the right sides of the boat, and you shall encounter (this). Therefore they cast it out (in this way), but then they were no longer strong enough to draw it in, because of the multitude of fishes.

Before unveiling the initiatory meaning here, some key words need to be briefly noted:

"right sides of the boat": the Greek actually states exactly this impossibility; obviously a boat can have only one right side and one left side. Scholars have concluded that this phrase is an unsolvable riddle, (but it has a specific esoteric meaning; see below). Regarding the two right 'sides' of the boat, it was noted with Jn. 2:23 and 5:1 (the 'Jerusalems'), that the plural is used wherever a very substantial spiritual significance or power is present.

"sides": this Greek word 'merae' (μέρη) has another meaning, 'portions' or 'parts', which is what is meant here.

'right': the word right 'dexia' (δεξιὰ) also means honoured or honourable (in Koine Greek) and in Hellenistic-Attic Greek, "assured, assurance, trusted". Moreover, it also means a fortunate or spiritual state of

---

[369] Godet, *Evangelium Johannes*, p. 634.

being, which can be the gift of a god, e.g., "Undoubtedly the god is bringing your happy (blessed) state to you."[370]

So the "right sides of the boat" can also be understood as 'the finer, nobler aspect of the soul or soul-body' (which the boat represents). And there is the implication these nobler qualities of the soul must be steering the soul.

Jesus is instructing them saying, try to take hold of the solar energies raying in from the direction of the constellation of Pisces, by extending your consciousness out from the higher, nobler quality of your soul (the Spiritual-soul). If you can be centred within your higher spiritual consciousness, then you **shall** encounter these cosmic influences. For it is with this sanctified consciousness quality, that the Christ can be cognized in spirit realms.

So v. 7 is communicating the following: the 'boat' is the soul-body, therefore **the right side(s) is the higher consciousness state** and because this is so crucial, it was put in the plural. This higher soul state has to be 'steering the soul'. The seven disciples are seeking to spiritually work together in an initiatory spiritual activity, as one unified group.[371]

By centering themselves on the Christ-presence within, and thus functioning from within their spiritual awareness, they sought to access and integrate these influences enveloping them in the Soul-world; in doing this, they were then successful.

But as they began to return to normal, earthly day-consciousness, they scarcely had enough empowerment from their higher self to absorb and integrate into their 'I' what they had encountered in the spirit realm. (However, Jesus is there monitoring, see below.)

The surface meaning here, of throwing a literal fishing net over the right side of a boat, reveals its deficiency, showing that the incident is not a physical

---

[370] In Grk. ho Theos nai sou pherae dexia (ὁ θεος νὰ(ι) σου φερῃ δεξιά). Milton-Moule *Vocab. Grk. NT*, δεξιός p. 141.

[371] That there are seven, may allude to seven of the zodiac influences (the same dynamic as in the feeding of the 5,000) to to the seven planets.

occurrence. For as Keener points out, the boat's right side is the wrong side to use. This is because a paddle was used to steer the boat and since most people are right-handed, this steering mechanism was placed on the right side of the boat. So this command is very unlikely to be feasible on the physical level, considering the boat's design. But for the surface level, it can be seen as a challenge to have faith in the command of Jesus; and to respect his advice, despite its impractical appearance.[372]

21:7 Consequently the disciple, that one whom Jesus loved, says to Peter; "It is the Lord !" Simon, thus, Peter, having heard that it was the Lord, girded himself around with the outer garment, for he was semi-clothed, and cast himself into the sea.

As a result of this successful encounter with divine influences in the Soul-world, through the help of Jesus, the disciple initiated by Jesus, that one whom Jesus loved (Lazaros-John), was able to perceive that this success was due to the presence of the Saviour, now their hierophant. So Lazaros then informs Peter, who could not perceive this; "It is the Lord !"

"Consequently": this word is revealing that since it actually is Jesus who was speaking, and because Lazaros had an initiatory seership, he was uniquely able to directly cognize that it was indeed the risen Jesus.

"thus, Peter": this unusual phrase in the text is affirming that this man is the one to whom Jesus had given the epithet Peter (meaning 'rock').

Simon Peter, having heard the call of Lazaros-John, strengthened the outer perimeter of his soul-body all around himself, and entered more intensely into a spiritual state of consciousness.[373] With his soul-body

---

[372] Keener, *The Gospel of John*, vol. 2, p. 1,218
[373] Meyer, *Gospel of John*, the middle voice of this verb diezoesatoe (διεζώσατο), with the accusative case of a garment 'epedutaen' (ἐπενδύτην), when referring to a garment usage, always means to "gird oneself therewith" (p. 395. vol 2).

(its aura) more protected, he then entered more securely into the Soul-world.

21:8 (Surface level)
The other disciples followed in the small boat, towing the net of fish, for they were not far from the shore, about 200 hundred cubits.

21:8: (Initiatory level, paraphrased)
The other disciples proceeded on after Peter, in a less impetuous manner; they were not very far from attaining to an 'I' state which also integrated awareness of the spirit realm. They were bringing along with them an awareness of the Christ-influence interwoven with Piscean influences, yet these were not fully integrated.

"200 cubits": Much debate has occurred as to what this measurement means. I have concluded that it signifies that the disciples, as acolytes on the spiritual quest, were much nearer to the Divine than is the general populace. For 200 cubits is one tenth of the distance of 2,000 cubits, that the general people had to maintain between themselves and the Ark of the Covenant, when the Israelites were marching in the desert during the Exodus. (Jos.3:4)
"net of fish": usually 'net full of fish'; but the Greek is literally 'the net (made) of fish'. This very unusual phrase is indicating that what the disciples were now bearing along within their souls, was a delicate 'tapestry' formed of Piscean-solar energies.
"the small boat": whereas in v. 3 the boat was simply 'the boat', here it is a smaller vessel. This boat is the soul-body of the disciples. The reason for this change is possibly that this is now being compared to the sheer glory and power presence of the divine influences they were now interwoven with.

21:9 When therefore they had disembarked on to the land, they see a charcoal fire laid, with a meal of fish provisions, lying upon {it}, and a bread-loaf.

"charcoal fire": the fish foodstuff is baked over the fire. This indicates that the fire of the will within the self, the

'I', has made enabled these cosmic forces to be assimilated.

"fish provisions" or a meal prepared from salted fish (which is washed or soaked to remove the salt, and then grilled.) The same kind of prepared fish 'provisions' is referred to in vs. 5 and 9. It is made from salted preserved fish; it can be regarded as the equivalent of one fish. This is very important because now the number of fish, or more accurately, fish foodstuff, which was 153, is now 154 (see below).

As they achieved this integrated seership state, they became aware that near to their consciousness were cosmic influences, mediated to them by Jesus Christ, and ready to be assimilated into their soul as soul-nourishment.

21:10 Jesus says to them, "bring forth from the fish provisions which you have just now taken hold of."

A remarkable sentence which contains the essence of the initiatory lesson.

"taken hold of": the verb means to seize or take hold of, and is not relevant to 'catching' a fish.

"fish provisions": again the word here is not 'fish' but 'fish provisions' (or foodstuff), as in vs. 5 and 9; that is, food prepared from salted fish. This is significant, because what is in the net was earlier described as 'large fish'. But now Jesus is in effect re-defining these Piscean-solar influences as no longer external influences, but as soul-nourishment; as something which has actually been absorbed by the disciples.

"bring forth": usually translated as 'bring', but the verb here, 'phero' (φέρω) means 'to bring forth' or 'to produce' or 'to offer'; so an inner effort is now asked of them by Jesus to produce, to make active, and manifest in their consciousness, these Piscean energies.

21:11 Consequently, Peter ascended, and dragged onto the land the net full of large fish – 153; and though there were so many, the net was not torn.

"ascended": this word points to the initiatory meaning, for it appears to mean that Peter had to make an effort to raise and direct his consciousness up to the cosmic solar forces which are now permeating his soul, and achieve mastery over them. (On the surface level, it can refer to dragging a fishing net up out the water onto the shore.)

"- 153": The Greeks assigned a numerical value to each letter; in codex Bezae this number 153 is emphasized by being written in just three letters after a pause (" - ργν ") that is, 'rng' which equals: 100, 50, 3. See below for an explanation of this number.

21:12 Jesus says to them, "Come, have the morning meal". But not one of the disciples dared to directly enquire, "Who are you?" - because they knew that it was the Lord.

Since this is not a physical event, there now rays into their consciousness from the Risen Jesus, the directive that, embraced by his guiding support, they may, and should, consciously absorb these cosmic energies into their souls.

"directly enquire": usually 'ask', but the verb here exetasoe (ἐξετάζω) means to really strongly enquire, to almost demand an answer.

For these seven souls it is a powerful seership experience, and they do not recognize Jesus in his form as a great empowered hierophant, as this is not how he appeared to their seership when he manifested to them shortly after the Resurrection. They intuited that this spirit-form in all its glory was Jesus, yet they were not fully confident of this.

21:13 Jesus appears to them, and takes the bread, blesses it, and gives this to them, as also the fish provisions.

So now the 153 fishes have become fish-foodstuff, and this number thereby increases, by the one that Jesus offers, to 154 (see below).

"blesses": this additional word is in codex Bezae, and appears to be a valid text.

The disciples now behold the spirit-form of the Saviour as near to them, and as passing over to them for their soul's sustenance, the spiritual sunlight (symbolized as bread, that comes from the grain, which grows in response to the sunlight); and also the Piscean influences, symbolized by the fish.

It was noted with v. 9, that this additional fish-foodstuff which Jesus has, is very important, because the number of fish(-foodstuff), which was 153, **is now 154**. Many and varied explanations of this number have been put forward over the centuries.

The 153 -> 154 fish

There is no unity about the meaning of this number. Most of the solutions as to the number 153 by various scholars, have been dismissed upon examination by other scholars.[374] My conclusion is as follows:

153 totals 9, but 154 totals 10. However, 10 is a number of great significance to the initiatory wisdom of Judaism; it represents a completed process. For example, in Genesis, when God creates the world, the Bible records that "God speaks" 10 times to bring creation about. As the wisdom of the great Jewish esoteric book, *The Zohar* states, "In 10 words the world was created" (II: fol. 14b-15a) and later, "Tenfold-ness in the work of Creation and tenfold-ness in the work of giving the Torah (the Law of Moses)..." (III: B. Mos. 3,1)[375]

For God gives the 10 commandments to Moses, after the Israelites have left Egypt; their exodus was made possible by the 10 plagues. Also as a result of this view of the number ten, and the view that the composition of our world is fourfold, there are many occasions where the number 40 (4 x 10) is emphasized in the Bible.

In v. 19:23 it was noted how the number 4 was central to Jewish thinking in regard to the world. This number refers to such realities as the 4 directions, the 4 life-waves (minerals, plant, animals, humans), and very prominently in the 4 cardinal zodiacal influences

---

[374] One theory is that complex shapes can be created if the numerical value of the words of key objects are arranged in a geometrical pattern. Another is that the phrase 'the Magdalene' equals 153. Both of these are irrelevant to the initiatory experience here.

[375] E. Müller, *Der Sohar, Das Heilige Buch der Kabbala*, 1932.

composing the multi-winged 'tetramorph', seen in the vision of Ezekiel. The number 40 represents a completion of a process or a cycle, but in regard to these aspects of life, or these cycles of time.

The significance of 10 as signifying the successful completion of a spiritual task involving Jesus, was already used in this Gospel (1:39) in regard to disciples discovering the spiritual home of Jesus 'at the 10th hour'.

So when the disciples had nearly reached the shore, and thus were drawing near to Jesus, the initiatory process was *nearly* completed (they had 153 fish-victuals = 9) but when they do reach the shore and are assisted by Jesus, then the number climbs to 154 = 10, because Jesus has a single plate of fish foodstuff. Then the disciples have completed their probationary challenge on the path to Christian initiation.

Here it is very important to note what was said by Jesus after the 153 "large fish" are mentioned;

21:10 **Jesus says to them, "bring forth from the fish foodstuff what you have just now taken hold of.**

Jesus has specifically re-defined the 153 fishes as 'fish foodstuff'; each one of these symbolic fish, are each now a portion of digestible processed (preserved) fish substance. That is, they are Piscean-solar influences which have been, or can be, 'digested' i.e., assimilated by the disciples. And so too is the single plate of fish foodstuff on the fire prepared by Jesus. So, now there are 153 + 1 "fish victuals" = 154. The disciples have achieved a state of awareness in which cosmic zodiacal influences in the spiritual realms, mediated by the sun-god Christ, can be experienced and integrated into their 'I'.

But moreover, in view of the above 'numerology', to ancient Jewish initiates, Creation was understood and experienced as a Tree of Life, with 10 spheres (called sephiroth). The 10th sephiroth (Malkuth) is understood as the physical world, and as Rudolf Steiner explains, Malkuth is also the earthly ego-state which we attain by living in the physical world. The disciples attained their goal of becoming co-workers consciously with the cosmic Christ energies.[376]

They were thereby spiritually functioning "in the sphere of the number 10, Malkuth": that is, they live in the physical realm, but have now attained a conscious experience of the cosmic Christ forces. In Malkuth, in the physical world, is where the self-conscious 'I' manifests. The story of the 'fishing trip' is a veiled narrative of an initiatory quest which was successfully completed by the disciples, with the help of the risen Jesus Christ.

21:14 This was already the third time that Jesus appeared to the disciples, after he was raised from the dead.

"already": this word implies that there were further occasions when Jesus appeared to the disciples.

21:15 Then, after they had eaten, Jesus said to Simon Peter, "Simon, son of John, do you love (agape) me, more than these?" He says to him, "Yes, Lord, You know that I love (phileo) you." Jesus said, "Feed my sheep."

"Son of John": as noted earlier, this is a ritual re-naming, in which Peter is given a sign of some success, or encouragement, in his spiritual development. For 'John' is a name which when used in an esoteric context, indicates that one's soul is nearing the Son of Man state.

"more than these": the Greek is ambiguous, so different interpretations have been proposed. To many other scholars, including myself, it means, "Do you love me more than these other disciples love me?"

"my sheep": most of the ancient texts have 'lambs' here, but I have followed Bezae, which has 'sheep'.

Jn 21:16 Again Jesus said, "Simon, son of John, do you love (agape) me?" He answered, "Yes, Lord, you know that I love you (phileo)." Jesus said, "Take care of my sheep."

---

[376] GA 123, lect., 8 Sept.1910.

Jn 21:17 The third time he said to him, "Simon, son of John, do you love (phileo) me?" Peter was hurt because Jesus asked him the third time, "Do you love (phileo) me?" He said, "Lord, you know all things; you know that I love (phileo) you." Jesus said, "Feed my sheep".

In the dialogue of these four verses, the risen Saviour has asked Peter if he has 'agape' (the profound, will-derived inner union or love) for Him, but Peter does not find it possible to comprehend and affirm this radical new love relationship between people, which Jesus had only very recently introduced into the Hellenistic world.

Instead Simon Peter answers, "I love you, as I do my closest friends". The dialogue is actually indicating that Jesus is attempting to get Peter to develop a deeper union with him, i.e., agape, but Peter is unable to reach to that level.[377]

So paraphrasing 21:15-18:

"When they had finished eating, Jesus said to Simon Peter, "Simon, son of John - in you something of the Divine (the IOA) can now be present - do you feel within you an **agape love** for me {*a higher-will unity* with me}, more than you have for these?" "Yes, Lord," he said, "You know that I **like** you (have a warm love for you)."[378] Jesus said, "Feed my sheep."

(As discussed earlier, the Greek name John has the vowels IOA in it, as does the name of God.)

21:16 Again Jesus said, "Simon son of John, do you have within a **divine love** for me {*a higher-will unity*} with me?" He answered, "Yes, Lord, you know that I **like** you." Jesus said, "Take care of my sheep."

---

[377] Various theologians, especially Catholic, dispute that agape and phileo refer to very different kinds of love. But I and many other scholars conclude, by assessing carefully how Lazaros uses this word, that there is indeed a very real difference, and this difference is a primary message in these verses.

[378] The core Greek text here is, …λέγει αὐτῷ πάλιν δεύτερον, Σίμων Ἰωάννου, **ἀγαπᾷς** με; λέγει αὐτῷ, ναὶ κύριε, σὺ οἶδας ὅτι **φιλῶ** σε.

21:17 The third time he said to him, "Simon son of John, do you like me?" Peter was hurt because Jesus asked him the third time, "Do you like me?" He said, "Lord, you know all things; you know that I like you." Jesus said, "Feed my sheep".

The NRSV has here, "Yes, Lord you know that I am *fond* of you...", in recognition of the difference in the two words.

21:18 Very truly, I tell you, when you were young, you used to fasten your own belt, and to go wherever you wished, but when you grow old, you shall stretch out your hands and someone else shall fasten a belt around you, and others shall take you where you do not wish to go.
21:19 This he said, to indicate the kind of death by which Peter would make powerfully manifest the Divine. After this, he said, "Follow me".

"powerfully manifest": usually, "glorify God".
Ancient church tradition records that Peter was crucified, but upside down, as he requested this, because he considered himself unworthy of the same death as that of Jesus.

21:20 So Peter, changed inwardly, directs his attention to the disciple following them, he whom Jesus loved; the one who had reclined next to Jesus at the supper, and said, "Lord, who is the one betraying you?"

"So": the little word 'de' (δέ) is omitted in some manuscripts, but included in codices Bezae and Sinaiticus. Here it is an important emphatic word, which introduces the next inner experience of Peter.
"changed inwardly": usually "having turned": however, this simple spatial meaning is unlikely to be meant. For the next verse suggests that there was an interval before Peter actually succeeded in perceiving Lazaros. So here it is not recorded that Peter immediately saw Lazaros. rather, that he is now wanting to understand the relevance and significance of Lazaros.

Since he is in a spiritual realm, where the spatial element is presumably not really a feature, Peter is having a similar experience to that of Mary Magdalene, who also had her awareness changed, after an encounter with Jesus. In other words, the text here means "his awareness having changed".

21:21 Then, having seen spiritually this person, Peter says to Jesus, "Lord, what about this man?"

"Then": the Greek word here (oun – οὖν) also means 'consequently'. The KJ version correctly has 'then', but the NIV and NSRV both have: "*When* Peter saw...", however, 'when' does not reflect clearly a time interval. Since the word here means 'then' or 'consequently' or 'accordingly' or 'in turn', this does suggest a time interval between the two verses.

"seen spiritually": the disciples with the Risen Jesus are in spiritual realms, and hence the verb here is horaoe (ὁράω), which is almost always used of clairvoyant perceiving, (or perceiving when in spirit realms), as noted earlier.

This supports the above interpretation of v. 20, wherein Peter is gradually orienting himself to perceiving the initiate Lazaros, and formulating the query he has about him. He then has a question about what could such an initiate be taking on as his task for the future.

21:22 Jesus says to him, "If I will that he remains in this same manner, until I am appearing, what is that to you; you, follow me !"

"in this same manner": this additional phrase (in Greek just one word in Greek, houtoes (οὕτως) is only recorded in Bezae. This is a crucial contribution, because the context here, i.e., 'the manner' in which this group of disciples now after the 'fishing' experience, are communicating with the Saviour, is directly transcendent or spiritual.

For they are communing or conversing with Jesus and with each other, with seership; i.e., they are in a higher consciousness state. Hence they are able to perceive each other and Jesus, as souls, each in a 'soul-body'. They have also just been seeking through the power of their consciousness to interact with divine influences from the Christ.

Jesus is here informing Peter that Lazaros-John shall continue on in this exalted 'spiritual work' from realms of spirit, for a long time; an activity which his initiatory consciousness permits him to do. The time of the re-appearing of Jesus (also known as the 'Second Coming') was not specified by Jesus, but it would not occur for many centuries.[379]

In just what way Lazaros would be discreetly assisting humanity over this time, is not made clear in this verse. But those with esoteric or mystical perspectives on this topic, accept that an esoteric stream of Christianity arose from his inspiring help.[380]

"I am appearing": the continuous present is used here, instead of a more definite end-point, 'until I appear'. This is supportive of Rudolf Steiner's view, that these words refer to the so-called 'Second Coming of Jesus'. In this process Jesus shall again appear to humanity, and this has commenced as of early in the 20th century, and shall continue to occur over several centuries, as more people develop some slight 'faith' i.e., capacity to perceive subtle ethereal energies, and thereby the presence of Jesus.[381]

21:23 So word spread out into the community, that this disciple would not die; yet Jesus did not say that he would not die, but "If I will that he remains until I am reappearing, what is that to you"?

---

[379] Rudolf Steiner taught that it would not occur until the 20th century, and continue on for some centuries. It would be on the level of the ethereal life-forces, not a physical re-birth. A study of the Greek text of Matthew's Gospel supports this interpretation.

[380] Rudolf Steiner taught that the medieval 'Rosicrucian' movement had its origin in this help, and in other culturally inspiring achievements. This includes the extraordinary fairy tale of J. W. von Goethe, "*The Green Snake and the Beautiful Lily*".

[381] He taught that the Re-appearing commenced early in the 20th century; many lectures in GA 118.

This is a reference to the above initiatory work of Lazaros; its full meaning remains somewhat veiled, but implies that Lazaros shall die at some point, and yet his transcendent spiritual work shall continue over the centuries.[382] This can indicate that Lazaros is to have a number of lives in which he carries out this work, or that he does this from within spiritual realms.

21:24 This is the disciple who is testifying to these things, and the one who has written them; and we know that his testimony is true.

"and *we* know": much debate has occurred about just what does 'we' refer to? The first part of the sentence confirms that 'the belovéd disciple', (who is to be identified with Lazaros), is the author of this Gospel. The reference to 'we' is enigmatic, but is probably referring to the writer Lazaros, who is giving himself a plural identity here, because of his awareness of inspiration from Jesus and other divine sources, just as Jesus does, in 3:11 and 3:32.

But it is also possible that it refers to a senior student, who has been instrumental in helping Lazaros getting the Gospel ready for distribution, now awkwardly inserts himself, here. However, that would mean that the 'I' in the next verse also refers to this student, and not to the Gospel writer.

21:25 But there are also many other things which Jesus did, which if they were written down, I suppose that the world itself could not contain the books which would be written.

****

---

[382] This is a profound disclosure about the initiatory attainments of Lazaros, (not, as some think, a later addition to the Gospel by those who are trying to validate conflicting ideas about Peter and Lazaros-John).

Appendix 1   (Part 1, Section 1)
Luke 16: 1-12: The Parable of the unsatisfactory estate manager

These verses include a section of the Gospel so enigmatic it has never been understood. Therefore, some pages of commentary are needed to reveal its meaning and showing why a very different translation is provided here. This parable has remained a riddle over the past two millennia, consequently current translations of these verses are not helpful.

These verses offer a parable about an estate manager whose work is unsatisfactory, so the wealthy landowner has decided to dismiss him. The parable is followed by statements from Jesus about the implications of the story he has just told. The translation of one of these statements about the parable in the NIV and other similar versions, reveal the dilemma here:

> Jesus said to his disciples, I tell you, if use worldly wealth to gain friends for yourselves, so that when it is gone, you will be welcomed into eternal dwellings.[383]

It is obvious that such a sentence does not convey any coherent meaning. In the NRSV, the misunderstanding has a disturbing aspect:

> Jesus said to his disciples, and I tell you, make friends for yourselves by means of dishonest wealth, so that when it is gone, they shall welcome you into eternal homes.

In the centuries-old King James and Luther versions, it is less confronting, but is still confusing. These both say in effect,
> "Make yourselves friends of unrighteous Mammon, so that when it is gone, they shall welcome you ...."

---

[383] Similar in the RSV, NEB, NKJV.

To whom the word 'they' refers has to remain unknown, until its esoteric message is discovered. Also, the term 'Mammon' is correct, for this Hebrew word is used in the Greek text. But the use by Jesus of the word 'Mammon' here is actually a pointer towards the Essenes, as this word is used as a negative term for wealth in their own writings and in two closely associated esoteric texts; the Book of Enoch, and the Book of Sirach. It is otherwise not used in the Old Testament. (However it does occur in other Jewish texts, but in a purely neutral sense.)

We saw in the Introduction that literary evidence from the Dead Sea Scrolls demonstrates that the Essenes were a very important esoteric group who played a significant role in the life and work of Jesus. We also noted that despite this, Jesus in the Gospels only ever dialogues with the Pharisees and Sadducees (apart from temple scribes). This absence of interaction with the Essenes is an astonishing omission, yet it is not generally noted; it shall become clear that this parable is about the Essenes.

St. Luke tells us that this parable was specifically told for the disciples. As we noted earlier, many of these were close to the Essenes, and no doubt in dialogue with them. As will be shown later, through this parable Jesus was cautioning the disciples about the negative aspect of the Essenes. Understanding of this context makes it possible for verses one to twelve to be accurately translated now, at last revealing their profound message.

Lk 16: 1-12: **The parable of the unsatisfactory estate manager**

Lk 16:1 Jesus told his disciples:
There was a rich man whose estate manager was being talked about as poorly managing his assets, wasting them.
Lk 16:2 So the rich man called him in and asked him, "What is this I am hearing about you? Provide me with the current (financial) status of my assets, because you cannot be my manager any longer.
Lk 16:3 The manager said to himself, What shall I do now? My master is taking away my job. I'm not strong enough to do manual labour, and I'm ashamed to beg.
Lk 16:4 Oh, I know what I'll do, so that people will welcome me into their houses when I lose my job here !
Lk 16:5 He called in each one of his master's debtors. He asked the first, 'How much do you owe my master?'
Lk 16:6 'Eight hundred gallons of olive oil,' he replied. The manager told him, 'Take your bill, sit down quickly, and make it four hundred.'
Lk 16:7 Then he asked the second, 'And how much do you owe?' 'A thousand bushels of wheat,' he replied. He told him, 'Take your bill and make it eight hundred.'
(These and other similar actions of this manager of the estate, came to the attention of the rich man.)
Lk 16:8 The rich man commended the incompetent estate manager in this matter, because he had acted in an intelligent, sensible way.
Lk 16:8b The people of this earthly world are more sensible in their dealings with their own kind, than are the 'People of the Light' in their dealings with each other.
Lk 16:9 So, I say to you, for yourselves' sake, make friends of the (un-spiritual) earthly goods and valuables, so that when this (your earthly existence) has ended, they shall welcome you into your dwelling-place in the heavenly realms.
Lk 16:10 For, the person who is perceptive regarding what is of little significance, is also perceptive regarding what is of greater significance. And whoever has poor

discernment with things of little significance, also has poor discernment of what is of greater significance.

Lk 16:11 If you were not discerning, regarding earthly assets and riches, who would entrust to you the true riches?

Lk 16:12 Indeed, if you were not spiritually discerning with (un-spiritual) earthly riches belonging to another person, who would give to you those true spiritual riches which belong to you (in the heavenly realms)?

Initial comments on the verses:
16:1 An estate manager had responsibility for a rich person's land holdings. Such a manager was often a slave or a freedman, and his responsibilities were substantial. He was in charge of all the slave labourers and the tenant farmers; he conducted the financial transactions, as well as the general administration of the estate. Called a 'villicus' during the Roman Empire, but referred to as a 'steward' in theological literature, he was in charge of the land holdings, so his task was to ensure that this flourished and was profitable. He was given a living by the landlord (who was probably absent), but he could also add to his wealth by increasing the amounts actually owed by tenant farmers and traders.

In the parable, the estate manager was not stealing from the wealth of the rich man, but he was ineffective and ethically dubious, so we may assume he was focussed more on improving his own financial situation than that of his employer. This caused the value of the assets to fall, or not to increase in value.[384] As the Greek indicates, he was rumoured to be 'squandering' the assets.

16:4 "Oh, I know what to....!" The Greek here (egnoen - ἔγνων) does specifically emphasize that this man had a

---

[384] A detailed account of the work of a villicus or farm manager is given by Marcus Cato (2nd cent BC) in his essay, *On Agriculture*.

solution suddenly light up in his mind. One could also translate it as, "I know !" or "I have it !"

16:6 and 7 the reduction by the estate manager of the value of the invoices held by the customers, is not a directly dishonest action. (See further Commentary on this parable, below.)

16:8a I conclude that the manager was called neither 'dishonest' nor 'unjust'; although the Greek word (adikias - ἀδικιας) often means un-ethical or un-spiritual, or 'unrighteous' in old Biblical language. From the words of the rich man here, it implies an inept manager, due in part to being self-focused, with ethically dubious attitudes, see Commentary.

Lk 16:8b The earthly people are more intelligent, more sensible, in their dealings....
The Greek (fronimoes - φρονίμως) can also mean 'wise', but here 'sensible' or 'intelligent' seems what is meant. The title, '*the People of the Light*' has long been regarded by Bible scholars as a general term for all good souls, but the following verses prove that it actually refers to the Essenes, for in the Dead Sea Scrolls this is their name for themselves. In the so-called *War Rule*, the Essenes are the 'Sons of Light' who are to engage with evil armies in a cataclysmic war which should end the rule of wickedness on the Earth, as the Messiah comes to humanity. So here we have a rare and highly significant reference by Jesus to the Essenes.[385]

Lk 16:9 This verse is the beginning of the seriously misunderstood section of the text. It is ambiguous in the Greek, this is because of a central word; a

---

[385] There are otherwise only two usages of this phrase in related literature; one is from Paul in his *Epistle to the Thessalonians* (1Thess.5:5-6), but there it is simply a poetic phrase, not a formal name for all Christians, and certainly not defining these Greek people as Essenes. The other is in a rare mystical text, the *Testament of Job,* 10:15 (written between 100 BC and AD 100) where an evil man is called "the son of darkness, not of light".

preposition, (ek - ἐκ), which can mean 'from'/'out of', or 'by means of', amongst other meanings. So this verse could be understood as saying in effect, "for yourselves' sake, make friends **from out of** worldly wealth" (KJ,Luth,EB), or "for yourselves' sake, gain friends **by means of** worldly wealth" (NSRV,RSV,NIV,NEB,NKJ). The next verses make clear that the meaning is the former; to 'make friends' of earthly goods, that is, to have a positive attitude towards earthly commercial things. Yet this should be done in order to achieve the best outcome for oneself, in spiritual realms. [386]

As we noted earlier, the Greek uses here a Hebrew term for wealth, 'mamona' (in English, 'Mammon'), which though generally a neutral term, amongst the Essenes meant sordid earthly riches. Its actual meaning in mainstream ancient Jewish writings is neutral, simply 'earthly riches'; and is only defined as a negative thing, if unethical circumstances are involved. The neutral nature of 'mammon' is made clear from this ancient Jewish text; "Rabbi Jose said: let the wealth (mamona/Mammon) of thy associates be as valuable to thee as thine own wealth."[387]

"they": this enigmatic plural word is explained in the Commentary. But note that what this word refers to, is not spelled out by Jesus, so its meaning must have been obvious to the disciples – not needing clarification. So the disciples do know who 'they' are. This enigma is discussed below.

Lk 16:10 The misunderstanding of these verses, and hence of the parable itself, is due to unawareness of the esoteric nuances involved, and therefore to ignoring the second meaning of the word 'pistos' (πίστος). As we saw in Chapter One, pistos does not only mean 'faithful' or 'trustworthy', it has a second, very different meaning;

---

[386] The verse does emphasize the phrase, 'for yourselves", i.e., for the sake of yourselves', by placing the pronoun "yourselves" (heautois - ἑαυτοῖ) first in the sentence: (ἑαυτοῖς ποινσατε φίλους).

[387] Pirke Aboth 2:16, in *The Pseudepigrapha and Apocrypha of the Old Testament*, edit. R.H.Charles, vol.2.

namely an intuitive-spiritual cognizing ability. This meaning points to being intuitive or perceptive, implying the capacity to be really discerning as to what one is perceiving.

Compare the difference in meaning between the two possibilities. The usual versions, lacking awareness of this second option, have:

"Whoever can be trusted with very little, can also be trusted with much..." (NIV, NEB, EB)   or,

"He that is faithful in that which is least, is faithful also in much..." (KJ, RSV, NRSV and Luth).

Comparing this now with my version,

> For, the person who is perceptive regarding what is of little significance, is also perceptive regarding what is of greater significance.

These concluding statements from Jesus are about the parable and how it relates to the disciples. So, for the estate manager to be 'faithful' in little and also in deeper matters, is quite irrelevant. Secondly, this age-old common version is obviously untrue; someone can be faithful or loyal in little matters, but yield to self-centred urges or temptations with larger, more potent, situations.

But if someone is actually perceptive, and therefore has real, inner discernment when facing a small, less important situation, then they are a discerning person. Hence he or she will also be perceptive when facing a larger, more potent situation. For if one is perceptive, then one is perceptive, in any situation. So what is meant by Jesus here is the condition of being spiritually perceptive or 'intuitive'. This will become clear in the next verses.

But furthermore. in its second part, verse 10 goes on to say, in most versions,

> ...and whoever is dishonest with very little shall also be dishonest with much.

However, as with the first part of verse 10, this is also an inaccurate rendering, because firstly, it is irrelevant to the parable, as the estate manager is not accused of being dishonest to varying degrees, but is accused primarily of incompetence; partly due to seeking to enrich himself as his first priority. Secondly, the usual understanding here is incorrect, because again it is not true that a person who is dishonest in small matters, will also be dishonest in larger, more serious, matters.

In modern terms, a person may be dishonest with regard to a small matter, such as parking restrictions or by keeping excess change given by accident to you in a shop. But she or he very likely will not defraud the government of large sums of money, nor hugely inflate the insurance value of a claimed item; this may be due to their conscience or to fear of punishment.
Consequently, in my version, 10b reads,

> And whoever has poor discernment with what is of little significance, also has poor discernment with what is of greater significance.

This is because part 'b' of verse 10 is connected to part 'a'; it is continuation of it. Both parts are about the same theme, which is discernment. We can conclude that discernment is meant, because the key word here is 'adikos' (ἄδικος) which although usually translated as 'dishonest' as shown above, has a second meaning. It is defined in Greek Bible dictionaries as dishonest or deceitful or immoral (often called 'unrighteous').

But like 'pistos' this word has another, less frequent meaning: an invalid, defective item, or a person who is in error and who makes mistakes, is not intelligent, or not perceptive. The famous Hellenistic scholar, Philo Judaeus, writing in the lifetime of Jesus, when referring to the laws and regulations announced by Moses, uses 'adikos' twice in one sentence, to refer to invalid or defective things used in commercial transactions, "No-one is to fraudulently substitute a *defective* scales-balance...nor are they to use any *invalid* currency."[388]

(trans. A.A.)   (emphasis mine, A.A.)

---

[388] Philo, *Hypothetica*, 7:8 Μὴ ζυγὸν ἄδικον ἀνθυποβαλλειν...μὴ νόμισμα ἄδικον...

Philo also used it to refer to unsatisfactory life circumstances: a father asks his daughters, who earlier had been bullied by some men, "Or did you not expect encounter such *difficulties* (defective behaviour) again?"[389]

But since the verse in Luke is about how we perceive people and circumstances, the word 'adikos' here means to have poor or defective perception, that is, to make mistakes in discerning, (i.e., to lack an intuitive capacity). Some examples of the word 'adikos' (or words directly derived from this) used in ancient Greek literature for 'being mistaken' or 'in error', or 'lacking discernment', include:

Plato in his *Charmides*, "for, if I am not *mistaken*, there is no-one present, who...."[390]

Pseudo-Phocylides, "The *ignorant* (unintelligent) do not comprehend the deeper teachings..."[391]

Polybius in his *Histories*, "Another very similar *mistake* people make is due to the appearance of the cities..."[392]

Philo Judaeus in his *Virtutatis*, "....it would be *foolish* for one man to labour, and for another man to reap the fruits of that labour.

Lk 16:11 Incorporating the deeper second meaning of 'faith', my translation, "not being discerning regarding earthly assets..." is accurate to the Greek even though it differs substantially from the common translations such as,

"if you have not been trustworthy in handling worldly wealth..." or "if you have not been trustworthy with

---

[389] Philo's Greek, in *Life of Moses* 1...,ἢ δεύτερον περιπεσεῖν ἀδίκοις οὐ προσδοκᾶτε;....(Greek in *Philonis Judaei* edit. E. Schwickerti, Lipsiae 1828.)

[390] Plato, (428-348 BC) *Charmides* 165a: ....ει μὴ ἀδικῶ γε...

[391] Lived between 100 BCE -100 CE. From his book of *Poetic Maxims*, (#89): ...οὐ χωρεῖ μεγάλην διδαχὴν ἀδίδακτος. in *Das Mahngedicht Phokylides*, edit. (Ger. & Grk.) 1833.

[392] Polybius, (200-118 BC) in his *Histories* 26a;7: ...και ἕτεπρον ἀδικνμα συμβαίνει ... (Grk. text made available in www.perseus.tufts.edu)

unrighteous mammon..." or "if you have not been faithful with the dishonest wealth..."

These versions miss the remarkably esoteric core message of the verse. (See the Commentary on this parable.)

Lk 16:12 "...if you were not spiritually discerning..." is accurate to the Greek since again the esoteric meaning of 'faith' is involved here.

Commentary: the Parable of the estate manager

Contemplation of the text with the Initiatory Quest approach, in conjunction with grammatical analysis and knowledge of the cultural context (academically called, *Sitz im Leben*), shows us that the parable is a cautionary message to the disciples about a negative aspect of the Essenes' attitude to material wealth and life. To confirm that this is the message, we first need to be informed about the cultural context of the times.

The estate manager had been working within the framework of the accepted custom of the times. It was customary for a person in such a position to be allocated a dwelling and his food and other needs, but no wages. So he could, within limits, place extra fees on transactions, as form of income.[393] (This was also done by tax collectors, but to a reprehensible degree.)

That is, when a tenant farmer or trader was due to pay a fee to the rich man for the use of his assets, or to hand over a share of the wealth generated by having used his agricultural land or other assets, estate managers could impose additional charges, which they then pocketed. This practice was kept within limits by various social and commercial factors, but could be abused.

So when the estate manager reduced the amounts owing to the rich man before he lost his job, he was reducing, or even removing, the percentage of the wealth intended for himself. This reduction in the

---

[393] S. Burder, *Oriental Customs illustrating Sacred Scripture*, p.126, 1840.

invoices is not a dishonest action, for it was not reducing the monies validly owed to his employer. It was an action which would make the estate manager more socially acceptable to his community. It is not stated, but we are to assume, that the rich man became aware of this prudent tactic.

The disciples are told in this parable that the rich man approved of this tactic, calling it 'sensible' or 'intelligent'. This message about being very 'grounded' or socially pragmatic, seems at first quite foreign to the teachings of Jesus, even to contradict these teachings, which are normally about achieving a highly compassionate and selfless attitude; and also an 'other-worldly' orientation, being mindful of what will be our destiny when life is over. The contradiction is resolved in the following verses.

For in verse 8 we read,

> The people of this earthly world are more sensible, in their dealings with their own kind, than are the 'People of the Light' in their dealings with each other.

Here the disciples are being told that the normal, earthly person is much more alert and sensible in relating to his peers, than are the Essenes to each other. The reason for the comparison to the Essenes becomes clear in the next verses.

After being told that the Essenes are less sensible, less 'earthed', than business people in their dealings with each other, the disciples are advised to develop a positive attitude towards earthly riches, and not to be like the Essenes in this regard. Some knowledge of the Essenes' attitude towards normal worldly assets (and to non-Essenes) helps to explain this teaching. Their attitude is shown for example, in their conviction that other people, "walk in the ways of wickedness....all their deeds are defilement (of God) and all their wealth is unclean".[394]

---

[394] Dead Sea Scrolls, *The Community Rule*: section 5., *The Dead Sea Scrolls in English*, transl. G. Vermes, 1987.

This view that the possessions or wealth of non-Essenes is inherently immoral, is emphasized in another statement, "They have wallowed in the ways of whoredom and wicked wealth (*mamona/Mammon*)...."[395] We can note that the associated attitude of avoiding people who accumulate unearned wealth, including tax collectors, is contradicted by Jesus in his own conduct and words during the three years of his ministry.

But furthermore, Jesus also tells the disciples that the way that the Essenes relate to each other socially is less intelligent, less sensible, than is the case with normal people in the community. This in turn implies that the soul blindness which condemns all earthly goods as inherently debased, has also influenced, and undermined, the social interaction prevailing in their own community. Again some statements from the Dead Sea scrolls affirm this.

One scroll decrees that if the owner of a bull which had already attacked a person, attacks again, this time fatally, the owner shall be executed.[396] Or if a person falls into a hole on the Sabbath day, another person may throw down their robe to the victim, as a way for him to climb up out, but one may not do more than that.[397]

A more potent example of unwise social regulation involves the rules around a Member who rebels against the community, and decides to give up being an Essene. If later on, this person decides to re-join the Essenes, he must spend ten years on probation, and, if he is rejected after that period, he shall be permanently banished. But if during those ten years another Essene had been kind to him, as in sharing his food for example, then that Member is to be expelled also.[398]

However this has terrible consequences, according to Josephus, because the expelled Essene was expected to stay loyal to various oaths he made, in which case he has to die of starvation, as he may not receive food other than that is provided in the ritualistic religious-

---

[395] Ibid., section 8.
[396] *Halakhah A - 4Q251*, Fragment 2. (*Dead Sea Scrolls Uncovered*, Eisenmann & Wise.
[397] Ibid.
[398] *DSS*, Community Rule (1QS), 7.

hygiene context of the Order.[399] (But we today assume that if he renounced his membership fully, then he can receive food and live in the normal community; but this may not have been the case.)

One can see that in these stipulations, an inner blindness to a reality, the reality of the dynamics needed to bring about wholesome social interaction between religiously committed, idealistic people living together in a community.

It is then relevant to learn from Rudolf Steiner, that Jesus, in his interaction with the Essenes prior to his Baptism in the Jordan, noticed with concern that the Essenes, by their self-imposed isolation, and social aloofness, living in secluded settlements, in effect were through their absence, withholding protection for people against influences from the various malignant spirit entities always active amidst the populace.[400] Consequently, in verse 9 we read,

> So, I say to you, for yourselves' sake, make friends of Mammon (earthly goods and valuables as defined by the Essenes), so that when this (your earthly existence) has ended, they shall welcome you into your dwelling-place in heavenly realms.

The reason for the advice to be positive and realistic regarding earthly wealth, cannot be grasped from a humanistic viewpoint. For now we see that the reason for this advice is to assist a spiritually oriented person to be welcomed into divine realms after death. But, to be welcomed in a way which enables a more alert, more profound cognizing, of those supernal realms.

At first, this makes the reader even more confused; how could a more balanced, positive, attitude towards worldly valuables bestow upon oneself a more meaningful dynamic, after death, in spiritual realms? Only through initiatory wisdom can that question be answered and thereby convey understand the message of the parable.

---

[399] Josephus, *Wars*, Bk. 2, chapt. 8)
[400] GA 148; many lectures in this volume.

Verse 10 then says,

> For, the person who is perceptive regarding what is of little significance, is also perceptive regarding what is of greater significance. And whoever is not perceptive with what is of little significance, is also not perceptive with what is of greater significance.

That is, Jesus is saying that if soul blindness is there, then it is operative in regard to matters small, or great. So, firstly this verse teaches that if you are not intuitive, not spiritually perceptive (that is, not possessing some wisdom from a sensitive, perceptive quality of mind) then you will not correctly assess or 'see into' the real nature of lesser things encountered in your earthly environment. For a person who is 'wise' is also an intuitive spiritually perceptive soul.

But if one is spiritually blind, then one also will not 'see into' – i.e., intuit the truth of – deeper, more profound realities which may be encountered. This is because an attitude which is acutely aware of 'things spiritual', but incapable of realizing that 'things earthly' have a valid place in the earthly world, results from a soul blindness, a distorted, limited cognizing; an unbalanced focus on things 'non-earthly'.

The implication here is, if like the Essenes, the disciples cannot realize that earthly goods and assets have a valid, essential role in earthly life, that is, if the disciples have a distorted antipathy (or inner blindness) to these, then that same blindness inherent in this 'flighty' attitude **will also limit them** when they encounter spiritual beings in higher realms.

We remind ourselves that such a directly esoteric theme is not being told to the crowds. St. Luke tells us that here Jesus is speaking to the disciples gathered near to him.

In verse 9 we had been told, "**they** shall welcome you into your dwelling-place in heavenly realms." It is now clear by verse 10, that the word 'they' refers to the divine beings ruling over the various spiritual realms. The Essenes were acutely aware, not only of the spiritual realms, but also the role of spirit beings dwelling in heavenly realms, especially Angels.

This is already shown in the Book of Enoch, but many other examples exist; one fragmentary text, *The Tree of Evil*, (4Q458) refers to an Angel being sent by God to the Earth. The entire theme of another fragment, *The Angels of Mastemoth and the Rule of Belial*, (4Q390) is the activity of various spirit beings. Another text, *The Vision of the Four Kingdoms*, (4Q457) refers multiple times to the Angels, and how brilliantly radiant they appear to clairvoyant vision.[401]

There are still other significant texts in regard to the acute awareness of spiritual beings amongst the Essenes. *The Testament of Amram* (4Q543, 545-548), directly refers to "The Watchers"; that is, stern, high spiritual beings who are guardians of the various spirit realms, and watch over the human souls in their realm. Two of these beings are described as battling over the soul of the Essene initiate who is recording this clairvoyant experience.

Another text is the report from Flavius Josephus, the ancient Roman historian, that a person who is admitted to the Essene Order is expressly "forbidden to reveal the names of the Angels".[402]

The word 'they' in verse 9 refers to divine beings active in spiritual realms. Now we come to another pointer to the Essenes as the focus of this parable; the expression "your dwelling-place" in verse 10,

> "...welcome you into your dwelling-place in heavenly realms".

The specific idea of the soul having a dwelling-place in spiritual realms after death was an important theme in the Essene community. It is found in *The Community Rule* (1QS:11), where God's chosen ones shall exist in community, in spiritual realms, with "the Sons of Heaven", in their assembly. In fact, this idea is found in apocryphal or esoteric Hebrew texts linked to the Old

---

[401] These fragmentary texts, with Q4 numbers, are published in *The Dead Sea Scrolls Uncovered* (Ref. 6)

[402] Josephus, *The Jewish War*, BK. chapt. 8.

Testament, and very closely associated with the writings of the Essenes.

One of these is *4 Ezra* which refers to "the souls of the righteous existing in their chambers (after death)" (4.35 & 7.95). Another relevant passage goes further, in conjunction with the Messiah (i.e., Christ), although it has not been accurately translated. Correctly understood, the seer records a high spirit being (the Sun-god Christ) saying,

> "For there was an occasion in the spiritual world, when for those human beings who now exist – before they were created – there was prepared by me, an Aeon (spiritual realm) in which they may have abode (in the future)."[403]   (trans. A.A.)

At least one scholar has stated that it is likely that *4 Ezra* is one of the sources of the Essene's own "Book of Mysteries".[404] In addition, in the *Book of Enoch*, the theme of a spiritual 'dwelling-place' is prominent. In chapter 38, the seer reports,

> "I saw the dwelling places of the holy ones, the resting place of the righteous. My eyes saw their dwellings, (together) with His holy Angels....there I wished to dwell, and (hence) **my spirit longed for that dwelling-place**."[405] (emphasis mine, AA)

Such apocryphal texts were not welcome in mainstream Judaism, but were obviously core texts for the Essenes. So in 16:10 is another indication that here Jesus was pointing to the Essenes.

---

[403] I have translated the term as 'Aion' or spiritual realm, (in Greek, 'αἰών') to distinguish it from 'Aeon', the usually spelling, meaning 'eternity'. But aeon as 'eternal Ages' here has no actual meaning. This same word as 'aeon' is used to mean a phase in the world's evolutionary history.

[404] A. Dupont-Sommers, *The Essene Writings from Qumran*, p.328, 1962.

[405] A very similar longing was expressed by Peter at the Transfiguration (Matt. 17:1-86) revealing how widespread was this initiatory attitude amongst the esoteric groups of Judaism.

The esoteric initiatory teaching behind this parable is taken even further in the next verses; we are now far beyond a humanistic, exoteric, religious view. For Jesus continues on, teaching an extraordinarily potent truth; that if this soul blindness or lack of wise discerning were the case, then, as both verses 11 and 12 caution, the divine beings in spiritual realms would not find it possible to allow awareness of the full divine reality prevailing in those realms to light up in such a soul after death.[406]

Verses 11 and 12:

> Lk 16:11 If you were not spiritually discerning regarding earthly assets and riches, who would entrust to you the true riches?
> Lk 16:12 Indeed, if you were not spiritually discerning with (un-spiritual) earthly riches belonging to another person, who would give to you those true spiritual riches which belong to you (in the heavenly realms)?

Now the meaning of this extraordinary parable is clear; that after our death, the divine-spiritual beings are prevented from revealing to a soul the glory of their own spirit in the heavenly realms, if that soul is ungrounded, and therefore limited in its ability to properly perceive reality. These divine beings cannot make perceptible "the true spiritual riches which belong to you".[407]

It is worthwhile to note here that, the same Greek word occurs in verse 4 and 9 for 'being welcome' (dexoenta - δεξωντά). In verse 4, the estate manager is hoping that "people will *welcome me* into their houses

---

[406] This same truth is presented in many forms in Rudolf Steiner's *Mystery Dramas*.

[407] This 'true riches' refers to the divine Spiritual-self, nearness to which, for the soul after death, is a profoundly uplifting and enriching experience. For those who have acquired knowledge of Steiner's teachings, this profound parable is cautioning about the danger of living an 'ungrounded' distorted, idealistic life, for it imposes limits on consciousness after death. This implies that entry into a 'luciferic' state may arise as a difficulty for the soul.

when I lose my job here". And in verse 9, Jesus informs the disciples that if the soul overcomes any flighty, ungrounded attitude, then "when this (earthly existence) has ended, they shall *welcome you* into your dwelling-place..."

No doubt Jesus chose to use the same word in these two places, in order to highlight the message of the parable, by linking the theme of 'being welcomed' in the neighbourhood, to 'being welcomed' in the spiritual realms.

Having finished cautioning his disciples about the limitation in the Essenes' worldview, Jesus now turns his attention outwards, to the larger group of people around him. He then, as from verse 13, addresses this wider group, in particular, the Pharisees. He speaks to them on the related theme of morality and wealth; but from a much less profound level.

Appendix 2   (Part 1, Sect.5)

The two 'Logoi' in Origenes

Here we assess an extremely important text from Origenes about the nature of 'Christ' and the Logos. It involves two paragraphs in his Commentary on the Gospel of St. John; these ancient texts have survived into the modern age, but they are a little unclear in places. I have established that when his meaning is discerned and his words translated accurately, they are the only texts which preserve evidence that in the early centuries of the new religion, Origenes, and possibly others following an esoteric Christianity, were aware that the word 'Christ' refers not to a man, but to a deity, indeed two deities.

Before we explore the actual texts of Origenes, it will be helpful to give a summary in advance of what he teaches in these texts. He declares that the term 'Christ' can be applied to not only the highest of a rank of divine beings, (the Sun-gods or Powers), but also to the high, primal Logos as well.

In addition, he writes that the term 'Logos' can be applied to both of these high beings, because to the ancient Greeks, a 'Logos' is a combined thought and will-impulse raying out through the cosmos, from a deity.

The implication here is that the term Logos, amongst Christians in esoteric groups, came to mean two powerful deities whose influences permeate creation. These are extraordinary teachings which go far beyond the perspective that became the basis of Christian theology.

However, as the reader may be aware, such teachings from Origenes are in fact not to be found in any presentation of the works of Origenes. The reason for this is that the actual meaning of the two paragraphs in which Origenes presented this, has not been noticed by earlier translators, or if noted, is glossed over.

In my translation, I have endeavoured to bring clarity to some difficult phrases. This text is somewhat degraded, making a few phrases obscure, as some linking words are evidently missing here.[408] Now the first of the paragraphs:

> And further, to acknowledge the (*solar*) Logos (*i.e., now, another Logos or Christ, not the high Logos*), as having its own definable, separate nature,[409] of the kind attaining to existence in itself, one must speak about "Powers", not only 'power'.

So Origenes is saying that solar Logos has a real individuated existence, so one has to refer to the Powers, i.e., that rank of deities; and not just to 'power' as a general divine quality.

> For frequently (*in Scripture*) it is set forth, "For thus says the Lord of the Powers (or, Lord of *Spirit Hosts*)".[410] This phrase refers to certain individuated (*i.e., specifically existing*) beings: spirits high and divine, who are designated "Powers" – of whom Christ (*or the solar Logos*) was the highest and the finest.

So Origenes is saying that the Bible refers to the rank of beings known as 'Powers' as the hosts of deities who surround God (Christ-JHVH). Then he states that the cosmic Christ or solar Logos, is very much an individuated entity; it is the most spiritual, the highest, of these Powers.

---

[408] This is a similar problem to a passage in Bk.2, 1:1,8 where he refers suddenly, without explanation, to the initiatory letters 'IAO' when referring to Isaiah. These letters were viewed in Hellenistic Mysteries as a sacred name for God, or to signify that a divine presence exists in initiated human being. It is also embedded in the name Jehovah. So is quite evident that in this passage the text has been corrupted.

[409] In his Greek, perigrafaen – περιγραφὴν.

[410] In the Hebrew Scriptures or Old Testament, God is sometimes called in Hebrew, 'Yahweh who has an army or host of powerful spirits'. But only once (in the Septuagint) is the version, the "Lord of Powers" used (at 2Kgs. 19:20).

> Therefore he (*the Christ-Logos*) is designated as not only the wisdom of God, but (as *another Christ-Logos is*) also the Power of God.

Here Origenes is teaching that 'the Logos' is a term which can be applied to the great primal Logos who embodies the wisdom of God, but also this same title of 'Logos' can be applied to the solar Logos, who is a one of the 'Powers'.

In this extraordinary passage, Origenes is validating not only the existence of other deities, but is also saying in effect that this Christ is uniquely individuated, in that it is the highest of this particular rank of gods or spiritual beings. So he declares this Logos-Christ to be "individuated" or having a real, specific existence.

He emphasizes this because he shall soon be declaring that the Logos in the beginning of the Prologue of John's Gospel is also an individuated, specific being, and is not just another way of identifying God. That is, Origenes is affirming that the Logos of the Prologue, was a god, not simply a part of God.

In the last sentence he is saying that there is the primal Christ-Logos, whom he regards as the wisdom of God,[411] and yet there is also that other Christ-Logos, who is the 'power of God', that is, the leader of the Powers. He continues on, and as he does so, it becomes clear that he now wishes to refer to the high, primal Logos as also somehow having a uniquely real individuated nature.

He wants to say that, just as the Logos-Christ, the leader of the Powers, is an individual deity, for he is the most sublime amongst his rank of spirits, so too the high, primal Logos is also somehow uniquely a separate entity.

The background to his statements is that non-esoteric church leaders were viewing the Logos in the Prologue as a part of God, "...and the Logos was God". Whereas

---

[411] When Origenes quotes Proverbs 8:22 in his *Commentary on John's Gospel* (Bk.1:39), he identifies the 'Wisdom' entity of the Hebrew Wisdom literature with the 'wisdom-Logos'. But that may be corrupted passage, since 'Wisdom' of Proverbs is not otherwise identified with the Logos, but with Jahve.

Origenes (and myself, and other scholars) translate, "...and the Logos was a god." Naturally in the non-esoteric view, this Logos is not considered to be a specific, individuated being, because it is seen as part of God.

But as a second theme, amongst Greek initiates, this high Logos was viewed as not being individuated, because it was understood to be what Plato refers to as, the 'Soul of the World'. Such a deity is spread out, immanent throughout Creation, as a diffuse entity.

Yet Origenes insists, despite this all-present, everywhere diffused quality, that the great primal Logos undoubtedly is a specific, individuated being. Why does he come to the conclusion?

It is because, as he points out regarding the Prologue of the Gospel, the Logos is described as being active as a separate creator-deity, in the primordial Beginning, with God, as His wisdom. Now here is the next paragraph,

> **Therefore, just as** many divine Powers exist, (*the Spirit-hosts*), each one of whom has individualization, yet all of whom are excelled by the Saviour (*i.e., the Christ-Logos unique amongst this rank of beings*) – **so too** the (*high, primal*) Logos is individuated, even if it is not individualized anywhere, outside of us humans.

So here we are told that the solar Logos is an individual deity, and is thus identifiable as being the highest of the Powers, and so too, the primal Logos is individuated. Origenes supports his argument in two ways. He argues, firstly, that this Logos is identified in the Prologue as a separate entity, near to God:

> This is because the Christ (*the primal Logos*) will be understood, through our elucidations in previous pages, as (*uniquely*) possessing real (*individuated*) being-ness, namely as divine Wisdom, in the Beginning (*of Creation with God*).

But then in a powerful, deeply spiritual statement, Origenes argues from his insight into the Christ mystery, that this Logos is also to be viewed as individuated – in a preliminary sense – **in that it is slumbering within every human being**.

So the great primal Logos was in the ancient Beginning, a separate entity close to God, and it is also a separate entity, potentially, in that it is slumbering in every person. These are profound insights from this sage. So here we find an invaluable presentation of the cosmic nature of 'Christ': that two distinct deities can each be called the Christ, or the Logos.

However, the mainstream view of this text does not perceive what is being said in these two paragraphs. As a result, in various translations of these paragraphs, the two 'Christs' or Logoi deities are merged into one being, resulting in a contradictory text.

This confusion has arisen partly because scholars have not seen that Origenes is referring to Christ as a member of a rank of hierarchical beings, and that these are associated with the sun-sphere. The mainstream interpretation of these words from Origenes is consequently erroneous.

This is shown in that various translations have to conclude that the many Powers (or Mights) around God (i.e., Jehovah) also existed in the Beginning, with the primal, uncaused God.[412] But since only the primal Logos was with God, this is not an accurate presentation of what Origenes is saying.

The mainstream interpretation of this text also thereby implies that the primal Logos is one amongst many deities of the same rank, all of whom were existing "in the Beginning". This is also obviously incorrect.

Reviewing these words of Origenes

Before writing these two paragraphs, Origenes' concern was to show that the high, primal Logos, as referred to in the Prologue to the Gospel, is a real being, a deity with a specific, individuated, nature.

---

[412] Allan Menzies, *The Ante-Nicene Fathers*, Eerdmans, edit. 1978; Ronald Heine, *Origen, Fathers of the Church*, C.U. of A, 1989, Cecile Blanc, *Commentaire sur S. Jean*, Tome 1, p.209-10, Editions Du Cerf, 1996, Paris.

But then as he begins paragraph 291, we are given no notice that he will now compare the two 'Logos' entities or Christ entities. This sudden and confusing situation is due to the poor quality of the text, (perhaps a gap where some words are missing).

Origenes wrote that the 'Logos' has a real, individuated existence, and in writing this, he is referring to the 'Christ-Logos' – but meaning the leader of the many deities belonging to a particular group or rank: the Powers, or Exousiai in Greek.

These words show that such a 'Logos' is not the high, primal Logos, for that Logos is a unique deity, alone with the Godhead in the Beginning; and far beyond the rank of any hierarchical deity. It has never been the 'most excellent' within any rank or group of hierarchical gods.

So we can conclude that Origenes is referring to a second 'Christ' deity who can also be regarded as a 'Logos'. He then proceeds in the second paragraph (#292), to say that there is a parallel between these two 'Logoi'.

Firstly, he says, the hierarchical Christ-Logos is an individual deity; it is the finest of the group of deities to whom it belongs. Likewise, the high primal Logos of the Prologue, is also individualized, that is, it has a real specific being-ness – even though it is nowhere individualized in today's world, and hence would not usually be identified as individuated.

Origenes is arguing firstly that the Logos was a specific, real, individuated deity in the Beginning, as divine wisdom; and yet it can still be defined today as having, in some subtle sense, an identifiable, individuated self. Because secondly, there is the implication that the primal Logos is what the Platonic wisdom refers to as the World-soul: this is the divine being who is immanent throughout all Creation. This World-soul is indicated when, in his second argument Origenes writes that this Logos is individuated, by existing within human beings.

This is a revolutionary new statement; for now the Logos is no longer just an individuated entity back in the Beginning, with God. It is also now an individuated entity, because, through the deed of Christ, it is slumbering within the human being. So it is present in Creation as an individuated deity, in a rudimentary and subtle sense, for it is a potential within the human being.

This is a potent, truly deep Christian statement; even though the human soul has not yet realized this presence in itself of the Logos (except some initiates, as the Prologue indicates).[413]

The two paragraphs from Origenes transliterated from the Greek
Paragraph 291

In order to let the reader assess the basis of my interpretation of these texts from Origenes, a literal translation of the two paragraphs follow. Firstly in the Greek, then in a literal rendering, (note that the word-order is jumbled compared to the English). These two versions are set in brackets, for clarity; then a final translation is given.

[Καὶ ἔτι εἰς τὸ παραδέξασθαι τὸν λόγον ἰδίαν]
[And further, to acknowledge the (solar) Logos its own]

And further, to acknowledge the (solar) Logos having its own

[περιγραφὴν ἔχοντα, οἷον τυγχάνοντα ζῆν καθ' ἑαυτόν]
[defined, separate-being having, of the kind attaining to]
[existence of itself,]

definable separate nature of the kind attaining to existence in itself,

[λεκτέον καὶ περὶ δυνάμεων οὐ μόνον δυάμεως· «Τάδε]
[one must speak also about Mights/Powers, not only]

---

[413] Here are his words, with a literal translation (note that the word order is different to that of English). From paragraph 291: ὁ παρ' ἡμῖν οὐκ ἔστι κατά περιγραφήν, ἐκτός ἡμιν

ho par haemin ouk esti kata preigraphaen, ektos haemin

"even if this Logos, except for us, is not individualized outside us" or, "even if this Logos, in us, is not individualized outside us" The phrase "παρ' ἡμῖν" is ambiguous; "in us" as a normal dative, or "except for us" if the comparative force of the preceding text is factored in.

[Might/Power; "For thus says]

one must speak about "Mights/Powers", not only 'power'.

[γὰρ λέγει κύριος τῶν δυνάμεων « πολλαχοῦ κεῖταν]
[the Lord of Powers (mighty Spirit-hosts)" {is} frequently [set forth;]

For "thus says the Lord of the Mights/Powers (*spirit Hosts*)" is frequently set forth (in Scripture)

[λογικῶν τινων θείων ζώων δυνάμεων]
[spiritual certain ones, divine, existing, "Mights/Powers "]

(*This phrase refers to*) certain,[414] really existing beings, spirits high and divine,

[ὀνομαζουενὼν; ὧν ἡ ἀνωτέρω καί χρέιττων Χριστος ἥν,]
[referred to as; of whom the highest and finest Christ]
[was]

who are designated "Mights/Powers" – of whom Christ (*or the Logos*) was the highest and the finest.

[οὐ μόνον σοθία Θεοῦ ἀλλά καί δύναμις προσαγορευόμενος]
[not only the Wisdom of God, but (also) the Might/Power]
[(of God) being designated.]

Therefore (*the Christ-Logos*) is designated as not only as to the wisdom of God, but also the Might/Power of God.

Paragraph 292

Here is all of paragraph 292, again in the Greek and a literal version, followed by a final translation.

['Ωσπερ οὖν δυνάμει Θεοῦ πλειονές εἰσιν,]
[Just as therefore Powers of God (spirit Hosts) many are]

Therefore, just as many (Hosts) Powers of God exist,

[ὧν ἑκαστη κατὰ περιγραφήν, ὧν διαφέπει]

---

[414] Here Zoeoen (ζώων) means 'existing' rather than 'living', to indicate they are truly specific beings, (i.e., they do have ontological validity).

[whom each one having individualization, (of) whom excels]

each one of whom has individualization, yet all of whom are excelled by

[ὁ σωτήρ, οὕτω καὶ λόγος - εἰ καὶ ὁ παρ']
[the Saviour, so too [the] Logos - even if this one except]

the Saviour; **so too** this, (*the high, primal*) Logos (is individuated)

[ἡμῖν οὐκ ἔστι κατά περιγραφήν, ἐκτὸ ἡμιν]
[for us, not is individualized outside us -]

even if it is not individualized anywhere outside of us humans,

[νοηθήσεται ὁ Χριστὸς διὰ τὰ προεξητασμένα]
[(it) will be understood (that) the Christ through the] foregoing elucidations]

for the Christ (*the primal Logos*) will be understood, through our elucidations in previous pages

[ἐν ἀρχῇ, τῇ σοθίᾳ τήν ὑπόστασιν ἔχων.]
[in the beginning, in Wisdom, (as) having real being-ness.]

as possessing real (*individuated*) being-ness, as Wisdom, in the Beginning (*of Creation*).

Appendix 3   (Part 1, Sect.7)

Faith - its second meaning in the Pistis Sophia

Another example of the word 'pistis' being used to mean an inner intuitive perceiving, and not religious faith, although usually translated as meaning 'faith', is in the highly unusual, esoteric text, the *Pistis Sophia*. So this title means, *Spiritually Perceptive Wisdom,* not 'Faithful Wisdom'.

In this text, the soul's intuitive, perceptive wisdom, which makes a human being spiritually aware, or intuitively cognizing, is personified. On one occasion (35:5), we read in the usual translations, that this wisdom quality,

> "has faith in the spiritual Light which brought it into existence, ever since it was brought into existence".

But it is unclear thinking which concludes that a spiritual perceiving ability in the soul can ever have, or dismally fail to have, the human trait of 'faith'. The Greek verb here (pisteuein - πιστευέιν) derives from 'pistis' and in this context, it can only refer to being intuitive or spiritual perceiving. So the ancient text is really saying that the wisdom capacity of the soul says of itself that,

> "I have intuitively perceived the spiritual Light which brought me into existence, ever since it brought me into existence".

In other words, the high spiritual faculty of being spiritually perceptive has an inherent awareness of Divine spiritual realities. This sentence obviously should not be interpreted as declaring that perceptive wisdom has 'faith' in its own creator. This high soul-quality or strand of human consciousness (personified in the text), existing body-free in spirit realms, does not need to affirm its ability to have faith in its own spiritual creator.

Nor does this soul quality - as presented in the usual translation of other parts of this text - need to confess that it is suffering from a lack of religious faith. This implies that in a spiritual being or capacity there exists an inability to feel and believe, both emotionally and intellectually.

Another example from a similar text (*The Books of Jeu*) shows how the word pistis, or its verb pisteuoe, is often erroneously translated, as 'faith' or 'believing'. It is in a passage where sublime spirit Powers are being described as to their influence on the human soul seeking higher consciousness. In my translation,

> The third Power is called "intuitive cognizing" (for) through it a human being (undergoing initiation) has intuitive cognizing of the Mysteries of the Indescribable.[415]

We are to understand that the Mysteries of the Indescribable are especially sublime. The high spirit Power mentioned here, is inspiring the spiritual consciousness of the acolyte, seeking to assist that person to attain to an intuitive perception of the remote lofty Mystery. But the usual translation of this text is,

> The third Power is called "Faith" (for) through it a human being (undergoing initiation) has faith in the Mysteries of the Indescribable.

It is scarcely meaningful to declare that an acolyte in the initiatory path is given 'faith' in the lofty Mysteries by a high deity. These words are about the ability to intuitively cognize or discern those spiritual dynamics that a particular Mystery requires of the acolyte. The alternative meaning of 'pistis' has not been perceived in the usual translations of this text, and likewise is at times not perceived in Gospel passages.

---

[415] The Second Book of Jeu, chapt.10:2,3.

Appendix 4 (Part 1, Sect.5)

Texts understood as showing Jesus to be the Logos

1: A major reason for identifying Jesus with the Logos is confusion about the expression, "The Son of God". This term in Hellenistic literature identifies initiates or sages who have attained to their Higher-self. It was not applied in earlier Hebrew literature to the Logos (or similar deity). But, church scholars erroneously began to identify Jesus as the Logos through a misinterpretation of the Prologue (vs. 1:14, 18).

Because 'The Son of God' is a term used of Jesus, scholars concluded erroneously that the Logos is also the same entity as 'The Son of God'. Since esoteric or initiatory wisdom is not part of theology, this situation led to other passages in the New Testament becoming understood as identifying Jesus as the Logos.

It will be helpful for the reader if the difference between the traditional theological view and the esoteric understanding is directly and clearly presented here. This involves partially re-visiting what was presented in earlier chapters. The traditional church view is that Jesus, before he became incarnate, was God – the Primal Weltengrund – for he is the Logos, which is understood to be an aspect of God.

By contrast, the understanding from a direct initiatory perception, as well as from an esoteric reading of the Greek Gospels, considers Jesus to be a human being – the holiest of all humans – whereas the Logos is a deity, a divine being of sublime, lofty status. Such a deity can never become conceived and born as a human being. Yet the difference is not so decisive, in that esoteric wisdom regards the Logos, through the Baptism of Jesus in the Jordan, as achieving a direct and deep interweaving with the being of Jesus: his body, soul and spirit.

Colossians 1:15-18
Several verses in Colossians (1: 15-18) appear to specifically declare that Jesus is the Logos. In the NIV translation they are,

1:15 The Son is the image of the invisible God, the firstborn ^(over) all creation.
1:16 For by him all things were created: things in heaven and on earth, visible and invisible, whether Thrones or Powers or Rulers or Authorities; all things were created by him and for him.
1:17 He is before all things, and in him all things hold together.
1:18 And he is the head of the body, the church; he is the beginning and the firstborn from among the dead, so that in everything he might have the supremacy.

Here verse 18 proclaims the unique nature of Jesus as the vessel of the Christ, and hence as the first of a new type of human being. But verses 15-17, especially verse 16, are entirely incompatible with esoteric knowledge. To dismiss this verse may at first appear disrespectful, but in fact, many theologians do not regard this text as from Paul. Many (but not all) have concluded that this Epistle is not an authentic text from Paul.

Scholars refer to the difference in the usage of the Greek language in this text to that of Paul.[416] This is also my conclusion, for it is very doubtful that Paul, with his esoteric knowledge and spiritual experiences, would identify the man Jesus with the Logos, a deity so sublime as to tower up beyond even the Seraphine, the highest of the nine ranks of deities. So this widespread doubt as to the authenticity of these verses, undermines

---

[416] This conclusion is presented in the 35 volume German EEK series in, *Kommentar zum Neuen Testament*. Prof. Schweizer, *Der Brief an die Kolosser*, p.23, 1997, points out the absence of any reference to the Law, Commandments or Righteousness - very unusual for Paul. Also the 'pagan' heresies are reacted to differently compared to Judaic Laws, again very unlikely. He also mentions that grammatically, synonymous expressions are strung together and explanations of these are then attached; all this in such a way as to make a living interaction with listeners nearly impossible (these Epistles were primarily meant to be read out aloud).

the validity of using them to support the traditional viewpoint.

Epistle of John 1:1-2
1:1 That which was from the beginning, which we have heard, which we have seen with our eyes, which we have looked at and our hands have touched – this we proclaim concerning the Word of life.
1:2 The life appeared; we have seen it and testify to it, and we proclaim to you the eternal life, which was with the Father and has appeared to us.

These verses do not specifically identify the Saviour with the Logos. They emphasize that within the words and deeds of Jesus, the Logos was present.

Revelation 19:13
Rev. 19:11 I saw heaven being open and there before me was a white horse, whose rider is called Faithful and True. With justice he judges and makes war.
Rev 19:12 His eyes are like blazing fire, and on his head are many crowns. He has a name written on him that no one knows but he himself.
Rev 19:13 He is dressed in a robe dipped in blood, and his name is the Word of God.

These verses do not specify that Jesus is the Logos, on the contrary, they refer to a spiritual being as an entity who is manifesting the dictates of God.

Philippians 2:5-7
2:5 Your attitude should be the same as that of Christ Jesus:
2:6 Who, being in very nature God, did not consider equality with God something to be utilized (*for his own advantage or enjoyment*).
Phil 2:7 but made himself nothing, taking the very nature of a servant, being made in human likeness.

It is verse 6 which has been used to identify Jesus with God, but in fact the Greek text is much more correctly as,

"Who, existing in a divine-spiritual form (*i.e., an appearance perceptible to spirit vision*), did not consider (*this state of*) existing in a condition which was consistent with the Divine-spiritual, as something to be utilized, but instead..."

This tells us that Jesus, when existing in spiritual realms, was in a form or appearance appropriate to those divine realms. But instead of regarding this condition as something to be kept for himself, as a privilege, he descended into flesh, to appear in bodily form. So this verse cannot be used as irrefutable evidence that Jesus is God.

Hebrews 1:1-2
In many versions it is translated like this:

1:1 In the past, God spoke to our forefathers through the prophets at many times and in various ways,
1:2 but in these last days he has spoken to us by his Son, whom he appointed heir of all things, and *through whom* he made the universe.

Although verse 2, in the form given, may be used as proof that Jesus is the Logos, this verse cannot in fact be used as proof of this view. This is because the Greek text is ambiguous (but only for those who think that a god can be conceived, as can a human). For the Greek word 'dia' translated here as 'through', has in fact a number of other meanings. Meanings well established and commonly used in the New Testament, such as 'for the sake of'. It is used in this way in Mark 2:27,
"Then he said to them, The Sabbath was made for (*the sake of*) people, not people for the Sabbath".

So Hebrews 1:2, is much more correctly translated, by myself and various other scholars, as:

"But in these last days he has spoken to us by his Son, whom he appointed heir of all things, and *for the sake of whom* he made the universe."

That this translation is correct is shown in the same Epistle to the Hebrews, where Jesus is in effect defined as a human being, as someone created "a little lower than the Angels",

Heb 2:7, "But we see Jesus, who was made a little lower than the angels, now crowned with glory and honor because he suffered death, so that by the grace of God he might taste death for everyone."

Then here this status of Jesus, as a man, being lower than the Angels, is emphasized further when we are told that after the Resurrection, Jesus is raised up above them,

1:3 "After he had provided purification for sin (of human beings), he sat down at the right hand of the Majesty in heaven."
1:4 "So he became as much superior to the Angels as the name he has inherited is superior to theirs."

So Jesus, through his union with the Christ, rose up above the Angels – from his human state – becoming deified through the presence of the cosmic Christ. The term 'name' here means one's core spiritual nature. Again the rank of Jesus is defined as that of human, not of the sublime Logos, which transcends even the Seraphine.

John 1:34
Finally, there is a text in the Prologue, verses 33-34, where John the Baptist declares, in the NIV version,
"......The man on whom you see the Spirit come down and remain, is he who will baptize with the Holy Spirit.'
1:34 I have seen, and I testify, that this is the Son of God."

We have already noted that to describe the Logos as the 'Son of God' is not a valid use of mystical language, if by 'Son' one means a human being. But it is valid if used for Jesus. It was otherwise a phrase reserved for revered persons or initiates, not for deities. This expression was an age-old term for describing revered people or powerful rulers. In ancient Egyptian times, pharaohs were regarded as vessels of a deity, and Augustus

Caesar was called The Son of God, so too was the initiate, Apollonius of Tyana.

Jesus himself used this phrase both of himself and with reference to other ennobled human beings. So this verse is not stating that Jesus was the Logos; it is stating that Jesus was a human being ennobled and sanctified, a state known as 'The Son of Man' in Hellenistic Mystery language. We have noted that all these key Scripture passages used to establish the traditional view are in fact not valid evidence; it is similar with this verse, which is saying,

1:34 I have seen, and I testify, that this (man, Jesus) is The Son of God."

These words are taking the esoteric term 'Son of God', used for initiates who have attained to their Higher-self or Spiritual-self, and applying it to Jesus. But it is applied to Jesus with the implication that after his Baptism, he has the divine Spiritual-self to a much greater degree than the initiates of olden times. For at the Baptism, the cosmic source of our Spiritual-self – the solar Logos or cosmic Christ – permeated Jesus.

Furthermore, with regard to this verse, various very old and reliable manuscripts, such as Codex Sinaiticus, do not have the "Son of God" here, but "the person selected by God" instead. (Unfortunately, in codex Bezae, Jn. 1:17 to 3:15 are missing.)

It is very likely that this is the correct version; in any event, this alternative version reinforces the fact that Jesus is not being defined here as the Logos, but as a man. So the text in these ancient alternative documents is actually saying,

"I have seen and I testify, that this is the person selected by the Divine (or by 'God')."

But the Committee formed of the scholars who were creating the definitive edition of the Greek New Testament, when deciding on which ancient versions or variations of New Testament texts should be regarded as the right one for this verse, decided on the version "The Son of God". This edition of the Greek New

Testament, the result of work by K. & B. Aland and others, is regarded world-wide as the definitive, most accurate version of the Greek.)[417]

The Committee noted that the majority of early texts had "The Son of God" not the "person selected by God". However, as they are aware, this is not proof of correctness. So there had to be another reason for choosing "The Son of God".

As the report on their work states, "This version is also in harmony with the theological terminology of the Fourth Evangelist".[418] They are referring to the fact that the expression, 'the Son of God' occurs several times in the Gospel. But, as I have pointed out, these passages do not declare that Jesus is the Logos. So the Committee was misled by the context of their own theology. That is they were in a circular argument, using the traditional interpretation of the Gospel of John, which itself was incorrect.

---

[417] It is published by the United Bible Societies and the Deutsche Bibelgesellschaft, Münster.
[418] B. Metzger, *A Textual Commentary on the Greek New Testament*, 2nd edition, 1994, p.172.

Appendix 5 (Part 1, Sect. 4)

Christ as a cosmic deity of the Sun-sphere

One: in the Gospel of Luke.

We noted earlier, that at the beginning of his Gospel, by freely utilizing texts from the Hebrew Scriptures, St. Luke gives a veiled indication about the cosmic aspect of the Messiah. The NIV renders this passage as,

"Salvation (is coming) because of the tender mercy of our God, by which the rising sun will come to us from Heaven, to shine upon those living in darkness and in the shadow of death, to guide our feet into the path of peace." (1:78-79)

This passage is understood as referring to Jesus, who is described as 'the rising Sun'. It may be considered simply as a fine piece of poetry, as are the texts of the Hebrew Scriptures from which it is taken, (Psalm 107:10,14 and Isaiah 9:2; 59:9-10). But by varying the Hebrew text, Luke intends it to discreetly refer to a mission of the cosmic Christ, involving the dead. The accepted translations miss various fine points of grammar, which veil a message which, when perceived, directly reveal an initiatory message.

In the version given above, we read, "the rising sun will come to us from heaven", this may give the reader the impression that this refers to the man Jesus. However this common understanding is grammatically incorrect. For Luke carefully, but discreetly, avoids presenting the rising sun as a metaphor of a human Messiah coming to earthly humanity.

The Initiatory Quest approach to scriptural assessment shows that the text is declaring a "something", which is called 'a rising' which brings radiance, shall visit humanity, from spiritual heights. There is here, grammatically, no reference to a human Messiah at all. The reason that a personal Messiah is not specified here, is that the being who is going to 'visit' the Earth, is not the Messiah nor a prophet, rather it is 'a rising'. Now that is a significant statement, because a radiant 'rising' must be of either the sun or a star, but not of a person. Further, this 'rising' is described here as a reality which comes from spirit realms.

There is also the implication that this 'rising' results in an increasing radiance for the Earth when it arrives. Since this radiance comes 'from above', in the sense of having its origin in a spiritual realm, we can again conclude that Luke is referring to a source of spiritual illumination, rather than to a person. Further, the Greek verb 'to visit' used here means to specifically, dynamically, seek out something to visit, not just casual visiting.

So, this means that 'It', the radiance, will be dynamically 'manifesting' or 'appearing' to people who are in a certain situation; it is not simply passively seen. The word used for 'heights' also has this connotation of a high, heavenly world in Ephesians 4:7 and in an ancient non-canonical text known as 1Clement 36:2.[419]

Moreover, the verb is also in the 'aorist' tense, which is a grammatical device in Greek, to show that what it refers to is a once-only event, rather than an ongoing, repeated process. So it is a unique event involving a radiant 'rising'. It is clear that these strange allusions cannot be simply regarded as a poetic way to describe the advent of the (human) Messiah. The Greek text is referring in a veiled manner, to an illumination that descends from the heights, a spiritual 'appearing' to a lower state of existence is meant, suggesting a descending to the level of human consciousness.

There is a milieu of darkness implied here; as Meyer comments, it is as if "there shall be the rising of a bright-beaming star of the night" (rather than a person), from a heavenly realm." [420]

The above understanding becomes confirmed when these verses are further examined. Firstly, to speak of

---

[419] It is also used in this same way in other Greek literature, especially in regard to the 'appearing' of the god Artemis in the Mysteries. (Moulton, James and Milligan, George, *The Vocabulary Of The Greek Testament illustrated from the Papyri and other non-literary Sources.* 1930.

[420] *Critical and Exegetical Handbook to the Gospels of Mark and Luke*, H.A.W. Meyer, trans. R. Wallis, 1883.

people existing "in the shadow of death" is a rather melodramatic expression to use for the people of Israel early in the first century CE, but it is certainly not so for the dead in the Soul-world, called Sheol in the Hebrew Scriptures.

For enforced inactivity, or existing in a state of disempowerment, accords very well to the understanding of the state of the dead in Hellenistic times. Furthermore, the usual translation refers to the people as "living" in the shadow of death, yet it is quite erroneous to translate the Greek word here ('kathaemenois') as 'living ones'.

For if Luke had wanted to refer to earthly people living their lives, he would have used the Greek verb zaoe (ζάω) which means 'to live'. This verb is used almost exclusively in the New Testament for precisely this sense. Or, he could have used the verb katoikeo (κατοικέω) which means 'to reside, to dwell'.

But the verb used here (kathmai - κάθμαι) means primarily to sit; it rarely refers to 'living', and when it does, it implies a very passive sense, indeed conveying the meaning of being useless, or being in a state of disempowerment, or living in a particularly sedentary manner.[421]

So, the people are not living in the shadow of death, they are 'seated', which means they are in a disempowered state. Furthermore the people are in 'skia thanatou' which means, in "death's shadow". Now this can be viewed as a poetic reference to living people, but in fact the dead are thought of in Hellenistic Jewish traditions as 'shadows'; their realm is called 'the realm of the shadows'. More significantly, in Hellenistic cultures, the about to depart soul of an aged person,

---

[421] Moulton, James and Milligan, George. *The Vocabulary of The Greek Testament illustrated from the Papyri and other non-literary Sources*. 1930. *Critical and exegetical Handbook to the gospels of Mark and Luke*, H.A.W. Meyer, trans. R. Wallis, 1883.

seen somewhat exteriorised about their body, was actually called a 'shade'[422]

Furthermore the word for darkness, used here, skotos, also refers to the darkness that exists in oceanic depths. Now, the Jewish and Greek Hellenistic understanding of the realm of the dead was that, qualitatively, it resembles a deep ocean or a deep sea. The dead languished there in torpor and, further down, below them, evil beings lurked. For example, the Book of Job (26:5) speaks of "the dead in deep anguish – those beneath the waters, and {those} that live in them."

So in summary, Luke is here discreetly revealing that a primary mission of the great Sun-god, the cosmic Christ, is to bring spiritual light to the souls of the dead, languishing within the periphery of the Earth, in the dark, dismal Soul-world. So this is how these verses should be translated, (Luke 1:78-79) showing that the cosmic Christ is to bring an empowering light to the souls in the Underworld,

Salvation {is coming} …
through the fervent compassion of our God,
by which a Dawning-Radiance from the heights of Heaven shall make visitation to us,
in order to dynamically appear (hence to give light)
to the people in the oceanic Netherworld darkness
and languishing disempowered in death's Shade –
    (i.e., in the shadowy 'soul-body')
in order to guide our feet into the path of peace.

These words of Luke become more clearly understood with the understanding of the cosmic Christ as the great leader of the Elohim, which are of the same rank of deity as the Powers. These gods have their area of activity in the Sun-sphere, hence they are in effect, sun-gods.

---

[422] Article "skiav" in '*A Greek-English Lexicon of the New Testament*', W. Bauer; trans. W. Arndt & W. Gingrich, 2nd edit, 1979, p. 755.

TWO The Gospel of John: The healing of the blind man.

The next Gospel passage to consider is in John (9:5), wherein 'Christ' heals a man who was born blind. As noted earlier, in the many translations, Christ says, "While I am in the world, I am the light of the world." So this sentence is understood theologically as meaning that the ethics of all good people derive somehow from the man Jesus when he was, on that one occasion, in the world; on that one occasion only when he was living in the world, he gave ethical 'light' to humanity.

But in fact here the Gospel text can be understood as saying that each time it re-occurs that 'Christ' is in the world, this same being is the source of illumination for the planet. Because the Greek word here (hotan – ὅταν) can also mean a multitude of times. So this word can mean "whensoever' not just 'when'; so 'every time that such and such happens'. Thus, verse 16 can also mean,

"Every time it is the case that I am in the world, I am the world's light".

This indication that it is the Sun-god Christ who illumines the world in a recurring manner, takes on more meaning when one notes the context of these words.[423] A man who was born blind is about to be given his sight, so he is someone who has never seen the sunlight; for when we see something, we are seeing the sunlight reflected off objects. As the Christ power, via the actions of Jesus, prepares to give sight to this man, Jesus says words which refer directly to the Sun, and for which there is no convincing theological explanation.

He declares that he must carry out this miracle before the Sun sets; "We must do the work of Him who sent me, while it is daytime." The Gospel writer wishes to convey the message that it is the Sun-god Christ who is active here, in conjunction with the Messiah, Jesus. (Some manuscripts have "I must" not 'we must': see under 9:4 where this is discussed.)

---

[423] Or, one may say, as the Greek is ambiguous here, "a light to the world", or "the light of the world".

This association of the Christ with the Sun shows affiliation with many earlier religions, whose central deity was the Sun-spirit, such as in Egypt and Persia. The priesthoods of most earlier religions were composed, at least in the higher ranks, of people who had been initiated. These priests experienced the reality that just as the Sun is the most significant physical body in the solar system, so too the leading spiritual beings in the Sun-sphere are the most significant in the solar system for humanity.

Christ as a cosmic Deity

John 8:51, and 57-58: The eternal I within the cosmic Christ as manifesting through Jesus
8:51 Very truly, I say to you, whoever keeps my words within their heart, shall never experience death (in spirit realms)…..
8:57 The Jewish leaders therefore said to him, "You are not yet fifty years old, and yet you have seen Abraham?"
8:58 Jesus said to them, Very truly, I say to you: before Abraham existed, **I am the 'I am'**.

V.8:58 brings to a culmination what is said in earlier verses. It aroused intense antagonism amongst the listeners, who question the credentials of Jesus, and this eventually results in the cosmic Christ declaring through Jesus,
"Before Abraham existed, I am the I am" (v.58)

When verse 51 is contemplated with the Initiatory Quest assessment method, it is saying in effect, whoever keeps secure within their soul what is intoning in the words of Jesus, shall never experience death in the heavenly realms. So this person has achieved an eternal 'I'.

This is itself a concept beyond the boundaries of non-esoteric or humanistic thinking. It concerns the capacity to maintain an ego-ic awareness in the spirit realms, instead of a 'sleep' condition. Verse 58 confirms v. 51, and likewise has a deeper meaning than the usual translations allow.

Here the word 'I' refers to the higher, eternal sense of self (the Spiritual-self or Son of Man) which slumbers as a potential in everyone, and which has existed since remote times. Secondly, this 'I am' - this higher divine self - is held within the being of the cosmic Christ. In traditional language one would say, 'it is held in the being of God'. This is the meaning of the words spoken to Moses in the burning bush. Thirdly, through the mediating work of Jesus Christ - after the Resurrection - the way has opened for everyone to develop this higher 'I".

Rev. 13:8 "...the Lamb who was slain from the foundation of the world"

Since this term is used without explanation, it is very likely that is an esoteric name used in esoteric groups for the cosmic Christ. The verse refers to an event in a remote aeon when the cosmic Christ, the leader of the Powers, (the solar Logos) restrained its own potential for further development. It does not refer to the man Jesus, for that would be implying that he existed before the solar system was even created.

The purpose of the sacrificial act of the great Sun-god was to align its own evolutionary pathway, so as to be closer to that of human beings in the far future. From this proximity, its influences (which are referred to as Grace) could more effectively assist humanity.

John 13:18 "lifting up his heel across me"

Rudolf Steiner often taught that in a deeper, cosmic understanding of the Gospels, one can see that the Earth became the body of Christ. The Earth is also alive, like us; so it has a life-force and a soul. The Earth-soul envelops the planet as a glowing aura, similar to what human beings have. To offer some Biblical evidence for this, Steiner would quote a verse from the Gospel for St. John.

He explained that this verse provides affirmation, if not precisely proof, of his teaching on this theme. This verse reads as follows in the NIV, "I am not referring to all of you; I know those I have chosen. But this is to fulfil the Scripture:

"He who shares my bread has lifted up his heel against me.'" (13:18)

A careful contemplative study of this verse reveals that it has some very complex structures grammatically, and these are indeed veiling a statement about the cosmic Christ as the indwelling spirit of our planet. (See the Appendix 15 for a commentary on 13:18)

Appendix 6   (v.1:5)

Verse 5 of the Prologue as starting from the Past

"**1:5** And the Light shone in the darkness, and is shining, but the darkness does not perceive it, and has not conquered it.

Beasley-Murray states that, "The present tense (phainei) is unexpected. (For) the verse embraces history and (also) the present time of the Evangelist. The light of the Logos *shone* in the primal darkness at creation and continued amidst the darkness of fallen mankind..."[424]

The eminent scholar, Prof. F. Godet, re-phrased the verse as, "This Logos, the Light of the World, *shone* in a world which was immersed in darkness of sins, it was not recognized and rejected by the world..."[425]

Another scholar, H. Ewald, concludes that here, the present tense is in effect in the 'gnomic aorist' condition, meaning that the past and the present tenses are merged into one, so that a past dynamic is also occurring in the present, if it repeats itself continually; "The present tense here represents the era in which the Light, that long ago since Creation, had been enlightening human beings from afar, had now suddenly come down into the (present) world..."[426]

---

[424] G.R. Beasley-Murray, *John*, Word Biblical Commentary, T. Nelson, Nashville, USA, 1999, p.11.
[425] Godet, F. Kommentar zu dem Evangelium Johannes, 1902, p. 30.
[426] H. Ewald, *Johann. Schriften*, quoted by H.A.W. Meyer, in *Handbook to the Gospel of John*, 1883, p 73.

Appendix 7 (v.1:12)

Photius against Clement of Alexandria re the Logos

A valuable mention of Clement's view of the Logos is presented by Edwards, in his essay, *Clement of Alexandria and His Doctrine of the Logos*. Edwards quotes words allegedly from Clement, words spoken by Patriarch Photius (AD 810-895) at a church council. Photius was a prominent clergyman, involved in major doctrinal disputes between Constantinople and Rome. He quotes these words as from Clement, and as constituting a serious heresy, (although the actual originator of these words is not fully established),

"...It was not (*directly*) the Logos of the Father, but a certain power of God, a 'flowing-down' from his Logos, (*which*) on becoming 'intelligence' permeated the hearts of human beings."[427] (trans. A.A.)

Clement is saying here that the holy qualities in such exalted persons, although ultimately derived from the primal Logos, did not come directly from it, but were mediated by hierarchical deities to receptive human beings. He is explaining that the sublime consciousness of the Logos had to be 'stepped-down' to what human beings can experience and then be absorbed as spiritual wisdom by initiates.

These comments are quite insightful, and in harmony with a spiritually informed perspective. The word 'intelligence' in this literature did not mean intellectuality, but what we now call spiritual wisdom.

---

[427] Photius in, *Bibliotheca 109*, from the text edited by R. Henry, in *Photius, Bibliotheque II* Paris, 1960. In an essay, *Clement of Alexandria and His Doctrine of the Logos* M. J. Edwards in *Vigiliae Christianae* Vol. 54, No.2 (2000) pp. 159-177, E.J. Brill.
The Greek of Photius is "οὐδὲ μὴν ὁ πατρῷος λόγος ἀλλὰ δύναμίς τις τοῦ Θεοῦ οἷον ἀπόρροια τοῦ λόγου αυτοῦ, νοῦς γενόμενος τὰς τῶν ἀνθρώπων καρδίας διαπεφοίτηκε."

This process transformed the souls of sages in antiquity, and enabled the birth of their radiant Spiritual-self. In Biblical terms, they achieved this by becoming vessels of 'the Christ-light', through raising their consciousness to higher realms, where the Christ-Logos (the Sun-god Christ) exists. In this way they became 'Sons of God'.

For scholars who wish to consider the arguments against Clement by Photius, the following observations may be of interest. Edwards argues, unconvincingly, that the implication here – of two Logoi – is not intended, for the terminology is somewhat imprecise. So the one Logos is the divine primal Logos, whereas the other 'Logos' is, according to Edwards, simply referring to the power of reason and speech, as given to human beings by the Creator. Edwards refers to another text from Clement, it is in Bk.5:1,4 (he erroneously states Bk.5:6,3) where two Logoi also are mentioned. One usage of the word logos in this other, well-known passage, simply means reason and speech, as it did in normal secular Greek; the other usage refers to the primal Logos of God.

But the above disputed passage (apparently) from Clement, quoted by Photius, has an entirely different context. It is saying that the primal Logos is a divine reality, but not (directly) a manifestation of what we humans possess as speech: "For the Logos of the Father of All is not this (humanly) 'uttered word'."[428]

Clement here is clearly saying that the usual meaning of logos, i.e., 'a word', is not what the Prologue in the Gospel is referring to. Rather, in the Prologue it refers to a high, divine being. (He is not thinking of how human speech may derive ultimately from the Divine.)

Whereas the passage from Clement quoted by Photius is specifically declaring that a spiritual influence, coming from the Logos, but not fully identical with it, entered into the world via Jesus; it is called a "power of God". Clement here may be referring to the Sun-god

---

[428] Clement's Greek, ὁ γὰρ τοῦ πατρὸς τῶν ὅλων λόγος οὐχ οὗτός ἐστιν ὁ προφορικός.

Christ, the solar Logos, who is not the primal Logos, (yet there is an interweaving between the two beings).

Appendix 8 (v.1:18)

Verse 1:18: attempts to identify the Logos as God and as Jesus.

The confusion that arises when the Logos is seen as God is shown in these sentences,

"No one has ever seen God, but God the One and Only, who is at the Father's side, has made him known." (NIV, 1984) Or, "No one has ever seen God, but the One and Only Son, who is himself God, and is in closest relationship with Father, has made him known." (NIV, 2011).

With these versions, the Logos is God, but is also not God (!), and thus somehow can be at the side of God. But some translations are still adhering to the inaccurate, but traditional, Greek text where the word 'deity' was replaced by 'son'. This is less contradictory than the above versions, but is still incorrect.

The King James Version is not contradictory, but uses the humanistic version, 'Son': "No man hath seen God at any time; the only begotten Son, which is in the bosom of the Father, he hath declared him". In this way, the KJ version avoids the involvement of the Logos, and instead identifies Jesus as the entity who declares the nature of God.

There is also much truth in such a statement, however this is a secondary theme in the verse, hovering in the background. For the correct Greek text, found in papyri already from about AD 150, states that the Logos, not 'the son', is the entity who in its nature is close to God, and hence has rapport with the uncreated God. Therefore the Logos is the only being who can explain and present the nature of God.

Appendix 9   (v.1:14)

Steiner interpreting Prologue 1:14 as about Jesus

1:14 Thus the Logos became flesh, and dwelt amongst us: and we beheld its splendour, that of the Uniquely-begotten from the Father, full of Grace and Truth.

One some occasions Steiner used the correct Greek text, and from this he explains that it refers to ancient initiates manifesting the glory of the Logos. On other occasions, he gave another interpretation, in which he refers this verse to Jesus, not the Logos, as do the mainstream theologians. But this requires the correct Greek text to be by-passed. He does still imply that 'glory' in v. 14 derives from the cosmic Christ or solar Logos, but now may be viewed as over-shadowing Jesus. He explains that this radiant glory is the same cosmic Christ whom Moses had seen in the burning bush.[429]

On another occasion, Steiner again interpreted this verse as referring to Jesus, but from a different viewpoint. He was utilizing the prevailing venerated (erroneous) theological viewpoint, but he grafted on to it a deeper, somewhat esoteric interpretation. But in the effort to do this, he had to ignore in several places, the actual meaning of the Greek. He translated it as,

"And the Word became flesh and has dwelt amongst us, and we have heard his teachings; the teachings from the only-begotten son of the Father, filled with devotedness and truth." [430]

A: 'heard': but the verb 'theaomai' (θεάομαι) means 'to see', 'to behold', and does not ever mean, 'to hear'.[431]

B: 'teachings': the verse is referring to a deity, the Logos, and its glory or radiant splendour ('doxa' in Greek). But in fact, the word doxa can also mean 'teachings', so selecting this rare meaning of 'doxa' is correct to the Greek.

---

[429] GA 103, lect., 29 May 1908.
[430] In GA 97, lect., 2 Dec.,1906.
[431] Its most 'refined' usage is in Plato's *Phaedrus* (84b), where he used it to mean 'to contemplate' (i.e., to see with the mind.)

C: 'devotedness': instead of 'Grace', Rudolf Steiner specifies 'devotedness', since 'Grace' alludes more to a deity bestowing this upon others, whereas the word 'devotion/devotedness' is more applicable to the inner self-surrender to God by a person; in this case, Jesus. But the Greek text has 'charitos' (χάριτος) which does not have the meaning of 'devotion', but of grace, charm, beauty or kindliness.[432]

D: 'Son': instead of 'Uniquely-begotten deity' Rudolf Steiner uses "once-begotten son", commenting that in esoteric usage of the period, a 'twice-born' human being is derived from its two parents, whereas a 'once-born' person is 'born' from the Spirit; meaning here, Jesus. Both 'uniquely-begotten' and 'once-born' are correct to the adjective used in Greek. It was understood in the Hellenistic Age as "begotten by one alone", as well as 'uniquely-begotten'.[433]

However, the full expression "once-begotten **son**" as used by Rudolf Steiner, is not in the Greek, for it states neither 'son' nor 'deity'. Yet of these two words, 'deity' would be the correct word (if something were specified), because in verse 18 the same being is identified as a deity in the oldest and most reliable papyrus texts, not a 'son' (papyrus #66 and #75).

The word 'son' only occurs in a later, less reliable codex, but it eventually pushed out the earlier, correct text. This no doubt happened because it was less confronting to the developing humanistic attitudes: see in v. 18.

Rudolf Steiner was seeking on this occasion to present a deeper perspective on an understanding which, though inadequate and humanistic, had become

---

[432] Devotedness is an uncommon word in modern times, and in the Hellenistic world too; the nearest occurs in the Greek Septuagint translation of the Book of Leviticus (27:28) where 'being devoted' (in Hebrew, charam - הָרֳמ) is translated as the Greek term, 'anathae' (ἀναθῆ) implying the (now extinct) positive nuance of the verb to anathematize: anathamatizoe (ἀναθεματιζω).

[433] G.R. Beasley-Murray, *John*, in Word Biblical Commentary series, 1999, p.14.

hallowed through time; it therefore exercised a huge impact on Christian thought.

Appendix 10

Rudolf Steiner's commentary on v. 18

As with verse 14, Steiner's commentary seeks to make use of the non-esoteric level of the text, and to provide a deeper understanding of the traditional viewpoint. His version is:
"No-one has ever physically beheld God, however the once-born Son, who rests in the inner being of the Father, he has become the leader in this beholding."

He explains that in much earlier times, people could clairvoyantly behold, at least in the Mysteries, divine realities (which is called 'God', in traditional language). But this capacity dwindled over millennia, as people became evermore immersed in the material world. By the Hellenistic Age, the soul was primarily cognizing sensory experiences.

So the need arose for a way to enable people to behold 'God' with only physical vision (but therefore in a proxy manner only). For people who were now limited to physically perceiving, and for whom the initiatory experience would become ever less possible, still yearned to experience the presence – subtly, indirectly – of a divine reality.

In encountering Jesus, people could have an inner perceiving of a divine-spiritual reality or 'God' enveloping Jesus. This opportunity, this experience, is what the incarnate Jesus Christ offered.[434] This points to the fact that for this, 'faith', in its second, esoteric sense, was needed.

On the basis of the now rejected Greek text of this verse, (which used 'Son', not 'deity') Rudolf Steiner's perspective here is still valid, and is based on a deeper, spiritually informed view of history. It does have some basis in the Greek. For the verb here is also used of physical cognizing, not only clairvoyant-spiritual perceiving.

---

[434] in GA 103, Lect. of 22nd May 1908.

Moreover, the last verb here, 'to explain' or 'make known' or 'instruct' has no object; that is, to what or to whom it refers, is actually left unsaid. So in the correct version, which states 'deity', the verb is referring to God. But in the version which states 'son', it can be interpreted as referring to 'physically beholding God'.

Appendix 11   (v.6:63)

The Naasseni Hymn

The first section of this hymn is not included here. It presents a Gnostic view of primordial phases of creation; which is not relevant to understanding an esoteric Christian view of the advent of Jesus.

Preserved in a large third century manuscript, this hymn presents an exoteric Christian view of Hellenistic esoteric groups, and general philosophical and religious ideas. Called *Refutation of All Heresies*, the author of this large work is unknown, but was possibly Hippolytos of Rome.[435] His lack of esoteric insight led him to view the hymn with contempt, and to preserve it as an example of Gnostic nonsense for posterity.[436] This wonderful text is however, not in any way an illusory 'semblance' as the Hippolytos thinks,

...Jesus said, "Behold, O Father,
how this being (upon the Earth)
The victim and target of all evil wanders
Far from your breath.
It seeks to flee the bitter Chaos,
Not sensing how to pass through,
For this reason, send me, O Father,
Bearing with me the Seals (of the Mysteries)
I shall descend,
Every Aeon I shall traverse,
All Mysteries I shall unveil,
and reveal the forms of the Gods.
The deep secrets of the Path of Holiness
I shall bestow on you;
Gnosis it is now called.

(transl. A.A.)

---

[435] An excellent dual-language version of *Refutation of All Heresies* is available, by M. David Litwa (SBL Press, 2016)
[436] illusory or 'seeming' Mysteries – Μυστήρια δοκοῦσι.

Appendix 12

8:25: The confusion around this verse

"They were saying to Jesus, "You, who are you?" Jesus said to them, "I am the One who, in fact since the Beginning, has been intoning to you."
The Greek is totally baffling unless one perceives that here the cosmic Christ is speaking. Lacking this perspective, many scholars conclude that the verse is too obscure to ever understand. Keener and Morris write, "The meaning of Jesus' answer is not clear" and Plummer comments, "the meaning of this obscure text cannot be determined with certainty...**every word here is unclear**, except one."[437] Westcott points out, scholars have been aware for some time that the traditional interpretation,[438] suggested by Augustine, is invalid to the Greek. Augustine (who did not know Greek) proposed an interpretation which was accepted for many centuries in the church: "Believe me to be the Beginning because, I am even speaking with you, because, that is, I have become humble for your sake."

Then 19th century German scholars came nearer with, "I am, from the Beginning, *that* nature which I also profess to you to be." (Fritsche and Hengstenberg, quoted by Meyer, *Gospel of John*, p .27.) Meyer comments, though rejecting their view, that this does imply "that Jesus is the Logos"; an understanding which, whilst erroneous, could lead one near to the actual meaning. As I have noted earlier, instead of implying that Jesus is the Logos, the verse is actually spoken by the Logos or Christ.

The Greek here is preserved in two versions as regards the little word 'hoti': either 'ho ti' or 'hoti'.

A: Τὴν ἀρχὴν ὅ τι καὶ λαλῶ ὑμῖν
  (ὅ τι = who/what what/one)
  taen archaen ho ti kai laloe humin

---

[437] That word is 'humin' (ὑμῖν) which means 'you'.

[438] B. Westcott, *Gospel of St. John*, p. 142.

and
B: Τὴν ἀρχὴν ὅτι καὶ λαλῶ ὑμῖν
(ὅτι = that, that which)
taen archaen hoti kai laloe humin

This first version A is recorded in Bezae, amongst others, and to me this is the correct version of the Greek text, giving a meaning which is both clear and deep:

"I am the One who, in fact since the Beginning, has been intoning to you."

Whereas version 'B' results in complicated possibilities that do not lead to meaningful solutions.

Appendix 13

The complex Greek in 8:28

My translation is:
8:28 So Jesus said to them,[439] **Whenever you have exalted the Son of Man, then you will know that I am the I am (in you); you will then also experience 'from myself I do nothing, but only as the Father taught me'.**

But in the NIV, this verse reads,

So Jesus said, "When you have lifted up the Son of Man, then you will know that I am the one I claim to be, and that I do nothing on my own, but speak just what the Father has taught me."

However, the word 'when' (hotan - ὅταν) can mean 'each time' or 'whensoever it happens', and not just 'when' (i.e., a one-off event). This more flexible nuance implies that Jesus is referring to multiple occasions; so whenever any spiritualized human being attains to the Spiritual-self, that person then becomes The Son of Man.

Also the verb "to lift up", (hupsoe - ὑψοώ) is not an appropriate verb for lifting up an object, for its main meaning is to **make exalted** something or someone; but since the evangelist seeks to veil the initiatory level of meaning, this verb can 'scrape by' as a word for physically raising upwards something.

Moreover, the Greek text includes the especial phrase, "ego eimi", (ἐγώ εἰμι) which often means when Jesus uses it, "***I am the I am***". In other words the people are told by Jesus:

I (Christ Jesus) *am the I-am* (in your human soul) – but only when you have developed the Spiritual-self or "Son of Man".

The usual translations avoid this esoteric meaning, and therefore to find a meaning, they have to add such

---

[439] In the NIV Bible, the word "that" has been inserted, although it is not there in the Greek.

words as, "the one I claim to be", which are not in the Greek. Thirdly, the usual translations of v.28 end with, "*but I speak these things which the Father has taught me*", however some of these words don't belong in this sentence. They are part of the next verse (v.29).

My conclusion here is supported by an examination of the very earliest Greek papyri and codices, especially Papyrus 75 (dated as of about AD 175). This early papyrus has outstanding punctuation marks, the result of thoughtful contemplation of the sentences.

It uses a particular dot for the full stop, and a different kind of dot for a pause; whereas some early papyrus texts have only scanty and ambiguous punctuation. An examination of the original papyrus (available online) shows that in verse 28, the scribe placed a full stop after "taught me"; this is clearly visible in the papyrus, and is noted in relevant publications.[440] So in the light of these considerations I have inserted into v. 29 that part of what is usually assigned to the end of v. 28.

---

[440] See, P. Comfort and D. Barrett, *The Complete Texts of the Earliest New Testament Manuscripts*, p.581.

Appendix 14

v.13:1 loved them with regard to the goal

We noted earlier that this verse is either saying,
1: Jesus loved his disciples 'to the uttermost',
or 2: until 'the end of his life';
or 3: he had brought about an inner union with them; so deep was this love that it went beyond the emotions, and encompassed the will. Furthermore, this was specifically achieved with regard to that goal which his close students were pursuing: initiatory spirituality.

Option 1 implies a gradation of agape love (i.e., inner unity of will), being achieved by Jesus over time; various scholars reject this, for it implies that Jesus gradually became more capable of loving over the years.

Option 2 implies his love ended when he died, which again is very unlikely; indeed it can be dismissed.

Whereas Option 3 is confirmed by many passages in the Gospels and in the Epistles, which spell out that the goal of the followers of Christ was to achieve high spirituality, including The Son of Man state. A passage by St. Paul in Corinthians (1Cor. 2:6-8) shows that telos was used to mean achieving initiation; in fact Paul deliberately used this meaning to convey his message that Christians also may achieve what the Mysteries bestow – that is a sanctified spirituality or higher consciousness – although in a different way, and through seeking nearness to the Christ;

> But wisdom we speak among the initiated (*teleiois*). A wisdom which is not of this Age, nor of the Rulers (Archons) of this Age, who are becoming negligible. Instead, we speak God's wisdom in a Mystery which (until now) has been concealed, but which God predestined before the Ages, for our divine empowerment.

"the initiated": usually translated as 'the mature', which is a valid rendering, but the word here (teleiois) also means the initiated; and I conclude that this is what Paul is directly referring to.

"in a Mystery": again Paul is using a word directly alluding to the initiatory Mysteries of the times.

"the Archons": translated as 'the Rulers'; but Paul is using esoteric Gnostic language which both Platonists and esoterically aware Christians used.

"speak": the verb here (laleoe – λαλέω) can also be used for intoning utterances in a mantric sense.

A passage in Matthew also shows how the word 'telos' was used in a veiled way amongst the esoterically aware Hebrews, not only the Greeks, to refer to becoming initiated. In Matt. 19:16-22 a young man asks Jesus a very significant question: how to achieve "eternal life" i.e., aeonic existence or a consciousness which is of the aeons or spiritual realms.

In the course of the dialogue, Jesus re-states this young man's goal as "to be teleios", which is usually translated innocuously as 'to be perfect'. The verb also means to complete or perfect something, but in this context where the young man is seeking a consciousness which is of the aeons, it actually means to be initiated, just as it did among esoteric Hellenistic groups.

Herodotus (4:79) speaks of someone being "initiated (teleios) into the Mysteries of Dionysos", Plato does likewise in his Phaedro (#249) as did various other Grecian writers.

Some words from Clement of Alexandria are relevant here, as he declares that initiatory spirituality was the goal of esoterically informed Christians; "The goal (telos) of Christian spiritual knowing (gnostikos), is that power of spiritual knowing, which in accordance with the laws of the spirit, confers spiritual beholding of the Other Side (i.e., into the realms of spirit)."[441]

In addition, in this verse 13:1, the verb for agape occurs **(He had brought about an inner union (agape) with the souls of his own....)** and both times the verb is in the 'aorist' state, which means that the agape inner union condition was a one-off, completed achievement. If agape is erroneously interpreted as friendship or emotive love, this has to be nurtured in an on-going

---

[441] Clement, *Miscellanies* Bk.3, paragraph 72.

manner. But this is not the case when agape is correctly understood as attaining an inner union of the deep soul qualities; for once achieved, this does not have to be perpetually re-attained.

As Bernard comments, "...if the intended meaning were 'he continued to love them', we should expect the simple past tense, not the aorist. The aorist indicates a definite (completed) act, not an on-going emotion."[442]

So with understanding that 'telos' means the goal of being initiated, we are being told here by Lazaros, that prior to his death on Golgotha, Jesus had spiritually helped his disciples to achieve a specific stage of their initiatory goal. This is a very important achievement, as the disciples will be inspired towards further sanctification (or initiatory stages) by the Risen Jesus, to enable them to meet their tasks of spreading the Gospel message.

Since Lazaros himself had been especially initiated by Jesus, he was acutely aware that this activity was of great importance to the future of Christianity. For Lazaros was aware that he had attained an 'agape' state (inner attunement) with Jesus. It was this which made possible his initiation, and as a result of this, his activity on behalf of Christianity in future centuries and millennia, became possible.

---

[442] Bernard, *St. John*, p. 455.

Appendix 15

Verse 13:18 The Initiatory Level: Christ as the Earth-spirit

Rudolf Steiner emphasized that in esoteric, cosmic Christianity, it is understood that through the events on Golgotha hill, the Earth, or Earth-soul, became united to the cosmic Christ. That is, that the Earth is also alive like us, so it has a life-force and a soul. The Earth-soul envelops the planet as a glowing aura, similar to what human beings have; and this is now permeated by the Christ. To offer some Biblical evidence for this, Steiner would quote a verse from the Gospel of John. He explained that this verse provides affirmation, if not precisely proof, of his teaching on this theme,

> 13:18, 'He who is eating my bread has lifted up his heel against me.'

The question here is, how can Rudolf Steiner validly use this verse as evidence for his assertion that a cosmic Christ being united to the Earth? To find its hidden meaning, we need to go back to the old Hebrew text of the Psalm which Lazaros has quoted, in a changed form. Psalm 41:9 contains a complex, subtle Hebrew idiomatic phrase, which however simply reads, in most translations,

> Even my close friend, whom I trusted, he who shared my bread, **has lifted up his heel** against me.

What the original Hebrew phrase means

Such translations are not quite accurate. For what does this Hebrew text in Psalm 41; 9 actually say? It says, mysteriously, when correctly translated, in an expression found only here in the Old Testament,

> "....**my friend**....he has *made-great* a heel against me."
> (trans.A.A.)
> Gam ish shelovmi asher batachi vov ovchel lachmi higdil alai akev.   (the Hebrew, transliterated)
> (גַּם־אִישׁ־שְׁלוֹמִי אֲשֶׁר־בָּטַחְתִּי בוֹ אוֹכֵל לַחְמִי הִגְדִּיל עָלַי עָקֵב׃)
> (the original Hebrew)

The verb used here for this strange expression '*made-great*' is gadal (גִּדַל), and it means **to magnify, exalt, to increase in power**. And it is used in a negative sense here in Psalm 41. It means that someone hostilely increases their potential to impact on another person.[443] (He has 'magnified it'.) This same verb is also found in a negative usage in Psalm 35:26 but without the use of 'heel'.[444] In non-esoteric thinking it is generally understood to mean that someone has magnified, or enhanced in a threatening way, their potential to harm you.[445]

So, it is not actually saying that someone has literally 'lifted up his heel', it is actually about the over-all lower self of someone becoming stronger, against you. The true meaning of the unusual Hebrew idiom was recognized by the translators of the Hebrew Scriptures about 300 BC when they produced the famous Septuagint. This is a Greek version of the Hebrew Scriptures for Greek-speaking Jews. For in the Septuagint this sentence in the psalm, reads in my translation of the passage,

"The one eating my foods {with me}, he has **exalted** himself against me **with craftiness**."[446]

ho esthioen artous mou, emegalunen epi eme pternismon
(ὁ ἐσθίων ἄρτους μου ἐμεγάλυνεν ἐπ' ἐμὲ πτερνισμόν.)[447]

---

[443] Dr. Julius Fürst, *Hebräisches und Chaldäisches Handwörterbuch über das Alte Testament*, Vlg. von Bernhard Tauchnitz, Leipzig 1863; and Gesenius's *Hebrew and Chaldee Lexicon to the Old Testament*, trans. S. P. Tregelles, S. Bagster & and Sons, London, 1857.
[444] Namely, '...they magnify themselves against me'
[445] This unique expression is highly esoteric, with other complex meanings we cannot elucidate here.
[446] Septuaginta id est Vetus Testamentus Graece iuxta LXX interpretes; edidit, Alfred Rahlfs, Privilegierte Würtembergische Bibelanstalt, Stuttgart, no date.
[447] From Psalm 40: 10 in the Septuagint, which has a slightly different numbering sequence of the Psalms to that of the Old Testament.

It is not about a physical heel being lifted up. But in fact the term 'craftiness' used here (pternismon) was actually created from the word for 'heel'. And thus this sentence really means in its underlying structure, something like, 'he has exalted himself against me in a '*heel-ish* way. So the Septuagint still preserves, in a weaker subtle way, the reference to 'heel'. The word 'heel' is still understood as a symbol of the lower self, and not as a part of the real foot. What is important here is to note that the phrase, "has lifted up his heel" should read, 'has made great his heel against me'.

So Greek words used by St. John retain, in a weak way, the original strange Hebrew image, namely that a person's over-all lower self, (symbolized as a heel), has been intensified against someone,

> The one eating my bread has lifted up against me his heel.
> Ho trogoen mou ton artov epaeren ep' eme taev pternan autou
> (ὁ τρώγων μου τὸν ἄρτον ἐπῆρεν ἐπ" ἐμὲ τὴν πτέρναν αὐτοῦ.)

The alteration made by Lazaros-John

But note that the Greek text from John's Gospel is actually a slightly weaker form of the Hebrew, for John says, "has lifted up", he does not say, "*made-great*" (a heel against me). Yet the Hebrew does **not** actually suggest a trampling of an enemy. If that were the meaning which John had in mind, then his text would just say quite clearly, and straightforwardly, that 'Judas has trampled on me'. Instead he uses the old Psalm 41 imagery, although in a slightly weakened form, which indeed does allow perhaps for some broader interpretation, but not so broad as trampling.

But, although John's Gospel has a weakened version of the Hebrew phrase in the Psalm, this verse, (John 13:18) is naturally understood around the Christian world to mean that Judas has become antagonistic to Jesus. So consequently, in all usual English and German translations of John 13:18, Christ says in effect, alluding to the Psalm, that his enemy has heightened his hostility; and this is poetically described as 'raising up his heel'.

> "{Judas whom I trusted,} He who eats my bread, {right now, the sop}, has lifted up his heel against me."

However in the Luther Bible, the German readers are told that Christ is saying, in an allusion to the same Psalmic text, that his enemy has heightened his hostility, but in the narrow sense of trampling upon him. The idea of trampling arises with Luther, because the word 'feet' replaces the correct word, 'heel'. So in an expanded translation Luther's version is this,

> "He {Judas whom I trusted,} who eats my bread {right now, the sop}, is trampling on me (treads on me with his feet)."

This Luther translation is not correct to the Greek. However, Rudolf Steiner is suggesting that this is not a sentence about a hostile trampling at all, but about a harmless walking around activity.

Rudolf Steiner's use of Luther

This verse in Luther's Bible reads,

"Even my friend, whom I trusted, the one who ate my bread, **tramples on me.**"

Rudolf Steiner used this sentence in Luther's version, as an indication that Christ is referring to people walking around on the Earth which has become the vessel for Christ, but Luther's version is a less accurate version of the words given in John as compared to any other translations in German or English.

Furthermore, John's words in Greek are themselves an altered version, a weaker version, of the original Hebrew. How can Steiner then interpret this sentence as accurate and indeed as something positive, by saying that it has nothing to do with an attack by Judas?

We now know that the phrase, as originally given in the Old Testament, should read when put into the Gospels, (unless there is esoteric reason to change it), 'he has made great his heel against me', and not "he has

lifted up his heel". But in fact in his version of the Old Testament, Luther also translated Psalm 41 in this same way,
> "Even my friend, whom I trusted, the one who ate my bread, **tramples on me.**"
> „Auch mein Freund, dem ich mich vertrauete, der mein Brot aß, *tritt mich unter die Füße.*"
> (literally, '*treads me under the feet*'.)   Psalm 41

Compare this with the normal English versions,
> Even my close friend, whom I trusted, he who shared my bread, **has magnified his heel** against me.

So Luther has weakened the esoteric meaning of this unusual Hebrew phrase in the Old Testament, because he has removed the reference to a heel. He narrowed it down to an act of metaphorically trampling on someone. Luther then uses his narrower view of this complex Hebrew idiom when translating the Greek of John. But as we shall see later, his less accurate version is actually a fortunate error.

Like everyone else, Luther thought that one could regard Judas's actions, as described by John, to be hostile, because it is directly alluding to Psalm 41, and of course since it is about Judas's betrayal, it must be about hostility. Perhaps Luther thought that the original old Hebrew text really did mean attacking someone with one's feet.

Luther's translation of this passage suffers from ignoring the underlying meaning of the Hebrew idiom about 'raising the heel', and provides only a narrow version of its true meaning, which is, "The one who eats my bread has strengthened his evil intentions against me".

But this simple clarification about the difference between the standard translations and the Luther version, only brings clarity to the elementary meaning here, about Judas and his political actions. The above explanation, so far, does seem to imply that Rudolf Steiner's interpretation is wrong, that it is less accurate than the standard interpretation in most Bibles. But we have laid the groundwork for actually getting to the solution.

It is quite clear that we have not yet resolved the enigma of how such a sentence can be understood to be referring to the incorporation of the cosmic Christ into the Earth's soul. It appears quite undeniable that, since the Hebrew psalm is about an attack on David, and the Gospel account at the Last Supper is about an attack on Jesus, then the 'lifting up of the feet', or the heel, also has to mean **to attack** someone. It seems to be a reference to the man Judas, not to all of humanity – and especially not in some **positive** way. So just how can this text be seen by Rudolf Steiner as referring to something positive; and also to something which refers to all humanity?

To properly explore Steiner's viewpoint, one has to find a way of understanding the Greek text which no longer refers to either the negative nuance of the sentence as normally understood, nor the specific historical reference to Judas being hostile to Jesus Christ. And grammatically it must also allow a **positive** walking activity, not an ill-will trampling. We shall now explore further, without the reader needing knowledge of ancient Greek.

Secrets hidden in the Greek script
As we proceed, it will be necessary that we note a few points about this wonderful ancient language. Firstly we need to remind ourselves that this passage is of course, about eating, and it is also about the imminent death of Jesus. However, the verb used by John in the phrase, 'eats my bread' is the word troegein (τρώγειν) which in fact, as mentioned earlier, is not the normal verb for eating.

To the esoterically perceptive person, this fact is very significant. The usual verbs for eating are either esthiein (ἐσθίειν) or phagein (φαγεῖν). And that is why, when the Septuagint was written, the translators used the normal Greek verb, esthiein.

So it is very significant that some 350 years later, Lazaros specifically rejected this usual verb and used instead a very strange verb. Secondly, although he does

indeed use the usual verb phagein quite often for the general act of eating, he uses 'troegein' only five times. But each time it refers solely to the very potent and very esoteric idea of **humanity somehow consuming (that is, absorbing) Christ.** As was noted in chapter 6, this usage is to be found in v.56,
6:56 The person nourished by the life-force of my 'body' and drinking in the vitality of my 'blood' abides in me, and I in that person.

This is usually translated as, **Whoever eats my flesh and drinks my blood remains in me, and I in him.** So the usage of this special verb in verse 13:18 is intended to direct the meditant's attention to the sacred theme of the inner absorption (or 'consuming') of Christ. And this of course must mean, absorbing spiritual energies from Christ; Christ as a deity. This is itself a sacred and potent idea,[448] it cannot be referring to a human being.

But this same verb also has two other special nuances. When used by ancient Greek writers of eating in the general sense, it points specifically to the process of really setting out to eat something; of really going through the process of taking nutrient into oneself **actively**, such as by chewing or biting off a portion of the foodstuff.

For example, when it was used of animals eating, it meant the actual process of crunching, chewing or munching, and also then the swallowing. So it would be used in ancient Greek texts, to mean 'the cow was chewing the grass' or 'the horse is biting off a portion of carrot', etc.

Also in an older usage of this verb, it was used almost exclusively **for the eating of plant substances**, that is, fruit and vegetables. So when used of people, it almost always referred to eating (chewing and swallowing)

---

[448] This idea or rather deep spiritual truth exists in ancient Egyptian texts about Osiris, whom many scholars consider to be an experience of the cosmic aspect of Christ, long before the Christian era began.

vegetables or fruit, and when even used of animals, it referred to herbivores munching, chewing, etc. [449]

But plant foods were seen as an expression of the Earth's life-forces, because plants grow and derive from the Earth's etheric energy field. So the phrase, *"The one 'eating' my bread"* directs the meditative attention of the reader attuned to the Christ mysteries, to people who are actively absorbing, as **soul** nutrient, through specific inner effort, something that has living energies within it, something associated with the edible plants that manifest the inner life of our planet. In fact, it hints at the eating of plants, but plants **as symbols of the Earth's life-forces**.

But it is used in John's Gospel **only in reference to absorbing Christ into one's soul** (absorbing the 'cosmic bread of life'). So here in John 13:18, the 'living thing' or life energies being consumed or absorbed, can only be those life-forces that come from Christ. And indeed it is Christ who is speaking these words. Bread of course is derived from grain, and the grains are from living plants. The bread is described as belonging to Christ. So Christ here **is directly linking himself to the Earth's life-forces**.

The first veiled point that has emerged is that the Earth's life-forces are permeated by Christ. The second teaching now unveiled is, human beings, in eating plant substances, are absorbing Christ. Now before we take a larger step to discover the next sacred message in this sentence, and thereby discover the deeper meaning of this sentence, we have to know about a special feature of ancient Greek grammar. Let's see the sentence in John 13:18 again, and focus on the next part, about raising the heel. In both the NIV and a non-Luther German version (the Elberfeld version) it reads,

> 'He who shares my bread **has lifted up** his heel against me.'

---

[449] Walter Bauer, *A Greek-English Lexicon of the New Testament*, edit. trans. Arndt & Gingrich, 2nd, edit., University of Chicago, Chicago, 1979 and A Greek- English Lexicon, comp. H.G. Liddell & R. Scott, Clarendon Press, Oxford, 1996.

Der mit mir das Brot ißt, hat seine Ferse wider mich aufgehoben.
ho trogon mou ton arton **epaeren** epi eme taen pternan autou
(ὁ τρώγων μου τὸν ἄρτον ἐπῆρεν ἐπ" ἐμὲ τὴν πτέρναν αὐτοῦ.)

We need to note that the verb used here in the Hebrew original of Psalm 41 ('*gadal*'), "my friend....he has *made-great* a heel against me" has been put into the imperfect tense, that is, the simple past tense (higdil, הִגְדִיל). And so following on from this, the Greek version in the Septuagint **also uses** the simple past tense, "...he has exalted himself against me, with craftiness (emegalunen, ἐμεγάλυνεν)."

But in the Gospel of John, the Greek verb used here '**has *lifted-up*'** (epaeren - ἐπῆρεν) **has been specifically put into a remarkable tense or condition, known as the Aorist condition. It is no longer in the simple everyday past tense.** What is the aorist condition of a verb? The word 'aorist' itself means 'indefinite' in Greek; and this grammatical feature is the key to unveiling the deeper hidden meaning of this sentence, and to thereby discover the core message of esoteric Christianity.

The timeless aorist condition
This verb condition is not found in any modern language. It is usually defined as being the past tense, especially a one-off past event. In this way the ancient Greek language can indicate whether an action was ongoing, or a one-off act. For example, if one writes that someone cut down a tree in the past, then the aorist is used, because that has to be a one-off event. But if a river overflowed its banks, then the simple past tense is used, as this action can re-occur.

But this aorist state can also signify other things, as we shall see. So the first question arises; why did Lazaros use here this special condition, the aorist state? Why not stay with the simple past tense? It is also very important to note that Lazaros has thereby **changed** the Hebrew in two ways. Firstly, as we saw earlier, the

Hebrew says,"....he has **made-great** ('gadal') a heel against me." but Lazaros has changed 'made-great' to 'lifted up'. This is the same alteration which Luther made when he translated the Psalm.

When Lazaros used 'lifted up' instead of a Greek equivalent to the Hebrew verb 'to magnify one's impact', he was doing this from high initiatory consciousness. And yet 'lifting up' is implied to some extent in the Hebrew, because this can be a poetic way of describing from the viewpoint of the observer, the effect when the enhanced potency of someone's hostility is manifested.

So firstly, why was 'lifting up' used and not 'making-great'? Secondly, why was this verb put into this aorist condition? The answer to the first question is, the use of 'lifting up' of the heel, (or the foot as Luther has it), rather than 'making-great', **introduces the possibility of the motion of walking**. So we can say at this point, that we have the suggestion of people walking, even if this seems quite accidental, even irrelevant, in the light of our earlier comments.

But we still have the second question, why is the verb in this unusual aorist condition? If we can answer this, we can discover how Rudolf Steiner is validated in identifying this sentence as evidence of Scriptural indications about the cosmic Christ as the spirit for the Earth. But let's just review what we have discovered so far.

Firstly, scholars would say that the aorist is very often a simple past tense, and so the whole sentence here simply means that Judas, who is eating bread with Jesus, has already planned to betray him. So he has lifted up his heel (or foot) symbolizing hostility, and it is quite clear that it is in the simple past tense, for it is an action that Judas had already planned.

But also we have seen that the sentence discreetly suggests two intriguing things, by the choice of special Greek words; this has not previously noticed by scholars. Namely, that people could somehow be taking up Christ into themselves, as a kind of living nutrient.

Now here we realize something very important has become clear; on this deeper level of meaning, deliberately put into the Gospel, about absorbing Christ,

actually has to *exclude* Judas! On this level of meaning, about the absorbing of Christ spiritually, the sentence refers not to one individual, but to many people.

For it is now about people, lots of people, who are absorbing energies from the cosmic Christ. But is this statement correct? It is actually allowed in the grammar? Yes, it is; for the word, 'the one' (eating my bread....") in Greek, 'ho' (ὁ), can refer to either a single person, or to many people. It is itself singular, but it can and very often does, refer to many people; it literally says one person, but it means numerous people. For example in Luke 6:49 it used in this way,

> The person (in Greek, 'ho') hearing, but not taking action, is like a man who has built a house on the ground without a foundation..."

Here, as in so many other places in the New Testament, this word is singular, but actually implies a lot of people. So is Rudolf Steiner right, seeing that the reference to lifting the heel or foot is indeed about walking? If so, something else has to be resolved, namely that negative word at the end of the sentence, 'against'; which implies an attack,

> 'He who shares my bread has lifted up his heel **against** me.'

Not against, but 'across'

This word 'against' is a preposition, in Greek (epi - ἐπι). But in Hellenistic Greek, the meaning that a preposition has in a particular sentence depends upon its grammatical context. When used with what is called the dative case, 'epi' does indeed mean 'against'. But here in this sentence it is used with the accusative case; and in this situation 'epi' almost always means **'across or upon', not 'against'**.[450] More precisely stated, the word

---

[450] A. T. Robertson, *A Grammar of the Greek New Testament in the Light of Historical Research,* Broadman Press, Tennessee, 1934 and D. Wallace, *Greek Grammar beyond the basics*, Zondervan, Grand Rapids, 1996 and *A Grammar of New Testament Greek,* James H. Moulton, Vol. III, T & T Clark, Edinburgh, 1963.

'epi' in the accusative case can sometimes mean 'against', but only rarely; nearly always it means 'across' (or on, or upon).

If the ancient Greeks wanted to say 'against' by using 'epi' then they would normally use the dative case. For example, of the 476 times that 'epi' occurs in the New Testament in an accusative context, it nearly always means 'upon'. In fact, it only means 'against' in just 30 cases out 476.[451] So this word means primarily 'across', 'on' or 'upon'; depending on the grammatical context ![452] So, now we can take a very significant new step; the last part of the sentence **is far more correctly translated** as, '*across* **me**', and not '*against* me'.

> 'He who shares my bread has lifted up his heel **across me**.

So now we can proceed further. We need to examine briefly the truly remarkable ways in which the aorist condition of a verb was used. When we do this, we shall discover that it is not limited to the past tense. It has a truly unique quality, a quality which modern languages no longer possess. There are a few sentences in the New Testament where the other, truly unusual meanings of this Aorist condition can be seen.

A past action continued on into the present

Consider this sentence from St. Mark, about how at the baptism in the Jordan, a voice from heaven declared that God was 'well-pleased' with Jesus; that is saying in effect that the divine could be fully manifested in Jesus.

> Mk 1:11 And a voice came from heaven: "You are my Son, whom I love; with you I am well pleased."

---

[451] R. Morgenthaler, *Statistik des Neutestamentlichen Wortschatzes*, Gotthelf-Vlg, Zürich, 1958.

[452] It is interesting to note that just as the Greek preposition means 'across' or 'upon' (or at times 'against'), the Hebrew preposition in Psalm 41, (ala-i - עָלַי), also means 'across' or 'upon' as well as 'against'.

Now in fact the verb 'am well-pleased' used here (in all three of the synoptic gospels), is in the aorist condition, and so it would normally have to mean,

> "You are my Son, whom I love; I **was once on one occasion**, well pleased with you." (!)

This implies that God is now no longer well-pleased with Jesus, even right now. Quite a problem for translators, so they have come to different conclusions; but the consensus is that here this aorist state must have its special timeless quality. So, here it could mean that God was well-pleased with Jesus already in the remote times before Jesus was conceived, and continues to be so now. Theologians conclude that this could show that Jesus was in unity with God before the world was created. [453]

And it is indeed true that the aorist condition is simply not always a past tense, even though it accidentally became a kind of past tense. For it is actually about a process becoming completed, any process, but the process can also still be ongoing, right now in the present; it does not have to be only in the past.

The aorist can be used for processes that continuously bring to completion various smaller actions that together create an on-going contemporary process. This is a very strange perspective by our standards. But this is what is going on here in this sentence.

We are told that God has become 'pleased with' Jesus as a one-off completed act (in the past), **and yet this state of union continues on as a completed reality,** and continually renews itself. This we call the gnomic aorist condition; it is well-known to scholars. So therefore, more correctly translated this sentence reads,

---

[453] Ezra. P. Gould, Internat. Critical Commentary; *Gospel Mark*, T. & T. Clark, Edinburgh, 1897, p. 216 and Joachim Gnilka, EKK, *Das Evangelium nach Markus*, II/2, Benziger Vlg, Zurich, 1999, p.135.

> Mk 1:11 And a voice came from heaven: "You are my Son, whom I love; with you I became well pleased and this is constantly re-affirmed."

When a verb is in the aorist condition it can refer to a process which happened long ago, but which is still livingly active in the present. So it ignores the earthly flow of time. The past is viewed as part of the present.

However, the aorist can also be used in another strange way. It can be used for the reverse of this, for a process which has not yet happened but which is nevertheless regarded as already being a real, living reality in the present.

Consider another sentence from Scripture. Normally it is translated in the present tense, and yet it is definitely about a future event. This sentence really helps us to understand how sophisticated and subtle is the Greek language. The following is obviously a divine prophecy, and so it is about a future event. It occurs in the description of the Last Supper as in the Gospel of John, and in the NIV is,

> Jn. 13:31 When Judas had departed, Jesus said, "Now the Son of Man is glorified and God is glorified in him."

However the verb here ('glorified') **is twice in the aorist condition, and so it should actually be translated as a completed action (and thus in effect a past deed), i.e.,**

> "Now the Son of Man has been glorified and God has been glorified in him."

But this would be absurd, as the Resurrection of Jesus has not yet occurred. So, the normal translations simplify the situation and put it in the present tense. Yet the verb, being aorist, can be neither in the future nor in the present tense.

So here translators usually adopt the compromise of using the present tense in such a way as to suggest the future. Yet the aorist has nothing to do with the present or future tenses at all. So this is baffling, since the future is obviously meant, but just how does the aorist do this?

The answer is that the aorist condition here is saying that, so utterly certain in the mind of Christ is his prophecy about what shall happen, that it can be regarded as already being completed. So the aorist is indicating that the process of the Son of Man being glorified shall most assuredly be fully completed soon, and indeed, it is so utterly certain to be completed, that it is presented (through the aorist condition) as an action that has already been completed, with no regard to the flow of time, (for it is still to happen).

There is no grammatical feature in our language that can do this. So if one were to try to render the meaning here, it would be a very awkward version; perhaps,

> Jn 13:31 When he was gone, Jesus said, "Now indeed the Son of Man shall have already been glorified, and indeed God shall have already been glorified in him.

So, here something which is definitely to occur in the future is to be regarded as having already been completed. So we actually encounter an intriguing grammatical feature of this language; to present as a truth already in the here-and-now, something which lies in the future. This is known to scholars as a gnomic aorist, which means a timeless indefinite condition.

So 13:31 means,
"Now the Son of Man is as if glorified, and God as if glorified in him."

Then, if the word 'glorified' is replaced with a more meaningful phrase, it then is,

"Now the Son of Man is as if empowered, and God is as if empowered in him."

Spiritually, this situation is quite understandable. For where is something already in existence but is not yet manifest in the flow of time? For the ancient Greek people the answer would be, in the spiritual realms.

It is there where the past, present and future exist side by side, so to speak, as is implied in the name of God, when Jahve speaks to Moses (I was, am and will be). In these realms important truths of the future (and the past) exist as 'thought-forms'. The timeless (gnomic) aorist is an ancient literary device giving expression to the awareness of spiritual realities that the ancients possessed.

We have seen that the aorist can be used of an event in the future as if it had already happened, because in the spiritual realms, in the intentions of the gods, it is a reality, regardless of the flow of earthly time. And secondly, it can used of a process in which actions are continually being completed or past, but the action carries on in the present time. [454]

So, the aorist can also be used to refer to a process whose components recede off into the past, but which also keep repeating themselves as part of a bigger procedure, so the over-all process itself **remains in the present time**. In Lk. 7.35 we find another remarkable example of this,

> [NIV] But wisdom is proved right by all her children.
> [NKJ] But wisdom is justified by all her children.

The verb here is actually aorist and thus would usually mean something that occurred once in the past, as it does with Luther, who translates,

> But wisdom was proved right by all her children

But it is aorist and therefore a gnomic aorist is correct here, because a simple past comparison ignores the present and future possibilities, and is thus wrong. So I translate it as follows,

> "Wisdom has been, and repeatedly becomes, justified by all her children."

So here Luke is saying that the process of wisdom being affirmed through the experience and the actions of

---

[454] A. T. Robertson and D. Wallace (8) and H.P.V. Nunn, *A Short Syntax of New Testament Greek*, Cambridge Univ. Press, 1975, p.87 and Samuel Green, *Handbook to the Grammar of the Greek Testament*, The Religious Tract Society, London, 1897, p. 304.

sages has occurred in the ancient past, and is also occurring when his text was written, and shall occur in the future.

Spiritual processes via the aorist in Homer

And in the ancient Classic Greek of Homer, some 800 years before the Gospel, we find this same kind of suspension of time, and reference to actions which do occur, are completed, but are nevertheless in the present and the future. For example in his great story, The Iliad, in book 16, v. 401, where the death of a hero is mentioned, we find,

>haeripe d' hoes hote tis drus   hearipen
>ἤριπε δ'ὣς ὅτε τίς δρῦς ἤριπεν

This is usually translated something like this,
>"…..and he fell like an oak tree falling."

But the verb is in the aorist, and thus it would normally have to read,
>"….and he fell as when an oak tree did once fall."

This is very odd, comparing the death of the fighter with a long past event that once happened, namely when an oak tree fell. But since it is a gnomic aorist, it actually means, when correctly translated, and esoterically understood,
>"…. and he fell, as when every time an oak tree has fallen, or ever shall fall."

From an spiritual understanding of the text, one can conclude that here Homer as an initiate, is hinting at a Mars activity, as oak trees are associated with the planet Mars. So that, as the martial hero died, Mars forces were released, and these always will be released whenever a strong Mars organism collapses, whether a human fighter or the oak tree, which is traditionally associated with Mars forces.

So here again is an action which is completed, but which constantly re-occurs and thus can be considered as being past or completed, yet happening now in the present, and on into the future. Now, after these examples, consider again the sentence that Rudolf

Steiner has used as an example of how Scripture points to the union of the cosmic Christ to the Earth, namely,

> "The one eating my bread, he has **lifted-up** his heel *across* me"

Let's recollect at this point that we have already seen that in the lifting up of *the heel* there is a faint reference to people walking. And in Luther, the allusion to walking is much stronger; lifting up *the foot*. And this change was made possible because the verb 'to magnify' was replaced by St. John with the verb 'to lift up'. And we saw that there is also a veiled reference to being nourished, by taking up living plant nourishment. And we noted that plants symbolize the life-forces of our planet. But also we have discovered that the taking up of this living nourishment is about taking up of Christ, since the verb is ever only used by St. John for the absorbing of Christ.

Lifting up the heel or foot
Now here we remind ourselves that the verb 'lifted up' is in the aorist condition. So, it does not have to be seen as just a simple past tense. It can also be seen as a timeless process, a continuous completing of s**omething which nevertheless remains in the present time**. What could that be? Here that something **is walking**. For what do we do when walking?

We lift up our heel (or better, foot) and then we place it down onto the ground; but no sooner is this action completed, than we lift up the other foot and complete the next action of lifting up our foot and then putting it down, before starting all over again with the other leg. Walking is a process of **continuously completing the lifting up of the foot or heel**.

Although it is a present action, it contains the past, namely, the continual completing of the process of lifting up the foot ! For this type of action the aorist condition is an ideal device, as we have seen above. So now the esoteric Christian meditant realizes that the sentence is saying here, on this level,

> "The one 'eating' my bread, he is **continually completing the act of lifting-up, and then putting down, his heel** (foot) *across* me."

And in fact this therefore means, when translated, with spiritual insight,

"The one 'eating' the bread, he **is walking *across* me**".

Now we need to bring all of this together. The deeper level of meaning can now be seen. For John 13:18 has become a sentence prophesying what shall soon come to pass – but as a direct result of the betrayal by Judas. For what does it now mean to a deeper insight into this sacred text? It now can be seen as conveying the following meaning to spiritually aware Christians,

"The one who is consuming living plant foods ....
digesting nourishment from the Earth's life-forces –
is eating that which belongs to me;
is absorbing Christ's divine life-force in the plants that he sustains,
and those same persons are walking
(*continually completing the process of lifting up his heel, and putting it down again.*)
across me."
across the surface of the Earth, which has (shall soon) become my body.

> "Those who are consuming living plant foods are eating that which belongs to me; and those same persons are walking and those same persons are walking across me."
>
> John 13:18

All of this implies that *the Earth is about to become the body of Christ.* The Earth and Christ have become united, and hence people are walking across or upon Christ. This translation is entirely accurate to the Greek, and indeed is much more correct to the subtle nuances of meaning than all the normal versions.

The cosmic Gospel
We have just seen the answer to the question, how can this sentence in the gospel of St. John actually mean what Rudolf Steiner taught. Is there any other evidence that this research here is correct? In the other Gospels the Last Supper includes a very special section; it is the passage where Jesus Christ offers bread and wine to the disciples. The words He speaks there, about the bread being his body and the wine his blood, became the basis for the church's holiest sacrament, the Eucharist or the Mass. The words used then are (Matt. 26:26-28),

> While they were eating, Jesus took bread, gave thanks and broke it, and gave it to his disciples, saying, "Take and eat; this is my body."
> Then he took the cup, gave thanks and offered it to them, saying, "Drink from it, all of you.
> This is my blood of the covenant, which is poured out for many for the forgiveness of sins.

These words are understood to mean that the individual worshipper may share spiritually in the very being of Jesus. Hence the sacredness of these words. So it is very striking to discover that these words and the associated action of passing around bread and wine, **are entirely omitted** in the Gospel of John. This omission has caused serious difficulties for theologians for many centuries. It seems to be a very serious defect in this Gospel. But once the deeper spiritual message in 13:18 is discovered, then this omission becomes understandable.

Instead of affirming the spiritual union of **individual Christians with Jesus** (and his associated, but undefined, divine-ness), St. John has affirmed, in a veiled way, the initiatory understanding of the spiritual union of the **cosmic Christ** with the **Earth-soul, and through this process with all humanity.** For this reason Lazaros omitted the sacramental words from the Last Supper about taking and eating the bread or drinking the wine, because those words are directed to individuals in an ecclesiastical setting, wherein the congregation becomes the 'body', that is a part of the spiritual essence of Jesus Christ.

But this description is about the larger cosmic perspective wherein all individuals, even if unaware of this, are to become people who, in living on the planet, and so of course walking over it, shall become part of the body of the great cosmic Christ spirit who is to about to become the indwelling spiritual essence of planet Earth.[455] There is therefore an underlying teaching in this sentence, which I would put in this way;

> **"The Earth has become my body, which is shed for ye."**

That is, the Earth has been created to enable humanity to evolve towards the Spirit. But one last objection could be raised; how can this be the secret deeper meaning of this sentence, because it is spoken **before** Jesus is killed. At the time when this statement is made, it is apparently not true. The answer is that the entire sentence is a spiritual statement of just that kind which the aorist makes possible. A statement that is above the flow of time. We saw how the aorist condition for the verb 'to lift up' implies walking, by hinting at a repeated finishing of an action going on continuously in the present.

But as we have also seen, the aorist enables one to point to events which transcend time, especially if the intention is very important. It points to events or intentions which live as ideas or 'thought-forms' of the gods. It is quite true that when this sentence was spoken, the union of the cosmic Christ with the Earth **had not taken place.**

But to Christ and many Christians, there is no intention or planned event, formulated by divine beings, greater than the Mystery of Golgotha. It is from the viewpoint of Lazaros, the very basis for the Earth's future existence. Consequently Christ can indeed proclaim, **before** the event, that He is the spirit of the Earth, because in this passage from the Gospel of John, He is pointing to the imminent occurrence of this

---

[455] There are references to this cosmic dimension in this Gospel, through the recording of the washing of the feet incident, which has to do with Piscean energies.

supreme event. And to Him, this event is a truth already, for it is an intention in the spirit realms planned by God, and which no power was able to prevent. An intention already planned as in remote ages.[456]

So at the Last Supper, Christ proclaimed it as already a truth spiritually, even though it was not yet embedded in the flow of earthly time. And similarly, as we saw earlier, some short time before this, He had proclaimed the glorification of the Son of Man, even though the event was still to occur in the flow of time. The aorist condition makes exactly this sort of language possible.

Review
The first level of meaning is historical, and concerns hostility from Judas Iscariot. In the English versions it appears as, **'The one eating my bread, he has lifted-up his heel against me.'** The surface meaning here is that Judas has become antagonistic to Jesus. In the Martin Luther version it appears as, **"He who eats my bread, is trampling on me."** This version means that Judas is regarded as metaphorically trampling on Jesus.

But when a deeper level of meaning in the sacred text is accessed, we see it is hinting that people, in digesting plant foods, are in effect absorbing energies from Christ. Because the verb used here means to really digest living (plant-based) food, but yet it is only ever used by Lazaros of absorbing or receiving into oneself the light of Christ. So it means that people can absorb life-enfilled nourishment from Christ. That points us to the subtle life-forces of the planet, and to the presence of Christ in these. This initiatory or inspired level of meaning in the gospel also then is in harmony with such other words of Christ, as "I am the bread of life".

And the people who are doing this, they are all incarnate people, because they are walking along over the Earth. Lastly, human beings, in walking along, across the planet, are walking across the deity Christ who is to permeate the Earth's soul. John 13:18 is saying that

---

[456] In anthroposophical teachings, this preparation occurred long ago in what is known as the Sun aeon, see my *Rudolf Steiner Handbook*, for more about this.

soon people shall be walking over Christ, absorbing the life-forces of the great cosmic god, because He shall soon become the indwelling guiding spirit of the planet.

To point towards this layer of meaning, Rudolf Steiner has used Luther's translation because Luther's German idiom for trampling is literally, "....tread on me with their feet". And by taking this idiom literally one can take a kind of short-cut to the third level of meaning, since it points to people walking along. And this was no doubt an appropriate decision by Rudolf Steiner at the time, and for his purposes.[457]

But it is more defensible to take the long route which I have given here. I have attempted to establish the accuracy of Steiner's insights, and that the deepest meaning of the sophisticated Greek grammar in John 13:18 accords fully with Rudolf Steiner's explanation, and confirms his understanding of a merging of the deity with the planet,

> "Those persons who are consuming plant foods are absorbing living nourishment from Christ, from within the planet's life-forces, and all such people, in walking over the planet's surface, are walking across Him (for He is to become the indwelling Earth-Spirit)."

And this shall be the case as a direct result of the betrayal by Judas. Christ is shortly to become the indwelling, guiding spirit of the planet. The last meaning is dependent upon the first meaning, upon the death of Jesus, through the Mystery of Golgotha. These conclusions also explain the absence of the Eucharist rite at the Last Supper, in the Gospel of John.

---

[457] In 1908, Steiner faced a question after a lecture as to why he insisted that this sentence in John 13:18 revealed that a cosmic Christ being would unite to the Earth, when obviously the Greek did not say that. He replied, "Yes it is a shame that this has not been seen correctly, but in the future someone shall appear who shall establish that this sentence does refer to the union of Christ to the Earth." (unpublished Archive document, Frag.-Beantw. #1789, published in a longer version in GA 244, p. 250.)

Appendix 16

17:3 That the verse with the name 'Jesus Christ' or Jesus the Anointed One, was not spoken by Jesus.

v.3: "And this is aeonic existence: that they cognize You as the only true God, and that they cognize Jesus the Anointed One as the one You sent forth (into this world)."

One conclusion reached by theologians to explain this strange situation that Jesus apparently refers to himself as someone else, is that Jesus did not speak these words, but rather it is an editorial insertion by the Gospel writer. However, this theory is on very tenuous grounds, because this would not be normal editorial work, such as the Gospels elsewhere contain.

For this is a potent insertion of words, which are very liable to be misunderstood by most readers, who naturally think that they were actually spoken by Jesus. So it is almost alleging incompetence by Lazaros-John to say that he inserted them. It is contrary to the work-ethic of this Gospel writer, who declared himself to be a true witness (21; 24), to allege that he would insert his own commentary, in such a confusing manner.

Of course at times a speaker can speak in the third person (using their name as if they were not that person), but to myself and many other scholars, this figure of speech is not being used here. Here is how various renowned scholars view this sentence, as I have noted elsewhere.[458] For example, Heinrich A.W. Meyer, in his *Commentary on the New Testament*, (1881) thinks that Jesus used his own name here, because "it is a kind of confessional prayer". And Prof. F. Godet, in his *Commentary to the Gospel of John*, (Kommentar zu dem Evangelium Johannes, 1903) concludes that here Jesus felt he should "state clearly for once that he is the Messiah, before he dies". Prof. T. Zahn, in *The Gospel of John*, (*Das Evangelium Johannes*, 1921) concludes that Jesus is here educating his listeners (readers) as to how to understand him, and thus how to eventually address

---

[458] In *Rudolf Steiner on Leonardo's Last Supper.* (2017)

him, once the church has been formed (in the decades to come).

But A. Plummer, *The Gospel according to S. John*, (1881) concludes that these words are "not without difficulty", and are an insertion from the Gospel writer and "perhaps abbreviated from {*now unknown*} words of Jesus".

B. F. Westcott, *The Gospel of St. John*, (1908) observes that these words "present a great difficulty", and remain a puzzle.

Prof. Dr. Prelate Franz Pölzl in his *Short Commentary to the Gospel of John*, (𝔎𝔲𝔯𝔷𝔤𝔢𝔣𝔞𝔰𝔰𝔱𝔢𝔯 𝔎𝔬𝔪𝔪𝔢𝔫𝔱𝔞𝔯 𝔷𝔲𝔪 𝔈𝔳𝔞𝔫𝔤𝔢𝔩𝔦𝔲𝔪 𝔍𝔬𝔥𝔞𝔫𝔫𝔢𝔰, 1914), brings a complex Catholic perspective, namely that "the one-ness and unity of God does not exclude a plurality of divine 'Persons'." Consequently Jesus can be thought of as separate from, yet also as part of, God. This allows Jesus, despite being God, in this instance, to set himself aside from God and "require cognisance of God and of himself {*as part of God*}, as objects to be cognized..."

Prof. C. K. Barrett, in *The Gospel according to John*, (1955) states that "this verse must be regarded as parenthetical". (That is, Lazaros-John added these words.) For "John felt the necessity of giving a definition of eternal life to the readers..."

Dr. L. Morris, *The Gospel according to John*, (1995) concludes that it cannot be John who wrote these words, because "why would he do this so late in the Gospel. But {*also it is a puzzle*} why Jesus would not simply say, 'me'." But Morris says anyway, "this 3rd person usage from Jesus here does harmonize with the 2nd person usage ('your son', 'him') in the 1st and 2nd verses" {*where again he should have said "me"*.) So therefore all these verses are a puzzle for Morris.

Prof. Craig Keener, *The Gospel of John - a Commentary*, (2003) concludes that the 'narrator', John, has added this verse, to bring about "a close association of Jesus and the Father".

The primary source of confusion in the Church over the centuries has been the lack of knowledge of, or the non-perceiving of, the complex and cosmic nature of the Christ-reality; the clearest exponent of which is Rudolf

Steiner. This involves the man Jesus, and various aspects of divine reality, in particular the solar Logos and the great primal Logos. As from the early centuries, persons not esoterically aware became the leading church authorities, so this more complex and highly transcendent aspect of Christianity was lost.

The Easter sequence of events in John

THURSDAY 2nd April AD 33   (13th Nisan)
Maundy Thursday
Evening: the LAST SUPPER occurs, this was also the preparation day for the Jewish Passover

The Foot-washing rite occurs
  (In the synoptics, a sharing of the bread & wine)
A: The traitor is pointed out, Judas goes out into the night
B: Jesus goes to the Mt. Olives, to pray in the Garden of Gethsemane

FRIDAY 3rd April Easter/Paschal Friday (14th Nisan)
Early morning: the kiss of Judas...arrest of Jesus
Morning: Jesus is questioned before Pilate
He is scourged, and Barabbas released
Jesus is lead to Golgotha to his death
by NOON he is **CRUCIFIED**
From noon to 3 pm: mysterious darkness falls
and earthquakes occur

3pm : THE DEATH OF JESUS,

6 pm: The centurion pierces his body, releasing the divine energies into the earth
Jesus is taken down from the cross
Buried: lies in the tomb
Earthquakes continue intermittently
SUNSET The Hebrew **PASSOVER** Festival starts now

SATURDAY   4th April   (15th Nisan)
* IN THE TOMB / Descent into Hades

SUNDAY   5th April   (16th Nisan)
THE RESURRECTION occurs
Before dawn, in the twilight, Mary Magdalene arrives at the tomb. Sees the risen Saviour in his densified etheric body, so she does not recognize Him until he speaks. She hurries off to tell Peter and John.

Appendix 18

Concerning Mary Magdalene

Various baseless theories have been spread in connection with Mary Magdalene and a life in ancient France, often with Jesus, who is alleged to have lived on after Golgotha. These theories are without any historical basis, ignore the available evidence, and also the testimony of the Gospels. They also show little understanding of the nature of Jesus Christ, as the human vessel of the sublime solar Logos.[459]

This myth was concocted by an over-zealous priest, in the ninth century, Rabanus Maurus, a pupil of Alcuin, at the court of Charlemagne. Maurus created the fantasy about 810 AD in his *Life of Mary Magdalene*. This myth was taken up in the 13th century by Vincent Beauvais, and spread from there. Church historians investigated this story thoroughly, and dismissed it as a fantasy. If she had been in France this would have been known to Gregory the Great and Gregory of Tours, back in the 6th century.

This situation was partly brought about by a misleading translation of a section of a Nag Hammadi text, *The Gospel of Philip* concerning Mary Magdalene. This text was translated as "Jesus kissed Mary Magdalene on the *mouth*", whereas actually the word 'mouth' is not there; the papyrus has a small section of papyrus missing in that line: it reads, "Jesus loved Mary and kissed her on the ----".

But the mouth would not have been the place meant; it would have been the forehead or the top of the head. This was common practice with spiritual teachers of that time. The true nuance of this text has been badly misrepresented, especially since in the preceding sentence it is said that Jesus 'loved' Mary Magdalene;

---

[459] Rabanus Maurus, a pupil of Alcuin, once ordered a monk be flogged for disseminating ideas about predistination that were not fully orthodox.

but the verb in this Coptic text is the equivalent of the Greek agapaeoe, so the love here is agape.

There are three women involved when exploring the mystery of Mary Magdalene.

A: the woman of Lk. 7:37-38; described as a 'sinful' woman. She anointed the feet of Jesus with perfume, and lived in the city of Jerusalem. She did this from feelings of penitence, sorrow and hope.

B: Mary Magdalene; she is first mentioned by Luke (see below) but then she is not mentioned again until the time of the Crucifixion.

C: Mary of Bethany, the sister of Lazaros and Martha; she lived with them outside of Jerusalem, in Bethany. That two different women could carry out a similar action, whether from penitence or reverence is quite possible.[460] But Mary of Bethany did the anointing because she was so perceptive about the life of Jesus, that, as Jesus stated, she knew he would soon be dying (12:3). Her anointing was done as a ritual anticipation of his death (the body was always anointed before burial.) So the sinful woman and Mary of Bethany are indeed two separate people.

Now, soon after the 'sinful' woman is mentioned in Luke's Gospel, a Mary, called 'the Magdalene' is mentioned. I have concluded that Mary Magdalene is not the previously mentioned 'sinful' woman, for several reasons. One reason is that Luke would have made it clear if these two were the same person, if that were the case.

But before proceeding further, we note that there is an argument against the above conclusion, because some theories presume that Mary Magdalene was also Mary of Bethany, who also anointed Jesus with expensive perfume. Consequently, on this theory, the Gospels have refrained from pointing out that all three are the same person.

However, the first woman with an alabaster jar is described as a sinner; she is now repentant, and her sins are 'forgiven'. Hence she is not Mary of Bethany, for this

---

[460] The village of Bethany was not part of Jerusalem, as some have argued, for it is distinctly identified as a separate village in the Gospels.

Mary carried out an anointing for a very different reason, as noted above; (see below for further reasons.)

But is she Mary Magdalene? Here one has to note that some other scholars have concluded that Mary Magdalene was the sister of Lazaros; meaning that she was also Mary of Bethany, but that she was not the sinful woman.

The textual fact is that the Gospels do not provide any concrete evidence for Mary Magdalene and Mary of Bethany being the same person. Lazaros in his Gospel never made any reference to Mary as his sibling; this silence remains a major counter-argument. Before considering the Magdalene further, the similarity of the sinful woman and Mary Magdalene needs to be considered again from another angle.

The 'sinful woman' has changed, and is now regretting her past; Jesus tells her that her sins are forgiven. Then one learns from Luke, that Mary Magdalene has seven apparently 'evil spirits' removed from her soul. Then we naturally think that perhaps she is also the sinful woman mentioned earlier. Firstly one needs to consider what Luke wrote this about 'the Magdalene' (8:2):

"The twelve were with him, and some women who had been healed from evil spirits and infirmities; Mary called 'the Magdalene' from whom seven spirits had gone out, and Joanna, wife of Chuza and Suzanna, and many others…"

So some of the women helping Jesus were healed of illnesses or had 'evil spirits' cast out of their soul. But it is not definitely the case that Mary Magdalene had seven 'evil spirits' removed, because, as my translation above shows, the Greek word 'daemonions' (δαιμόνια) was used with regard to the Magdalene. This word means 'spirits' – either evil spirits or good spirits.

Luke specifically refrains from identifying these seven spirits as evil, by using this ambiguous word here. This contrasts with his words just before, when he states 'evil spirits' in regard to other unspecified people.[461] But perhaps Luke was just being imprecise and did mean evil spirits; or he actually meant spirits which were not evil, but neutral, hence he chooses an ambiguous word.

The comments by Luke are unusual in their brevity, and cannot be clarified. There is a strong possibility that the number seven relates to the seven classical planets, and therefore it is just possible in regard to this Mary, that some kind of neutral spirit entities are meant, as part of a mysterious preliminary initiatory process.[462]

So the situation with Mary Magdalene remains unclear in this matter, but the basis for identifying Mary Magdalene with the 'sinful' woman is weak, yet still possible.[463] Likewise the case for identifying the sinful woman with Mary of Bethany is weak; indeed to me, is without any basis.

A: The sinful woman: generally understood to mean a prostitute.
Was a sinner who was full of regret, sadness and was hoping that all shall go well with her now.
She was comforted by Jesus who told her that her sins were forgiven.
The perfume was not enormously expensive.
She lived in Jerusalem.

B: Mary of Bethany:
Was full of reverence for Jesus,

---

[461] In this regard it is very difficult to know whether Luke's words, "certain women, healed of evil spirits and infirmities", just before he mentions the Magdalene, (and Johanna and Suzanna), are referring to these three named women, or not. They could be in a second category; if they are in that first category ("certain women, healed of evil spirits and infirmities") then since Luke says "daemonions' and not 'evil spirits' these three women did not have evil spirits in them, but lesser lowly spirits.

[462] Perhaps Luke is alluding to spiritual energies from the planetary spheres, which in the Hellenistic Age were understood to have a major role in the human soul.

[463] There is a brief comment from R. Steiner which seems to affirm that Mary of Bethany and the Magdalene are the same person (GA 244, p. 435) but this comment is of uncertain validity.

Was not a sinner hoping for forgiveness
Had especially acquired extremely expensive ointment
Her purpose was to honour the sacrifice of Jesus; the anointing being ritually made in anticipation of the day of embalming his body, after his death.
Lived in Bethany.
Her brother was wealthy and religious, she would have had no compelling financial reason to become a prostitute – and many reasons to maintain a high social status, as well as a deep religiosity.

The identifying of her in the Gospel (11:2) as the one who anointed Jesus, even though this had not yet happened, does not refer the reader back to the sinful women episode, since the two anointings were so different. It is a pattern in this Gospel that if someone has a noteworthy feature, that they are identified by that, even if they have not been mentioned in the Gospel.

There is also speculation that Mary Magdalene was 'the Beloved Disciple'. This view is erroneous; in 20:3 both Mary Magdalene and 'the other disciple' are present, as two separate persons. The counter argument that someone has falsified the Gospel verse, to create the impression that there are two separate persons when really they are but one, is simply a theory that creates more problems than it solves, which points to its lack of validity.

Magdalene: The epithet 'Magdalene' is of unclear origin, but, despite ideas to the contrary, it probably does not refer to her alleged birthplace. Linguistically, 'Magdalene' might mean 'of Magdala' and this might refer to a town of that name. But no such town was mentioned at the time of Jesus, in contemporary literature, except possibly in Matt. 15:39, where a 'Magadan' is mentioned, but this place is also elusive; with no such town ever being identified.

Consequently, many scholars are not at all certain that she was from any such town. There is a town of the name Magdala, which is now being excavated in Israel, but it appears to have begun as a settlement only about 100 BCE, and was insignificant until the time of

Josephus (writing about CE 70-100). Some scholars assert that it was known as Tarichaea at the time of Jesus, and only later as Magdala.[464] So the evidence indicates that at the time of Jesus, it is most unlikely that anyone would be called 'someone of Magdala" as a way to identify their origin or especial local characteristics.

It is much more likely that this epithet refers in a veiled way to initiatory processes. For in the Gospels, Mary Magdalene is presented primarily as being involved in scenes of death and resurrection. Linguistically, Magdalene is much more likely to be derived from an Aramaic word, 'Mighdol' or 'Migdal', which means 'tower' or 'the elevated one'. I conclude that the meaning is 'tower'.

In the time of Jesus, villages with simple towers were common around the Roman Empire; these were places where soldiers could keep a look-out for enemy troops, or where farmers could keep an eye on their crops. But in Egypt, in the Hellenistic Age, (and probably long before) there was a town with a tower on the west bank of the Nile, just south of Cairo. This place was consequently known to the Greeks as 'Magdola'.[465]

The tower would have been looking to the west, but in ancient Egypt, the west bank of the Nile was the realm of the Dead. Consequently the focus of all clusters of buildings (for convenience called 'towns') on the west bank was religious; their buildings were temples, which were dedicated to the After-life and the Gods. The site of a very large and splendid city was recently discovered on the west bank, built by Amenhotep III (14th century BCE); it was built specifically to honour the sun-god, Aten. So a tower in such a site was very likely ritualistic, not pragmatic; that is, to do with the cult of the After-life.

Evidence exists for various kinds of contact between ancient Egypt and Palestine already by the Egyptian Middle Kingdom (2025-1075 BC). As Offord makes clear,

---

[464] Prof. Joan Taylor, King's College, London, in *Sight* magazine, 8 Jan. 2022.

[465] This ancient place was known as Magdola and Medinet Nahas, situated in the Nile delta region.

there was considerable interaction between Palestine and Egypt for centuries, with regard to 'migdol' or towers. There is an Egyptian inscription in hieroglyphs mentioning various Syrian 'Migdols' (or Migdals) located in the Holy Lands.[466]

It was noted earlier that there is an undercurrent of ancient Egyptian themes and characters in the Gospels. To the ancient Egyptians, looking into the distance from a tower on the west bank of the Nile was quite possibly a metaphor for gazing into the realm of the Dead. In view of the connection of Egyptian initiatory wisdom with that of the Essenes and other groups, the epithet 'Magdalene' probably meant, 'she of Migdal'. This signified a Migdal tower, and may have alluded to that one on the west bank of the Nile, near Cairo.

This suggests that this woman Mary was an acolyte learning to perceive and to understand the realm of the Dead. It is a key feature of the personality of Mary Magdalene that she had to engage with the death and resurrection of Jesus.

---

[466] J. Offord, *Some migdols of Palestine and Egypt*, The American and Oriental Journal (1880-1914), vol. 25 Iss.2, 1903. One such inscription for Palestine is referred to, at Medinet Habou.

Selected Bibliography

Abbott, T. *Ephesians and Colossians*, ICC, Edinburgh, T & T Clark, 1897.
Alford, H. *Greek Testament*, Chicago, Moody Press, 1958.
Allberry, edit. *Manichaean Psalm-Book*, Stuttgart, Kohlhammer Vlg, 1938.
Angus, S. *The Mystery Religions,* New York, Dover, 1975
Assmann, Jan and Bommas, M. edits, *Ägyptische Mysterien?* Munich, W. Fink Verlag, 2002.
Athenagoras: Writings of, Edinburgh, T & T Clarke, 1868.
Aune, D. *Revelation 1-5* Word Biblical Commentary, Nashville, Thomas Nelson,1998.
Bacchiocchi, S. *Anti-Judaism and the origin of Sunday*, Rome, Pontifical Gregorian Univ. Press, 1975.
Barrett, C.K. *The Gospel according to St. John* London, SPCK, 1955.
Borsch, F. H. *The Son of Man in Myth and History*, London, SCM Press, 1967.
Beasley-Murray, G.R. *John*, Biblical Word Commentary, Thomas Nelson, Nashville, USA, 1999.
Bengel, J. A. *New Testament Word Studies*, Grand Rapids, Kregel, 1971.
Bernard, J.H. *A Critical and Exegetical commentary on the Gospel according to St. John*, ICC, Edinburgh, T & T Clark, 1972.
Black, M. *An Aramaic Approach to the Gospels*,
Box, G.H. *The Ezra-Apocalypse*, Pitman, London, 1912.
Bruce, F.F. *The Epistle to the Hebrews*, NICNT, Grand Rapids, Eerdmans, 1990.
Burder, S. *Oriental Customs illustrating Sacred Scripture,* London, T. Teg, 1840.
Burrows, M. *The Dead Sea Scrolls*, London, Secker & Warburg, 1956.
H.J. Cadbury, *The Style and Literary Method of Luke,* 2001, Wipf and Stock-Harvard UP.
Charlesworth J., edit. *Jesus and the Dead Sea Scrolls*, N.Y. Doubleday, 1992.
Charlesworth J. & Crabbe, L. edit. *Critical Reflections on the Odes of Solomon*, Sheffield Academic Press, 1998.

Cyril of Alexandria, *Commentary on John*, edit. J. Elowsky, trans. D. Maxwell, IVP Acad. Illinois, 2013.
Clement of Alexandria, The Ante-Nicene Greek Library, translations of the Church Fathers, vol. 12, Edinburgh, T & T Clarke,1882.
ΚΛΗΜΕΝΤΟΣ ΤΟΓ ΑΛΕΞΑΝΔΡΕΩΣ ·Λογος Προτρεπτικος, Stählin, O. edit., *Die Griechischen Christlichen Schriftsteller der erste drei Jahrhunderte*; Leipzig, J.C. Hinrich'sche Verlag, 1906.
Daniélou, J. *Theology of early Christianity*, London, Westminster, no date.
Daniélou, J. *Theology of Jewish Christianity*, London, Westminster, 1964.
Davies, E. *The Mythology and Rites of the British Druids*, London, J. Booth, 1809.
Dupont-Sommers, A. *The Essene Writings from Qumran*, Cleveland World Publ. Co., 1962.
Eisenmann and Wise, *Dead Sea Scrolls Uncovered*, Shaftesbury, Dorset, Element Books, 1992.
Svans, E. *The Books of Jeu and the Pistis Sophia*, Leiden, Brill, 2015.
Gnilka, Joachim EKK, *Das Evangelium nach Markus*, II/2, Zurich, Benziger Vlg, 1999.
Godet, F. *Kommentar zu dem Evangelium Johannes*, Hannover/Berlin, 1903.
Goethe, J. W. von, *Faust,* Hamburger Ausgabe (HA), edit. Trunz, Erich. Hamburg: Christian Wegner Verlag, 1955.
Goethe, J.W. von, *Das Märchen* in "Unterhaltungen Deutscher Ausgewanderten" Hamburger Ausgabe (HA), edit. Trunz, Erich. Hamburg: Christian Wegner Verlag, 1955.
Goethe, *The Fairy Tale of the Green Snake and the Beautiful Lily*" trans. Carlyle, T. Edinburgh, Floris Bks, 1979.
Gould, Ezra. P. *Gospel of Mark,* Internat. Critical Commentary, Edinburgh, T. & T. Clark, 1897.
Grässer, *An die Hebräer*, EKK, Zürich, Benzinger, 1990.
Green, Samuel. *Handbook to the Grammar of the Greek Testament*, London, The Religious Tract Society, 1897.
Gregorovius, F. *Eudocia*, in Athenais, Leipzig, F. A. Brockhaus, 1882.
Harris, J. R *Codex Bezae*, Cambridge UP, 1893.

Heine, Ronald. trans. *Origen, Fathers of the Church*, C.U. of A, 1989.
Hill, C.E. *Who wrote the gospels?* Oxford, UP, 2010.
Hippolytus, *Refutation of All Heresies,* trans. M. David Litwa SBL Press, 2016.
Holmes, M. *Apostolic Fathers*, Grand Rapids, Baker Books, 1999.
Isho'dad of Merv, *The Commentaries*, trans. Gibson, M. Cambridge, UP, 1916.
ΕΙΣ ΤΟΝ ΒΑΣΙΛΕΑ ΗΛΙΟΝ ΠΡΟΣ ΣΑΛΛΟΥΣΤΙΟΝ (Julian the Apostate, *To King Helios, for Sallust*) The Loeb Classical Library.
Justin Martyr & Athenagoras, trans. Dodds, M. & Reith, G. Edinburgh, T & T Clark, 1867.
Käsemann, *The Testament of Jesus*, trans. Krodel, Philadelphia, Fortress Press, 1968.
Keener, Craig. *The Gospel of John*, Peabody, Hendrickson, 2003.
Luz, U. *Das Evangelium nach Matthäus*, EKK, Zürich, Benzinger, 2002.
Meyer, H.A.W. *Handbook to the Gospel of John*, trans. Urwick, W. Edinburgh, T & T Clark, 1881.
Meyer, H.A.W. *Critical and Exegetical Handbook to the Gospels of Mark and Luke*, trans. R. Wallis, Edinburgh, T & T Clark, 1883.
Metzger, B. *Textual Commentary on the Greek New Testament*, United Bible Societies, 1994.
Metzger, B. *The Text of the New Testament*, Oxford, OUP, 1964.
Metzger, B. *The Apocrypha*, Oxford, UP, 1965.
Metzger, B. *An Introduction to The Apocrypha*, New York, OUP, 1957.
Moffat, J. *Epistle to the Hebrews*, ICC, Edinburgh, T & T Clark, 1968.
Morgenthaler, R. *Statistik des Neutestamentlichen Wortschatzes*, Zürich, Gotthelf-Vlg, 1958.
Morris, L. *The Gospel according to John*, NICNT, Grand Rapids, Eerdmans, 1995.
Marjanen, A. *The Woman Jesus loved*, Leiden, E.J. Brill,1996.
Meyer, M. edit. *The Ancient Mysteries*, Upenn. Press 1987.

Moffat, J. *Epistle to the Hebrews,* ICC, T & T Clark, Edinburgh, 1968.
Moulton, J. and Milligan, G. *The Vocabulary Of The Greek Testament illustrated from the Papyri and other non-literary Sources.* London, Hodder & Stoughton, 1930.
Moulton, James H. *A Grammar of New Testament Greek,* Vol. III, Edinburgh, T & T Clark, 1963.
Müller, E. *Der Sohar, Das Heilige Buch der Kabbala,* Wien, Vlg. H. Glanz, 1932.
Novalis: Werke, Tagebücher and Briefe, Bk. 1, edit. R. Samuel, Carl Hanser Vlg. 1978.
Oesterley, W. *Introduction to the Apocrypha,* London, SPCK,1958.
Origeneswerke: Matthäus-erklärung, edit. E. Klostermann, Leipzig, J.C: Hinrichs Vlg, 1941.
Origenes, *Exhortation to Martyrdom,* trans. R. Greer, New York, Paulist, 1979.
Origenes, *Treatise on the Passover,* trans. R. Daly, Paulist, 1992
ΟΙΓΕΝΟΥΣ Περὶ ἀρχῶν (Origenes, *On First Principles*), edit. Crouzel, H. & Simonetti, M. Paris, Editions Du Cerf, 1978.
ΟΙΓΕΝΟΥΣ, ΤΩΝ ΕΙΣ ΤΟ ΚΑΤΑ ΙΩΑΝΝΗΝ ΕΥΑΓΓΕΛΙΟΝ ΕΞΗΓΤΙΚΩΝ (Origenes, *Commentary on the Gospel of John*) Cecile Blanc, edit. Editions Du Cerf, Paris, 1996.
Origen: On First Principles, Lubac, H. edit, Butterworth G. trans. Gloucester, Mass. P. Smith Press, 1973.
Philips, J. *The Disciple whom Jesus Loved,* Philips, Lockport Il, 2010.
Philonis Judaei *Omnia Opera,* Patrum Ecclesiae Graecorum, edit. E. Schwickerti, Lipsiae 1828.
Philo, The Works of. trans. C.D. Yonge, Hendrickson, 1997
Phokylides, Das Mahngedicht. edit. Ger. & Grk. Joseph Nickel, Mainz, J. Rauch Vlg, 1833.
Photius, *Bibliotheque II* Paris, in *Bibliotheca 109,* edit. R. Henry, 1960.
Plummer, *The Gospel according to John,* Cambridge, CUP,1889.
Pölzl, F. Kurzgefaßter Kommentar zum Evangelium des Hl. Johannes, Graz und Wien, 1914.

Polybius. *Histories*, (Greek text at www.perseus.tufts.edu.)
Purl, F. *Der Pantocrator*, Hamburg, H-R/Evangelischer Vlg, 1969.
Robertson, A. T. *A Grammar of the Greek New Testament in the Light of Historical Research,* Tennessee, Broadman Press, 1934.
Schmidt, C. *Die Pistis Sophia*, Berlin, Akademie Vlg, 1959.
Schweizer, E. *Kommentar zum Neuen Testament, Der Brief an die Kolosser*, Benziger, 1997.
Scipio, Dream of, trans. P. Bullock, Wellingborough, Aquarian Press, 1983.
Scott, Walter. trans./edit. *Hermetica*, Boston, Shambala, 1985.
Smith, M. *Clement of Alexandria and a Secret Gospel of St. Mark*, Harvard, Harvard UP, 1973.
Souter, A. *The Text and Canon of the New Testament*, revised edition, London, G. Duckworth & Co, 1954.
Steiner, Rudolf. *Das Christentum als Mystische Tatsache.* Dornach: RSV, 1976.
Steiner, Rudolf. *Das Ewige in der Menschenseele.* Dornach: VRSN, 1962.
Steiner Rudolf. *Das Johannes Evangelium im Verhältnis zu den drei anderen Evangelien.* Dornach: RSV, 1975.
Steiner Rudolf. *Das Johannes Evangelium.* Dornach: RSV, 1981.
Steiner, Rudolf. *Das Wesen der Ewigkeit und die Natur der Menschenseele im Lichte der Geisteswissenschaft.* RSV, 1912.
Steiner, Rudolf. *Die Geheimwissenschaft im Umriss.* Dornach: RSV, 1977.
Steiner, Rudolf. *Die neue Geistigkeit und das Christus Erlebnis des zwanzigsten Jahrhunderts.* Dornach: VRSN, 1970.
Steiner, Rudolf. *Die Philosophie der Freiheit.* Dornach: RSV, 1973.
Steiner, Rudolf. *Die Rätsel der Philosophie.* Dornach; VRSN, 1961.
Steiner, Rudolf. *Goethes Geheime Offenbarung In Seinem Märchen von der Grünen Schlange und der Schonen Lilien.* Dornach: RSV, 1982.

Steiner, Rudolf. *Goethes Naturwissenschaftliches Schriften*. Dornach: RSV, 1973.
Steiner, Rudolf. *Goethes Weltanschauung*. Dornach: RSV, 1979.
Steiner, Rudolf. *Mein Lebensgang*. Stuttgart: Verlag Freies Geistesleben, 1975.
Steiner, Rudolf. *Vorträge und Kurse über Christlich Religiöse Wirken*. Dornach: RSV,1993.
Thiede C. & D'Ancona, *The Jesus Papyrus*, London, Weidenfeld & Nicolson, 1996.
Themistius: *on Aristotle On the Soul*. Todd, R. (trans.) Bristol Classic Press, 1996.
Vermes, G. *The Dead Sea Scrolls*, London, Penguin,1987.
Vincent, M.R. *Word Studies of the New Testament*, Peabody, Hendrickson, no date.
Wallace, D. *Greek Grammar beyond the Basics*, Grand Rapids, Zondervan, 1996.
Wallis-Budge, E.A. *The Gods of the Egyptians*, New York, Dover Press, 1969.
Wallis-Budge, E.A. trans. The *Egyptian Book of the Dead*, London, RKP, 1969.
Wallis-Budge, E.A. *The Egyptian Heaven and Hell*, La Salle, USA, Open Court Publishing, 1989.
Westcott, B. F. *The Gospel of St. John*, London, J. Murray, 1908.
West, A. *Alcuin*, W. Heinemann, London, 1893.
Westcott, B. F. *The Canon of the New Testament*, London, Macmillan & Co., 1881.
ZAHN, T. *Das Evangelium Johannes,* Deichert Vlg, Leipzig, 1908.

BIBLES & NEW TESTAMENT

New International Version	NIV
King James	KJ
New King James	NKJ
Revised Standard Version	RSV
New English Bible	NEB
New Revised Standard Version	NRSV
Die Bibel - Martin Luther	ML
Das Neue Testament - Emil Bock	EB
Holy Bible - G. Lamsa	GL

New Greek-English Interlinear NT
Novum Testamentum Graece: 28th rev. edit. Aland
The Greek New Testament 4th rev. edit. Aland
Holy Scriptures of the Old Testament Hebrew & English

REFERENCE WORKS

The Apocrypha and Pseudepigrapha of the Old Testament, edit. Charles, R.H. Oxford, OUP, 1978.
Apocrypha – New Testament, edit. W. Schneemelcher, trans. R. Wilson, Philadelphia, Westminster Press, 1964.
Apocryphal New Testament, edit. James. M. Oxford, UP, 1975.
The Complete Text of the Earliest NT Manuscripts, edit. Comfort & Barrett, Baker Books, Grand Rapids, 1999.
Gesenius: Hebrew and Chaldee Lexicon to the Old Testament, trans. S. P. Tregelles, London, S. Bagster & and Sons, 1857.
Greek-English Lexicon of the New Testament, W. Bauer; trans. W. Arndt & W. Gingrich, 2nd edit, Univ. Chicago, Chicago, 1979.
Greek-English Lexicon, comp. H.G. Liddell & R. Scott, Oxford, Clarendon Press, 1996.
Hebräisches und Chaldäisches Handwörter-buch über das Alte Testament, Fürst, Julius. Leipzig, Vlg. von Bernhard Tauchnitz, 1863.
Josephus, *Works*, trans. W. Whiston, Ward, Lock & Co.
Migne: Patrologia, vol. CCX (V) METANOIA TOU AGIOU KUPRIANOU, ps. 296 – 329.
Lives of the Saints, Butler, edit. Thurston-Attwater, London, Burns & Oats,1981.
Nag Hammadi Deutsch, 1. Band, NHC 1-1-V,1 edit. Schenke, Bethge, Kaiser, Berlin, De Gruyter, 2001.
Nag Hammadi Library, edit. Robinson, J., Leiden, E.J. Brill 1977.
New Documents Illustrating Early Christianity, Horsley, G. edit. Macquarie Univ. 1978+, vols. 1-7.
Septuagint: Septuaginta id est Vetus Testamentus Graece iuxta LXX interpretes; edidit, Alfred Rahlfs, Stuttgart, Privilegierte Würtembergische Bibelanstalt, (no date, ca. 1932).
Septuagint: Η ΠΑΛΑΙΑ ΔΙΑΘΗΚΗ κατα τους ʽΕΒΔΟΜΗΚΟΝΤΑ sixti qvinti pontificus maximi Lipsiae, 1824.
Theologisches Wörterbuch, vols. 1-13, edit. Kittel, Stuttgart, Kohlhammer Vlg, 1953.
Thomas, Gospel of, trans. Guillaumont /Puech /Quispel /Till/ Yassah/ Masih. Leiden, E.J. Brill, 1959.

Zohar, 5 vols. trans. Sperling H. & Simon, M. London, Soncino, 1970.

INTERNET ARTICLES
Labourt, J. and Batiffol, P. *Les Odes de Salomon Texte*, in Revue Biblique Vol.8 No.1 (Janvier 1911).
J. Schmitt, "*The Virgin of Israel...*" in The Catholic Biblical Quarterly; jstor.org.stable/43718279
Zimmer, S and Mattison M. (trans.), *The Odes of Solomon, the Nuhra version.* www.academia.edu

JOURNALS
Canaan, T. "*Haunted Springs and Water Demons in Palestine*" Journal of the Palestine Oriental Society, 1 (1922) 23.
Edwards, M. J. *Clement of Alexandria and His Doctrine of the Logos* in *Vigiliae Christianae* Vol. 54, No.2 (2000) pp. 159-177, E.J. Brill.
Knowling, R. *The Medical Language of St. Luke*, in The Biblical World journal, Chicago, 1902.
Lattke, M. "*Eine übersehene Textvariante in den Oden Salomos*, in the Zeitschrift für Antikes Christentum 8[2] Jan. 2004.
Offord, J. *Some migdols of Palestine and Egypt*, The American and Oriental Journal (1880-1914), vol. 25 Iss.2, 1903.
Taylor, Joan. King's College, London, *Sight*, 8.Jan.2022.

INDEX (For often repeated terms, only the most significant are listed.)

2 Baruch, 27
4 Ezra, 275, 285, 542
accurately discerning, 93
aeonic existence, 68
agape, 66, 288, 291
Alexandrinos Codex, 232
almighty, 79, 80
ambiguous, 224, 228, 254, 520
Amen, amen, 279
Am-Tuat, 406
ancient initiates, 222
Ancient of Days, 30
Apollonios of Tyana, 224
Aristotle, 60
Ascension of Isaiah, 424
Athanasian Creed, 206
Athenagoras, 44
Augustine, 80
autumn, 356
Baptism in the Jordan, 64
Beliar, 383
Bethphage, 19
blossoms of Shu, 327
bodily resurrection, 65
Book of Amos, 12
Book of Daniel, 258
Book of Enoch, 15, 30, 541
Book of Ezekiel, 29, 30
Book of Job, 566
Book of Sirach, 38, 343
butterfly, 396
canon, 5
catenae, 51
Charlesworth, 16, 37
Christ, 63
Christianity, 62
clairvoyance, 95
clairvoyant cognizing, 92
Clement, 6, 28, 40, 81, 87, 221, 409
cloud of dew, 25
conscience, 66, 362
cosmic Christ, 75, 566
Court of the Women, 356
Crucifixion, 66
Cyprian and Justina, 200
David Flusser, 18
Dead Sea Scrolls, 326, 365
deliberately ambiguous, 371
dew, 27
Dialogue of the Saviour, 493
Dionysian, 265
Dionysos the Areopagite, 43
divine Hierarchies, 43
docetic, 77
dove-like shape, 246, 248
doxa, 22,5 426
Dead Sea Scrolls, 41
Earth-soul, 66, 214
ego eimi, 32
ego-ic awareness, 568
Egyptian, 7
Egyptian Book of the Dead, 406, 408
Eleusis, 100, 390
Elijah, 228, 238
Elohim, 75, 80, 205, 566

energetic template, 496
energy template, 491
Essene, 17, 24
Essenes, 199, 528, 537
eternal life, 67, 68, 285, 587
Eudocia, 200
Faith, 87, 92
fallen spirits, 238
Father, 84, 85, 222
Father-God, 77, 85
fig-tree, 19
Folk-spirit, 258, 417
freedom, 370
Galilee of the Gentiles, 270
God, 79, 80, 82, 220
Goethe, 26, 438, 525
Golgotha hill, 66
Gospel of Philip, 616
Gospel of Thomas, 102
Grace, 227, 569
Greek Folk-spirit, 418
Grimm, 37
Harrowing of Hades, 312
Harrowing of Hell, 36
have faith, 92
Heimarmene, 35
Heliopolis, 112
Hermetica, 198, 228
hierarchical Christ-Logos, 550
hierophant, 399
hierophantic, 6, 470
hierophantic teaching, 103
Hippolytos, 581
historic present, 197
Ignatius, 45
in this same manner, 106
indwelling spirit, 376

initiated, 586
initiatory spirituality, 587
initiatory teaching, 432
intoning, 367, 427
IOA, 190, 215
Jahve, 80, 209, 287
Jehovah, 83
Jerome, 50
Jerusalems, 274
Jeshua Ben-Pandira, 14
Jesus, 61, 66
Jonah, 36, 39, 391
Joseph and Asenath, 34
Josephus, 16, 246
Julian the Apostate, 363
karma, 52, 375
karmically, 361
katabasis, 36, 39, 41, 390
Kyridwen, 39, 391
Kyrios, 241
Lazaros-John, 192, 194, 208
life-forces, 67, 211, 311
Life-spirit, 33, 34, 67, 222
living cameos, 195
living water, 16, 299, 302
Logos, 77, 203, 206, 545, 548, 553
Logos-Christ, 547
love, 288
Luke, chapter 16, 18
Malachi, 215
Manichaean, 27
mantric, 295
Mary Magdalene, 616
Messiah, 62
Mighdol, 621
Mysteries, 7

Mystery of Golgotha, 64
Myvyrian Archaiology, 390
Naasseni, 402, 581
Naasseni Psalm, 348
name, 317
name of God, 31
Nazarene, 22
Nazarene sect, 21
Nazareth, 10
Nazarites, 12
Nazaritic Essene, 257
Nazir, 13
Nazirite, 252
Nephesch, 59
Neschamah, 59
nine hierarchies, 44
nine ranks, 207
Novalis, 418
oak tree, 605
Ode 36, 24
ode 42, 36
Odes of Solomon, 24
Origenes, 5, 50, 52, 254, 275, 403, 545
pantokrator, 79
papyrus 75, 232
Paraclete, 448
Paradise, 423
perceptive cognizing, 94
perceptive spiritually, 340
Philo Judaeus, 52, 199, 534
Photius, 221, 573
Pisces, 322
pistis, 215, 349
Pistis Sophia, 54, 408, 554
planetary spheres, 58, 444
Pleroma, 227

Powers, 71, 80, 566
Prayer of the High Priest, 67
primal Logos, 76, 77, 217, 550
Prince of the Air, 384
Psalm 104, 405
Psalm 110, 28
Psalm 82, 387
Pythagoras, 390
Qumran, 15, 38
Ra-Osiris, 326
reincarnation, 47, 50, 53, 238, 375
re-naming, 191, 256, 521
Resurrection, 64
Resurrection memory, 194
Ruach, 59
Rudolf Steiner, 592, 593, 594, 598, 606, 611
Sabaoth, 76, 80
Salvation, 56, 57, 74, 563
Saying 72, 102
secret Gospel, 6
see, 84
seership, 94
sephiroth, 520
Septuagint, 288, 590, 591 594, 597
serpent, 283
shaddai, 79
sigils, 361
Sinaiticus, 264, 315
solar Logos, 217, 569
Son of God, 33, 34, 35, 38, 206
Son of Man, 30, 31
Sons of Light, 531
Soul of the World, 548
soul-body, 19
spiritual cognizing, 88

spiritual Sun, 363
Spiritual-self, 29, 221, 569
Sunday, 500
sun-god Christ, 74, 567
Sun-spirit, 568
Sun-spirits, 364
take up his cross, 420
Taliesin, 39, 391
tenth, 254
Testament of Abraham, 46
Testament of Levi, 383
the Ancient of Days, 30, 31
The Books of Jeu, 555
The Dream of Scipio, 486
The Festival of Booths, 356
The Mysteries, 220
The Nine Hierarchies, 49
The Odes to Solomon, 326
The Shepherd of Hermas, 40
the solar Logos, 76
The Son of Man, 28, 284
The Testament of Adam, 44
The Watchers, 15
The Way, 20, 21

The Wisdom of Solomon, 52
Themistios, 200
Theodore Beza, 97
Thothmes III, 197
three aspects, 35
Three Kings, 223
three-day initiatory sleep, 390
Thrones, 318
Thummin, 323, 324
tracing out imagery, 361
Trinity, 207
triune soul, 59
tuning fork, 286
Two Enoch, 275
Underworld, 39, 390
unripe figs, 19
Urien Rheged, 39, 391
Urim and Thummin, 323
virgin birth, 221
Watchers, 199
water pitcher, 17
water-spirits, 306
Weltengrund, 81
Wisdom of Solomon, 240
Wisdom, Power and Love, 80
World-soul, 550
zodiac, 321, 323, 409, 432
Zohar, 519

For other books by the author see website:

www.rudolfsteinerstudies.com

www.ingramcontent.com/pod-product-compliance
Lightning Source LLC
Chambersburg PA
CBHW021712300426
44114CB00009B/116